W9-BCI-306

An Introduction to Special Education

An Introduction to Special Education

A. Edward Blackhurst and William H. Berdine, Editors
University of Kentucky, Lexington

 Little, Brown and Company
Boston   Toronto

This text is dedicated to our students, who have taught us much about teaching.

Copyright © 1981 by Little, Brown and Company (Inc.)

All rights reserved. No part of this book may be reproduced in any form or by any electronic or mechanical means including information storage and retrieval systems without permission in writing from the publisher, except by a reviewer who may quote brief passages in a review.

Library of Congress Catalog Card No. 80-82551

9 8 7 6 5 4 3   ISBN 0-316-09060-3

HAL

Published simultaneously in Canada by Little, Brown & Company (Canada) Limited

Printed in the United States of America

We would like to thank the following people and organizations for their contributions to the photo essays in this book: Judith Sedwick for the photos, and the Development Evaluation Clinic of Children's Hospital in Boston, Massachusetts, and John Lappen for assistance in the essay on assessment; Alan Carey for the photos in the essays on hearing disorders and physical disabilities; and Alan J. Brightman for the photos, and Marianna Smith and West House, a community residence for the mentally retarded in Pittsfield, Massachusetts, for participation in the essay on mental retardation. Special thanks are due all the parents and children who appear in the photo essays, for their time, generosity, and warmth of spirit.

CREDITS

Title page: Alan Carey.

Part I opening photo: Reprinted by permission of Camp Kysoc, Kentucky Easter Seal Society. Photo by W. J. Wells.

Chapter 1. *Excerpt, p. 10:* From M. Satchell, "Ladies, Start Your Engines," *Parade* Magazine, May 6, 1979. Reprinted by permission. *Fig. 1–1:* Based on figure from M. Reynolds, "A framework for considering some issues in special education," *Exceptional Children,* 28 (7), 1962, p. 368. Originally adapted from E. Deno, "Special education as developmental capital," *Exceptional Children,* 39, 1973. *Excerpt, pp. 31–32:* From *Bluegrass Association for Retarded Citizens, Newsletter,* July 1979. Reprinted by permission.

Photo essay, pp. 52–53: Judith Sedwick.

Chapter 2. *Fig. 2–1:* From W. J. Robbins et al, *Growth* (New Haven, Connecticut: Yale University Press, 1928). Reprinted by permission. *Fig. 2–2:* Adapted from H. Knoblock and P. Pasamanick (eds.), *Gesell and Amatruda's Developmental Diagnosis,* 3d ed. Copyright © 1974 Harper & Row, Publishers, Inc. *Fig. 2–3:* From Rhoda Priest Erhardt, "Sequential Levels in Development of Prehension." Reprinted with the permission of the American Occupational Therapy Association, Inc., Copyright, 1974, *American Journal of Occupational Therapy,* Vol. 28, No. 10, p. 594.

Chapter 3. *Fig. 3–1:* From Paul Skinner and Ralph Shelton, *Speech, Language, and Hearing: Normal Processes and Disorders,* Chapter 3, p. 57, Fig. 3.3 © 1978, Addison-Wesley Publishing Company, Inc. Reprinted with

(continued on page 611)

371.9
A53

84-2383

Preface

This text is designed to introduce you to the field of special education. Special education is that branch of education directed to the learning needs of exceptional children — those who are very bright or those who have intellectual, physical, emotional, or sensory impairments. We will examine the nature and characteristics of exceptional children and describe the educational programs and services that have been developed to help these children realize their maximum potential. Although this book is not a methods of teaching text, some specific teaching techniques will be described to give you a glimpse of some common special education practices.

Whether you are a student just entering a program to prepare you to become a special education teacher or a person interested simply in broadening your knowledge of exceptional individuals, you will find the information in this book useful. After completing the reading of the text, you should be able to

define terms that are commonly used in special education

describe the educationally relevant characteristics of exceptional children

define the various traditional categories of exceptionality and explain reasons for de-emphasizing categorical labels

describe the major issues and trends in special education and explain how these relate to general education and other fields

explain the various educational provisions for services to exceptional children

ORGANIZATION

The fourteen chapters making up this book are divided into four parts. Part I, the first three chapters, contains information critical to an understanding of all areas of special education. In Chapter 1 we introduce you to definitions of major terms, legal requirements, and key issues that special educators must face. We explore the basic principles of child development within the context of early childhood special education in Chapter 2. It is our contention that knowledge of normal child development is a prerequisite to understanding abnormal development. Also, since the achievement of communication skills pervades all areas of special education, speech and language development as well as communication disorders are discussed in Chapter 3.

Part II, building on the broad foundation of the first three chapters, covers sensori-motor exceptionalities. In three chapters we discuss hearing disorders, visual impairments, and physical disabilities.

In Part III we examine individual differences in learning and behavior. Chapters on mental retardation, learning disabilities, behavior disorders, the severely and profoundly handicapped, and the gifted and talented are included. Although we believe that the type of educational services created should not be determined only by the the type of exceptional children being addressed, we cover the various categories of exceptionality in

v

separate chapters to facilitate your understanding of the different nature and characteristics of exceptional children. As you study these chapters, you will notice that certain educational programs or strategies can be used or adopted to fit the needs of various exceptionalities.

To complete a comprehensive overview of special education, we offer, in Part IV, chapters on career and vocational education for the handicapped, the critical role of parents in the education of exceptional children, and the importance of continued development of professional skills.

FORMAT

This book has a number of distinctive features that will help you master the content.

Competency statements. In each chapter we identify key principles that we believe you should learn in an introductory course in special education. These competency statements, set off in the text by a shaded background, are followed by discussion of related content. The competency statements will help focus your attention as you read through each chapter.

Probes. Lists of questions, called probes, appear at various points within the chapters. In general, there is usually one probe or set of questions for each competency statement. The probes will enable you to check whether you have learned the material that has been presented. You are encouraged to answer each probe as you come to it. You should write your answers to the probes directly in the spaces provided in the text. This will enhance your learning and retention of the material and will become an invaluable tool for reviewing chapters. Answers to the probes are provided at the end of each chapter.

Task sheets. Each chapter concludes with a task sheet. The task sheets contain activities that are designed to supplement the information presented in the text. Generally, the activities involve some sort of field experience, such as observing actual special education programs or interacting with people who work with exceptional children. The variety of possible field experiences will depend on your access to children and the time you will be able to allocate. For those of you who are unable to schedule field experiences, an alternative such as library research is included.

Human interest features. Examples, anecdotes, and excerpts from popular literature have been incorporated into the text. They will give you insight into some of the unique problems that exceptional people face in their everyday lives. We hope that these human interest features will help you to develop positive attitudes toward the handicapped and gifted.

STYLE

We have tried to write the text in a relatively informal style that should make reading it an enjoyable, as well as an educational, experience for you.

SEX ROLE STEREOTYPING

In dealing with the perplexing problem of using personal pronouns, we elected to alternate the use of "his" and "her". Any sex role stereotyping that may have occurred is strictly the result of alternating these personal pronouns. We flipped a coin to see which gender would be mentioned first.

FIELD TESTING

Each chapter has been field tested with our own undergraduate and beginning graduate students over a period of two years. As a result of countless suggestions, we have made two complete revisions in the content, format, and writing style.

ACKNOWLEDGMENTS

A text such as this, covering an enormous amount and diversity of information, is the product of a team effort in the best sense. We would like to thank our contributors, identified in the Brief Contents, for their cooperation and willingness to make the numerous revisions recommended by the reviewers of the manuscript. A special note of recognition goes to Barbara Tymitz of Indiana University at Bloomington who read the entire manuscript several times. Much of the sharpening of content and the "teaching" qualities of this book resulted from her valuable critiques and thoughtful insight into how students learn. We also wish to thank Herbert Prehm, Arizona State University, Melvyn Semmel, University of California at Santa Barbara, Thomas M. Skrtic, The University of Kansas, and Linda Blanton, Appalachian State University, who reviewed the entire manuscript. We also express our gratitude to our colleagues who critiqued selected chapters: Gary M. Clark, The University of Kansas; S. C. Ashcroft, Peabody College of Vanderbilt University; Jack W. Birch, University of Pittsburgh; Nancy J. Fennick, University of Oregon; Carolyn Callahan, University of Virginia; Verna Hart, University of Pittsburgh; and Albert Fink, Indiana University.

The development of this book was also significantly assisted by Henry Schlotzhauer, Lori Kennedy, Linda Shaw, Barbara Reeves, and Monica Brown, who organized and revised the glossary and bibliography. Therese Serhus and Janie Kelley typed two pre-publication revisions of the manuscript. Blanche Williams completed the index. The illustration program was created by Art Editor Tina Schwinder at Little, Brown and photographers Alan J. Brightman, Alan Carey, and Judith Sedwick. Dan Otis helped us to convey our ideas clearly by making the writing style smooth and consistent. Our book editor, Dana Norton, carefully coordinated the many steps in producing the book from manuscript. We are particularly indebted to Mylan Jaixen, Editor in the College Division of Little, Brown and Company, who patiently taught us how to pull together a text of this scope into a comprehensive whole.

A.E.B.
W.H.B.

Brief Contents

Contents

Foundations of Special Education

Special education is a part of regular education, not a separate entity. Many people imagine that the techniques and materials used in special education cannot be used in other areas of education as well. By the same token, some believe that the practices of regular education are unsuitable for teaching the exceptional child.

Neither belief is true. The same procedures, with modifications, are used to educate both groups of children, and many concepts and fields of knowledge have relevance for *all* children. For example, concepts that guide the teaching of normal children are also used to develop individual education plans for exceptional pupils. Similarly, a knowledge of speech and language development is needed in both types of education. Most important, you must understand normal child development if you hope to understand deviations in this process.

We hope you will keep in mind this close relationship between general and special education throughout your career. The view that special education is only distantly related to general education can create a distance between the two groups of personnel that ultimately lowers the quality of service children receive.

Just as a building needs a solid foundation to be structurally sound, you need a solid understanding of the concepts, issues, and social forces that underlie current practices in special education. Your familiarity with the interplay of these factors will then serve as a foundation for further study.

The three chapters in Part I of this text are intended to provide the foundation. An overview of each follows.

1. Basic Concepts. In this chapter we will discuss definitions, terminology, and the origins and historical development of special education. We will also describe the federal legislation that has had an impact on the field, and the major issues facing special educators today.

2. Early Childhood Education. Whereas educational research has long shown that early intervention is critical for exceptional children, legislation was required to raise the field of early childhood education to the position it deserves in special education's array of services. This chapter offers the rationale for providing special education services to young handicapped children and describes related issues and historical precedents. Of special importance is the discussion of normal child development, accompanied by illustrations of how various developmental milestones relate to exceptional children. Methods of identifying young handicapped children are also presented. The chapter concludes with a description of the different methods of delivering special education to preschool children.

3. Communication Disorders. More children are potentially affected by communication disorders than by any other type of impairment. In this chapter, we define and differentiate speech and language and describe the development of each. Four types of language disorders and three types of speech disorders are also discussed. The chapter closes with a discussion of the role of speech-language pathologists and classroom teachers in providing therapeutic services to children with communication disorders.

We hold these truths to be self-evident, that all people are created equal, that they are endowed by their Creator with certain unalienable rights, that among these are Life, Liberty, and the pursuit of Happiness. We further declare that for the handicapped, the paramount right is to be a person made whole by exercising human potentialities, most notably: . . .

The Right to Educate Oneself

No handicapped person shall be denied equal opportunity to utilize educational institutions, libraries, museums, or other means of pursuing knowledge by reason of architectural, traditional, or attitudinal barriers.

The Right to an Occupation or Profession

No person shall be denied the right to enter any occupation or profession solely for reasons of disability, provided he or she can perform the duties of the occupation creditably.

The Right to Maintain Health and Physical Well Being

Medical facilities shall provide equal access to all persons regardless of physical or other disabilities; moreover, public facilities shall be made generally available, identifiable, and accessible to handicapped persons including food service, restrooms, and places to have a drink of water or to rest when tired. . . .

The Right to Independent Living

Handicapped persons shall not be denied accommodations in houses, apartments, hotels, dormitories, or barracks open to other persons, and shall be free to live with other persons of their choice. . . .

The Right to Love

No citizen, agency, or any legislative, executive, or judicial branch of government shall deny to handicapped persons the relationships of friendship, love, and marriage through any means not applicable to all other persons. . . .

Source: Adapted from Charles M. Westle, *A Bicentennial Declaration of Human Rights for Handicapped Persons.* Central Michigan University, Office of Career Development for Handicapped Persons, 1976.

1

Basic Concepts
of
Special Education

A. Edward Blackhurst
and William H. Berdine

A. Edward Blackhurst is a Professor and past Chairman of the Department of Special Education at the University of Kentucky. He has taught mildly mentally retarded adolescents and was principal of a school for mentally retarded children. William H. Berdine is an Associate Professor and Coordinator of the certification program for teachers of the trainable mentally handicapped at the University of Kentucky. He has taught classes for the mentally retarded in both primary and secondary settings.

The declaration of rights at the beginning of this chapter, written in 1976 for the bicentennial celebration of the United States, reflects the mood of handicapped people during the 1970s. During that decade, the search for human rights culminated in court decisions and legislation that marked the beginning of a new era for the handicapped and those who work with them.

In the 1980s we will see direct results of the legal advances that were made. No longer will people be denied jobs because of disabilities they may have. Colleges and universities will admit more handicapped students and offer improved services to support their education. Communities will provide more modifications such as ramps, curb cut-outs, and buses with wheelchair lifts that will facilitate travel for the handicapped. New buildings will be designed and old buildings will be renovated to make them accessible to the handicapped. The most significant developments, however, will occur in special education programs for exceptional children in public schools.

The influence of the activism of the handicapped will be evident in the treatment of the subjects in this chapter. Here, special education will be defined and placed in historical perspective. A summary of the legislation related to special education will be presented. These will be followed by a discussion of some of the major issues facing special educators today.

DEFINITIONS AND TERMINOLOGY

You should be able to define special education and related terminology.

If you asked a teacher or school administrator how schools should serve children, the response would probably include the comment that school programs should respond to the individual differences of the children who are enrolled. Almost everyone thinks this is a desirable goal for a school system.

It is easy to state a goal. Achieving it can be another matter. If you think back to your elementary and secondary school career, you will undoubtedly recall many examples of individual differences. Some of your classmates were better than you in some subjects, while you were better in others. These differences *between* students are called *interindividual differences*. Similarly, you were probably better in some subjects than in others and enjoyed some more than others. These differences *within* students are called *intraindividual differences*.

Your school probably responded to these differences by grouping in elementary school and by providing different electives and tracks in secondary school. In fourth grade, for example, you may have been a member of the Eagles reading group or the Buzzards math group. In high school you may have taken an academic rather than a vocational curriculum, and you may have taken several courses in subjects you were particularly interested in. Such arrangements are adequate to respond to the interindividual and intraindividual differences of most students.

For other students, however, these arrangements are not enough. Students who take longer to learn, who have severe difficulty in learning, who exhibit disruptive behavior, who have severe physical problems that interfere with learning, who are exceptionally intelligent or talented — all have needs that are not met by the general education program. They need programs designed to meet their needs individually. Special education exists to provide such programs.

Special education, then, is *instruction designed to respond to the unique characteristics of children who have needs that cannot be met by the standard school curriculum*.

A child's individualized education program is typically a modification of the standard school curriculum. The program may call for changes in content, methods of instruction, instructional materials, and expected rate of progress. It may also call for supportive services from speech pathologists, audiologists, physical and occupational therapists, psychologists, physicians, counselors, and others. Special education is delivered to each child according to an individualized educational program that has been developed for that child.

Special education can be delivered in a variety of settings, depending on the needs of a particular child. Some special children can be enrolled in regular classes where the teacher receives help from specialists. Some receive instruction for part of the day in resource rooms. Some require placement in a full-time special education class. Others need to be placed in homebound, hospital, or residential school programs. These options will be discussed in more detail later in this chapter.

TERMINOLOGY

The term most often associated with special education is "exceptional children." Many people believe this term refers only to very intelligent children, whereas others believe it refers only to the handicapped. Both beliefs are misconceptions; the term encompasses both groups of children.

Exceptional children are children who have physical, mental, behavioral, or sensory characteristics that differ from the majority of children such that they require special education and related services to develop to their maximum capacity. The category includes children with communication disorders, hearing disorders, visual impairments, physical disabilities, mental retardation, learning disabilities, behavior disorders, multiple handicaps, high intelligence, and unique talents. More precise definitions of these categories will be presented in the chapters that follow.

Several other terms are also used to refer to children who receive special education services. Although the use of varying terminology is quite common in special education, there are technical differences in meaning among a number of terms. In attempting to develop a system for classification of special education concepts, Stevens (1962) differentiated among the following terms:

Impairment refers to diseased or defective tissue. For example, lack of oxygen at birth may cause brain damage or neurological impairment that will result in cerebral palsy. Similarly, a birthmark could be considered an impairment because it is different from the tissues that surround it.

Disability refers to the reduction of function, or the absence, of a particular body part or organ. A person who has an arm or leg missing has a physical disability. Similarly, someone who cannot control the muscles required for speech has a disability in communication. The terms *disorder* and *dysfunction* are frequently used as synonyms for disability.

Handicap refers to the problems that impaired or disabled people have when interacting with their environment. A Vietnam veteran who is confined to a wheelchair put it this way: "Sure I have a disability; but I'm not handicapped — until I try to get into a building that has a flight of steps and revolving door as its only entrance."

It should be noted that many people treat these terms as synonyms. In this book we will reflect the common practice of occasionally referring to impaired and disabled children as handicapped. This practice came about largely because federal legislation directs our public schools to provide special education to all "handicapped children."

Generally, however, there are distinct differences between impairment, disability, and handicap. A person can be handicapped in one situation and not in another. A boy with a birthmark on his face may be impaired, but he is not disabled. He may, however, be handicapped in getting dates. A musician may have a visual disability but not be handicapped when it comes to producing music. Consider the case of Kitty O'Neil described in *Parade* magazine:

If Kitty O'Neil merely parked cars for a living instead of driving them at 600 mph and faster, she would still be a very unusual person. At one time or another, she has held 22 speed records. As a teenager, she was an Olympic class diving champion. She plays the cello and piano. And she's one of Hollywood's top stuntwomen.

She also is totally deaf.

Parade caught up with the 33-year-old Kitty at her home in Glendale, Cal. Communicating with her is easy. Her mother spent years teaching her to read lips and to speak. She does not know sign language and she doesn't need it.

Kitty was raised in Wichita Falls, Tex., born to a part Cherokee Indian mother and an Irish father. At 4 months, she almost died from the simultaneous onslaught of chicken pox, measles and mumps—illnesses that robbed her of her hearing.

At the age of 12, she began competitive swimming and diving, becoming an AAU Junior Olympic diving champion and earning a wallfull of medals. Obsessed with speed and motion — "I love to go fast and I love danger" — Kitty began racing in any vehicle she could climb onto or into: production sports cars, motorcycles, drag racers, speedboats, dune buggies and snowmobiles. She tried skydiving, scuba diving and hang gliding. At one time Kitty held the world's record for women's water skiing, zipping across the water at better than 104 mph. She tackled anything to prove that a stone deaf, 95-pound, 5-foot-3 slip of a woman could do as well as anyone, male or female. Eventually, she turned inward and began competing against herself. Her vehicle: the rocket car.

At 38 feet long and developing 48,000 horsepower, the rocket car she drove was little more than an earthbound guided missile made principally of aluminum and fiberglass. After testing on the Bonneville Salt Flats in Utah, Kitty and her crew went to the Alvord Dry Lake in Oregon to try and beat the women's land speed record of 308 mph.

On Dec. 6, 1976, she was strapped into the cockpit of the rocket car and attained an average speed of 512.7 mph. Later that day she made another run and hit an incredible 618.3 mph — just 4 miles an hour under the world record held by Gary Gabelich.

Kitty supports herself these days as a movie stuntwoman. If you've ever watched *The Bionic Woman, Police Woman, Baretta, ABC Superstars* and a host of other television shows, or caught the movies *Airport '77* and *Omen II*, you may have seen her [Satchell, 1979].

Does Kitty have an impairment? Probably. Her various childhood diseases probably damaged her auditory nerve or central nervous system. Does she have a disability? Yes. She cannot hear. Is she handicapped? Certainly not when she is racing or working as a stuntwoman. Yet she would be handicapped if she attempted to use a telephone.

What should be noted is that a person's having an impairment or disability does not mean she will be handicapped in all situations. Similarly, the severity of the disability may have little relationship to the severity of the ensuing handicap. The physical environment and psychological situation of the impaired or disabled person are crucial in dealing with them. As Gearhart (1974) put it:

> The degree of the disability does not necessarily determine the degree of the handicap. Most children with special needs are more normal than abnormal and will likely spend most of their lives in a basically nonhandicapped world. They, therefore, must have programming that will help them to adjust to their social and physical environment and minimize the handicapping effect of their disability [pp. 22–23].

Terms have also been developed to refer to specialty areas of special education. Thus, children with speech and language problems are said to have "communication disorders"; those with visual problems are "visually impaired"; children in wheelchairs have "physical disabilities"; and those who are seriously mentally retarded with other physical problems are referred to as "severely [or profoundly] handicapped." The commonly used terminology is reflected in the chapter titles in this text.

INCIDENCE AND PREVALENCE

To plan for the provision of special education services it is important to know how many exceptional children there are at present and how many can be expected at a given point in the future. Accurate estimates can be used to get funds for programs and to determine how many teachers and other professionals will be needed to staff them.

But the exact number of children who need special education services is difficult to determine. There are several reasons. First, there are many different definitions of the categories used to group children — especially those with learning problems. A child placed in one category by one authority might be placed in another by a different authority. A child who has severe problems with academic subjects and who is very disruptive in class because of inability to do academic work may be classified as learning disabled by one diagnostician and emotionally disturbed by another. Second, categories often overlap. Children with more than one problem may be arbitrarily placed in one category or another. A child who has cerebral palsy, is confined to a wheelchair, and has difficulty reading may be classified in one school district as physically disabled, in

Table 1-1
Estimated Prevalence of Handicapped Children Under Age 19

Category	Percentage	Prevalence
Speech impaired	3.5	2,293,000
Mentally retarded	2.3	1,507,000
Learning disabled	3.0	1,966,000
Behavior disordered	2.0	1,310,000
Hearing impaired	.575	372,000
Orthopedically handicapped	.5	328,000
Visually impaired	.1	66,000
Multiply handicapped	.06	40,000
TOTAL	12.035	7,887,000

Source: Aid to States Branch, Bureau of Education for the Handicapped, U.S. Office of Education, 1976.

another as learning disabled, and in a third as multiply handicapped. Third, school officials simply have not identified all of the children who require special services.

The terms "incidence" and "prevalence" are used in discussing the number of exceptional children in a population. The *incidence* of a given characteristic is the estimated number of people in a population who exhibit the characteristic at some point during their lives. The *prevalence* of a characteristic is the number of people who currently exhibit it. Incidence figures are either equal to or higher than prevalence figures. Because they have more immediate implications for the practice of special education prevalence figures will be used in this text unless otherwise noted.

Although they are frequently used as synonyms, the difference between incidence and prevalence is very important. For example, if you were planning services for people who had hangnails and you used the incidence figure of 10 percent, this would mean that at some point in their lives, 10 percent of the population will have had a hangnail. However, if the prevalence of hangnail is only 5 percent at any given point in time, only 5 percent of the population have hangnails. If you were planning a treatment program on the basis of the 10 percent figure, you would overestimate the number of fingernail clippers you would need at any given time by 100 percent.

Estimates of the proportion of school-aged children needing special education services have ranged from 10 to 15 percent. In 1976 the prevalence of handicapped children in the United States was estimated by the Bureau of Education for the Handicapped in the United States Office of Education. By surveying various special education organizations, they were able to estimate the percentage of the population that had different types of handicaps. The percentages used and the resulting estimated prevalence figures for children under nineteen years of age are reported in Table 1-1. If the estimated 1.5 million gifted children in this age group are added to the total prevalence figures in Table 1-1, we arrive at an estimated total of more than 9 million exceptional children in the United States.

Theoretically, the prevalence for a given year could be estimated by multiplying the population under nineteen by the percentages in Table 1-1. It should be emphasized, however, that the percentages given are estimates; the exceptional children in this country have never actually been counted. It should also be noted that the estimates are intended to be applied to the population as a whole. The actual prevalence for a particular population may vary according to the sex of the children being studied, the population's ethnic makeup and geographical region, and many other factors. Because of this variation, prevalence figures are used primarily for the early stages of planning. To accurately project service needs, the exceptional children in the area to be served must actually be located. Estimated projections of prevalence often differ considerably from the number of people who actually need services.

PROBE 1-1
Definitions and Terminology

1. What is your definition of special education? _____

_____

_____

_____

2. T   F   The term "exceptional children" refers primarily to the gifted and talented.

3. Differentiate between "disability" and "handicap." _____

_____

_____

_____

4. Why are incidence figures higher than prevalence figures? _____

_____

_____

_____

5. There are approximately _____ handicapped children and _____ gifted children in the United States.

HISTORICAL DEVELOPMENTS

> **You should be able to describe the effect that historical developments have had on special education.**

A knowledge of history helps one to understand present practices and to plan improvements. When we examine the historical forces that have influenced special education, we realize that the programs, practices, and facilities that were established at any given time reflected the prevailing social climate. People's attitudes have been particularly important; as attitudes have changed, so have the services that have been provided. For example, when people believed the mentally retarded were a genetic threat to the future of the human race, there was a dramatic increase in the practice of sterilizing the retarded. Similarly, when the prevailing attitude was that it was wrong to deny physically disabled people access to buildings, legislation to require the removal of architectural barriers was developed. Efforts to foster positive attitudes toward exceptional people are crucial in improving the services provided them. The history of these attitudes and the developments they reflected can be divided into distinct periods.[1]

EARLY PRACTICES: 1552 B.C.-A.D. 1740

We know little about how early cultures dealt with the handicapped. The significance of the few reports that are available has been exaggerated. Saint Nicholas Thaumaturgos, for example, has been described as a champion of the mentally retarded. Kanner (1964) pointed out, however, that although "he may well have put in a good word for them now and then, . . . he is also regarded as the patron saint of *all* children, of sailors, and — of pawn brokers; the fact that at a much later date he was made to serve as the prototype of 'Santa Claus' certainly does not qualify him to figure in the chronicles of mental deficiency" (p. 3).

An Egyptian papyrus dated 1552 B.C. (known as the therapeutic Papyrus of Thebes) contains the first known written reference to the handicapped. Other references, entreating people to care for the handicapped, are found in the Bible, the Talmud, and the Koran, but at the time those works were written many were forced to beg for food and shelter.

Treatment had not improved in classical times. The ancient Greeks and some of the Romans thought the handicapped were cursed, and sometimes drowned them in efforts to preserve the strength of their races. At other times those who

---

[1] The events examined in this section were drawn from the following authorities: Doll, 1962; Kanner, 1964; Nazzaro, 1977; Payne, Kauffman, Patton, Brown, DeMott, 1979.

could not care for themselves were simply allowed to perish. Some Romans did employ the handicapped in high positions — as "fools" who performed for the elite.

During the Middle Ages, the handicapped were viewed with a mixture of fear and reverence, because they were thought to be somehow connected with the unknown. Some were wandering beggars, whereas others were used as jesters in castles.

The Renaissance and the Reformation brought a change for the worse. Exorcism, demonology, and persecution of the handicapped flourished. Martin Luther and John Calvin, for example, accused the mentally retarded of being "filled with Satan," and many were put in chains and thrown into dungeons.

By the early 1600s, however, there were indications that attitudes toward the handicapped were beginning to change. A hospital in Paris began to provide treatment for the emotionally disturbed. The first manual alphabet for the deaf was developed. John Locke became the first person to differentiate between persons who were mentally retarded and those who were emotionally disturbed.

Change occurred slowly. In colonial America people with mental disorders that made them violent were treated as criminals. Those who were harmless were generally treated as paupers. The retarded, for example, were subjected to one of three treatments: (1) kept at home and provided partial public support, (2) put in poorhouses, or (3) auctioned off to the bidder who would support them at the lowest cost to the community, in return for whatever work the bidder could extract from them. The last practice was eventually halted by public outrage. The retarded were then put in poorhouses, where conditions were often worse than those provided by the person who had won the bid for their services.

THE MOVEMENT FOR TRAINING: 1798–1890

One of the first persons to investigate methods of educating the exceptional child was the French physician Jean Marc Itard. Itard's initial contribution was the result of his effort to alter the wildly uncivilized behavior of a boy who had been found living naked and alone in the woods near Aveyron, France, in 1799 (Itard, 1932; Lane, 1976). Although Itard did not consider his efforts completely successful, the techniques he documented and promoted gave the initial impetus to the movement to train the mentally retarded.

Itard's investigations exerted a strong influence on special educators working in the United States in the early 1800s. Two of the most important are Thomas Hopkins Gallaudet and Samuel Gridley Howe. In 1817 Gallaudet founded the first school for the deaf in Hartford, Connecticut. Howe, a physician turned political and social reformer, was instrumental in founding the Perkins School for the Blind in Watertown, Massachusetts, in 1829.

During the middle of the 1800s major contributions were made by two special educators, Jacob Guggenbuhl and Edward Seguin. In the 1840s Guggenbuhl opened, in Switzerland, a facility for the mentally retarded with thyroid conditions (cretins) that was to become world-famous. Although he was later discredited and drummed out of business, he is acknowledged as the originator of institutional care for the retarded.

Seguin was a student of Itard's who emigrated to the United States in 1848. After completing his medical training in 1861 he worked with Howe, Gallaudet, and other American educators and continued to develop Itard's scientific techniques. Seguin's text, *Idiocy and the Treatment by the Physiological Method*, was published in 1866.

By the 1870s the movement to establish institutions had begun. An organization that urged the establishment of institutions was formed in 1876, with Seguin as its president. This organization, originally called the Association of Medical Officers of American Institutions for Idiotic and Feeble-minded Persons, later became the American Association on Mental Deficiency.

Although they were designed to be used for education, institutions during this period came to be used primarily for custodial care. By 1890 it was generally accepted that the states had the responsibility for providing institutional services for the handicapped.

MEASUREMENT AND SOCIAL CONTROL: 1890-1919

The first standardized test of intelligence was published in 1908 by Alfred Binet, a Frenchman. The test was developed to identify mentally retarded children. It was then standardized on American populations by Goddard and published in the United States in 1910. The intelligence quotient (IQ) was introduced by Terman in a 1916 revision of the test. IQ tests have been used ever since to identify persons with retarded or advanced intellectual development.

Unfortunately, IQ tests have been subject to much abuse. Many people have ignored Binet's warning that the results of IQ tests are not to be trusted without taking into account other information about a child's performance. Abuses have led to federal legislation that prohibits the placement of exceptional children in special education programs solely on the basis of an intelligence test score.

Maria Montessori's work also began in the early 1900s. An Italian physician concerned with early childhood education, Montessori further developed Seguin's elaboration of Itard's techniques. Her methods text, published in 1912, detailed a sequence of instructional procedures for working with the retarded child. The so-called Montessori methods are still an important part of the curriculums of many regular and special preschool education programs.[2]

---

[2] Throughout this text, we will consider school-age children to be those between the ages of six and seventeen. Preschool children will be those aged five or under.

In 1912 a famous psychologist, Henry Goddard, published a study about the Kallikak family which traced five generations of the offspring of a man who had fathered both a legitimate and an illegitimate child. A large percentage of the descendents of the illegitimate child were mentally retarded, whereas the descendents of the legitimate child were reported to have average or superior intelligence. Goddard's report led to the belief that mental retardation was an inherited trait and therefore a threat to the human race. The so-called Eugenic Scare that followed prompted many states to enact laws authorizing the sterilization of retarded people and criminals.

Other trends were more encouraging, however. At the same time that many of the mentally retarded were being institutionalized and sterilized, the number of special education programs in the public schools was gradually being increased. The first college programs for the preparation of special education teachers were also established during this period.

EXPANSION OF SERVICES: 1920–1949

There were a number of new developments in the United States during the 1920s, 1930s, and 1940s. Many of them were good. Halfway houses were established to bridge the gap between institution and community; followup studies were performed to examine the relative effectiveness of various programs; outpatient clinics were established in hospitals; the use of social workers and other support personnel was increased; new diagnostic instruments were discovered; and comprehensive statewide programs were developed.

The periods of progress proved to be of short duration in some areas, however. The number of special education programs begun in public schools increased fairly rapidly until 1930 and then began to fall. The impetus of the 1920s toward humane, effective treatment for the handicapped died out in the 1930s and 1940s. These decades were a period of stagnation, characterized by large-scale institutionalization and segregation of the handicapped from the rest of society. The economic depression was one cause. Another was the widespread dissatisfaction with poorly planned programs staffed by inadequately trained teachers.

Even while the number and quality of services were being cut back, however, important changes in attitude and awareness were occurring. Cruickshank and Johnson (1975) pointed out that the massive screening of young men and women for service in World Wars I and II made it clear how many people were physically, mentally, or behaviorally handicapped or disabled. Few people had expected to find that such a large segment of the population had significant disabilities. The return of physically disabled soldiers from the wars also made the public more sensitive to the problems of the handicapped, and the acceptance offered them was extended to other groups in the population. The same phenomenon was to occur following the wars in Korea and Vietnam.

ADVOCACY AND LITIGATION: 1950-1974

Of all the factors that were significant in the rapid growth and expansion of special education during the period, three stand out: (1) parent activism, (2) professional research and development regarding deviant human growth and development, and (3) changes in teacher education practices. More will be said about the latter two later in this text. The advocacy of parent activists and the effects of the litigation they instigated will be discussed in this section.

The majority of activities related to advocacy and litigation were initiated by parent groups and have been nurtured and supported by professional organizations. In 1950 the National Association for Retarded Children (NARC) was formed. This agency (later renamed the National Association for Retarded Citizens) pressured public schools to initiate programs for the moderately retarded and to expand other special education services. The next twenty-five years saw a rapid growth in services.

Residential institutions were also subjected to pressures, partly as a result of Burton Blatt's *Christmas in Purgatory* (1966). In this exposé of the squalid conditions in many American institutions for the handicapped, Blatt presented photographs of some of the most deplorable conditions imaginable and then contrasted them with photos of an institution in which humane treatment was provided. (We recommend this work for a perspective on some of the conditions and practices that existed as late as the mid-twentieth century.)

A different tactic was used by a parents' group to fight for public support of services for severely handicapped children. In January 1971 the Pennsylvania Association for Retarded Children filed a class action suit against the Commonwealth of Pennsylvania for failing to provide free and appropriate public education for all mentally retarded citizens residing in the state. (*Pennsylvania Association for Retarded Children* v. *the Commonwealth of Pennsylvania, 1971.*) The plaintiffs in this suit, which came to be known as the PARC case, were thirteen mentally retarded school-age children and all other school-age children of their class in Pennsylvania. The plaintiffs contended that the state had not given them due process before denying them "life, liberty and property" (Fifth Amendment). It was also argued that they were not afforded equal protection under the law (Fourteenth Amendment). To support their position the plaintiffs provided expert testimony regarding the educability of all mentally retarded children, regardless of the severity of their retardation.

Conceding defeat, the Commonwealth of Pennsylvania entered into a court-approved consent agreement with the plaintiffs. This agreement defined the commonwealth's obligation to provide all mentally retarded children between the ages of six and twenty-one with a publicly supported, appropriate education, effective September 1972. Included in the agreement were procedures for reevaluation, placement, and due process. Ages of attendance were established, as were regulations calling for homebound and preschool instruction.

PROBE 1-2
Historical Developments

1. Match the item on the left with the appropriate name.

Contribution	*Name*
_____ First school for the deaf	a. Itard
_____ Preschool educational methods	b. Howe
_____ Worked with a "wild boy"	c. Gallaudet
_____ First school for the blind	d. Seguin
_____ Brought special education to the United States	e. Montessori
	f. Guggenbuhl
_____ First intelligence test	g. Terman
_____ Introduced the IQ	h. Binet

2. List four concepts developed by early contributors to special education that are relevant today:

   a. _____

   b. _____

   c. _____

   d. _____

3. T   F   There has been a steady, even growth in special education services since the early 1900s.

4. T   F   Institutions were originally set up for custodial purposes.

5. The name of the parent organization that fought for more public school services is the _____

   _____

6. Contrast the PARC and Mills right-to-education cases.

   _____

   _____

   _____

LEGISLATIVE IMPLICATIONS

> **You should be able to describe the impact of legislation on special education practices.**

The delivery of special education services in public schools is governed primarily by state laws. These vary from state to state. For example, some states mandate special education services for preschool children; others do not. Funding patterns for special education programs also differ considerably across the country.

Once laws are passed, regulations follow. They describe the procedures necessary to comply with the laws, and like laws they are not uniform among states. For example, all states have laws requiring teacher certification in special education, but the regulations that specify requirements for certification are not the same. This situation is due to different philosophies about what is needed to be a special education teacher.

At the local level boards of education handle direct delivery of special education services, and their policies reflect the state laws and regulations. Each board's policies are also a product of local attitudes and biases.

If you plan to become a special education teacher, you should be familiar with the laws, regulations, and policies that affect special education in your school district. You can obtain information from your state Department of Education or Department of Public Instruction, which includes a unit that administers programs for exceptional children. Regardless of where you work, you should also be aware of all federal laws that concern special education practices. Chart 1-1 describes some of this legislation.

Chart 1-1
Major Milestones in Federal Legislation for the Handicapped

1879   Funds to produce braille materials are granted to the American Printing House for the Blind (PL 45–186[a]).

1918   Vocational rehabilitation services are authorized for World War I veterans (PL 65–178).

1920   Vocational rehabilitation services are extended to civilians (PL 66–236).

1936   Blind persons are authorized to operate vending stands in Federal buildings (PL 74–732).

1943   Mentally retarded and mentally ill become eligible for services under the Barden-LaFollette Vocational Rehabilitation Act (PL 78–113).

1958   Colleges and universities receive funds to aid in preparing teachers of the mentally retarded (PL 85-926).

1962   Provisions are made for production and distribution of captioned films for the deaf (PL 87-715).

1963   Funds are provided to train teachers for all disabilities; research and demonstration projects are established to study education of exceptional children (PL 88-164).

1965   Elementary and Secondary Education Act provides funds for local school districts to attack problems of educating disadvantaged and handicapped children (PL 89-10); support is provided to aid handicapped children in state institutions (PL 89-313); National Technical Institute for the Deaf is established (PL 89-36).

1966   Authorization is provided for establishing the Bureau of Education for the Handicapped and a National Advisory Committee on the Handicapped (PL 89-750); talking book services for the visually impaired are expanded to include the physically handicapped who are unable to handle printed material (PL 89-522).

1968   Experimental demonstration centers for preschool handicapped are established (PL 90-538); ten percent of vocational education funds are earmarked for the handicapped (PL 90-576); provisions are made for deaf-blind centers, resource centers, and expansion of media services for the handicapped (PL 90-247).

1969   National Center on Educational Media and Materials for the Handicapped is authorized (PL 91-61).

1970   Facilities constructed with federal funds are required to be accessible to the physically handicapped (PL 91-205).

1972   Ten percent of enrollment opportunities in Head Start must be available to handicapped children (PL 92-424).

1973   Rights of the handicapped in employment and educational institutions receiving federal funds are guaranteed through Section 504 of the Rehabilitation Amendments (PL 93-112).

1974   Due process procedures in placement, nondiscriminatory testing, and confidentiality of school records are guaranteed; programs for the gifted and talented are authorized (PL 93-380).

1975   Free appropriate public education and other procedural guarantees are mandated for all handicapped children (PL 94-142).

Source: Nazzaro (1977)

[a] The PL stands for "Public Law." The first two digits represent the number of the congressional session in which the law was passed. Thus, PL 94-142 was the 142nd law that was passed by the Ninety-fourth Congress.

Of the legislation mentioned in the chart, two acts have been of outstanding importance: Section 504 of The Vocational Rehabilitation Act of 1973, and PL 94–142, the Education for All Handicapped Children Act.

SECTION 504 OF THE VOCATIONAL REHABILITATION ACT OF 1973

> No otherwise qualified handicapped individual in the United States . . . shall, solely by reason of his handicap, be excluded from the participation in, be denied the benefits of, or be subjected to discrimination under any program or activity receiving Federal financial assistance.

This rather awkward sentence, Section 504 of the Rehabilitation Act of 1973, is perhaps the most important ever written regarding the handicapped. It is the first federal civil rights law that protects the rights of handicapped persons.

The language is almost identical to that of the Civil Rights Act of 1964, which applied to racial discrimination, and of Title IX of the Education Amendments of 1972, which dealt with discrimination in education on the basis of sex. The enactment of Section 504 reflects the realization that the handicapped, too, had been subjected to discrimination for many years.

Ending discrimination is an extremely difficult task; it took nearly four years to develop the federal regulations to implement this law. When he issued the regulations in 1977, Secretary of Health, Education and Welfare Joseph Califano stated,

> The 504 Regulation attacks the discrimination, the demeaning practices and the injustices that have afflicted the nation's handicapped citizens. It reflects the recognition of the Congress that most handicapped persons can lead proud and productive lives, despite their disabilities. It will usher in a new era of equality for handicapped individuals in which unfair barriers to self-sufficiency and decent treatment will begin to fall before the force of law.

As a result of these regulations (Nondiscrimination on Basis of Handicap, 1977) the following changes have occurred:

— Employers are required to provide equal recruitment, employment compensation, job assignments, and fringe benefits for the handicapped.
— All new public facilities are required to be accessible to the handicapped.
— Handicapped children of school age are entitled to a free and appropriate public education.
— Discrimination in admission to institutions of higher education is prohibited.
— Discrimination is forbidden in providing health, welfare, and other social service programs.

As you can see, Section 504 opened up a whole spectrum of new opportunities for the handicapped. The next important step in ending discrimination was the enactment of PL 94–142, which provided for the education of all handicapped children.

PL 94–142: THE EDUCATION FOR
ALL HANDICAPPED CHILDREN ACT

At about the time Section 504 was being enacted, Congress was investigating other aspects of the lives of the handicapped. In 1975 it reported that

— There are more than 8 million handicapped children in the United States.
— More than half of the handicapped children in the United States do not receive the educational services necessary to give them an equal opportunity.
— One million of the handicapped children in the United States are excluded entirely from the public school system and will not be educated with their peers.
— Many handicapped children have undetected handicaps that prevent them from being successfully educated.
— The lack of adequate services within the public school system often forces families to find services elsewhere, often at great distances from their homes, and at their own expense.
— Developments in teacher training and in diagnostic and instructional procedures have advanced to the point that, given sufficient funding, state and local educational agencies could provide effective special education.

Congress also determined that state and local educational agencies have a responsibility to provide education for all handicapped children, even though present financial resources are inadequate. Finally, it determined that the national interest is served by the federal government's assisting state and local efforts to provide special education programs, thereby assuring handicapped children of equal protection under the law (PL 94–142, 89 Stat. pp. 774–75).

As a result of the congressional studies and pressures by advocacy groups, PL 94–142 was passed and signed into law by President Gerald Ford on November 29, 1975. This law, commonly referred to as the *Education for All Handicapped Children Act*, establishes the right of all handicapped children to an education. It also explains the procedures for distributing federal resources to state and local agencies for the development and operation of special education programs. It is the most important federal mandate of services for children with special needs. The act is intended to

1. ensure that a free, appropriate education be made available to all handicapped children

2. assist state and local education agencies in providing this education
3. assess the effectiveness of these educational efforts
4. provide handicapped children and their parents the assurances of due process

The effect of PL 94–142 on both state and federal policy for special education service delivery was reviewed by Abeson and Ballard (1976). A summary of its provisions follows.

Due Process. Handicapped children and their parents are guaranteed procedural safeguards in all matters related to identification, evaluation, and educational placement. This means that parents must be notified when their children are to be tested, and they must give permission for the test to be given. Parents must also be actively involved in any decision about the educational placement of their handicapped children.

Least Restrictive Environment. When appropriate, handicapped children are to be educated with children who are not handicapped. This provision has resulted in major changes in the organization of school programs for the handicapped. Many self-contained special education classes have been eliminated in favor of integrating mildly handicapped children into regular classes for much of the school day, with part-time instruction in resource rooms.

Nondiscriminatory Assessment. When children are tested to determine whether they are eligible for special education services, the tests and testing procedures must not be culturally or racially biased. Under this provision, all testing must be done in the native language of the child. In addition, no educational decisions can be made solely on the basis of a single test score. The use of a number of assessment techniques is required.

Individualization. An individualized educational program (IEP) must be developed for each child who is enrolled in a special education program. The plan is to be developed in consultation with the child's parents and based on the information obtained from assessment. The IEP must also be reviewed at least once a year and revised if necessary.

Confidentiality and Record Keeping. The confidentiality provision reiterates the provisions of the Family Educational Rights and Privacy Act (PL 93–380), also known as the Buckley Amendment, which guarantees parental control of school records. No one may have access to the records of handicapped children without specific written parental permission. In addition the Buckley Amendment guarantees parents the right to examine all the school records of their children.

Parent Surrogate. If the parents or guardians of handicapped children are either unknown or unavailable, someone else can be appointed to work on behalf of the handicapped child. The parent surrogate is responsible for approving the testing and placement of the child. He also serves on the committee that develops the individualized educational program. The parent surrogate is, in effect, an advocate for the child.

Categorical Priorities. The law determines priorities in the provision of services. The first priority is for handicapped children currently receiving no services. Second are those who are the most severely handicapped and who are receiving inadequate services. This means that schools must identify and serve both the handicapped children in school and those not in school. They must also identify those who are in an inappropriate educational program.

Age Levels. The law requires that all handicapped children between the ages of three and twenty-one be served by 1980, unless those aged three to five are excluded from services by state law or court decision. Special incentive grants are available to the states that provide special education and related services to their preschool handicapped children.

Private Settings. Any child placed in or referred to a private school or institution by the state or local education agency must receive special education services at no cost to the parents. The agency receiving the child must also meet state and local education standards. In addition, the children served by these private agencies must be accorded the same educational rights they would have if they were being served by the public agency directly. Thus, all the conditions we are discussing in this section must be adhered to by private agencies that provide services under contract to local school districts.

Finances. The law establishes a formula according to which the federal government substantially increases its monetary contribution to state and local education agencies for their compliance with the act. Funds received by local districts must be used only for the extra costs of educating handicapped children. That is, a district must spend as much of its own revenue for educating a handicapped child as it does for educating a nonhandicapped child if it is to be eligible for PL 94-142 funds.

Planning. Each state Department of Education must submit to the United States Commissioner of Education a plan describing in detail how it proposes to provide a free and appropriate education to all its handicapped children. A similar plan must be submitted by local school districts to the state educational agency. These plans must be examined and revised annually. The plans are also subject to public review and comment prior to their submission.

CONCLUSIONS

The provisions of Section 504 and PL 94–142 have brought about tremendous changes. They put great pressure on schools to change their special education service systems.

As might be expected, the laws are controversial. Critics argue that the federal government should not meddle in what is essentially a local concern. In response, advocates for the handicapped point out that local school districts neglected the needs of the handicapped for years. Without federal legislation, they argue, most of the changes that have revolutionized life for the handicapped would not have occurred.

PROBE 1-3
Legislative Implications

1. What is the difference between a law and a regulation?

_____

_____

_____

2. Circle the law that relates to each statement:
   a. Civil rights for the handicapped   504   94–142
   b. Requires an IEP for all handicapped children   504   94–142
   c. Ensures due process safeguards   504   94–142
   d. Mandates building accessibility   504   94–142
   e. First to require a free, appropriate education for handicapped   504   94–142
   f. Provides for a parent surrogate   504   94–142
   g. Prohibits discrimination in higher education   504   94–142
   h. Mandates fair employment practices   504   94–142
   i. Nondiscriminatory assessment   504   94–142

3. T   F   All states must educate handicapped children between the ages of three and five.

4. Which of the following established the right of privacy of educational records?
   a. Section 504
   b. The Buckley Amendment
   c. PL 94–142

ISSUES IN SPECIAL EDUCATION

> **You should be able to demonstrate awareness of the major issues currently confronting special educators.**

As you saw in the preceding section, many issues in special education came to a head in the 1970s. Parental activism often provided the impetus. The movement began in earnest in the late 1940s. Learning valuable lessons about collective efforts from the civil rights actions of the 1950s and 1960s, activists for exceptional children increased in strength in the 1970s. They were the driving force behind most of the legislation guaranteeing quality public school education for everyone.

The issues have not been completely resolved, of course. There are still many areas of controversy that special educators should be familiar with. The most important are discussed briefly in the following pages, and at greater length later in the book.

LABELING

Consider the image you see when you visualize the following terms:

idiot	spastic
bookworm	epileptic fit
crippled	crazy
deaf and dumb	

If you are like most people, each of these terms conjures up an image of a person who has a certain physical appearance or who is behaving in a certain way. Generally, the images are negative and stereotypical. We learn them from television, literature, and other media. For example, a person who does something unusual is called "crazy"; a bright child is often portrayed as a frail individual who wears glasses; stories sometimes have a "village idiot" as a character; an umpire may be referred to as "blind." The stereotypes that result are reinforced by daily conversations and the attitudes of the people we grew up with.

Labels of a different sort have been used for many years to categorize handicapped children. Children have been identified, diagnosed, and labeled as emotionally disturbed, learning disabled, and educable mentally retarded, for example. It was argued that placing children in categories helped in the effective delivery of instruction. Further, labeling was helpful in obtaining funds.

Today the trend is to reduce diagnostic labeling, particularly of children with mild disabilities. In addition to the obvious humanitarian reasons, there are some very pragmatic ones. Gillung and Rucker (1977), for example, found that regular educators and some special education teachers had lower expectations for children who were labeled than for children with identical behaviors who were not labeled. A label can thus become a self-fulfilling prophecy. Even if the label were incorrectly assigned, children might eventually behave as the label said they would, simply because people expected them to. Although research on the effect of labeling has yielded mixed results, this at least seems clear: most people tend to view a labeled person differently than a nonlabeled one.

Controversy about labeling reached such proportions in the early 1970s that the eminent psychologist Nicholas Hobbs was commissioned to begin a study called the Project on Classification of Exceptional Children. In his summary report Hobbs (1975) described some problems with current diagnostic categories. His conclusion included the following points: (1) labels are applied imprecisely; (2) labeled children are stigmatized; (3) labels yield too little information for planning; (4) the classification of children with multiple problems in terms of a dominant set of attributes leads to the neglect of other conditions; (5) classification tends to be deviance oriented; (6) classification systems are insensitive to the rapid changes that take place in children; (7) classification of a child can result in the disregard of important etiological (causative) factors.

In favor of labeling, one could argue that administrators need to be able to categorize children in order to qualify for state financial support. Labels can also help focus public attention and legislation on a particular problem. One could argue further that if one set of labels were eliminated it would soon be replaced by another, and that labels are useful in discussing children with similar characteristics.

As much as we might like to do away with them, the use of labels is almost inevitable. Labels and categories are used whenever something is being organized. For example, we organized the information in this text into categorical areas to present it in the most efficient manner.

The important thing to remember is that labeling can have bad effects if used incorrectly. Labels should be used only when necessary. The focus of attention should always be an individual, not a group or class. For special educators the crucial question is, "How should this particular child's strengths and weaknesses influence the teaching strategy I've devised for her?"

NORMALIZATION

Normalization can be defined as the philosophy that all handicapped people should have the opportunity to obtain an existence as close to the normal as possible; making available to them patterns and conditions of everyday life which are as close as possible to the norms and patterns of the mainstream of society

(Nirje, 1969). It evolved in the late 1960s and early 1970s as a result of parental dissatisfaction with the placement of their handicapped children. Many were being placed in isolated residential institutions or in programs in public schools that were segregated from the nonhandicapped.

Normalization has resulted in the greater integration of the handicapped population into business and social activities. Its greatest influence on special education, however, has been the promotion of two practices, deinstitutionalization and mainstreaming.

Deinstitutionalization. Deinstitutionalization refers to the movement to eliminate large institutions, particularly those for the retarded. Wolfensberger (1972), an early advocate of normalization, proposed that long-term, total life care institutions be replaced by small, community-based group homes that would permit residents to participate in local activities and be closer to their families. The establishment of group homes is being encouraged by many parents and special education professionals.

Deinstitutionalization has its problems, however. It is often difficult to find qualified staff for group homes. States that have invested large sums to build or renovate institutions are reluctant to support moves to other facilities. What is more, the establishment of some group homes is opposed by the communities in which they hope to locate. Such community attitudes have prompted articles such as this:

> Despite current-day myths about community resistence to group homes for mentally retarded there's much more community support *for* them than most of us realize.
>
> That's the surprising finding of a study of the myths and facts about community acceptance of group homes, conducted by three researchers from Texas Tech University and reported in a recent *Journal of Rehabilitation.*
>
> Here are highlights of four myths and some facts:
>
> *Myth One*
>
> Handicapped people in group homes are likely to engage in criminal activities. Therefore, keep them out.
>
> *The Facts*
>
> A two-year follow-up of 105 group homes with nearly 2,000 developmentally disabled residents showed that fewer than one percent had ever run afoul of the law.
>
> A study of a community home for retarded juvenile offenders disclosed not a single event that disturbed the neighborhood.
>
> *Myth Two*
>
> If a group home moves into a community, surrounding property values will go downhill.

The Facts

A study of Washington State group homes showed that property values actually rose — because of superior care given to the group homes.

The Crofton House study showed "no significant change" in the asking price of surrounding homes sold before or after the group home opened.

In Stockton, Cal., 200 neighbors of community homes for elderly people were asked whether the homes would have an adverse impact on housing prices. Eighty-four percent thought not.

Myth Three

Group homes create upheavals in neighborhood lifestyles. Everybody's living comfortably in single-family units and along comes this group home. . . .

The Facts

The California Department of Planning found that 93 percent of neighbors of foster homes for elderly people reported no traffic problems; 80 percent, no restrictions on children's play; 75 percent, no unusual activity in the neighborhood.

A Fresno, Cal., study of 20 community homes for mentally retarded people showed that 96 percent of the area's residents had no difficulties at all with their retarded neighbors.

Myth Four

People living near group homes will never come to like their mentally retarded neighbors, no matter how long they live together.

The Facts

A national study of group homes for developmentally disabled people showed that in 89 percent of the cases community opposition decreased after the homes opened.

A Fresno, Cal., study concluded that "once mentally retarded residents have lived in a neighborhood, they tend to be accepted."

A Warning

Utopia still isn't here for mentally handicapped people in group homes. It isn't even around the corner.

But these studies, and others like them, are rays of hope.

Source: Blue Grass Association for Retarded Citizens Newsletter, July, 1979.

Mainstreaming. The second aspect of normalization that relates to special education is a reflection of a provision of PL 94–142. The provision stipulates that handicapped children be educated in "the least restrictive environment." This means that handicapped children are to be educated with nonhandicapped children whenever possible, in as nearly normal an environment as possible. This process is known as mainstreaming.

Exceptional children may be placed in a variety of educational settings, *depending on their educational needs*. The options are illustrated in Figure 1-1. These options are frequently referred to as the "continuum of special education services" or the "cascade of services" (Deno, 1973). You will note that there are ten educational settings listed. The least restrictive setting is at the bottom and the most restrictive is at the top. The arrows on the right illustrate that children should only be placed in a more restrictive setting if it is to their educational advantage; however, they should be moved to a less restrictive setting as soon as they are capable of being educated in that environment. You should also note that, in general, the more restrictive environment will have fewer children, and these will have more severe disabilities.

Levels 1 through 4 are all variations of the regular class. The level 1 class resembles the one you probably attended. In level 2 classes specialists provide consulting services to the regular class teacher but do not work directly with children. In level 3 classes itinerant specialists such as speech therapists and mobility instructors for the blind assist children directly. In level 4 classes children leave the regular classroom for part of the day to obtain direct instruction individually or in small groups from a resource teacher. The resource teacher usually provides consultation help to the regular class teacher as well.

Although mainstreaming does result in more appropriate services for most children, it can cause problems. Some educators have interpreted the "least restrictive environment" provision of PL 94–142 to mean that handicapped children can be placed in regular classes without being provided the support services they need. We think the phrase "most facilitative environment" more clearly embodies the provision's intent.

The use of that phrase alone would not eliminate the problem, of course. The development of criteria for determining the best setting for variously handicapped children is one of the most important tasks facing special educators today. Accordingly, each chapter of this text concludes with a discussion of some of the factors related to educating a given exceptional child in the least restrictive environment.

ASSESSMENT

The many methods of assessing the educational performance of exceptional children can be divided into two categories, informal and formal.

Informal assessment relies on (1) teachers' observations of children's varying skills in different areas, which may be recorded in what are called anecdotal records; and (2) teacher-constructed tests designed to determine whether a child has learned what is being taught.

Formal assessment relies on tests developed by test publishers. These may

Figure 1-1
Continuum of Special Education Services

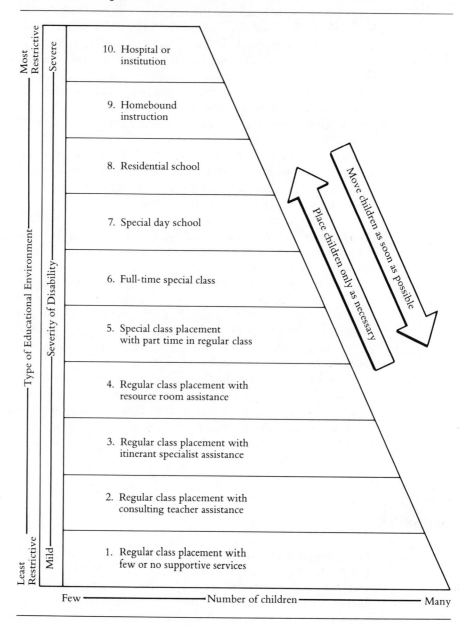

include achievement tests to measure academic attainment; intelligence tests to estimate level of ability, and parent interviews to obtain information about social skills. Language, personality, creativity, physical ability, vocational interest, and other tests may also be warranted.

Most of the tests available from test publishers are *standardized*. This means the test has been given to a large number of people under identical conditions: all people received the same instructions and had the same amount of time to complete the test. In addition, all the tests have been scored the same way. According to test publishers, the test must be administered and scored precisely as the directions indicate for the results to be useful.

Some tests are *norm-referenced*, whereas others are *criterion-referenced*. Norm-referenced tests are those which compare a particular student's performance to that of the norm group, the group of people on which the test was standardized. For example, a score at the 2.0 level in reading on an achievement test indicates that the child reads about as well as most children at the beginning of the second grade. Most of the achievement tests you took in school are norm-referenced tests.

A criterion-referenced test, on the other hand, does not compare one child's performance with that of other children. Instead, the child's performance is compared to some standard, called a criterion. For example, a teacher giving a multiplication test on the sevens tables is interested only in whether a child can correctly multiply the numbers 0 through 10 by 7. The criterion would be 100 percent correct responses. Criterion-referenced tests are used to determine whether a child can perform a particular task, and not how well her performance compares to other children's.

All of the tests mentioned can have varying *validity*. A test is valid when it measures what it purports to measure. Standardization alone does not ensure validity. The test administration manual for publisher-made tests usually includes information about test validity; it should be studied before test results are interpreted.

The assessment of most exceptional children requires the use of formal and informal techniques, standardized and teacher-made tests, and norm- and criterion-referenced tests. Children are assessed for two primary purposes: (1) for identification, to determine who needs special education services; and (2) for teaching, to determine what and how a child should be taught.

Assessment for Identification. For most children in school, assessment for identification begins with the regular classroom teacher. If the teacher notices a child is doing very poorly or especially well in a particular area, the child may be referred to a specialist for in-depth assessment. The specialists are selected on the basis of the child's suspected problem and may include educational diagnosticians, psychologists, physicians, speech-language pathologists, or others.

Many schools and health agencies prefer not to rely exclusively on teachers to discover exceptional children; there is always a chance that someone will be missed. As a result, systematic procedures to *screen* children have been developed. The vision screening program most schools conduct is a good example. In this program children are given a quick, easy eye examination every two years or so. When the results show that a child may have a problem, she is referred to a vision specialist. The best identification programs rely on a combination of teacher observation and screening.

Once a child is referred, the specialist determines whether she meets the eligibility criteria for one of the categories of special education services. If she does, the child is labeled. For example, if the child meets the criteria for the category of learning disabilities, she is labeled a learning disabled child.

Whereas a child's visual acuity, hearing, physical ability, and speech can be measured fairly accurately, traits such as intelligence, personality, emotional stability, academic achievement, social adjustment, and creativity are very difficult to assess. One reason is that many of the tests used to identify them are imprecise. Tests are sometimes used inappropriately, as well. For example, the administration of an English IQ test to a child whose primary language is Spanish may produce a very low IQ score, one that does not accurately reflect the child's ability to perform academic tasks. The use of inappropriate tests and testing practices such as this has resulted in laws forbidding the identification and placement of children on the basis of a single test score. Ideally, assessment for identification should be based on the results of a number of tests, in combination with the anecdotal records of teachers, the observations of parents, and the findings of physicians and other professionals who come in contact with the child.

Assessment for Teaching. The purpose of assessment for teaching is to provide information useful in planning what to teach (content) and how to teach it (methods).

In this kind of assessment, teacher-made tests and observations are generally more helpful than the more sophisticated standardized tests. Similarly, a teacher is more likely to use a teacher-made or commercial criterion-referenced test than a norm-referenced test. This may surprise you, but which would help you *teach* a child best — an hour-long IQ test or a five-minute session in which the child was asked to identify the initial consonants of words presented on flash cards? The IQ score would indicate the child's intellectual ability relative to that of a group of children of the same chronological age. The flash card test, on the other hand, would indicate which consonants the child could pronounce and which needed to be taught. What's more, by paying careful attention to the type of errors the child makes, the teacher should get some insight into how the consonants the child didn't know should be taught.

Effective teachers generally assess children regularly, not just at fixed times of the year such as at the beginning and end of the grading period. It is best to adopt the "test-teach-test" principle, according to which a concept is assessed, taught, and then reassessed. If the concept has been learned, the teacher can move on. If not, the concept is taught again — perhaps using different methods after the teacher has determined why the child did not learn during the first instructional sequence. For additional information on assessment you may want to refer to Wallace and Larsen (1978).

Once again we want to emphasize that the teacher should not rely solely on formal test data to make educational decisions. Although the data may provide insight into a child's strengths and weaknesses, they can also be imprecise and inaccurate. They should be considered only in conjunction with observations of the child in the classroom. Ideally, the assessment process should result in an individualized education program such as the one discussed in the section immediately following.

INDIVIDUALIZED INSTRUCTION

One of the most important provisions of PL 94–142 requires that an individual education program be developed for each child receiving special education services. The IEP, as it is called, is the foundation on which the child's education is built. It is a written document developed by a committee of school personnel, at least one of the parents, and when appropriate the child himself. It must include the following:

1. A statement of the child's present levels of educational performance.
2. A statement of annual goals — to be achieved by the end of the school year — including short-term instructional objectives.
3. A statement of the specific special education and related services to be provided to the child, and of the extent of the child's participation in regular education environments.
4. The projected date for initiation of services and the anticipated duration of services.
5. Objective criteria, evaluation procedures, and schedules for determining at least once a year whether short-term instructional objectives are being achieved.

Figure 1-2 shows a sample IEP. Most IEPs are far less detailed than this sample, largely because the principals, special educators, parents, and others who generate them have trouble finding time to develop them this completely. This shouldn't surprise you if you remember that IEPs must be written for *all* children receiving special education services, both those being newly admitted and those already enrolled. In addition, IEPs must be reviewed and revised at least once a year.

Figure 1–2
A Sample Individual Education Program

Individual Education Program

Date _January 5_

(1) Student	(2) Committee		(3) Present Level of Educational Functioning	(4) Annual Goal Statements	(5) Instructional Objectives	(6) Objective Criteria and Evaluation

(1) Student

Name: Joe S.

School: Tall Trees Elementary

Grade: 5-7

Current Placement: Regular class

Date of Birth: 11/4/64   Age: 13-1

(2) Committee

Name	Position	Initial
Mr. Havlichek	Principal	
Mr. White	Regular Teacher	
Mrs. Jones	Regular Teacher	
Mrs. Green	Resource Teacher	
Mrs. S.	Parent	

IEP From _1/20/77_ To _6/1/77_

(3) Present Level of Educational Functioning

MATH

Strengths

Can successfully compute 3-digit addition and subtraction facts without regrouping. Can complete an oral or written sequence of 4 digit numbers.

Weaknesses

Frequently makes computational errors on problems with which he has had a great deal of experience.
Cannot successfully compute division problems.

(4) Annual Goal Statements

MATH

1. To complete an oral or written sequence of 5-digit numbers with 0 in 10's, 100's or 1000's place.
2. To correctly add a 3-digit plus a 3-digit number with carrying in the 10's and 100's place.

(5) Instructional Objectives

MATH

1. Will complete oral and written sequence with 4, 5-digit number with no zeroes, with 90% accuracy.
2. Will complete oral and written sequence with 4-digit numbers with 0 in the 10's place and 0 in the 100's place, with 90% accuracy.
3. Will complete an oral and written sequence of 5-digit numbers with 0 in 10's place, 0 in 100's place and 0 in 1000's place. These tasks must be completed, with 90% accuracy.
4. Solves addition problems of 1-digit plus 2-digit numbers with carrying, with 90% accuracy.
5. Solves addition problems of 2-digit plus 2-digit numbers with carrying, with 90% accuracy.

(6) Objective Criteria and Evaluation

MATH

1. Key math at beginning and end of this 2-month period
2. Teacher-made CRT
3. Teacher observation

Individual Education Program cont'd.

Present Level of Intellectual Functioning	Annual Goal Statements	Instructional Objectives	Objective Criteria and Evaluation
SCIENCE Strengths Demonstrates knowledge about plants through discussion and by successful development of small plants from seeds. Demonstrates great enthusiasm and curiosity for science by listening well and following verbal instructions correctly. Weaknesses Ability in carrying out experiments is restricted by inability to read instructions.	SCIENCE 1. Joe will be able to classify different types of trees correctly. 2. Joe will be able to classify different types of plants (flowering) and discuss reproduction.	SCIENCE 1. Joe will identify characteristics of evergreen trees, with 90% accuracy. 2. Joe will identify characteristics of deciduous trees, with 90% accuracy. 3. Joe will classify trees into reproduction type: (a) self-pollination and (b) pollination through the air from another plant, with 90% accuracy. 4. Joe will classify different types of flowering plants: (a) flowering trees; (b) flowering bushes; and (c) flowers, with 90% accuracy. 5. Joe will classify how different types of flowering plants reproduce: (a) self-pollination; (b) pollination through air from another plant; (c) bulbs, with 90% accuracy.	SCIENCE Teacher-made CRT Observation Discussion Discussion Discussion
PHYS. ED. Strengths Demonstrates highly developed gross motor coordination by successfully playing in team games. Weaknesses Writes poorly and illegibly at times; fine motor skills need practice.	PHYS. ED. 1. Joe will be able to participate successfully in the team game of volleyball. 2. Joe will be able to identify the rules of this game correctly.	PHYS. ED. 1. Joe will demonstrate proficiency with the underhand serve by serving it over the net into the opposing court on 5 out of 10 trials. 2. Joe will return a volley by using the two hand underhand pass or the two hand overhand pass on 5 out of 10 trials. 3. Joe will demonstrate the ability to score a game correctly by doing so in a game situation, with 90% accuracy. 4. Joe will answer correctly 6 out of 9 questions about the 9 rules of the game.	PHYS. ED. Teacher-made tests Observation
SOCIAL COMPETENCE Strengths Joins in team games with enthusiasm. Is able to cooperate with team members appropriately during team games. Weaknesses Demonstrates poor self-concept by making derogatory statements about himself. Lacks respect for other classmates doing quiet work periods by talking out loud. Demonstrates lack of self-discipline with out-of-seat behaviors during work periods.	SOCIAL COMPETENCE 1. Joe will develop desirable behaviors (good manners, responsibility & self-discipline) such that he is able to interact appropriately with teachers & peers. 2. Joe will increase positive interpersonal behavior such that he is able to make friends in his class.	SOCIAL COMPETENCE 1. Joe will give examples of and use socially acceptable language 90% of the time. 2. Joe will give rules of and practice etiquette in these situations: in the classroom, in cafeteria, on playground, as a guest, in a store, 90% of the time. 3. Joe will display self-discipline when placed in a tempting situation (e.g., finishing work before play, returning or reporting found articles) 90% of the time. 4. Joe will demonstrate that he can be trusted by successfully completing a task without delay or persuasion 90% of the time.	SOCIAL COMPETENCE Observation Teacher-made written tests Discussion with teacher Role play Observation

Figure 1-2 (continued)
A Sample Individual Education Program

Present Level of Intellectual Functioning	Annual Goal Statements	Instructional Objectives	Objective Criteria and Evaluation
	3. Joe will develop a more positive self-concept by increasing his success experiences.	5. Joe will give 6 examples of good friendship while practicing new and positive behaviors toward peers during 80% of the school day.	Teacher-made tests
		6. Joe will discuss and give 5 examples of good and bad family relations between parents & children with 80% accuracy.	Role play and discussion.
READING Strengths Can identify the main idea of a paragraph from a 2nd grade reader. Comprehends written reading material at 2nd grade level. Reads 90% of words from Durrell Reading List at 2nd grade level. Weaknesses Cannot identify the meaning of certain words after having read them in a sentence. Unable to sound out an unknown word successfully when seeing it for the first time. Has difficulty with the comprehension skills of sequencing and inferring details when reading 2nd grade material.	READING 1. Joe will read paragraphs correctly and demonstrate comprehension skills. 2. Joe will demonstrate understanding of the visual clues to long & short vowel sounds by identifying correctly letters that are clues to vowel sounds.	READING 1. Given paragraphs and matching sets of multiple choice questions, he will complete the questions with 90% accuracy. 2. Given a 3-paragraph story, he will number the sentences in the order in which they sequentially occurred. 3. Given a paragraph containing clues to character's emotions, he will identify the emotions of the character correctly. 4. Will complete study sheets on O, E, and Y in final syllable or end of word, with 90% accuracy. 5. Will complete study sheets on ai, ay, ea, ei, ie, oa, and oe in the accented syllable, with 90% accuracy. 6. Will complete study sheets on identifying one consonant preceding a final ie, with 90% accuracy.	READING Teacher-made questions Teacher-made material Teacher-made material Teacher-made CRT Teacher-made CRT Teacher-made CRT

Individual Education Program cont'd.

(7) Educational Services to Be Provided

Services Required	Date Initiated	Duration of Service	Individual Responsible for the Service
Regular Reading—Adapt	4/10/77	6/1/77	Mrs. Jones
Resource Room	4/10/77	6/1/77	Mrs. Green
Counselor Consultant	To be arranged		Not available at present

Extent of time in the regular education program:　　60% increasing to 80%

Justification of the educational placement:

It is felt that the structure of the resource room can best meet the goals stated for Joe; especially coordinated with the regular classroom.

It is also felt that Joe could profit enormously from talking with a counselor. He needs someone with whom to talk and with whom he can share his feelings.

(8) I have had the opportunity to participate in the development of the Individual Education Program.
I agree with the Individual Education Program　( )
I disagree with the Individual Education Program　( )

_____
Parent's Signature

CULTURAL DIVERSITY

We often find a disproportionately large number of children from minority groups in programs for exceptional children. Martin (c. 1976), for example, reported the results of a 1973 study of the placement of blacks, Spanish-surnamed Americans, Asian Americans, and American Indians in 2908 school districts. The survey, which represented almost half the school-age population of the United States, indicated that 37 percent of those enrolled in special education programs were from minorities. The study also found that

> Minority children participate in educable mentally retarded programs at a rate that is 62 percent higher than would normally be expected. Their participation in trainable mentally handicapped programs was 20 percent higher and in other special education 34 percent higher. Thus for total special education, the rate of minority representation was 35 percent higher than would normally be expected [p. 6].

This does not mean that minority children are handicapped more frequently than other children. It is a reflection, rather, of both improper assessment techniques and diagnoses, and, in some cases, of actual cultural or ethnic differences in behavior or performance expectations. We mentioned earlier, for example, that many students were placed in special education programs because they did not perform well on standardized tests administered in a language they did not understand. As you remember, this resulted in federal legislation requiring that tests for special education placement be given in the child's native language.

The enactment of that legislation reflects the increased emphasis of the last twenty years on meeting the educational needs of children from diverse cultural groups. The change was brought about by a variety of factors. The civil rights movement of the 1960s and the Johnson administration's War on Poverty focused attention on the problems of minorities. Shifting populations raised the issue of busing. More members of minorities were elected to school boards and other public offices. Interesting multicultural education was also stimulated by the increasing academic interest in the sociology, anthropology, and linguistics of various cultural groups (Taylor, 1973).

But what exactly is a cultural group? According to Aragon (1973), members of a cultural group share the same characteristics in five areas: (1) language and communication, (2) diet and food preparation customs, (3) dress, (4) socialization patterns, particularly within families, and (5) values, beliefs, and ethics. When a child's cultural orientation differs from that of her school's personnel, a cultural conflict exists. The child is usually the loser.

Cultural conflicts based on language are the most evident and have the most serious consequences. For example, Taylor (1973) suggested some questions a teacher should consider when dealing with the language of some black students:

— Is language used to make inaccurate statements about cultures and miseducate children?
— What is the mismatch between the language accepted by schools and the language that a substantial portion of black children bring to schools?
— What is the impact of language diversity on the performance of black children on standardized tests?
— How does language diversity affect the attitudes of teachers?
— Is an awareness of language diversity reflected in educational materials?
— [To what extent are] inaccurate diagnoses . . . related to an ignorance of the unique linguistic features of large numbers of blacks? [p. 39].

The point to be emphasized is that educators should be familiar with and sensitive to the special needs of children from different cultures. Extra care is especially important in interpreting test data on children not represented in the group on which the test was standardized. For example, if there were no Chicano children in the norm group of a reading test you are using, you should view with caution the test scores of any Chicano children in your class. If you use criterion-referenced tests, you should be certain your assessment is not biased by conflicts between the criterion you establish and the culture of the child being tested.

CHILD ABUSE AND NEGLECT

In Section 3 of the Child Abuse Prevention and Treatment Act (PL 93–247), child abuse and neglect are defined as "the physical or mental injury, sexual abuse, negligent treatment, or maltreatment of a child under the age of eighteen by a person who is responsible for the child's welfare under circumstances which indicate that the child's health or welfare is harmed or threatened thereby." Some symptoms that might indicate abuse or neglect have been described by Kline (1977) and are shown in Chart 1-2. (He also published a checklist worth examining if you want to develop a program to combat child abuse and neglect in a school system.) It is important to note that only nonaccidental or deliberate injuries are considered abusive.

Approximately 1 million children are abused, neglected, or sexually molested each year, according to the National Center for Child Abuse and Neglect. The causes are hard to determine. Child abusers come from all income levels, geographic areas, family settings, religious backgrounds, ethnic groups, and residential environments. They do not necessarily use drugs or alcohol.

There is one factor that seems related to child abuse: many child abusers were themselves abused as children. And, although a cause-effect sequence has not been demonstrated, Kline has reported a clear relationship between child abuse and

Chart 1-2
Symptoms of Abuse and Neglect

Symptoms of Abuse	*Symptoms of Neglect*
Evidence of repeated injury	Clothing inappropriate for weather
New injuries before previous ones have healed	Torn, tattered, unwashed clothing
Frequent complaints of abdominal pain	Poor skin hygiene
Evidence of bruises	Rejection by other children because of body odor
Bruises of different ages	Need for glasses, dental work, hearing aid, or other
Welts	health services
Wounds, cuts, or punctures	Lack of proper nourishment
Scalding liquid burns with well-defined parameters	Consistent tiredness or sleepiness in class
Caustic burns	Consistent, very early school arrival
Frostbite	Frequent absenteeism or chronic tardiness
Cigarette burns	Tendency to hang around school after dismissal

handicapping conditions. His research found that of children judged to be abused or neglected, 27 percent were subsequently enrolled in special education classes. Many of these children had symptoms resembling those of behavior disorders. PL 94-142 programs designed to locate handicapped children will probably identify a number of children who have been abused or neglected.

Obviously, cases of child abuse should be identified and reported as soon as possible to treat existing injuries and to ensure that the child is protected from further injury. Teachers have not only humane and professional responsibilities to report possible cases of abuse; in at least thirty-six states they have a legal responsibility as well. In the other states, persons or institutions providing social services are similarly obliged. Failure to report a suspected case is a misdemeanor in nearly half the states (Kline, 1977).

You should note, however, that providing proof of abuse is not the responsibility of the teacher; that is done by the agency that receives the report. In fact, every state except Oklahoma provides immunity from civil or criminal liability to those who report cases in good faith (Kline, 1977).

ACCESS TO THE COMMUNITY

Most of us can do everyday things like open doors, climb stairs, answer the phone, and use the lavatory without giving it a thought. But consider the problems you would face in these situations:

— You are blind and must find a certain office or house number.

— You are in a wheelchair and must get into a building that has only stairs and revolving doors, or you are in an elevator and cannot reach the button for the floor you want.
— You are on crutches and can't carry your groceries or push a grocery cart.

As you can see, tasks most of us accomplish easily can present impenetrable barriers to the handicapped. Some obstacles just cause minor inconveniences — being late for an appointment, perhaps. Others can have grave consequences. What if you are deaf and can't hear the fire alarm in your apartment building?

The situation is improving, however. As we mentioned earlier, Section 504 required that buildings built in part with federal funds be accessible to the handicapped. Colleges and universities, too, are prohibited from discriminating against the handicapped; many are renovating their physical plants to give the handicapped access to previously inaccessible facilities.

With respect to school programs, it is important to remember that *all parts* of all buildings need not be accessible; rather, all *programs* must be accessible. Thus, access to a second-floor science class need not be provided to a student in a wheelchair. The science class may, however, have to be moved to the first floor to make the science program accessible to her.

The Council for Exceptional Children publishes a useful resource for planning facilities for handicapped children (Aiello, 1976). In it are listed a number of other resources that deal with barrier-free environments.

Heightened sensitivity to the needs of the handicapped is also reflected in the use of the international symbol of access for the handicapped (Figure 1-3A).

Figure 1-3

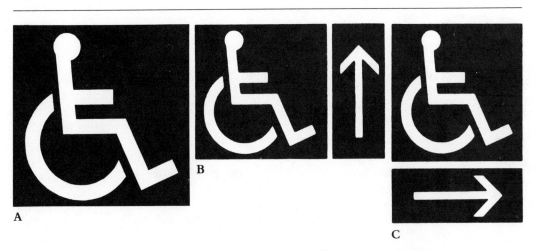

Figure 1-4

You've probably seen it along highways, where it is used to indicate restrooms equipped for the disabled. You may also have seen the signs in Figure 1-3B and C, which indicate the route a handicapped person should take to enter or leave a building. The sign in Figure 1-3B means "straight ahead," whereas the one in Figure 1-3C means turn right.

What do you think the signs in Figure 1-4 represent? The first indicates a ramp; the second, a telephone; the third, parking; and the fourth, an elevator accessible to the handicapped.

Although few people would argue that access for the handicapped is undesirable, it is controversial because it is so expensive. For example, Wieck (1979) reported that it cost $15,000 to outfit a bus with a lift or ramp. High costs such as this influenced the National Council of Mayors' decision to state their preference for alternative services, such as dial-a-van. Some groups of handicapped have gone to court to force full access to buses.

Wieck also reported that there were 404,000 people in wheelchairs in urban areas in 1979 and that the Department of Transportation estimated the cost of providing full access to buses, subways, railcars, and trolleys at $1.7 billion. This figure was challenged by the American Public Transportation Association, which claimed it would cost $3–6 billion just to adapt the subway systems of nine major cities. Whichever figure you accept, the cost of providing access is staggering.

PROBE 1-4
Issues in Special Education

1. Give three reasons why labels should be deemphasized.

   a. _____

   b. _____

   c. _____

2. Name five items included in an IEP.

   a. _____

   b. _____

   c. _____

   d. _____

   e. _____

3. Describe the instructional setting alternatives of the continuum of services model.

   Setting 1 _____

   Setting 2 _____

   Setting 3 _____

   Setting 4 _____

   Setting 5 _____

   Setting 6 _____

   Setting 7 _____

   Setting 8 _____

Setting 9 _____

Setting 10 _____

4. Mainstreaming is _____

_____.

5. The move to small-group homes from large residential facilities is called

_____.

6. T   F   Mildly handicapped children should always be educated in regular classes.

7. T   F   There are relatively more handicapped children in minority cultures than there are in the general population.

8. T   F   In most states teachers have a legal responsibility to report suspected cases of child abuse and neglect.

9. T   F   Although there may be architectural barriers in a given school, all programs must be accessible to the handicapped.

10. List 3 symptoms of child abuse.

   a. _____

   b. _____

   c. _____

11. List 3 symptoms of child neglect.

   a. _____

   b. _____

   c. _____

SUMMARY

1. Special education is individually planned instruction designed to respond to the unique characteristics of children who have needs that cannot be met by the standard school curriculum.
2. In addition to the gifted and talented, the category of exceptional children

includes those with communication disorders, hearing disorders, visual impairments, physical disabilities, mental retardation, learning disabilities, behavior disorders, and multiple handicaps.

3. Handicaps are the result of a person's interaction with the environment. A child with an impairment or disability may be handicapped in some situations but not in others.
4. It is estimated that between 10 and 15 percent of the children under the age of twenty-one need special education services. Thus, there are approximately 8 million handicapped children and 1.5 million gifted children in the United States.
5. In the past the handicapped have sometimes been cared for and sometimes abused and persecuted. The development of genuinely beneficial programs began in 1950 with the founding of the National Association for Retarded Children.
6. Litigation has resulted in court determinations that affirm the right of all handicapped children to a publicly supported education.
7. Section 504 of the Rehabilitation Act of 1973 prohibits discrimination against the handicapped in employment, accessibility to facilities, education, and other social services. It is essentially civil rights legislation for the handicapped.
8. Public Law 94–142 guarantees a free and appropriate public education to all handicapped children.
9. The assignment of labels to exceptional children can lead to improper practices and should be avoided whenever possible.
10. Deinstitutionalization and mainstreaming are efforts to provide the handicapped with opportunities and environments that resemble those normal for the nonhandicapped.
11. Exceptional children are assessed to identify those who need special education programs and to determine where instruction should be begun. Assessment is a difficult process that often yields imprecise results.
12. Exceptional children are educated in a variety of environments, including regular classrooms, resource rooms, special schools, residential facilities, homes, and hospitals. It is best to place the child in the least restrictive educational environment that meets the child's needs.
13. An individualized educational program must be developed for every exceptional child who is enrolled in a publicly supported educational setting.
14. Special educators should be particularly sensitive to the unique characteristics and needs of exceptional children from minority cultures.
15. There are many abused and neglected children in special education programs. Teachers need to be particularly alert for signs of child abuse and neglect.
16. Efforts are being intensified to remove architectural barriers that prevent people with physical disabilities from gaining access to community facilities.

TASK SHEET 1
Simulation of Disability

Select one of the following simulations of disabilities and perform the required tasks for a minimum of three hours. *Do not* spend the majority of this time resting or studying, or you will defeat the purpose of the simulation.

1. *Hearing Impairment:* Wear a pair of foam rubber ear plugs. During this simulation you should attempt to communicate with someone. Also try to watch part of a TV show with the sound turned off. Spend a portion of your time outdoors.
2. *Blindness:* Blindfold yourself so that you can see no light. Try to perform several routine tasks, including grooming, dressing, and eating. Make a brief venture out of doors, but take a companion with you to protect you from injury.
3. *Physical Disability:* Do *one* of the following:
   a. Wrap your hands so that you cannot use your fingers.
   b. Use a pair of crutches.
   c. Spend several hours in a wheelchair.
   d. Restrain your dominant arm by tying your wrist to your belt or waist. During the above simulations, attempt tasks that you perform every day, such as preparing food, eating, dressing, grooming, performing your job, studying, etc.

Following this experience, write a brief report. It should include descriptions of the following:

1. The disability you selected.
2. The activities you engaged in during the simulation.
3. The things you could do without difficulty during the simulation.
4. The problems you encountered and how you attempted to solve them.
5. The feelings you had while simulating the disability.
6. The effect that this experience had on you.

Probe Answers

Probe 1-1

1. Components of the definition should include:
   —instruction that is part of the regular education program
   —instruction that is individually designed to meet the needs of exceptional children
   —designed for children whose needs cannot be met by the regular school curriculum
   —may call for supportive services
2. False
3. Disability refers to reduction of function or absence of a particular body part or organ; handicap refers to problems a disabled person may have as a result of interacting with the environment.

4. Incidence includes all persons who may have a condition during their lifetime; prevalence includes only those who have the condition at a specific point in time.
5. 8 million; 1.5 million

Probe 1-2

1. 1. c;   2. e;   3. a;   4. b;   5. d;   6. h;   7. g
2. a. Education should be individualized.
   b. Tasks should be sequenced from easy to difficult.
   c. Students should be active learners.
   d. Learning environments should be structured.
3. False
4. False
5. National Association for Retarded Citizens (NARC)
6. PARC verified that mentally retarded children were entitled to a publicly supported education. Mills extended this right to all exceptional children.

Probe 1-3

1. A law is made by elected representatives and generally represents broad policy. A regulation is written by appointed officials and specifies the procedures to be followed in the implementation of a law.
2. a. 504;   b. 94–142;   c. 94–142;   d. 504;   e. 504;   f. 94–142;   g. 504;   h. 504;   i. 94–142
3. False
4. b

Probe 1-4

1. a. Labels lower the expectations of teachers.
   b. Labels have little relevance for educational practice.
   c. Children do not fit neatly into categories.
2. Any 5 of the following:
   a. statement of child's level of performance
   b. annual goals
   c. short-term objectives
   d. time spent in regular education environments

   e. related services required
   f. dates for services
   g. procedures for evaluation
3. 1. regular class placement with little or no supportive services
   2. regular class placement with consulting teacher assistance
   3. regular class placement with itinerant specialist assistance
   4. regular class placement with resource room assistance
   5. special class placement with part time in regular class
   6. full-time special class
   7. special day school
   8. residential school
   9. homebound instruction
   10. hospital or institution
4. The educational placement of the child in the least restrictive environment. Mainstreaming does not mean always placing exceptional children in regular classes.
5. de-institutionalization
6. False
7. False
8. True
9. True
10. Any 3 of the following:
    a. bruises, cuts, welts, or punctures
    b. new injuries before previous ones have healed
    c. frostbite
    d. abdominal pain
    e. cigarette, caustic, or scalding liquid burns
11. Any 3 of the following:
    a. clothing that is inappropriate for the weather
    b. torn, tattered, unwashed clothing
    c. body odor/poor skin hygiene
    d. need for glasses, hearing aid, or other health services
    e. lack of proper nourishment
    f. tiredness or sluggishness in class
    g. consistent early arrival or tendency to stay at school after dismissal
    h. frequent absenteeism or chronic tardiness

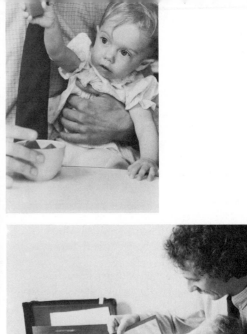

Early identification of children's problems greatly increases the chances of correcting them through education or medical treatment. From birth, this sixteen-month-old girl had feeding problems that resulted in her very small stature. Her parents were concerned about whether other areas of development were also affected.

Here, the examiner is administering tasks from the Bayley Scales of Infant Development. The tasks assess psychomotor development, social responsiveness, gross and fine motor functioning, language development, and conceptual abilities.

The child's performance was compared to norms for infants and toddlers between two and thirty months old. Although she was physically small, it was found that her psychomotor skills were developing normally. Had her performance been significantly below the norms, suggestions would have been made for activities to stimulate her development.

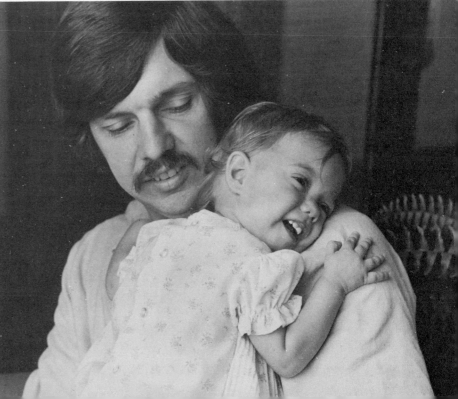

Robbie's mother first noticed his hearing impairment when he was ten months old. At the mother-infant class at the preschool for the hearing impaired, she learned to work with Robbie at home. From the time he was a year old, Robbie wore two hearing aids. He learned to understand and use language. When Robbie entered kindergarten, he had a vocabulary of about 300 words.

Ann was hospitalized for meningitis at age three. After she returned home, she was more quiet. Instead of full sentences, she now used fragments. Six months later, her language had all but disappeared. Her parents bought her a hearing aid, but they never learned to work with her. Ann did not talk to her parents, and they believed she did not listen. After Ann tried to flush her hearing aid down the toilet, her parents took it away from her. When she entered kindergarten, Ann had no speaking vocabulary.

During Paige's birth brain damage occurred, resulting in cerebral palsy. As Paige developed, she appeared to understand events in her environment, but she did not speak clearly and had great difficulty grasping and moving. Paige was enrolled in a preschool program operated by the local Easter Seal Society, where she was taught self-help skills and given physical therapy and special speech instruction. Although she continued to have difficulty speaking and moving, she was enrolled in kindergarten, where she was able to succeed with the support of continued physical therapy and special education.

Scott was diagnosed as having Down's syndrome. The parents desperately searched for services for him, but their small town could not provide assistance. Scott's parents placed him in a residential institution for the mentally retarded. Scott was confined to a crib and received very little stimulation. During the parents' visits, Scott became increasingly less communicative. He had no speech or language, no bowel or bladder control, and spent most of his time rocking back and forth, biting his fingers, and screeching.

2
Early Childhood Education

Susan M. Kershman

Susan M. Kershman is an Assistant Professor in the Department of Special Education and Coordinator for the Program in Education of the Visually Handicapped at Temple University in Philadelphia. She is an experienced teacher of the deaf and of the blind and former program director of a deaf-blind early intervention program. Dr. Kershman received her PhD (1975) in special education from the University of Pittsburgh.

The education of exceptional children in the age range from birth to five or six is currently undergoing great changes. Like Robbie and Paige in the anecdotes on the previous page, more young exceptional children and their families are receiving services than ever before. Unfortunately, however, there are still many like Ann and Scott who do not receive appropriate services. In fact, approximately three-fourths of the handicapped preschoolers who need services do not receive them (Ackerman and Moore, 1976).

Why are so few handicapped preschoolers served? There are several reasons: funds are lacking, trained personnel are scarce, and decision makers are often badly informed. Public attitudes are also important; for example, it used to be widely believed that all young children should be kept at home with their mothers, rather than being placed in day care or educational settings. Since the 1930s however, our understanding of the effectiveness of early intervention has grown tremendously. There is now little doubt that exceptional children can benefit from educational intervention begun as soon as a problem is diagnosed. As a result, additional funds are being made available and personnel are being educated to work specifically with exceptional preschoolers. But until the rationale for early education is broadly understood and the effectiveness of programs demonstrated, there won't be universal support for the education of exceptional children in their first few years of life.

FACTORS INFLUENCING DEVELOPMENT OF EARLY CHILDHOOD PROGRAMS

> **You should be able to describe factors that have contributed to the development of early childhood education of exceptional children.**

Among the many factors that have influenced the development of early childhood special education programs, three stand out. These factors are (1) research, (2) the contributions of professionals, and (3) federal legislation.

RESEARCH STUDIES

One of the most dramatic studies of the long-range effectiveness of early intervention was designed by Skeels and Dye (1939) and followed up by Skeels (1966). The plan for the study came from an accidental discovery of IQ gains in two young "hopeless" children, institutionalized with older retarded women who cared for them and played with them. An experimental group of thirteen young children was transferred from an orphanage to the institution, while a control group of twelve babies in the same age and IQ range remained at the orphanage. The older retarded women on the ward stimulated and cared for the young children in the experimental group. A year and a half later the IQs of the experimental group children had gained about twenty-eight points. Those of the control group had lost about twenty-six points. At the time that these results were published, the Skeels and Dye study was severely criticized, but it is recognized today as one of the earliest empirical studies of the effectiveness of early intervention.

Many years later Skeels reported on what had happened to the two groups of children. Of the experimental group of thirteen, all were self-supporting adults. Their median level of education was twelfth grade. Four persons from this group had attended one or more years of college, and one had graduate training. Of the original control group of twelve, four were still wards of an institution, and one had died in adolescence. The median level of education for the control group was third grade. Of the 50 percent employed, all but one were unskilled laborers.

Another important early study was conducted by Kirk (1958). For this study two groups of mentally retarded institutionalized children between three and five years of age, with IQs between 40 and 60, were compared. The experimental group was given two years of preschool training, while the control group was not trained. Both groups were retested two years after the preschool training had ended. The trained group had accelerated in mental and social maturity, but the control group's scores had dropped on all tests.

The results of these studies suggest the importance of early experiences on a child's development. The failure to provide early stimulation can lead not just to a developmental standstill, but to real regression. In both studies children in the control groups did not remain at the level of achievement they started with but actually grew worse in comparison with other children of the same age.

As we will explain, an early beginning to educational services for young exceptional children and their families is important in all categories of special education.

Hearing Impaired. By far the most serious effect of early significant hearing impairment is that it limits language development. The early years are a critical period for language learning; if hearing impairment is not detected and special education not begun, the handicapping potential of hearing impairment is compounded. If, during the early years, hearing impaired children do not learn to use and understand language, their intellectual and educational growth is retarded (Horton, 1976).

Visually Impaired. Infants who are blind from birth often have problems relating to adults and to objects. Blindness also delays control of the hands and gross motor development. Studies have indicated that blind children who received early education services show smaller developmental delays than other blind children (Adelson and Fraiberg, 1975, Fraiberg, 1975).

Physically Disabled. Scherzer (1974) noted that, although cerebral palsy is a difficult condition to diagnose in infants, it is no longer acceptable to adopt a "wait and see" policy before planning intervention. Both parents and physical therapists need to be included in the educational programs for such children. The value of such programs was demonstrated by Koch (1958), who did a follow-up study of cerebral palsied children who had participated in a nursery school program. His results showed that better long-term results were achieved by children who had early treatment than by those for whom treatment was postponed.

Mentally Retarded. LaCrosse (1976) stated that sending mentally retarded children to nursery school can encourage them to enter group activities at a time when their differences from the normal group are not very distinct or severe, and when society is more willing to accept them. Parent-child relationships are likely to improve as young mentally retarded children become less dependent, less fearful, and less burdensome.

The early studies of mentally retarded children (Kirk, 1958; Skeels, 1966;

Skeels and Dye, 1939) provide convincing evidence of the effectiveness of early education in raising IQ scores and improving social behavior. More recently the multidisciplinary preschool program for Down's syndrome children at the University of Washington has provided a model of effective early childhood educational practices for children whose mental retardation stems from an organic cause. In this program each child serves as her own control; current performances are compared to earlier progress, so that all identified children may participate fully. The mean developmental lag was reduced from 21 to 5.6 months for children in the program, and participating children mastered designated tasks as well (Hayden and Dmitriev, 1975). In 1977 Hayden, Morris, and Bailey reported that 34 percent of the program's graduates were doing well in their regular public school classes. This program has clearly established not only the effectiveness of early and continuous education, but also its cost effectiveness and efficiency in terms of the children's later placements.

Learning Disabled. Although it has been argued that identifying learning disabled children at an early age may lead to unnecessary labeling and stigmatizing (Hayden and Edgar, 1977), there have been efforts to define the characteristics of this population and begin early intervention (Keogh, 1970). Learning disabilities are suspected when a written or spoken language problem has no obvious cause, such as deafness or mental retardation. Most young children are not expected to read, spell, or do arithmetic, but their problems may be no less apparent in their thinking, talking, or listening (Wallace and McLaughlin, 1975).

Early childhood education may eliminate or reduce the severity of specific learning disabilities before children are required to learn academic subjects (Wallace and McLaughlin, 1975). But despite the need for services, especially for children with severe problems, programs for children with early symptoms of learning disabilities are very scarce.

Behavior Disordered. Children who have behavior disorders present particular difficulties at home. For this reason, early intervention programs for these children place a special emphasis on the role of parents. One such program is at the Rutland Center in Athens, Georgia. In this program parents are provided information about the children's progress and needs and assisted in implementing complementary home programs (Shearer and Shearer, 1977). Of the graduates from this program, 65 percent were placed in regular elementary classes and the remainder were placed in nurseries, kindergartens, and special classes (Karnes and Zehrbach, 1977a).

Multiply Handicapped. Appell (1977) reported that deaf-blind children are extremely vulnerable to developmental delay. Without early diagnosis and intervention most will never achieve their full potential. Despite the expense and other requirements of early instruction Appell stated, "Saving an infant and family in crisis from further deprivation, dissolution and disruption more than justifies the cost and the effort expended" (p. 163).

Gifted. Efforts to help gifted children achieve to the extent of their abilities are just as important as efforts to help other exceptional children. Because children establish their individuality and a strong healthy identity in their early years (Torrance, 1974), educational services should be begun as soon as children reveal their distinctiveness. Gifted children among the handicapped may be particularly hard to identify, but the results of serving them may be outstanding.

In addition to the studies just mentioned, early childhood education for exceptional children also provides assistance and support to parents of the children. They can receive emotional support from other parents, models for working with their own children, and specific suggestions for ways that they can assist in the education of their children.

CONTRIBUTING INDIVIDUALS

Many people from the areas of child development and psychology have contributed to the development of early childhood programs for all children. From the field of early childhood education has come the concern for the "whole child" that is so basic to the field of special education. The marriage of early childhood education and special education is permeated by the fundamental view that the preschool exceptional child has the same basic needs, desires, and problems in growing up as other children, but he also has additional difficulties to overcome. In this section of the chapter we will discuss some of the major people who have contributed to the field and briefly describe some of their contributions.

Maria Montessori. One of the major figures in the early history of the education of young children was Maria Montessori. Her work in Europe during the late nineteenth and the early twentieth centuries has had a great influence on current practices for three to six year olds. Her techniques and didactic materials were developed for use by children in mental institutions and slum areas. One of Montessori's many contributions to the field of early childhood education was her emphasis on the teacher's role as a highly skilled observer. According to Montessori's philosophy the teacher's observations enabled her to collaborate with the child in designing his learning activities (Evans, 1971).

Alfred Binet. Binet, the originator of intelligence testing, was by no means convinced of the fixed nature of intelligence. In fact he started classes for the mentally retarded in Paris in 1909 and 1910 in an attempt to raise intelligence levels (Kirk, 1977). Nevertheless, American psychologists and society as a whole have only slowly begun to accept the concept that intelligence is modifiable.

Jean Piaget. Born in 1896, the Swiss psychologist Jean Piaget became well known for his theory of cognitive or intellectual development. Like Montessori and others, Piaget derived his theory from observations of children. At the core of Piaget's theory is the idea that all children progress through the same sequence of stages of cognitive development. The stages are only loosely tied to chronological ages. When and how these stages are reached depends on the quality of learning opportunities in the child's environment (Flavell, 1977).

One of the most striking features of Piaget's work is his method of interviewing children. The purpose of this method is to probe the mind of the individual child rather than to determine what large numbers of children do under standardized conditions. For many years, particularly in the 1930s in the United States, Piaget's work was dismissed as not rigorous enough to be important (Hein, 1979). Today, however, Piaget is highly regarded as the originator of the major theory of cognitive development that psychology has so far produced.

Arnold Gesell. In the second and third decades of this century, nursery schools and child study laboratories were proliferating around the United States. The Clinic of Child Development at Yale University was begun in 1911 under the direction of Arnold Gesell, a physician and psychologist. Gesell collected filmed observations of thousands of children. By studying these films he was able to describe the behaviors of young children and the ages at which they appeared. This work resulted in his Schedules of Development and many other publications.

Gesell believed that the early years were the most important biologically and mentally, since they laid the foundation for all subsequent development (Gesell and Ilg, 1943). Probably because of his medical training and background he also believed that genetic endowment and biological maturation were responsible for both the changes or "unfolding" of children in their early years and their ultimate achievement and IQ levels. Unlike Piaget, Gesell attached great importance to the development of skills at particular chronological ages.

Gesell was also interested in children with emotional problems and other handicaps. Staff work at the Yale clinic emphasized the diagnostic evaluation of each child and work with parents (Braun and Edwards, 1972).

Jerome S. Bruner. The Russian launching of Sputnik and an important conference at Woods Hole (reported by Bruner, 1960) resulted in an effort to improve American education. One part of this effort was the search for the beginnings of cognitive development. Bruner was concerned with the presentation and sequencing of information to children in the manner most appropriate to the child's level of understanding (Bruner, 1971). Like Piaget and Montessori, Bruner felt that the environment of the child could be arranged in ways that enhanced or retarded cognitive growth. He identified the schools as one of the most important causes of differences in cognitive development (Warren, 1979). Although Bruner's work has ranged over many areas, his chief concern has always remained the processes of education.

J. McVicker Hunt. In his survey of literature dealing with the influence of experience on intelligence, J. McVicker Hunt (1961) provided evidence that challenged belief in fixed intelligence. Hunt's work focused attention on Piaget's theories and reinterpreted the concept of intelligence. In so doing Hunt drew public attention to the early years of life. He became a strong advocate for preschool enrichment programs for the poor to ensure equality of opportunity (Braun and Edwards, 1972).

Benjamin Bloom. In his important review of child development research, Benjamin Bloom described periods of *Stability and Change in Human Characteristics* (1964). He suggested that experience has its greatest effect during periods of rapid change such as the first few years of life. As a result, he argued, stimulating and enriching experiences have the greatest effect on very young children. One of Bloom's most striking statements was that 50 percent of intelligence, as measured at age seventeen, is fully developed by the age of four (Bloom, 1964).

LEGISLATION

The development of early education programs for exceptional children has been influenced by a great deal of state and federal legislation. Because state legislation varies considerably, only federal legislation will be discussed in this section.

Head Start and First Chance. Legislation for the Head Start program was passed in 1965 as part of President Johnson's War on Poverty. Its purpose was to provide preschool education to children from culturally disadvantaged environments, to give them a "head start" on school. In 1974 Head Start was amended (PL 93–644) to require that at least 10 percent of the enrollment opportunities in each state be made available to handicapped children. As a result many handicapped preschoolers have been placed in programs that were previously unavailable to them.

In 1968 the Handicapped Children's Early Education Assistance Act (PL 90–538) was passed by Congress. The purpose of this act, which came to be known as the First Chance Program, or HCEEP, was to develop experimental demonstration projects for preschool handicapped children. The program called for the possible replication of projects that proved to be successful. There are now

First Chance Programs, or local programs based on practices developed in First Chance Programs, in every state in the country. The federal law required that each of these projects educate parents and decision makers as well as the enrolled children. As a result there is an increased awareness of the importance of early education for the handicapped.

An amendment to HCEEP in 1974 established funding for State Implementation Grants. These grants were to be used by State Departments of Education to develop comprehensive plans for the education of young handicapped children.

Section 504 and PL 94–142. In the previous chapter we described the importance of Section 504 of the rehabilitation amendments and PL 94–142. Under the provisions of these laws it is illegal to discriminate against the handicapped in the area of education. There are several provisions of these laws, however, that relate specifically to early education. These are summarized here:

— If a state provides education to any preschool nonhandicapped children, then similar services must be made available to preschool handicapped children.
— Any state that provides services to preschool handicapped children is eligible for a special incentive grant from the federal government for each child who is enrolled. Although this program was only partially funded, the law authorizes up to $300 for each child per year.
— Although the provisions of PL 94–142 include handicapped children down to age three, a state that has a law or court order excluding children of preschool age from educational services is not required to provide such services.
— Preschool children receiving special education under the provisions of PL 94–142 are entitled to the same benefits as school-age children (due process, IEPs, nondiscriminatory testing, parent involvement in planning, etc.).

Conclusion. Despite the unevenness of the development of educational opportunities for young handicapped children, significant progress has been made. Although some requirements of these legislative acts, such as parental involvement and diagnostic evaluations, originated in legislation designed for young children, they are now accepted practices for all exceptional children. One result has been the increase in the number of infant programs, day care programs, and kindergartens for the children of working and teenage mothers.

In many states preschool services are provided by state agencies other than the departments of education (e.g., Mental Health/Mental Retardation; Department of Human Resources or Social Welfare). Major national agencies (e.g., National Association for Retarded Citizens, National Easter Seals, United Cerebral Palsy) continue to provide needed services to young handicapped children and their families.

PROBE 2-1
Factors Influencing Early Childhood Development

1. List six reasons for establishing broader educational opportunities for handicapped children of preschool age.

   a. _____

   b. _____

   c. _____

   d. _____

   e. _____

   f. _____

2. T F Young handicapped children who do not attend early childhood education programs are more likely to show declining achievement over time than other children of their age.

3. *Matching*

   _____ 1. Montessori

   _____ 2. Binet

   _____ 3. Piaget

   _____ 4. Gesell

   _____ 5. Bruner

   _____ 6. Hunt

   _____ 7. Bloom

   a. Developed major theory of cognitive development

   b. Believed that most intelligence is fully developed by age four

   c. Provided evidence to challenge the idea of fixed intelligence

   d. Emphasized the role of the teacher as observer

   e. Originated the intelligence test

   f. Developed schedules of child development

   g. Was concerned about the way information was sequenced and made appropriate for learning

   h. Studied the effects of drugs on intelligence

4. _____ was the first law designed to provide educational services to children who were culturally disadvantaged.

5. What percentage of enrollments in Head Start should be available to handicapped preschoolers? _____

6. The First Chance Program was designed to _____

_____ .

7. T F State Implementation Grants were designed to provide funds to states to develop comprehensive plans for services to the preschool handicapped.

8. T F If a state does not provide services to three and four year olds because they are excluded from the mandatory attendance law, then the provisions of PL 94–142 do not apply to handicapped children of the same age.

HUMAN GROWTH AND DEVELOPMENT

You should be able to describe the principles of human growth and development and how they relate to educational programming for young handicapped children.

Developmental theory is based on the assumption that individuals change throughout their lives. One of the most obvious changes in infants and young children is the change in physical size and proportions. For example, during the first two years of life, both the absolute size of the human body and the size of the head compared to the trunk and limbs undergo very rapid growth (Figure 2-1). Growth may be defined as an increase in physical size of the whole or any of its parts.

Changes in size, however, produce corresponding changes in function. These changes in function are often referred to as development. But the exact definition of the term "development" varies depending on the type of development that is being described. For example, motor development is an increase in skill and complexity of movement. Cognitive development, on the other hand, is the process of gaining abilities related to knowing, perceiving, and recognizing. Development results from both growth and learning. The terms "growth" and "development" do not mean the same thing, but they are obviously related. For our purposes, development will be regarded as a continuous, cumulative process.

Neither growth nor development is a smooth, uniform process. Each is characterized by spurts of rapid change, periods of apparent rest or "plateaus," and even, at some stages, decline. For example, in old age growth becomes insufficient to replace lost cells and the body may become inefficient. Similarly, certain

FIGURE 2-1
Relative Proportions of Head, Trunk, and Extremities for Different Ages

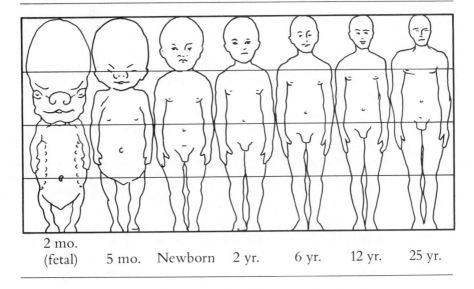

| 2 mo. (fetal) | 5 mo. | Newborn | 2 yr. | 6 yr. | 12 yr. | 25 yr. |

behavioral skills may decline as other skills are learned as in the following anecdote:

> Kristen was one of the youngest of several hearing impaired children who, with their parents, received individualized educational services from a teacher in a hospital clinic. At the age of six months Kristen had been fitted with hearing aids, and her mother brought her regularly to the clinic, where language teaching techniques were explained and demonstrated.
>
> By the time she was about eleven months of age, her mother and teacher noticed a plateau in Kristen's babbling. One week her mother complained to the teacher that Kristen was not babbling much and was not using any new sounds. Mother and teacher together tried to develop some exciting new approaches to be implemented at home. The second week, as her mother continued to complain, the teacher noticed that instead of being carried into the therapy room, Kristen had walked quite independently. It then became apparent to both adults that for the past several weeks walking was what Kristen had been interested in learning, and with only a minimum of enthusiasm from the adults around her for her latest accomplishment!

The various physiological systems of the body change at different but related rates, too. For example, the reproductive system of the young child changes very slowly during the first three years, whereas the motor system changes very quickly.

Specific behaviors that typically occur at certain ages are called "milestones." These have been identified either by studying the same children over a long period of time or by examining the behaviors of children of different ages. The milestones usually represent a particular behavior, such as walking without assistance, which is characteristic of young children at a certain level of development. Sample milestones of development are presented in Charts 2-1 through 2-10.

The average ages at which milestones occur are called *norms*. It should be emphasized, however, that wide variations of age for any given milestone should be expected. For example, a child who does not pull herself to a standing position using furniture for support at exactly eleven months is not necessarily retarded in this area. The child's lateness could simply mean that her rate of development is different from the average. Nevertheless, greater variation from norms are found among handicapped than nonhandicapped children.

Information on normal development is based on the fact that sequences of early development milestones are *uniform* and *universal*. Remarkable though it may seem, the sequences described by Gesell, Piaget, and others are found in numerous cultures around the world, and children everywhere move through them in about the same way.

PRINCIPLES OF NORMAL DEVELOPMENT

Normal early development involves a myriad of behaviors and changes in behaviors. Unless one understands the principles of normal development, it is impossible to work effectively with children who are developing abnormally. Several general principles are associated with developmental change:

1. The sequence of development is, in general, the same for all children, but each child develops at his own rate and to his own level (Meier, 1976).
2. Rates of growth and development vary between individuals and between different developmental areas within the same individual.
3. Progress in development is often uneven; the rate of change in one skill area may vary while other skills are being learned.
4. Individual differences are apparent in young children at a very early age; they also tend to remain apparent over time (for example, see Neilon, 1948).
5. Early development proceeds by processes of increasing *differentiation* and *integration*. When the newborn is startled, his whole body tenses in reaction. This mass activity is gradually replaced by more specific activity; a startled three year old only tenses his shoulders and neck muscles, or blinks his eyes

rapidly shut. Thus, early mass responsiveness has become differentiated into responsiveness that is more localized and specific. Furthermore, as development proceeds, small units of behavior (for example, hand movements) are combined and integrated into larger, functional behaviors (for example, reaching for and grasping objects.

6. Children progress step by step in orderly sequences of development. Each accomplishment prepares the way for the next one. Regardless of chronological age, the mastery of later milestones generally depends on the achievement of earlier ones. One such early example is head and neck control, which is used later in walking.

7. Motor development progresses in a *cephalocaudal* and *proximodistal* direction. This means that control of voluntary movement in the infant proceeds from the head downward and from the trunk outward, respectively. This is illustrated in the following summary of early motor development:

> In the first quarter of the first year, the infant gains control of the six sets of muscles that move his eyes; in the second quarter, the muscles that support his head and move his arms. He reaches out for the objects he sees. In the third quarter, the controlled use of his hands improves; in sitting, he grasps, transfers, and manipulates objects. In the fourth quarter, he stands on legs and feet. Using his forefinger and thumb, he pokes and plucks. In the second year, he walks and runs [adapted from Gesell and Amatruda, 1974, p. 10].

8. There are times during which children show that they are "ready" for new learning. During these times particular kinds of learning may be cultivated or damaged relatively easily. Before or beyond this point (sometimes referred to as a "critical period"), learning of the particular skill or process may be more difficult.

9. Children (including very young infants) give those taking care of them subtle behavioral cues about their needs, rhythms, and readiness for new learning. Professionals and parents can be taught to recognize these cues. Progress is best when the stimulation provided matches the child's readiness to learn.

10. As children develop increasing capacities for learning and doing, they tend to use these capacities. Conversely, especially with regard to the senses, what you do not use, you lose.

11. All areas of development are interrelated. Although we often speak of motor development or conceptual development as a separate entity, in the normal child all areas are related to each other.

12. The processes and outcome of development are influenced by children's genetic inheritances, their social and cultural backgrounds, and their families.

13. Development results from both growth and learning, each of which continually influences the other. The challenge of education is to provide the influences necessary to achieve the child's full potential.

USES OF DEVELOPMENTAL NORMS

Information about normal development is used in many educational settings for many different purposes. The purpose of screening is to identify children who may have problems, so that, if appropriate, special education services can be provided. Developmental norms are also considered in the *assessment* of a child's strengths and weaknesses. This information is used to plan instruction that uses the child's areas of strength to compensate for, or help build up, areas of weakness.

The milestones identified in developmental norms are also used as the basis for *curriculum development* in preschool programs. Unlike school-age subject matter, which is neatly divided into such disciplines as reading, writing, arithmetic, geography, and history, the skills that should be taught in early education have not been widely agreed on. Generally, however, the early milestones of development are considered prerequisites of academic skill building.

SEVEN AREAS OF CHILD DEVELOPMENT

The behavioral changes young children go through can be categorized into distinct but related areas of development. Seven areas will be discussed in this chapter:

1. *Gross motor development* deals with reflexes, postures, and changes in postures, including locomotion and other whole body movements.
2. *Fine motor development* is concerned with the sequence of milestones in reaching for and obtaining objects, grasping, manipulating, and using objects such as puzzles, formboards, cubes, and drawing materials.
3. *Perceptual development* includes milestones related to the use of hearing and vision.
4. *Conceptual development* is concerned with the sequence of milestones in relating to objects, and in imitation; counting; recognition of colors; classification; knowledge of time and gender; and making analogies and comparisons.
5. *Social-emotional development* relates to a child's increasing attachment to persons and objects. It is also concerned with the child's increasing ability to differentiate between feelings; her different levels of play; the emergence of her independence; and her ability to delay gratification.
6. *Communication* is divided into receptive and expressive areas. More will be said about these in the next chapter.
7. *Self-help* consists of eating; dressing; bathing, and grooming; and toileting.

The normal child generally develops at about the same rate in all these areas. Consequently, it is important to see how behaviors in different areas are related to each other, to form an integrated picture of the child. For example, by about two years of age the average normal child is able to walk well and go up and down stairs alone (gross motor). At the same time, the child can turn doorknobs that are within reach and hold a pencil well enough to make vertical and circular strokes or dots on a page (fine motor). The achievement of important norms across a variety of areas is called parallel development.

The development of exceptional children often shows uneven progress across the different areas. For example, orthopedically handicapped children's levels of motor development may not match the functioning age of their communication or, similarly, blind children's visual-perceptual skills will not parallel their achievements in communication. The early childhood educator must be able to determine when the cause of a child's inability to do a task is his age, and when the cause is his impairment. To do this the educator must know what behaviors are appropriate for what ages, and what the effects are of various disabilities.

In the following discussions of the seven areas of development normal development sequences will be explained. We will also illustrate how these sequences relate to the education of handicapped children. Unfortunately, space limitations do not allow for the inclusion of a complete listing of skills in each area of development. References are provided in each section for those who may want to obtain additional information.

PROBE 2-2
Human Growth and Development

1. T F All children develop at the same rate.

2. T F Development does not proceed in a smooth, continuous manner.

3. Which of the following does *not* characterize normal development?
   a. cephalocaudal direction
   b. increasing differentiation
   c. increasing integration
   d. proximodistal direction
   e. universal and uniform rates
   f. interaction between heredity and environmental experiences

4. T F Developmental information

   _____ may be used to screen children.

   _____ may be used to assess handicapped children.

   _____ may be used to build preschool curricula.

   _____ is not observable or measurable.

   _____ is incompatible with professions other than early education.

   _____ may be applied to low-functioning children.

GROSS AND FINE MOTOR DEVELOPMENT

You should be able to describe the sequences of gross and fine motor development and identify examples of abnormal development.

GROSS MOTOR DEVELOPMENT

Some of the sequences of gross motor development are described in Figure 2-2. These sequences illustrate how the large muscles of the body gradually come under increasing control.

In a study by Pikler (1971) of the emergence of milestones related to movement it was reported that, without any urging from adults, children changed their postures (turning to prone, turning back, rising on all fours, kneeling, sitting up, standing, and getting down from all these positions) an average of 53.3 times in 30 minutes. These changes are most frequent in a child in the developmental periods between sitting up, kneeling up, and standing up. This means that the normal young developing child moves and changes position almost twice every minute with no particular adult inducement to do so. (Having read that, try sitting perfectly still for as long as you can. It is more difficult to be still than you may realize.) Normally developing young children are remarkably active creatures, a fact many parents sorely regret. You may have heard the anecdote about the professional athlete who tried to imitate the movements of a toddler — he collapsed halfway through the day. Even before children begin to walk, they are "into" everything; they can become a danger to themselves as well as to their environments, particularly if their surroundings have not been "babyproofed."

Chart 2-1, an excerpt from a gross motor development checklist, illustrates the range of milestone behaviors that children can exhibit in an eighteen-month period. From the time they begin to change positions voluntarily, normal developing infants are learning many things. Aside from what they learn about the environment through exploration, they learn how to use their own bodies, how to move in a coordinated fashion, how it feels to touch different textures and surfaces, and how their movements can lead to new explorations. As you can see, motor development is related to the development of concepts.

Why do children put themselves through the trouble of learning to walk, when crawling and creeping seem so much easier and efficient? Reinforcement by parents is probably of secondary importance. What the child probably enjoys most is the ability to see new levels of the adult world. Walking also frees the hands to manipulate the ever-increasing number of items within reach. With increasing motor skills, shifts in attention become more rapid and more diversified.

FIGURE 2-2
Gross Motor Development

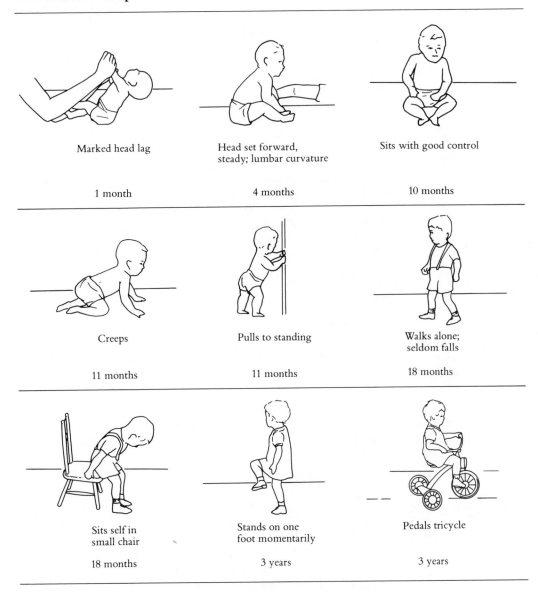

Marked head lag

1 month

Head set forward,
steady; lumbar curvature

4 months

Sits with good control

10 months

Creeps

11 months

Pulls to standing

11 months

Walks alone;
seldom falls

18 months

Sits self in
small chair

18 months

Stands on one
foot momentarily

3 years

Pedals tricycle

3 years

For children with motor impairments this learning is altered or limited. If a
child's ability to explore is limited, so is the number of new experiences he can
have. What is more, handicapped children have less success and fewer rewards

Chart 2-1
Sample Gross Motor Milestones

19 mo.	stairs: walks down, one hand held, 2 feet per step
	walks fast, runs stiffly
20 mo.	walks, carrying large objects
	climbs on furniture
	walks, pushing toy
21 mo.	stairs: walks up alone, 2 feet per step
	stairs: creeps down backwards
22 mo.	raises self from sitting position with hips first, then head
	walks with stability
23 mo.	when walking, makes short turns and sudden stops
2 yrs.	runs well, without falling
	kicks ball without overbalancing
	stairs: goes up and down alone, 2 feet per step
	jumps from first step without help, with one foot leading
	walks with heel to toe gait
2½ yrs.	jumps with both feet in place
	walks on tiptoes briefly
	picks up objects from floor
3 yrs.	stairs: goes up, one foot per step, and down, two feet per step
	stands on one foot for one second
	runs and gallops; takes short running steps on his toes
	rides a tricycle
	jumps from bottom step with both feet together

when they try. This may decrease their motivation to keep active. As you can see, problems in motor impairment have implications for other areas of development as well. Children who can't walk see only what others put in front of them, and they have trouble investigating the source of sounds. Although their language development may appear to be normal, closer investigation often reveals that the concepts behind the words they use are not the same as for children with normal motor functioning.

Because children with motor impairments are generally imprecise or restricted in their movements, their parents often feel they need to be protected. As a result many children who can move around somewhat are prevented by their parents from developing their abilities. This attitude is common in the parents of young children with many handicaps. Although the attitude is understandable, parents should be made to understand the importance of exploration, or the child will be further handicapped by her lack of experiences. Real limitations in self-help skills are often seen in children with spina bifida and cerebral palsy, when bowel and bladder control are impossible or late in developing. Motor impairments may also affect the child's level of independence, as seen in dressing and self-feeding skills.

According to Finnie (1975), one of the foremost authorities in early intervention for cerebral palsied children, those who cannot move by themselves should not be left in any one physical position for more than twenty minutes. In current intervention practices appropriate handling, positioning, and movement are emphasized in order to inhibit abnormal movement patterns, to facilitate the development of more mature patterns, and to prevent stiffness or contractures in the physically handicapped young child. This often means that teachers spend part of their day moving children from one position to another, feeding, and changing diapers. It should be remembered, however, that these services are as important to the overall welfare of the child as any teaching the teachers may wish to do. By carrying out the appropriate techniques of physical management, teachers help to minimize the long-range effects of physical disability.

FINE MOTOR DEVELOPMENT

Figure 2-3 depicts the sequence of milestones related to grasp (prehension) and release. Obviously, children who have difficulty with these fine motor skills will also have difficulty in other areas, such as feeding, dressing, and writing. The column headed "stimulation" provides some suggestions that teachers could use to teach these skills to children.

In addition to grasping and release, a host of other fine motor skills is developed by young children. Chart 2-2 illustrates those typically developed between the ages of two and five years.

It is important for teachers not to jump to conclusions when a child is delayed in reaching a milestone. Particularly where there is no preschool, many children enter nursery, kindergarten, or the first year of academic work with only a minimum of experience with books, pencils, and crayons, and with hardly any idea of how they should behave. For the child with poor fine motor control, the teacher must ask, "How much opportunity and experience has this child had in these activities?" The lack of hand dominance, for example, is not necessarily an early predictor of learning disabilities.

The child who has problems with tasks requiring fine motor development may try to avoid them if the teacher does not give her enough opportunities to do them successfully. The child may also prefer to do tasks requiring gross motor skills, sometimes to the extent that she is labeled hyperactive or learning disabled.

Children with fine motor development problems should be screened for vision problems. A child with poor visual acuity from birth will not be aware of or communicate her problem, but may show it in specific fine motor behaviors. For

FIGURE 2-3
Sequential Development of Prehension

Age (weeks)	Description	Stimulation
12	Reflexive, ulnar side strongest; no reaching before eye contact.	Place objects in hand; hang toys in crib to stimulate eye contact and tracking.
16	Mouthing of fingers and mutual fingering; retains object placed in hand; no visually directed grasp until both hand and object in field of vision.	Toys hanging within swiping reach; toys on floor within visual field and hand reach.
20	Primitive squeeze, raking; fingers only, no thumb nor palm involved, immediate approach and grasp on sight.	Toys of varied textures, colors, sizes, shapes and weights.
24	Palmar or squeeze grasp; still no thumb participation; eyes and hands combine in joint action.	Place toys in different positions and distances so eyes and hands must search.
28	Radial-palmar or whole-hand grasp; radial side stronger; thumb begins to adduct; unilateral approach; transfer from one hand to the other.	Toys that can be picked up and transferred by one hand; must be washable and safe (mouthing).
32	Inferior scissors or superior-palm grasp; known as monkey grasp because thumb is adducted, not opposed.	Toys with smaller and thinner circumferences to strengthen thumb adductor.
36	Radial-digital or inferior forefinger grasp; fingers on radial side provide pressure on object; thumb begins to move toward opposition by pressing toward PIP joint of forefinger; finer adjustment of digits.	More pliable materials, including sand, clay, yarn, tissue paper, tape, and many types of finger food for self-feeding and exploration.
40	Inferior-pincer grasp; thumb moves toward DIP joint of forefinger; poking finger, inhibition of other four digits; beginning of voluntary release.	Many small objects with a variety of shapes to examine and palpate; toys with holes and indentations to poke and explore.
44	Neat pincer or forefinger grasp with slight extension of wrist.	Tiny objects to pick up and drop, such as dry cereal.
52	Opposition or superior-forefinger grasp; wrist extended and deviated to ulnar side for efficient prehension; release smooth for large objects, clumsy for small objects.	Toys that provide repeat motions of release, such as blocks and container, both becoming gradually smaller.

Chart 2-2
Sample Fine Motor Milestones

2 yrs.	turns pages of a book one at a time
	places two or more objects neatly in a row
	can string large beads with shoelace
	turns door knob, unscrews lids
2½ yrs.	overgrasps and overreleases
	holds object (pencil) in hand instead of fist
3 yrs.	closes fist and wiggles thumb
	can fold a piece of paper lengthwise and crosswise along a dotted line
	exhibits good wrist rotation
	snips with scissors
3½ yrs.	moves fingers with agility
	completes two-piece puzzle
	brings thumb into opposition and touches thumb to two or four fingers on same hand
4 yrs.	brings thumb into opposition with each finger on both right and left hands
	completes three-piece puzzle
	cuts with scissors fairly well
4½ yrs.	completes seven-piece puzzle
5 yrs.	can pluck a dozen pellets, one by one, drop into a bottle with speed and accuracy, usually with preferred hand
	can wind thread on a bobbin
	can manipulate clay into balls and other shapes

example, the use of utensils, drinking from a cup or glass, pouring from a pitcher, unbuttoning and buttoning, zipping, snapping, lacing, and tying shoes all require eye-hand coordination, as well as control and strength for fine motor movements. As with other skills, fine motor skills are integrated with the growth and development of the whole child.

PROBE 2-3
Gross and Fine Motor Development

1. T F When young children begin to creep and crawl, if they change their position more frequently than once every minute, they may be considered "hyperactive."

2. T F Learning to walk upright is not only socially reinforcing, it also opens new horizons and brings countless new objects within easier reach of the young child.

3. Ideally, orthopedically handicapped young children should not be left in any one physical position for more than _____ minutes.

4. One reason for the current emphasis on proper handling and positioning for young cerebral palsied children is _____

_____.

5. When a young child shows poor fine motor skills in the first year of preschool or school attendance, the teacher should consider _____

_____.

PERCEPTUAL DEVELOPMENT

You should be able to describe the sequence of development in vision and hearing and identify examples of abnormal development.

Perceptual development is related to vision and hearing. Because a separate chapter is devoted to each of these topics, this section will be relatively brief.

VISION

Knoblock and Pasamanick (1974) stated that seeing cannot be isolated from children's postures, manual skills, coordination, intelligence, or even their personalities. Some sample milestones in the area of vision are presented in Chart 2-3.

One of the most important of these milestones is the coordinated movement of both eyes at six months (twelve weeks, according to Knoblock and Pasamanick, 1974). If the two eyes fail to move in coordination they may appear to be crossed (one or both looking in toward the nose) or divergent (one or both looking out to the side). This condition is usually called *strabismus*.

Because the brain receives two uncoordinated visual images, one from each eye, most children with strabismus see "double" (two of everything). The brain will not tolerate double vision for long, and it suppresses the image being sent by the weaker eye. This is called *amblyopia* or "lazy eye blindness." The result is the loss of depth perception. Young children with faulty depth perception may miss the cup when pouring water from a pitcher, or walk into the door-frame instead of through the doorway. Earlier, one year olds may persistently fail to contact the object toward which they are reaching.

Chart 2-3
Sample Visual Milestones

4 mo.	regards hand
	can visually pursue circular movement
	immediately attends to a dangling object
5 mo.	visually pursues lost rattle
	smiles at mirror image
6 mo.	has completely developed conjugate movement of the eyes
	shifts visual attention from one object to another or to hand and back
	maintains voluntary fixation of stationary objects even in the presence of a moving object
7 mo.	pats own image in mirror
	fixates object, reaches for object, fixation relaxes, grasps for object, and fixation intensifies
8 mo.	watches intently movements of own hands in mirror

Typically, the young child with strabismus can be helped; surgery, eye exercises, patching, or prescriptive lenses may be recommended, depending on the cause of the condition. These remedial techniques, however, become progressively less effective the longer treatment is postponed. The longer the suppression goes untreated the more difficult the restoration of normal visual functioning will be. Reinforcement of bad visual habits can eventually reduce the chances for attaining full vision and straight, fully coordinated eyes (Windsor and Hurtt, 1974).

Strabismus is both *identifiable* and *preventable* in the early years. The National Society for the Prevention of Blindness, Inc. (79 Madison Avenue, New York, NY 10016) will send you a *Home Eye Test for Preschoolers* free of charge. It is intended for use by parents. Screening for strabismus is even less demanding than writing a letter. One need simply be aware of the six-month milestone for conjugate eye movements.

Most newborn babies cannot see well. About 80 percent of all babies are born hyperopic (farsighted), 5 percent are myopic (nearsighted), and about 15 percent have normal visual acuity (Vaughan, Asbury, and Cook, 1971). As the baby grows, the size and shape of his eyes are growing too. As a result, visual acuity changes may be very rapid in the early years of life.

The areas of development most seriously affected by the early lack of vision are gross and fine motor development. Specifically, the related actions of reaching out to objects and attaining independent locomotion are significantly delayed in the blind baby. One reason is that young blind children cannot see behaviors being performed by others, and as a result cannot model their own movements.

In her work with blind infants Fraiberg (1975) described efforts to substitute sound cues for visual cues to elicit reaching out and mobility. Theoretically, locating something by sound operates by allowing the listener to interpret very subtle differences in the times at which sounds coming from left or right reach each ear. However, when sound sources are directly in front or directly behind a listener, he cannot detect the source without the additional cues provided by head movement. Similarly, neither distances nor azimuth (up-down) positions can be detected without head movements, even by normal individuals. As a result the sound-making toys that may be used to induce reaching out and movement are of limited use and may take a long time to provide the desired effect.

Adelson and Fraiberg (1975) report that blind babies achieve postural milestones (elevation on arms in prone position; sitting and standing) within the norms established for sighted children. However, the blind infants were characterized by delays in initiating their own mobility. Interestingly, hand regard, which appears at approximately four months of age, is noted in blind as well as sighted infants (Bower, 1977; Illingworth, 1972). Hand regard is the process in which the infant holds her hands in front of her face and appears to be studying all aspects of the fingers and hands. It does not apparently require visual stimulation, however. Like the early babbling of deaf infants, this behavior is "built in."

Vision also helps develop the body image, a central aspect of the child's self-concept. Through vision, infants and young children achieve coordination and control of their movement (Barraga, 1978). Because blind babies are not reinforced by seeing their own movements, they often become quiet, passive, and undemanding; these behaviors are often mistakenly interpreted by parents as qualities of a "good" baby. Understandably, parents of blind infants are also often overprotective, which leads to deficits in experience and to immature social-emotional development.

To understand the severe delays in the cognitive development of blind children (Stephens, 1978), notice how many items in cognitive development (see Chart 2-5) depend on visual experience. These include items related to the knowledge that objects exist even when they are out of sight, the appropriate manipulation of objects, the mimicry of domestic activities, and other forms of imitation.

Problems in communication skills are also often noted in the visually handicapped population. Cutsforth (1932) coined the term "verbalism" to describe the use of words of which blind children could not have a firsthand understanding — color words, for example. Young blind children typically learn these verbal associations by rote memorization; they learn that sighted persons label the grass as green, the sky as blue, the sun as yellow, and so on. However, teachers must be aware that blind children can develop excessive dependence on verbal learning if they aren't given opportunities for concrete experiences with their other senses.

In John's first-grade class at the school for the blind, the topic of discussion was nature. As was often the case, John seemed to be more advanced than his classmates in his knowledge of vocabulary related to the topic. While other children reviewed terms such as "grass," "trees," "shrubs," and "leaves," John recited a long list that included the words "bark," "branches," "trunk," and "stems."

At lunchtime John's teacher asked him to accompany her to another building, to collect some materials for the afternoon. As they walked, John recited the directions for their walk and the number of stairs they encountered. Basing her actions on a suspicion, his teacher led John off the normal route, through the grass and toward a large tree. She placed his hands on the tree trunk and asked John what he was touching. John could not answer the question. He had apparently learned his advanced vocabulary without ever actually exploring a tree with his hands!

In dealing with blind children, teachers often depend heavily on verbal explanation and description. The value of providing blind children with firsthand experiences, which give information via the senses of touch, hearing, taste, and smell, cannot be overestimated. On the other hand, the use of language or concepts that are visually oriented (e.g., "Do you see what I mean?") should not be limited in teaching visually handicapped children. As Warren (1977) suggested, "The goal should be to bring the blind child to the point of maximal use of the language used by the surrounding culture so that language can aid in meaningful and useful social interaction, in behavioral self-direction, and in progress in the educational system" (p. 161).

HEARING

Normal hearing functions on three levels (Ramsdell, 1965). On the *auditory background* level, hearing the quiet sounds of the surrounding environment contributes a sense of well-being to the individual. Adults who have lost their hearing report almost overwhelming feelings of isolation, despite their still being able to see the world around them. The sounds that contribute to an understanding and knowledge of distances are also considered part of this level. If you close your eyes for a moment, you will probably discover that you can hear many relatively quiet sounds in the distance, such as traffic noises and the sounds of others' voices. Although both hearing and vision are considered the "distance senses" (Myklebust, 1960), hearing keeps the individual in contact with the environment by functioning uninterruptedly.

The second level of hearing is the *signal/warning* level. The baby who approaches the stove hears Mother say, "No! Don't touch — that's hot!" and is warned by her tone to be careful. Many other sounds (cars honking, sirens, fire alarms) serve the same purpose. This function of hearing is important for survival as well as for the development of independence.

The third level of hearing is the *symbolic* level, through which normal communication skills are developed. What the young normal hearing child hears around him determines in large part what language he will produce. If, as an infant, he hears French spoken, then French is the language he will gradually begin to speak. If he hears English, he will speak English. If what he hears is muffled and unclear and makes no sense to him, he will gradually stop paying attention to it. This causes a serious delay in the development of language skills. Without early intervention efforts young profoundly deaf children often cease babbling entirely and become quite silent. The same principle that applied to amblyopia applies here: what you don't use, you lose.

The auditory perception milestones for the first two years of life are presented in Chart 2-4. In the normal developing infant, auditory *localization* skills develop during the first year. The ability correctly to identify the source of sound helps the child make associations between the sound and events in the environment. These associations are the basis on which later communication skills are built. By four months of age, an infant who hears the sound of a spoon in her bowl anticipates being fed.

The infant's own movements produce sounds, as do the actions of others. The normal developing infant experiments with producing sounds by using her voice and by using objects. These produce auditory as well as social consequences. By the age of eighteen months, young normal hearing children swing rhythmically with their whole bodies in response to music (Knoblock and Pasamanick, 1974, p. 292). Later, children can recognize melodies, sing songs and parts of songs, match and grade tones and sound blocks, and participate in rhythmic play. As a result, their rapport with their social environment is strengthened. When a child cannot hear, some of these activities may be imitated through vision, but their meaning and association to sounds may not be recognized.

Young children with significant hearing impairments may also show subtle problems in gross motor development. This is due partly to the loss of association between sounds and movement and partly to the loss of auditory feedback on their own movements. Moreover, the problems that cause hearing loss often affect the semicircular canals as well, which can affect the body's ability to balance.

Communications is the area of development most seriously affected by hearing impairment in the early years. Methods have been developed to help young deaf children develop communication skills. These include the use of appropriate amplification devices, to allow deaf children to use their residual hearing. For reviews of these educational programs and methods see the articles by Horton (1976), Moores (1976), and Northcott (1973a and b).

Along with the delay or lack of communication skills in young hearing impaired children come problems in conceptual, social-emotional, and self-help skills. The meaning of sounds in the environment is often misunderstood or missed completely by young hearing impaired children. Furthermore, because they cannot express themselves through language, they often resort to physical

Chart 2-4
Sample Auditory Perception Milestones

Birth	crying or startling in responses to loud noises; smiles or quiets to soft voice
1 mo.	quiets when bell is rung (or to soft pleasing sounds)
2 mo.	accepts loud sounds as part of environment; doesn't react violently
3 mo.	turns head and eyes in direction of sound source
5 mo.	localizes horizontally and up, horizontally and down
7 mo.	localizes using curving arc
8 mo.	localizes diagonally and directly
11 mo.	imitation indicates he can hear sounds and match them with his own sound production
15 mo.	investigates sounds
18 mo.	swings rhythmically in response to music
2 yrs.	responds to sound blocks and simple sound patterns (such as Mother Goose)
	can distinguish sounds that are very different and begins to guess their source (example: verbal response)
	repeats 2 digits

means to satisfy their desires. Teachers of hearing impaired preschool children are frequently asked whether their students are also "emotionally disturbed." This highlights the importance of teaching deaf children the language necessary to express their moods and feelings. The lack of adequate language for understanding and expression, combined with the common overprotective attitudes of parents, can cause serious problems in the development of independence and self-help skills in young hearing impaired children. (For a developmental model applied to problems of deafness, see Schlesinger and Meadow, 1972.)

PROBE 2-4
Perceptual Development

1. The coordinated movements of the two eyes are normally established by ____ (age). The condition of deviating eyes is usually called _____; if it is not corrected, it may lead to

_____

2. T F At birth, most newborns have normal visual acuity.

3. T F Hand regard appears in both sighted and blind infants at about four months of age.

4. T F Presenting a sound from *directly behind* the child facilitates auditory localization.

5. Auditory localization skills normally develop during the _____ year of life.

6. The area most seriously affected by hearing impairment in the young child is

_____ .

7. T F Young blind babies in intervention programs have been shown to have less difficulty achieving postural milestones (e.g., sitting, standing) than achieving self-initiated mobility.

CONCEPTUAL, SOCIAL-EMOTIONAL, AND COMMUNICATION DEVELOPMENT

You should be able to describe the sequences of conceptual, social-emotional, and communication development and identify examples of abnormal development.

CONCEPTUAL DEVELOPMENT

A concept can be a thought, an opinion, an idea, or a mental image. The word can also be used to refer to the attributes a class or group of things has in common (Good, 1959). Red, yellow, and blue, for example, have in common the fact that they are all colors. There are other kinds of concepts, too. The concept of object permanence is the knowledge that objects continue to exist even when they can no longer be seen (Wadsworth, 1978). The concept of motor meaning is the knowledge that an object can be used for a particular purpose, such as cups for drinking or hair brushes for grooming.

Concepts are useful because they help us bring order to the things in our environment (Sigel, 1975). They reduce the ambiguity in our lives and allow us to function more efficiently, because we do not have to relearn something when we encounter a member of that class of concept.

Concepts are associated with and expressed in observable behaviors. For example, infants suck, look around, listen, make noises, grasp, and move their trunks and limbs. Between the ages of four and eight months, they learn that their actions can produce effects. They can, for example, move the mobiles over their cribs by hitting them or shaking their cribs. The concept that they learn as a result is cause and effect. It signifies the child's moving her body to achieve a purpose (Sigel, 1975). Later examples of the same concept are the activation of a mechanical toy after demonstration and, still later, before demonstration. Illustrations of other concepts that are developed at different ages are included in Chart 2-5.

As a result of studies of the ages at which children from different cultures achieved object permanence, Hunt, Paraskevopoulos, Schickedanz, and Uzgiris (1975) introduced the concept of the "range of reaction." The range of reaction is the span between the highest and the lowest average ages at which children raised under different conditions achieve a particular milestone. For example, the range of reaction in achieving object permanence is 109 weeks, or over 2 years (Hunt et al., 1975). An understanding of the concept of range of reaction helps one develop perspective on development. Inherent in the concept are the assumptions that intervention can hasten the accomplishment of conceptual milestones and that some children develop concepts sooner than others.

Problems in conceptual development have been reported in brain injured children and children with communicative disorders (Johnson, 1975), in deaf children (Hicks, 1975), in learning disabled children (McCarthy, 1975), in

Chart 2-5
Sample Conceptual Milestones

3–3½ yrs.	matches colors
	names one color
	counts 2 blocks
	correctly tells gender to question, "Are you a boy or a girl?"
	names own drawing
	counts by rote to 10
	chooses between 2 alternatives using concrete objects
3½–4 yrs.	matches pictures
	gives "heavy" block from comparison of two differently weighted blocks
	classifies objects by physical attributes (e.g., color, shape, size) one class at a time.
4–5 yrs.	discriminates colors when named
	names 3 primary colors
	classifies by groups (e.g., animals vs. toys)
	counts 3 objects with correct pointing
	counts 4 objects and tells how many
	when shown 2 pictures, tells which is prettier
	distinguishes between day and night
	can finish opposite analogies (Brother = boy; sister = ____)
	names a penny in response to "What is this?"
	matches sound blocks by loudness
	tells which of 2 is "bigger," "slower," "heavier"

visually handicapped children (Stephens, 1978; Umsted, 1975), and in children with mental retardation (Moss and Mayer, 1975). Safford (1978) reported that the mentally retarded children he studied proceeded through the same developmental progression as nonretarded youngsters, although their rates of progress and their levels of highest attainment were different.

Persons interested in additional literature related to concept development may examine the works of DeVries and Kohlberg (1977), Furth (1970), Kamii (1973), Sigel (1975), and Wadsworth (1978).

SOCIAL-EMOTIONAL DEVELOPMENT

Children's social behaviors are developed through interactions with people and other parts of the environment (Corter, 1977). The components of these behaviors that the child internalizes are referred to as "feelings" (Lewis and Rosenblum, 1978). Samples of such behaviors in children ranging from fifteen months to four years are included in Chart 2-6.

This area of development is the most difficult one to evaluate objectively, because it is very difficult to define "normal" social-emotional behavior. In addition, there is controversy about the ages of achievement of many social-emotional milestones.

Furthermore, cultural factors are especially influential in this area. Most norms for social-emotional development are based on observations of predominantly white, middle-class, suburban children. There is some question about their applicability to children from other cultural backgrounds.

Because of these many variables, special educators who work with children who may be socially or emotionally disturbed are faced with an especially difficult task. On the one hand, they do not want to prematurely apply a label such as "emotionally disturbed" or "socially maladjusted," because such a label can become a self-fulfilling prophecy. On the other hand, children with real problems need to be diagnosed and labeled before they can receive special services.

Behavioral problems in young handicapped children often result from frustration caused by another problem. The behavioral problems can often be relieved by eliminating the frustration. For example, teaching young deaf children language to express themselves may help to keep them from acting inappropriately.

Safford (1978) described several symptoms that could indicate a social or emotional problem. Each symptom could be temporary or indicate a serious problem. Safford emphasized the need for preschool teachers to record behaviors *objectively* if they are to develop effective intervention strategies. Symptoms that may indicate problems are (1) great difficulty in separating from parents, (2) extreme withdrawal, (3) extreme aggressive behavior, and (4) infantile patterns

Chart 2-6
Sample Social-Emotional Milestones

15 mo.	beginning to claim possessions and to make distinctions between "yours" and "mine"
	makes social contact with other children, smiles and looks
2 yrs.	arousal is sudden, brief, intense
	uses language to communicate with others
	parallel play, with one other child
	smiles when praised: hangs head when reprimanded
2½ yrs.	attached to object such as toys or blanket (e.g., carries them around, talks to them)
	shows pride in ability to accomplish tasks (do it myself, Mommy; watch me, Mommy)
3 yrs.	beginning of imaginative play/make believe
	begins to use words to express feelings
	beginning of cooperative play: one other child, shares toys, takes turns
	talks to himself
	will sacrifice immediate satisfaction for promise of later gain (delayed gratification)
	shows sympathy (projects feelings to others)
	may show jealousy of new baby, dog
3½ yrs.	lying becomes common (difficult for child to distinguish wish and truth)
	decline of attachment to objects (plays more with other children)
4 yrs.	may have imaginary friends and playmates
	cooperative play: common goal, evidence of social organization
	shares toys brought from home
	shows humor by silly words and rhymes
	tells stories, fabricates, rationalizes
	goes on errands outside home

of behavior (pp. 160–61). In each of these areas beginning school may cause a child to behave mildly "abnormal." For example, nursery school teachers often notice regressions in toilet training of children separated from their parents for the first time. In this as in the other areas described earlier, teachers need to be able to observe and systematically document children's behaviors; they must also be acutely aware of how their responses reinforce or discourage a behavior. The most obvious approach to take is simply to tell the child what is expected of him.

Additional information related to this topic is covered in the chapter on behavior disorders, in Garfunkel's (1976) review, "Early Childhood Special Education for Children with Social and Emotional Disturbances," and in the First Chance publication edited by Enzer and Goin (1978).

COMMUNICATION

Communication may be defined as "the passing of meaning from one source to another" (DuBose, 1978). Subjects considered under this general heading are receptive language (understanding), expressive language (speaking), and speech (the articulation of specific speech sounds). It is important to understand the distinctions between these three areas to accurately identify young children's problems.

Speech and language will be discussed in the next chapter. However, some milestones for receptive and expressive communication are listed in Chart 2-7.

Receptive language development precedes and exceeds expressive language development. By the time a child begins to use her first word, she has already been listening for approximately ten to twelve months. This "listening age" (Northcott, 1972) is important because of the number of skills that must develop before the child begins to use words.

Auditory association is only one of the processes underlying the early development of language. The infant must also be skilled in *auditory discrimination,* the ability to distinguish between the sounds she hears, including the very subtle differences between speech sounds; and in *auditory memory,* the ability to remember sequences of auditory events, both at the level of individual speech sounds (dog versus god) and at the level of entire sentences. As you can see, the *comprehension* and *interpretation* of language are complex receptive processes, and the rate at which they develop help determine when the child begins to speak.

Some of the sequences in the normal development of both expressive language and speech sounds are grouped under "expressive communication" in Chart 2-7. When analyzing a child's expressive language, a teacher should consider the following questions: (1) Is the child's language adequate in quantity for his age? (2) Is the child's intelligibility appropriate for his age? If the teacher cannot understand a child's utterances, the problem may be the teacher's limited experience with children of this age and development, and not the child's manner of

Chart 2-7
Sample Receptive and Expressive Milestones

Receptive

11 mo.	understands a few words
1 yr.	points to one named body part on request
	stops activity to name and/or "no"
15 mo.	points to familiar persons, animals, toys on request
	follows one-step simple commands (give me the ____; get the ____)
17 mo.	points to 3 named body parts on request
20 mo.	follows 2-step command

21 mo.	points to 5 or 6 pictures of common objects on request
22 mo.	points to 5 body parts on self or doll
2 yrs.	follows 3-step commands given in one long utterance
	understands 200 to 400 words
	follows prepositional commands using *in, on, under*
3 yrs.	understands 800 words
	demonstrates *first* and *last, next to, between, in front of, behind*
	responds to "or" questions
	verbalizes past experiences
	points to *big, little, soft, loud*
4 yrs.	follows commands with 2–3 actions
	understands approximately 1500 words

Expressive

10 mo.	says first word (crude approximations: "mama," etc.)
11 mo.	imitates phonemes — head: baba, kaka
	shakes head "no-no"
1 yr.	echolalia begins (child imitates the sounds of others: dada, mama)
	sometimes will imitate dogs, clocks, cows, or other adult exclamations
	shakes head "no-no"
	speech accompanies gestures
13 mo.	uses three words in speaking vocabulary besides mama and dada
	words are likely to be nouns since the child usually hears more nouns than other parts of speech
14 mo.	use of verbs appears, followed by adjectives and adverbs
	points/gestures and vocalizes to indicate wants
17 mo.	uses at least 6 words
23 mo.	uses "me," "you," and refers to self by name
2 yrs.	says 50 to 200 words
	knows full name, uses "I"
	begins to name things, to suit words to actions and action to words: "bring me the spoon, cup, shoe, etc."
	uses plurals
2½ yrs.	rhythm of speech is often broken and varied
	answers "What do you do with a ____?"
	uses negatives in speech
	asks questions spontaneously
	speech is about 65% intelligible, in context
3 yrs.	enunciates all vowel sounds, diphthongs, and the consonants m, l, ng, p, t, b, d, g, f
	speech is 70–80% intelligible, in context
4 yrs.	has mastery of inflection (can change volume and rate)
	uses 3- and 4-syllable words
	says 6- to 8-word sentences
	uses adj., adv., prep., and conj., and complex sentences
	speech is about 90–95% intelligible in context

speaking. A reasonable third question is: How familiar am I with the speech and language of children of this age?

Disorders in communication are not uncommon in young handicapped children. They influence the development of other skills in a variety of ways. For gross and fine motor instruction, the young child needs to be able to understand and follow verbal directions. When a child begins school, her ability to understand language and concepts becomes increasingly important; she may become socially isolated as young normal children become increasingly verbal in their play.

When children fail to acquire language normally, their families often begin speaking to them less frequently. The substitution of gestures and nonverbal forms of communication might help, but many of the same children who don't understand oral language also have difficulty interpreting nonverbal symbols such as facial expressions and vocal inflections (Johnson, 1975). As a result, the child may not be able to go on errands that involve verbal requests or the use of a telephone. All of these problems tend to retard the growth of the communication-impaired child's independence from his family. As was true of the other areas of development, a problem in developing communication skills affects all aspects of a child's development.

PROBE 2-5
Conceptual, Social-Emotional,
and Communication Development

1. The baby who throws her bottle from her high chair, cries for someone to pick it up, then throws it again, once it is returned to her is demonstrating
   a. the concept of object permanence
   b. the concept of motor meaning
   c. the concept of same and different
   d. the concept of cause and effect
   e. the concept of range of reaction

2. T F Mentally retarded children have been shown to progress through sequences of Piagetian tasks in the same developmental sequence but with different rates of progress and different levels of attainments from those of normal children.

3. T F Beginning to attend school is often sufficient cause for mild forms of expression of abnormal social-emotional behaviors.

4. T F Disturbances in the behaviors of young handicapped children may frequently result from the failure to provide intervention for primary handicapping conditions.

5. T F Disorders in communication are uncommon in young handicapped children.

6. T F Expressive language always exceeds receptive language development.

SELF-HELP SKILLS

You should be able to describe the development of self-help skills and identify areas of abnormal development.

The ability to care for one's self is fundamental in achieving independence and self-sufficiency. The collected norms in self-help skills have been divided into those related to eating; dressing, bathing, and grooming; and toileting. These will be discussed in three sections.

EATING

The earliest self-help behaviors are those related to feeding and eating. When the cheek is lightly touched, normal newborns turn their heads toward the stimulus and purse their lips (rooting reflex). Normal newborns also have sucking and swallowing reflexes. The sucking reflex is lost when spoon or cup feeding is begun (Knoblock and Pasamanick, 1974). The sight of food or the sounds of food preparation produce excitement and anticipation in the normal four month old. By six months of age, biting and chewing begin to replace the earlier mouthing of objects or foods (Knoblock and Pasamanick, 1974). Finger foods are usually introduced when the child can sit and grasp objects.

According to Knoblock and Pasamanick the movements of eating (biting, chewing, control of salivary overflow, swallowing with a minimum of air) and drinking (command of lips, tongue and jaws) are well differentiated and well coordinated by eighteen months of age. By five years children can handle a knife and fork quite well, although they may need occasional help.

During the second or third year of life, the rapid growth that characterized infancy declines; the rate of weight gain and metabolic rate also decline, and the child often refuses to eat (Lowrey, 1973). It is during this period that behavior problems often begin. These problems can be exacerbated by parent's excessive concern with the child's decreased appetite. Although it has not been clearly established, there is some evidence that learned attitudes about food can cause overweight and obesity, which can affect the development of gross motor skills and social acceptance by peers. In addition, overweight children often have weight problems as adults (Erickson, 1976).

Milestones for eating are listed in Chart 2-8.

DRESSING, BATHING, AND GROOMING

Dressing, bathing, and grooming skills begin to develop in young normal children at about two years of age. At this point, they begin to assume more responsibility for themselves, although they are still somewhat dependent on their caregivers. Their earlier passiveness begins to be replaced by more active participation in bathing and getting into and out of their clothing.

Norms of dressing, bathing, and grooming are included in Chart 2-9.

TOILETING

Although wide variations appear in the literature, children are considered physiologically capable of inhibiting bowel and bladder release by the time they are approximately fifteen months old. By eighteen months of age they indicate wet pants. They use their newly developed ability to express themselves to tell about the product of urination or a bowel movement after the fact. Gradually they begin to associate internal sensation with language; at approximately two years they tell as they act. The next stage is to tell before they act, but not soon enough to be taken to a toilet. Finally, they tell of a need for the toilet in advance. The level of maturity for toilet training can be estimated by measuring and recording the length of time between one bowel movement or urination and the next. After a few days a pattern will emerge. The child is ready for toilet training if he is dry for periods of two hours or more. Unless a child is dry for at least two hours at a time, he will not have a sensation of relief as he uses the toilet. Toileting milestones are listed in Chart 2-10.

Disturbances in toilet training may appear with the beginning of school attendance or during other periods of anxiety or excitement. The progress of toilet training may be slowed if the child finds it is more rewarding not to be toilet trained because of the play and social interaction surrounding the changing of diapers (Hart, 1974, p. 21).

Since toilet training is as much a parental activity as a child's, parental readiness should also be assessed. This may be done by exploring parents' attitudes about past toilet training efforts, the advantages of toilet training, the time investment required, and the convenience. Toilet training can be accomplished more quickly and easily if both parents and child are ready as determined by the criteria we have mentioned.

For exceptional young children the appearances of milestones of development in each of the seven areas we have described may not proceed "on schedule."

Chart 2-8
Milestones for Eating Skills

Birth	sucks and swallows liquids
	reflexes: rooting, sucking, swallowing, gagging
2 mo.	sucks and swallows liquids from spoon
3 mo.	eats strained foods from spoon
	brings hands against bottle while drinking
4 mo.	sips from cup, with spilling, if held for him
	anticipates on sight of food or sound of food preparation
5 mo.	holds spoon, cannot use alone
6 mo.	feeds self cracker, begins to bite and chew
7 mo.	holds own bottle
8 mo.	chews small lumps
9 mo.	removes bottle and replaces it
10 mo.	finger feeds self part of meal with ease
11 mo.	holds bottle momentarily alone, using 2 hands
1 yr.	holds cup, 2 hands
14 mo.	chews table food
15 mo.	grasps spoon, inserts into mouth, uses rotation, spilling much
	holds cup, digital grasp
1½ yrs.	manages spoon well, a little spilling
	uses cup (2 hands), drinks without spilling
21 mo.	replaces cup after use
23 mo.	requests food when hungry, water when thirsty
2 yrs.	holds and uses small glass, one hand
	uses spoon well, no spilling
3 yrs.	uses fork for spearing
	spreads butter/jam on bread with knife
4 yrs.	uses knife for pulling meat apart
	helps set the table
	pours from pitcher
5 yrs.	cuts with knife
6 yrs.	sets table without help

Although achievements in one area may progress normally, a handicapping condition may affect achievements in other areas. Familiarity with the sequences of normal early development can help both parents and professionals identify developmental delays and provide services to overcome them.

When parents know their child has a handicap, they often alter their expectations of the child's progress in ways that are detrimental to the child's attaining his full potential. Both parents and professionals can learn to differentiate between what exceptional children are unable to perform due to their age and what

Chart 2-9
Milestones for Dressing, Bathing, and Grooming

Dressing

3 mo.	pulls at clothing
1 yr.	cooperates in dressing: holds out arms for sleeves, foot for shoe
14 mo.	takes shoes off
1½ yrs.	pulls on simple garments (mitts, socks, hat)
	pulls up pants, unzips only
	tries to put on shoes
2 yrs.	helps in dressing: puts arms in sleeves
	pulls up and pushes down pants
2½ yrs.	undresses completely
	puts on shirt and coat
	puts on shoes (may be wrong feet)
3 yrs.	chooses own clothes
	unbuttons (except back)
3½ yrs.	distinguishes front from back of clothing
4 yrs.	dresses and undresses with supervision, except difficult fasteners
	laces (does not tie) shoes
4½ yrs.	buttons front buttons
5 yrs.	zips zippers and snaps snaps
5½ yrs.	ties shoes with bow
	buckles, unbuckles, laces, and unlaces shoes
	dresses and undresses completely

Bathing and Grooming

5 mo.	holds onto side of tub and cries when taken out
6 mo.	splashes with hands and feet during bath, closes eyes at sight of washcloth
8 mo.	puts arm in front of face to avoid being washed
1½ yrs.	opens doors, pulls out drawers
2 yrs.	washes hands and face, neither well
	washes front of body in bath
2½ yrs.	brushes hair, rumpling it
3½ yrs.	brushes teeth, needs help
4 yrs.	washes and dries face without help
	brushes teeth, no help
	puts away toys after play, with some supervision
	can hang coat if hook is used
4½ yrs.	dries self after bath
5 yrs.	brushes hair well independently
	hangs up clothes
	washes face and hands alone
6 yrs.	bathes self if tub is prepared

Chart 2-10
Milestones in Toileting

1 mo.	bowel movements 3–4 times a day, associated with waking
2 mo.	2 bowel movements a day, either at waking or after feeding
4 mo.	delay between feeding and elimination
7 mo.	stays dry for 1–2 hour intervals
10 mo.	may be dry after short naps
1½ yrs.	may awaken at night and cry to be changed
	may respond with utterance or nod when asked if she wants to go to toilet, or may tell you
	indicates wet pants
22 mo.	begins to tell need of toilet and usually uses same word for both functions
	only occasional accidents
2 yrs.	verbally differentiates bowel and bladder functions
	may stay dry at night if taken up
2½ yrs.	climbs onto lavatory seat
	can control bladder up to 5 hours
3 yrs.	uses routine times for elimination
3½ yrs.	attempts to wipe herself, usually not successful
	stays dry at night
4 yrs.	goes to toilet herself, manages clothes alone
5 yrs.	toilets self, washes and dries hands
	may have few accidents and needs reminding during the day
	one bowel movement a day

they cannot do because of their impairment. A knowledge of normal early development and familiarity with the effects of a variety of handicapping conditions forms a solid basis for working with exceptional young children.

PROBE 2-6
Self-Help Skills

1. T F The child's refusal to eat during the second or third year of life is caused by a change in his temperament at this time.

2. Except when thumb-sucking persists, mouthing of hands and toys usually disappears by approximately ____ (age).

3. T F Dressing skills begin to become possible in most children at about 24 months of age.

4. T F All children reach the maturity required for toilet-training at the same time, twelve months of age.

5. T F Toilet-training may be delayed if parents, as well as the child, are not "ready" for this activity.

IDENTIFYING YOUNG CHILDREN WHO NEED SPECIAL SERVICES

You should be able to define and give examples of activities used to identify young children who need special services: casefinding, screening, diagnosis, and assessment.

As services for young exceptional children and their families are expanded, many states are involved in efforts to locate and identify this target population. However, these efforts present some unique problems; to make matters worse, there is often confusion about the terminology used in these efforts. The following definitions and descriptions may provide helpful clarification.

CASEFINDING, CHILD FIND, AND EARLY IDENTIFICATION

The term *casefinding* refers to the activities designed to make initial contact with a target population and increase the public's awareness of the services that are available (L. Cross, 1977a). Casefinding activities can include circulating brochures, presenting radio or television announcements, preparing newspaper articles, sending notes home with children already in programs, making personal contacts with agencies (including health, civic, religious, and community organizations), and door-to-door canvassing. The relative effectiveness of each of these approaches depends on a variety of factors, but it is crucial that the target population (ages of children, types of handicapping conditions, geographic boundaries) be decided on before casefinding efforts begin. Zehrbach (1975) reported that no one approach is effective in all areas.

The term *child find* is applied to many of these same activities when they are implemented by states and local educational agencies as a result of federal legislation requiring that all handicapped children be identified and served (Safford, 1978). Each state has its own definitions of handicapping conditions and ages of eligibility for services. Thus, child find efforts and activities, particularly those related to very young children, vary from one place to another.

Identification is the process of establishing an awareness that a problem exists (Hayden and Edgar, 1977). Certain kinds of problems or potential problems can be identified very early. For example, *genetic counseling* may make prospective parents aware of risk factors indicated by their own genetic makeup or histories. Using this information, prospective parents can decide whether or not to risk the birth of a child who may be handicapped. During pregnancy, certain conditions such as Tay-Sachs disease and Down's syndrome may be detected by *amniocentesis*. This procedure, which involves testing the amniotic fluid surrounding the fetus, may allow parents to decide to terminate the pregnancy rather than give birth to a handicapped child.

Beck (1977) stated that 6.8 percent of all handicapped children could and should be identified at birth or shortly after birth. Examples of conditions identifiable at birth are galactosemia and phenylketonuria (PKU) (genetic disorders); these are identified by urine tests. The harmful effects of these two conditions can be avoided by special diets for the infants.

Some children develop handicapping conditions through accidents, illnesses, or poisoning. Many young children have handicapping conditions that go unnoticed. In the period between birth and school age, there are procedures to identify children who need special services, but they are not universally applied (Kakalik, Brewer, Dougherty, Fleischauer, and Genensky, 1973). Pediatricians (when they are consulted) often lack the time or techniques to notice developmental problems (Hayden, 1978). Thus, many children who could benefit from early identification do not receive the services they need. Suggestions to remedy this situation have included the establishment of a national registry for all births (Caldwell, 1976), the maintenance of "high risk" registries (Conference on Newborn Hearing Screening, 1971), and the use of public information programs and mass mandatory screening programs (Karnes and Zehrbach, 1977b).

SCREENING

As you know from the brief description in Chapter 1, screening is the testing of a large number of children to identify those most likely to exhibit a handicap. The children who are identified as possibly having handicaps are then referred to a professional for a more in-depth assessment. Ideally, screening should be accomplished by administering a standardized, quick, easy to administer, and efficient assessment test (or tests) to the population being screened. This keeps the screening effort as economical as possible. It is also helpful if the screening instrument is acceptable not only to the professionals who do the follow-up, but also to parents and the general public. One example of a screening procedure is the urine test for PKU, mandated by law in many states. For young children a variety of screening instruments have been developed. Many of these are discussed by Hayden and Edgar (1977).

There are several important issues to consider in developing a screening program. Some have argued that if the necessary diagnostic follow-up personnel and educational services are not available to help suspected or identified children, the screening effort should not be undertaken. On the other hand, if the number of children needing services is not known, funds for their services are not likely to be allocated. Particular attention should be given to the accuracy of the selected instruments. Obviously, if the screening instrument does not accurately select the target group from the larger population, it will not provide accurate data on the number of children needing services.

Other important factors that help determine the value of a screening effort are (1) whether the condition being screened for improves with treatment, (2) whether early treatment improves the prognosis more than treatment at the usual time, and (3) whether the condition can be adequately diagnosed through the use of further tests. It is important to remember that when children are selected through the screening process (that is, they fail the screening test), their parents should be made aware of the need for further diagnosis before decisions are made about their suspected problems. If this is not done, and the other factors we have mentioned are not considered, parents may be caused unnecessary anxiety. Screening should *not* result in the application of a label without further diagnostic study.

In 1967 the Early and Periodic Screening, Diagnosis, and Treatment (EPSDT) program was established by an amendment to Title 19 of the Social Security Act. The purpose of this legislation was to make these services available to all children eligible for Medicaid, up to age twenty-one. The program began in 1972; in 1976, it was reported that of the 12 million eligible children, about 4.5 million were enrolled in EPSDT. There were wide variations from state to state in how this program was being run and in its quality (Special Report: Public Policy, NAEYC-EPSDT, 1976).

The importance of identifying exceptional children as early as possible has been emphasized throughout this chapter. Teachers of young children in early childhood programs should be a part of this early identification process. According to Safford (1978) teachers should (1) be familiar with normal developmental processes, (2) know the symptoms of specific handicapping conditions, (3) be skilled observers and recorders of individual children's behavior, (4) be able to use informal procedures to diagnose educational problems, (5) be familiar with and able to use resource persons in the community and the school, and (6) be able to communicate effectively and continuously with parents (p. 31). Teachers of young children see them longer and more continuously than other professionals, such as pediatricians or psychologists; although they cannot make final diagnoses, their efforts to identify children with problems are very important.

DIAGNOSIS

Screening for the genetic disorders we have mentioned is conducted largely to determine whether a child needs medical attention. When a child is referred from screening for diagnosis of an educational problem, the process is more complicated. The purposes of diagnosis are (1) to determine whether a problem exists and if it is serious enough to require remediation, and (2) to clarify the nature of the problem.

Diagnosis is best carried out by a multidisciplinary team selected on the basis of the child's suspected problem. The team may include doctors, psychologists, social workers, teachers, and other education personnel. The ultimate purpose of diagnosis of a suspected education problem is to determine what is hindering a child's development and how best to help her. Once the relevant information on a child's problem is collected and analyzed, a conference should be arranged with her parents to discuss placement and treatment.

ASSESSMENT

After a child is placed in a program, he is assessed to determine (1) specific strengths and weaknesses in the child's abilities; (2) his level of functioning in a number of developmental areas, and (3) his learning characteristics. This information allows teachers to plan specific instructional objectives in the child's curriculum. The use of assessment (including diagnostic) information ensures that a child's overall program is based on his individual needs, strengths, and weaknesses.

Assessment can involve the use of criterion-referenced measures, norm-referenced measures, Piagetian devices, anecdotal records, daily logs, observational records, and videotapes.

PROBE 2-7
Identifying Young Children
Who Need Special Services

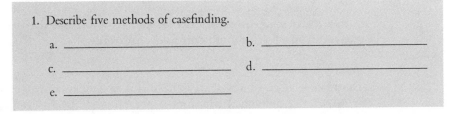

1. Describe five methods of casefinding.

   a. _____   b. _____

   c. _____   d. _____

   e. _____

2. How may certain handicapping conditions be identified before or at the time of the birth of the child?

_____.

3. T   F   The purpose of screening young children is to make diagnoses of their handicapping conditions; this may be done through the screening procedures.

4. Give one reason why the accuracy of the screening instrument is an important consideration.

_____.

5. Give one example of a condition that may be screened for at the preschool level. What are the benefits to the identified children? _____

_____.

6. Why are teachers in a good position to screen the young children in their early childhood programs? _____

_____.

7. Describe the differences between diagnosis and assessment, in purposes, personnel involved, and outcomes.

	diagnosis	*assessment*
purpose	_____	_____
personnel	_____	_____
outcome	_____	_____

8. Name 3 assessment procedures.

a. _____   b. _____   c. _____

ALTERNATIVE SERVICE DELIVERY SYSTEMS

You should be able to describe the implications the "least restrictive environment" clause of PL 94-142 has for the education of young exceptional children.

The processes of casefinding, screening, diagnosis, and assessment culminate in the preparation of individual educational programs (IEPs) for young exceptional children. These programs are implemented and delivered to children and their families in many different ways. Several of the alternatives are discussed in the following section. For more detailed information, you are referred to texts by Allen et al. (1978); Day and Parker (1977); Ellis and Cross (1977); Jordan, Hayden, Karnes, and Wood, (1977); Lillie and Trohanis (1976); and Tjossem (1976).

FACTORS IN PLANNING

Several important factors must be considered in determining how best to serve young exceptional children and their families. Program planners must consider the age range, types and degrees of handicapping conditions, and the variety of services needed by the target population in the particular geographic area (Lillie, 1977b).

Other factors that should be considered are the philosophy of the intervention program, the administration of the program, the amount of funding available, the number of children the program may serve, the target population for training, and the physical location of the program (Ackerman and Moore, 1976). Although all these factors are important, we will focus in this chapter on the physical locations of the various service delivery systems.

ALTERNATIVE DELIVERY SYSTEMS

Center-Based Service Delivery. Among programs developed under HCEEP funding, the center-based models (those in which services are provided in a central location) are the most numerous (Ackerman and Moore, 1976). These programs tend to be for older preschool children and for those with relatively severe or multiple handicaps, who benefit most from special equipment and specialized personnel assembled at the central location (Karnes and Zehrbach, 1977a). Although staff members may only rarely visit the children's homes, parent participation at the center is considered important, and parents are encouraged to use what they've learned at home.

One example of a center-based program is the Model Preschool Center for Handicapped Children at the University of Washington, mentioned earlier. This program serves Down's syndrome and other handicapped children of all ages, including the newborn and the very young. The Preschool Center is part of the Experimental Education Unit of the College of Education and the Child Development and Mental Retardation Center; it is supported by a combination of federal, state, and private funds (Hayden and Haring, 1976).

Children in this program may be placed in one of several classrooms, depending on their needs and levels of functioning. Individual instruction is based on initial and ongoing assessment and behavioral information. Parents and staff work together to formulate each child's objectives.

Another example of a center-based program for young exceptional children and their families is the UNISTAPS Project in Minneapolis, Minnesota. This program serves hearing impaired children in the public schools from birth onward. Parent involvement is also one of the strengths of this program (Freedman, Warner, and Cook, 1973).

Center- and Home-Based Service Delivery. Many programs provide services coordinated between an instructional center and children's homes. Parents may receive training at the center as well as home visits from teachers who conduct parent conferences, observe parent-child interactions, and educate parents about appropriate teaching methods.

The PEECH (Precise Early Education of Children with Handicaps) Project at the University of Illinois is a combined home- and center-based service delivery system. The program is supported by state, local and university funds. Services to handicapped children from the age of three years are mandatory in Illinois, so the program must meet state requirements for certification, size of class, length of school day, eligibility criteria, teacher-pupil ratio, and length of the school year. This program serves children who are mildly to moderately multiply handicapped.

The PEECH program uses eight different classrooms, each with a maximum of ten handicapped and five normal children, who act as models. It is staffed with educators, psychologists, speech and language therapists, and social workers. Parents are encouraged to teach at home, attend parent group meetings, use the parent library and toy-lending library, speak at public gatherings, work with other parents, construct instructional materials and make policies (Karnes and Zehrbach, 1977a and b).

Other examples of combined center- and home-based programs include the Rutland Center in Athens, Georgia, the Chapel Hill Training Outreach Project in North Carolina, and the Preschool and Early Education Project (PEEP), in Starkville, Mississippi. More complete descriptions of these programs may be found in the text by Jordan, Hayden, Karnes, and Wood (1977).

Home-Based Service Delivery. Home-based programs are particularly well suited to sparsely populated areas and clusters of small towns. They do not necessarily serve only those with relatively uncommon handicaps, such as hearing or visual impairment or severe multihandicaps. Home-based services are also appropriate when parents are reluctant to leave their homes or send their children away. Many home-based programs begin with children in the birth to three-year-old age range.

In home-based early education programs, parents are viewed as their children's primary teachers. Paraprofessionals or professionals provide instruction and demonstrations for parents on a regular schedule of home visits.

One example of a home-based program is the Portage Project. This program serves children with a variety of handicapping conditions from birth to age six in the large rural area surrounding Portage, Wisconsin. Although the program began as a First Chance project, it is now supported by the public schools.

Children in the Portage program must exhibit a one year lag in development to be enrolled. No child is considered too severely handicapped to participate. Each full-time home visiting teacher serves approximately fourteen children. The frequency of visits is decreased as parents learn to plan objectives and teach their own children. Initial and ongoing assessments are made in a number of developmental areas, and curriculum objectives are designed to suit individual children's needs. Parents are encouraged to spend time working with their child each day (Shearer and Shearer, 1977).

Other examples of home-based programs with unique approaches to service delivery include the Telstar Project in Alpena, Michigan, which places handicapped children with normal children in day care homes located near the children's usual homes. In Projecta Casa, the homebound component of Edgewood School's Early Childhood Education for the Handicapped Program in San Antonio, Texas, high school students work in pairs under the direction of a homebound teacher. They serve Mexican American exceptional children from six months to six years of age. More information on these and other programs may be found in Jordan's (1977) text.

In addition to the three alternatives for service delivery just described, many programs provide a sequence of home-based instruction for children under a certain age (usually three years), followed by center-based preschool. Yet another alternative is provided by the itinerant (traveling) consultant or resource teacher. These teachers provide assistance to other preschool teachers who have identified exceptional children in their classrooms. The purpose of the consultant teacher is to help with the integration of young exceptional children in classes with normal children. An excellent resource on the topic of mainstreaming young exceptional children is Guralnick's (1978) text, *Early Intervention and the Integration of Handicapped and Nonhandicapped Children.*

INFANT PROGRAMS

Several authors (such as Caldwell, 1971; Bronfenbrenner, 1975) have suggested that the earlier intervention begins and the longer it continues, the better are the results. Yet exceptional infants present many unique problems, particularly in diagnosis and assessment. Even normal infants respond differently than toddlers and young children. The presence of handicapping conditions in infants compounds the difficulties in making clear diagnoses and interpreting behavioral information.

Yet the number of programs serving exceptional infants continues to grow, and research is helping determine the best methods of serving this population. An excellent resource text describing the issues and several exemplary service programs for infants is Caldwell and Stedman's (1977) book, *Infant Education: A Guide for Helping Handicapped Children in the First Three Years.* Connor, Williamson, and Siepp (1978) recently provided another useful resource, the *Program Guide for Infants and Toddlers with Neuromotor and Other Developmental Disabilities.*

PARENTS

One reason home-based programs and programs dealing with children under the age of three are so effective is that they emphasize the involvement of parents. When parents are interested in enhancing their children's development, the children are more likely to gain from the early intervention program. Furthermore, the gains made by the target child often have beneficial effects on the child's siblings (Klaus and Gray, 1968).

Parent involvement was required in the First Chance Network programs. In their survey of parent involvement in these programs, Shearer and Shearer (1977) reported that parents filled the following roles: they acted as administrators, disseminators, staff members, primary teachers, recruiters, curriculum developers, counselors, assessors of skills, evaluators, and record keepers. This variety of parent roles contributed to the projects' overall operations tremendously. Parents have also been effective in changing the role of the state in providing services (Luterman, 1971). Parents should not, however, substitute involvement in programs or political activity for direct involvement with their children. Parents are their children's first, most enduring, and most influential teachers. Nobody else can teach as effectively; as a result, educators of young exceptional children must be prepared to teach parents to teach their own child. Lillie and Trohanis' (1976) *Teaching Parents to Teach* is a valuable resource for this effort.

PROBE 2-8
Alternative Service Delivery Systems

1. Name five factors which should be considered in planning programs for young exceptional children.

   1. _____   2. _____

3. _____   4. _____

5. _____

2. Describe the advantages of center-based programs. Give one example of this type of program. _____

_____

_____.

3. One example of a combination center- and home-based program for young exceptional children is: _____.
Describe this program.

_____

_____

_____.

4. Under what circumstances are home-based services for young exceptional children appropriate? Name one such program. _____

_____

_____.

5. What is the most important role that a parent of an exceptional young child can take in the early childhood intervention program? _____

_____

_____.

SUMMARY

1. Many research studies have demonstrated the importance of providing early education for exceptional children. In fact, those exceptional children who do not receive early education may actually decline in their development.
2. The preschool exceptional child has the same needs, wants, and problems as all other children, but she also has additional difficulties to overcome.
3. Intelligence is not fixed but can be modified by environment.
4. Ten percent of the vacancies in Head Start programs for the disadvantaged must be made available to the handicapped.

5. Special incentive grants are available to states that serve preschool handicapped children. Other federal legislation funds experimental demonstration projects for the young handicapped.
6. Exceptional children go through the same developmental stages as other children.
7. Developmental norms are useful in screening, assessing, and developing curricula for young exceptional children.
8. The areas of development of most importance in young exceptional children are gross motor, fine motor, perception, conceptual, social-emotional, communication, and self-help.
9. State and local officials are involved in casefinding, child find, and early identification projects. The purpose of these projects is to identify young handicapped children who need services.
10. Screening is the testing of a large number of children to identify those who need additional in-depth diagnosis and assessment; these activities can result in the provision of special services.
11. Services are most frequently delivered to young handicapped children in centrally located service-delivery centers, in the children's homes, or in both centers and the children's homes.
12. There is a trend to develop and offer infant intervention projects for very young children to reduce the effects of disabling conditions on later development.
13. It is extremely important to include parents in the education programs for their young handicapped children.

TASK SHEET 2
Field Experiences in Early Childhood Special Education

Select *one* of the following and complete the assigned tasks:

Program Visitation

Visit a preschool program for exceptional children. This could be a center-based program, a kindergarten, or a home-based program. Describe in a paper of no more than three pages the program that you visited, the curriculum that was being used, the interactions that you had with the staff or the students, and your general reactions to the program.

Professional Interview

Arrange to visit a professional who works with preschool exceptional children. This could be a teacher, pediatrician, physical therapist, or director of a preschool. Discuss the job with the person you choose and write a paper that answers the following questions.

1. Where did you visit?
2. Whom did you interview?
3. What were the responsibilites of the person being interviewed?
4. What types of training were necessary to enter that profession?
5. What types of problems does the person encounter?
6. What are the rewards that the person receives?
7. What did you learn from this experience and what was your reaction?

Parent Interview

Interview the parents of a preschool exceptional child. Using great tact, inquire about the types of services that they have received for themselves and their child, and the types of services that they would like to receive. Try to determine some of the problems and rewards of being the parent of an exceptional child. In a paper of no more than three pages, summarize your findings. Include your reactions and a description of what you learned from this experience.

Home Inventory

Obtain the inventory included in the following article and evaluate your home. Then, summarize your evaluation and indicate what you would need to do in order to make it safe for a young child.

Wolinsky, G. F. and Walker, S. A Home Safety Inventory for Parents of Preschool Handicapped Children, *Teaching Exceptional Children*, 1975, 7 (3), 82–86.

Library Study

Select three articles from your library that relate to the education of preschool exceptional children. Write a one-page abstract of each.

Design Your Own Field Experience

If you know of a unique experience you can have with young exceptional children, or do not want to do any of the above alternatives, discuss your alternative with your instructor and complete the tasks that you agree on.

Probe Answers

Probe 2-1

1. a. prevent secondary problems
    b. increase acceptance of the handicapped
    c. enhance probability of regular school attendance
    d. be cost efficient
    e. improve parent-child relations
    f. help the family and parents
2. True
3. 1. d; 2. e; 3. a; 4. f; 5. g; 6. c; 7. b

4. The Head Start program or PL 93-644
5. 10%
6. develop experimental demonstration projects for preschool handicapped children
7. True
8. True

Probe 2-2

1. False

2. True
3. e
4. True; True; True; False; False; True

Probe 2-3

1. False
2. True
3. 20
4. Either of the following:
   — to prevent contractures
   — to facilitate normal movement patterns
5. previous experience with fine motor skills

Probe 2-4

1. 6 months; strabismus; amblyopia
2. False
3. True
4. False
5. first
6. communications
7. True

Probe 2-5

1. d
2. True
3. True
4. True
5. False
6. False

Probe 2-6

1. False
2. one year
3. True
4. False
5. True

Probe 2-7

1. a. brochures; b. radio/television announcements; c. newspaper articles; d. sending notes home with children in programs; e. personal contacts with agencies
2. Before birth: amniocentesis for Tay Sachs disease or Down's syndrome; at birth: urine tests for galactosemia or PKU

3. False
4. It must be accurate in order to provide information on the number of children needing services.
5. Amblyopia. Early treatment can save vision in the deviated eye.
6. They see the children more continuously and for longer periods of time than pediatricians.
7. *Diagnosis*
   Purpose: to substantiate the existence of the problem or to disprove it
   Personnel: medical, psychological, educational
   Outcome: placement and/or treatment, conference with parents
   Assessment
   Purpose: to identify strengths, weaknesses, functioning levels, and learning style
   Personnel: educational
   Outcome: individualized educational program
8. Any 3 of the following:
   a. norm-referenced devices
   b. criterion-referenced devices
   c. Piagetian measures
   d. observation
   e. logs
   f. anecdotal records

Probe 2-8

1. age range; types and degrees of handicapping conditions; geographic area; funds available; numbers of children
2. Specialized personnel and/or equipment can be assembled in a central location. Example: Model Preschool Center, University of Washington
3. the PEECH Program. It serves 3-5 year old handicapped children along with normal children and is funded by a combination of state, local, and university resources. Includes parent involvement activities.
4. In rural and sparsely populated areas. Example: Portage Program, Wisconsin.
5. teaching his or her own child

Brian, six, was repeating words and phrases. He was certain that he couldn't talk like everyone else. The children at school teased him unmercifully. He began to develop "stomachaches" and "headaches." His parents, in an attempt to help, suggested to Brian that his stuttering handicap was something he had to learn to live with. It certainly did not affect their love for him or make him a lesser person. After three months of speech therapy, Brian was speaking normally. He was looking forward to school each day and could demonstrate to his classmates and his parents that he could talk just like everyone else.

Martha, six, could not move her tongue, lips, and jaws on command to talk. Even though she clearly understood all that was said and could gesture or point to appropriate responses, she was unable to use spoken language. Her IQ when tested with instruments that did not require speech placed her in the average to bright group. Much to her parents' concern and after many futile attempts to train Martha to use spoken language, her speech pathologist introduced an electronic communication device that Martha could program to say for her some of the things she could not say for herself.

Walter's mother spent countless hours training him to repeat the letters of the alphabet, name body parts, and identify colors, hoping that he would be placed in a class with normal seven year olds. Walter learned his letters and words but repeated them in a parrotlike way with no understanding of their meaning. He could not understand simple directions or even use his memorized words appropriately. A speech-language pathologist counseled Walter's family and helped them to realize that before his language could be meaningful, Walter had to learn what words meant. Currently Walter is in a class for mildly retarded children where the teacher in cooperation with the speech-language pathologist is providing him with the enriched experiences he needs to learn how to use language.

3

Communication Disorders

Richard Culatta
and Barbara K. Culatta

Richard Culatta is Associate Professor of Speech-Language Pathology and Audiology at the University of Kentucky. Current areas of interest are disfluency in children and adults and clinical supervision. Dr. Culatta has functioned as a speech-language pathologist in public schools, hospitals, rehabilitation centers, and university clinics. Barbara K. Culatta is Assistant Professor at the University of Kentucky. Currently the coordinator of an early childhood program for handicapped children, Dr. Culatta has developed several language intervention programs. Her primary research interest is the relationship between perceptual and linguistic deficits in hyperactive and autistic children.

The three children and their communication disorders described on the facing page represent success stories in the diagnosis and treatment of speech and language problems. Unfortunately, these success stories are not nearly as common an occurrence as we would like to see. Most of us can speak as easily as we breathe. Our children can tell us quite clearly of the worlds they are discovering as they grow. Although we may have to struggle for words occasionally, and sometimes we can't express what we would like precisely, we can almost always make someone understand what we are trying to say.

For more than 20 million people in this country, about 10 percent of the population, communication is much more difficult (Human Communication and Its Disorders — An Overview, 1969). Some people have mild disorders, sources of occasional embarrassment and annoyance. Others have problems so severe that it is impossible for them to live normal lives, especially in a society like ours that places great emphasis on the ability to communicate.

This chapter is about the processes of communication and the causes and effects of communication problems. When you are finished, you should know how to tell the difference between speech and language; how speech and language are acquired; how to define a "communication problem"; what the characteristics of some common speech and language disorders are; and what the responsibilities of the speech-language pathologist are.

It is important to remember that communication problems, like the other disorders discussed in this book, cannot be considered in isolation. The ability or inability to communicate can have an effect on every other area of development. You should always regard a child's problem in the context of the whole child.

BASIC CONCEPTS OF SPEECH AND LANGUAGE

> **You should be able to define speech and language, differentiate between them, and describe how each develops.**

WHAT IS A COMMUNICATION PROBLEM?

There have been many attempts to describe what constitutes a communication disorder. According to Van Riper (1978), a person has a communication problem when his speech differs from the speech of others to the extent that it calls attention to itself, interferes with the intended message, or causes the speaker or listener to be distressed. More concisely, impaired speech is conspicuous, unintelligible, or unpleasant. Perkins (1977) adds that speech is impaired when it is ungrammatical, culturally or personally unsatisfactory, or injurious to the speech-producing mechanism. Johnson (1967) stresses the importance of listener reactions and the speaker's feelings about himself.

Perhaps the best way to determine whether a person has a speech problem is to ask yourself the following questions:

1. *Can I understand this person?* This is the simplest judgment you will have to make. If you cannot understand or can understand only with difficulty what a person is saying, she has a communication disorder.

2. *Does this person sound strange?* If you can understand someone, but he doesn't sound like you expect him to, he has a problem. An adult who sounds like Elmer Fudd, a 200-pound adult male who sounds like a nine-year-old girl, and a person who has a flat, expressionless manner of speaking all have communication problems.

3. *Does this person have any peculiar physical characteristics when speaking?* A person who has distracting mannerisms that interfere with his message has a problem. These mannerisms might include unnecessary or unexpected movements of the lips, tongue, nostrils, arms, legs, or posture.

4. *Is the communication in a style inappropriate to the situation?* We do not expect the president of the United States to greet Congress before his annual State of the Union address by saying, "Hey, baby, what's happenin'? It's cool at my pad, what's goin' down here?" Nor do we expect a baseball manager to confront an umpire with "I strenuously object to the judgmental process in which you have recently indulged. It would be to our mutual benefit if you would reconsider

your opinion and its ramifications." Our point is that we normally shift our style of communicating to fit a given situation. A speaker unable to do this may have a problem.

5. *Do I enjoy listening to this speaker?* This is a judgment we all feel comfortable making. If the reason we don't enjoy a speaker is that we don't like her message, the speaker doesn't have a problem. If, on the other hand, we don't enjoy a speaker for one of the reasons mentioned here, she probably does have a problem. It is said that a true diplomat can tell you to go to hell in such a way that you'll look forward to the trip. Speakers who can alienate people merely by introducing themselves need help.

6. *Is this speaker damaging his communication mechanisms?* Like most other parts of the body, the organs used in communication can be misused. Although diagnoses of physiological abuse can be made only by specialists, listeners can often detect signs of strain in a speaker. Teachers should always refer to professionals children they think may be injuring their voices. An unnecessary referral hurts no one, but overlooking a symptom can have disastrous consequences.

7. *Does the speaker suffer when attempting to communicate?* This is difficult to judge, because a listener cannot usually determine how a person feels about her efforts to communicate. Many people considered normal communicators by their peers suffer emotionally as a result of shortcomings they imagine. Communication problems such as these that do not have obvious symptoms are among the most difficult to treat.

As you've probably realized, many speakers with problems will have more than one of the characteristics in this list. As always, your emphasis should be on the speaker as a whole, and not exclusively on a particular behavior.

THE DIFFERENCE BETWEEN SPEECH AND LANGUAGE

Speech and language are related, but they are not the same thing. Speech is the physical process of making the sounds and sound combinations of a language. Language is much more complex than speech; speech production is one of its components. Language is essentially the system according to which a people agree to talk about or represent environmental events. Once a group of people agree on a system for representing objects, events, and the relationships among objects and events, the system can be used to communicate all their experiences. The language system consists of words and word combinations.

Whereas the meaning of language is contained in its words and word combinations, it is speech that permits the transmission of meaning. Speech sounds are not meaningful in themselves, of course. They acquire meaning only if the speaker or listener knows their relationship to real events. To state it very simply, speech sounds are a medium for carrying messages.

Language, however, does not have to be transmitted via speech. Gestures that have some agreed-on relation to environmental events, such as the American Sign Language used by the deaf, can also be used to transmit messages. Similarly, words can be transmitted in writing. A person cannot learn to interpret written words, however, unless she knows what objects, actions, or events the words stand for. The distinction between the sounds used in words and the meanings of words is very important. The ability to make speech sounds is worthless unless we understand the meaning of the sounds. A parrot can be taught to produce words, but it cannot be taught to communicate with them.

We must remember that speech is a purely expressive activity, whereas language has both a receptive component and an expressive component. Our ability to receive language develops before our ability to express it. Furthermore, we all understand more language than we can say: we've all been unable to pronounce or define a word that we feel quite comfortable reading. In fact, our receptive skills, the ability to process and derive meaning from language, are a necessary prerequisite for expressive language. The person who cannot develop a receptive language will not produce an expressive one.

SPEECH MECHANISMS

Our ability to speak involves the coordination of three physical systems: the respiratory system, the sound-production system, and the articulatory mechanism.

The respiratory system permits us to draw air into our lungs; our actions on this air as it is slowly exhaled result in speech. The lungs consist of passive, spongy, elastic tissue. They are located in the rib cage above the diaphragm. (See Figure 3-1.) When we inhale, the diaphragm flattens out and the rib cage moves up and out, which increases the volume of the chest cavity and decreases the air pressure within the lungs, causing air to rush in. When the process is reversed, air is exhaled through the bronchial tubes and the trachea.

This exhaled air then encounters the sound-producing structure, the larynx (Figure 3-2). The larynx, a complex arrangement of cartilages, ligaments, muscles, and membranes, guards the passage to the lungs and contains a pair of soft tissue folds called the vocal folds. These folds can be brought together over the trachea; sound is produced when air rushes past and vibrates them. You can feel this vibration if you place your fingers beside your Adam's apple and say "ZZZZZZZZZ." Sounds that require the vibration of the vocal cords are said to be *voiced*.

The sound produced in the larynx is then acted upon by the third speech-producing system, the articulatory mechanism (Figure 3-3). This consists of the throat (pharynx), the mouth (oral cavity), the nose (nasal cavities), the jaw (mandible), the soft palate (velum), the lips, and the tongue, each of which affects the sound.

Figure 3-1
The Respiratory System

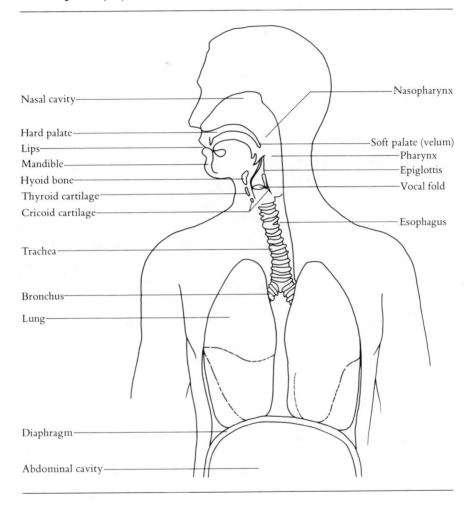

Nasal cavity

Hard palate

Lips

Mandible

Hyoid bone

Thyroid cartilage

Cricoid cartilage

Trachea

Bronchus

Lung

Diaphragm

Abdominal cavity

Nasopharynx

Soft palate (velum)

Pharynx

Epiglottis

Vocal fold

Esophagus

These complicated systems are all coordinated by the neurological system. Damage to the brain or nerves can drastically affect how they function, as we will discuss in the section on cerebral palsy.

Detailed accounts of the workings of the physical systems used in speech can be found in James Curtis's *Processes and Disorders of Human Communication* (1978), DeuPrec's "The Muscles of Voice and Speech" (1971) or Robert West's "The Neurophysiology of Speech." The latter two appear in the *Handbook of Speech Pathology and Audiology* (1971), edited by Lee Travis.

Figure 3-2
The Sound-Producing Structure

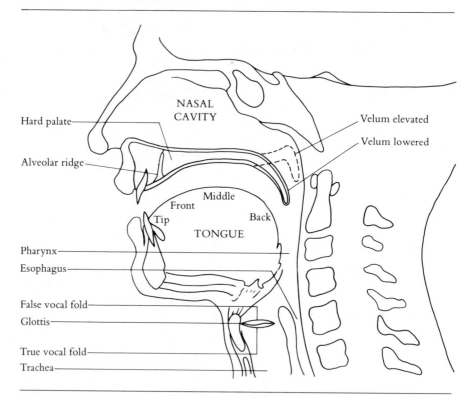

THE THREE TYPES OF SPEECH SOUNDS

There are three basic types of sounds in our language: vowels, diphthongs, and consonants. The symbols of these sounds and examples of words in which they appear are listed in Table 3-1.

Vowels are speech sounds that require voicing (the vibration of the vocal folds) and shaping by the tongue and lips. Try saying each of the vowels in Table 3-1, paying particular attention to your lips and tongue. For example, compare /i/ as in be to /u/ as in pool. /i/ is made with the tongue tip up and the lips in a grin. (The /i/ sound is in "cheese," which is why we smile when we say that word for a photographer.) By contrast, /u/ is made with the lips rounded and the airway modified by the back of the tongue.

Diphthongs (pronounced difthongs) are combinations of two vowels in a single syllable. Like vowels, they require voicing. Compare the single vowel /ɔ/

Figure 3-3
The Articulatory Mechanism

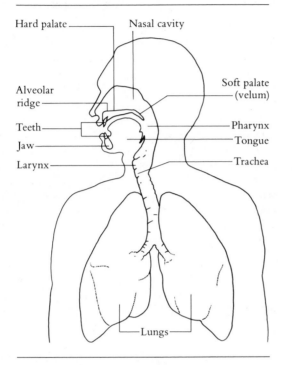

in the word h*a*ll to the diphthong /ɔɪ/ in the word t*oi*l. Can you hear the difference? Try saying the diphthong words in Table 3-1 aloud, listening carefully until you can hear the two vowels.

Consonants can be made with or without voicing. They are produced by specific movements of the articulators. Three factors determine how consonants sound. They are: (1) the manner in which the sound is made; (2) the major places where the articulators come in contact; and (3) whether the sound is voiced or not. These three factors are examined more closely in the following section.

Producing Consonant Sounds. We will consider the following manners of making sounds: (1) plosive, (2) fricative, (3) affricate, (4) nasal, (5) lateral, and (6) glide.

A *plosive* sound is made by building up pressure behind a complete articulatory closure and then suddenly releasing it in an ex*plosive* manner. Examples are /p/,/b/,/t/,/d/,/k/,/g/ (these are phonetic symbols representing sounds, not

Table 3-1
Phonetic Symbols

Vowels		Diphthongs		Consonants	
Symbol	Key	Symbol	Key	Symbol	Key
i	be	eɪ	paid	p	pill
I	lip	aɪ	time	b	ball
e	day	aʊ	couch	t	tip
ɛ	bed	ɔɪ	boil	d	down
æ	fad			k	kick
u	took			g	go
ʊ	pool			tʃ	charm
o	odor			dʒ	judge
ɔ	ball			f	fall
a	hot			v	vast
ɝ	girl			θ	thank
ə	ago			ð	this
ʌ	up			s	kiss
				z	zipper
				ʃ	shoe
				ʒ	usual
				h	hot
				m	mild
				n	never
				ŋ	bring
				l	light
				w	wish
				r	rule
				j	yesteryear

letters). Consider, for example, the different movements necessary to say /p/. First, you seal your lips. Then you allow air pressure to build, and finally you release it in a burst. That is a plosive. Try saying the other plosive sounds, paying particular attention to their plosive manner of production.

A *fricative* sound is made when the articulators do not completely stop the flow of air, but merely dam it up in a way that causes a friction-like noise. Examples of the fricative sounds are /f/,/v/,/θ/,/ð/,/s/,/z/,/ʃ/,/ʒ/,/h/. Try making a prolonged /f/ sound. You should be able to feel the air rushing over your lower lip and below your upper teeth in a continuous stream. See if you can feel the fricative manner of the other speech sounds.

An *affricate* is a combination of a plosive and a fricative. There are two affricate sounds: /tʃ/ and /dʒ/.

For all but three sounds in our language, the soft palate, or velum, comes in contact with the back of the throat, or pharynx. This closes the passage to the nasal cavity and forces the sound out through the mouth. Sounds produced this way are called *oral* sounds. When we make the other kinds of sound, the soft palate does not block the passage to the nose, so the sound passes through the nasal cavity. These are called *nasal* sounds. The three nasal sounds are /m/,/n/, and /ŋ/ (ng).

A *lateral* sound results when you fix an articulator in a certain position and allow air to escape around its sides. The sound /l/ is an example. Notice how your tongue tip touches the upper gum ridge while the air stream escapes from the sides.

A *glide* sound results from moving the articulators while the sound is being produced. The three glides we are most concerned with are /w/, /r/, and /j/.

The second way of describing sounds concerns the places where the articulators contact each other. There are seven contact points. We make sounds with both lips (bilabial) as in /p/, /b/, /m/, and /w/; with the lips and teeth in contact (labio-dental) as in /f/ and /v/; with the tongue and teeth in contact (lingua-dental) as in /θ/. Sounds are also made with the tongue against the gum ridge (lingua-alveolar) as in /t/, /d/, /n/, /s/, /z/, /and /l/; with the tongue touching the hard palate (lingua-palatal) as in /j/, /ʒ/,/ʃ/, and /r/ with the tongue and soft palate in contact (lingua-velar) as in /k/, and /g/; and finally by the action of the vocal folds (glottal) as in /h/.

The third factor that affects a sound is whether it is voiced or not. All sounds that use vocal fold vibration are voiced. Those which do not are voiceless. For example /s/ is voiceless, /z/ is voiced; /p/ is voiceless, /b/ is voiced. You should be able to go down the list of sounds on Chart 3-1 and determine which are voiced and which voiceless.

The three factors in saying consonants, manner of articulation, place of articulation, and voicing, are presented in Chart 3-1. For example, /m/ is a bilabial, voiced nasal, whereas /p/ is a bilabial, voiceless plosive. What would /f/ be? By using Chart 3-1 you should be able to describe the three characteristics of all the consonants.

THE DEVELOPMENT OF SPEECH

We don't learn all the sounds of our language at the same time. Some estimates suggest that many children are still acquiring the sounds of speech after the age of seven. Some sounds, however, are generally learned much earlier. The ages at which children in our culture generally master the sounds of consonants are illustrated in Chart 3-2. In the chart, the solid bar corresponding to each sound starts at the median age of customary articulation; it stops at an age level at which 90 percent of all children are customarily producing the sound.

Chart 3-1
Description of Consonant Sounds
by Place of Articulation

Manner of Articulation	Bilabial		Labio-Dental		Lingua-Dental		Lingua-Alveolar		Lingua-Palatal		Lingua-Velar		Glottal	
	V	VL	V	VL	V	VL	V	VL	V	VL	V	VL	V	VL
PLOSIVE	b	p					d	t			g	k		
FRICATIVE			v	f	ð	θ	z	s	ʒ	ʃ				h
AFFRICATE									dʒ	tʃ				
NASAL	m						n				ŋ			
LATERAL							l							
GLIDE	w								r	j				

V = Voiced   VL = Voiceless

THE DEVELOPMENT OF LANGUAGE

Like speech, language takes a long time to acquire. There is a well-defined pattern that children go through in the acquisition of language.

Children usually begin to attach meaning to words when they are eight to ten months old. At this age the child probably does not know the meanings of individual words, but he may associate whole phrases with whole experiences. He might, for example, anticipate going to bed when he hears the phrase "night-night time." Children at this stage also associate words or phrases with specifically taught gestures. For example, a child may begin waving when he hears "wave bye-bye" or begin clapping when told "patty cake."

At about ten to twelve months, the child begins to comprehend what people say to her if she has environmental information to help her figure it out. She might, for example, respond to the request "give me your shoe" if her shoe is in front of her. The same child, however, would probably not respond to the same request if she heard it just before dinner time, or if her shoe was not in front of her. At this stage the child learns language by using her knowledge of the event she is experiencing to figure out the meanings of the words and word combinations she hears.

At about the same time, the child begins to produce his own first words. The first words learned generally refer to specific familiar people or objects, "mama" or "doggie," for example. The child of this age does not generalize words to new

Chart 3-2
Average Age Estimates and Upper Age Limits of Customary Consonant Production

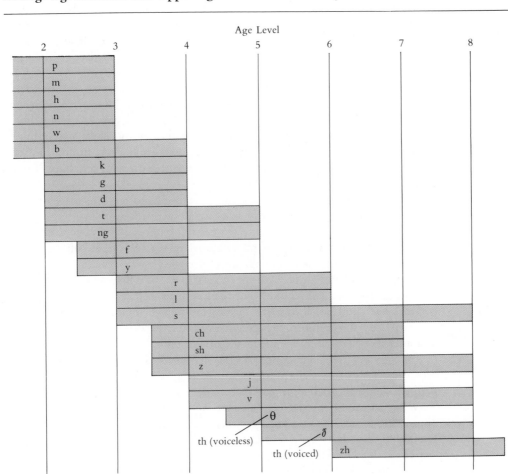

Source: Eric K. Sander, When Are Speech Sounds Learned? *Journal of Speech and Hearing Disorders,* 12 February 1972, *23* (1). Reprinted by permission.

situations. The child may, for example, produce an approximation of "water" to indicate he wants a drink from the kitchen faucet, but it may be some time before he says "water" when he sees it in a bird bath, toilet, or water fountain.

Between twelve and eighteen months the child begins to use words to refer to classes of objects and events instead of just specific events. "Hot," "more," "go," and "shoe" are words of this sort.

Until the child is approximately two years old, she usually uses single words and may acquire a fairly large single-word vocabulary. She will probably use some single words inappropriately, however. She may, for example, overgeneralize and apply the same words to different people or events, calling all animals "doggie" or all men "da-da." Overgeneralization indicates that the child is trying to figure out the relationship between words and experiences. It also indicates that the child knows that words stand for classes of events, and not just specific events. When a child reaches this point she can begin to use words to communicate in any situation.

At two years, the child begins to learn to combine words. His very first attempts are simple two-word phrases, in which the words are combined, not at random, but in an organized manner that indicates the child has begun to understand the importance of word order. The child now begins to signal relationships between people, actions, and objects, with sentences like, "Daddy go," "Mommy eat," or "Eat cookie."

At two and a half to three years, the child begins to use three-word combinations. At this stage, he can specify more than one relationship in a single phrase. The child who says "Get my cookie" is specifying not only what he wants but is also pointing out the nature of his relationship to the cookie (object). These children can combine words in all sorts of creative ways. With his increasing vocabulary and knowledge of how to signal relationships among people and objects, he can even talk about events he has never before experienced.

Once the child has learned to specify most basic meanings in simple word combinations, she begins to include some of the less crucial parts of speech in her sentences. For example, at about three years the child begins to add words such as "is," "the," and "an." She begins to speak in very simple, grammatically correct sentences. The process of adding grammatical parts of speech such as word endings continues gradually until the age of five or six.

While the child is acquiring rules for combining words into sentences, he is continuing to develop vocabulary. In fact, vocabulary development is a never-ending process. By two years of age a child learns words that stand for familiar objects, actions, and simple events, such as "car," "get," "cup," "milk," "shoe," "no," "more," "all gone," "put away," "pick up," "bear," "chair," "look," and "come." The three year old learns words for less common actions. The child might, for example, add the word "press" or "scatter" to his vocabulary. The three-year-old child also begins to add words that describe particular aspects of experiences, such as "same" or "soft."

By the time most children are five or six years old, they have mastered language well enough to produce grammatically correct sentences like those used by adults.

It should be emphasized that the ages quoted may vary considerably with a particular child. Some children pass through these stages slower or faster and still develop normal speech and language. The norms we mention are generally accurate, however, and any child who develops at a rate significantly different from them should be closely monitored by trained professionals. There is no penalty for unnecessarily checking a pattern of development that turns out to be normal, but ignoring a real problem can have serious consequences.

Language development is a fascinating and complex subject. If you'd like to develop a greater understanding of it, we suggest Lois Bloom and Margaret Lahey's *Language Development and Language Disorders* (1978).

PROBE 3–1
Basic Concepts of Speech and Language

1. _____ percent of the population of the United States have communication disorders.

2. T F Only people who sound unusual have communication problems.

3. A sound is called a voiced sound when there is _____.

4. We speak on air that is _____.

5. We produce the different vowels of our language by changing the shape and position of our _____ and

   _____.

6. /p/, /b/, and /t/ are examples of _____ consonants.

7. *Matching*

Linguistic Event	*Age*
_____ three-word combinations	a. 8–10 months
_____ use of words	b. 10–12 months
_____ two-word combinations	c. 12–18 months
_____ comprehension of sentences	d. 24 months
_____ meaning attached to familiar words	e. 30–36 months

8. T F Speech and language are essentially the same.

9. T F Speech is part of language.

10. T F Language is part of speech.

11. T F Speech is acquired prior to language.

12. T F Language and speech are developmental processes.

13. T F By age six, children should be producing adult-like sentences that are grammatically sound.

14. T F Language develops at the same rate for all children.

LANGUAGE DISORDERS

You should be able to describe the components of a language disorder.

Of all the communication problems we will discuss, language disorders are the most complex and the most serious. Between 1 and 5 percent of this country's population have language disorders — perhaps as many as 12 million people (Perkins, 1977).

Language disorders vary as much as the people who possess them. They may occur in every population discussed in this book. To thoroughly understand a particular child's disorder, we must know his levels of linguistic and nonlinguistic functioning, his physical and perceptual skills, and what aspects of language he is not able to use. The purpose of this section is to give you the background necessary to develop the ability to make such determinations. We will discuss the nature and assessment of language disorders and specific methods of remediating them.

TYPES OF LANGUAGE PROBLEMS

A child has a language problem when she cannot adequately receive and send messages about her world. Such children do possess knowledge of themselves and their environments, but they cannot talk about them meaningfully or understand when other people do.

A child does not have a language problem if his level of language functioning equals his level of nonlanguage functioning. For example a six-year-old child who functions developmentally at the level of a three year old should be expected to have the language development of a three year old. This does not mean that developmentally delayed children cannot benefit from language teaching; rather, it means that their expected level of achievement should be commensurate with their nonlanguage functioning. Parents of retarded children often correctly believe that their child's other problems would be less handicapping if they could speak. They sometimes don't recognize, however, that the child's other problems are what keeps him from speaking.

There are three primary types of language disorders that result from differences between language and nonlanguage functioning. These are receptive, expressive, and mixed receptive and expressive.

Receptive Language Problem. When a child's ability to comprehend questions and follow commands is below her mental age, she has a receptive language problem. A thirty-month-old child, for example, can demonstrate her level of development by re-creating familiar events in play, such as feeding or fixing her toys. She may also throw away broken or dirty objects, put things where they belong, match objects, or give people things that belong to them. If the same child does not understand age-appropriate words and sentences, such as "Show me your shoe," "Throw away the paper," or "Give baby some milk," she may have a receptive language problem.

Expressive Language Problem. Adults as well as children understand more words than we can produce. But when a child's ability to send messages is significantly below his ability to receive them, he may have an expressive language problem. A three-year-old child, for example, may know the meanings of "big," "little," "chin," "socks," "hers," "his," "heavy," "one," "all," "under," "show me the baby's not sleeping," "make the baby kiss the bear," and "make the bear kiss the baby." If the same child can express only a few words, however, his expressive skills may be assessed to be those of a one year old. The gap between a three-year level of receptive skills and a one-year level of expressive skills indicates an expressive language problem.

Mixed Receptive/Expressive Problems. A child may show both a receptive and an expressive language delay. This is indicated when her receptive language age is below her mental age, *and* her level of expressive language is lower still. An example would be a child who functions as a four year old while doing nonlinguistic tasks, who understands language at the two-year-old level, and who expresses language at the level of a one year old. This child would understand simple language such as "get your coat" and "do you want more milk?" but be able to say only a few single words, such as "milk," "mama," or "go."

PHYSICAL AND PERCEPTUAL SKILLS
NEEDED TO LEARN LANGUAGE

Problems such as those just described can result from deficits in any of the processes necessary to learn language. The four most important are the ability to hear, auditory perceptual abilities, recall or retrieval skills, and motor skills.

Hearing.   The problems of the deaf and hearing impaired will be discussed in Chapter 4. Suffice it to say that the child who does not hear will have a language problem that requires intensive treatment.

Auditory Perception.   To learn language, a child must be able not only to hear, but to associate aspects of her environment with specific sounds. A child who cannot, for example, associate a coarse texture with the word "rough," may have an auditory perception problem. Auditory perception, the ability to recognize sounds and associate them with environmental events, can be broken into four categories: (1) auditory integration, (2) auditory figure/ground perception, (3) auditory discrimination, and (4) auditory analysis.

Auditory integration is the ability to associate a sound or sound combination (words and sentences) with an experience. The child who cannot, for example, integrate the visual sight of a ball with the word "ball" will have language difficulties. *Auditory figure-ground perception* is the ability to isolate a word from a sentence or a particular sound from all other sounds. You will understand the importance of this ability if you have ever tape recorded a lecture in a classroom. During the actual lecture, you may have easily understood what the speaker was saying, only to find when you played back the tape that it was difficult to distinguish the lecturer's voice from other sounds in the classroom. The difference is the result of normal figure-ground perception. If a child cannot make such distinctions and isolate a speaker's voice from background noises, she may be unable to learn the rules of language. *Auditory discrimination* is the ability to detect differences among sounds. A child who cannot distinguish between the words "ball" and "doll," for example, will not be able to associate these words with the appropriate object. Children with auditory discrimination problems have an especially difficult time when there is a great deal of background noise, when their language model does not speak clearly, or when a message is distorted or unclear. Their understanding also tends to rely on situational cues to a greater extent than that of people with normal auditory discrimination. *Auditory analysis* is the ability to rapidly process and understand the sounds and rules of language. A child whose processing is slow may have trouble understanding what is being said.

Retrieval Skills.   In addition to auditory perception, children must possess retrieval skills to develop language normally. Retrieval is the ability to summon words from our memories. Children with retrieval problems have trouble selecting appropriate words, even though they may understand the word they are seeking. Such a child might be unable to recall the word "break" when trying to describe a broken pencil. Nevertheless, he would recognize and understand the word "break" if it were spoken to him.

Motor Skills.   A child must also be physically able to send messages to have normal language. Even if a child knows words and syntax, she will not be able to communicate verbally unless she can physically shape and transmit sounds. This type of language disorder will be explained more thoroughly later in this chapter.

ASSESSING LANGUAGE DISORDERS

Individual language-disordered children have problems with different aspects of language. Before a particular child can be helped, his knowledge of language (receptive skills) and use of language (expressive skills) must be assessed. By comparing the child's receptive and expressive language levels to his mental age, we can differentiate between a language problem and a developmental delay. IQ tests that are language based are of little use in this effort, because a child with a language problem will do poorly on them, regardless of his intellectual abilities.

Observations of how a child responds to verbal instruction can indicate his receptive language age. Properly recorded samples of how the child uses language to communicate are useful in evaluating a child's expressive language abilities. Barre–Blackey, Musselwhite, and Rogister (1978) have described how to do this successfully.

There is no shortcut to thorough effective language assessment. The skills being tested must be thoroughly understood, and the results of testing carefully considered, before an appropriate strategy of language intervention can be formulated.

APHASIA

Unlike the disorders we've already described, aphasia generally affects adults who have already mastered language. It is usually caused by a stroke (a cerebral vascular accident, or CVA) or by direct destruction of brain tissue. A CVA occurs when the flow of blood to the brain is suddenly interrupted by a blocked or burst blood vessel. Without oxygen, the brain tissue is very quickly destroyed. If the CVA occurs in an area of the brain that deals with communication, a language disorder may result. Car accidents, gunshot wounds, and other sources of cranial impalement can also destroy brain tissue and result in aphasia. Many war veterans have aphasia as a result of their wounds.

Aphasia is a general term used to describe a variety of problems. According to Darley and Spriestersbach (1978), "Aphasia is a disorder of language function — a disturbance of the ability to recognize and use the symbols by means of which we relate to our surroundings and other people ... questioning and testing will probably reveal the language difficulty is both receptive and expressive in nature." Aphasics may have difficulty expressing themselves or understanding what is said to them; they may hear well enough but not understand the meanings of words. Their situation is somewhat analogous to what yours would be if you had to communicate using a foreign language you understood very poorly. This analogy is not completely appropriate, however, because you would be able to trust your understanding of the words you could communicate with, whereas an aphasic, with part of her brain damaged, cannot.

Aphasia can be predominantly expressive or predominantly receptive. Expressive aphasics have difficulty in using language symbolically. They do not lack the physical ability to speak; rather, they have trouble formulating and editing what they are trying to say. They may have trouble recalling specific words and grammatical constructions necessary to convey messages.

Receptive aphasics have trouble understanding spoken and sometimes written language. This often leads to an inability to talk coherently.

Aphasics are not retarded; they are just as intelligent as they were before they became aphasic. IQ tests cannot be administered to them, of course, because most of these tests are based on verbal skills.

Aphasia, caused by cranial impalement or CVAs, is rarely found in children. Thus, aphasic children are infrequently encountered in schools.

PROBE 3–2
Language Disorders

1. The three types of language disorder are: _____

   _____ , _____ ,

   _____ .

2. T   F   Children are not perceived as having language problems if their language functioning is equal to their mental age.

3. Receptive language : Expressive language :: understanding : _____

4. T   F   Deaf children automatically have language problems.

5. Name the four critical processes necessary to learn language.

   a. _____

   b. _____

   c. _____

   d. _____

6. CVA stands for _____

7. What are two ways a person might become aphasic?

   a. _____

   b. _____

SPEECH DISORDERS

> **You should be able to describe different types of speech disorders.**

Speech disorders can disrupt a person's ability to communicate as seriously as language disorders. It should be emphasized that speech and language disorders are not necessarily separate entities. Children often have severe language problems complicated by speech disorders. The focus of attention should always be on the whole child.

Speech disorders can be either organic or functional. Organic problems are caused by a physical or neurological abnormality. Functional problems are not the result of physical problems; they can be caused by improper learning.

Organic problems can be regarded as having three components. First, there is the symptom — what we hear. With the child who says "shoup" for "soup," we hear /ʃ/ (sh) substituted for /s/. Second, there is a physical explanation for the symptom. The child who says "shoup" is producing a voiceless lingua-palatal fricative rather than a voiceless lingua-alveolar fricative. (Refer back to Chart 3-1 if you don't remember the consonant classifications.) Third, there is an underlying neurological or physiological reason for the symptom's physical explanation. In this case, it might be cerebral palsy, resulting in poor muscular control.

Functional problems also have symptoms that have physical explanations, but they lack an underlying physiological cause.

The difference between these two kinds of problems affects how we attempt to remediate them. Obviously it would be pointless to ignore a serious organic problem when planning speech therapy.

The types of speech disorder we will discuss are (1) disorders of articulation (speech sound production), (2) disorders of voice, (3) disorders of fluency.

ARTICULATION DISORDERS

Organic Causes. Among the most common organic causes of articulation disorders are cleft palate and cerebral palsy.

Clefts can actually be of three types — clefts of the lip only, clefts of the palate only, or clefts of both the lip and the palate. They are caused by the failure of the lip or palate to grow together during the child's fetal development. It is uncertain why this happens. It occurs during the first three months of pregnancy in one of every 600 births in the United States.

As you can see in Figure 3-4, the palate forms the roof of the mouth and the bottom of the nasal cavity. The front two-thirds is called the hard palate, and the back third is called the soft palate. You will remember from our discussion of sound production that all but three of the sounds in our language (/m/, /n/, and /ŋ/) require that the soft palate contact the throat, thereby sealing off the nasal cavity. Many children with cleft palates cannot do this; as a result their speech may be excessively nasal, breathy, and difficult to understand.

Lip clefts usually involve only the upper lip. A cleft may appear on either side of the nose, or on both sides.

Treatment of clefts and the resulting articulation disorders is a long-term, coordinated effort made by a team of speech-language pathologists, doctors, and dentists. The repair of physical structures is undertaken by surgeons. Surgery for cleft lips is usually performed when the child is one and a half to three months old. Surgery for cleft palate problems is postponed until the surgeon is certain that it will not alter facial growth. A child may be fitted with a prosthesis that closes the opening in the palate during the period before surgery (Figure 3-5). Figure 3-6 shows a patient's surgical result.

Articulation disorders are found much more frequently among those with cleft palates than cleft lips. Unfortunately, surgery alone does not usually lead to normal articulation. In addition to excessive nasality those with cleft palates may have trouble making sounds that require the damming up of air pressure, such as plosives and fricatives. They need to be taught to take full advantage of the tissue they do have, or to use their prostheses effectively. With effective education a

Figure 3-4
Different Types of Clefts. A: Cleft of hard and soft palates. B: Unilateral cleft of palate and lip. C: Bilateral cleft of palate and lip.

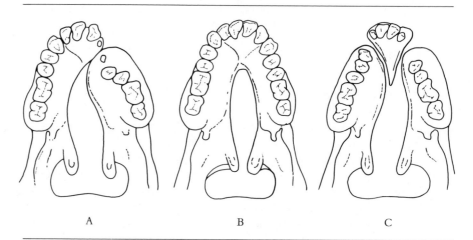

A   B   C

Figure 3-5
A Velo-pharyngeal Prosthesis and How It Is Fitted

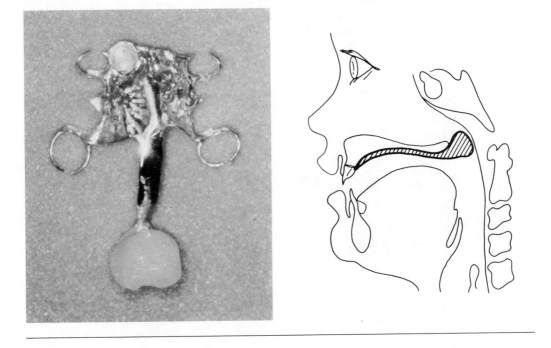

child can be taught to reduce excessive nasality and develop the air pressure necessary to produce plosives and fricatives. Postsurgical muscular training may also help improve speech.

Some articulation problems are the result of the soft palate's inability to reach the throat, rather than the absence of soft palate tissue altogether. When this is the case, the adenoids (tissue located where the back of the throat and the nasal cavity join) are sometimes used to fill the gap. Before the adenoids are removed surgically, it is very important to determine their role in closing off the nasal cavity. Careless removal of adenoidal tissue can result in articulation problems that could have been avoided.

Additional information on cleft palates is sometimes available from university and teaching hospitals, many of which maintain cleft palate teams.

Cerebral palsy, like cleft disorders, is not itself a communication problem; it is, rather, the cause of one. Its severity is related to the extent of the brain damage that causes it. This brain damage impairs the ability to control the articulators (the tongue, lips, soft palate, and so forth), which results in an articulation disorder.

Figure 3–6
A: Complete unilateral cleft of lip and palate. B: Three years later, the scars have camouflaged positions and there is symmetry of the lip. C: Wide complete unilateral cleft of lip and palate with distortion and absence of tissue. D: Two months after surgery. E: Incomplete unilateral cleft of the lip with minor nasal deformity. F: Two years later, symmetry and scar camouflage have been achieved.

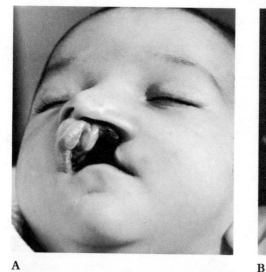

A

B

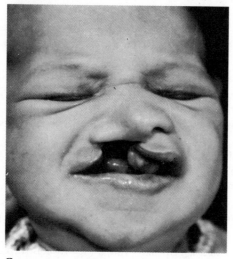

C

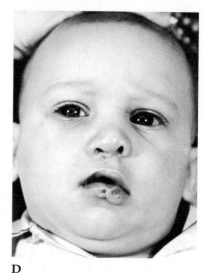

D

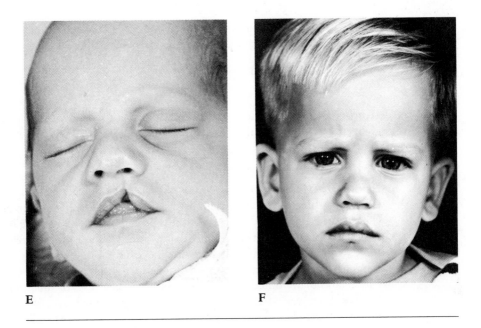

E   F

People with cerebral palsy are likely to have slow, labored speech, to articulate words imprecisely, and to slur sounds together or omit them completely. They may also expel air too quickly or not be able to exhale enough air to speak smoothly. One effect of these factors is a distortion of the rhythmic patterns we associate with normal speech. Until one becomes familiar with these distorted patterns, a cerebral palsied person's speech may be unintelligible.

The reason people with cerebral palsy speak as they do is basically their inability to bring together the complex movements necessary for speech with the speed needed to speak normally. Normal speakers make the rapid adjustments necessary to travel from one sound to another without having to think about them. In fact, we make these adjustments so quickly that we must "cheat" a little to keep up with our thoughts. For example, try saying the /p/ sound, as in "pay," and then the /p/ sound in "play," paying close attention to the different positions of the tongue. You will notice in the latter case that your tongue has anticipated the next sound almost before you had finished the first. These rapid movements can be seen clearly in x-ray motion pictures of the mouth. If you have access to a cleft palate team, you should ask them to show you a sample film.

Although the effects of cerebral palsy cannot be reversed because brain tissue will not regenerate, it is possible to teach a person to compensate for his deficits. Most cerebral palsied people can be helped to become more intelligible, although few will develop normal articulation. For some, oral communication will be impossible, and tools such as communication boards and picture cards may be their best option.

Other aspects of cerebral palsy will be described in Chapter 6.

Hearing Disorders.   A severe hearing impairment will obviously affect a child's ability to learn to articulate correctly. This will be discussed in detail in Chapter 4.

Functional Causes.   Between 2 and 20 percent of all articulation disorders are classified as functional rather than organic in origin. The higher percentage is for children in primary grades, whereas the 2 percent figure is for those in or beyond secondary school. Functional articulation disorders, as you will remember, are those which have no identifiable organic cause. They may be the result of improper learning, short auditory memory span, problems in phonetic discrimination, and many other factors. Research into the causes of functional disorders has not been very fruitful. Unlike organically caused articulation disorders, however, functional disorders can often be completely cured. Effective diagnosis and remediation efforts usually result in normal articulation.

Testing and Classifying Articulation Disorders.   People with articulation problems tend to make four kinds of mistakes when speaking. These are substitution, omission, distortion, and addition. The acronym "SODA" may help you remember them.

Substitution is the replacement of one sound for another. For example, a person who says "thoup" for "soup" is substituting a voiceless θ (th) for /s/. Saying "wabbit" for "rabbit" is another example. *Omission* is leaving a sound out altogether, saying "_oup" for "soup" or "_abbit" for "rabbit," for example. *Distortion* is the replacement of an acceptable sound with one that doesn't exist in our language. The slushy Daffy Duck kind of /s/ sound is a good example of a distortion. *Addition* is the addition of a sound that doesn't normally occur in a word, saying "warsh" for "wash" or "atpple" for "apple," for example.

The speech of some speakers with problems such as those described above is obviously disordered; when this is true, it is easy to diagnose a speaker as having an articulation problem. Effective guidelines for diagnosing less conspicuous cases have been provided by Tomblin (1978):

> Even the most careful speakers will occasionally misarticulate sounds. Therefore, we cannot reasonably propose that a person making any error in articulation has an articulation disorder. Although no definition exists that is universally accepted by speech pathologists, we propose that a disorder of articulation involves the following characteristics:

1. There must be rather frequent and recurring misarticulations of one or more speech sound units.
2. The sound units considered to be in error must be elements of the phonemic system of the person's linguistic community.
3. It is reasonable to expect that the misarticulated sound elements would be articulated acceptably by most persons of the same age.

Even if these characteristics are not met, individuals could be considered to have an articulation problem if their articulation causes them to believe that they are inadequate speakers.

Once it has been determined that a person has an articulation problem, a speech sample must be obtained and analyzed before treatment can be planned. The method that seems most obvious, listening to a person speak for a while, is not very effective. The examiner must listen to content to determine what the person is saying, and she must also listen to the pronunciation of specific sounds. To do both at once is very difficult. Furthermore, an examiner would have to listen to a speaker for a long time to be certain she heard all the sounds of our language produced.

To overcome such problems articulation tests that require the person being tested to say specific sounds have been developed. Most of these tests rely on easily recognizable pictures of objects that contain the target sound. The person being tested is asked to name the objects, and the examiner listens for specific sounds. Generally the same sound is tested three times — once at the beginning of a word, once in the middle, and once at the end. Thus, for the sound /s/, a person might be shown pictures of a *saw*, a *baseball*, and a *glass*. By going through sounds and sound combinations in this way, the examiner can discover errors. After this the examiner can attempt to assess a sample of spontaneous communication, because she will know what sort of errors to listen for. It is important to listen to a sample of conversational speech, because we say words differently in sentences than we do when we pronounce them individually. As you can see, correctly administering an articulation test takes a good deal of skill and practice.

Additional information on this subject can be found in Charles Van Riper's *Speech Correction: Principles and Methods* (1978). Chapter 6 of that text deals with disorders of articulation; pages 173–216 explain how to remediate them and where to find more information.

PROBE 3-3
Articulation Disorders

1. List three characteristics of an organic problem. Put an asterisk next to the characteristics that are also representative of a functional problem.

   a. _____

b. _____

c. _____

2. The most common communication problem with speakers who have cleft palates is _____.

3. What is a cleft palate prosthetic device? _____

_____

4. How might cerebral palsy cause an articulation disorder? _____

_____

_____

5. The four types of articulation disorders are:

S_____

O_____

D_____

A_____

6. Identify the articulation errors in the following statement and describe the sounds being misarticulated. You may want to refer back to Charts 3-1 and 3-2.

"Ven I come to varsh the vindoes, I ave fount dey vas donet."

_____

_____

_____

_____

_____

_____

VOICE DISORDERS

Approximately one percent of the population of this country, or more than 2 million people, have voice disorders (Perkins, 1977). Although some are organic in origin, the result of changing tissue or structural inadequacies, most problems are caused by abuse of a normal voice. However, if a normal mechanism is misused it may show physical signs of abuse. These signs can be seen as the organic result of functional misuse.

Pitch Disorders. The sound you hear when someone laughs or clears her throat is that person's optimal pitch, the sound she can produce most efficiently. Ideally, optimal pitch is the same as habitual pitch, the pitch we use most frequently. When a person's optimal pitch differs severely from her habitual pitch by being too high, too low, or lacking in variation, she probably has a pitch disorder.

In our society, men with very high voices and women with very low voices may pay severe social penalties. Although these disorders are sometimes organic, they are generally functional, the result of improper use. In men the disorders usually begin during adolescence, when, for reasons ranging from psychosexual fixation to poor learning, their voices fail to change and they retain the high-pitched voices of youth. This condition is generally remediable.

A related disorder is pitch breaks. These are the sudden shifts in pitch that occur primarily in the voices of pubescent males. Pitch breaks are associated with growth spurts and rarely last more than six months. Although a period of pitch breaks is normal, the condition may have destructive effects if it becomes chronic, or if a person develops bad vocal habits in an effort to disguise or avoid them. A person who has pitch breaks for more than six months should be referred to a speech-language pathologist.

People whose voices lack the variation in tone we expect from a normal speaker may also have pitch disorders. Pure monotone or monopitch voices are very rare, but there are many people who alter their tone very little, or alter it in a predictable pattern. This condition can be caused by hearing loss or by the use of a habitual pitch level that doesn't permit pitch variation. It can also be caused by emotional problems, when, for example, a person tries to hide powerful emotions by speaking in a flat, calm, controlled voice. This behavior is sometimes appropriate, but when it becomes the dominant manner of speaking, it indicates a problem. As you can see, a person's voice is frequently an accurate indicator of his psychological condition; how a person presents a message can be as important as the message itself.

Loudness Disorders. Inappropriately loud or soft voices are another type of voice disorder. Some loudness problems are caused by the lack of control that results from impaired hearing or cerebral palsy. In some cases, however, an excessive loudness is the result of a family's communication problem. For example, children who have to shout to get attention from their parents may also speak very loudly at other times. If this continues over a long period, the child may develop "screamer's nodes," growths on the vocal cords that lead to a harsh-sounding voice. It is usually the family that needs treatment in these situations, and not only the child.

Weak or very soft voices are also usually the result of psychological or environmental problems, rather than organic disorders. A person who is frequently punished when speaking or drawing attention to herself may learn to speak in a barely audible voice. At times, of course, this is appropriate, but a person who tries to be unobtrusive by rarely speaking or speaking inaudibly has a serious problem. As was true of loudness problems, the child herself may not benefit from treatment unless the situation which caused her to develop the habit is changed.

Problems with Voice Quality. Voice quality defects are among the most common and the most difficult to describe. Four of the most common are excessive or insufficient nasality, breathiness, harshness or stridency, and hoarseness.

Nasality problems result from the inability to control the flow of air into the mouth and nasal cavity. As we described in the section on cleft palates, excessive nasality is usually an organic problem best controlled by a team of doctors, dentists, and speech-language pathologists. Sometimes, however, it results from improper learning and can be cured without surgical intervention.

Insufficient nasality is the cause of the sounds we associate with having colds, allergies, or enlarged adenoids. These blockages and swollen tissues hamper normal resonance and result in a flat-sounding voice.

To clarify the difference between the two nasality disorders, try saying "time and tide wait for no man" first with excessive and then with insufficient nasality.

People with nasality problems that persist after their organic causes have been remedied should be referred to speech-language pathologists.

Breathiness can be caused by a number of organic and functional disorders. It is the result of the vocal folds not coming together correctly, which allows air to rush past them without vibrating them as it does in normal speakers. This can be the result of callus-like nodes developing on the folds, due to chronic vocal abuse, or it can be caused by vocal fold paralysis. Breathiness can also result from functional problems and poor vocal habits.

The voices of people with breathiness problems have a whisper-like quality because of excessive air flow. This can be very distracting to a listener. Except when caused by paralysis or irrevocable tissue damage, it can usually be cured.

Harshness is usually the result of tension or strain. Some speakers develop harsh voices because they have to strain to be heard where they work; others have personality conflicts. The condition can also have organic causes. If eliminating the source of stress does not resolve the problem, and a medical examination reveals little or no pathology, a psychological examination may be appropriate.

Hoarseness is familiar to everyone. It is usually the result of cheering or shouting too loudly. Another common cause is laryngitis, a swelling of the area around the larynx. Hoarseness should only last for a few days. If it lasts longer, a physician should be consulted; hoarseness is the first symptom of a number of potentially dangerous disorders.

Disorders Resulting from Laryngectomy. The final voice disorder we will discuss is that of the person whose larynx has been removed, generally to keep cancer from spreading (Figure 3-7). This procedure involves changing the position of the trachea, which normally carries air from the nose and throat to the lungs. During surgery, the trachea is redirected to a stoma, or opening, in the lower part of the neck. It is through this stoma that the person breathes.

When the larynx is removed, the vocal folds are removed as well; as a result, a laryngectomized person can no longer speak with vocal fold vibrations. These people, generally older adults, can be rehabilitated, however. The easiest way for them to produce understandable speech is to use a substitute sound generator, commonly called an electrolarynx. This instrument is placed beside the neck, and the speaker articulates the buzz that the device produces (Figure 3-8).

Although the device is easy to use, many people find the sound produced by an electrolarynx highly artificial and unpleasant. A method known as esophageal speech is a preferred alternative. The esophageal speaker forces air from his mouth into the area where the pharynx and esophogeous join. This area, known

Figure 3-7
After Laryngectomy

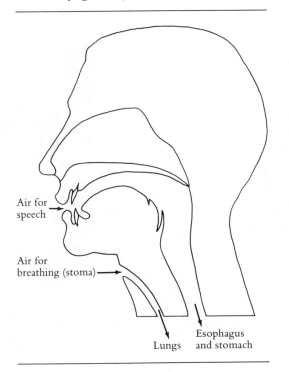

as the PE segment, vibrates when the air is released, and the vibrations are used to shape sounds. Esophageal speech takes a relatively long time to learn, but the resulting speech is closer to normal than that produced by the electrolarynx devices.

The Role of the Physician. Because many voice disorders are caused by changing tissue, it is very important that a person with symptoms of a problem get a medical examination before vocal rehabilitation is attempted. An examination by an Ear, Nose, and Throat (ENT) specialist, officially called an otorhino-laryngologist, can determine whether the patient has a serious degenerative disease. As we mentioned earlier, vocal disorders are sometimes symptoms of diseases that can lead to serious disabilities or even death.

Additional information on alaryngeal speech is available in *Alaryngeal Speech,* by W. Diedrich and Youngstrom (1966). For more information on speech disorders in general, we recommend Charles Van Riper's *Speech Correction: Principles and Methods* (1978).

Figure 3-8
How the Electrolarynx Is Used

PROBE 3-4
Voice Disorders

1. How can a functional voice problem become an organic voice problem?

   _____

   _____

   _____

2. People with hay fever may sound _____,
   whereas a person who is unable to block off the nasal cavity will sound
   excessively _____.

3. What does ENT stand for? _____

4. What does an otorhinolaryngologist do? _____

   _____

5. How does a laryngectomized person breathe? _____

   _____

6. T F Occasional pitch breaks in adolescent males should be a cause for
   concern.

7. Four voice quality defects are _____,

   _____, _____, and

   _____.

FLUENCY DISORDERS

Disfluency, the preferred term for stuttering, is a disorder that begins and usually
ends in childhood.[1] The age of onset is typically between two and seven years,
with its highest incidence occurring among two and a half to three and a half
year olds. It affects about 1 percent of the total population (R. Milisen, 1971).

Disfluent adults who did not begin stuttering during childhood are quite rare.
Most experts agree that it is a learned disorder that results from the continuation
of the disfluency many children experience as part of their verbal development.

---

[1] Parts of this segment are reprinted from "Stuttering as an aftereffect of normal developmental
disfluency" (Rubin and Culatta, 1974).

Normal and Developmental Disfluency. A child's first words are almost always free from disfluency. They are usually a source of pride for both child and parents. When the child begins to put words together, however, and must learn the rules for sequencing words while selecting them, she hesitates, in order to edit and revise what she intends to say. Adults also pause to revise and edit their speech; such pauses in a speaker's verbal flow are considered normal disfluency.

Normal disfluency differs from developmental disfluency in several respects. In the former case, the speaker pauses or inserts a phrase or a sound such as "uh." Developmental disfluency, on the other hand, is characterized by the *repetition* of words, parts of words, or phrases during editing time (Davis, 1939). They also differ in that developmental disfluency may begin suddenly, without apparent explanation, and without the child's being aware that his speech has changed. Distinctions such as these are sometimes hard to make, however, and the boundary between the normal and the abnormal is hard to define precisely. The speech of either kind of disfluent is relaxed and apparently effortless. The speaker is, in effect, saying, "Don't interrupt me. I'm not finished yet."

The period of developmental disfluency normally lasts from a few weeks to a few months. Parents can be assured that it is normal behavior, the result of a child's not knowing the conventional methods of gaining time to organize her words. She hasn't learned to say "let me see" or "you know" yet; the easiest way to hold the floor is to continue saying a word she has already uttered fluently. For example, she might say, "Can, can, can, can I go with you?" Most children go through the disfluent stage at about the same period of language development, one that is characterized by many inconsistent displays of disfluency.

Adult disfluency can grow out of the normal developmental disfluency of childhood. Each instance of disfluency can be the occasion for parents to react unusually to the child's speech. Any acknowledgement a parent makes of a child's disfluency may make the behavior more likely to appear again. This acknowledgement need not be anything obvious. For example, a parent who stops raking leaves or fixing dinner when the child is disfluent, but not when he speaks fluently, may draw the child's attention to his unusual speech. Even parents who are not worried about their child's disfluency, but are merely trying to help by saying "Slow down" or "Think before you speak," can affect a child's verbal behavior. Ideally, parents should react in the same manner when the child is fluent and when he is disfluent.

Stress-Induced Disfluency. Shames (1968) makes a distinction between the normal disfluency, which results from editing, and disfluency caused by environmental pressure. If the child has unconsciously recognized during a period of developmental disfluency that her being disfluent serves a purpose, she may revert to disfluency when making requests, answering direct questions, and during other stressful situations. If her parents reinforce this behavior, it may become ingrained in their child. However, both the child who stutters and the parents who reinforce stuttering are unconscious of the effect of their behavior.

Purposes for Disfluency. A child may use disfluency for three possible purposes: to secure attention, to express hostility, and to control the behavior of others.

— *Securing Attention.* Disfluency draws attention to itself. A child who is not getting enough attention may prefer even negative comments to no attention at all. Disfluency is no longer normal if a child has learned to use it to make his parents notice him.

Parents who are unaware that a period of disfluency is frequently part of a child's normal language development are especially susceptible to apprehension about their child's disfluency. This apprehension may take the form of worry, empathy, or sympathy — all forms of caring that the child may be seeking.

Adults may also feel threatened by a child's disfluency, imagining that it reflects on their ability as parents. These feelings may be reinforced by the social embarrassment they suffer if they are subjected to unsolicited and unhelpful comments from friends and relatives. As a result, parents may be irritated with their child, sometimes to the point of anger; they may even punish him if they believe his behavior is willful. More frequently, however, parents regard their child's disfluency as beyond his control, and sublimate their irritation into feelings of concern.

— *Expressing Hostility.* Any child who faces restrictions and controls will be frustrated and sometimes angry at the parents who control her. If she cannot express her anger through name calling or physical aggression, she may have to express it indirectly. If she is already disfluent and her parents are unduly concerned, she may become more disfluent to elicit further concern.

Every child faces restrictions, of course, and can be expected to rebel against them occasionally. Disfluency may result only when the child cannot express her frustration, and when her parents are made uncomfortable by her speech problem. Even relatively secure children may be so hesitant to antagonize an adult that they may habitually use their disfluency to irritate, inconvenience, frighten, embarrass, or intimidate threatening adults. Neither parent nor child is usually aware that the disfluency is being used aggressively.

— *Controlling the Behavior of Others.* Once a child's disfluency is labeled (i.e., identified by both the parents and the child), it undergoes a rapid series of changes. It ceases to be a relaxed repetition of words, syllables, and other sounds, and becomes very tense (W. Johnson, 1959). The child may have periods when he utters no sound; repetitions may become very tense; and pitch and loudness may vary frequently. The child generally begins to show signs of anxiety as well. He may circumlocute, substitute some words for others, or go to the extreme of avoiding speaking altogether. In addition, his disfluency is likely to become more predictable in certain situations, although he may retain his fluency when not under stress — when he is alone, with other children, or when he is singing, for example.

Once a child's disfluency becomes habitual, parent and child alike begin to anticipate and prepare for it in the situations where it has appeared most consistently. The child is identified as different from other children and treated accordingly. Even if the child struggles to speak fluently, he will probably lack confidence in his ability to change. Parents who regard their child's problem as organic in origin, rather than caused by his environment, are likely to begin adjusting to it rather than trying to eliminate it. Because they believe they themselves can do nothing to cure the condition, parents often turn to a specialist for advice.

The Treatment of Disfluency. Unnecessary parental concern about disfluency, and the pressure on children that often results from it, can frequently be eliminated by informing parents that a period of developmental disfluency is normal.

Those who tend to worry excessively or who have already labeled their child as disfluent, however, should seek professional help as quickly as possible. The longer a child is disfluent, the harder her condition is to cure. Early diagnosis and treatment are also important because the environmental factors that cause disfluency are harder to control once a child has started school. Because it is difficult for parents to assess their effect on a child's behavior objectively, they should be referred to a speech pathologist.

Some speech pathologists prefer to work exclusively with parents, basing their strategies on restructuring the child's environment rather than the child herself. Others view disfluency as a family problem and prefer to involve the child along with the parents in treatment of the problem. The speech pathologist may also have to impress parents with the fact that disfluency is acquired and to explain that environmental changes are crucial if their child is to speak normally.

An understanding of the circumstances that perpetuate a child's disfluency often provides the insights necessary to change a child's speech. An analysis of the child's home, and of the circumstances during which a child is most fluent and disfluent, can be very helpful. Once parents understand what may have been very subtle and confusing environmental influences, they can help adjust the home environment to change their child's speech.

For example, they may decide not to ask their child questions or otherwise encourage her to speak in situations where she has been consistently disfluent. Conversely, she should be encouraged to speak in situations where she is consistently fluent. If family members have to compete for speaking time at the dinner table, they might adopt a policy that allows time for everyone. If the child's schedule is such that she is always under pressure, it should be changed. Because at this age children spend most of their time in the home, parents can manipulate much of what their children experience and can provide occasions for fluent speech.

Disfluent Adults. Although we have stressed childhood disfluency in the preceding section, there are many disfluent adults as well. A great deal can be done to help them. Whether their speech problem is caused by improper learning, psychic trauma, or one of the other factors that we discussed earlier, it can be treated effectively.

For further information on disfluency, we recommend the chapter titled "Stuttering," by Dean Williams, in *Processes and Disorders of Communication* (1978), and Oliver Bloodstein's *A Handbook on Stuttering* (1975). The latter book, an inexpensive paperback, is the most comprehensive available on the subject of disfluency. The author writes so clearly that even the most complex theories are easily understandable.

Other works of interest are Williams (1957), Kent (1961), Rubin and Culatta (1971), Culatta and Rubin (1973), and Culatta (1976).

PROBE 3-5
Fluency Disorders

1. Why is disfluency called a disorder of childhood? _____

   _____

   _____

2. Most children pass through a stage called normal developmental disfluency at approximately _____ to _____ years of age.

3. What are three purposes disfluency may serve for a young child?

   a. _____

   b. _____

   c. _____

4. T   F   Adults who are disfluent cannot be helped because their problem is so deeply ingrained in them.

EDUCATING CHILDREN WITH COMMUNICATION DISORDERS

> **You should be able to describe implications of the "least restrictive environment" clause of PL 94–142 for the education of children with communication disorders.**

THE ROLE OF THE CLASSROOM TEACHER

Along with most schools' communication disorder screening programs, the responsibility for identifying children who may need speech or language therapy is shared by the teacher. The teacher should ask himself the seven questions presented at the beginning of the chapter when evaluating a child's speech and language.

A child who may have a problem should be referred to a speech-language pathologist. Detailed records of the child's verbal behavior can help the speech pathologist make a diagnosis. Teachers should note the type of problem they suspect, examples of the child's problem, and the context in which the problem was observed.

Since the majority of children with speech or language problems are in regular classrooms, their teachers can be of great help in stabilizing the gains made during the predominantly tutorial speech therapy sessions. By cooperating with each other, the speech-language pathologist and classroom teacher can arrange experiences in the real world communication of the classroom that have been learned in the pathologist's office. The classroom teacher can encourage the child to use his newly gained skills. She can reward attempts at adequate communication and defuse potential penalties a child might suffer because of inadequate communication skills. This transfer from the therapy room to the classroom can serve to reinforce the child's growing awareness of the value of normal communication. The actions of the classroom teacher as a facilitator can go a long way toward ensuring that behavior mastered in therapy will be maintained and valued by the child.

THE SPEECH-LANGUAGE PATHOLOGIST

The professionals who work with children who have communication disorders may be called speech therapists, speech clinicians, and speech teachers, as well as speech-language pathologists. The education required before such people can practice in a school or private clinic varies from state to state. Some states require only a bachelors degree for state certification; others require that a person have a masters degree and pass a national examination and receive the Certificate of Clinical Competence awarded by the American Speech and Hearing Association (ASHA). Do not hesitate to ask about a speech-language pathologist's credentials. The ASHA believes that only those who can qualify for the Certificate of Clinical Competence are qualified to provide clinical services to the public.

Although many speech-language pathologists work in hospitals, university clinics, rehabilitation centers, and private clinics, they are predominantly employed in public school programs. There, they generally take children from their regular classes and administer therapy in a separate environment. Children are seen either individually or in small groups, usually for thirty or forty minutes. Speech-language pathologists may serve more than one school and may see as many as sixty or seventy children regularly. They also perform diagnostic speech and language evaluations and help develop IEPs. In addition, they advise teachers about ways to incorporate language development activities into the regular classroom programs of children with verbal problems.

Speech-language pathology has been an organized profession only for fifty years, but it has made great progress in the treatment of communication disorders. It has never been a stronger or more exciting profession. The ASHA presently has about 30,000 members, and there are at least as many new professionals in training. Although treatment must still be considered experimental in many areas, more information about its effectiveness is available every year. There is every reason to believe that further important advances will be made in the future.

As is true of most areas of special education, the key to successful speech and language therapy is catching problems as early as possible. The effects of many communication disorders can be dramatically reduced if they are recognized early enough, and some can be avoided altogether.

As you can see, curing speech disorders is a group effort that involves parents, teachers, doctors, and others, in addition to the speech-language pathologist. Therapy will not be successful unless the prescribed program is carried out in the child's home and regular classroom as well as the therapy session itself. The speech pathologist will accomplish little without the active involvement of both parents and teachers.

SUMMARY

1. Communication is disordered when it deviates from accepted norms such that it calls attention to itself, interferes with the message, or distresses the speaker or listener.
2. Speech results from many organs of the body working cooperatively to produce sound.
3. The three major types of sounds in our language are vowels, diphthongs, and consonants.
4. The sounds of our language may be characterized by the manner in which they are made, and the primary place in the oral cavity where they are articulated.
5. Speech and language are developmental processes acquired over time.
6. Language disorders are the most complex and most serious of all communication problems.
7. Most speech disorders involve problems with speech sound production, voice, or fluency.
8. Speech problems may have an organic cause, or they may not. Problems of the latter type are called functional problems.

9. Speech-language pathologists are the professionals trained to deal with communication disorders.
10. The classroom teacher has an important role in the early identification of communication disorders.
11. Gains made in therapy sessions must be reinforced in the home and classroom for speech therapy to be effective.

TASK SHEET 3
Field Experiences with Communication Disorders

Select *one* of the following alternatives and complete the required activities:

Program Visitation

Arrange to visit a program that provides diagnostic or therapeutic services to children with communication disorders. In no more than three pages, describe the program you visited and what you observed. If you saw children being treated, describe the treatment that was being administered and the problem it was intended to help cure. Describe your general reaction to the program.

Professional Interview

Interview one of the people listed below and determine his or her job responsibilities, the training necessary for the job, the problems encountered, and the rewards of the work. If observation facilities are available, ask to observe the person working with a client.
   a. Speech-language pathologist
   b. Director of a speech clinic at a hospital or private clinic
   c. Member of a cleft palate team at a hospital
   d. An otorhinolaryngologist

Interview with a Communication-Disordered Person

Using great tact and discretion, either interview or observe a person who has a communication disorder. This may be someone who has had a stroke, a member of The Lost Cord Club (for laryngectomized speakers), a stutterer, or a person with a cleft palate, cerebral palsy, or an articulation problem. In your interview or observation, pay particular attention to the person's communication. Describe your experience and your reaction to it in no more than three pages.

Speech and Language Analysis

   a. Ask a child of nursery school age (2½–3½) to tell you a story such as *The Three Bears,* and then ask a child who is two or three years older to tell you the same story. Aside from linguistic sophistication, note the difference in the fluency of the speakers. Compare the number of repetitions of words, hesitations, and false starts for the two children, and describe your conclusions and reactions.

b. Locate two children of different ages, tell them a fairly complex story, then ask them to retell it to you. Describe the differences in the children's linguistic development, especially differences in sentence length, sentence complexity, embellishments of the story, vocal inflection, and general storytelling ability. It may be helpful to tape record the stories.

Library Study

Select three articles concerning communication disorders and write a one-page synopsis of each.

Probe Answers

Probe 3-1

1. Ten
2. False
3. vocal fold vibration
4. exhaled
5. lips and tongue
6. plosive
7. e; c; d; b; a
8. False
9. True
10. False
11. False
12. True
13. True
14. False

Probe 3-2

1. receptive language problems; expressive language problems; mixed expressive and receptive language problems
2. True
3. transmission
4. True
5. a. auditory acuity
   b. auditory-perceptual abilities
   c. retrieval skills
   d. motor skills
6. cerebral vascular accident
7. Any 2 of the following:
   a. blocked blood vessel to the brain
   b. burst blood vessel to the brain
   c. injury to the brain

Probe 3-3

1. a. symptoms★
   b. physical explanation★
   c. underlying neurological or physiological cause
2. excess nasality
3. a device that is inserted in the mouth to block off the air to the nasal cavity
4. Lack of motor coordination may prohibit rapid enough movement of the articulators.
5. substitution
   omission
   distortion
   addition
6. Ven: /v/ substituted for /w/ (/v/ is a labio-dental voiced fricative being substituted for a bi-labial voiced glide)

   Varsh: /v/ substituted for /w/ as above
   /r/ addition (/r/ is a lingua-alveolar voiced glide)

   Vindows: /v/substituted for /w/ as above

   Ave: /h/ omission (/h/ is a glottal voiceless fricative)

Fount: /t/ substituted for /d/ (/t/ is a lingua-alveolar voiceless plosive for /d/ lingua-alveolar voiced plosive)

Dey: /d/ substituted for /ð/ (/d/ is a lingua-alveolar voiced plosive and /ð/ is a lingua-dental voiced fricative)

Vas: /v/ for /w/ as above

Donet: /t/ addition

Probe 3-4

1. If a normal voice mechanism is misused, it may break down and show the results of physical damage, which may be interpreted as an organic problem.

2. denasal; nasal
3. Ear, Nose, and Throat specialist
4. He or she specializes in the treatment of problems of the ear, nose, and throat.
5. through a stoma (hole in the neck)
6. False (unless they last longer than 6 months)
7. excess or deficient nasality; breathiness; harshness; hoarseness

Probe 3-5

1. It starts in childhood after a child begins to put words together.
2. 2½; 3½
3. a. securing attention
   b. expressing hostility
   c. controlling the behavior of others
4. False

Sensorimotor Exceptionalities

The subject of Part II is children who have impairments that affect their ability to hear, see, or move. Problems of this sort, called sensorimotor problems, are usually (but not always) easier to identify than learning problems. They can generally be measured more precisely as well. For example, a child's visual acuity or hearing loss can be measured accurately; it is more difficult to assess such characteristics as intelligence and learning ability. This does not mean, however, that the needs of children with sensorimotor problems are easy to meet.

Sensorimotor disorders do not necessarily affect children's intellectual abilities. The great majority of children with these problems can learn and do school work as well as children without disabilities. We hope you will remember this throughout your professional career.

Although the three types of sensorimotor impairments are presented in separate chapters, you should be aware that children often have more than one type of disability. Whether a child has one disability or several, her education will probably involve a number of specialists, who must be able to work together as a team to be effective. The education of children with sensorimotor problems can involve audiologists, who evaluate hearing; peripatologists, who offer mobility training to the blind; physical therapists, who assist in the rehabilitation of the physically handicapped; and medical personnel, such as orthopedic surgeons, psychiatrists, and nurses. Special education teachers themselves must also have highly specialized skills. Teachers of the deaf, for example, may have to know sign language, and teachers of the blind must be able to use braille. Decisions about the education and treatment of a child with cerebral palsy may involve a physician, special education teacher, speech-language pathologist, physical therapist, nurse, principal, and the child's parents. The roles of these and other specialists will be explained in the following chapters.

As you can see, cooperation among specialists is very important. It has been our experience, however, that some special education teachers, particularly those who are just beginning their careers, occasionally feel intimidated by physicians and other specialists. You should remember that just as physicians are specialists in the treatment of children's physical needs, teachers are specialists in meeting children's educational needs. A professionally well-prepared teacher has no reason to feel intimidated.

Following is an overview of each of the chapters related to sensorimotor exceptionalities.

Hearing Disorders. The nature of sound and how we hear are presented in this chapter. Five conditions that can lead to hearing loss are also explained, and the procedures used by audiologists to measure hearing loss are described. The effects of hearing loss are also presented, followed by a discussion of the treatments and classroom techniques used with the hearing impaired. Finally, the roles of the different professionals who work with the hearing impaired are described, and the operation and maintenance of hearing aids are discussed.

Visual Impairments. The identification and characteristics of visual impairments are presented in this chapter. The effects of visual impairment on children are also described, and the procedures used to educate the visually impaired are explained. A discussion of braille and other teaching aids is also included.

Physical Disabilities. The physical disabilities encountered in schools are described in this chapter, and related terminology is defined. Disabilities that affect children's health are also discussed, with particular emphasis on cerebral palsy and epilepsy. The significance of architectural barriers and ways to eliminate them are also explained. The chapter closes with a description of the equipment used to help children adapt to their disabilities.

In 1934, a handsome fifteen-year-old boy was brought to school in Danville for the first time. His parents explained that they had been unable to part with him when he became old enough for school and thus he had grown up entirely uneducated and had never learned to obey, or live under restrictions of a regular school.

The school administration had to admit this boy, but foresaw the difficulty of training him, also teaching him.

They got an older boy to be his "Big brother" and help keep him in line. This proved quite difficult, since the new boy was powerfully built and showed great distaste for the life at school.

Despite the difficulties encountered, most of the school population were of the opinion that the new pupil would gradually adjust to the new life and surroundings.

One Saturday afternoon, the older boys were allowed to attend the movies in town and took this boy with them in hopes he would have a good afternoon. By some . . . ruse, the boy gave his big brother and the other boys the slip and disappeared in the darkened theatre.

It was later discovered that he had left the theatre, unobserved and gone to the bus station. Since he couldn't read or write, he in some unexplained way, had bought a ticket to a town where they had recently had a bank robbery, arriving at midnight.

The boy got off the bus and being in a strange darkened town, made for a lighted window. This happened to be the bank where an armed guard was stationed. . . .

The boy banged on the bank door seeking to gain admittance. This alarmed the guard who drew his gun. . . .

Seeing the guard with his gun pointed at him, the boy took flight and was shot to death when he failed to halt when ordered to do so.

Identification was easily established because in his coat pocket was a letter written to him at the school by his mother, in which she told him to be a good boy and do as he was told.

This is only one of the many tragedies attributed to deafness which could be recounted in our history, but is a true story and explains why our educators are so determined in getting young deaf children in school.

Source: From J. B. Beauchamp, "A Tragedy of Deafness," *The Kentucky Standard,* Danville: Kentucky School For The Deaf, February 1979. Used by permission.

4

Hearing Disorders

William W. Green

William W. Green is Professor of Pediatrics and Special Education and Director of the Clinic for Communicative Disorders at the University of Kentucky. Current areas of interest include audiological evaluations of infants, noise-induced hearing loss in industrial settings, and environmental hearing conservation.

The tragedy described on the facing page is, of course, an exaggeration of the dilemma most deaf persons are confronted with, an invisible handicap that the public can easily misunderstand and react to inappropriately. The interpersonal disabilities that hearing disorders often bring about are staggering when one considers the high rate of oral language used in most societies. Helen Keller, renowned author, educator, and advocate for the deaf and hard of hearing succinctly describes the multiple dilemmas of being deaf:

> I am just as deaf as I am blind. The problems of deafness are deeper and more complex; if not more important than those of blindness. Deafness is a much worse misfortune. For it means the loss of the most vital stimulus — the sound of the voice that brings language, sets thoughts astir, and keeps us in the intellectual company of men [Keller, 1933].

That statement was made by Helen Keller when she was asked to describe the effects of her problems of deafness and blindness. It might surprise you: many of us assume that a loss of vision would have a deeper and more disruptive influence on our daily lives than a loss of hearing. One reason we make that assumption could be that vision problems are relatively easy to imagine — almost everyone has played games that involve being blindfolded or tried to maneuver in the dark. But how many people have ever tried to function without hearing, even for a little while? Almost no one. We generally take our hearing for granted, and we often remain unaware of the subtle and the not-so-subtle ways we are affected by the sounds that pervade our environment.

By the end of this chapter you should have an increased understanding of the importance of hearing. Specifically, we will discuss normal hearing and hearing disorders, particularly as they relate to the education of children. In addition, we hope to motivate you to seek more information to help you to better understand hearing and to enhance your abilities as an educator.

SOUND AND HUMAN HEARING

You should be able to describe the nature of sound and the different ways we use our hearing.

Unless you are reading in a soundproof room, it is almost impossible for you not to be hearing something. If you stop for a moment, close your eyes, and just listen, you may hear a number of simple and complex sounds: a clock ticking, a bird chirping, the hum of a light or heater, wind rustling through the trees, rain hitting the window, the radio or television, traffic noise, people talking, and so on. Our environment is filled with sounds. We are accustomed to them; they are part of our feeling of well-being or annoyance, of our participation in a world full of life.

THE NATURE OF SOUND

Before we discuss hearing and hearing disorders, it is important that you understand what a sound is. Although physicists and acoustic engineers refer to different aspects of sound in many different and often complicated ways, a simple description best serves our purposes. The basic parts of a sound system are identified in Figure 4-1. This configuration is called the TMR system.

A sound is created by the vibration of an object, a transmitter (T). It may be a string, reed, or column of air, as in a musical instrument, or it may be metal, wood, or some other object. The human vocal folds consist of highly specialized vibrating tissue. Vibration, however, becomes sound only if there is a surrounding medium (M) that can carry it. The most common carrying medium is air, but it is also possible for water, metal, or other substances to carry the vibration. The final link in the sound system is something to receive the sound. This receiver (R) may be electronic in the case of radio or TV, but one of the most sensitive receivers is the ear.

Figure 4-1
A Sound System

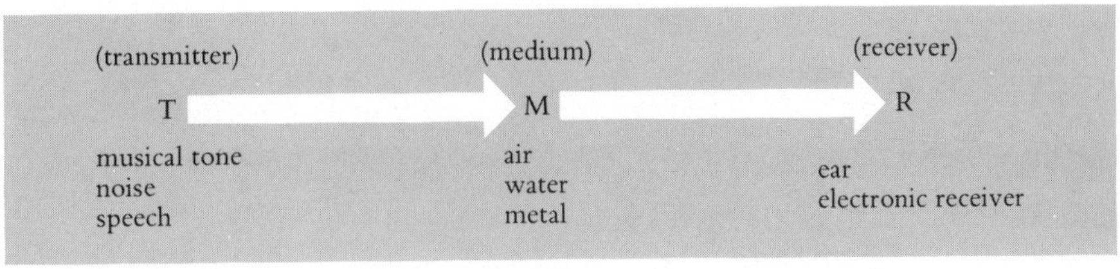

HOW WE USE OUR HEARING

A normal, healthy human ear can hear sounds over a remarkable range of frequencies and intensities. Frequency and intensity are two of the measurable physical characteristics of sound. Pitch is the ears' perception of frequency, and loudness is the ears' perception of intensity. A good way to understand the difference is to regard the lowest and highest keys of a piano keyboard as somewhat representative of the range of frequencies and pitches that the ear can hear, while the intensity and loudness of the sounds are related to how hard the keys are pressed.

The frequency of sounds is expressed in a unit called the Hertz (abbreviated Hz). This is an internationally recognized notation and replaces the use of cycles per second that has predominated in the United States. The human ear can generally hear sounds ranging from 20 to 20,000 Hz, but most sounds in our environment fall between 125 and 8000 Hz. The frequencies of speech sounds fall in the range from 300 to 4000 Hz; it is especially important that the ear be able to hear this range. Frequencies above 8000 Hz are not crucial to hearing speech, but we do use them to enjoy high fidelity music.

The intensity of a sound is directly related to the energy or force of the vibration that caused it. Since the human ear is capable of responding to an enormous range of sound energy, a ratio scale is used to describe intensity. The unit of intensity is the decibel (dB). Zero dB represents the intensity of the softest sound that the normal young adult ear can hear, and 140 dB represents a level so loud it is painful. Table 4-1 gives the intensities of some common environmental sounds.

Levels of Hearing. As we mentioned in the opening paragraphs, most people do not understand how much they depend on their hearing. Ramsdell (1970) describes hearing as having three psychological levels: (1) the *symbolic level,* (2) the *signal* or *warning level,* and (3) the *auditory background* or *primitive level.* An

Table 4-1
Typical Sound Intensities

Intensity in Decibels (dB)	Communication	Environmental	Industrial
140		jet airplane at takeoff (80 ft. from tail)	
130			foundry
120		auto horn	jackhammer
110		discotheque	punch press
105			bulldozer
100		chain saw	
90		heavy city street traffic	noisy factory
85	loud shout at 5 ft.		
80			printing press
75		auto at 65 mph	average quiet factory
70		average restaurant	
65		window air conditioner	stenographic room
60		quiet typewriter	
50	average conversational speech at 5 ft.	washing machine	average office
45			
40		residential area at night	
35		quiet office	
30		average dwelling	
20	whisper at 5 ft.	broadcast studio	
10		rustle of leaves	
0	threshold of normal hearing		

understanding of these three levels will enable us to appreciate the practical implications of hearing loss and the psychological changes that accompany it.

The symbolic level of hearing is the level we use to understand words, which are the symbols of objects and concepts. Good hearing is essential for learning speech and language.

The second level is used as a signal or warning system. We constantly rely on hearing to signal us of changes in our environment and to warn us of approaching danger (e.g., a car horn, a train whistle, or an approaching storm). Our use of this level is generally unconscious, but nevertheless it is important. A loss of hearing places an additional burden on the other senses, which sometimes cannot compensate adequately.

Finally, the ear functions on a so-called primitive or background level by constantly monitoring sounds in our environment, thereby keeping us in touch with it. People who have lost the ability to hear background noises often experience almost overwhelming feelings of isolation. These feelings and the frustration that accompanies them can have serious psychological consequences.

We might also consider these levels of hearing from the perspective of the special education teacher. Many mentally retarded, learning disabled, and emotionally disturbed children have delayed speech or language development. Although this delay may not be the direct effect of a hearing loss, it can result from central auditory perceptual or processing problems. These children are likely to have trouble with the symbolic level of functioning.

These special children may also have problems with the signal/warning level or the background level. They are often easily distracted and have trouble adjusting to sudden environmental changes. They may, for example, be distracted or even alarmed by the ringing of the bell to signal class changes, or by the public address system. As a result, the special education teacher may have to control background noises and signal/warning-level sounds.

PROBE 4-1
Sound and Human Hearing

1. What are the three basic components of a sound system?

   a. _____

   b. _____

   c. _____

2. How would you define sound? _____

   _____

3. Two measurable aspects of sound are _____
   measured in _____ and _____ measured in

   _____.

4. What is the intensity range for average conversational speech?

   _____

5. List Ramsdell's three psychological levels of hearing.

   a. _____

   b. _____

   c. _____

HOW WE HEAR

You should be able to describe how we hear.

ANATOMY AND PHYSIOLOGY OF THE EAR

To understand hearing disorders, it is necessary to understand the structures and processes involved in normal hearing. It is helpful to consider the ear in three parts, *the outer ear, the middle ear,* and *the inner ear.* The parts of the human ear are illustrated in Figure 4-2.

Figure 4-2
The human ear. The pathways for sound waves to be transmitted to the inner ear are shown.

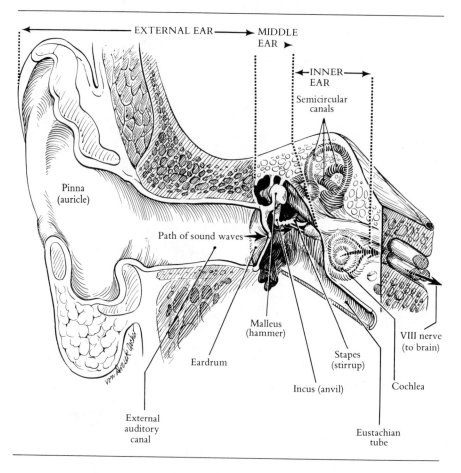

Outer Ear. The outer ear consists of the pinna or auricle (the cartilagenous structure on the side of the head) and the external auditory canal. Since the pinna is the only outwardly visible part of the ear, many people think it is more important than it actually is. The function of the pinna is to collect sound waves arriving at the ear and direct them into the auditory canal. If you have a dog or a cat, you have probably noticed that they can move their pinnae to improve their hearing. Humans retain only a vestige of this ability. We must turn our entire head to focus the ear on a particular sound.

The auditory canal protects the sensitive internal structures in the ear from damage and foreign objects. It is one to two inches long and has stiff hairs at its outer edge to help keep objects from entering. In addition, the skin lining the outer third of the canal secretes a bitter-tasting wax called cerumen that traps foreign material and keeps the ear canal and eardrum from drying out. Earwax is not dirt, and the process of removing it can sometimes result in irritation and infection. The old adage that you shouldn't put anything smaller than your elbow in your ear is still good advice. A doctor should be consulted if you have a problem with wax buildup.

Middle Ear. The outer and middle ear are separated by the eardrum. The eardrum is a membrane that vibrates when it is struck by sound waves; the vibration is then transmitted by a series of three small bones, the malleus (hammer), incus (anvil), and stapes (stirrup). These bones, which are named for the objects they resemble, carry the vibration across the middle ear cavity to the entrance to the inner ear.

Another important structure generally considered part of the middle ear system is the eustachian tube, which extends between the back wall of the throat and the middle ear cavity. This structure opens and closes to equalize the air pressure on the inside of the eardrum with that on the outside. The eustachian tube is the structure that relieves the feeling of pressure or stoppage we feel when descending in an airplane or swimming under water. By swallowing, yawning, or using normal muscle action, we cause the tube to pop open, which allows air to enter the middle ear cavity (Davis and Silverman, 1970; Newby, 1972).

Inner Ear. The inner ear is a remarkably intricate structure. The cochlea of the inner ear contains thousands of hair cells (12,000 in the human ear). The two major structures of the inner ear can be differentiated by their function. The vestibular mechanism is used for balance; the cochlea is used for hearing. Both structures are filled with fluid and are joined by the vestibule, the open area into which sound waves enter from the middle ear.

The vestibular mechanism is the structure that enables us to maintain our balance. It consists of three loop-like structures, the membranous semicircular canals. The angles of the loops correspond to horizontal, vertical, and lateral planes. The canals and two other structures, the utricle and the saccule, relay information about head movement, body movement, and acceleration to the brain, which then adjusts the body to maintain balance (Martin, 1975; Newby, 1972).

The cochlea, which lies just below the semicircular canals, is important for hearing. This organ, which is shaped like a snail shell, contains the endings of the auditory nerve (Cranial Nerve VIII) in a central channel called the cochlear duct. The movements of the stapes in and out of the opening to the inner ear create waves in the fluid in the cochlea. These waves then stimulate the nerve endings of the auditory nerve, which sends an electrical impulse to the brain (Davis and Silverman, 1970; Martin, 1975).

These structures are all considered part of the peripheral hearing mechanism, to distinguish them from the central auditory mechanism, which consists of those parts of the brain involved with sound. The peripheral hearing mechanism serves as an extremely efficient sound transmitter. To repeat the steps: a transmission starts with a vibration in air (sound wave), which travels down the auditory canal and causes the eardrum to vibrate. This vibration is then carried across the middle ear cavity mechanically by the three bones of the ossicular chain, to the opening of the inner ear. There the vibration is transferred to a fluid movement that travels through the cochlea. The fluid, vibratory energy is finally changed to electrical energy by the stimulation of the nerve endings of the auditory nerve.

Central Auditory Processing. The operations involved in the central processing of auditory signals are far too complex to discuss in detail in this text. You need only understand that sounds in the form of electrical energy travel along the auditory nerve through several complex lower brainstem areas to the cortex, which is the covering of the brain. One area of the cortex is adapted to manage sound; it is there that the interpretation and perception of sound take place. This area, called the auditory cortex, is responsible for the gross and fine discrimination necessary to understand speech and language (Ades, 1959; Northern and Downs, 1974).

The function of the auditory cortex and the rest of the central auditory system is roughly comparable to that of a computer. It interprets and analyzes the sounds that are fed into it, organizing them into a pattern that we can understand and use as a language. The analogy is only partially accurate, however — only humans can interpret the emotions, subtleties, and intentions expressed in speech.

You may be surprised to learn that a five-month-old human fetus can hear sounds. At birth, the newborn has been hearing, albeit passively, for four months. After the child is born he begins learning the basic building blocks of language. He gradually refines his cooing, gurgling, and babbling by listening to his own sounds and the sounds of those around him, a process known as an "auditory feedback loop." The child with normal hearing usually produces his first words when he is about one year old, and his language develops very quickly thereafter.

This process is delayed by several years in deaf children, and the words these children learn must be acquired by other means than hearing.

As you can see, learning is a complex process that takes place formally and informally throughout our lives. It depends on the senses, particularly vision and hearing. These senses are so basic that problems with any component in their complex arrangement can interfere with learning.

Auditory learning requires an intact peripheral auditory mechanism. The hearing losses that result from problems at this level preclude the processing of raw data (sounds). A partial hearing loss can retard auditory learning, and complete deafness stops auditory learning altogether and requires a heavy emphasis on visual skills. If the peripheral hearing mechanism functions as it should, the central auditory system is the crucial mechanism in auditory learning and speech/language development.

PROBE 4-2
How We Hear

1. Match each item on the left with the appropriate selection on the right.

   ____ 1. incus

   ____ 2. sense organ of hearing

   ____ 3. outer ear

   ____ 4. ventilation

   ____ 5. balance

   ____ 6. earwax

   ____ 7. transmits sound to brain

   ____ 8. hammer

   a. cerumen
   b. malleus
   c. stapes
   d. semicircular canals
   e. anvil
   f. pinna
   g. eardrum
   h. cochlea
   i. auditory nerve (VIII)
   j. eustachian tube

2. T F Earwax is dirt and should be cleaned from the ears.

3. Trace the pathway of sound through the structures of the ear.

   _____

   _____

   _____

4. The part of the brain most important to hearing is the _____.

5. The human ear begins responding to sound at what age? _____

HEARING LOSS

> **You should be able to define hearing loss, describe its prevalence among children, and know its major classifications and causes.**

DEFINITION AND CLASSIFICATION

Many different systems have been proposed to define and classify hearing loss. Some of these systems are physiologically oriented and focus only on the measurable amount of hearing loss, whereas others focus on the extent to which the hearing loss affects speech/language development, educational achievement, and psychological adjustment (Myklebust, 1964; Newby, 1972). Another consideration is the age at which the hearing loss occurred. Very early loss of hearing affects a child's development more than a later loss (Myklebust, 1964). A classification system designed to aid teachers and counselors of the hearing impaired must take into account all of these factors.

An important distinction must be made between the term "deafness" and other more general terms such as "hearing loss," "hearing disorder," and "hard of hearing." *Deafness* means a hearing loss so great that hearing cannot be used for the normal purposes of life, whereas the other terms are used to describe any deviation from normal hearing, regardless of its severity. For the educator of deaf or hard-of-hearing children, the definitions proposed by the Conference of Executives of American Schools for the Deaf can be used effectively. This group first proposed definitions in 1938, as follows:

1. *The deaf.* Those in whom the sense of hearing is nonfunctional for the ordinary purposes of life. Based on the age at which the deafness occurred, the deaf were grouped into two distinct classes:
   a. The *congenitally deaf.* Those who were born deaf.
   b. The *adventitiously deaf.* Those who were born with normal hearing but in whom the sense of hearing became nonfunctional later through illness or accident.
2. *The hard of hearing.* Those in whom the sense of hearing, although defective, is functional either with or without a hearing aid.

These definitions were more recently refined to reflect the importance of hearing in language acquisition, as follows:

Hearing Impairment — A generic term indicating a hearing disability that may range in severity from mild to profound. It consists of two groups, the *deaf* and the *hard of hearing:*

A *deaf* person is one whose hearing disability precludes successful processing of linguistic information through audition, with or without a hearing aid.

A *hard-of-hearing* person is one who, generally with the use of a hearing aid, has residual hearing sufficient to enable successful processing of linguistic information through audition (Report of the Ad Hoc Committee to Define Deaf and Hard of Hearing, 1975).

The educator should be very careful not to classify a child as deaf or hearing impaired until her hearing has been thoroughly assessed. Even after assessment, professionals should remain flexible about a child's classification. New evidence about a child's ability to hear or speak with proper stimulation, education, or amplification may dictate that she be reclassified (Silverman, 1971).

PREVALENCE

Approximately 14 million Americans, including 500,000 to 700,000 children, have impaired hearing. About 40,000 children with severe impairments attend schools for the deaf, and another 100,000 need special education classes. In addition, there are between 250,000 and 500,000 children with some type of hearing impairment in regular classes. It has been predicted that at least one of every 2000 newborns can be expected to be deaf or hard of hearing (National Advisory Neurological Diseases and Stroke Council, 1969; U.S. Dept. of HEW, 1964).

You may remember the prevalence study cited in Chapter 1. In this study, it was estimated that there are 49,000 deaf children and 328,000 hard-of-hearing children in the nation's schools. The study also indicated that 80 percent of hard-of-hearing children and 60 percent of those with multiple handicaps were not receiving special services. It is to be hoped that the passage of PL 94-142 will enable a greater number of those needing services to be reached.

CAUSES OF HEARING LOSS

To this point we have considered the nature and process of hearing and its importance in the development of speech/language and auditory learning. Those of us with normal hearing pay little attention to the complexities of these processes. It is more difficult for a person with a hearing impairment. Hearing losses can result from a number of conditions and illness. There are five major types: conductive, sensorineural, mixed, functional, and central.

Conductive Hearing Loss. A conductive hearing loss results from problems with the structures in the outer or middle ear, generally a blockage in the mechanical conduction of sound. Sounds must be amplified to overcome the blockage.

The leading cause of conductive hearing loss is middle ear infection, or otitis media. This condition usually results from a malfunction of the eustachian tube.

If this organ does not allow enough air into the middle ear to equal the air pressure on the outside of the eardrum, the oxygen in the air trapped in the middle ear is gradually absorbed by the middle ear cavity tissue. This causes a partial vacuum, which pulls the eardrum into the middle ear cavity. Next, the tissues of the middle ear secrete fluid to fill the void created by the absorbed oxygen. This fluid may become infected. If the condition is unchecked, the fluid may build up sufficiently to rupture the eardrum.

Children have smaller, more horizontal eustachian tubes than adults, and more frequent colds and allergies which affect the eustachian tube openings. As a result they have more eustachian tube problems and much more frequent middle ear infections. Teachers should be aware that this is a common problem. Children who appear to be daydreaming or don't understand assignments may have mild hearing losses caused by ear infections.

Another cause of conductive loss is the blockage of the auditory canal by excessive earwax or a foreign body. If the ear canal is completely blocked, a mild conductive hearing loss can result. Earwax buildup is not as common a problem as many people think, however; even a tiny opening through a plug of earwax is sufficient for relatively normal hearing. Often a condition assumed to be caused by earwax has an entirely different cause. Children may have a mild hearing loss as a result of putting a foreign object, such as a bean or part of a toy, in the auditory canal.

Another cause of conductive hearing loss is a condition called otosclerosis. This results from the formation of a spongy-bony growth around the stapes, which progressively impedes its movement and causes gradual deterioration of hearing. This condition can often be overcome by a surgical procedure called a stapedectomy.

Conductive hearing losses are usually temporary, and the amount of hearing loss varies, depending on the medical condition that causes it. These losses are seldom severe enough to prevent one from hearing speech entirely, but they can cause a child to miss sounds and words and delay the development of speech and language. Most, but not all, conductive hearing losses can be successfully treated with medicine or surgery. Specific treatments will be discussed later in this chapter.

Sensorineural Hearing Loss. Sensorineural hearing losses result from damage to the cochlea or the auditory nerve. This damage is caused by illness or disease. Sensorineural hearing losses are usually greater than those caused by conductive disorders, and they require more extensive treatment.

Viral diseases are a major cause of hearing loss, particularly in children. These can occur either before or after birth and may cause problems ranging from mild hearing loss to deafness. There is a high probability that a pregnant woman who contracts rubella (German measles) during her first three months of pregnancy will give birth to a child with some sensorineural hearing loss. It is estimated that 10,000 to 20,000 children were born deaf as a result of the rubella epidemics of the early and mid 1960s (Northern and Downs, 1974). Severe hearing loss or deafness can also result from infectious meningitis, mumps, measles, chicken pox, and influenza. Viral conditions may also result in malformed body parts, retardation, nervous system damage, and congenital heart disease.

Rh incompatibility is the cause of impairment in about 3 percent of the children who have hearing loss (Northern and Downs, 1974). This condition, called erythroblastosis fetalis, is the result of the destruction of fetal Rh positive blood cells by maternal antibodies. The condition kills some of the afflicted infants during the first week of life. Of those who survive, 80 percent have partial or complete deafness. Like viral diseases, Rh incompatibility can cause other problems, such as cerebral palsy, mental retardation, epilepsy, aphasia, and behavioral disorders.

Other hearing problems are caused by ototoxic medications, medicines that destroy or damage hair cells in the cochlea. Kanamycin, neomycin, gentamycin, streptomycin and vancomycin are some of the drugs known to be ototoxic. These drugs can cause partial or complete hearing loss when taken by the child or the pregnant mother. The fetus is particularly susceptible during the first three months of its development, especially the sixth and seventh weeks. The use of drugs by expectant mothers and young children should be carefully controlled.

Hereditary factors can also cause hearing loss. Proctor and Proctor (1967) report that hereditary deafness occurs in one of 2000 to one of 6000 live births. In many cases hearing loss is only one of several symptoms of a genetic problem. A specific group of symptoms may be classified as a syndrome, which may be identified by facial appearance, physical anomalies, mental retardation, sensory deficit, and motor weakness. Alport's syndrome, Treacher-Colling syndrome and Down's syndrome are examples of genetic conditions that may result in hearing loss. The child with a hereditary deficit often presents complex multiple problems that challenge the background and resourcefulness of the special educator.

Although we have emphasized conditions that result in sensorineural hearing loss in children, two other important causes of sensorineural loss should be mentioned — exposure to noise, and aging. The recognition that noise can damage hearing has led to government regulation of acceptable noise levels in industry and the environment. Most of us can expect our hearing to deteriorate as we grow older. Both aging and excessive noise initially affect our ability to hear high-frequency sounds; the loss may gradually progress until we have problems understanding speech.

Unlike conductive hearing losses, sensorineural losses are not medically or surgically treatable. They are usually quite severe and require long-term rehabilitation efforts, which will be discussed later in this chapter.

Mixed Hearing Loss. A mixed hearing loss is one caused by both sensorineural and conductive problems. Such losses can create particularly serious problems for schoolchildren: a physician may focus on the conductive, medically treatable part of the loss, and be unaware of the sensorineural component. As a result, a child may not receive proper treatment for a problem that affects his classroom performance.

Most hearing losses are caused by conductive, sensorineural, or mixed problems. However, all three types of problems may affect only one ear, or may affect one ear more severely than the other. When this is the case, the child relies on her better ear and may turn that ear toward the speaker; she also has trouble determining the source of a sound. Generally, however, a child with good hearing in one ear acquires speech and language without difficulty.

Functional Hearing Loss. Functional problems are those which are not organic in origin, as you will remember from the last chapter. Functional hearing losses are generally affected to (1) gain attention, (2) explain a poor performance, (3) avoid a responsibility, or (4) collect insurance money. In some cases, functional hearing loss may be psychosomatic or hysterical in origin and the person may not be conscious of the assumed loss.

Among children, functional hearing losses occur most frequently between the ages of nine and thirteen. The losses are usually discovered in hearing tests given in school. It is not unusual to discover that a child with a functional loss is upset or unhappy. There might, for example, be a new baby in the family who diverts parental attention; there may be a divorce or friction between the child's parents; there may be problems with the child's siblings or peer group; or the child may be receiving poor grades. Any of these conditions could cause a child to assume a hearing loss. Once the loss was assumed, it would be awkward and threatening to admit that it was all a game:

> Sonja was an attractive, alert nine-year-old child from a Middle-Eastern country who was brought to the clinic by her aunt. She had been seen by a local otologist whose tests showed moderate hearing loss. The otologist could find no ear pathology, however. The aunt explained that Sonja had failed one subject, dictation, and under the educational system in her country she was required to repeat the entire year. Her family was upper class and ambitious and when Sonja was questioned about the failure, she stated that she could not hear the teacher. This triggered a chain of events that led to a trip to America to visit her aunt for medical treatment and/or a hearing aid. The first test in the clinic showed a moderate loss, but after considerable counselling and with the aunt's help, testing finally revealed normal hearing. Sonja then admitted that she failed dictation because she didn't like the teacher, not because she didn't hear her. Once she had fallen into the trap of having a "hearing loss," she couldn't find a comfortable way out. Apparently, no one wondered why she had trouble hearing one of her teachers and not the others.

Among adults, functional hearing loss is often consciously intended, and can generally be considered malingering. The purpose is usually to make money, from an automobile or industrial accident, for example. When there was a military draft, it was not uncommon for a hearing loss to be "faked" to avoid induction. There were also attempts to obtain disability payments at discharge by assuming a hearing loss. There are functional hearing losses that are not intentional, of course. A functional loss can result from emotional or psychological problems. Most adult losses, though, are intentionally assumed. Audiologists have several tests designed to detect malingering.

Central Auditory Disorders. Central auditory disorders are those in which there is no measurable peripheral hearing loss. Children with this type of disorder may display problems with auditory comprehension and discrimination, auditory learning, and language development. These disorders are the result of lesions or damage to the central nervous system, but specific causes are hard to pinpoint. Children with central auditory disorders have trouble learning, and are often considered learning disabled. Interest in children with these disorders is growing. They have serious long-term problems and are difficult to treat effectively.

PROBE 4-3
Hearing Loss

1. A person who had a hearing loss severe enough that he cannot learn language through hearing is classified as _____.

2. As many as ____ percent of schoolchildren have some degree of hearing loss.

3. List the five major types of hearing loss.

    a. _____

    b. _____

    c. _____

    d. _____

    e. _____

4. Otitis media is the most common cause of _____ hearing loss. Other possible causes for this condition are _____ and _____.

5. When a "hearing loss" is assumed to explain poor school performance, the "loss" would be termed _____.

6. When there is damage or deterioration of the cochlea or VIII nerve, the hearing loss is termed _____.
A major cause of this type of problem is _____ disease. One of these diseases, _____, is a major cause of deafness in children.

7. When a child displays weakness in auditory skills and yet shows no measurable hearing loss, a _____ should be suspected.

EVALUATING HEARING LOSS

You should be able to discuss how hearing loss is identified and evaluated and be able to read an audiogram.

The hearing problems of children are identified at different ages and by a variety of different people. Children are generally referred first to a physician or otologist, who may in turn refer the child to an audiologist if she finds no obvious problem that can be resolved medically or surgically. The audiologist can perform many different types of tests to determine whether a child has a problem, what kind of problem he has, and how it should be remediated.

As is true of other types of disorders, hearing disorders are treated most effectively if they are discovered early. In fact, there is sometimes concern about a child's hearing before he is born, if there is a hereditary factor predisposing the child to a hearing problem or if the mother has had an illness such as rubella or meningitis. There may also be concern if the mother has taken ototoxic drugs or had a traumatic accident, or if there is Rh incompatibility. Hearing evaluations are sometimes difficult to perform with very young children, but evaluations must be begun early to give the child every possible advantage.

Hearing problems are often discovered when the child is older, however. Parents may notice that a child does not react to loud sounds, does not turn his head when he hears a voice, does not engage in vocal play, or is delayed in speech and language development. Hearing problems may also be identified in hearing screening programs offered through health departments, speech and hearing centers, or school systems. Attentive teachers who notice that a child doesn't pay attention or frequently asks to have things repeated sometimes uncover hearing problems as well. However a problem is discovered, it should be promptly and thoroughly evaluated.

This evaluation is generally medical and audiological. The pediatrician or otologist takes a thorough medical history of the child, examines him, and looks at the auditory canal and eardrum with a small light called an otoscope. If the child has an obvious middle ear infection, the doctor may be able to cure the problem. She may request audiometry to determine the effects of treatment. If the doctor cannot find the cause of the problem, she should refer the parents and child to an audiologist.

AUDIOMETRIC EVALUATION

Special educators should have some knowledge of the means and purposes of audiometric testings, and should be able to read an audiogram. A thorough discussion of audiometric testing can be found in Newby (1972) and Martin (1975).

Some types of hearing evaluation that yield gross information do not require the use of sophisticated equipment. Observations by parents and doctors provide some information, as do the child's medical history and otoscopic examination. Even something as simple as the child's reaction to loud noises such as hand clapping and rustling paper can help determine the need for further evaluation. The relatively refined methods of formal audiometric testing, some of which are described in this section, are necessary to determine the precise extent of the hearing problem and the best methods of auditory rehabilitation.

Pure Tone Audiometric Screening. Pure tone audiometric screening is usually a child's first encounter with formal hearing testing. Most school systems provide a regular schedule of hearing screening through the school speech pathologist or school nurse. Group hearing screening tests (Newby, 1972) offer the advantage of testing more than one child at a time, but they are less susceptible to control and less reliable than individual tests.

Pure tone screening of individual students, often referred to as sweep testing, is performed with a pure tone audiometer (Newby, 1972). In this test the child is presented with pure tones over the frequency range from 250 Hz through 8000 Hz, and at a set intensity level of 20 or 25 dB. The child is asked to respond if she hears a tone, usually by raising her hand; children who cannot hear sounds at two or more frequencies are referred for more extensive evaluation.

Pure Tone Threshold Audiometry. Pure tone audiometry is a testing method that requires a child to raise his hand or push a button each time he hears a tone. The audiologist gives the child tones of different frequencies, ranging from 125 Hz to 8000 Hz, and determines the lowest intensity the child can hear, his threshold, at each frequency. This testing is done through earphones (air conduction) or through a vibrator placed on the mastoid bone behind the ear (bone conduction). The air conduction (AC) test reveals the presence of hearing loss, and shows the amount of the loss. Bone conduction (BC) testing measures the response of the sensorineural mechanism of the inner ear, bypassing the outer and middle ear systems. A comparison of air conduction and bone conduction thresholds reveals the loss as conductive, sensorineural, or mixed as follows:

Conductive loss is indicated when AC testing reveals some loss of hearing in the outer or middle ear, but BC testing shows normal hearing because the auditory nerve is functioning properly.

Sensorineural loss is indicated when AC and BC testing show the same amount of loss, which signifies that the outer and middle ear are intact and the inner ear is affected.

Mixed loss is indicated when BC testing shows a loss resulting from a sensorineural problem, and AC testing shows further loss resulting from a middle ear problem.

Speech Audiometry. Speech audiometry is a technique used to determine a child's ability to hear and understand speech. The threshold for speech (that is, the lowest intensity at which words are heard), is called the speech reception threshold, abbreviated SRT. The SRT is discovered by asking the child to repeat two-syllable words that she hears, while the audiologist reduces the intensity of the words until they are barely heard. To determine how well the child can understand or discriminate among words that she hears at a comfortable loudness level, the child is presented with a recorded list of one-syllable words and asked to respond. The child is expected to respond to all words whether she understands them or not. The purpose of the test is to determine how many correct responses she makes in a given word list (usually twenty-five or fifty words). The number of correct responses is converted to a percentage score, and this is her speech discrimination score. Both the SRT and speech discrimination measures require the use of earphones.

In some cases it is necessary to keep one ear "busy" to accurately test the other ear. This occurs primarily when one ear is better than the other. This technique, called masking, involves transmitting a noise to the good ear to keep the good ear from hearing a sound being presented to the bad ear.

Special Audiometric Tests. Pure tone and speech audiometry constitute the standard test battery used to determine what type of hearing loss a child has and how extensive it is. Both tests require that the person being tested understand the test instructions and give a voluntary response, such as pushing a button, raising a hand, or repeating words. Some children cannot be evaluated with these tests, however, because they are too young (less than two), have motor or emotional problems, are mentally retarded, or present other difficulties. For these children special tests and test variations have been devised.

Sound field audiometry. If a child is too young to understand test instructions or is unwilling to wear earphones, his hearing can be evaluated by observing the intensity levels at which he responds to sounds broadcast through speakers. Using this method the audiologist presents speech, noise, or pure tones, and notes whether the child pays attention to the sounds or consistently turns to determine the sound source. The speech reception threshold of very young children can sometimes be determined by asking them to point to pictures or parts of the body as they are named. The same method can also be used to get an impression of a child's ability to discriminate speech (Northern and Downs, 1974).

Behavioral play audiometry. Various techniques can be used to entice a frightened or reticent child to participate in testing by setting up a game or challenge (Newby, 1972; Northern and Downs, 1974). This "play" audiometry involves the child in a series of activities that reward her for responding appropriately to tone or speech. The game might involve putting a block in a bucket, activating a moving toy, turning on a light, or completing a puzzle.

Impedance audiometry. The impedance audiometer is used to obtain information about the functioning of the middle ear system to assist the physician in treating otitis media and other middle ear problems. The two major impedance audiometry tests are *tympanometry,* which gives information about the compliance or resistance of the eardrum, and *stapedial reflex testing,* which measures the reflex response of the stapedial muscle to pure tone signals. These tests do not require a behavioral response from the child and are therefore useful with very young and difficult-to-test children (Northern and Downs, 1974).

Evoked response audiometry. The evoked response technique requires the use of an electroencephalograph and a computer. It is used to measure the changes in brainwave-electrical activity in response to sound. Like impedance audiometry, this type of testing does not require a behavioral response from the child; it can also be performed when the child is asleep or sedated. It is used with infants who are suspected of being deaf and with children who have multiple handicaps (Martin, 1975; Northern and Downs, 1974).

INTERPRETATION OF AUDIOGRAMS

Pure tone air conduction and bone conduction results are generally charted on a grid, or audiogram, that has the frequencies tested noted at the top and the amount of loss in decibels noted down the side (see Figure 4-3). The type of test and the ear being tested are noted in symbols:

O — right ear, air conduction (△ when masking is applied to the left ear)
X — left ear, air conduction (□ when masking is applied to the right ear)
< — right ear, bone conduction ([when masking is applied to the left ear)
> — left ear, bone conduction (] when masking is applied to the right ear)

The extent of a hearing loss can be categorized as normal, mild, moderate, severe, or profound (Figure 4-3), based on the average pure tone air conduction loss at 500, 1000, and 2000 Hz (the frequencies of speech) for each ear (see How We Use Our Hearing earlier in this chapter). The type of loss and its extent determine whether medical treatment or rehabilitation is necessary. Examples of typical audiograms are found in Figure 4-4A–E.

Figure 4-4A shows the test results for a six-year-old boy who has had a recurrent ear infection. His teacher thinks he doesn't pay attention, and he is having problems in school. This hearing test was requested by his pediatrician. It indicates a mild conductive hearing loss in both ears, which was treated with medication.

Figure 4-4B shows test results for the same six-year-old boy following his medical treatment. His hearing has returned to normal for both ears. His mother was urged to take her child to a doctor if she suspected a recurrence of the problem. The child's teacher was asked to seat him in the front of the classroom so he would not miss instructions if his problem returned.

Figure 4-4C is the audiogram for a four-year-old deaf boy whose mother had rubella during the first three months of her pregnancy with him. His pediatrician

Figure 4-3
Extent of Hearing Loss

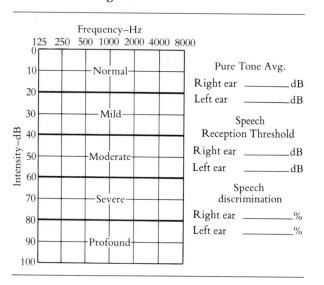

Figure 4–4
Examples of Typical Audiograms

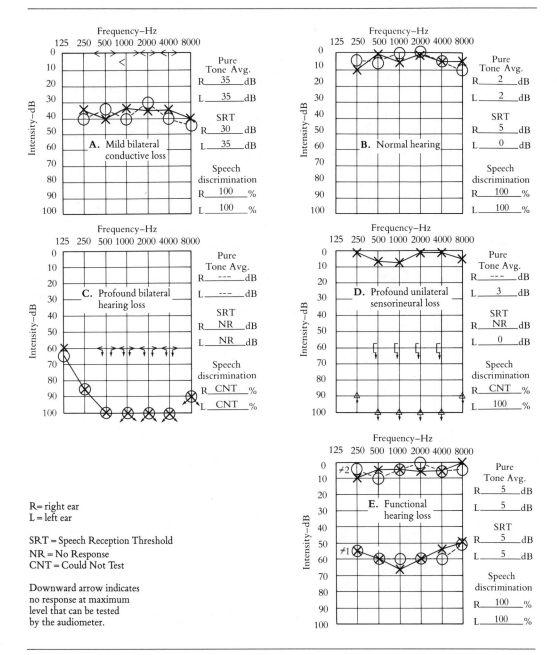

sent him for testing at three months of age, and he has had several tests since. He was fitted with a hearing aid when he was fourteen months old. He was first enrolled in a preschool program for the deaf and later in a residential program, where he did very well.

Figure 4-4D represents the hearing of a nine-year-old girl who was referred for evaluation because a problem with her right ear was discovered in a school screening program. The family doctor found no medically treatable condition and sent her to an audiologist for a complete evaluation. The evaluation indicated that she had normal hearing in her left ear and a profound sensorineural loss in her right ear. Her mother was surprised to learn of the loss, because her daughter had had no trouble learning speech and language, got good grades in school, and was an able conversationalist. Her normal hearing in one ear accounts for these abilities. This child did, however, have trouble determining where sounds were coming from, because we rely on differences in the time of arrival of sounds at our two ears to determine their direction of origin. Favorable classroom seating was requested for this child. In her case favorable seating was on the front right side of the room, so her good left ear was toward the teacher.

Figure 4-4E is the audiogram for Sonja, the nine-year-old Middle Eastern child discussed earlier in this chapter. The pure tone responses labeled #1 are results of the first attempt to test; they represent the functional moderate-to-severe "loss." The pattern labeled #2 represents the true responses, which show normal hearing. During all the tests Sonja took, her responses to speech were normal and she had excellent understanding and discrimination. As with all functional hearing losses affecting children, it was necessary to resolve the problem that prompted the child to "need" the hearing loss.

PROBE 4-4
Evaluating Hearing Loss

1. What are four signs that might indicate a hearing loss?

   a. _____

   b. _____

   c. _____

   d. _____

2. A graphic portrayal of a person's hearing is called an _____
   _____.

3. T   F   An otoscopic examination will determine whether a child has a sensorineural hearing loss.

4. List the different types of audiometric test.

   a. _____

   b. _____

   c. _____

   d. _____

   e. _____

   f. _____

5. T   F   Children's hearing cannot be tested accurately until they are six years of age.

6. Match the audiometric symbol on the right with the correct category listed on the left.

   ____ 1. right ear, bone conduction   O

   ____ 2. right ear, air conduction (masked)   X

   ____ 3. left ear, air conduction   >

   ____ 4. right ear, air conduction   <

   ____ 5. left ear, bone conduction (masked)   △

   ____ 6. left ear, air conduction (masked)   □

   ____ 7. right ear, bone conduction (masked)   ]

   ____ 8. left ear, bone conduction   [

7. The speech frequencies on the audiogram are ____, ____, and ____ Hz.

8. Match the amount of average loss on the right to the descriptive word on the left.

   ____ 1. mild   0-20 dB

   ____ 2. profound   20-40 dB

   ____ 3. moderate   40-60 dB

   ____ 4. normal   60-80 dB

   ____ 5. severe   80+ dB

9. The audiometric test that measures a person's ability to understand speech is called _____.

THE EFFECTS OF HEARING LOSS

> **You should be able to discuss the effects of hearing loss.**

A hearing loss is a major sensory deficit, and it can affect many different abilities. Its effects vary depending on a number of factors, including the severity of the loss, the age at which it occurred, and the hearing impaired person's determination to adapt. Those who teach and treat the hearing impaired must consider the extent of the handicap that results from the hearing loss, and whether the handicap is exclusively the result of the loss, or of societal expectations and pressures as well. In this section we will discuss some of the issues that relate to the development and adjustment of the hearing impaired.

INFLUENCE OF AGE OF ONSET
AND SEVERITY OF HEARING LOSS

Myklebust (1969) stressed the importance of the age of onset and severity of hearing loss on the personality development and emotional adjustment of the hearing impaired. These factors are also crucial in developing language and speech skills, in educational achievement, and in vocational, social, personality, and emotional adjustment. Tables 4-2 and 4-3 summarize some of the effects of these variables. You should refer to them as we discuss the characteristics and needs of the hearing impaired.

LANGUAGE AND SPEECH DEVELOPMENT

One of the most serious consequences of a hearing loss is the effect it can have on the development of speech and language. Language is crucial to personal and societal development. As Northern and Downs put it,

> All the progress that man has made, if one can call a highly technologic society progress, is due to sophistication in the manipulation of language. . . . It follows that language deprivation is the most serious of all deprivations, for it robs us of a measure of our own human-ness. Whether caused by sensory deprivation, by experimental deprivation, or by central disordering, in some degree it keeps one from the complete fulfillment of one's powers [1974, p. 264].

To understand the effects of a hearing loss, you must understand normal speech and language development. The role of hearing in this process was discussed in Chapter 3. For our purposes it is sufficient to reiterate the importance of the auditory feedback loop. As you will remember, an auditory feedback loop is

Table 4-2
Hearing Loss: Effects of Age of Onset

Age of Onset	Speech/Language Development	Educational Adjustment	Vocational Adjustment	Social Adjustment	Personality and Emotional Adjustment
birth to 2 yrs.	Deafness prevents normal development of speech and language. Hearing loss may retard speech/language and may require some therapy.	Deafness requires early special education. Parents need counseling. Child with hearing loss may be held back by early influence of loss.	Not crucial at this age, except for deaf whose vocational future is limited.	Child may begin to notice he is different and environments restricted.	Feeling of isolation, frustration, and fear may begin to develop. Problems mostly at signal level.
2-6 yrs.	Deaf child will need therapy to develop speech/language. Hearing impaired child will need therapy for speech/language development delay.	Deaf child should attend daily special preschool. Hearing impaired child will need some preschool special services.	Deafness will restrict later vocational choices. Not crucial for mild to moderate hearing impaired.	Children may tease or be impateint with the deaf child. Adults may lack the necessary patience. Child with mild loss may not be affected.	Continuation of problems identified above. Problems mostly at signal and symbolic levels.
6-18 yrs.	Deafness/hearing loss may not affect already developed speech and language; therapy may be needed to prevent regression of speech/language skills.	Deaf child may need day or residential school; young adult needs auditory rehabilitation and possibly vocational training.	Deafness restricts vocational choices. Moderate-severe loss may cause change in career goals.	Deaf child will have peer-group problems. Hearing loss may Cause social withdrawal or affect marital status.	Deafness and severe loss may result in friendship and peer-group identity problems. Problems at signal and background levels.
18-60 yrs.	Same as for 6-18. Speech and language needs likely center on vocational and social concerns.	Deaf or hearing impaired may need formal or informal education and job training.	Crucial vocational period for deafened or hearing impaired. Hearing loss may require change in work setting or career goals.	Deafness or hearing loss may cause traumatic social changes, withdrawal, marital upheaval.	Basic personality may not change, but frustration, isolation, and insecurity may develop.
60+ yrs.	Same as for 18-60. Speech and language needs determined by social and family concerns.	Deaf or hearing impaired may need informal education to better understand hearing loss and to help with social adjustment.	Person close to retirement age, so hearing loss may not affect vocation.	Deafness or severe hearing loss may cause withdrawal and isolation from family and friends.	Deafened and severely hearing impaired may withdraw, feel isolated or be insecure or bitter. Problems at background and signal levels.

Table 4-3
Hearing Loss: Effects of Degree and Type

Average Hearing Loss (500–2000 Hz)	Probable Causes	Ability to Hear Speech Without a Hearing Aid	Extent of Communicative Handicap	Auditory Rehabilitative Considerations
0–20 dB *Normal Range*	May have slight, fluctuating conductive loss. Child with central auditory disorder will show normal hearing.	No difficulty in any conversational setting. Child with central auditory disorder will seem to hear but not understand.	None, except for child with central auditory disorder or with speech/language disorders from other causes.	Probably needs no rehabilitative treatment. Child with central auditory disorder will need intensive therapy.
20–40 dB *Mild Loss*	Most likely conductive from otitis media. Sensorineural loss may result from mild illness or disease.	Hears in most settings, misses soft or whispered speech, will hear vowels but may miss unvoiced consonants, says "huh?" wants TV turned up loud.	Mild handicap, may have speech disorder or mild language delay, may omit final and voiceless consonants.	If conductive and medically or surgically treatable, needs favorable classroom seating. Child with sensorineural problem may need hearing aid, speech reading, and auditory training.
40–60 dB *Moderate Loss*	Conductive from otitis media or middle ear problem; maximum conductive loss is 60 dB. Sensorineural loss from ear disease or illness.	Hearing is a problem in most conversational settings, groups, or when there is background noise; hears louder voiced consonants, may need TV and radio up loud, and have difficulty on the phone.	Possible disorder in auditory learning, mild to moderate language delay; articulation problems with final and voiceless consonants; may not pay attention.	All of the above may apply. May also need special class for the hearing impaired or special tutoring.
60–80 dB *Severe Loss*	Probably sensorineural, although mixed is also possible. Rubella, meningitis, Rh, heredity are possible causes.	Misses all but very loud speech, unable to function in conversation without help, can't use telephone.	Probable severe language and speech disorder; learning disorder; may have no intelligible speech.	All of the above may apply. May need placement in school for the deaf.
80 dB or more *Profound Loss*	Sensorineural, or mixed with large sensorineural component. Rubella, meningitis, Rh, heredity, ear disease, etc. are causes.	Unable to hear speech except loud shout, does not understand spoken language, can't hear TV or radio, can't use the telephone.	Severe speech and language deficit, probably no oral speech, learning disorder, "deaf-like" speech and voice.	All of the above may apply. Will need placement in deaf-oral school or school for the deaf.

a process beginning at birth whereby the child monitors her own utterances as well as those of people around her, and the child is reinforced as she learns correct speech and language (Northern and Downs, 1974). This process may result in speech-like sounds when the child is two months old and in the first meaningful words at about one year. Although we never stop learning language, the early months and years are especially crucial (Lenneberg; 1967, Menyuk, 1972).

The interruption of this vital auditory feedback loop, or its absence in the case of a child born deaf, can slow speech/language development or preclude it altogether. The earlier the onset and the more severe the loss, the greater the developmental deficit. A child with mild to moderate loss will probably develop speech/language skills slowly, but she can usually learn to speak and use language effectively with therapy and adequate amplification from a hearing aid (Holm and Kunze, 1969; Quigley, 1970). A child born deaf, on the other hand, generally grows up without acquiring adequate speech or language skills (Carhart, 1970).

Those who become deaf after even a brief exposure to speech and language are much more likely to develop communications abilities than those who were deaf at birth. According to Lenneberg (1967), "It seems as if even a short exposure to language, a brief moment in which the curtain has been lifted and oral communication established, is sufficient to give a child some foundation on which much later language may be based" (p. 239). Helen Keller, who became deaf and blind from meningitis at age two, is the classic example. The "lifting of the curtain" for the first two years of her life undoubtedly provided the basis for the excellent communication skills she later developed.

EDUCATIONAL ACHIEVEMENT

Most education systems use spoken and written language as the vehicle for learning. As a result individuals with hearing loss, especially if it is severe or profound, are at a distinct disadvantage in the learning process. This is not because the education of the hearing impaired has been consistently inadequate; on the contrary, there has been much progress in the field. There is, however, a tendency to inappropriately judge the hearing impaired by the standards used to measure the achievement of their hearing peers. Similarly, some of the techniques used to teach those with hearing problems are variations of the methods used to teach those who hear normally. More innovative techniques would often be more effective.

The areas of greatest concern in educating the hearing impaired are their intellectual ability and their ability to learn to read.

Intellectual Ability. The intellectual ability of hearing impaired children has been the subject of controversy for many years. The question of the relationship between intelligence and deafness was first raised in a 1920 study by Pintner and

Reamer. In that study it was concluded that deaf children were two years retarded mentally and five years retarded educationally as compared to their hearing peers. It also suggested that two years of the educational lag could be attributed to mental inferiority and three years to language handicap. The debate has continued ever since.

Myklebust (1969) pointed out that the conclusions of the early Pintner and Reamer study were biased by the nature of the test materials, which required verbal ability, and also by the fact that a group test was used. Pintner (1941) himself eventually concluded that education for the hearing impaired should stress motor skills. As test techniques have become more sophisticated, the reported differences between the intellectual abilities of deaf and normal-hearing individuals have been shown to be largely due to test error. Using more appropriate nonverbal tests, Vernon and Brown (1964) and Lenneberg (1967) have reported relatively insignificant intellectual differences between deaf children and their hearing peers. This view is further reinforced by the findings of the Annual Survey of Hearing Impaired Children and Youth of Gallaudet College, which reviewed the cases of almost 20,000 hearing impaired children and found an average IQ close to the norm for normal-hearing individuals (McConnell, 1973).

Reading Ability. Over the past few decades there have been several studies of the reading skills of hearing impaired children. Myklebust (1964) reported that deaf children had a much smaller reading vocabulary than their normal-hearing counterparts. Deaf children the age of high school seniors were reported to have reading vocabularies at the level of nine year olds — an eight- to nine-year lag in reading skills. A 1963 survey by Wrightstone, Aranow, and Moskowitz of hearing impaired students between the ages of 10.5 and 16.5 years indicated that the average reading achievement level was that expected of a third grader. The reading skills deficit indicated in this study is between three and eight years. Williams and Vernon (1970) reported on a study that included 93 percent of the deaf students over sixteen years old in the United States and found that 60 percent were below grade level and 30 percent were functionally illiterate.

If one considers the direct relationship between speaking and reading abilities, these findings are not surprising. It is the underlying language problems of deaf people that cause their serious lag in reading skills. People with minor hearing losses can be expected to have reading levels closer to the norm than those with severe losses.

VOCATIONAL AND SOCIAL ADJUSTMENT

Most of the vocational and social adjustment problems of the hearing impaired are the result of their having to live in a society that relies heavily on spoken and written language. This creates barriers, and as a group they experience more marital, social, and vocational problems than those with normal hearing (Meadow, 1975).

Probably the most serious social problem for those with severe hearing loss is isolation. The young deaf child cannot communicate easily with his hearing peers or with most adults who have normal hearing. Many deaf people interact socially almost exclusively with other deaf people. Interaction with people who hear normally can be very demanding; it is much easier for the deaf to find social acceptance among people with similar disabilities.

Deafness also affects an individual's choice of vocation. The deaf are often restricted to manual jobs where there is relatively little verbal interaction. Williams and Vernon (1970) note that the vocational trend toward more white-collar jobs and greater technical knowledge and education requirements increasingly limits the job market for the hearing impaired.

PERSONALITY AND EMOTIONAL ADJUSTMENT

The loss of any sensory capability can result in emotional and personality adjustment problems. The emotional impact of a loss is not always directly related to the severity of the loss, but greater losses do tend to cause greater isolation and hence more serious adjustment problems. It has been suggested but not proven that those who are born deaf or lose their hearing early in life have fewer adjustment problems because they never acquired a dependence on hearing.

The isolation mentioned in the last section can cause emotional as well as social and vocational problems. Those who sustain severe hearing loss sometimes feel rejected and frustrated (Meadow, 1975; Myklebust, 1969). They also frequently report feelings of living in a "dead" world. The loss of the primitive or background sense of hearing may have a greater effect than the loss of the signal or symbolic levels.

Many hearing impaired individuals could relieve their feelings of isolation by wearing a hearing aid. It is not unusual, however, for a person to refuse to wear an aid because she feels it stigmatizes her. Adults are sometimes concerned that their aid will be considered a sign of old age, whereas children may be afraid of the reaction of their classmates. Both cases may require emotional adjustment.

PROBE 4-5
The Effects of Hearing Loss

1. What are some major areas of development and adjustment for those with hearing loss?

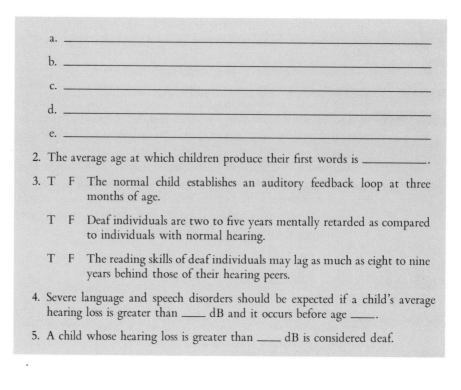

a. _____

b. _____

c. _____

d. _____

e. _____

2. The average age at which children produce their first words is _____.

3. T F The normal child establishes an auditory feedback loop at three months of age.

   T F Deaf individuals are two to five years mentally retarded as compared to individuals with normal hearing.

   T F The reading skills of deaf individuals may lag as much as eight to nine years behind those of their hearing peers.

4. Severe language and speech disorders should be expected if a child's average hearing loss is greater than ____ dB and it occurs before age ____.

5. A child whose hearing loss is greater than ____ dB is considered deaf.

TREATMENT FOR HEARING DISORDERS

You should be able to describe the different types of treatment for hearing loss.

There are many different ways to treat hearing disorders. In some cases the appropriate treatment is medical or surgical; in others longer-term rehabilitative procedures are required. Although we cannot discuss all types of treatment in detail, we will describe some of the common, basic treatments, emphasizing those which are frequently used with children.

MEDICAL AND SURGICAL TREATMENT

In most cases conductive hearing loss in children can be overcome by appropriate medical or surgical treatment. The conductive component of a mixed hearing loss may also respond to this type of remedy. Children suffer from more conductive hearing disorders than any other age group. The most common cause is otitis media, or middle ear infection (Davis and Silverman, 1970; Newby, 1972; Paparella and Juhn, 1979). As you will remember, blockage of the external auditory canal and otosclerosis can also cause conductive loss, but these disorders are relatively uncommon.

Otitis media can be cured with medication (Paradise, 1979). If the condition recurs frequently, the doctor may insert a small tube through the tympanic membranes, to act as a substitute for poorly functioning eustachian tubes, and to help ventilate the middle ear (Paparella, 1979). These tubes tend to work out of the eardrums every few months, and it is sometimes necessary to reinsert them. Physicians can also remove excessive earwax and objects that have become lodged in the auditory canal. Parents should not attempt this operation with cotton-tipped sticks, because of the risk of damage to the ear canal.

Sensorineural hearing problems, on the other hand, are not yet medically treatable. There are some experimental efforts to surgically implant a small device resembling a hearing aid in the cochlea or auditory nerve, bypassing the damaged nerve area and thereby overcoming the sensorineural loss (Michelson, Merzenich, and Shindler, 1975; Porter, Lynn, and Maddox, 1979). This technique holds great promise, but it will probably not be perfected for many years.

AUDITORY REHABILITATIVE TREATMENT

Sensorineural losses and central auditory disorders are relatively complex and require long-term intensive treatment. Auditory rehabilitation can include the use of hearing aids as well as auditory training and speech reading (Davis and Silverman, 1970; Sanders, 1971). It is usually a team effort involving an audiologist, a speech pathologist, and a special teacher, as well as a psychologist and a social worker in many cases.

The goal of all auditory rehabilitative treatment should be to develop an individual's communication skills. In the case of young children, language development is particularly important (Northern and Downs, 1974). This is done most effectively by using a variety of different techniques and approaches, as illustrated in Figure 4-5.

Hearing Aids. Hearing aids are electronic devices that make sounds louder to assist in communication (Northern and Downs, 1974; Rubin, 1976; Sanders, 1971). The use of a hearing aid does not result in normal hearing, but it often greatly improves communications skills. Hearing aids may be considered for children with mild to severe sensorineural losses. They may even help deaf children by allowing them to detect some environmental sounds.

In recent years technological advances have resulted in smaller, more powerful aids with improved sound quality and fidelity. There are many brands and types

Figure 4–5
Development of Communication Language Skills

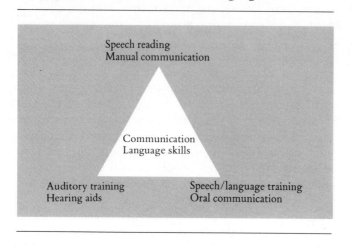

Speech reading
Manual communication

Communication
Language skills

Auditory training   Speech/language training
Hearing aids   Oral communication

on the market. The very young child with a severe or profound hearing loss will probably first use a body hearing aid because it is both powerful and durable. The child may later be able to change to a strong-gain ear-level aid. The aid used most commonly is the over-the-ear or behind-the-ear model. There are also aids that are built into glasses or into an earmold that fits into the external auditory canal. These types of aids are illustrated in Chart 4-1.

Before seeing a hearing aid dealer, it is important that adults and especially children receive a thorough audiological evaluation and medical clearance. This procedure is required by federal regulations, and by many state laws as well. The different considerations in selecting an appropriate aid are too involved to discuss in this chapter; the reader who seeks additional information is directed to Northern and Downs (1974) and Rubin (1976).

Those who work with children who use a hearing aid should know the parts of the aid and how to take care of it (Chart 4-1).

A discussion of hearing aids would not be complete without mentioning some of the misconceptions that prevent people from trying amplification. Sanders (1971) and Northern and Downs (1974) discuss several. One such misconception is that people with sensorineural hearing loss cannot benefit from amplification. This misconception is based on the assumption that damaged nerves cannot be stimulated or regenerated, and amplification is therefore pointless. But most people with sensorineural losses retain the ability to hear some sounds through the parts of the auditory nerve that function correctly, and amplified sound can travel along these structures. In fact, over 95 percent of hearing aid

Chart 4-1
The Hearing Aid

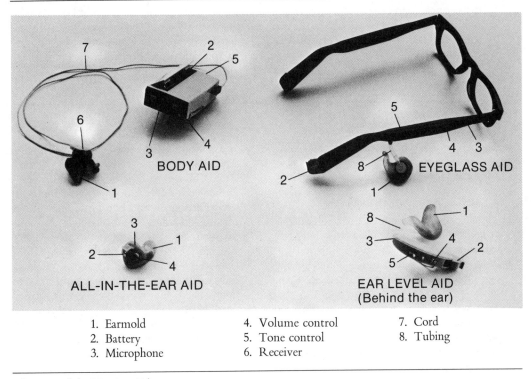

1. Earmold
2. Battery
3. Microphone

4. Volume control
5. Tone control
6. Receiver

7. Cord
8. Tubing

The Parts of the Hearing Aid

1. The *earmold* fits into the ear canal. In body aids, the earmold holds the receiver; in ear-level aids, it is connected directly to the rest of the aid through a piece of clear tubing. The earmold should fit snugly but comfortably. It should be checked immediately if the ear becomes sore or if the hearing aid squeals. The earmold should be cleaned at least once a week using lukewarm soapy water. A pipecleaner can be used to remove earwax.

2. The *battery* supplies the power which operates the hearing aid. When the battery is weak, the sound will be weak. Most hearing aids require only one battery. The battery must be put in such that its terminals line up correctly or the hearing aid will not operate. The battery

should be taken out of the aid when it is not going to be used for several hours.

3. The *microphone* is usually located on the front, tip, or sides of the case. Clothing that rubs the case of the body-type hearing aid can cause noises which interfere with hearing, so the aid is best worn outside the clothing.

4. The *volume control* is a wheel that can be turned to increase or decrease the loudness of sound. In some hearing aids this wheel also controls the on-off switch.

5. A *tone control* switch, not found on all hearing aids, allows the tone to be adjusted. The audiologist will recommend the best setting.

6. The *receiver* is the button that can be attached to the earmold on body-type hearing aids. It

Chart 4-1 Continued

should fit the earmold tightly. If the hearing aid squeals when the volume is turned up, it usually means either that the receiver does not fit the earmold tightly enough, or that the earmold does not fit tightly enough in the ear. Although the receiver is small, it is expensive to repair or replace.

The receiver of an ear-level aid is inside the instrument's case.

7. The *cord,* found only on body aids, connects the receiver with the hearing aid case. It should be cleaned frequently to make certain it connects correctly. The cord should be replaced if it becomes worn. The wires in a worn cord are likely to break, which may cause the sound to be transmitted intermittently or not at all.

General Suggestions for Hearing Aid Use

---

1. The parents or teacher should check the child's hearing aid every morning. They should know what the various controls do, where the battery is inserted, and how to fit the earmold properly in the child's ear.
2. The child should have spare batteries available at home and at school. Those who use body aids should also have at least one spare cord.
3. *Never* attempt major repairs on the hearing aid. Only the manufacturer can make them correctly.
4. Preschool children with impaired hearing should have annual audiological and hearing aid reevaluations. Older children should receive such checks at least once every two years.
5. It's important to remember that a child who wears a hearing aid does *not* hear normally. The aid's effectiveness will vary with the situation. Children with normal hearing may easily understand speech in a noisy environment; a child dependent on a hearing aid may find it impossible to understand speech in the same situation.
6. Teachers and parents must be sensitive to a child's need to adjust socially and psychologically to a hearing aid. It is sometimes best to begin a child's hearing aid use in gradual stages, with the eventual goal of the child's using the aid during most of the time he is awake. The child's classmates should be told about hearing loss and hearing aids to help them understand and accept the child.

Hearing Aid Problems and How to Solve Them

Problem
1. Squealing, or feedback, is a high-pitched noise that may occur when the child moves her head or may be constant. In the classroom this feedback can disrupt the work of other students. Although the hearing impaired student may not hear the feedback herself, it usually means that her aid is functioning less efficiently than it should.
   What to do about it
   a. Be sure the earmold is placed correctly in the ear and is the proper size for the child and is not too loose. Arrange to get a new earmold made if it is loose or does not fit properly.

   b. With body aids, check that the earmold is snapped firmly to the nub of the receiver.
   c. With ear-level aids, be sure the hollow plastic tube from the earmold fits tightly over the receiver opening.
   Problem
2. The hearing aid does not work or only works intermittently. This problem may be indicated if the child fails to respond or has an unusually hard time with assignments. The hearing aid can be checked by holding the earmold or receiver to the teacher's ear.
   What to do about it
   a. Replace battery.
   b. Make sure that positive (+) and negative

(−) ends of battery are placed correctly in the battery compartment and that the battery is held firmly in its compartment.

c. Check for corrosion on battery contacts. This can be removed with a pencil eraser.

d. Be sure the canal of the earmold is not plugged with earwax.

e. If the aid is the body type, turn it on and wiggle the cord where it fits into the receiver and where it enters the case.

f. Be sure the aid is not switched to "telephone" position.

Problem

3. The signal is weak, distorted, or scratchy. This

problem may come to light when the child reports it to the teacher, or the teacher may notice a reduction in the child's performance. It can also be checked by listening to the child's aid.

What to do about it

a. Change the battery, even if it is new or checks normal on battery tester.

b. With a body aid, try another receiver if one is available.

c. Turn the volume control up and down and listen for scratchiness or dead spot.

d. Make sure the tone control, if there is one, is set properly.

---

users have sensorineural rather than conductive losses. Those with conductive hearing loss can, of course, benefit from amplification, because their auditory nerves are intact. These individuals can usually be helped medically or surgically, however, and they don't need hearing aids. Everyone with a sensorineural hearing loss should have an opportunity to try amplification.

A second misconception is that a hearing aid will restore hearing to normal. A hearing aid is an amplifying system that makes things louder. It does not heal the ear, and most hearing aid users initially report that the sound through the hearing aid is artificial. Hearing aid technology is improving, however, and with a reasonable effort the hearing aid user will adjust to the artificial quality of the sound.

Some people believe that a hearing aid will result in increased hearing damage. This misconception is derived from the understanding that very loud noise can damage the ear, particularly the sensorineural component that hears high frequency sounds. It would be possible for damage to result from the use of an aid that was far too powerful. It is doubtful, though, that the hearing aid user would tolerate such overcompensation. The danger is further reduced by relying on the guidance of an audiologist.

Fourth, it is believed that hearing aids do not help those with mild or severe losses. No hearing loss is so mild or so severe that hearing aid use should not be attempted. Although people with mild losses do not always find an aid helpful, many like to use them in school, at work, or in social settings. The profoundly deaf can also use aids to help them communicate. Although a hearing aid will not allow them to understand speech, it can be used to supplement their speech-reading.

Auditory Training. Auditory training is intended to teach the hearing impaired to use their residual hearing to the greatest extent possible (Sanders, 1971). It is usually provided by an audiologist or speech pathologist in individual or group therapy sessions, and reinforced in the regular classroom and at home. In auditory training, the child is taught to use and care for a hearing aid; to use environmental cues in conversation; and to sharpen his ability to discriminate among sounds and words. The goals of an auditory training problem include the following:

1. To familiarize the child and parents with the nature and extent of the loss. This involves explaining how the normal ear functions; describing how various types and amounts of hearing loss affect communication, and specifically how the loss will affect the child's communication; and explaining the child's audiogram.
2. To familiarize the child and parents with hearing aids and hearing aid maintenance. This involves explaining that hearing aids make things louder, not necessarily clearer; explaining the controls and settings of the hearing aid; and providing the child and parents with information on the care and maintenance of the hearing aid.
3. To familiarize the child and parents with the methods and goals of the auditory training plan. This includes developing an awareness of sounds and the basic meanings of sounds; teaching the child to discriminate among sounds; and encouraging the child to make full use of his auditory abilities.
4. To carry out the program designed to meet the individual child's needs. This requires regularly scheduled therapy sessions with an audiologist or speech pathologist; active involvement of the child's regular classroom or special teacher in reinforcing the auditory training; and active involvement of the parents in reinforcing auditory training in the home and family.

Speech Reading. A child who has had a hearing loss naturally becomes more attentive to a speaker's lips and facial movements. Most hearing impaired people are not even aware that they are doing so. Such "lip reading" or "speech reading" can be a valuable skill, but it can be used only to supplement communication, not as a complete communication system. Only 30 to 40 percent of the sounds in our language are produced with visible lip movements, so the speech reader has many gaps to fill in.

Nevertheless, many hearing impaired children do benefit from formal speech reading training. It is typically provided by audiologists and speech pathologists in group or individual therapy sessions. These usually take place through speech and hearing clinics or in the school. Speech reading therapy is most effective when it is part of a rehabilitation program that includes auditory training and the use of a hearing aid. Speech reading lessons are most productive when they take advantage of the child's interests and experiences.

Some people cannot become good speech readers even with formal training. It requires considerable concentration to speech read successfully.

A communications system based on speech reading has the same components as the TMR system described in Figure 4-1. The transmitter is the person speaking, the receiver is the speech reader, and the medium is the environment in which the communication occurs. As with other communications systems, successful communication depends on the proper functioning of the three components, as we will now describe (Berger, 1972).

Speech reading is usually easier if one is familiar with the speaker. Ideally, the speech reader should be able to see the speaker's entire face from the front. This allows the speech reader to distinguish both lip movements and facial expressions. As much of the speaker's body as possible should be in view of the speech reader, since body gestures are a part of communication. The speaker's lip movements are crucial. A lack of normal movement or exaggerated movement makes speech reading more difficult. Also, the speaker should speak at a normal pace.

The second component in our system is the environment. The distance between the speaker and the speech reader is very important. The greater the distance, the more difficult it is to speech read effectively. To speech read, one must be able to see the speaker's face. Therefore, good lighting is also important. Even when the speaker is clearly seen, however, it is sometimes difficult to read speech if the environment is filled with distractions.

The speech reader herself can also affect the quality of the communication and may be the most crucial component. Intelligence, age, and educational background do not appear to have a serious effect on the ability of an individual to speech read effectively. However, it is usually easier for younger people to learn speech reading than it is for older people, and the speech reader's attitude, ability to pay attention, and motivation are crucial. Good visual acuity is also necessary for successful speech reading.

PROBE 4-6
Treatment for Hearing Disorders

1. The medical specialist who typically deals exclusively with children is called a _____. The medical professional who specializes in treating ear disorders is the _____.

2. Small tubes may be inserted in the tympanic membrane to _____ the ear.

3. T F Hearing aids are electronic devices that always make sound clearer.

4. The young child with a severe hearing loss will probably require a _____ type hearing aid.

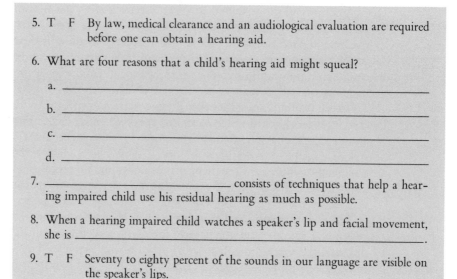

5. T   F   By law, medical clearance and an audiological evaluation are required before one can obtain a hearing aid.

6. What are four reasons that a child's hearing aid might squeal?

    a. _____

    b. _____

    c. _____

    d. _____

7. _____ consists of techniques that help a hearing impaired child use his residual hearing as much as possible.

8. When a hearing impaired child watches a speaker's lip and facial movement, she is _____.

9. T   F   Seventy to eighty percent of the sounds in our language are visible on the speaker's lips.

EDUCATIONAL NEEDS OF THE HEARING IMPAIRED

You should be able to describe the educational needs of hearing impaired children and the implications of mainstreaming practices.

IDENTIFICATION

Many children are identified as having a hearing loss before they enter school, particularly if their loss is severe enough to delay speech and language development. The loss is generally first recognized by a doctor or by the child's parents. A doctor may be especially alert for hearing problems because of (1) a history of hereditary hearing loss; (2) infections or illnesses of the mother during pregnancy; (3) defects of the child's ears, nose, or throat; (4) low birth weight; (5) prematurity; or (6) infections, diseases, or accidents sustained by the child (Northern and Downs, 1974). Parents may discover a hearing loss by observing that their child does not respond normally to sounds. Children whose hearing problems have been discovered very early have probably undergone audiological evaluation and treatment before they entered school.

Children with hearing losses that have not been discovered when they entered school are frequently identified by their teacher. One of the most common indications of a hearing problem is a child's failure to pay attention. Other signs that may indicate a hearing disorder include the following (Duffy, 1967):

— The child complains of frequent earaches or has a discharge from the ears.
— Articulation of speech sounds is poor, or consonant sounds are omitted.
— Easy questions are answered incorrectly.
— The child fails to respond or pay attention when spoken to in a normal manner.
— "Hearing" appears to be better when the child faces the speaker.
— The child often asks the speaker to repeat what was just said.
— When listening to the radio, TV, or other audiovisual equipment, the child turns up the volume to a level that is uncomfortable to those with normal hearing.

Although some of these signs may indicate problems other than hearing disorders, any child displaying them should be observed carefully. A child thought to have a hearing disorder should be referred to an audiologist.

Most school systems have regularly scheduled hearing screenings. They are usually conducted by the school speech pathologist, audiologist, or nurse, sometimes with the assistance of parent volunteers. Some schools' screening programs make use of university-based audiology training programs. Whoever staffs them, screening programs are an effective method of discovering undetected hearing problems.

EDUCATIONAL NEEDS OF THE CHILD
WITH MILD TO MODERATE HEARING LOSS

The treatment and educational requirements of a school-age child will depend on the nature and severity of the child's hearing loss.

Mild to moderate conductive losses that result from recurrent ear infection can often be successfully treated medically or surgically. Although most children with this type of disorder can function in a regular classroom, the teacher should not assume that the child requires no special attention. The child should at least be given favorable seating. The teacher should also know that recurrent otitis media may result in delayed speech and language development (Holm and Kunze, 1969; Lewis, 1976; and Needleman, 1977). If it does, the child will need regular speech and language therapy. Children with mild to moderate conductive losses will benefit from the use of a hearing aid only in the uncommon cases that are not curable.

Most children with mild to moderate sensorineural hearing loss can also function in regular classrooms. In fact, the school-related problems of these children are sometimes not thought to be the result of hearing loss, because they can usually hear and understand conversational speech. These children will probably need a hearing aid, preferential seating in the classroom, speech/language therapy, and possibly speech reading and auditory training therapy. In some cases the child with mild to moderate sensorineural hearing loss may benefit most from being placed in a special class. This is determined by audiological and educational assessment.

Suggestions for the Classroom Teacher. There are many children with mild to moderate hearing loss in regular classrooms. The following suggestions may help the teacher work with them effectively.

1. If the teacher generally teaches from the front of the room, the hard-of-hearing child should be seated in the front, preferably slightly off center toward the windows. This allows the child to hear better and read lips more effectively. Light should be directed toward the teacher's face and away from the speech reader's eyes.
2. If the child's hearing impairment involves only one ear, or if the impairment is greater in one ear than the other, the child should be seated in the front corner seat such that his better ear is toward the teacher.
3. The teacher should pay attention to the posture of the hearing impaired child's head. The habits of extending the head or twisting the neck to hear better can become firmly fixed.
4. The child should be encouraged to watch the face of the teacher whenever she is talking to the child. The teacher should speak at the speech reader's eye level whenever possible.
5. The teacher should try to face the hard-of-hearing child as much as possible when speaking to the class. An effort should be made to give all important instructions from a position close to the child. It's best not to speak between the child and the windows, which may prove distracting.
6. The teacher should not speak loudly or use exaggerated lip movements when speaking to the hard-of-hearing child.
7. The hearing impaired child should be encouraged to turn around to watch the faces of children who are reciting.
8. It is easy to overestimate the hearing efficiency of a child. It should be remembered that it takes a greater effort for a hearing impaired child to hear than it does for a normal child. It may as a result be more difficult to hold the hearing impaired child's attention.
9. A hearing loss of long duration can cause a person's voice to become dull and monotonous. It can also result in poor diction. The hearing impaired child and the rest of the class should be encouraged to speak clearly and distinctly.
10. An interest in music and participation in vocal music should be encouraged.
11. Since a hearing loss affects all the language processes, the child should be

encouraged to compensate by taking a greater interest in reading, grammar, spelling, original writing, and other activities that involve language.

12. The hard-of-hearing child should be observed carefully to ensure that he doesn't withdraw or suffer emotionally as a direct or indirect result of his hearing.
13. The hard-of-hearing child should participate actively in all plays and other activities which involve speech.
14. Teachers should watch carefully for illnesses in hearing impaired children. Colds, influenza, throat and nose infections, tonsilitis, and other ailments should be treated as soon as possible.
15. The teacher should be able to assist the child who wears a hearing aid in the classroom.

EDUCATIONAL NEEDS OF THE CHILD WITH MODERATE TO SEVERE LOSS

A hearing loss in the moderate to severe range has a much greater effect on a child's education than a mild to moderate loss. Most of the more serious losses are caused by irreversible sensorineural problems present at birth or from a very early age. There are some moderate conductive hearing losses, but they are relatively uncommon and can usually be successfully cured.

Auditory Rehabilitative Considerations. The child with a moderate to severe sensorineural loss will probably use a hearing aid. The teachers of such children must be familiar with the information on aids presented earlier. These children may also need special therapy, reinforced by classroom drills. If there are several children with hearing loss in a classroom, the teacher may need to use a group auditory training unit. These units enable a teacher to speak to a large number of children through an amplifying device that is connected to earphones or the children's hearing aids (Davis and Silverman, 1970; Sanders, 1971).

The child with a moderate to severe loss may also need to learn speech reading. As mentioned earlier, most hearing impaired people speechread to some extent without being aware of it and without having been taught (Berger, 1972). Formal training in speech reading will help the hearing impaired in general communication, in the classroom, and in maintaining speech.

Communicative Considerations. The techniques of auditory training and speech reading we have described are associated with what is known as the *oral approach* to teaching communication skills to the severely hearing impaired and the deaf. For the child with moderate hearing loss, oral speech and language skills can usually be taught through long-term, regularly scheduled auditory training sessions, speech reading, and speech-language therapy. When a child's hearing loss is in the severe to profound range, the development of oral speech and language is a more difficult process, and what is known as the *manual approach* may be considered most appropriate. These two approaches have historically been considered separate and mutually exclusive, and oralists and manualists have been debating the relative effectiveness of the two approaches for many years.

Supporters of the oral approach focus their efforts on teaching the child to speak and speech read. The use of gestures is discouraged and manual signing is prohibited (Furth, 1973). Strict oralists contend that a manual system tends to isolate those who use it, arguing that the deaf child should adapt to our speech- and hearing-oriented society. Manualism has been the preferred method for a long time, but oralism began gaining popularity in Europe during the mid-nineteenth century (Sanders, 1971). The oral approach has worked very effectively for many people with severe impairments, but some have trouble learning it and never develop intelligible oral speech.

Proponents of the manual approach believe that sign language is the common, natural language of the deaf. Manualists contend that deaf children learn language best by using their vision. Garretson (1963) cites some of the other arguments for the manual approach:

1. Denying a child the use of fingers and hands in the communicative process can lead to anxiety and emotional stress.
2. The use of manual systems of signs and finger spelling in conjunction with speech enhances communication. The manual alphabet is illustrated in Figure 4-6.
3. Signs are clearer, larger, and more easily visible than lip movements.
4. Children's individual skills in oral communication vary widely. Fingerspelling and signs are easier to learn. Thus, these manual systems might be considered less discriminatory, permitting children equal opportunity to participate in and learn from classroom activities.

The realization that no single method is appropriate for all children has recently broken down some of the barriers between proponents of the two methods and given rise to a philosophy known as *total communication*. This increasingly influential philosophy advocates the use of every possible method to develop a base for language learning, including combinations of the oral and manual approaches (McConnell, 1973).

Educational Settings for the Hearing Impaired. Children with severe to profound hearing loss have traditionally been placed either in *residential settings* or *day schools*. Most residential schools are state-supported and usually stress the manual approach, whereas most day schools are privately funded and emphasize oralism (Meadow, 1972). There is a current trend toward a philosophy of total communication in both settings. Since the late 1950s there has been a tendency to place children in day schools rather than residential settings (McConnell, 1973).

Figure 4-6
The Manual Alphabet

The manual alphabet as the receiver sees it

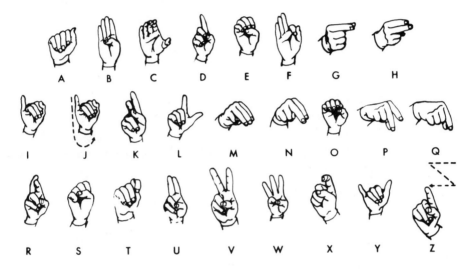

The manual alphabet as the sender sees it

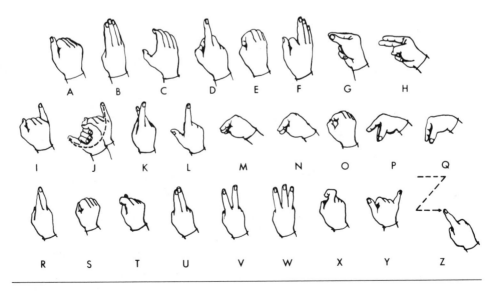

The contemporary emphasis on providing education in the least restrictive environment is reflected in several educational settings for the hearing impaired. These include the *special class* and the *resource room.* In a special class with other hearing impaired children, a child is given training designed to permit her eventually to enter a regular classroom. Once this step is made, the child may receive individual help for part of the day in a resource room. The goal is to integrate the child to the greatest extent possible into the "mainstream" of the educational process that children with normal hearing pass through.

PROBE 4-7
Educational Needs of the Hearing Impaired

1. What are four reasons a physician might suspect a hearing loss in a newborn baby?

   a. _____

   b. _____

   c. _____

   d. _____

2. Name five signs of possible hearing loss that a classroom teacher should watch for.

   a. _____

   b. _____

   c. _____

   d. _____

   e. _____

3. T   F   Language and speech delay can result from recurrent ear infections.

   T   F   Hearing aids are never appropriate for children with conductive hearing loss.

   T   F   The classroom teacher should use exaggerated lip movement and speak loudly to assist the hearing impaired child.

   T   F   The manual approach to communication stresses speech reading and auditory training.

4. Educators of the deaf who prohibit the use of gestures by the child are called

   _____.

5. Educational settings for the severely hearing impaired include the

_____, _____,

_____, and _____.

SUMMARY

1. A person with a substantial hearing loss at the frequencies in the 300–4000 Hz range will be severely handicapped in hearing other people's speech.
2. The intensity, or loudness, of normal conversational speech at a distance of five feet is between 40 and 60 decibels.
3. In normal hearing, sound waves are collected by the outer ear and mechanically transferred by the eardrum to the hammer, anvil and stirrup bones of the middle ear. These bones carry the sound vibration across the middle ear to the inner ear, where fluid motion within the cochlea stimulates the auditory nerve. This nerve transmits electrical impulses to the brain, where they are interpreted.
4. One of the most serious consequences of hearing loss is that it can hamper the development of speech and language in young children.
5. Hearing losses are due to conductive, sensorineural, mixed, functional, and central auditory problems. The conductive loss, which is usually caused by middle ear infections, is the easiest to correct.
6. It is estimated that there are 49,000 deaf children and 328,000 hard of hearing children in the nation's schools.
7. The professionals who evaluate hearing by means of audiometric testing are called audiologists.
8. A hearing loss of between 20 and 40 decibels is considered mild. A loss of between 40 and 60 decibels is considered moderate. A 60- to 80-decibel loss is considered severe, and losses of more than 80 decibels are considered profound.
9. Hearing loss can affect speech and language development, and educational, vocational, social, and emotional adjustment.
10. Hearing aids make sounds louder. They do not make sounds clearer.
11. For educational purposes, children with hearing disorders are classified as either hard of hearing or deaf.
12. The philosophy of total communication makes use of both oral and manual procedures to teach deaf children.
13. Regular class teachers should be able to recognize signs that may indicate hearing disorders so that they can refer children for hearing evaluations. Teachers can help keep children with hearing disorders in the regular classroom in many different ways.

14. Children with severe hearing impairment are best educated in a variety of settings, depending on the severity of their problem. These settings include the residential school, day school, special class, and resource room.

TASK SHEET 4
Field Experiences with Hearing Disorders

Select *one* of the following alternatives and complete the activities that are described. Do a report of no more than three pages on the alternative that you choose.

Professional Interview

Interview a professional who provides hearing services and answer the following:
1. Who did you interview?
2. What services does this person provide?
3. What questions did you ask?
4. What did you learn from the interview?

Observation of an Audiometric Examination

Observe an audiometric testing of a child or adult and respond to the following:
1. Where did you observe the examination?
2. Describe the person being tested.
3. What did the tester do?
4. What tests were administered?
5. What problem was identified by the tests?
6. What follow-up was recommended?
7. Describe your reaction to the experience.

Observation of a Program for Hearing Impaired Children

Visit an educational program for hard-of-hearing or deaf children and respond to the following:
1. Where did you observe?
2. Describe the physical setting.
3. Describe the activities that were being conducted.
4. Interview the teacher about the purposes of the program and what kind of problems are encountered.
5. Describe your reactions to the experience.

Library Study

Use the library to locate three articles related to a topic associated with hearing disorders. Write a one-page abstract of each.

Design Your Own Field Experience

If you know of a unique experience you can have with hearing disabled persons, discuss your alternative with your instructor and complete the task that you agree on.

Probe Answers

Probe 4-1

1. a. transmitter; b. medium; c. receiver
2. Sound is created by the vibration of some object. This vibration is carried across some medium and can be heard by the ear.
3. frequency; Hz; intensity; dB
4. 40–65 dB
5. a. symbolic level; b. signal level; c. background or primitive level

Probe 4-2

1. 1. e; 2. h; 3. f; 4. j; 5. d; 6. a; 7. i; 8. b
2. False
3. The sound wave is collected by the pinna (auricle) and funneled into the auditory canal, causing the eardrum to vibrate. This vibration is mechanically carried across the middle ear via the hammer, anvil, and stirrup; the movement of the stirrup sets up a wave motion in fluid that stimulates nerve endings of the auditory nerve, which carries the impulses to the brain for processing.
4. cortex
5. fifth month of fetal development

Probe 4-3

1. deaf
2. .5%
3. conductive; sensori-neural; mixed; functional; central
4. conductive; a blocked auditory canal; otosclerosis
5. functional
6. sensori-neural; viral; rubella
7. central auditory disorder

Probe 4-4

1. Any 4 of the following:
   a. illness or disease for mother during pregnancy
   b. child does not react to sounds
   c. child does not engage in normal amount of vocal play
   d. child does not pay attention in class
   e. child says "huh" in response to questions
   f. child cannot localize sound
2. audiogram
3. False
4. a. pure tone audiometric screening; b. pure tone threshold audiometry; c. speech audiometry; d. sound field audiometry; e. behavioral play audiometry; f. impedance audiometry; g. evoked response audiometry
5. False
6. 1. <; 2. △; 3. X; 4. ○; 5.]; 6. □; 7. [; 8. >
7. 500; 1000; 2000
8. 1. 20–40 dB; 2. 80+ dB; 3. 40–60 dB; 4. 0–20 dB; 5. 60–80 dB
9. speech discrimination

Probe 4-5

1. a. language/speech development; b. educational adjustment; c. vocational adjustment; d. social adjustment; e. personality and emotional adjustment
2. 12 months
3. False; False; True
4. 60–80; 2 years
5. 80

Probe 4-6

1. pediatrician; otologist
2. ventilate
3. False
4. body
5. True
6. Any 4 of the following:
   a. earmold not seated properly in the ear
   b. earmold is too loose
   c. may need new earmold
   d. earmold and receiver not firmly attached
   e. plastic tubing loose on ear-level aid
7. Auditory training
8. lip reading or speech reading
9. False

Probe 4-7

1. Any 4 of the following:
   a. history of hereditary hearing loss
   b. infection or illness of the mother during pregnancy
   c. defects of ears, nose, or throat
   d. low birth weight
   e. prematurity
   f. accident, infections, or illness of the child
2. Any 5 of the following:
   a. frequent earaches or ear discharge
   b. poor articulation, consonant sounds omitted
   c. wrong answers given to easy questions
   d. child often doesn't respond when called
   e. hearing appears better when child faces speaker
   f. child asks to have things repeated
   g. child turns TV or radio up too loud
3. True; False; False; False
4. oralists
5. residential setting; day school; special class; resource room

This little boy, pictured at age 2½, has a severe sensorineural hearing loss that was discovered when he was three months old. Almost totally deaf, he has been using sign language since he was two. His first signed word was "cookie" and his first spoken word was "mama." The entire family uses sign language and has participated in a speech and language development program for preschool deaf children.

The child is now enrolled in a communication disorders program that includes an evaluation of the effectiveness of his body hearing aid. Recent tests indicate that his language comprehension is appropriate for his age, his vocalizing is good, and his signing has improved. He has begun to speak in complete sentences, and his parents are thrilled at his progress.

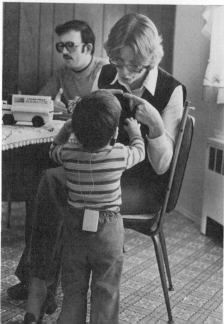

...JoAnn has been blind since she was born at Des Moines, Iowa. She went to special schools until her sophomore year in high school, when she was "main-streamed" — put into a regular high school. There, she says, her biggest trouble was that "I didn't have a very good self-image."

That, she says, is the major problem of the nation's half-million people who are totally blind, and probably the million more Americans whose sight is so impaired they can't read.

Two years ago JoAnn was a student at a Des Moines school run by the Iowa Commission for the Blind, which she says operates "the best program for the blind in the country." The commission bought a Kurzweil Reading Machine for the Blind, the second such machine purchased in the nation. . . .

The Kurzweil machine has opened a new world to her. It is the world of books, of *any* printed material. Now, says JoAnn, "I want to be a lawyer."

The machine is described by its inventor, Raymond Kurzweil, 30:

"A camera scans the print. A small computer recognizes the letters, *all* type styles — that's the heart of the problem. The computer groups letters into words. A thousand linguistic rules and 1,500 exceptions to the rules are fed into the computer's memory. This enables the machine to change the letters to phonemes, the sounds of words pronounced phonetically. There are 64 phonemes, and these are fed into a speech synthesizer which produces speech."

Result: JoAnn Guidicessi now "reads" about 210 words a minute, faster than most sighted persons can read. . . .

The first Kurzweil machine was installed at the end of 1976. Since then about 50 have been installed and Kurzweil has orders on hand for another 100 from as far away as Sydney, Australia.

The U.S. Bureau of Education for the Handicapped picked up on the Kurzweil machine after its first installation. It funded research for its improvement and has ordered 64 of the new models. . . .

Source: From William Steif, Machine Can Open Reading World to the Blind. *The Albuquerque Tribune,* March 2, 1979. Reprinted by permission.

5

Visual Impairments

Hilda R. Caton

Hilda R. Caton is Associate Professor in the Vision Impairment Program at the University of Louisville and Director of the Primary Braille Reading Projects at the American Printing House for the Blind. Dr. Caton has also worked as a resource and itinerant teacher of the visually impaired in elementary and secondary day school programs. Current areas of interest are research and curriculum development in braille reading and development of teacher training modules for teachers of deaf/blind children.

Most of us who can see take our vision for granted. We watch television, read books and newspapers, use the library, walk from place to place without difficulty, and engage in a host of other activities that depend on our ability to see.

But think what your life would be like if you lost your ability to read. The information in newspapers, magazines, textbooks, even letters from your friends would be lost to you. For you the worlds described in poetry and fiction might not exist. A device such as the Kurzweil Reader described on the facing page could have an enormous effect on you. Whole realms of thought previously only partially available in the form of braille or audio tapes would be opened up. The extent of the handicap that results from blindness could be greatly reduced.

That is the goal of special education for the visually impaired — the reduction of vision-related handicaps to the greatest extent possible. In this chapter we will describe visually impaired children and the different degrees of visual impairment. We will explain the visual system and some of its common disorders and discuss the developmental characteristics of visually impaired children, as well as some of their educational alternatives. Finally, we will illustrate methods of educational assessment and describe some of the instructional methods and equipment used to reduce the effects of visual impairment.

THE VISUAL SYSTEM

> **You should be able to identify the parts of the visual system and describe how we see.**

The most obvious characteristic of the visually impaired child is that his vision is in some way abnormal. Normal, or unimpaired, vision has four basic components: (1) the object to be viewed; (2) light that reflects from the object; (3) an intact visual organ (the eye); and (4) the occipital lobes of the brain, where visual stimuli are interpreted and "seeing" takes place (Chalkley, 1974).

PARTS OF THE VISUAL SYSTEM

The visual system consists of the eye and the parts of the brain responsible for seeing. The eye itself is a complex organ consisting of a number of structures. Although each structure has its own specific and unique function, the functions of all the structures are closely related. The eye is illustrated in Figure 5-1. The discussion of the parts of the eye is based on the work of Allen (1963), Chalkley (1974), and Vaughn and Asbury (1974).

The bony socket, sclera, eyelids, eyebrows, and conjunctiva all serve as protection for the eye. The bony socket provides a strong outer protection from severe blows, sharp objects, or other wounds. The sclera is the tough outer layer of the eyeball, which holds and protects its contents. The eyelids, eyelashes, and eyebrows trap dust and other particles and keep them from entering the eye, where infection and damage can occur. Further protection from dust and particles is provided by the conjunctiva, a thin, transparent layer that lines the eyelids and covers the front of the eye. The tears protect by washing out particles that have entered the eye. They also contain an enzyme that helps prevent infection.

The cornea, aqueous, iris, lens, ciliary body, and vitreous are responsible for making sure that light rays reach the exact point on the retina of the eye that will result in distinct vision. The cornea, aqueous, lens, and vitreous refract (bend) the light rays that enter the eye and direct them to that point. Part of the function of the iris, the colored part of the eye, is to screen out a portion of the entering light rays. The iris is controlled by muscles that contract to allow less light through the pupil or expand to allow more light.

The ciliary body has two parts and two functions. One part, the ciliary processes, produces the aqueous fluid. The other part, the ciliary muscle, changes the shape of the lens so that light is focused correctly on the retina.

The retina is the "nerve-layer" of the eye. It consists of a thin layer of tissue

FIGURE 5-1
Cross-section of the Human Eye

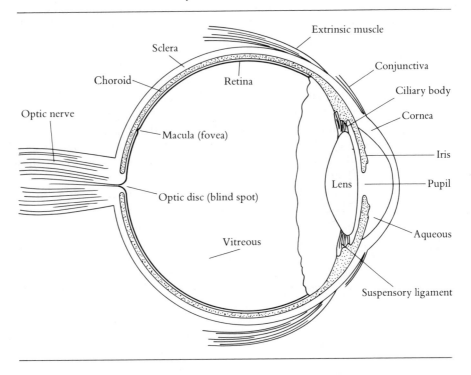

and nerves that lines the inside of the eyeball. It is actually an extension of the optic nerve, which enters the back of the eye, coming directly from the brain. For a person to have a clear, distinct vision, the light rays, having been refracted by the structures just described, must strike a small spot on the retina called the macular area. When this occurs, nerve impulses are sent out of the eye through the optic nerve along another nerve system to the occipital area of the brain. There the visual stimuli are interpreted and "seeing" takes place.

The retina receives its nourishment from the blood vessels in the choroid, the layer of the eye between the sclera and the retina.

The movement of the eye is controlled by its extrinsic, or external, muscles. These muscles turn the eyes to enable them to focus simultaneously on specific objects. There are six external muscles, located on each side of the eyeball and above and below it. These muscles move the eye to the left, to the right, upward, and downward. The failure of the muscles to function properly can result in crossed eyes (strabismus) and double vision.

HOW WE SEE

Seeing is a complex process, with the efficient functioning of one part of the visual system often dependent on the efficient functioning of the other parts. The process is illustrated in Figure 5-2.

Basically, the process of seeing involves the following sequence of events:

1. Light rays are reflected from an object and enter the eye.
2. The light rays pass through the cornea, which refracts, or bends, them.
3. The light rays, properly refracted, pass through the anterior, or aqueous, chamber, where they are again slightly refracted.
4. From the anterior chamber, the light rays pass through the pupil. The size of the pupil can be changed by the movement of the iris to allow more or less light as needed.
5. The light rays pass through the lens, the major refracting structure of the eye. The shape of the lens can be changed by the suspensary ligament to focus the light rays on exactly the right place in the eye. This process is called accommodation.
6. The light passes through the vitreous chamber. Its content, the vitreous humor, also has a slightly refractive effect.
7. The light rays are focused on the fovea, a small spot on the macula that produces the clearest, most distinct vision.
8. Light energy is changed to electrical impulses, which are carried by the optic nerve to the occipital lobe of the brain, where "seeing" takes place.

FIGURE 5-2
The Process of "Seeing"

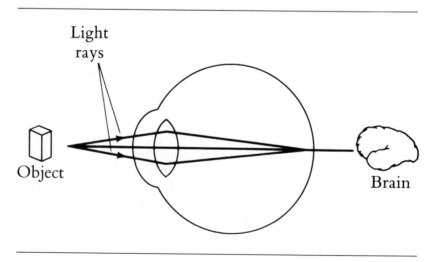

PROBE 5-1
The Visual System

1. The two parts of the visual system are the _____ and the _____.

2. Indicate whether each of the following is (a) a protective part of the eye; (b) a refractive part; or (c) a receptive part, by placing the appropriate letter in the blank preceding each item.

   ____ bony socket   ____ optic nerve

   ____ retina   ____ tears

   ____ cornea   ____ lens

   ____ eyelid   ____ vitreous

   ____ aqueous   ____ conjunctiva

   ____ eyebrow

3. Describe, in your own words, the process of "seeing."

   _____

   _____

   _____

   _____

   _____

DISORDERS OF THE VISUAL SYSTEM

You should be familiar with some common disorders of the visual system.

REFRACTIVE DISORDERS

Disorders of the refractive structures of the eye are among the most common encountered in children today. The so-called refractive errors are hyperopia (farsightedness), myopia (nearsightedness), and astigmatism. The state of the eyeball in each of these conditions is illustrated in Figure 5-3.

FIGURE 5-3
Refractive Errors of the Eye

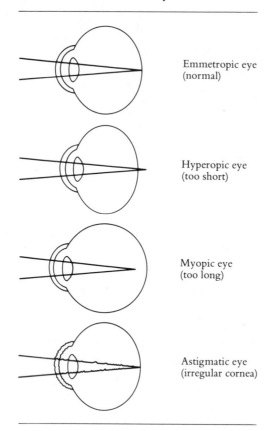

Emmetropic eye
(normal)

Hyperopic eye
(too short)

Myopic eye
(too long)

Astigmatic eye
(irregular cornea)

Hyperopia, or farsightedness, occurs when the eye is too short and the rays of light from *near* objects are not focused on the retina. Myopia, or nearsightedness, occurs when the eye is too long and the rays of light from *distant* objects are not focused on the retina. The hyperopic eye can see objects more clearly at a distance, whereas the myopic eye can see them more clearly at close range. Astigmatism is "blurred" vision caused by uneven curvature of the cornea or lens. This curvature prevents light rays from focusing correctly on the retina. Except in extreme cases, all of these disorders can be corrected with spectacles or contact lenses, so children with refractive errors are not often placed in special programs. These problems are found very frequently in regular classrooms, however, and can cause serious problems unless they are detected and corrected.

Cataracts, a common disorder of a refractive structure, often does result in the need for special education placement. Cataracts are not, as many believe, growths on the eye. They result, rather, when the semifluid substance in the lens gradually becomes opaque and the vision is obscured. Cataracts can result in severe visual loss. They are an especially serious problem in young children, since the opacity prevents light rays from focusing on the retina. This can result in the retina's failure to develop. Surgical procedures for the treatment of cataracts are quite advanced, however, and visual losses can usually be prevented.

RETINAL AND OPTIC NERVE DISORDERS

Common problems of the receptive parts of the eye include degeneration of the retina and the optic nerve, and detachment of the retina.

Although some forms of optic nerve degeneration result from infections, and some forms of retinal degeneration are linked to recessive gene traits, the cause of most cases is unknown. The severity of the visual loss varies widely, since the pace of the structure's degeneration is different for each person affected. Total blindness occurs in many cases, but not in all. These degenerative conditions are extremely difficult to cope with, both medically and educationally, since little is known about their causes or rate of progress and there is no known treatment for them. Children with these eye conditions are almost always placed in special educational programs.

Retinal detachment is a separation of the retina from the adjacent layers of the eye, the choroid and the sclera. This disorder is sometimes associated with extreme cases of myopia, or nearsightedness, where the eyeball becomes excessively long and pulls the retina away from surrounding tissues. Retinal detachments can also result from retinal degeneration, glaucoma, and other disorders. Although it is now possible to reattach the retina through various surgical techniques, this must be done immediately or total blindness will occur (Chalkley, 1974). Children with retinal detachment are almost always placed in special education programs, because of their visual loss and because they must be protected from sharp blows on the head, falls, and other actions that could cause further detachment.

MUSCLE DISORDERS

Disorders of the extrinsic muscles are very common in young children. They are usually the result of the muscles being imbalanced. As noted earlier, such an imbalance creates a condition known as strabismus, or "crossed eyes." When this occurs, the eyes cannot focus simultaneously on the same object. As a result, the child sees a double image of the object. Normally, the brain reacts by suppressing the image in one eye, and when that eye is not used its vision is lost. Amblyopia is a condition of this kind. Fortunately, it can be prevented if detected early and properly treated. The treatment sometimes consists of placing a patch over the unaffected eye to bring the affected eye into focus. A simple surgical procedure to straighten the muscles involved can also be used. Because muscle disorders are easily corrected and rarely impair vision severely, children who suffer from them do not often need special education.

GLAUCOMA

Glaucoma is a common disorder that is not related to one specific structure of the eye. It is caused by the failure of the aqueous fluid to circulate properly, which results in an elevation of pressure in the eye. This pressure very gradually destroys the optic nerve. The result can be total blindness. Glaucoma can be treated, however, and if the treatment occurs early, visual loss can be prevented. Because their eyes are not fully developed, however, young children are especially susceptible to harm from glaucoma, and many have severe visual losses. Those who do usually need special education.

RETROLENTAL FIBROPLASIA

One of the most devastating eye disorders affecting young children is retrolental fibroplasia. Found almost exclusively in premature babies, this disorder first appeared in the 1940s. It became progressively more prevalent for ten years, with its highest incidence occurring in 1952–53. The cause was finally discovered to be the use of too much oxygen in the incubators of premature babies.

Once the cause was identified and the use of oxygen controlled, the number of children affected dramatically decreased. Large numbers of children were affected before this occurred, however, and at one time the majority of visually impaired children in special education programs were victims of retrolental fibroplasia.

When these children were first placed in educational programs, it was thought that only their vision was affected. Evaluations conducted when the children were ten to fifteen years old, however, indicated that many of them also had neurological and behavioral disorders, as well as some speech problems (Bender and Andermann, 1965). A related problem that has surfaced in recent years is that reduced levels of oxygen in incubators have caused cerebral palsy in some premature babies (Silverman, 1970). Problems resulting from the reduced oxygen levels have ultimately had an effect on the number of multihandicapped, visually impaired children to be served in educational programs and has required the development of new techniques and materials for these programs.

MATERNAL RUBELLA

Another disorder related to the visual system is that caused by maternal rubella. Women who have rubella (German measles) during the first trimester of pregnancy often have babies with severe multiple handicaps. Among these handicaps, visual impairment is very common. Montgomery (1969) has estimated that about 40 percent of the infants affected had visual handicaps in addition to other disabilities.

The last major rubella epidemic in the United States occurred in 1964. It resulted in the establishment of many educational programs and services to multihandicapped and deaf-blind children. Although much progress has been made in providing services to these children, a great deal remains to be learned about how they function and what services are most appropriate to them.

PROBE 5-2
Disorders of the Visual System

1. If detected early, amblyopia can be corrected by either _____ or_____.

2. T   F   Cataracts are growths on the eye.

3. Nearsightedness is to _____ as farsightedness is to hyperopia.

4. Two diseases that resulted in large numbers of multihandicapped blind children are _____ and _____.

5. _____ is the eye disorder caused by excessive oxygen in incubators of premature babies.

DEFINITIONS

You should know the definitions of visual impairment and the purposes for which they are used.

Definitions and descriptions of visually impaired children tend to vary considerably, depending on the purposes for which individuals or groups are being described. Generally, visually impaired children are defined as those who differ from normally seeing children to such a degree that they need specially trained teachers, specially designed or adapted curricular materials, and specially designed educational aids to achieve their full potential (Ashcroft, 1963).

Within this broad definition, visually impaired children are differentiated into two categories, the blind and the partially seeing or low-visioned (Ashcroft, 1963). Two definitions are accepted for both blind and partially seeing children, one based on visual acuity, and one on the educational media to be used.

DEFINITIONS BASED ON VISUAL ACUITY

Definitions based on visual acuity are used for legal and economic purposes and for the allocation of federal funds to purchase educational materials. They are called the "legal" definitions of visual impairment.

Legally blind children are defined as (1) those whose visual acuity is 20/200 or less in the better eye with the best possible correction, or (2) those whose field of vision is restricted to an angle subtending an arc of 20 degrees or less (American Foundation for the Blind, 1961). Partially seeing children are defined as (1) those whose visual acuity is between 20/200 and 20/70 in the better eye with the best possible correction, or (2) those who in the opinion of an eye specialist need either temporary or permanent special educational facilities.

Although these definitions are useful for the purposes we have mentioned, they do not provide enough information to deliver effective educational services to visually impaired children. It is important to understand what the definitions can and cannot tell educators about these children.

The first factor to be considered in both definitions is the concept of visual acuity itself. Visual acuity is simply a means of describing the sharpness or clearness of vision. It does not describe the efficiency with which particular individuals use their vision, nor does it take into account the variety of ways in which vision is used in an educational setting.

The visual acuities used in the legal definitions are measures of distance vision. These are almost always obtained through the use of the Snellen Chart, illustrated in Figure 5-4. This chart is designed so that the top letter, when seen from a distance of 200 feet, seems to be the same size as the standard letter when seen from a distance of 20 feet. The test distance of 20 feet was used because rays of light reflected from objects at that distance are parallel. When light rays entering the eye are parallel, the muscles of the normal eye are at rest, and the visual acuity obtained does not reflect the accommodative power of the eye (the ability of the eye muscles to change the shape of the lens to focus a clear image on the retina). As a result, the visual acuity obtained at 20 feet gives a truer picture of the sharpness and clearness of vision than it would at other distances.

FIGURE 5-4
Snellen Symbol Chart

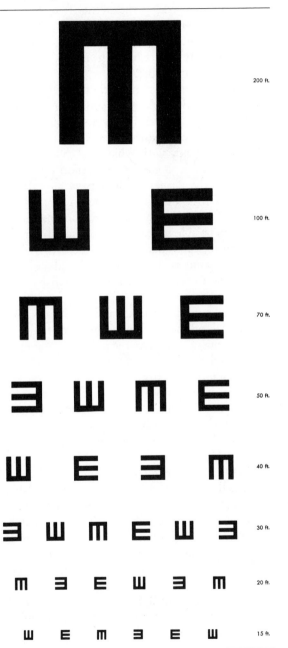

	200 ft.
	100 ft.
	70 ft.
	50 ft.
	40 ft.
	30 ft.
	20 ft.
	15 ft.

Visual acuity is expressed as an index, such as 20/20, 20/70, or 20/200. This index does not represent the fraction of remaining vision, as some people think. The top number in the index represents the twenty feet the person being tested stands from the chart. The bottom number is the distance at which a person with normal vision can distinguish the letters in the line being viewed. For example, if a person being tested can read at 20 feet what the person with normal vision can read at 200 feet, her visual acuity is 20/200.

Visual acuity actually tells educators very little about the child's ability to read or examine educational materials at close range. Barraga (1964) has illustrated that some children with visual acuities as low as 6/300 can learn to use their remaining vision quite efficiently. In educational planning then, the causes of the visual loss as well as the efficiency with which the child uses remaining vision must be considered. For example, a child with corneal opacities (small opaque areas scattered throughout the cornea) would have an extremely low visual acuity (around 8/400) as measured by the Snellen Chart, because the child would be unable to see through the opacities when looking directly at the chart. The child might, however, be able to read relatively small print held close to the eyes if he turned his head to see around the opacities. Many illustrations of this kind could be given. The point is that visual acuity alone is not an adequate measure of a child's ability to function in an educational setting. The limited value to teachers of definitions based on visual acuity should be clear.

The second factor to be considered in these definitions is the visual field, or peripheral vision. Peripheral, or "side," vision is measured in degrees of visual arc. The procedure for measurement is to place the individual about 39 inches from a square black chart and ask her to fix her eye on a central point on the chart. A round, white object is then moved in from the periphery of the chart in a circular pattern until the individual being tested can see it. The distance at which the stimulus can be seen is then measured. When the widest angle at which the stimulus can be seen is 20 degrees or less in the best eye with the best possible correction, the person is considered to be legally blind. Many educators would also consider the person educationally blind.

The field of vision is often reported on charts similar to those in Figure 5-5. A separate chart is provided for each eye. If you examine the fields of vision represented on the charts, you will note that an individual with a field of vision of less than 20 degrees can see little more than what is directly in front of the eye. People with this restricted field of vision are said to have "tunnel" vision.

Tunnel vision causes problems in mobility as well as in reading. The lack of peripheral vision makes it difficult for a person to see objects not directly in front of him. This severely limits the person's knowledge of the area he is traveling through. Reading problems are caused by the inability to see more than one letter at a time or letters too large for the visual field. Even when the visual acuity in the very small visual field is good, the restriction in the field severely impairs the vision.

FIGURE 5-5
Field of Vision Charts

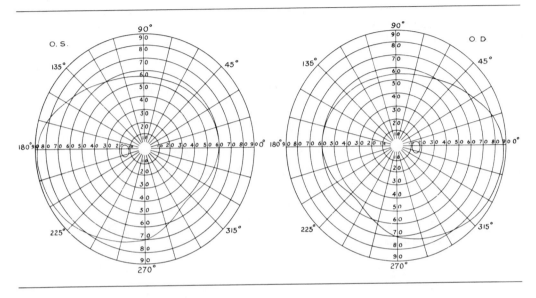

DEFINITIONS FOR EDUCATIONAL SERVICES

Although definitions based on visual acuity and field of vision are helpful, definitions that describe children in terms of the type of education they receive are most appropriate for educational planning. This kind of definition, first proposed in 1957 (American Foundation for the Blind, 1957), is now widely accepted by educators of visually impaired children. Educationally defined, the blind child is one whose visual loss indicates that she should be educated chiefly through the use of braille and other tactile and auditory materials. The partially seeing child is defined as one who has some remaining useful vision and can use print and other visual materials as part of the educational program.

PROBLEMS WITH DEFINITIONS

Obviously, neither a definition based on visual acuity nor an educational definition should be used as the sole criterion for deciding how and in what programs a child should be educated. Such factors as the cause of the visual loss (etiology), age of onset of visual impairment, experiential background, intellectual ability, and chronological age must also be considered (Harley, 1973).

The most important considerations are the etiology and age of onset. The etiology is crucial because some eye conditions require the use of a particular teaching method or set of materials. For example, a child affected by atrophy of the optic nerve requires a great deal of light and materials with good contrast. He might eventually need to learn braille. Children with visual losses from other causes might require different methods and materials.

The experience a child had before she lost her vision and the age at which she lost it are also important. An early visual loss obviously limits what was learned through seeing to a much greater extent than a later visual loss. The knowledge of how much a child knew when her vision became impaired can help a teacher decide what the child needs to learn and how it should be taught to her.

Intellectual ability and chronological age, though also important in determining how a child should be educated, are not as significant as the factors already discussed. They will be discussed in the section on the developmental characteristics of visually impaired children.

PROBE 5-3
Definitions

1. Define visually impaired children. _____
   _____
   _____
   _____

2. Visually impaired children are classified as either _____
   or _____.

3. With correction, a legally blind child has visual acuity of 20/200. A partially seeing child has visual acuity between _____ and _____.

4. T   F   Visual acuity is a term for sharpness and clearness of vision.

5. Explain the meaning of an index of visual acuity that is stated as 20/150.
   _____

6. Field of vision is measured in terms of _____.

7. From the perspective of educational definitions, how would you differentiate between a blind and partially seeing child?
   _____
   _____
   _____

IDENTIFICATION AND PREVALENCE

You should be able to describe the procedures used in identifying visually impaired children.

To plan for the education of visually impaired children, the children must first be identified. As was pointed out in the preceding section, a knowledge of visual acuity alone is of limited value. The children who actually need services can only be discovered by careful, systematic identification procedures such as those carried out by school systems. The planner must also know the numbers and types of visual problems to determine how many and what kinds of programs are needed.

IDENTIFICATION

Systematic identification procedures include coordinated preschool and school vision screening programs, as well as national, state, and regional child-find programs. These programs are team efforts by teachers, doctors, and other people. According to Ashcroft (1963), a good identification program includes (1) comprehensive screenings, (2) referral for complete eye examinations of those who appear to have problems, and (3) follow-ups to ensure that the recommendations resulting from the examination are carried out. The eye specialist, and not the people doing the screening, make the final diagnosis.

Ideally, every child should have a complete eye examination every year. Unfortunately, most children don't. As a result, preschool and school vision screening programs tend to be the most effective means of identification.

The agency most active in preschool and school vision screening programs is the National Society for the Prevention of Blindness. All across the United States its branches train volunteers, who then conduct the actual screening sessions. Their basic screening program consists of an annual test for distance visual acuity using the Snellen Chart and careful instructions to teachers describing symptoms that may indicate eye disorders (National Society for the Prevention of Blindness, 1969). The test for visual acuity is used because it has proven to be an effective indicator of children with eye problems, when they are later examined by ophthalmologists. The society recommends that children be referred for an eye examination if they are unable to read the following lines on the Snellen Chart:

Three year olds	20/50 or less
Four year olds through third grade	20/40 or less
Fourth grade and above	20/30 or less

Very strict standards have been set up for the actual testing session. They must be followed exactly in order to obtain valid results. These standards are described in the society's *Vision Screening in Schools* (1969), which is available through the organization's national, state, and regional offices. Standards and procedures for correct screening are also illustrated in a film, *Before We Are Six,* which is available through the national office.

Observations by teachers, parents, and others closely associated with the children are also important in the identification of eye problems. Some symptoms which might suggest an eye problem are

1. Clumsiness and trouble walking in a new environment.
2. Having to hold one's head in an awkward position, or having to hold material very close to one's eyes, in order to see.
3. "Tuning out" when information is written on the blackboard or somewhere else a child might have trouble seeing.
4. Constant requests for someone to tell the child what is going on.
5. Being inordinately affected by glare, or not being able to see things at certain times of the day.
6. A pronounced squint.
7. Excessive rubbing of the eyes.
8. Pushing the eyeballs with fingers or knuckles.
9. Obvious physical anomalies such as red, swollen lids, crusts on the eyes, crossed eyes, etc. (National Society for the Prevention of Blindness, 1969)

Children who exhibit any of these symptoms should be referred to an eye specialist for a thorough eye examination.

Visually impaired children are identified through other means than vision screening programs, of course. Doctors discover the problems of many children. In addition, many cities and school systems and most states now have agencies whose major responsibility is the identification and appropriate referral of the visually impaired.

Once a child has been identified as possibly having an eye problem, he is referred to the appropriate eye specialist. Generally this is an ophthalmologist or an optometrist. The ophthalmologist is a licensed physician who specializes in eye disorders. The optometrist is not a physician; her practice is limited to the prescription and fitting of corrective lenses and the treatment of optical defects without drugs or surgery. Other specialists are the optician, who grinds lenses or makes glasses, and the orthoptist, who provides eye exercises when they are prescribed by an ophthalmologist.

Because they are most familiar with all possible eye defects, it is generally best to refer a child who has vision problems to an ophthalmologist. All these eye specialists have important roles in eye care, however, and educators should acquaint themselves with the specific services that each of them provides (Ashcroft, 1963).

PREVALENCE

It is very difficult to get an accurate count of the number of visually impaired children. There are several reasons for this. Definitions of visual impairment vary from state to state, as do the methods of collecting and reporting prevalence data. The accuracy of the data collected varies as a consequence. In addition, a national census of visually impaired children has never been taken. As a result of these factors, prevalence figures are usually estimates based on a variety of sources.

The most often quoted prevalence figures state that approximately one in every 1000 school-age children, or about 0.1 percent, is either blind or partially sighted. This figure, arrived at independently by Jones and Collins (1966) and Meyen (1978) is considered fairly accurate. According to population estimates, then, there are about 55,000 visually impaired children in the United States today. This figure matches that projected by the United States Department of Education in 1971–72, a fact that further argues for the figure's accuracy.

Another source of information regarding numbers of visually impaired children is the annual registration of legally blind children by the American Printing House for the Blind. Although this registration does not tell us what percentage of all children are visually impaired, it does give an accurate count of the legally blind children enrolled in school programs throughout the country. In 1977 a total of 30,587 legally blind children were registered. Of these, approximately 21 percent had to use braille as their reading medium, and approximately 43 percent had sufficient vision to read large type. These percentages do not include children with visual acuities better than 20/70 and do not therefore reflect the overall prevalence of visually impaired children.

Even though the accuracy of these estimates is subject to disagreement, it is clear that visually impaired children make up one of the smallest groups of exceptional children. It should also be noted that more visually impaired children are partially seeing (read print) than blind (read braille). The most accurate prevalence figure, which states that 0.1 percent of the school-age population is visually impaired, is the one that should probably be used in planning educational services.

From this discussion it is obvious that a great variety of disorders can affect the vision of children. Unfortunately, there are no recent figures on the relative prevalence of specific eye disorders. The latest figures that are available are furnished by the United States Department of Health, Education, and Welfare (1976). These figures show that among visually impaired persons who are not legally blind the leading causes of impairment are cataract, refractive errors, and glaucoma. Among the legally blind and totally blind the leading causes of impairment are retinal disorders, glaucoma, and cataract. Most of the visually impaired children in special educational programs have one of these disorders.

PROBE 5-4
Identification and Prevalence

1. *Matching*

   profession   *function*

   _____ ophthalmologist   a. provides eye exercises

   _____ optician   b. physician specializing in the eye

   _____ optometrist   c. grinds lenses and makes glasses

   _____ orthoptist   d. prescribes glasses

2. The name of the most common instrument for screening visual impairments in children is the _____.

3. List five symptoms that may indicate eye problems:

   a. _____

   b. _____

   c. _____

   d. _____

   e. _____

4. The most widely accepted prevalence estimate for visually impaired is ____%.

5. T   F   Visually impaired children are one of the smallest groups of exceptional children.

DEVELOPMENTAL CHARACTERISTICS

You should be familiar with the physical, learning, and social-emotional characteristics of visually impaired children.

To plan effectively, persons concerned with the education of visually impaired children should be familiar with their physical, learning (mental, cognitive, etc.), and social-emotional characteristics.

There is little agreement on the effect of blindness on the physical, mental, and emotional development of children. On one end of the spectrum of opinion are Cutsforth (1951), who states that "no single mental activity of the congenitally blind child is not distorted by the absence of sight" (p. 3), and Carroll (1961), who states that when vision is lost "the sighted man dies" (p. 11). On the other end are Ashcroft (1963) and Scholl (1973), who state that the visually impaired child is like other children in many more ways than she is different from them.

The latter statement is probably the most accurate. It is worth remembering in educational planning, because it points out that "other" children are not alike; they are individuals, each with their own individual characteristics and developmental patterns. The statement that visually impaired children are more like other children than different from them simply means that they are not a homogeneous group who fit easily into a carefully delineated "category." They are just as varied a group as sighted children, and their educational needs vary just as greatly. It is extremely important to keep this in mind during the discussion that follows, since the emphasis on aspects of development unique to these children may appear to set them apart from other children.

PHYSICAL CHARACTERISTICS

In general, the physical development of visually impaired children resembles that of children who see normally. They do not tend to be taller, shorter, fatter, thinner, etc., than other children simply because they are visually impaired. However, visual impairment often does have indirect effects on their physical development (Scholl, 1973). This is true largely because the physical activity of many visually impaired children is severely limited.

Some visually impaired children are overly protected or neglected by parents and do not have the opportunity to move about and develop physical skills. When these children enter school, the overprotection and neglect may continue, because teachers and peers sometimes fail to understand that these children can do many of the same physical activities that normally seeing children do. As a result, the physical skills of these children may not develop at a normal rate. An additional problem results from these children's not being able to observe the physical activities of others. They cannot develop certain physical skills through imitation, as seeing children do.

To overcome these problems, the visually impaired must be allowed the freedom to move about in their environment and to participate in the physical activities normal for all children. They can be taught directly many of the physical skills normally learned through visual observation. When they are given this training and a rich, stimulating environment, their physical development will follow the same pattern as that of their seeing peers.

LEARNING CHARACTERISTICS

Because there is no generally accepted definition of learning, it is difficult to discuss the many factors that influence it. Most experts acknowledge, however, that a child's ability to learn is significantly affected by two factors: intelligence and the ability to develop concepts. Accordingly, our discussion will focus on these two qualities and how and why they affect the child's school achievement.

Intelligence. The results of research on the intelligence of the visually impaired must be viewed with caution, for several reasons. First, the children studied have been enrolled either in segregated residential school programs or in special education programs in public schools. Second, most of the intelligence tests used were originally developed for use by children with normal vision. Third, a child's score on an intelligence test reflects not only her intellectual potential, but also the opportunities the child has had to develop that potential. Each of these factors could have an effect on a child's intelligence test score.

Nevertheless, a number of studies of the intelligence of the visually impaired have been undertaken. Although the evidence is inconclusive, many studies indicate no significant differences between the intelligence of the blind and that of those who see normally. The small differences that are sometimes found are probably attributable to the three factors we have mentioned. Students interested in specific studies are directed to Dauterman, Shapiro, and Swinn, 1967; Davis, 1970; Goldman, 1970; Hammill, Crandell, and Colarusso, 1970; Hayes, 1941; Parker, 1969; Scholl and Schnur, 1976; Tillman and Osborne, 1969; and Warren, 1977.

Studies of the intelligence of those with partial vision have yielded similar results. Livingston (1958), for example, found the average IQ of partially seeing children to be 98.6, and Pintner, Eisenson, and Stanton (1941) also found intelligence levels in the normal range. Other studies by Bateman (1963) and Birch, Tisdall, Peabody, and Sterrett (1966) came to the same conclusions.

It seems likely, then, that the intellectual development of children is not directly affected by visual loss. Intelligence quotients alone, however, are an inadequate measure of a child's ability to learn.

Concept Development. Like intelligence, concept development is affected by the restrictions that result from visual loss, rather than by visual loss itself. A visually impaired child has a smaller range and variety of experiences, has trouble moving about freely, and has a more difficult time interacting with the environment (Lowenfeld, 1973). Many visually impaired children have never visited a farm, a grocery store, a park, and many other places familiar to most of us, and thus have little understanding of what their world is like. They may as a result have a poor understanding of spatial relationships, faulty impressions of distance, and little concept of form, size, position, and so on (Nolan, 1978). The visually impaired are further handicapped by their inability to learn through imitation of what they see. They must learn through direct experiences which, as mentioned, they often don't have.

Visually impaired children do, however, progress through the same sequence of developmental stages as other children, albeit at a much slower pace. This is indicated by a number of studies that compared the performance of visually impaired children on Piagetian tasks with that of seeing children (Friedman and Pasnak, 1973; Gottesman, 1971, 1973, 1976; Higgins, 1973; Miller, 1969; Simpkins and Stephens, 1974; and Tobin, 1972). Piaget's theory of stages of development is based on the belief that a child progresses through active interaction with his environment. This argues further that it is the restricted environmental involvement of the child that causes his delayed conceptual development, and not his visual impairment itself. It should be noted that the age of onset of the loss of vision will significantly affect the child's concept development.

School Achievement. As you might expect, visually impaired children tend to lag behind children with normal vision in school. Children with partial vision are average in their grade placement and somewhat below grade level in academic achievement, according to studies by Bateman (1963) and Birch et al. (1966). The same pattern of achievement is found among blind students who read braille (Caton and Rankin, 1978; Lowenfeld, Abel, and Hatlen, 1969). The children studied in the Caton and Rankin research were from two to four years over age for grade placement and from one and a half to two years below grade level in reading achievement.

This does not mean that a vision impairment necessarily leads to underachievement in school. Ashcroft (1963) suggests that the academic lag may be the consequence of many factors, including the following:

1. Visually impaired children usually enter school at a later age than other children.
2. Many children with vision problems are educated in inappropriate programs.
3. Many children miss a great deal of school due to surgery or treatment for eye conditions.
4. Many do not have any opportunity to attend school.
5. All children with severe impairments must use braille or large-type editions of books, which retards their ability to gather information.

As you can see, then, school underachievement, too, is an indirect rather than a direct result of visual impairment.

Though we have considered only a few of the factors that can influence learning, we can draw two general conclusions: (1) visual impairment does not necessarily result in mental retardation; and (2) the delays that are found in the intellectual development of the visually impaired are the result of inadequate opportunities to explore the environment (Harley, 1973). It should be noted that these conclusions do not take into account visually impaired children who also have other handicaps.

SOCIAL-EMOTIONAL CHARACTERISTICS

The prevailing opinion is that most of the social and emotional problems of the visually impaired are caused by the attitudes and reactions of those who can see. Cutsforth (1951), in fact, stated that society's negative attitudes were entirely responsible for their social and emotional problems. A number of studies (Bauman, 1964; Cowen, Underberg, Verrillo, and Benham, 1961; Gowman, 1957; Spivey, 1967) reveal that visually impaired children either accept the opinions and expectations conveyed to them by society or suffer isolation as a result of rejecting them. In general, children with partial visual impairment tend to be more isolated by their seeing peers than those who are totally blind. This appears to be true because less severely handicapped children do not elicit the sympathy accorded totally blind children. Harley (1973) suggests that this is at least partially due to the practice of placing the visually impaired in special schools and classes.

Another factor that causes persons with normal vision to react negatively toward the visually impaired is the lack of contact between the two groups. This results in misunderstanding by both groups and the formation of unrealistic ideas about the effects of visual impairment on children. For example, a typical attitude of seeing persons toward the visually impaired is that all persons with visual losses are totally blind and that, as a result, they are basically helpless and dependent. This is, of course, not true. It is this kind of misconception which causes social and emotional problems in visually impaired children.

It is possible to improve attitudes, however, as Bateman (1964) found when she studied the attitudes of seeing children who were enrolled in classes with visually impaired children. She found that these children had much higher estimations of the abilities of visually impaired children than children who had not had direct associations with them. This implies that greater integration of the visually impaired into classes with seeing children, and more training about the capabilities of the visually impaired for regular classroom teachers would result in improved attitudes toward the visually impaired, and more appropriate educational planning and placement as well.

PROBE 5-5
Developmental Characteristics

1. T   F   Although blind children may have delayed physical development due to their inability to do some physical activities, they typically do not differ in physical ability from normally seeing children.

2. List three possible causes of apparent retardation in the intellectual development, school achievement, and concept development of blind children:

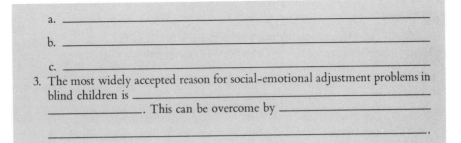

a. _____

b. _____

c. _____
3. The most widely accepted reason for social-emotional adjustment problems in blind children is _____ _____. This can be overcome by _____ _____.

INSTRUCTIONAL METHODS AND MATERIALS

You should be familiar with the methods and materials used to educate visually impaired children.

Once a child has been placed in the most suitable educational environment, the educator must consider the curriculum that will best meet her needs. The term "curriculum" means "the total experiences a learner has under the supervision of the school" (Smith, Krouse, and Atkinson, 1961, p. 969). The curriculum includes the subjects to be taught and the methods and materials used to teach them. The educator must consider the needs that the visually impaired share with other children, as well as the needs unique to the visually impaired.

Children with visual problems are usually taught the same sequence of subjects as children with normal vision, because they need to master the same basic skills. Unlike children with normal vision, however, they will need to be taught special skills in addition, such as how to orient themselves, how to attain mobility, and how to take care of themselves. Visually impaired children will also need to be taught certain skills to learn academic subjects — how to read braille, how to use an optacon, and how to use recording equipment, for example. Although the responsibility for implementing the total curriculum plan lies with the regular classroom teacher, the assistance of a specially trained teacher of the visually impaired will be necessary to teach children the special skills just mentioned.

Many educators believe that the methods of teaching the visually impaired should not differ from the methods of teaching those with normal vision. Others contend that the instruction of the visually impaired requires significantly different strategies. Both positions possess some validity (Napier, 1973). When adjustments or adaptations are made, they involve changing the media and the manner in which material is presented.

The media through which visually impaired children obtain information are tactile, visual, and auditory. The selection of the appropriate medium for a particular child was mentioned earlier in this chapter. You will remember that a measurement of visual acuity alone does not provide enough information to decide what medium is best for a child. Some children with extremely low visual acuity can use visual materials quite efficiently, whereas others will need tactile materials, and still others may be able to use both. Decisions about the best medium for a child should be made only after thorough assessment by specially trained professionals. This assessment can be accomplished with the use of the Visual Efficiency Scale (Barraga, 1970); the careful observations of teachers are also helpful. Once the primary medium for learning has been selected, teachers should keep in mind that some children can use both tactile and visual materials, and that all children can and should use auditory materials. In other words, a "total communication" approach for visually impaired children should be employed.

SPECIAL SKILLS

Children with visual impairments need to learn certain special skills not included in the curriculum of children with normal vision. Broadly defined, the two most important such areas are orientation and mobility, and daily living skills.

Orientation and Mobility. The ability of a child to move about in his environment and interact with it has important educational and social effects (Lowenfeld, 1971). Educationally, it allows him to develop realistic concepts about his environment and thus enables him to participate more fully in learning experiences with seeing children. Socially, it helps to dispel the notion that visually impaired persons are helpless and dependent, and fosters the notion they can become fully participating and contributing members of society. Thus, it is very important that schools provide orientation and mobility training for all children who need it (Graham, 1965).

Orientation training involves teaching the visually impaired child to understand her environment and to recognize her surroundings and her relationship to them. Mobility training involves teaching the child to move efficiently from place to place in the environment (Lyndon and McGraw, 1973). These types of training are generally taught by specially trained instructors, although some preliminary skills can be taught by the regular classroom teacher of the visually impaired. Orientation and mobility training should not be considered only for the child who is totally blind; many children with partial vision can also benefit from it. The training should begin as early as possible to avoid the formation of unrealistic concepts and attitudes.

A number of new and exciting devices to aid in mobility training have recently been developed. Galton (1978) describes the laser cane, developed by Bionic Instruments, Lynwood, California. This cane uses beams of light to probe the environment, sending auditory and tactile signals to warn of obstacles, stairs, curbs, etc. Wormald International Sensory Aids produces two electronic mobility devices for the visually impaired, the Mowat Sensor and the Sonic Guide (Figure 5-6). The Mowat Sensor is a hand-held electronic probe that uses vibration signals to indicate the distance to objects that fall within its narrow beam (Wormald International Sensory Aids, 1979). The Sonic Guide is an electronic aid in the form of spectacles, which emits sounds to convey spatial information (Wormald International Sensory Aids, 1979). Other electronic mobility aids continue to be developed. They hold great promise for the visually impaired.

Daily Living Skills. Daily living skills include such things as eating, bathing, toileting, dressing, grooming, and household chores. Most of these skills are acquired by seeing children through visual observation alone and are not directly taught in school programs. However, it is usually necessary to teach them directly

FIGURE 5-6
Electronic Mobility Devices. Left: Sonic Guide. Right: Mowat Sensor.

to visually impaired children. Ideally, most of these skills should be acquired at home before the child enters school, but this doesn't often occur; thus, the responsibility for teaching the skills is left with the school. In most cases, the special teacher of the visually impaired provides the training, although regular classroom teachers can also do so with assistance from special teachers. To provide training in a particular daily living task, the task is analyzed, and programmed lessons leading the child through the task in steps are developed, with the emphasis on the use of senses other than vision. Lowenfeld (1971) provides some guidelines for developing these skills for preschool children, and O'Brien (1976) includes a number of developmental scales in her study of preschool children. The latter are excellent references for planning lessons in daily living skills.

SKILLS NECESSARY TO LEARN ACADEMIC SUBJECTS

In addition to the skills just described, visually impaired children need to learn how to use the techniques that have been designed to compensate for their loss of vision. These techniques involve the use of tactile, visual, or auditory media. Children with visual problems acquire information through reading and listening. The two media used for reading are braille and print.

Braille. The primary tactile medium used by visually impaired persons is the braille code, developed by Louis Braille in 1829 when he was student at the Paris School for the Blind. The code is based on a braille "cell," which consists of six raised dots:

Sixty-three combinations of these six dots are possible. With these sixty-three combinations, three braille codes have been developed — one for presenting literary material, one for mathematics and science, and one for music. Since the braille cell occupies a great deal of space (each cell takes up a quarter inch), the original code has been altered to make it more compact. For example, many of the single braille units that represent alphabet letters (see Figure 5-7) also represent whole words. Many words are also represented by abbreviations, shortened forms of words, and nonalphabetic symbols. The total number of meanings assigned to the sixty-three configurations is 263. All of the duplicate meanings of a single configuration were assigned to conserve space (American Printing House for the Blind, 1972).

The changes in the braille code designed to save space have created problems

FIGURE 5-7
The Braille Alphabet

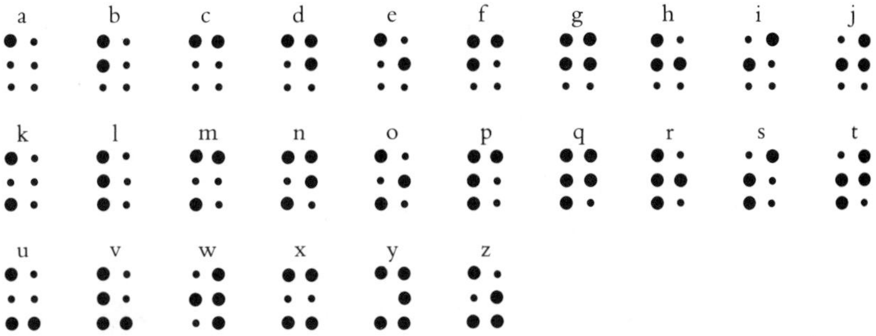

for children who must use the code to learn how to read. Most material used to teach reading to the visually impaired is transcribed directly from material designed to teach print reading. The problems unique to the braille code are not taken into consideration. For example, words sequenced in order of their difficulty for a child who can see may be sequenced inappropriately when transcribed into braille (Caton, 1979; Caton and Bradley, 1978-79).

Because of the problems just discussed, it is absolutely essential that those who teach reading to children who use braille be well trained. When the basic skills of reading and the braille code have been mastered, most braille readers can participate successfully in reading classes with children who read print.

The "paperless" brailler is another innovative approach to the problems of braille readers (see Figure 5-8). Although there are none on the market at present, several types are currently being developed. The information for a paperless brailler is stored on small cassettes and can be projected onto displays. The different types print between twelve and twenty braille lines; some also have audio components, and one type can index and place-find. Although these machines save the cost of books by storing large amounts of information on a small cassette, they are themselves expensive. There are other disadvantages, too: they are limited in what they can display, and they project short lines, which may affect the reading process. Nevertheless, their use in education has exciting possibilities.

Writing in braille is accomplished with a braille writer, illustrated in Figure 5-9, or a slate and stylus, illustrated in Figure 5-10.

The braille writer is a hand-operated machine with six keys, one to correspond to each dot in the braille cell. When a key is pressed, a dot is embossed on the paper that is inserted in the back of the machine. The other parts of the machine are labeled in Figure 5-9.

FIGURE 5-8
The Telesensory "Paperless" Brailler

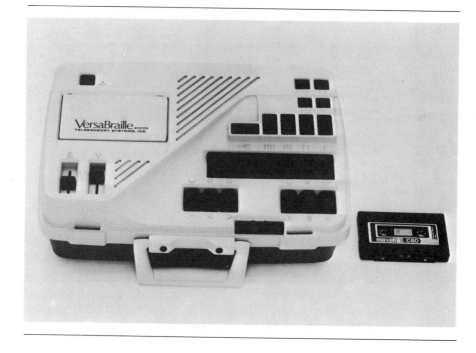

There are many different braille slates. The chief variation among the various types is in their size. All slates consist of a metal or plastic frame, which is sometimes mounted on a board. A pointed steel stylus is used to hand-punch braille dots. Each slate has two parts connected by a hinge on the left side. The bottom part has several rows of braille cells indented on its top. The top part has holes that correspond to the indentations. The paper is placed between the two parts, and the stylus is used to punch in the dots from the top.

The braille writer and the slate have been in use for many years. They are rather slow methods of communicating, but they are the only devices presently available.

Print Reading. Children with partial vision can read print if it is presented to them appropriately. Such conditions as proper lighting, reduction of glare, print size, spacing, and the use of low-vision aids must be considered to ensure that the child is reading as efficiently as possible.

The best print size for a particular child will probably fall between 12 and 24 points, although there is some evidence that normal-sized type is just as efficient

FIGURE 5-9
The Perkins Brailler

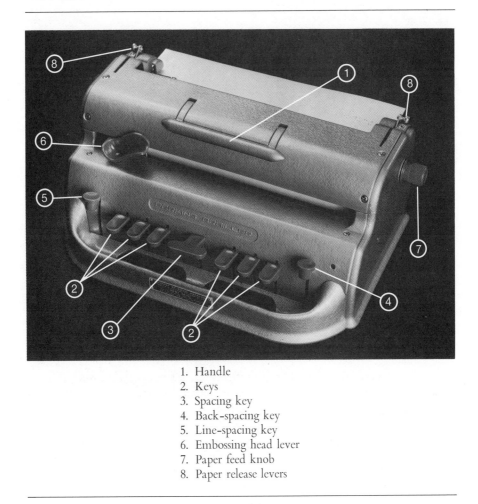

1. Handle
2. Keys
3. Spacing key
4. Back-spacing key
5. Line-spacing key
6. Embossing head lever
7. Paper feed knob
8. Paper release levers

if read with the proper optical aid (Peabody and Birch, 1967; Sykes, 1971). The most effective print size will vary with the particular child. Studies have indicated that 18 point type may be the most efficient size for most visually impaired children (Eakin, Pratt, and McFarland, 1961). Most of the large-type books published by the American Printing House for the Blind are printed in this size. Examples of 12, 18, and 24 point type are illustrated in Figure 5-11.

When an optical aid is called for, the user may choose from among several

FIGURE 5-10
Slate and Stylus

types. These are (1) magnifiers attached to eyeglass frames, or part of the eyeglass lenses themselves; (2) stand magnifiers, which are mounted on a base to maintain a particular viewing distance; (3) hand-held magnifiers; (4) telescopic aids, which are used like binoculars; and (5) television viewers, which magnify print and project it onto a television screen. The type of aid selected will depend on the user's preference and the task for which the device is to be used. The strength of magnification is best determined by a professional in a low-vision clinic, or by a suitably trained teacher (Harley and Lawrence, 1977).

The child's reading environment is just as important to her reading efficiency as print size and the use of optical aids. The chief environmental considerations are the brightness of the lighting and the contrast between the writing itself and its background (Harley and Lawrence, 1977).

The amount of illumination required for comfortable reading will vary considerably from child to child but, generally speaking, the best quality lighting is from fluorescent bulbs evenly distributed throughout the room. Children with optic atrophy will require intense illumination, whereas those with vision problems resulting from albinism will require less illumination. In all cases, care must be taken to avoid glare.

FIGURE 5-11
Samples of Three Type Sizes

---

12 Point

When darkness fell, the women began preparing a great heap of wood for the circle of ceremonial fires. Then Chanuka slipped into the river and swam silently

18 Point

When darkness fell, the women preparing a great heap of wood circle of ceremonial fires. Then Ch slipped into the river and swam s

24 Point

When darkness fell, th preparing a great heap circle of ceremonial fires slipped into the river an

---

Children with partial vision are able to read most efficiently when the print they are reading contrasts sharply with the material on which the letters are printed. Most children read dark print on buff-colored paper best, but some prefer dark print on white paper. Buff-colored paper is used because it reduces glare. Contrast is also important when chalkboards are being used. White chalk on a black chalkboard provides the best contrast, but white chalk on a green board is acceptable for some children. In general, contrast is best when the background is clear and uncluttered, and when the shade of the material to be viewed is sufficiently different to stand out clearly.

Most visually impaired children who read print do so at a much slower rate than children who see normally. Those who read large print typically progress at less than half the rate of children with good vision. Those who use optical aids also read relatively slowly. Several factors retard the rate of reading. Some eye disorders permit the reader to see only one or two letters at a time. The reading of large type is slower because it takes longer to pass the eye over larger letters and words. The use of an optical aid reduces the field of vision and requires that the aid be frequently moved or adjusted.

Many children who read large print need to hold material closer to their eyes or at different angles than children with normal vision. These practices do not harm vision and should not be discouraged if they help children see properly. Children with vision disorders should be seated close to the chalkboard and other areas where visual material is displayed.

Once the many factors that influence how the visually impaired read have been considered, the child can be taught to read using normal instructional methods. Visually impaired children can usually be taught in the regular classroom if the teacher is assisted by a special teacher in setting up an appropriate environment.

Reading Machines. There are two new technological alternatives to the reading methods and techniques just discussed. They are called direct print reading systems, and involve the use of machines — the optacon, illustrated in Figure 5-12, and the Kurzweil Reading Machine, described at the beginning of this chapter.

The optacon (optical-to-tactile converter) "reads" print and reproduces the form of the print letters with a series of small wires. The reader fits one hand into an opening in the machine and touches the panel where the letters are formed. With his other hand he scans a page of print with a small camera. The optacon is especially useful to visually impaired persons who must read print for their jobs. It has also been used extensively with schoolchildren, but its educational effect has not yet been evaluated thoroughly.

The Kurzweil Reading Machine, introduced in 1975, converts printed words into synthetic speech. It provides access to a great deal of printed matter that was previously unavailable to the visually impaired.

Listening. There are, of course, means of acquiring information that do not involve reading. Listening is one of the most effective. Accordingly, listening skills have been increasingly emphasized in recent years. A number of guides to developing listening skills have been produced. One of the most valuable is available through the Illinois Instructional Materials Center, where it was developed (Alber, 1978). Listening is not a solution to all academic problems, but it is effective in such areas as literature and social studies. It is crucial in the education of children who can read neither print nor braille.

FIGURE 5-12
Reading with an Optacon

SPECIAL EDUCATIONAL AIDS

A number of instructional materials have been designed to meet the needs of the visually impaired. These include diagrams, charts, and maps available with large print, or in tactile form; sets of materials to replace pictures or visual displays in textbooks; mathematics aids such as specially adapted abacuses and tactile graph boards; braille writers; special bold-line paper for writing both braille and print; and many others.

Most of these aids are available from the American Printing House for the Blind in Louisville, Kentucky. Federal funds for purchasing materials produced by the American Printing House for the Blind are available to children who meet the legal definition of blindness given at the beginning of this chapter. These children must be registered at the American Printing House for the Blind by the first Monday in January of each year. Specific information about registration and ordering procedures can be obtained from special education departments, state departments of education, state residential schools for the blind, or the American Printing House for the Blind.

Organizations other than the American Printing House for the Blind have developed materials to be used in teaching specific subjects to the visually impaired. The MAVIS program is used to teach social sciences, for example, and the SAVI program describes activities to be used in teaching science (Lawrence Hall of Science, 1978; Social Science Consortium, 1978). In both cases the materials are adaptations of curricula originally designed for children with normal vision.

The work of Dr. Natalie Barraga (1964) has had a strong effect on the materials and planning procedures used to educate the visually impaired. Dr. Barraga's work has demonstrated that visually impaired children can be trained to use their residual vision to a much greater extent than was formerly thought possible, even if the impairment is very severe. A set of materials based on Dr. Barraga's work is available through the American Printing House for the Blind. It includes the Visual Efficiency Scale used to assess visual functioning (mentioned earlier), and a set of lessons to provide training in the efficient use of vision. Dr. Barraga and the American Printing House for the Blind are currently working on a revision of these materials, which should substantially increase the effectiveness of training in the efficient use of residual visual vision.

The use of special methods and materials alone will not adequately compensate for a child's loss of vision. Regardless of the subject being taught, the child must, whenever possible, be given the opportunity to learn through direct experience with his environment. These experiences should be accompanied by thorough verbal explanations by the teacher. In addition, the visually impaired child should be encouraged to interact with seeing members of his environment. A child who is given these opportunities and who makes appropriate use of the methods and materials discussed previously can be regarded as having a completely developed curriculum.

PROBE 5-6
Instructional Methods and Materials

1. T   F   Visually handicapped children are usually taught the same sequence of subjects as children with normal vision.

2. T   F   Many instructional procedures that are effective for normal children are also effective for visually impaired children.

3. List some optical aids that can be used by partially seeing children to assist them in reading.

   _____

   _____

4. The most important areas included in the curriculum of the visually impaired but not in the curriculum of those with normal vision are _____ and _____.

5. T   F   Partially seeing children who hold their books close to their eyes when reading should be instructed not to hold the materials so close.

6. The media through which visually impaired children obtain information are _____, _____, and _____.

7. Technological advances have resulted in the development of a number of exciting new devices for the visually impaired. List three devices related to reading that blind people can use.

a. _____

b. _____

c. _____

EDUCATIONAL PROGRAMMING

You should be able to describe the implications of PL 94-142 for educating visually impaired children in the least restrictive environment.

To understand current practices in educating visually impaired children, it is necessary to understand their history and development.

The first formal educational program for visually impaired children was a residential school, primarily for totally blind children, established by Valentin Hauy in Paris in 1784. Hauy was extremely influential in the development of educational programs for the visually impaired in Europe. Residential schools for the blind were eventually begun in several European cities.

The first educational programs for the visually impaired in the United States were also residential schools. These schools were designed for totally blind children, but children with partial vision were eventually enrolled in them as well. The earliest schools, which both opened in 1832, were the Perkins School for the Blind, in Boston, and the New York Institute for the Blind, in New York City. In 1833 the Pennsylvania Institution for the Instruction of the Blind was opened in Philadelphia. This later became the Overbrook School for the Blind. Other residential schools were gradually established in other states. The founders of many of these schools saw the value of educating visually impaired children in classes with their seeing peers. Many of them advocated that residential schools be established only when absolutely necessary.

The first local day school classes for blind children were set up in Chicago in 1900, followed by a day school program for those with partial vision in Roxbury, Massachusetts, in 1913. As you can see, the practice of separating blind and partially seeing children in local day school classes was established early. It has continued in some areas until the present. The current trend, however, is to combine programs for blind and partially seeing children. Taylor (1973) states that in 1968 about 89 percent of the programs listed in the *Directory of School Programs for Visually Handicapped Children* had classes in which both blind and partially seeing children were enrolled. Today there is a variety of educational alternatives for the visually impaired, including the residential school and five types of administrative plans in local day schools.

RESIDENTIAL SCHOOLS

The residential school has traditionally provided a total educational program for visually impaired children. This program usually has a complete range of grades from kindergarten through twelfth, and teaches the same curriculum taught in other schools in the state or region. Most residential school students do not attend classes integrated with children with normal vision, although some residential schools have an agreement with the local school system that allows some visually impaired students to attend regular classes. Most children who attend residential schools live at home and attend classes during the day.

The role of the residential school has changed during the past decade. Some residential schools now function as educational resource centers for the visually impaired. They may provide activities that involve the visually impaired with sighted children outside the school, and services to local school programs that serve visually impaired children. These services can involve storing materials and resources and developing special summer programs to train children in orientation and mobility, daily living skills, and other special skills. Other residential schools serve as centers for visually impaired children with additional handicaps. These schools offer extensive support services, such as physical therapy, occupational therapy, and speech therapy for severely handicapped children, as well as regular education programs. Of the four residential schools established during the last four years, two have been of this type (Bledsoe, 1971). This reflects the current trend of placing children in local day schools whenever possible, and reserving space in residential programs for those who cannot function successfully in other environments. The effectiveness of such residential programs cannot be assessed until they have been in operation for a longer period of time.

LOCAL DAY SCHOOLS

Local day schools for the visually impaired are currently run according to one of five basic administrative plans. These are

1. *The special class plan.* Students are enrolled in a special class for the visually impaired and receive most of their instruction in that class. They may par-

ticipate in some nonacademic activities with sighted children, but they usually do not receive academic instruction outside the special class.

2. *The cooperative class plan.* Students are enrolled in a special class for the visually impaired in a public school. They do some of their academic work in this room, and some in the regular classroom. They also participate in nonacademic activities in the regular classroom.
3. *The resource room plan.* Students are enrolled in the regular classroom and come to a special classroom for the visually impaired for special help in difficult academic areas. They spend as much time as possible in the regular classroom and leave only when help is necessary.
4. *The itinerant teacher plan.* Students are enrolled in the regular classroom, and a specially trained teacher of the visually impaired, who most often serves several different schools, provides them with special instruction and materials.
5. *The teacher-consultant plan.* Students are enrolled in regular classrooms and receive basically the same services as those offered under the itinerant teacher plan. The major difference between the teacher-consultant plan and the itinerant teacher plan is that the teacher-consultant spends a greater part of her time working with the regular classroom teacher or other school personnel to assist them in providing appropriate services (Harley, 1973).

All of these plans require a specially trained teacher of the visually impaired, as well as special equipment and materials for both blind and partially seeing children. The major differences among them involve their administrative organization and the instructional duties of the teachers. In the special class plan, for example, the child is enrolled in a special classroom, and the teacher of the visually impaired is responsible for most of the academic instruction and grading. In the resource room, itinerant teacher, and teacher-consultant plans, on the other hand, the child is enrolled in the regular classroom, and the regular classroom teacher is responsible for most of the instruction and for grading. Under these plans the teacher of the visually impaired assists the regular teacher in obtaining materials and provides instruction in subjects in which the child is having difficulty.

The resource room, itinerant teacher, and teacher-consultant plans are preferred today because they permit greater integration of visually impaired children into regular classrooms. In actual practice, many school districts use combinations and adaptations of the plans to suit their needs. This is desirable, of course, since the goal of all educational programming is to provide each child with a program that will meet his individual needs. It is very important that program planning remain flexible. The selection of the least restrictive alternative should *not* be based on existing administrative plans. It must be based on the needs of the individual child.

SELECTING THE LEAST RESTRICTIVE ENVIRONMENT

PL 94-142 requires that the least restrictive environment for a particular child be selected by an admissions and release committee. This committee can be regional — the Administrative Admissions and Release Committee — or it can be local — the School Based Admissions and Release Committee. The committee must be furnished with a variety of evaluation data, including (1) an eye examination report, (2) a medical report, (3) a developmental and social history, (4) reports of behavioral observations by parents and teachers, and (5) any other information that might be helpful. The committee reviews the data and then decides what type of educational environment is best suited to the child's needs.

The decision to place a child in a particular program should be based on the child's level of independence and the kind of services the program makes available. Generally speaking, the more independent the child, the less structured her program needs to be. A high school student who can travel independently and succeed academically with only occasional help from the special teacher may do best in an itinerant teacher program or with the help of a teacher consultant. Young children who are acquiring basic skills will probably require daily contact with a teacher of the visually impaired and may be best educated under the resource room plan. Children who have severe impairments or handicaps in addition to blindness will probably function best under the special or cooperative class plans. For some students, residential school placement may be most appropriate.

Because children's needs change as they develop, it is important to remain flexible in determining what program best fulfills a child's needs. A program well suited to a six-year-old child may be inappropriate for the child at age eight. As Taylor (1947) states, "The facility should be selected which fulfills a particular need, at the time of the need, and for only as long as — in light of the total situation — it is fullfilling this need" (pp. 118-20). Children should be educated as much as possible in the classes they would be attending if they were not visually impaired, and they should spend as much time as possible in classes with children who have normal vision.

There are several other important factors to be considered in choosing the program best suited to an individual child's needs. The most important is that the child's parents should be made familiar with all the data on their child and should play an important role in selecting the child's program. Even though the final decision on a child's placement rests with the Admissions and Release Committee of the local school system, parental consent for such placement is required by law. Parents must also consent to the collection of evaluation data (Abeson, Bolick, and Haff, 1976).

It is also very important that placement recommendations be based on *all* the available information on a child. All too frequently a measurement of the child's visual acuity is used as the primary criterion for placement. Although visual acuity is important, it should be considered in conjunction with other information about the child's level of functioning.

Finally, the availability of appropriate programs should be considered. Unfortunately, there is sometimes a shortage of programs for the visually impaired, particularly in sparsely populated areas. Federal legislation states, however, that the fact that no program exists in a particular community does not relieve the school district of the responsibility to provide such a program. This means that the recommendations of an Admissions and Release Committee should be based solely on the needs of the child, and not on the availability of a particular program. In some communities, however, it may be impossible to provide the full range of programs that are available in major population centers.

PLANNING FOR DIRECT INSTRUCTION

In addition to selecting the best program for a child, the Admissions and Release Committee is responsible for developing an Individual Educational Program (IEP) for each child who is referred to them. The IEP is used as the basis for planning direct instruction. To plan effectively the teacher must be familiar with the characteristics of visually impaired children and know what types of assessment tools are available, and how to interpret their results.

Characteristics Relevant to Educational Planning. Persons involved in assessment should pay particular attention to the effect of visual loss on the formation of concepts. A visually impaired child whose ability to interact with his environment is restricted will not perform well on tests that assess concepts usually formed visually. The child's formation of visual concepts is also affected by the age at which his loss of vision occurred, whether the loss occurred gradually or suddenly, and, of course, the severity of the loss. The last-named will influence what reading medium the child uses, how efficiently he uses his remaining vision, and whether he uses optical aids (Scholl and Schnur, 1976).

Assessment Data Needed. Visually impaired children vary as much as other children. Thus, the data used to plan their education should be derived from a variety of formal and informal assessment techniques. DeMott (1974) suggests that information in the following areas be included in any educational assessment of the visually impaired:

1. Visual efficiency — the use the child makes of any remaining vision.
2. Sensory abilities — the ability to hear, perceive through touch, and use the senses of taste and smell to acquire information.

3. Other impairments — the identification of impairments in abilities other than vision which might affect the child's ability to learn.
4. Motor performance — the ability to move about to gain information.
5. Language — the ability to use speech and listening skills to learn.
6. Intelligence — the intellectual ability to learn.
7. Achievement — academic progress and ability.

Bauman (1974) suggests that the child's personality, social competency, vocational interests and eptitudes, and readiness to learn be assessed as well. Areas of assessment have also been discussed by Scholl and Schnur (1976).

Assessment Instruments. There are three basic types of assessment instruments available for visually impaired children:

1. Those developed specifically for the visually impaired.
2. Those developed for a seeing population, but adapted for use by the visually impaired.
3. Those developed for seeing population and used in their original form by the visually impaired.

Assessment instruments are described by a number of authors, including Bauman (1977); Chase (1977); Scholl and Schnur (1976); Spungin and Swallow (1977); and Swallow, Mangold, and Mangold (1978). The American Foundation for the Blind and the American Printing House for the Blind can also provide valuable assistance in selecting assessment instruments.

Interpretation of Assessment Data. Although the interpretation of assessment data is too complicated a topic to cover adequately in this chapter, the student should be familiar with two general guidelines.

1. Assessment data should only be interpreted by specially trained persons who are familiar with the characteristics of the visually impaired.
2. Information about norms (i.e., the population used to establish standards for a test) should be used with caution. If the norm data were based on a sample of visually impaired children, it is important to know whether the children were enrolled in public schools or in residential school programs. Most of the children in residential schools today have multiple handicaps, and norms based on such children may not be valid for children with visual impairment alone. Norm data based on a sample of children with normal vision will not be valid for the visually impaired unless they have been modified for an adapted form of the test.

To restate the most important considerations in providing the best education for a particular child: the least restrictive environment consists of the program the child is placed in and the direct instruction that occurs in that program. The best program for a child is the one the child would normally be placed in if she were not visually impaired. As much as possible, visually impaired children should be educated with children who have normal vision. Ideally, there should be a continuum of services so that a child can be moved from one program to another as her needs change. The educator should never regard a child's placement as final; he should, rather, be willing to move the child to a different program if the child's needs change.

PROBE 5-7
Educational Programming

1. The first schools established for the visually impaired in Europe and the United States were _____ schools.

2. T   F   The residential school traditionally follows the same curriculum as other schools in the same state or region.

3. How has the role of residential schools changed in recent years? _____

_____

_____

_____

4. List the five types of local day school programs provided for visually impaired children.

   a. _____

   b. _____

   c. _____

   d. _____

   e. _____

5. T   F   Once a child has been placed in a particular type of program, it is safe to assume that the child will remain in that program throughout her school career.

6. T   F   The school principal makes the decision about the type of program that a visually impaired child should be placed in.

7. List three types of information that are used to make placement decisions for visually impaired children.

   a. _____

   b._____

   c. _____

8. T F   Parents must consent to the collection of evaluation data and to the placement of their visually impaired child in a particular program.

9. Persons involved in assessing visually impaired children should pay particular attention to the effects of the loss of vision on _____ development.

10. DeMott suggests that information about a number of areas be included in the educational assessment of the visually impaired. List four of these areas.

    a. _____

    b. _____

    c. _____

    d. _____

11. What three types of instruments are used to assess visually impaired children?

    a. _____

    b. _____

    c. _____

12. T F   Normative data provided for standardized tests are appropriate for use with visually impaired children.

SUMMARY

1. Normal, or unimpaired, vision has four basic components: (a) the object to be viewed, (b) light that reflects from the object, (c) an intact visual organ (the eye), and (d) the occipital lobes of the brain, where visual stimuli are interpreted and "seeing" takes place.
2. The leading causes of visual impairment among those who are not legally

blind are cataracts, refractive problems, and glaucoma. Among totally blind persons, the leading causes of blindness are retinal disorders, glaucoma, and cataract.

3. Definitions of visual impairment based on visual acuity are used primarily for legal and economic purposes, and for the allocation of federal funds for the purchase of educational materials.

4. Educational definitions of visual impairment are based on the media through which the child learns rather than on visual acuity.

5. The incidence of visually impaired children in the school-age population is generally considered to be one in every 1000.

6. Most visually impaired children are not totally blind. Approximately two-thirds of all visually impaired children have some remaining vision.

7. The physical characteristics of visually impaired children other than vision are the same as those of children who are not visually impaired.

8. The intellectual development of children is not directly affected by visual impairment or blindness.

9. Because the loss of vision leads to restrictions in the child's range and variety of experiences, in her ability to get about, and in her interaction with the environment, the visually impaired child has problems in concept development.

10. Visually impaired children tend to lag behind their seeing peers in school achievement.

11. The most widely accepted view is that the social/emotional problems of visually impaired children are the result of the attitudes and reactions of persons with normal vision, and not the result of the loss of vision itself.

12. The curriculum for programs for the visually impaired is usually the same as that for the other school programs in a particular state or region.

13. In considering basic instructional methods for visually impaired children, it is important to remember that many of the techniques and strategies that are effective with seeing children are also appropriate for the visually impaired.

14. Visually impaired children do have some unique instructional needs, and will require help from specially trained teachers of the visually impaired in some academic areas.

15. In the United States, visually impaired children are educated in residential schools and a number of different types of programs in local day schools.

16. Those involved in educational planning should remain flexible in their approach to placement.

17. It is important to remember that the most appropriate, least restrictive environment for visually impaired children is the one in which they would normally be enrolled if they were not visually impaired. They should be educated to the greatest extent possible with children who are not visually impaired.

TASK SHEET 5
Field Experiences Related to the Visually Impaired

Select *one* of the following and perform the assigned tasks:

Program Visitation

Visit either a residential school, a local day school (self-contained) program, or a resource program for the visually impaired. In a paper of no more than three pages, describe the program you visited, the curriculum that was being used, the interactions you had with the staff and students, and your general reactions and impressions of the program. How did it differ from programs for normally seeing children?

Professional Interview

Arrange to visit one of the following professionals, and discuss his job with him: ophthalmologist, optometrist, optician, orthoptist, teacher of the visually impaired, rehabilitation counselor for the visually impaired, or director of a facility for the visually impaired. In a paper of no more than three pages, answer the following questions:

1. Where did you visit?
2. What were the responsibilities of the person you interviewed?
3. What type of training was necessary to enter this profession?
4. What types of problems does the person encounter?
5. What did you learn from this experience, and what was your reaction to it?

Interview with a Visually Disabled Person

Interview a visually impaired person, or the parents of a visually impaired person, and determine the types of problem they encounter, their attitude toward their disability, and their attitude toward people with normal vision. Describe your findings and the feelings you had during the interview.

Library Study

Use the library to find three articles related to the visually impaired. Write a one-page abstract of each.

Design Your Own Field Experience

If you know of a unique experience you can have with visually impaired people or do not want to do any of the listed alternatives, discuss your alternative with your instructor and complete the task that you agree on.

Probe Answers

Probe 5-1

1. eye; brain
2. a; c; b; a; b; a; c; a; b; b; a
3. The process of seeing begins when light is reflected from an object and enters the eye. As the light rays pass through the cornea, aqueous, lens, and vitreous, they are bent, or refracted, so that they will strike the retina in the macular area. From there, nerve impulses relay the

impressions of visual stimuli to the brain, where "seeing" takes place.

Probe 5-2

1. placing a patch over the unaffected eye; surgery to straighten the eye muscles.
2. False
3. myopia
4. retrolental fibroplasia; maternal rubella
5. Retrolental fibroplasia

Probe 5-3

1. Visually impaired children are those who differ from normally seeing children to such an extent that it is necessary to provide them with specially trained teachers, specially designed or adapted curricular materials, and specially designed educational aids, so that they can realize their full potential.
2. blind; partially seeing
3. 20/200; 20/70
4. True
5. The index of 20/150 means that an object which can be seen clearly from a distance of 150 feet by a normally seeing person must be 20 feet from the visually impaired person to be seen clearly.
6. visual arc
7. A blind child is one whose visual loss indicates that he must use braille and other tactile and auditory materials to learn. A partially seeing child has some useful vision and uses print and other visual materials in his educational program.

Probe 5-4

1. b; c; d; a
2. Snellen Chart
3. Any five of the following:
   a. Child appears clumsy in a new situation and has trouble walking.
   b. Child holds head in awkward position or holds material close to eyes.
   c. Child "tunes out" when information is on chalkboard or books he cannot read.
   d. Child constantly asks someone to tell him what is going on.

e. Child is inordinately affected by glare from sun and not able to see things at certain times of day.
   f. Child has a pronounced squint.
   g. Child rubs eyes excessively.
   h. Child pushes eyeball with finger or knuckle.
   i. Child has obvious physiological anomalies or signs of eye disease, such as red swollen lids, crusts on lids, or crossed eyes.
4. 0.1
5. True

Probe 5-5

1. True
2. a. restrictions in the range and variety of experiences they have had
   b. restrictions in the ability to move about in the environment and observe people and objects around them
   c. restrictions in their integration into all aspects of their environment
3. the negative attitudes of those who can see; the integration of blind children with seeing peers and inservice training for teachers

Probe 5-6

1. True
2. True
3. eyeglass magnifiers; stand magnifiers; hand-held magnifiers; telescopic aids; television viewers.
4. orientation; mobility
5. False
6. tactile; visual; auditory
7. Any three of the following:
   a. braille
   b. paperless brailler
   c. optacon (optical-to-tactile converter)
   d. Kurzweil Reading Machine

Probe 5-7

1. residential
2. True
3. In recent years some residential schools have

functioned as educational centers for visually impaired children, and have provided activities and experiences for their students that involve interaction with sighted children outside their school. Residential schools have also provided consultative services to local school programs. In addition, some residential schools are functioning as centers for multiply handicapped visually impaired children.

4. a. special class plan
   b. cooperative class plan
   c. resource room plan
   d. itinerant teacher plan
   e. teacher consultant plan
5. False
6. False
7. Any three of the following:
   a. eye examination report
   b. medical report
   c. educational assessments
   d. reports of behavioral observations by parents and teachers
   e. any assessment information that might be helpful in placement
8. True
9. concept
10. Any four of the following:
    visual efficiency
    sensory abilities
    other impairments
    motor performance
    language
    intelligence
    achievement
11. a. those developed for visually impaired
    b. those adapted for use with visually impaired
    c. those developed for use with seeing population and used as is for visually impaired
12. False

. . . Emmett is a paraplegic — paralyzed from the neck down from a tackle that broke his neck in a junior high football game.

In the months since the accident, Emmett and his parents have learned how to cope with his disability from therapists at Cardinal Hill Hospital. . . .

To Emmett's parents, Mr. and Mrs. Everett Land, it's meant traveling back and forth several hundred miles each week from their tiny hometown. . . .

And to Emmett, it's meant depending on someone to guide his wheelchair, and to do things most people take for granted, like adjusting the volume on a radio.

But this week Emmett came back to Cardinal Hill for some magic — magic in the form of an electronically-powered wheelchair. By using his chin to push buttons placed near his neck and head, he can go forward, backward, maneuver around objects, and control the speed of the chair at the same time.

By bringing the right picture on the screen [on the front of the chair], Emmett's head controls can activate a remote control system that includes a radio, television and lamp. He can also "dial" a telephone by pushing out the numbers on his chin button. . . .

The base for all of this magic is a regular, though comfortable, wheelchair. But a sophisticated electronic device developed by the Romich, Beery and Bayer Co., in Shreve, Ohio, enables Emmett to perform the extra functions. . . .

"I don't have to wait for anyone else to go as fast or slow as I want," he said, comparing the new chair to his old one that had to be pushed. "And now I have my own telephone, I've always wanted that. I don't have to depend on someone else to dial for me and hang up when I'm through."

But Mrs. Land sees the chair in a different light. "This is the first time in so long that we've seen Emmett able to move on his own. It's a great feeling that he can do things alone."

Source: From Judi Joseph, Thanks, But Emmett Doesn't Need Help Now. *The Lexington Leader,* January 25, 1979. Reprinted by permission.

6

Physical Disabilities

Donald P. Cross

Donald P. Cross is Associate Professor, Faculty Chairperson of the Learning and Behavioral Disorders program, and Director of the Educational Assessment Clinic in the Department of Special Education, University of Kentucky. Dr. Cross is a member of the Division for Physically Handicapped (DPH), the Division for Children with Learning Disabilities (DCLD), and the Teacher Education Division (TED) of the Council for Exceptional Children.

The story about Emmett on the facing page illustrates one of the most dramatic types of change that has occurred recently in the care of the physically disabled. The evolution of educational programming has been more subtle, but great progress has been made since the turn of the century. Consider the following statement, written in 1898:

> Inherited physical deformity means mental deformity, particularly when the former is an affection of the cerebral or sensory nerves, or even of the motor organism. So positively has this been demonstrated that in the treatment of feeble-minded and insane children, as well as of adults, physicians attempt to correct physical disorder first. With the normal physical functions restored, mental equilibrium also ordinarily returns [Taylor, 1898, p. 184].

As this statement indicates, children with visible physical disabilities were perceived at that time as being mentally defective, and it was thought that the mental problem could be cured by correcting the physical problem.

At the beginning of the twentieth century, children with physical disabilities either stayed at home or were institutionalized. Gradually, however, educators began to admit the physically disabled into the schools, and special schools and hospital classes were developed. Later, programs for the physically disabled were incorporated into public schools through the establishment of self-contained special classes, but they were frequently housed in substandard facilities, such as church basements or old houses.

Like children with other disorders, the physically disabled are typically grouped in categories. In this chapter we will discuss children who are grouped according to their abilities to function in a particular area, and children who are grouped according to a medical diagnosis. The functional categories are *ambulation,* which refers to the child's ability to move from place to place, and *vitality,* which refers to the child's health and ability to sustain life. In the medical category, we will discuss convulsive disorders. We will also discuss architectural barriers, and devices designed to assist the physically disabled.

Categories are useful in grouping children for education, funding, and research. At the same time, however, children who have been placed in a category for the physically disabled tend to be isolated from other children. The current trend is to eliminate categorical labels that can prevent the physically disabled from attending regular education programs.

TERMINOLOGY RELATED TO PHYSICAL FUNCTIONING

You should be able to define physical disabilities and related terminology.

For our purposes, a physically disabled child will be defined as *one whose physical or health problems result in an impairment of normal interaction with society to the extent that specialized services and programs are required.* This group does not include persons with visual or hearing impairments or persons who can be labeled severely or profoundly handicapped.

The disabilities we will discuss in this chapter are presented separately, and each of them is described separately in medical literature. This does not mean, however, that children with one type of disability should be separated from children with a different type, or from children who have no disability. Children with disabilities resemble one another in more ways than they differ from one another. Particular disorders are discussed separately simply because that is the most efficient method of presenting the material relevant to each of them.

TERMINOLOGY BASED ON ANATOMY

Most of the terms used to describe physical disabilities are based on medical usage, which is itself derived from Greek and Latin. Areas of the body are frequently designated with prefixes, whereas suffixes are used to designate conditions of the body. For example, the prefix "hemi" refers to one side of the body, whereas the suffix "plegia" refers to paralysis or the inability to move (Johnston and Magrab, 1976). Thus, the term "hemiplegia" refers to the paralysis of one side of the body. The serious student of physical disabilities is advised to take a class in medical terminology.

Other common terms are listed here:

Term	*Body Area Involved*
Monoplegia	One limb
Hemiplegia	Both limbs on the same side of the body
Paraplegia	The lower limbs
Diplegia	All four limbs, but the lower limbs more seriously than the upper
Triplegia	Three limbs
Quadriplegia	All four limbs
Double hemiplegia	Upper limbs more seriously affected than the lower
Anterior	Front
Posterior	Back
Medial	Nearest the middle
Lateral	Farthest from the middle
Superior	Nearer to the head
Inferior	Farther from the head

There are a number of other terms used to describe the physically disabled. The terms *proximodistal* and *cephalocaudal* are used to describe the growth of children, as you may remember from the chapter on early childhood development. The term *proximodistal* is used to describe the sequence of development that begins with the child's gaining control of muscles close to the trunk (proximo) and progresses gradually until the child gains control of muscles located farther away (distal). For example, a child can control shoulder and elbow movements before controlling finger movements. The term *cephalocaudal* refers to the maturation of the nervous system, which begins at the head (cephalo) and progresses down the trunk to the more distant parts of the body to the tail, or anterior end (caudal). Thus, a child can control head movements before arm movements (Johnston and Magrab, 1976).

Other terms and concepts will be explained as they are used. For those who would like further reading, Bleck (1975, pp. 1–20) is a good source of information on terminology, growth, and anatomical structure. The Johnston and Magrab text presents an excellent description of normal motor development and cerebral palsy (Johnston and Magrab, 1976, pp. 15–55).

PROBE 6-1
Terminology Related to Physical Functioning

1. T F The term "proximodistal" is used to refer to the process whereby the child gains control of the muscles in the trunk before gaining control of muscles in the fingers.

2. The suffix that means paralysis, or inability to move, is _____.

3. In the illustration below, write the appropriate word in the space next to the part of the figure that it represents.

Anterior   Monoplegia
Cephalad   Paraplegia
Caudal   Posterior
Hemiplegia   Quadraplegia
Inferior   Superior

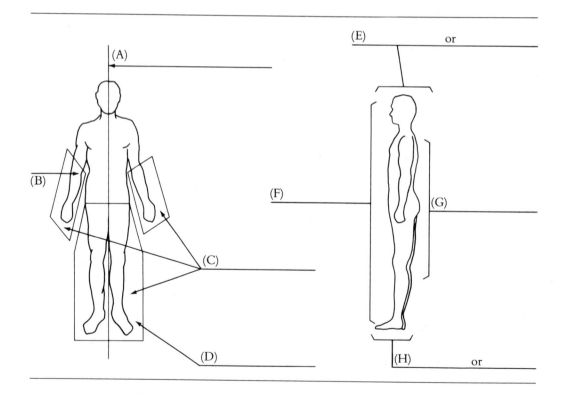

CEREBRAL PALSY

> **You should be able to describe ambulation disabilities that are cerebral in origin.**

Physical disabilities that prevent a child from entering a building, traveling easily from room to room, using toilet facilities, moving from one floor to another, or traveling in a crowded hallway all cause serious problems. It is this type of impairment that has restricted the physically disabled to special schools and modified self-contained classrooms. We cannot discuss all of the disabilities that affect ambulation, but must restrict ourselves to those most commonly encountered in the classroom. Some ambulatory problems that result from other disabling conditions will be discussed in other parts of this chapter.

Cerebral palsy is caused by damage to the brain. It is a nonprogressive disorder (that is, it does not become progressively more debilitating) that affects gross and fine motor coordination. It is often associated with convulsions, speech disorders, hearing defects, vision problems, deficits in measured intelligence, or combinations of these problems. Cerebral palsy was originally called "Little's Disease," after the English surgeon who first described it. The condition was first called cerebral palsy by Sir William Osler (Wolf, 1969), and the name was brought to common usage by Dr. Winthrop Phelps, a doctor who studied cerebral palsy in the 1930s and demonstrated that cerebral palsied children can be helped.

PREVALENCE

Although the individuals with cerebral palsy have never actually been counted, figures suggest that it affects 1.5 per 1000 persons of all ages (Hallahan and Kauffman, 1978). The different types of cerebral palsy are classified according to the physiological, topographical, and etiological characteristics they exhibit (Keats, 1965). Bleck's citation of a statement by Phelps is useful in placing cerebral palsy in perspective:

> Seven children per 100,000 are born with cerebral palsy. Of those seven, one dies the first year. Of the remaining six, two are so severe as to require institutional treatment. Of the four left for treatment, one will receive only home care or day care center treatment. Two are moderately involved and benefit from treatment while the remaining one is so mild that no special treatment is required [Bleck, 1975, p. 38].

Today, however, the description would be somewhat different, largely because of deinstitutionalization and the current emphasis on services for the multiply handicapped. Many of those who would once have been placed in institutions or kept at home are now being educated in public schools, and many children who would once have died are now being saved. These factors could result in an increase in the measured prevalence of cerebral palsy, but improved medical care has reduced the number of children stricken by cerebral palsy. As you can see, a definitive prevalence rate is difficult to establish.

CLASSIFICATIONS OF CEREBRAL PALSY

Persons with cerebral palsy can be classified and described in several different manners. One way is to describe the limbs that are affected, as discussed in the previous section. The most frequently used classification system, the physiological system, is based on the person's body functioning. According to this system, there are six types of cerebral palsy.

1. *Spastic.* The spastic type is characterized by a loss of voluntary motor control. Without this control, the extensor muscles, which are used to extend the arm, and the flexor muscles, which are used to pull the arm toward the body, contract at the same time. This causes movements to be tense, jerky, and poorly coordinated. The spastic may be easily startled by sudden noises or movements, which can cause rigid extension or flexion of the muscles. As a result, the spastic child may become fixed in a rigid position, which gradually relaxes as the child regains composure. As the child grows, the spastic muscles become shorter, which can cause limb deformities. For this and other reasons it is important that the spastic child receive physical therapy. Spastic characteristics are found in about 50 percent of the cerebral palsied population.

2. *Athetosis.* Athetoid cerebral palsy is characterized by involuntary, purposeless movements of the limbs, especially at the extremities. Fluctuating muscle tone affects deliberate muscle exertions, which results in uncontrolled writhing and irregular movements. The throat and diaphragm muscles are also affected, which causes drooling and labored speech. The hands are affected most frequently, followed by the lips and tongue, and then the feet. Excitement and concentrated efforts to control movement generally result in increased tension and spasticity; by contrast, athetoid movement stops during relaxation or sleep. There are at least two major types of athetosis, tension and nontension. The tension athetoid's muscles are always tense, which tends to reduce the contorted movement of the limb. The nontension athetoid has contorted movements without muscle tightness. Athetosis affects 15 to 20 percent of the cerebral palsied population. It is not uncommon for spasticity and athetosis to be found in the same individual.

3. *Ataxia.* Ataxia is caused by damage to the cerebellum, which results in

balance problems. Ataxics have poor fine and gross motor movements, poor depth perception, slurred speech, and a staggering gait. They frequently fall. About 25 percent of the cerebral palsied population is ataxic.

4. *Rigidity*. Rigidity cerebral palsy has been described as a severe form of spasticity (Bleck, 1975). It is characterized by continual, diffuse tension of the flexor and extensor muscles. This "equal pull" of the two muscles renders the limb rigid and hard to bend; once a limb is bent, it tends to stay in that position, like a lead pipe. The words "lead pipe" are frequently used to describe this type of cerebral palsy.

5. *Tremor*. Tremor cerebral palsy is characterized by the shakiness of a limb, which may be evident only when one is attempting a specific movement. This is called intentional tremor. The shakiness of the limb is caused by alternating contractions of the flexor and extensor muscles. Tremor cerebral palsy is differentiated from athetoid by the extent of the limb movement: athetoid motor movements are large and changeable, whereas tremor movements are small and rhythmic.

6. *Mixed*. Most cerebral palsied individuals have more than one type of palsy; they are labeled according to the predominant type. A typical combination involves spasticity and athetosis.

ETIOLOGY

Cerebral palsy can be caused by a number of disorders, which can arise before birth (prenatal), during birth (perinatal), or after birth (postnatal). Prenatal causes include German measles (rubella), prematurity, Rh incompatability, lack of oxygen to the brain of the fetus, and metabolic disorders such as maternal diabetes. Perinatal causes include prolonged labor, breech (feet first) delivery, asphyxia of the fetus, and some obstetric procedures. After birth, cerebral palsy can be caused by infections such as encephalitis, lack of oxygen, and injuries to the head. Postnatal causes are said to be "acquired," whereas those which are present at birth are "congenital."

Certain types of cerebral palsy are caused by damage to the pyramidal, extrapyramidal, and cerebellar traits of the brain. Damage to the pyramidal tract, located between the motor and sensory areas of the cortex, affects the nerve cells that initiate motor impulses to the muscles. Damage to the extrapyramidal system, located in the basal ganglia in the midbrain, results in athetosis, rigidity, and tremor in varying degrees. Damage to the cerebellum affects the ability to maintain balance and coordinated movement; it can also cause ataxia. More information on the physiology and anatomy of cerebral palsy is found in Capute (1975, pp. 151–56) and Denhoff (1966, pp. 24–77).

ASSOCIATED CONDITIONS

Many people with cerebral palsy have problems in a number of areas, including disorders in communication, sensory systems, and intellectual disabilities, and convulsive disorders. These associated disorders can sometimes have effects as serious as the cerebral palsy itself.

1. *Communication disorders.* Disorders in speech are found in 70 percent of the cerebral palsied population. Studies indicate that speech defects are found in 88 percent of persons with athetosis, 85 percent of those with ataxia, and 52 percent of those who are spastic. Most of the speech problems are caused by problems controlling the muscles used to make speech sounds (dysarthria). Delayed speech may also be caused by either mental retardation or the cerebral dysfunction. Other communications problems are voice disorders, stuttering, and aphasia.

2. *Sensory disorders.* Thirteen percent of the cerebral palsied population have hearing defects (Hopkins, Bice, and Colton, 1954). These defects are found in 7 percent of those with spastic disorders, 13 percent of the ataxic population, and 22 percent of those with athetosis. Athetoids are affected more frequently because athetosis is often caused by Rh incompatibility, which also caused hearing disorders.

Twenty-eight percent of those with cerebral palsy have defective or questionable vision (Hopkins et al., 1954). Forty-two percent of ataxics had vision defects, compared with 27 percent of spastics and 20 percent of athetoids. Oculomotor defects, which involve muscle incoordination and imbalance, are found in 50 percent of the cerebral palsied population.

3. *Intellectual ability.* Studies indicate that 50 percent of the people with cerebral palsy have IQs below 70 (Hohman and Freedheim, 1958; Hopkins et al., 1954). It is important to recognize that accurate measures of the intelligence of the cerebral palsied are difficult to achieve. Motor and communications problems interfere with the administration of the tests, and tests such as the Stanford Binet and the WISC are not standardized on a cerebral palsied population. Although it has been reported that adaptations of tests to accommodate a physical disability do not significantly affect test scores (Allen and Jefferson, 1962), the skill with which the test is adapted and the expertise of the examiner may influence the outcome. If a child does better in the classroom than an IQ score leads one to expect, the IQ score should be disregarded in favor of more reliable data about the child's performance.

4. *Convulsive disorders.* Estimates of the percentage of the cerebral palsied population that have convulsive disorders vary considerably. Denhoff (1966) estimates that 30 to 60 percent of the population have convulsive disorders, whereas Keats (1965) finds that 86 percent of the spastic population and 12 percent of the athetoid population have them.

As you can see, cerebral palsy can cause a wide variety of problems, some very serious, some relatively easy to adapt to. Those who suffer from it can be expected to attend school in regular classrooms, in classes for the orthopedically handicapped, or in programs for the severely or multiply handicapped. These children may need physical, occupational, and speech therapy. Some will need minimal extra attention, whereas others will need a great deal of assistance to develop to their full potential.

PROBE 6-2
Concepts Related to Cerebral Palsy

1. T   F   Cerebral palsy is caused by brain damage.

2. *Matching*

   _____ Tense and jerky movements   a. Athetosis

   _____ Involuntary, writing movements   b. Rigidity

   _____ Staggering gait   c. Spastic

   _____ "Lead pipe" stiffness   d. Tremor

   _____ Shakiness   e. Ataxia

3. _____-natal means before birth, _____-natal means during birth, and _____-natal means after birth.

4. T   F   There is a higher incidence of speech disorders, sensory disorders, and mental retardation in the cerebral palsied population than in the "normal" population.

5. T   F   Cerebral palsy is rarely accompanied by convulsive disorders.

6. T   F   Cerebral palsied children do not attend public schools.

OTHER DISORDERS THAT AFFECT AMBULATION

You should be able to describe ambulation disabilities caused by noncerebral factors.

MUSCULAR DYSTROPHY

Muscular dystrophy is a disease in which the voluntary muscles progressively weaken and degenerate until they can no longer function. The age of onset can vary widely; cases have been identified in people ranging in age from one through eighty. There are several types. The Duchenne type, which is the most common, frequently affects young children. It is transmitted to male offspring by the mother, who is the carrier of the condition. Some children are afflicted when there is no family history; this is thought to be caused by gene mutation. The Duchenne type of muscular dystrophy usually appears first between the ages of three and six. Growth and development are normal before the initial onset.

Progression. Muscular dystrophy progresses slowly. In the early stages it is painless and its symptoms are nearly unnoticeable. The first symptoms can include delayed muscle functioning; difficulty walking and climbing stairs; abnormal gait, in which the trunk sways from side to side; difficulty rising from a sitting position; frequent falling; and difficulty in running (Bender, Schumacher, and Allen, 1976). Another early symptom is known as "Gower's Sign," the name given to the practice of placing the hands on the knees and thighs and literally "walking" the leg. To do this, the child must bend his upper body; because his back and stomach muscles are also affected, he may have trouble straightening up again. The child may also grasp something to pull himself up into a vertical position, or place his hands on top of his desk to push himself up. The child may also "tiptoe," a symptom caused by the weakening of the muscle that pulls the feet up to a level position.

In the disease's second stage the child has more difficulty rising from the floor when he falls, because of muscle degeneration in the calves, front thigh muscles, and the dorsiflexors of the feet. The child will also probably have a sway back and protruding abdomen (lordosis). The calf muscles will appear large and healthy (pseudohypertrophy: false enlargement).

During the third stage the child can no longer walk independently and gradually becomes completely confined to a wheelchair. Those who have Duchnene muscular dystrophy usually have reached this stage by age ten.

During the final stage, the child is bedridden and totally dependent. In some cases the child grows obese, which complicates the process of taking care of him. In other cases the muscles atrophy and the child becomes very thin. As the muscles weaken, contractures (shortenings of the muscles) occur, which can result in disfigurement and the loss of limb functioning. Death is caused most often by heart failure, when the heart muscles become weak, or lung infection due to the weakening of the muscles involved in breathing.

Treatment. There is no cure for muscular dystrophy. The primary treatment is physical therapy designed to control contractures. Bleck (1975) indicates that positioning the joints with sandbags or other equipment is more helpful than stretching or exercise. He also describes group games designed to promote good breathing and increase the limb's range of motion. Bracing can be used to prevent contractures, but it is rarely used after the child becomes confined to a wheelchair. Surgery can be used to correct deformities in some cases; treatment will vary from child to child.

Educational Implications. The goal of a school program for the child with muscular dystrophy should be to keep him as active as possible. The child should remain in the regular classroom as long as feasible. When necessary he may be moved to a special class or receive home-bound instruction. Despite reported IQ scores in the eighties (Bleck, 1975), and the fact that the child will not live beyond the second decade, the child should be given instruction appropriate to his level of functioning. The child, teacher, and the child's family may need counseling about the nature of the illness and the poor prognosis for improvement.

SPINAL MUSCULAR ATROPHY

Spinal muscular atrophy affects the spinal cord and results in progressive degeneration of the motor nerve cells (Koehler, 1975). It can be caused by a number of diseases (see Ford, 1966, pp. 188–312). The degeneration can cause problems ranging from slight weakness to symptoms similar to those of muscular dystrophy. The primary characteristic is the progressive weakness and atrophy of the proximal (trunk) muscles. This may cause delayed motor skill acquisition, and the child may be easily fatigued and appear clumsy. The atrophy of muscles may cause muscle tightening and joint contractures. Bone substance may be lost due to muscle and joint disuse.

Spinal muscular atrophy is known to be inherited. If both parents are carriers of the defective gene, there is a 25 percent chance that the offspring will have spinal muscular atrophy, and a 50 percent chance that the child will be a carrier of the defective gene.

Although there is no cure for spinal muscular atrophy, therapy is used to prevent or reduce joint contractures and other bone complications. Physical therapy is very important. Respiratory infections and the aspiration of food must be carefully avoided.

Children with this disorder have normal intelligence but little or no motor strength. Some children are severely affected, whereas others are affected relatively mildly. In school, tasks that do not require muscular skill or strength should be emphasized. If the child's condition stabilizes, he or she may require vocational training.

POLIO

Poliomyelitis (infantile paralysis) is a viral infection that affects or destroys the anterior horn cells in the spinal cord. When these cells are destroyed, the muscles that they serve eventually die or become paralyzed. The paralysis may affect the entire body or just parts of the body. Some persons are kept alive only through the use of a lung machine that helps the person breathe. Many people with polio are bedridden, confined to wheelchairs, or dependent on braces and crutches for ambulation.

Polio was once a greatly feared disease that affected thousands of people each year, but the development of the Salk polio vaccine has almost eradicated it. Unfortunately, an increasing number of children are not being vaccinated, and they are extremely vulnerable to the disease. Although polio is not a major disabling disease today, it could become one again if children are not vaccinated.

SPINAL CORD INJURIES

Spinal cord injuries are most often caused by auto accidents, sports accidents, and accidents at work. In the past most of the victims have been male, but the increasing participation of women in hazardous sports and occupations may increase the number of women with spinal cord injuries. An injury may result in quadriplegia or paraplegia. Depending on the damage that occurs, the injured person may recover completely or may not recover at all.

If a person who has been in an accident complains of neck or back pain or can feel nothing in his legs, he should be treated on the assumption that his spinal cord has been injured. He should be required to lie flat, and not be allowed to turn his head or rise to a sitting position. The injured person should be moved without bending or twisting. Medical care and physical therapy both play a part in the treatment of spinal cord injuries.

Most children with injuries of this type will be served in hospital schools and home-bound education programs. Some may be able to return to the regular classroom, whereas others will be placed in classes for the orthopedically impaired, depending on the extent of the child's recovery. Intelligence is not affected by a spinal cord injury.

SPINA BIFIDA

Spina bifida is a congenital defect that results when the bones of a part of the spine fail to grow together. The defect, the cause of which is unknown, occurs during the first thirty days of pregnancy (Bleck, 1975). The gap in the spine can appear anywhere, but it is usually found in the lower part, the lumbar-sacral area. It can cause paraplegia and loss of bowel and bladder control.

There are three types of spina bifida. The most severe is called myelomeningocele (or meningomyelocele). In this type, part of the spinal cord protrudes through the gap in the bones of the spine into a sac-like structure that surrounds the gap, causing a neurological problem (see Figure 6-1). If the sac contains cerebrospinal fluid, but the spinal cord does not protrude and there is no neurological impairment, the condition is called meningocele. The least severe form is

FIGURE 6-1
A Myelomeningocele

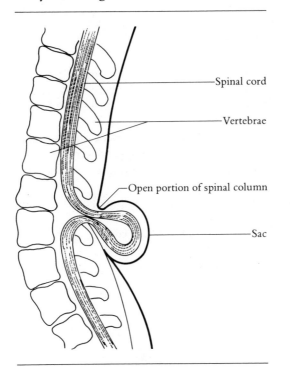

—Spinal cord

—Vertebrae

—Open portion of spinal column

—Sac

called spina bifida occulta. The only evidence of this form is a growth of hair covering the area of the defect. Myelomeningoceles are four to five times more common than meningoceles (Bleck, 1975).

Gearheart states that spina bifida is the third most common disability found in long-term education settings. Its incidence is estimated to be between 0.1 and 4.13 cases per 1000 live births (Bleck, 1975; Myers, 1975). The prevalence rate is somewhat lower than the incidence rate because some of the children die shortly after birth. Recent medical advances have decreased the mortality rate, but spina bifida is still a dangerous condition frequently accompanied by several other chronic disorders.

One of the most common is hydrocephalus, or "water on the brain." This condition occurs when the drainage of cerebrospinal fluid is blocked. The build-up of pressure that results can cause serious brain damage, including mental retardation. Kidney infections caused by poor urinary drainage are another condition associated with spina bifida. If untreated, these infections can lead to kidney failure. Pressure sores are a problem that results when the blood supply to an area of skin is cut off. Persons with normal feeling experience discomfort when this happens and shift their position to allow the blood to circulate normally. Those who are paralyzed, however, do not feel the discomfort. Pressure sores are very difficult to heal. Other disorders that may accompany spina bifida are dislocation of the hip, club foot, and when the child is older, scoliosis (spinal curvature), kyphosis (humpback), and lordosis (swayback).

Treatment. The initial treatment of spina bifida is surgery for the outpouch (sac) and hydrocephalus, if that is also a problem. Surgery for hydrocephalus involves placing a shunt to drain excess cerebrospinal fluid to the atria of the heart or to the abdominal cavity. When successful, there is no brain damage. Surgery for the outpouch frequently takes place during the first week after birth. Sharrard (1968) reports less paralysis and a lower mortality rate among those who receive surgery within forty-eight hours. Bleck (1975), however, reports that early surgery does not diminish paralysis.

Most people with spina bifida, particularly those with myelomeningocele, use crutches or wheelchairs, which may be a problem in school. A more serious problem is the lack of bowel and bladder control. In some cases, physical, occupational, and speech therapy will be part of the school program. Most cases require continual medical monitoring.

OSTEOGENESIS IMPERFECTA

Osteogenesis imperfecta is also known as *brittle bone disease.* The bones of children with this disorder break very easily; the many fractures cause the limbs to be small and bowed. The disorder is inherited and affects both male and female children. The bones of those with osteogenesis imperfecta have been described as being immature, like the bones of a developing fetus. Many children with this disorder are hard of hearing, because of defects in the bony structure of the ossicles.

There is no cure for this disorder. Surgery and bracing are used to straighten the legs and aid in ambulation. Many use a wheelchair as well. Since the intelligence of these children is normal, their educational prognosis is good. Great care must be exercised in working with these children, however, because their bones can be broken very easily — even when helping them change position in a wheelchair. The physical activity of these children will of course be severely restricted.

ARTHROGRYPHOSIS

This congenital disorder is characterized by stiff joints and weak muscles. In some cases the muscles of the limbs are missing or are smaller than normal. The stiff joints and subsequent restricted movement of the limbs will hinder the child in normal school programs. The disorder is not progressive, however, and the children can be expected to have a normal intellect. Educational goals should be geared toward tasks that do not involve the use of the impaired limbs. These children may need special classroom adaptations to meet their needs, depending on the severity of their problem.

JUVENILE RHEUMATOID ARTHRITIS

According to the Arthritis Foundation, there are five common forms of arthritis: rheumatoid, osteoarthritis, ankylosing spondylitis, rheumatic fever, and gout. Rheumatoid arthritis is the most common among school-age children. The first signs of the disease are general fatigue, stiffness, and aching of the joints as they swell and become tender. It is a chronic condition, but 60 to 70 percent of those affected are free of the disease after ten years (Miller, 1975). During the active phase, children experience severe pain whenever the affected joints are moved. If the condition first appears in childhood, most children recover completely. Those who first acquire the condition as adults have a much smaller chance of a permanent remission.

Arthritis cannot be cured. Aspirin is used to reduce the pain, and rest and exercise are also important parts of the treatment. The most severe complication of juvenile rheumatoid arthritis occurs when the heart muscle becomes inflamed, which can be fatal (Miller, 1975). Less severe complications are temporary hearing loss, which is caused by taking aspirin, and permanent damage to the joints, which can restrict their mobility. Some types of therapy have proven to have more harmful consequences than the disorder itself. Cortisone, for example, when administered frequently to children can halt growth, reduce resistance to infection, and cause obesity and brittleness of the bones.

In school, arthritic children may have difficulty remaining in one position for long periods of time. The child may also need extra time to get from one place to another.

OTHER MUSCULOSKELETAL DISORDERS

A problem in one part of the body frequently causes problems in another part. Children who have cerebral palsy, spina bifida, muscular disorders, or other disorders frequently have back problems as well. Muscles that pull too hard, or that are unequally balanced, can cause such disorders as scoliosis, lordosis, and kyphosis. Inadequate muscle tension sometimes results in the complete collapse of the skeletal system.

Scoliosis is lateral curvature of the spine. A person with scoliosis will appear to have an s-shaped spinal column when viewed from behind. *Lordosis* is a condition in which the spine is curved inward, resulting in a swayback and protruding abdomen. *Kyphosis* is a condition in which the area surrounding the shoulders is rounded. These disorders are treated with physical therapy, bracing, and in some cases, surgery. If not properly treated they can cause severe physical deformity and can threaten breathing and other life-sustaining functions. They may also increase pressure on a number of the body's organs.

A *club foot* is a disorder that can appear by itself or in conjunction with another problem. Children with this disorder are born with one or both feet turned down and in. The condition can be corrected with surgery, bracing, and casts, and children who have club feet learn to walk in the normal fashion. They are indistinguishable from their normal peers by the time they reach school age.

Amputation is another important disability. It can be partial or complete. Most amputations are necessary because of accidents, but some are required by life-threatening physiological disorders and diseases.

Limbs may also be missing as the result of disruptions in the early fetal development of the limbs. This sometimes occurs randomly, but it can also be caused by drugs such as *thalidomide,* which was taken by pregnant women as a relaxant. Depending on the time at which it was taken during the first trimester of pregnancy, it can cause a variety of congenital deformities, including extremely short or missing limbs (phocomelia). In this disorder, the hands and feet, which are deformed themselves, are attached directly to the torso and may resemble "seal flippers." Several thousand children with this deformity were born in Germany, where the drug was routinely prescribed in the late 1950s and early 1960s. Once the effects of the drug were established, the drug was taken off the market. Special schools for thalidomide children have been established in Europe. The United States Department of Health did not approve the medication, so the problem in this country was relatively uncommon. Some American women who did obtain thalidomide gave birth to children with birth defects. This tragedy underscores the fact that pregnant women must be very careful not to take drugs that may harm the fetus.

PROBE 6-3
Disorders That Affect Ambulation

1. Which type of supportive service is used to minimize muscular deterioration in children with diseases such as muscular dystrophy, spinal muscular atrophy, and polio?

_____

2. T   F   Children with muscular dystrophy generally recover completely.

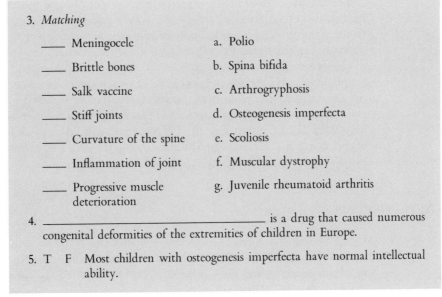

3. *Matching*

_____ Meningocele   a. Polio

_____ Brittle bones   b. Spina bifida

_____ Salk vaccine   c. Arthrogryphosis

_____ Stiff joints   d. Osteogenesis imperfecta

_____ Curvature of the spine   e. Scoliosis

_____ Inflammation of joint   f. Muscular dystrophy

_____ Progressive muscle   g. Juvenile rheumatoid arthritis
deterioration

4. _____ is a drug that caused numerous congenital deformities of the extremities of children in Europe.

5. T   F   Most children with osteogenesis imperfecta have normal intellectual ability.

DISABILITIES THAT AFFECT VITALITY

You should be able to describe disabilities that affect the vitality of children.

Children with disabilities that affect vitality are frequently placed in special classes or programs. Although all of these disorders are life-threatening, some are more dangerous than others. All children with these types of disorders will need special assistance from a primary care worker or teacher, and special educational, social, and vocational training as well.

CONGENITAL HEART DEFECTS

The symptoms exhibited by persons with congenital heart defect are shortness of breath, cyanosis (blue appearance of the skin), and low tolerance for exercise (Myers, 1975). Most congenital heart problems, which are generally recognized at birth or early childhood, are mechanical in nature (i.e., they do not involve infection or inflammation). They can frequently be repaired surgically.

Because these children are often restricted physically and have usually spent a lot of time in hospitals, they have not had the opportunity to participate in many of the normal activities of children. Although the intelligence of most of these children is in the normal range, they may not function academically at the level of their peers. The child's classroom activities may be restricted by orders from his physician, and the teacher will have to watch the child carefully for signs of overexertion. At the same time, however, the teacher should be aware that the child may try to use his condition as an excuse not to participate in activities that he is capable of participating in. The care and education of children with this disorder requires careful cooperation among the child's parents, teacher, and physician.

CYSTIC FIBROSIS

Cystic fibrosis is a chronic genetic disorder that affects the pancreas, the lungs, or both. When the lungs are affected, the mucus normally found in the lungs does not drain properly, and when it builds up, it blocks the passage of air to and from the affected area. When the pancreas is affected, digestion is impaired and the child may suffer from poor nutrition, even if he or she eats what would normally be an adequate amount of food. The disease, which is hereditary, is usually fatal in childhood. It is estimated that one in every twenty-five Caucasians carries the defective gene. It is the most common cause of death from a genetic disorder in the United States (Harvey, 1975). Proper treatment may slow the progress of the disease, however, and some children live to adulthood.

In school, the child may cough frequently, have an increased appetite, and have low physical stamina. She may also take multiple medications. The child may also need to be percussed periodically. This process, designed to dislodge mucus, involves placing the child in certain positions to enhance lung drainage, and vigorously clapping and vibrating her chest (Harvey, 1975). These children have normal intelligence; they will need special attention only for periods of treatment and restrictions in their physical activities.

DIABETES

Diabetes is an inherited metabolic disorder. The diabetic does not produce enough insulin to absorb the sugar in the blood stream. The disorder is treated with a special diet and injections of insulin, administered by the diabetic himself on a prescribed schedule. If properly treated, the condition can be adequately controlled. If too much insulin is taken, however, blood sugar may be consumed too readily, and the diabetic may go into insulin shock. When this occurs, the child must be given something sweet immediately. If the diabetic does not have enough insulin, he or she will go into diabetic coma.

Hypoglycemia, a related disorder, is caused when the body produces too much insulin. This may cause a condition similar to insulin shock, although it is usually not as severe.

The diabetic or hypoglycemic child may need to eat snacks during class time. Hypoglycemic children need to reduce their intake of carbohydrates, as well. Cooperation between the teacher and the child's parents is very important in dealing with these disorders effectively.

ASTHMA

Asthma is a chronic condition characterized by wheezing or labored breathing, which is caused by the constriction in the individual's air passages and by excessive secretion in the air tubes of the lungs. The decrease in the size of the air passage makes breathing — particularly exhalation — difficult (Harvey, 1975). The causes of the condition are not fully understood, but allergic reactions to foods (ingestants) or to particles in the air (inhalants) appear to precipitate it. Excessive emotionality is not considered a primary cause, although it is thought to influence the conditions that may bring on an asthmatic attack. Asthma tends to run in families. The severity and duration of asthma attacks vary considerably. Harvey reports that it is the fifth most common reason for a child to see a physician in the state of Washington. It is similarly prevalent in other states.

The treatment of asthma involves removing ingestants and inhalants from the child's environment. The child may also be given injections to increase her resistance to allergic reaction. Breathing exercises and mechanical drainage of the lungs may also be helpful. During an acute attack, medication can be used to relax the bronchial tree.

The treatment of asthma is a long-term process. The teacher should contact the child's parents to find out whether the child's environment or physical activities need to be controlled, or whether the child needs other special attention. Aside from these considerations, the asthmatic child should be treated like any other.

PROBE 6-4
Disabilities That Affect Vitality

1. A condition characterized by low tolerance for exercise is _____.

2. Children with asthma typically have difficulty _____.

3. Diabetes is controlled through _____

   _____.

4. T   F   Most children with cystic fibrosis die during childhood.

CONVULSIVE DISORDERS

You should be able to identify and treat the symptoms exhibited by children with convulsive disorders.

Epilepsy is caused by brain damage that impairs the ability of the brain to control its normal electrical activity. This can perhaps best be understood through an analogy: the electrical activity of the brain can be compared to a glass of water filled to just above the brim. The water may bulge slightly over the top of the glass, but it will not spill unless the surface tension is broken by a pin prick, a movement of the glass, or some other disturbance. When the brain has been damaged, electrical energy flows over the brain, and control of the resultant overload can be lost as a result of a minor disturbance. When control is lost, electrical energy stimulates many different parts of the brain at the same time, and the individual has a seizure. About one percent of the population has epilepsy. It affects males more frequently than females.

Epilepsy has been a recognized disorder for thousands of years. Hippocrates was the first to suggest that seizures were caused by brain malfunctions. The term "seizure" itself, which is used to describe the active motor states of epilepsy, is derived from Greek and Latin and means "seized by the gods." The Romans called epilepsy "the sacred disease."

Today, epilepsy and seizures are categorized under the general heading of *convulsive disorders*. Epilepsy can occur in anyone at any age. Young children may have convulsions during high fever, but these are considered "febrile seizures" rather than epilepsy. Prolonged high fever can cause brain damage that results in epilepsy, however. Epilepsy can also be caused by injuries when the child is being born, or, later, through head injuries. Epilepsy that has no apparent cause is called "idiopathic" epilepsy.

TYPES OF EPILEPSY

There are many types of epilepsy. The three major types will be discussed in this section. The different types of epilepsy are actually classified medically under four categories: partial seizures, generalized seizures, unilateral seizures, and unclassified seizures (Epilepsy Foundation of America, 1977). This classification system is relatively recent, however, and is not in universal use; we will use the traditional classifications now in common use. More information on epilepsy can be found in Livingston's 1963 book, *Living with Epileptic Seizures*.

Petit Mal. The petit mal seizure frequently goes unnoticed. It lasts five to ten seconds, and its only visible symptoms are staring, a momentary suspension of activity, a "frozen" posture, and perhaps a slight fluttering of the eyelids. The child may appear to be daydreaming or going to sleep. Petit mal seizures may occur as often as ten to fifteen times a minute, or they may occur only occasionally.

The main effect of a petit mal seizure is a momentary lapse of consciousness. It can be compared to a radio that has a short in its system such that only parts of the broadcast can be heard. The child may miss portions of the classroom instruction. Even when teachers notice that a child is behaving oddly, they may not realize what is happening. It is important that parents and teachers collect accurate data on the seizures to aid the doctor in prescribing treatment.

Grand Mal. The grand mal seizure is much more conspicuous. It is this type of seizure that is referred to by the uninformed as a fit, spell, attack, or convulsion. The child may fall to the ground, become stiff (tonic stage), begin to jerk or thrash (clonic stage), and cry out or make noises. The child may hurt himself from falling or biting his tongue, or by hitting objects when thrashing on the floor. The child may also lose bowel and bladder control momentarily. Grand mal seizures may last from a few seconds to five minutes or more. As the seizure progresses, the child's movements gradually slow and finally cease. When the epileptic regains consciousness, he will not remember the seizure or anything that happened during it. The child may also be confused and very tired, particularly if the seizure was a severe one. In some cases, however, the child simply gets up and continues his activities.

Grand mal seizures may be preceded by a warning, or aura, of some kind. An aura can be a sensation, a sound, a light perception, or some other indication. If the child is aware that he is about to have a seizure, he should be quickly taken to as safe a place as possible.

Psychomotor. The psychomotor seizure is characterized by automatic, stereotyped movements, which may be purposeless, inappropriate, or both. This type of seizure progresses through the following stages: suspension of activity, repetitions, automatic movements, incoherent or irrelevant speech, possibly followed by a display of rage or anger. Persons who have this type of seizure are often identified as emotionally disturbed or as having a temper tantrum. When the seizure is over, the individual will be confused.

FACTORS THAT CAN PRECIPITATE SEIZURES

Seizures are most likely to occur one to two hours after a person falls asleep, or one to two hours before awakening. Physicians use this knowledge to help diagnose epilepsy by comparing the results of electroencephalogram (EEG) testing, which is used to record brain wave activity, with observed abnormal motor activity.

Seizures can also be caused by *emotional disturbance* and *stress.* They are more common among women during the menstrual period. Drug withdrawal, hyperventilation, fever, photic stimulation (such as sunlight glittering through leaves or on water), television, and fluorescent lights have also been known to precipitate seizures. If an individual's seizures tend to be precipitated by a certain kind of environmental event, the seizures can sometimes be controlled by avoiding the events that precipitate them.

The following newspaper article illustrates some of the misconceptions held by the general public about epilepsy and the consequences of these misconceptions for the epilepctic.

> A young man wakes up from his epileptic seizure to find a woman bystander dancing over him, trying to exorcise what she believes is a devil that has possessed him. . . .
>
> Quoting from a national survey about charitable causes to which the public is most likely to contribute, the board president of the financially ailing Epilepsy Association of Kentucky says: "We're right down at the bottom, just one notch above venereal disease."
>
> Welcome to the uncertain, somewhat secret world of the epileptic.
>
> They are suffering — or have suffered sometime — seizures ranging from dramatic convulsions to brief lapses of consciousness. More than that, they have suffered from public ignorance and uneasiness over the ailment. . . .
>
> "The average citizen is not hostile to epilepsy. It's just they don't know very much about it, and sometimes they're scared about it," said E. Wayne Lee, a 27-year-old epileptic. . . .
>
> Greater understanding in the schools can prevent some of the embarrassment and ridicule faced by students who suffer from epilepsy.
>
> This embarrassment sometimes prompts teen-age epileptics not to take their seizure-preventing drugs in an attempt to prove they really are like everyone else. . . . [Peirce, 1979].

TREATMENT OF EPILEPSY

Epilepsy is treated primarily with chemotherapy, the administration of drugs. The drugs are used to prevent seizures or to reduce their frequency. Many of them have serious side effects, which vary with the child and the medication being taken. Dilantin, for example, causes a condition known as gingival hyperplasia, in which the gums become swollen and tender and grow over the teeth. The gums also bleed easily and are susceptible to infection. Other side effects of concern to the classroom teacher are lethargy and restlessness.

Another part of the treatment program involves classroom adjustment and efforts to ensure that the epileptic is accepted by the teacher and the child's peers. Children are much more likely to accept the epileptic child if seizures have been explained to them. The teacher may also have to control classroom activities that regularly precipitate grand mal seizures. If, for example, the child regularly has a seizure after heated classroom discussion, the discussion may have to be toned down, or the child may have to be occupied with another activity. The teacher should also know how drugs affect the child's school work.

How to Deal with Seizures. Although seizures can generally be controlled with medication, the teacher may occasionally have to manage seizures in the classroom or elsewhere. Petit mal seizures are more difficult to control than grand mal seizures. The teacher who has children who experience petit mal seizures may have to repeat instructions several times to be certain they are clearly understood. The teacher should also realize that the child is not merely daydreaming.

A child who experiences an aura or warning that precedes a grand mal seizure should be taken immediately to as safe a place as possible. If the child falls to the floor, these instructions should be followed:

1. Give the child room to thrash. The immediate area should be cleared of children and objects on which the child could hurt herself.
2. Allow the child to remain on the floor. The child should not be moved, restrained, or held during the seizure.
3. Protect the child's head by cradling it in your hands. Do not restrain head movement, however. Move with the child.
4. When possible, turn child's head to one side. This allows saliva to drain. If it flows back into the throat, the child may choke. Turning the head to one side also keeps the child from choking on his tongue, which may be caused by gravity forcing the tongue to the back of the throat if the child is lying face-upward.
5. Don't put your fingers in the child's mouth. The child could bite and seriously injure them. Tremendous strength is exerted during a seizure. If you have a chance, insert a soft object (folded hanky, belt, etc.) between the child's jaws. This can prevent the child from biting her tongue.
6. Don't lay the child on his stomach; to do so will impair his breathing. When possible, the child should be turned on his side.
7. Loosen tight clothing.
8. Get down on the floor with the child. Do not stand up and look down at the child.
9. Allow the child to remain lying down for a while after she has regained consciousness.

10. Talk to the child in a calm voice. Acknowledge the seizure, but don't make a major issue of it.
11. When the child is ready, help him stand up.
12. Allow the child to lie down or sit at a desk with her head down. The child should be permitted to go to sleep if she wants to.
13. Unless instructed otherwise, you need not call the physician. You should report the seizure to the parents and principal and note its severity and duration in the anecdotal seizure record.
14. The children in the classroom should be assigned the task of moving tables, chairs, and other objects away from the child, because they are closer than the teacher. Other children should be instructed to go on with their work.
15. Other children in the classroom should be prepared for the event. Discuss the appropriate procedures for dealing with seizures with the child's parents, and obtain parental and school permission to discuss seizures with the class. A discussion can perhaps be related to health instruction. After the child has regained consciousness, appropriate reactions (do not stare, do not avoid the child) should be discussed with the class.
16. Above all, try to remain calm.

Psychomotor seizures should generally be treated in the same way as grand mal seizures. It is important to recognize the emotional component and when necessary clear the room or take the individual from the room. The individual may resist attempts to move him, however; if he does, he should be allowed to remain.

If the child is still convulsing after five minutes, or seems to go from one seizure right into another, the child's parents and the physician (or school nurse if one is available) should be consulted immediately. There is a condition, called status epilepticus, which can cause death if allowed to continue. This condition requires immediate treatment by a physician (Walshe, 1963).

EDUCATIONAL IMPLICATIONS

Children with epilepsy will be found in the regular classroom and in the special class. Epilepsy alone is not sufficient reason to place a child in a special class or program, but it is often found in conjunction with other disabilities, such as mental retardation and cerebral palsy. The teacher must watch for the side effects of medication and adjust the classroom to reduce the effects of the seizure on both the child and her peers. He should also collect data on side effects and the incidence, duration, and severity of seizures, which should be reported to the child's physician to aid her in monitoring the child's disorder. Epilepsy is not a progressive disorder, nor does it cause mental retardation. It is not contagious. As noted, the child will require some adaptations and adjustment, but otherwise she should be treated as normally as possible.

PROBE 6-5
Convulsive Disorders

1. A temper tantrum may sometimes be confused with what type of seizure?

   _____

2. A child who falls to the ground, thrashes around, and loses bladder control may be suffering from a _____ seizure.

3. The type of seizure that often goes unnoticed is a _____.

4. T F Epilepsy is treated primarily through chemotherapy.

5. T F In treating a person having a grand mal seizure, it is wise to place a pencil or tongue depressor between the teeth to prevent swallowing of the tongue.

6. When is it necessary to call in professional help for a child having a grand mal seizure? _____

   _____

   _____

ASSISTIVE AND ADAPTIVE EQUIPMENT

You should become familiar with the devices used to aid the functioning of persons with physical disabilities.

There are many devices available to the physically disabled to help them overcome problems of everyday living. *Prosthetic* devices such as artificial arms and legs are used to replace missing body parts. *Orthotic* devices are attachments, such as a leg brace or a splint, that assist a body function. Other types of adaptive equipment, such as machines that turn pages, long forceps used to reach objects that would otherwise be out of reach, and wheelchairs, are also available.

Although devices such as these may be beneficial to the handicapped, they should not be recommended without a careful examination of their potential effect. In some cases the use of a device may lead to a dependency that adversely affects the disabled person's remaining physical functions. Those who do not use adaptive aids may become more independent, thereby preventing or retarding physical deterioration. What is more, some prosthetic devices actually hinder body functioning or motor movement, and tasks may be accomplished more efficiently without them. Questions about the use of a particular device should be referred to a physical therapist.

The many devices used to help the handicapped have been classified in an information storage and retrieval system called the Information System for Adaptive, Assistive, and Rehabilitation Equipment (ISAARE), which was developed by Melichar (1977, 1978). Under this system, *adaptive* equipment is defined as that which aids one in adapting to the environment through the use of supportive devices or materials. *Assistive* equipment is described as items designed to assist people to increase their functional capability by providing support or replacing the lost capability. *Rehabilitation* equipment is that used in physical therapy or in rehabilitating people who are trying to regain physical functioning they have lost. Under the ISAARE system, equipment is divided into six categories, according to the purpose for which it is used. These categories are existence, communication, *in situ* motion, travel, adaptation, and rehabilitation. These categories and an example of a piece of equipment in each are described in the following list. The examples are taken directly from the ISAARE manual.

EXISTENCE

Items in the existence category provide support, stabilization, and protection. They allow the disabled person to pursue activities necessary to sustain life. Aids in this category are used for feeding, elimination, bathing, grooming, sleeping, fastening clothing, and so on.

Example. *Dorsal feeding splints* provide assistance for independent feeding to the person who lacks wrist extension and flexion and who is unable to grasp.

The dorsal feeding splints are structured to support the palm, wrist, and forearm. An 8-inch-long band of lightweight metal or rubber with soft underpadding extends lengthwise on the dorsal side of the individual's forearm; three adjustable leather or Velcro straps are attached to the band winding around the user's palm, wrist, and mid-forearm. An adaptable utensil holder is usually inserted or otherwise attached to the palmar strap (Figure 6-2).

COMMUNICATION

Communication devices are used in the reception and expression of information. Included are specialized typewriters, hearing aids, braillewriters, magnifiers, and machines that help dial telephones.

FIGURE 6-2
Dorsal Feeding Splint

FIGURE 6-3
Automatic Page Turner

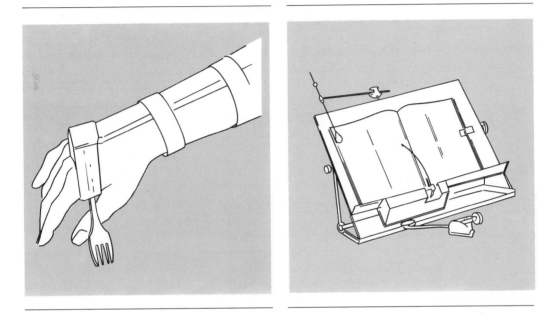

Example. The *automatic page turner* (Figure 6-3) is a device that enables the patient with impaired upper extremity function to turn magazine or book pages automatically. The device operates to turn pages with a slight momentary touch or movement of a sensitive switch mechanism by any part of the body.

The automatic page turner accommodates all sizes of magazines and books, and adjusts to hold positioned materials at any angle, depending on the reading position of the patient.

The automatic page turner is available in two models: a model that turns pages forward and backward, and a model that turns pages in only one direction.

An able-bodied person is required to set the machine for an individual book or magazine, and it takes some time to get the correct amount of pressure on the silicone arm.

IN SITU MOTION

Equipment related to in situ motion is designed to support a person's body. It can either stabilize the body so that it remains immobile (a splint, for example) or add support to facilitate movement (a brace).

Example. The *institutional relaxation chair* allows the person with no sitting balance and a severely involved trunk area to sit comfortably. These chairs are used in therapy units to accommodate patients who are too handicapped to utilize a conventional chair or wheelchair.

The chair is made of wood, plastic, or metal with two solid sides enclosing the user from the armrests to the base; a solid back extends from the headrest to the base with a bench-like seat. This chair tilts on a metal rod at the back of the platform on which the chair rests. The chair may be adjusted to a thirty-degree angle; the seat tilts to a full jackknifed position; the padded headrest is contoured; and the platform is on casters (Figure 6-4).

TRAVEL

Devices in the travel category help a person to move either vertically or horizontally. A wide variety of items is included in this category, including wheelchairs, hoists, canes, walkers, and crutches.

Example. The *stairclimbing wheelchair* provides greater mobility to the user than the standard wheelchair, as it will negotiate stairs. The stairclimbing wheelchair creeps along on caterpillar treads, is battery operated with push-button controls, and the seat tilts so the occupant is always in an upright position (Figure 6-5). On floors and level areas the chair rides on two power-drive front wheels with two trailing casters; the tracks are stationary and clear the ground. Both the tracks and wheels are driven in negotiating curbs; the rear wheels are retracted in climbing stairs.

ADAPTATION

Devices are available to help a person adapt to the environment. Included in this category are such things as cooking utensils that can be used by someone with one hand, aids for doing housework, and driving accessories.

Example. *Drive control* units basically consist of a hand lever, usually positioned on the left side and directly behind the steering wheel, which has been connected by long rods to the brake and accelerator (Figure 6-6). There are various types of mounting; some are attached to the steering column, some to the lower portion of the dashboard. Also located on the hand control is a headlight dimmer switch.

The hand control is operated by pushing it downward, toward the floor, to brake; and pulling it back in the direction of the lap of the driver to accelerate. In

FIGURE 6-4
Institutional Relaxation Chair

FIGURE 6-5
Stairclimbing Wheelchair

some models it is possible to brake and accelerate simultaneously, as would be used in starting on a hill.

REHABILITATION

The rehabilitation category includes devices and equipment used by medical personnel and physical therapists. Included are items that are used to exercise various body parts and to measure physical functioning.

Example. The *finger shoulder ladder* is a therapeutic device used to increase range of motion of the shoulder joint. The ladder is constructed of wood, 1½ × 2½ × 89 inches with grooved steps for the fingers to climb. It is mounted on a wall and may be positioned at a convenient level (Figure 6-7).

If you are interested in finding out more about the ISAARE system, you might read the article by Melichar (1978) or obtain a copy of the ISAARE retrieval system manual (Melichar, 1977).

FIGURE 6-6
Drive Control Unit

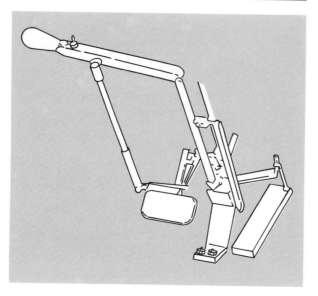

FIGURE 6-7
Finger Shoulder Ladder

PROBE 6-6
Assistive and Adaptive Equipment

1. *Matching*
   Place the letter of the category into which each piece of equipment would fit in the blank that precedes the name of that equipment.

Equipment	Category
____ Exercise stairs	a. Existence
____ Arm sling	b. In-situ motion
____ Adjustable head pointer	c. Rehabilitation
____ Bus wheelchair lift	d. Adaptation
____ Self-threading needle	e. Travel
____ Drinking straw holder	f. Communication

2. Differentiate between a prosthesis and an orthosis.

_____

_____

_____

3. When would it be inappropriate to recommend an assistive or adaptive device for use by a person with physical disabilities?

_____

_____

LEAST RESTRICTIVE ENVIRONMENT

You should be able to describe implications of Pl 94-142 for educating children with physical disabilities in the least restrictive environment.

Children with physical disabilities can frequently be educated in the regular classroom with the help of some of the devices mentioned in the previous section. Depending on the severity of the child's disability and the extent to which she requires special attention, the child might be placed in any of the environments described in Chapter 1. If a child with a physical disability or a health problem is assigned to your school program, you should contact the child's parents and those who have worked with the child in the past, and obtain answers to the questions in the following areas.

Medical Concerns

— In addition to the child's primary disorder, does the child have additional problems such as seizures or diabetes? Does the child have any sensory disorders?
— Does the child take medication? How frequently, and in what amounts?
— If medication is taken, is the school authorized to administer the medication during school hours?
— What are the expected side-effects of the medication? What are the other possible side-effects?
— What procedures should be followed, in the event of a seizure, insulin shock,

diabetic coma, or other problem, with regard to contacting the child's parents or medical personnel?
— Should the child's activities be restricted in any way?

Travel

— How will the child be transported to school?
— Will the child arrive at the usual arrival time?
— Will someone need to meet the child at the entrance to school to provide assistance in getting the child on and off the vehicle that transports him to school?
— Will the child need special accommodations to travel within the school building or the classroom?

Transfer and Lifting

— What methods are used to get the child on and off the school bus?
— What is the preferred way to lift and transfer the child out of a wheelchair and on to the school seat?
— What cautions or limitations are there regarding transfer and lifting?
— How much help does the child really need with movement and transfer?

Communication

In addition to finding answers to the following questions, the teacher of a child with a communications problem should consult a speech/language pathologist.

— If the child does not communicate verbally, what particular or unique means of communication does the child use?
— Does the child have a speech or language problem?
— Does the child use gestures? If so, what are they? Is a pointer used? Does the child use the same signal consistently for yes, no, or other common words?
— Can the child write? Type? How?
— Is an electronic communication aid used? If so, are there any special instructions necessary for the child to use it or the teacher to understand and maintain it?
— Can the child make his needs known to the teacher? How?

Self-Care

— What types of help does the child need with self-care activities such as feeding, dressing, toileting, etc.?
— What equipment, such as a special feeding tray, does the child need?

Positioning

If possible, the physical therapist should be involved in conversations with parents about this area of concern.

— What positioning aids or devices (braces, pillows, wedges, etc.) does the child use?

— What particular positions are most useful for specific academic activities? What positions for resting?
— What positions are best for toileting, feeding, dressing, and other activities?
— Are there any other special aids or devices that I should know about?

Sources of information about providing architectural accessibility include Aiello, 1976; Kliment, 1976; and Mace and Iaslett, 1977. Additional information on principles useful in mainstreaming the physically disabled is available in Cathey and Jansma (1979).

PROBE 6-7
Least Restrictive Environment

1. Describe the conditions under which you would recommend that children be placed in the regular classroom for their education.

_____

_____

_____

_____

_____

_____

2. What criteria would you propose for selecting physically disabled children for placement in a self-contained special class?

_____

_____

_____

_____

_____

3. List one question you should ask a physically disabled child's parents in each of the following areas to help develop procedures for caring for the child.

   a. Medical _____

   b. Travel _____

   c. Transfer _____

d. Communication _____

e. Self-care _____

f. Positioning _____

ARCHITECTURAL BARRIERS

You should be able to recognize ways that architectural barriers can be eliminated.

People with physical disabilities are frequently faced with architectural barriers that prevent them from using facilities easily accessible to people without disabilities. There have been several important laws passed by Congress, however, that are designed to reduce or eliminate architectural barriers, and it is now illegal to build facilities inaccessible to the handicapped with federal funds (PL 90-480). Another piece of legislation, the Urban Mass Transportation Act of 1964, was amended in 1970 to require that federally supported transportation be barrier-free. The Architectural and Transportation Barriers Compliance Board was created to monitor building and ensure that the intent of legislation on accessibility is being followed (PL 93-112).

A set of standards and specifications for making facilities accessible to the handicapped has been developed by the American National Standard Institute (ANSI). These standards are followed by planners and builders, and describe specifications for (1) parking and approaches to building entrances; (2) travel within hallways, and on elevators and stairs; (3) services such as public telephones, water fountains, and rest rooms; (4) hazardous places, gratings, and alarms; (5) special rooms, such as kitchens; (6) schoolrooms such as lecture halls, libraries, and physical education facilities; and (7) other buildings, such as churches, restaurants, and stadiums.

Useful resources for planning facilities for handicapped children have been published by the Council for Exceptional Children (CEC), the state of North Carolina, and the Rehabilitation Services Administration (Aiello, 1976; Kliment, 1976; Mace and Iaslett, 1977). The drawings and specifications in the following section are drawn from these sources.

The following narrative describes some of the barriers you might encounter on a trip to the dentist if you were in a wheelchair. The standards that should be met to overcome these barriers are also discussed.

Curbs Can Be Hazardous To Your Health

Especially if you are in a wheelchair, on crutches, have a heart condition, or suffer from other conditions such as the ageing process which hamper your mobility.

In an attempt to eliminate the hazardous conditions that curbs present this segment of the community, the Kentucky Department of Transportation has developed a design for curb ramps which is both safe and efficient, and meets all the requirements of the curb ramping laws.

Copies of these designs are available through the Department of Transportation, Division of Design, Frankfort, Kentucky 40601.

Mobility. A basic law which cannot be violated.

Poster funded by Department of Transportation, Office of Highway Safety Programs; Picture courtesy of Canadian Rehabilitation Council for the Disabled.

A TRIP TO THE DENTIST

Walkways

You will need to travel on sidewalks in order to get to the building. A walkway is defined as a predetermined, prepared surface that leads to or from a building and is on the same level as the adjacent ground. Walks should be at least 48 inches wide, and should have a continuous surface that is not interrupted by steps or abrupt changes of more than one-half inch. Larger vertical changes than this may obstruct the small wheels on wheelchairs and trip people who have trouble walking.

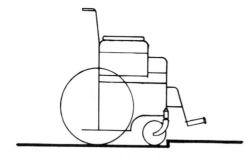

Ramps

You must get from the walk up the stairs to the entrance of the building. To do so, you must use a ramp. A ramp is a sloping walkway that enables one to move from one floor elevation to another without encountering any obstruction. Ramps should be at least 4 feet wide and should have a slope of not more than 8.33 percent, which is a drop of one inch in every 12 inches.

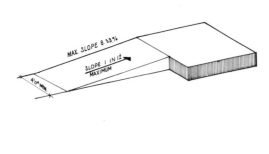

Doormats and Grates

After wheeling up the ramp, you encounter a grate that has been installed in front of the doorway to trap snow and sand. The grate should have grid openings of no more than three-eighths of an inch square. Larger openings will create hazards for those who use canes and will make wheelchair travel difficult.

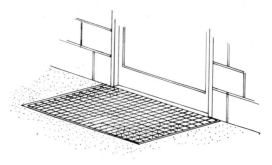

After you have traveled across the grate, you come to a door mat. Thick, bristly doormats of hemp or plastic bunch up under the small wheels of chairs and make the wheelchair difficult to push. Door mats more than one-half inch thick should be recessed into the surface, or thin mats of woven rubber should be used.

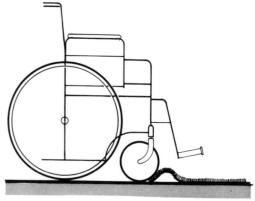

Entrances

You are successful in maneuvering over the grate and door mat and are now ready to open the door to the building. Revolving doors and turnstiles should have accessible doorways placed immediately beside them. The threshold at an exterior door should be beveled and have a maximum edge height of three-quarters of an inch so that you can get your chair over it without difficulty. You should be able to open the door with one hand, and the passageway with the door open should be at least 32 inches wide. An adult wheelchair is approximately 27 inches wide, so a 32-inch doorway allows 2½ inches on each side for the hands as they are used to turn the wheels.

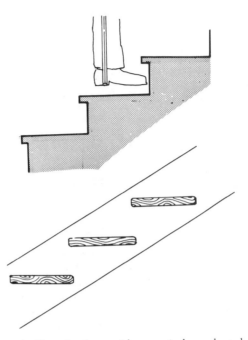

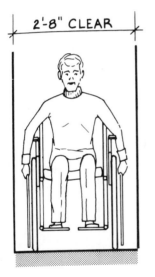

Stairways

Now you are in the building. Ideally, there would be an elevator to take you to the second floor where the dentist's office is located. If there were no elevator and you could ambulate with crutches or leg braces, you would have to use the stairs. Open riser stairs are attractive, but they are hazardous to a person wearing leg braces. People who wear braces also have a difficult time climbing stairs that have abrupt or square lips that stick out over the stair riser. The following two side views are examples of unacceptable stairs.

Acceptable stairs have either vertical or slanted risers. They could be used by someone who had to lift her legs straight up or drop them straight down without risk of the person's catching her toes on the top of each step. Two types are shown below.

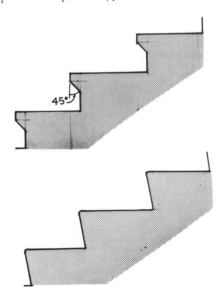

The handrails of stairways should also be modified to make it easier for someone with limited grasping power to hold on to them.

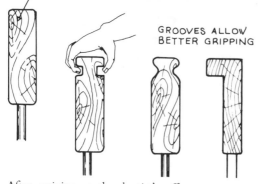

After arriving at the dentist's office, you must move from the wheelchair to the dental chair. You have of course chosen a dentist who has been trained in lifting and transfer techniques. He straddles one of your knees, places his wrists under your arms, and, bending his knees, leans you forward. Then, using his legs for lifting, the dentist pivots you 90 degrees so that you are seated in the chair. The same procedure is used to get you back in the wheelchair after the dentist informs you that you have no cavities.

Rest Rooms

If you need to go to the rest room after your visit to the dentist, you may encounter obstacles there as well. Most rest rooms have self-closing doors that can make toilet facilities inaccessible. Time-delay door closers and automatic, power-operated doors that slide or pivot should be used at major entrances, doorways, and rest rooms.

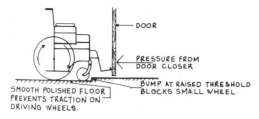

After you have gotten through the door, you must still gain access to the stall. Standards now require that one toilet room for men and one for women be accessible to the handicapped on every floor that has a rest room. Each rest room must have at least one accessible toilet as well. There are three basic techniques for transferring from a wheelchair to a toilet in a stall. The first two methods, used in ordinary stalls, are difficult or impossible for many people who have not had extensive training. You have probably seen the grab rails that have been installed in some stalls to assist the physically disabled with their toileting.

Method 1

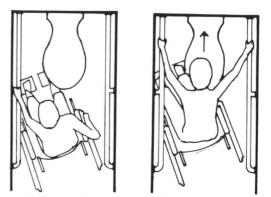

1. (Left) Enters stall, turns at an angle, placing footrests and feet to one side of the water closet.

2. (Right) Leans forward, placing hands on rails near wall, and pulls torso forward, sliding onto seat in sideways position.

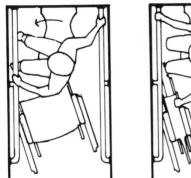

Method 2

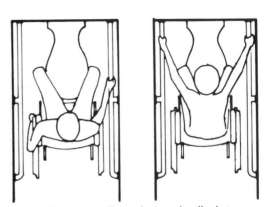

3. (Left) Switches right hand from right rail to left, arriving in side seated positon as in 4.

4. (Right) Maintains balance with right hand while using left to fold chair or push it back.

1. (Left) Enters stall straight in and pulls chair up to seat, placing legs to each side of water closet.

2. (Right) Leans forward, placing hands on bars near wall. Pulls torso forward, sliding onto seat.

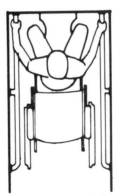

5. With chair folded or pushed back, swings legs around to front, switching left hand to opposite rail.

3. Remains in "backward" position facing wall.

Method 3

This side-approach method can be used by most people in wheelchairs. Stalls that allow space for this method are preferred.

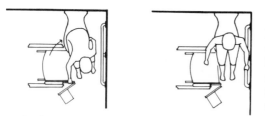

1. (Left) *Approaches water closet from side.*

2. (Right) *Removes arm rest and swings foot rest to side. Places one hand on seat or grab bar and other on chair.*

3. (Left) *With a lifting and sliding motion shifts torso onto seat.*

4. (Right) *Maintains balance by using grab bar and wheelchair.*

temperature of the water should not exceed 120 degrees Fahrenheit. Exposed hot water pipes should be insulated to avoid burning people who have no feeling in their legs.

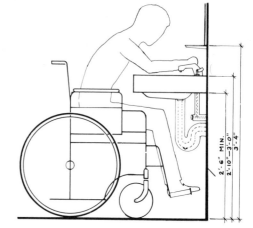

If the rest room contains mirrors and shelves, one of each should be placed above the sink for the handicapped. The shelf and the bottom of the mirror should be no more than 40 inches from the floor. The operating mechanisms (cranks, coin slots, buttons) of towel racks, dispensers, disposal units, vending machines and other appliances should be within 40 inches of the floor as well.

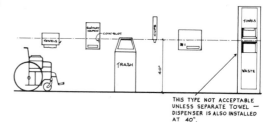

To complete your use of the rest room, you will need to wash and dry your hands. Each rest room should have a sink no more than 34 inches from the floor. There should be a space of at least 29 inches between the floor and the bottom of the sink so that a wheelchair can be pushed close to it. The

As you can see, a building designed to be accessible to the handicapped is significantly different from a traditional building in a number of respects. It is not necessary, however, that every building constructed prior to the enactment of access legislation be renovated. As you will remember from Chapter 1, Section 504 requires only that all *programs* be accessible. For example, every dormitory on a college campus does not have to be accessible, but some dormitories must be. Similarly, the entire building housing a math department need not be free of barriers, but the math program must be available to handicapped students. The expense of making accessible all buildings constructed before the middle 1970s would be enormous.

PROBE 6-8
Architectural Barriers

1. Standards for the elimination of architectural barriers have been developed by an organization called _____.

2. Doorways should be at least ____ inches wide to accommodate wheelchairs.

3. Ramps should be at least ____ feet wide.

4. T   F   A lavatory stall can be made accessible to all persons in wheelchairs by placing grab bars at convenient heights.

5. T   F   Thick door mats should be used in front of doors to give wheelchair travelers better traction on wet days.

6. T   F   Open-riser stairs are particularly well suited for persons who are wearing braces

7. Lavatory towel dispensers and other appliances should be mounted no more than ____ inches above the floor.

8. Obstructions on walkways should not be more than ____ high or they may cause travel problems.

SUMMARY

1. Physically disabled children are those whose physical or health problems result in an impairment of normal interaction with society to the extent that specialized services and programs are required for them.
2. Cerebral palsy is caused by damage to the brain. It is characterized by

impaired motor coordination. There are several types of cerebral palsy, including spastic, athetoid, ataxic, rigidity, tremor, and mixed.

3. Muscular dystrophy is a progressive weakening and degeneration of the voluntary muscles.

4. Other disorders that affect ambulation are spinal muscular atrophy, poliomyelitis, arthrogryphosis, arthritis, osteogenesis imperfecta, and spinal cord injuries.

5. Spina bifida is a congenital defect caused by the failure of the bones of the spine to grow together completely.

6. Thalidomide, a drug taken by pregnant mothers, caused a large number of children to be born with physical defects in the late 1950s and early 1960s.

7. Some of the disabilities that can affect the vitality of children are congenital heart defects, cystic fibrosis, diabetes, and asthma.

8. Epilepsy is caused by uncontrolled electrical discharges in the brain. The three primary types of seizures that result from epilepsy are grand mal, petit mal, and psychomotor seizures. Epilepsy can usually be controlled with medication.

9. Standards have been developed to aid in the elimination of the architectural barriers encountered by the physically disabled. Federal law now requires that buildings built in part with federal funds be barrier-free.

10. Many types of assistive and adaptive equipment have been developed to help physically disabled children in their day-to-day existence, travel, adaptation to their environment, and communication.

11. The great majority of physically disabled children can be educated in regular classrooms with the use of assistive equipment and special teaching aids.

TASK SHEET 6
Field Experiences with the Physically Disabled

Complete *one* of the following alternatives:

Building Accessibility Survey

Acquire a copy of the Accessibility Compliance Checklist included in Kliment's (1976) work, another appropriate checklist, or develop your own. Select a public building in your area and survey it for accessibility. Try to select a building that has been constructed relatively recently, since buildings constructed prior to the mid-1970s are less likely to be in compliance with accessibility standards. If you find areas out of compliance, try to talk to the building owner or supervisor. What was his or her reaction, and what problems did you encounter in your survey?

Program Visit

Arrange to visit an education program for the physically disabled. Describe the type of program that you visited, the physical setting, the assistive and adaptive equipment that was being used, the modifications that were made in the physical environment to adapt to the needs of the children, the type of lesson that you observed, and your general reaction to the program. If possible, interview the teacher and ask what types of problem are encountered in teaching children with physical disabilities. Describe what you learned and how you felt about the experience.

Professional Interview

Interview one of the following professionals: physical therapist; occupational therapist; orthopedic surgeon; prosthetist; orthotist; director of a facility serving the physically disabled; affirmative action officer or person responsible for supervising accessibility at the public school, university, or hospital; or anyone else who works with physically disabled people. Describe who you interviewed, the person's responsibilities, the problems encountered in performing the job, the type of training needed, what you learned from the interview, and how you felt about it.

Interaction with the Physically Disabled

Arrange to help a physically disabled person with a routine daily task such as traveling, shopping, etc. Describe who you helped, the activities you helped with, where you went, the problems you encountered, the adaptations that had to be made, and what you learned from the experience.

Library Study

Use the library to find three articles related to physical disabilities and write a one-page abstract of each.

Design Your Own Field Experience

If you prefer, design your own field experience and after discussing it with your instructor, perform the designated tasks.

Probe Answers

Probe 6-1

1. True
2. plegia
3. a. hemiplegia; b. monoplegia; c. quadraplegia; d. paraplegia; e. cephalad or superior; f. anterior; g. posterior; h. caudal or inferior

Probe 6-2

1. True
2. c; a; e; b; d
3. pre-natal; peri-natal; post-natal
4. True

5. False
6. False

Probe 6-3

1. physical therapy
2. False
3. b; d; a; c; e; g; f
4. Thalidomide
5. True

Probe 6-4

1. a congenital heart defect
2. breathing

3. diet and medication (insulin)
4. True

Probe 6-5

1. psychomotor
2. grand mal
3. petit mal seizure
4. True
5. False
6. when seizure activity continues for more than five minutes, or when it appears that the person is going into repeated grand mal seizures

Probe 6-6

1. c; b; f; e; d; a
2. An orthosis supports or assists the body, and a prothesis replaces a body part.
3. when a careful evaluation of the potential effect of the device has not been conducted

Probe 6-7

1. when medical, travel, transfer and lifting, self-care, and positioning needs can all be appropriately met in the regular classroom
2. the existence of specific problems that would seriously interfere with the children's educa-

tion in the regular classroom or medical, travel, transfer and lifting, self-care, or positioning needs that can only be met by placement in the self-contained special class

3. a. Does the child take medication? If so, how often and in what amounts?
   b. Does the child require special arrangements to travel within the school building or the classroom?
   c. How is the child transferred on and off the school bus?
   d. Can the child make his needs known to the teacher? How?
   e. What special equipment does the child need?
   f. What positions are best for specific academic activities?

Probe 6-8

1. ANSI
2. 32
3. 4
4. False
5. False
6. False
7. 40
8. ½ inch

This ten-year-old girl was born with spina bifida and has no feeling below her thighs. She wears braces and walks with the aid of crutches, although she sometimes uses a wheelchair. She often vacillates between wanting to use the wheelchair, which gives her speed, and wanting to use the crutches, which she perceives as giving her more social approval.

She attends public school classes and receives physical therapy once each week at a cerebral palsy center, doing follow-up exercises daily at school. (At times she balks at doing her exercises.) Her physical therapist believes that she may eventually be able to get along with only one crutch.

After a period of adjustment she has developed a very positive self-image and is well liked by the other children. As these photographs demonstrate, she is an active participant in school activities.

Individual
Differences
in Learning and
Behavior

In the section on sensorimotor exceptionalities, many of the characteristics of the children described were shown to have educational implications. For example, a child who is legally blind and cannot read print will probably use braille, and a child with a profound hearing loss may use sign language.

Among the disabilities discussed in this section, however, the category in which a child is placed does not have implications for her education. What is important is how the child performs in the educational setting. A child who cannot differentiate among initial consonants, for example, will be educated with the same techniques whether he or she is educable mentally retarded, learning disabled, or mildly emotionally disturbed. Those with sensorimotor disabilities will also be educated with the same techniques, once their disabilities have been corrected to the greatest extent possible.

You may be wondering why we include

chapters on retardation, learning disabilities, and behavior disorders if such categories are irrelevant to education. There are several reasons.

1. As you will read in Chapter 9, on behavior disorders, "classification is a process scientists go through to organize and systematize information, which permits them to make useful statements about the phenomenon being classified." Thus, we have chosen to present the material in these categories because that is the common practice. We do try, however, to limit use of a number of terms one frequently hears in special education circles, such as "neurotic," "psychotic," "dyslexic," "minimal brain dysfunction," "developmental retardation," and so on.
2. Most public school programs use categories in special education. For example, there are classes for the educable mentally retarded, resource rooms for the learning disabled, and

programs for the emotionally disturbed. Categorization is used because it is traditional (We've always done it this way."); because of funding. ("You have to label the kids to get the money."); and because of certification practices ("I'm certified to teach the emotionally disturbed.").

Fortunately, the placing of children in categories is becoming more flexible in public schools. The current trend in state funding is to permit groupings based on educational variables. In addition, some states have moved to teacher certification that is noncategorical or generic.

3. Many universities are still training teachers in categorical areas. Consequently, if we don't include chapters on the various categories, it is doubtful that anyone would adopt this text for use in their program.

We hope that by the time the next edition of this text is published, special education will have advanced to the point that we will not have to include categorical chapters. We have tried to focus on specific behavior and learning characteristics that have relevance for education in the following chapters, but the material has of necessity been organized into categories. You will notice as you read the chapters in this section that there is considerable overlap among the characteristics of children who have been categorized as mentally retarded, emotionally disturbed, learning disabled, or severely handicapped. We believe this repetition will reinforce some of the major concepts that are presented.

OVERVIEW

The five chapters presented in Part III deal with individual differences in learning and behavior. Following is a brief overview of each.

Mental Retardation. In Chapter 7 we describe issues related to the identification and appropriate educational placement of mildly and moderately retarded children. Definitions and inci-

dence figures are also given. In addition, the genetic and environmental causes of retardation are described, as are some of the major methods of prevention and treatment. The chapter concludes with a discussion of trends in educational practices.

Learning Disabilities. Children with learning disabilities are the largest group currently receiving special education services. Chapter 8 provides an introduction to the basic concepts of learning disabilities and a discussion of four factors that can cause them: education, physical or organic problems, psychological problems, and environmental problems. The effects of using the label "learning disabilities" are also described, as are the characteristic behaviors of learning disabled children. In addition, instructional intervention programs and the roles of the classroom teacher and resource room teacher are presented. The chapter closes with a discussion of the increasing role of the regular classroom teacher and other current trends.

Behavior Disorders. Chapter 9 describes current practices of identifying children with behavior disorders, and discusses the effects of labeling such children. A behavioral definition of behavior disorders is given, and the different types of behavior disorders are described. Information about effective intervention procedures is also provided. The biological and environmental causes of behavior disorders are discussed as well, and the chapter concludes with a discussion of current educational service models and the continuum of services.

Severe Handicaps. The introduction of children with severe handicaps into the public schools is a recent phenomenon brought about by federal and state litigation and legislation. Chapter 10 describes the severely and profoundly handicapped population. The behaviors that characterize these children are discussed, and examples of effective intervention procedures and programs are provided. In addition, the relationship between mental retardation and severe or profound handicaps is also considered, and a definition is provided. Finally, the role and function of the public school teacher are analyzed, and specific teacher competencies are discussed.

Gifted and Talented. The education of the gifted and talented has long been neglected. The reasons for this neglect and many of the misconceptions about the gifted and talented are dealt with in this chapter. A definition of the gifted and talented that differentiates intellectual characteristics from other characteristics associated with gifted or talented behavior is offered. The underachieving gifted child is described, and intervention procedures are suggested. Gifted children from different cultures are discussed, and the need for flexibility in educating this group is explained. Of particular interest to special educators is the section on the gifted handicapped student. Techniques of assessment and identification of the gifted or talented are also presented, and effective educational practices are described.

A BEHAVIORAL ORIENTATION

The authors of the chapters in this section subscribe to the behavioral approach to instructing exceptional children. Although there is growing support for the behavioral approach, you should be aware that a number of other approaches are also advocated and used by special education teachers and researchers. The proponents of these models use them to explain and predict the learning and behavior of children and claim that the models have implications for educational programming. A brief description of several of these approaches, taken from Reeve and Kauffman (1978), is provided here.

The major models to be described are the humanistic, psychodynamic, psychoeducational, ecological, and behavioral models. Many educators draw on different parts of several approaches, depending on the demands of the task they are trying to accomplish. They do this partly because there is little data to support the contention that one approach is better than another. There is evidence that each of these approaches can be applied successfully.

The Humanistic Approach. Advocates of a humanistic approach believe that children's problems are caused by psychological or emotional conflicts that interfere with the ways they understand or cope with their feelings and emotions. Many humanists also claim that children so affected cannot learn in traditional school settings, and recommend that alternative school settings be developed. They may also recommend that teachers be nonauthoritarian in their relationships with pupils. School settings are designed to be "open," with many opportunities for self-directed activity. Humanists believe that the teacher should be a friend to the students and should serve as a resource for the students' self-directed activities. More information on this approach is available in the work of Peter Knoblock (1973).

The Psychodynamic Approach. The psychodynamic approach is based primarily on the work of Sigmund Freud. Advocates of this approach believe that a person's actions are governed by unconscious impulses that were formed by the emotional atmosphere in which the person grew up. Problems that arise are considered the result of conflicts the child went through during a previous stage of development. The goal of treatment is to discover the source of the conflict that underlies the problem and help the child to restructure his personality. A teacher with a psychodynamic orientation would favor a permissive atmosphere in which children could act out their impulses. Such teachers would not try to change the behavior of the children directly; rather, they would attempt to uncover the symbolic meaning of the behavior and help the children work through their conflicts. Bruno Bettelheim (1950, 1967) provides additional information on the psychodynamic approach.

The Psychoeducational Approach. The psychoeducational approach is an outgrowth of the psychodynamic approach. Advocates of the psychoeducational approach acknowledge the importance of children's behavior and try to strike a balance between psychiatric and educational concerns. Proponents of the psychoeducational approach, like those of the psychodynamic approach, search for the causes of behavior, but they also favor a structure in academics that results in highly individualized programs of instruction. Teachers who favor the psychoeducational approach are concerned with the mental processes involved in learning; diagnostic and educational techniques focus on the evaluation and remediation of these processes. Carl Fenichel (1966) explains how the psychoeducational approach can be applied in the classroom.

The Ecological Approach. Ecologists are concerned with how organisms interact with their environment. Advocates of an ecological approach to education contend that children with learning or behavior problems are out of balance with their ecosystem and believe that an imbalance in one part of the system affects all the other parts. Consequently, an education or treatment program must take into consideration family, school, community, and all other systems of which the child is a part, in addition to the child's classroom. As will be seen in chapters later in this section, the ecological approach can be combined with other approaches to education. More information about the ecological approach is available in the work of Nicholas Hobbs (1966, 1974).

The Behavioral Approach. The behavioral approach is based on the work of B. F. Skinner. Behaviorists believe that all behavior is learned and that searching for the causes of behavior is futile. Behaviorists focus their attention on behaviors that can be observed, measured, and recorded. Educational programs developed by behaviorists emphasize the modification of children's behavior by the manipulation of their environment, especially through altering the effects of particular behaviors. In recent years the influence of behaviorism on special education has perhaps been greater than that of any other approach; the remainder of this introduction is devoted to a discussion of some of behaviorism's basic concepts. Additional information is available in books by Frank Hewett (1968), and Norris Haring and Richard Schiefelbusch (1976), both of whom provide good examples of the application of the behavioral approach in special education.

PRINCIPLES ASSOCIATED WITH THE BEHAVIORAL APPROACH

The application of behaviorism in special education services is generally accomplished through intervention, therapy, or instruction — generally referred to collectively as behavior modification or applied behavior analysis. Behavior modification has been used with exceptional children from the time of ancient Greece to the present, as is documented by MacMillan and Forness (1973). There are many behavior modification procedures. O'Leary and O'Leary recommend that they be considered in two groups: those which are intended to increase performance or behavior and those which are intended to decrease behavior or performance (1972, p. 26). This dichotomy is somewhat arbitrary, but it does bring to the array of available procedures an order that allows the teacher to find an appropriate procedure quickly. Quick access such as this can be very important to a teacher who has children with severe behavior problems.

PROCEDURES USED TO "INCREASE" BEHAVIORS

Let us look at the procedures identified by O'Leary and O'Leary that are used to "increase" behavior (1972, pp. 26–31).

Praise and Approval. A positive response by the teacher to a desired student behavior can increase the frequency of the behavior. The response could involve verbal praise, gestures, giving the student a star, and some other expression of approval.

Modeling. Showing or demonstrating the desired behavior and then having the student repeat the behavior is an effective teaching technique. The effect of modeling is increased when it is accompanied by praise and other expressions of approval. The behavior to be modeled can be demonstrated by either the teacher or another pupil.

Shaping. A teacher using a shaping procedure rewards successive approximations of the desired behavior, rather than waiting for the pupil to make a completely correct response. This method is more efficient than working with the child until she has completely mastered a problem, and it allows the teacher to move on to other areas of need.

Passive Shaping. A passive shaping procedure is often used with children who cannot or will not imitate or model a behavior. The teacher demonstrates the desired behavior and then actively helps the student imitate the behavior.

Token Reinforcement. Another process involves the systematic use of either tangible reinforcers, such as food, tokens, or grades, or intangible reinforcers, such as satisfaction at completing a task, or a smile or praise from the teacher. Generally, a token reinforcement system, or "economy," involves (1) rules specifying which behaviors will be rewarded and which will not; (2) a system for issuing the tokens that does not disrupt the activity that is occurring; (3) a system for giving additional backup reinforcers for particular behaviors, such as special privileges, prizes, or paraphernalia. The effectiveness of "token economics" has been well documented, but the procedure is still subject to much debate.

Self-Specification of Contingencies. Allowing children to participate in the selection of backup reinforcers in a token economy can significantly improve the economy's effectiveness. This procedure can also help the teacher determine what a particular child enjoys doing; the teacher can often use this knowledge to encourage the child to do something he does not enjoy. For example, if reading is a low preference for a child, but listening to records with earphones is a high preference, the teacher can make listening to records contingent on the child's reading appropriately. This is called contingency contracting.

Programmed Instruction. Another practice involves instructing a pupil along a preprogrammed sequence of steps. The steps are progressively sequenced from easy problems or tasks to more difficult ones. The program steps are arranged to provide the user with feedback about the completion of each step and also to provide information that can be used in the next step. Contemporary teaching curricula using programmed instruction concepts and task analysis have revolutionized some types of special education services.

Self-Reinforcement. Although self-reinforcement is often thought of as the end result of a successful behavioral programming, it does require specific attention on the part of the teacher. As the student becomes familiar with the token economy and the effects of appropriate behavior, her behavior will gradually become influenced more by self-reward than by rewards from others. In addition, the student often begins to model herself on other authority figures. If those figures have clearly defined high standards of performance, the student will often adopt similar standards for herself.

Establishing Clear Rules and Directions. In all the behavior modification procedures described it is important that rules and directions be stated clearly. Students must be able to understand rules and directions to profit from them. The relationship between the class rules and conditions for reward must be understood by both teachers and students. The development of "contracts" between teachers and students is common in many special education settings, because contracts permit classroom rules and directions to be altered to meet individual children's needs. Contracts can also be made with the entire class to help establish an effective learning environment.

PROCEDURES USED TO "DECREASE" BEHAVIORS

Now we shall examine some of the procedures for "decreasing" behavior described by O'Leary and O'Leary (1972, pp. 32–38).

Extinction. The extinction procedure involves selectively ignoring inappropriate behavior. Extinction has been used effectively in a wide variety of settings; it is especially effective when coupled with the reinforcement of appropriate behavior. However, some inappropriate behaviors (self-mutilation, aggressive acts) cannot be safely ignored.

Reinforcing Behavior Incompatible with Undesirable Behavior. Reinforcement is often used with extinction. It is relatively easy to manage. Basically, it involves analyzing the undesirable behavior to determine what behaviors would decrease the probability that the undesirable behavior would occur. For example, a child's being out of his seat without permission is undesirable, and remaining seated is incompatible with being out of one's seat. The teacher can generally decrease the frequency with which the child leaves his seat by (1) reinforcing the child when he remains seated, and (2) ignoring the child when he is out of his seat.

Soft Reprimands. Often, teachers use unobtrusive reprimands in conjunction with extinction. By keeping the reprimand between the teacher and the child the teacher reduces the chances that the child will be reinforced by increased class attention.

Time-Out. The time-out procedure has been the subject of much research. It involves removing the student to a position in which she cannot be reinforced in any way for a specified period of time. Time-out procedures may involve removing the child to an isolation room, changing the child's seat to a remote area of the classroom, or seating the child in a carrell or cubicle. The specific technique used is often determined by school policy and the availability of resources.

Relaxation. Children who are easily frustrated, agitated, or angered often benefit from being taught how to relax. A relaxed child will often exhibit fewer symptoms of emotional or behavioral disorders than one who is not relaxed.

Gradual Presentation of Fearful Stimuli in Vivo. A gradual process is frequently used to decrease or eliminate unrealistic fears or phobias. For example, a child who has a fear of school might at first be placed in real-life (in vivo) situations that don't resemble school and then systematically brought into increasingly comparable situations and reinforced for appropriate behavior at each step along the way.

Desensitization. The desensitization procedure is not commonly used with young children, but it has been used with considerable success with young adults and older individuals. The procedure consists of completely relaxing a client and then asking him to talk about situations that arouse anxiety. It has been found that after repeated sessions the client is able to control his anxiety or fears and maintain his relaxed state.

Response Cost. Commonly used in contingency management or token economy programs, the response cost procedure involves establishing rules for removing or deducting tokens or rewards for inappropriate behavior. This type of system helps the child understand that a behavior can have either a positive or a negative consequence. The student quickly learns the effects of her behavior and begins to control how she acts.

This list of applied behavior analysis methods does not include all the procedures currently in use, but it does include most of those which are important in special education. The use of these procedures, in conjunction with the increase in educational technology, has had a great effect on special education as it is practiced today.

It is important to realize that applied behavior analysis is *not* used solely to eliminate undesirable social behavior or to develop socially acceptable behavior, as many people believe. Applied behavior analysis techniques are equally effective in improving academic skills.

After returning from a two weeks vacation, I was met by Bernie, a 55 year old former resident of the BGAMR group home. During my absence he had graduated from our program and along with another former resident moved into an apartment in the community. With a smile from ear to ear he shook my hand and said, "I'm out, you know. I have an apartment and I want you to come sometime for dinner. I'm happy." . . .

Bernie, unfortunately, spent 47 years of his life in one institution or another because there simply was no place else for him. When he was referred to us in February 1976, we were told by a state official that we were wasting our time. . . .

"Chalk one up for Bernie," I thought. . . . If one restricts an individual to his home, school or work with little or no time for recreation, responsibility, challenges or the dignity of risk and trying new things, then surely the mind is not being exercised and stimulated to its full potential and will probably remain dull.

After 47 years of institutionalization, Bernie arrived at the group home, still unable to write the first letter of his name. Since this time, 2 years and 3 months later, Bernie has learned to write his name by attending adult education classes. Bernie has learned to budget his money on a week-to-week money management system. He makes up his own menus using a pictorial cookbook, does his own laundry and grocery shopping, prepares his own meals and tends to all his own personal hygiene needs. . . .

Bernie was adjudicated incompetent when he was a child and after forty-seven years, on December 20, 1977, he was restored complete citizen rights by a Fayette County judge.

Bernie has held the same job as a kitchen helper at a local hotel for nearly five years. . . . Bernie has earned his dream — respect, trust, faith, and above all his freedom and the right to be a human being just like each of us. . . . He has paid a tremendously unfair price for being mentally retarded and a little different, when all he ever needed was . . . a little faith and someone who really cared. . . .

Source: From the *Blue Grass Association for Mental Retardation News,* June-July, 1978. Reprinted by permission.

7

Mental Retardation

William H. Berdine
and A. Edward Blackhurst

William H. Berdine is an Associate Professor and Coordinator of the certification program for teachers of the trainable mentally handicapped at the University of Kentucky. He has taught classes for the mentally retarded in both primary and secondary settings. A. Edward Blackhurst is a Professor and past Chairman of the Department of Special Education at the University of Kentucky. He has taught mildly mentally retarded adolescents and was principal of a school for mentally retarded children.

As you have undoubtedly noted, remarkable changes have occurred in special education research, program development, litigation, and legislation over the past two decades. Bernie's story exemplifies one of the changes in institutional services. In the area of mental retardation, the focus of the 1960s was on providing additional services to the mildly and moderately retarded. In the later half of the 1970s, however, the focus shifted to the provision of services to the severely and profoundly retarded. This shift of attention was so extensive that it led some professionals (e.g., Haywood, 1979) to wonder, "What happened to mild and moderate retardation?"

The shift of emphasis to the severely retarded can be attributed, in part, to federal legislation. For example, the preface to the Rehabilitation Act of 1973 (PL 93-112) states that there should be a "special emphasis on services to those with the most severe handicaps." The same act also states that those with the most severe handicaps should be served first. The highest priority of PL 94-142 is on serving unserved children and the most severely handicapped who are underserved. More recently, the Comprehensive Rehabilitation Services Amendments of 1978 (PL 95-1780) adds, "Comprehensive services [should be provided] to handicapped persons who may not be ready for vocational rehabilitation" (Haywood, 1979, p. 430). The intention of recent legislation is clearly to bring the more severely handicapped into programs they were previously ineligible for.

Although this change in emphasis has brought great benefits to a part of the population that was long denied equal services, it has had a fairly negative effect on study and research concerning the mildly and moderately retarded. This is an alarming and unfortunate trend. The population of mildly and moderately retarded people is much larger than that of the severely retarded, as Haywood (1979) points out:

> On a population base of 222 million persons (which the United States Bureau of the Census estimates will be our population in 1980) we shall have 110,000 persons with I.Q.s less than 20, and 444,000 with I.Q.'s between 20 and 50, but we shall have 6,693,940 individuals with I.Q.'s between 50 and 70. Thus in 1980 there will be more than 12 times as many mentally retarded persons in the I.Q. 50 to 70 range as there will be with I.Q.s less than 50 [pp. 430–31].

The size of the mildly and moderately retarded population alone should dictate that special educators continue to devote attention to this segment of the population. The emphasis of the 1970s on the needs of the severely and profoundly retarded was undoubtedly important in focusing attention on the services provided to them. During the 1980s, however, a more evenly balanced distribution of efforts should be made, without sacrificing any of the benefits acquired during the 1960s and 1970s. In this chapter, the identification, definition, and etiology (causes) of mental retardation will be emphasized. The delivery of education services to the severely and profoundly handicapped will be covered in Chapter 10.

INTELLIGENCE AND MENTAL RETARDATION

> **You should be able to discuss intellectual assessment as it relates to the identification of mentally retarded children.**

Defining the nature of "intelligence" is a central concern of most educational endeavors for the mentally retarded. Over the years numerous definitions of intelligence have been suggested (e.g., Bruner, 1964; Cattell, 1971; Guilford, 1956; Hebb, 1942; Piaget, 1950). These definitions have ranged from the simplistic "intelligence is what is measured by intelligence tests" to the complex conceptualization of Guilford (1956), who proposed a structure that describes 120 types of intelligence.

For the special education teacher it seems appropriate to define intelligence in terms of children's interactions with their environments: how well they meet the demands made on them by their school, family, community, and other social situations. A person who is consistently unable to meet those demands without some form of special assistance is generally considered mentally retarded. To be classified as "mentally retarded," a child must be unable to demonstrate behavior based on intellectual functioning that is appropriate for that person's age or social situation (Salvia, 1978). To put it another way, the mentally retarded are incompetent in behaviors that their society believes to be indicative of intellectual functioning.

It is important to distinguish between intellectual incompetence and other forms of behavioral incompetence. For example, blind children may be incapable of performing some academic or motor tasks at the age considered normal for seeing children, but this is due to their visual impairment, not to an intellectual defect. Mentally retarded children may be willing to perform a task and have all of the necessary senses, but be unable to perform it even with additional training. The concept of incompetence is also important in distinguishing the mentally retarded from those with deviant behavior. For example, a mentally retarded child may be willing to perform tasks appropriate for her age but be unable to do so. On the other hand, a child with a behavior disorder may be able to perform the same tasks but be unwilling to do so. Incompetence in adapting to the demands of the environment is another factor to be considered when distinguishing retarded children from those with normal intelligence.

ASSESSMENT OF INTELLECTUAL RETARDATION

For educational purposes, mental retardation is generally considered a child's inadequacy in performing certain behaviors that society values and that are appropriate for the child's age group. Intelligence tests are used to assess the intellectual ability that theoretically determines whether a person can perform educational tasks. The forms of different intelligence tests vary widely, but the majority are standardized. A standardized test is one that was developed and tried out on a group of children who all received the same instructions, who took the test under the same conditions, and whose responses were all interpreted the same way. The test items, which are devised by the test developers, are designed to determine the level of some aspect of intellectual functioning. If a particular culture believes that the test measures qualities that are important for that culture, the tests become a generally accepted means of measuring intellectual functioning in that culture.

The most frequently used intelligence tests yield two types of scores, an intelligence quotient (IQ), and a mental age (MA). Most of the commonly used IQ tests are designed such that the average IQ is 100. In theory, this means that if a test such as the Stanford-Binet Intelligence Scale (Terman and Merrill, 1973) were administered to a large number of children, the test scores would range from very low to very high, but the average, or mean, score would be 100. If the scores were plotted on a graph, the result would be a bell-shaped curve, called the normal curve (see Figure 7-1). A statistical computation yields a figure known as the standard deviation (SD), which can be used to determine where a person's

Figure 7-1
The Normal Curve

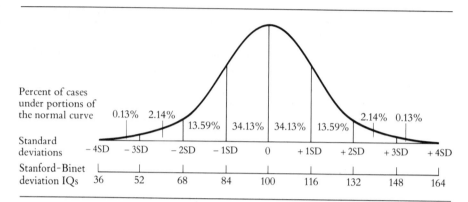

Percent of cases
under portions of
the normal curve

| 0.13% | 2.14% | 13.59% | 34.13% | 34.13% | 13.59% | 2.14% | 0.13% |

Standard
deviations

−4SD   −3SD   −2SD   −1SD   0   +1SD   +2SD   +3SD   +4SD

Stanford-Binet
deviation IQs   36   52   68   84   100   116   132   148   164

score falls in relation to others in the population. For example, the standard deviation for the Stanford-Binet is 16. If you look at Figure 7-1, you will see that one SD below the mean is 84. A person who receives a score of 100 on the Stanford-Binet is average; about 50 percent of the population scored below him and 50 percent scored above him. Between each pair of SD cutoff points is written the percentage of the population that falls between them. By starting at the left of the normal curve, you can estimate the number of people who fall below a particular score by adding the percentages. Thus, the child who scored 84 would have a score that was higher than about 16½ percent of the population.

The scores shown in Figure 7-1 represent plus or minus four standard deviations from the mean. In theory, however, the scores could go into infinity, because intelligence does not have absolute limits. Intelligence is viewed by most developers of intelligence tests as a continuum of abilities and not really a discrete or finite entity.

The determination of a score below which children are considered retarded is an issue of great social, political, and educational concern. As mentioned earlier, intellectual ability — behavior considered socially valuable and appropriate — is defined by the predominant cultural group, who as a result determine what will be considered normal intelligence as well. In special education, the IQ score of 67, adopted by the American Association on Mental Deficiency (Grossman, 1977) is generally considered the score below which children are described as mildly mentally retarded. Some variation in cutoff scores is found among different intelligence tests. For example, the standard deviation for the Wechsler Intelligence Scale for Children (WISC) is 15, and the cutoff for retardation is 69 (Wechsler, 1974). Table 7-1 illustrates the cutoff scores established by the American Association on Mental Deficiency (AAMD) for different levels of

Table 7-1
IQ Scores for Different Levels of Mental Retardation

Levels of Retardation	Stanford-Binet IQ Score (SD = 16)	Wechsler Intelligence Scale for Children IQ Score (SD = 15)
Mild	67–52	69–55
Moderate	51–36	54–40
Severe	35–20	39–25
Profound	19 and lower	24 and lower

Source: Grossman, H., *Manual on Terminology and Classification in Mental Retardation*, AAMD, 1977. Reprinted by permission.

mental retardation. Notice that the scores are different because of variations in the test's standard deviations.

PROBLEMS WITH USING IQ SCORES

The use of IQ test scores in education presents a number of problems.

1. To provide useful scores a test must have been tried out on a large enough normative group to reflect the cultural, social, and economic variables that affect the children in a given classroom.
2. The items in a particular test may measure a relatively small variety of behaviors. The IQ score derived from such a test should be considered in the context of the test items and the norm group.
3. A test score may be inaccurate and may not reflect a person's actual level of intellectual functioning.
4. An IQ score should be considered only in conjunction with information about the child's chronological age, her home life, the resources of her school, and other environmental variables.
5. An IQ score is not very useful for planning the education of a particular child. The knowledge that one pupil has an IQ score of 70 and another has an IQ score of 75 does not help a teacher develop appropriate instruction.

Teachers should not overemphasize the importance of IQ scores. The major function of determining the IQs of retarded children is to identify them and place them in special programs to obtain the funds necessary for operating them.

In spite of the limitations in their use, intelligence test scores remain one of the most reliable types of data on children's performances, and they will probably continue to be used in the assessment of mental retardation. Today, however, most professional organizations such as the American Association on Mental Deficiency require that IQ test scores be corroborated with assessment information on adaptive behavior.

MEASURING ADAPTIVE BEHAVIOR

The importance of adaptive behavior in determining whether a person should be diagnosed as mentally retarded has been recognized in the past ten years. Adaptive behavior can be defined as "the effectiveness or degree with which an individual meets the standards of personal independence and social responsibility expected for age and cultural group" (Grossman, 1977, p. 11). Salvia (1978) notes that industrialized societies value such things as academics, good interpersonal relationships, independence, and social skills.

Intelligence and adaptive behavior are related, but how closely and in what ways are not clearly understood. Intellectual functioning and adaptive behavior levels can change, and a change in either of them can bring about a change in the other. Furthermore, people at the same level of intellectual functioning may be at different levels of adaptive behavior (Grossman, 1977). All diagnoses of mental retardation should take into account both intellectual functioning and adaptive behavior.

The AAMD recognizes four levels of adaptive behavior impairment — mild, moderate, severe, and profound. You will notice that these degrees of impairment are described with the same terms as intelligence. Adaptive behavior impairment is generally considered the result of problems in maturation, learning capacity, and social adjustment (Sloan and Birch, 1955).

Adaptive behavior is very difficult to measure. Assessment of this characteristic presents all the problems encountered in assessing intelligence and additional problems caused by subjectivity in interpreting responses. The criterion against which the performance of a particular child is measured is the behavioral level considered appropriate to a specific age level. Mentally retarded children typically exhibit deficits in both quantity and quality of adaptive behavior. Parents and other family members are potentially more likely to make biased reports, which the professional needs to be prepared to account for.

Edgar Doll (1953) developed a system to measure adaptive behavior. This scale, called the Vineland Social Maturity Scale (VSMS), assesses adaptive behavior in eight areas: general self-help, eating self-help, dressing self-help, self-help direction, occupation, communication, locomotion, and socialization. The Vineland yields a social quotient (SQ) that can be interpreted in the same fashion as an IQ and provides a social age (SA) as well. Thus, it is theoretically possible to determine whether a person's adaptive behavior is at the same level as that of other people of the same chronological age. The mean score of the VSMS is 100.

The most widely used measure of adaptive behavior is the revised AAMD Adaptive Behavior Scale (ABS). The AAMD-ABS is probably the most comprehensive, thoroughly researched instrument available to the special educator (Nihira, Foster, Shellhars, & Leland, 1974). There are two parts to the AAMD-ABS, the components of which are delineated in Table 7-2. The ABS does not produce a single score such as an SQ or SA. The individual's performance scores are recorded on a profile sheet (Figure 7-2), which permits one to note a child's strengths and weaknesses.

Neither an intelligence test score nor an adaptive behavior assessment score is comprehensive enough to be used as a sole criterion for determining that a child is mentally retarded. The use of a single measure not only would be unwise professionally, it is illegal under the provisions of PL 94-142. The best procedure

Figure 7-2
AAMD-ABS Profile

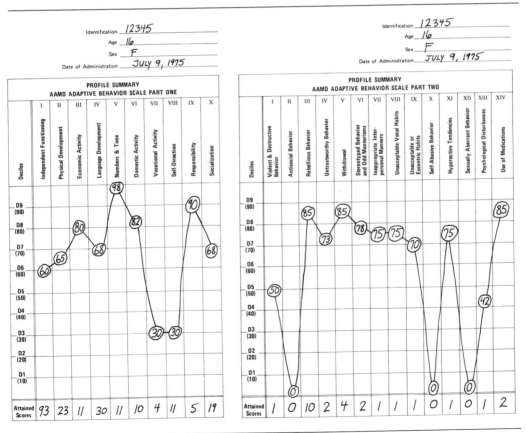

Table 7-2
Components of the AAMD Adaptive Behavior Scale

Part One	*Part Two*

I. Independent Functioning
  A. Eating
  B. Toilet Use
  C. Cleanliness
  D. Appearance
  E. Care of Clothing
  F. Dressing and Undressing
  G. Travel
  H. General Independent Functioning
II. Physical Development
  A. Sensory Development
  B. Motor Development
III. Economic Activity
  A. Money Handling and Budgeting
  B. Shopping Skills
IV. Language Development
  A. Expression
  B. Comprehension
  C. Social Language Development
V. Numbers and Time
VI. Domestic Activity
  A. Cleaning
  B. Kitchen Duties
  C. Other Domestic Activities
VII. Vocational Activity
VIII. Self-Direction
  A. Initiative
  B. Perseverance
  C. Leisure Time
IX. Responsibility
X. Socialization
	I. Violent and Destructive Behavior
	II. Antisocial Behavior
	III. Rebellious Behavior
	IV. Untrustworthy Behavior
	V. Withdrawal
	VI. Stereotyped Behavior and Odd Mannerisms
	VII. Inappropriate Interpersonal Manners
	VIII. Unacceptable Vocal Habits
	IX. Unacceptable or Eccentric Habits
	X. Self-abusive Behavior
	XI. Hyperactive Tendencies
	XII. Sexually Aberrant Behavior
	XIII. Psychological Disturbances
	XIV. Use of Medications

Source: ABS Manual (Fogleman, 1975, pp. 6–7).

is to use data from a variety of sources, including assessments of intelligence and adaptive behavior, anecdotal records from teachers, an analysis of the home and family situation, direct observation of the child's behavior in the classroom, and measures of school achievement.

Mercer (1979) has recently developed a system that he says can be used to interrelate all the variables considered in determining whether a person is mentally retarded. This system, called the System of Multicultural Pluralistic Assessment (SOMPA), objectively correlates measures of intelligence and adaptive behavior and statistically relates them to the child's cultural background; it also takes the child's physical health and abilities into consideration. The instrument yields an estimated learning potential (ELP) for each child. If the SOMPA is shown through research and validation studies to be valid, it will be an invaluable aid in the assessment of retarded children.

PROBE 7-1
Intelligence and Mental Retardation

1. T F   A diagnosis of mental retardation should never be made solely on the basis of an intelligence test.

2. The popularly used tests of intelligence generally report a summary of performance in the form of an _____ score.

3. The AAMD requires that a child's _____ and _____ be considered in diagnosing mental retardation.

4. What is the range of IQ scores for each of the following levels of retardation, according to the AAMD? Assume that the Stanford-Binet IQ test is being used, and disregard adaptive behavior considerations.

   Mild   _____

   Moderate   _____

   Severe   _____

   Profound   _____

5. T F   The AAMD-ABS yields an SQ and SA.

6. T F   All IQ tests have a mean score of 100 and a standard deviation of 16.

7. List four problems involved in the use and interpretation of IQ tests.

   a. _____

   b. _____

   c. _____

   d. _____

8. T   F   A special education teacher could not teach if he did not have the IQ scores of the mentally retarded children in the class.

9. Define adaptive behavior. _____

_____

_____

10. What is a problem encountered in measuring adaptive behavior that is not encountered in measuring intelligence?

_____

_____

11. List four components of adaptive behavior.

a. _____

b. _____

c. _____

d. _____

DEFINITIONS OF MENTAL RETARDATION

You should be able to define mental retardation.

The development of a satisfactory definition of mental retardation has proven to be a difficult task for several reasons. There is little agreement about the criteria that should be used to assess intelligence and adaptive behavior; measuring instruments are imprecise; and the needs of the different professional groups concerned with the mentally retarded vary widely.

The mentally retarded have educational, medical, psychological, and sociological problems, which require the services of teachers, physicians, psychologists, and social workers. Each of these professional groups considers the problems of the mentally retarded from a different perspective; and they rarely share a common training philosophy or similar goals. MacMillan has offered a schematic representation of the problem, illustrated in Figure 7-3. Only in a few instances — represented by the shaded area — will the four professional groups agree on a definition of mental retardation or on a preferred program of education or rehabilitation.

The problems between professional groups are not caused by disagreement

Figure 7-3
The Impact of Definitions of Mental
Retardation that Emphasize Different
Sets of Criteria

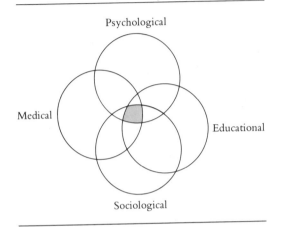

about the essential nature and characteristics of retardation; they are the result, rather, of the different groups' interest in some aspects of retardation and not in others. This can lead to conflicts that adversely affect the services offered to the retarded. Professionals from different fields should attempt to discover areas of common concern about which they can communicate, while retaining the orientation that best serves their own particular interests. Because of the different interests and orientations of the professional groups involved, it is unlikely that a universally acceptable definition will be developed.

According to MacMillan (1977) a definition of mental retardation should meet three criteria. First, the conditions that would result in a person's being classified as retarded should be specifically stated. Second, every retarded person must share the elements described in the definition. Third, those who are not classified as retarded must fail to exhibit at least one of the elements in the definition. For the educator, a definition of mental retardation should offer clear criteria that could be used to identify retarded children who need special education services.

TRADITIONAL DEFINITIONS OF MENTAL RETARDATION

Most early definitions of mental retardation did not offer precise criteria for determining whether or not a person was mentally retarded. This made it difficult to assess retardation accurately, particularly when the individual was only mildly retarded. The early definitions also tended to focus on adult behavior, and those who worked with children often had difficulty adjusting the definition to apply to a younger population.

Early definitions of mental retardation often used the terms "amentia" or "mental deficiency" to refer to retardation that was not associated with mental illness or brain injury. The various levels of retardation were differentiated with terms that are considered degrading today and are no longer used, such as moron, imbecile, idiot, feebleminded, dull, and mental defective. A comparison of these terms with those now in use has been made by Kauffman and Payne (1975).

The definitions proposed by Tredgold (1937), Doll (1941), and Kanner (1957), which are considered traditional, will now be discussed.

Amentia. One of the most commonly used definitions of mental retardation of its time was Tredgold's definition of amentia (1937):

> a state of incomplete mental development of such a kind and degree that the individual is incapable of adapting himself to the normal environment of his fellows in such a way as to maintain existence independently of supervision, control, or external support [p. 4].

Tredgold's definition emphasized the adaptive behavior of adults and their inability to independently cope with the environment. The source of the person's incompetence was thought to be an internal dysfunction that led to the underdevelopment of mental abilities.

Social Incompetence. Doll's (1941) definition of mental retardation stressed social or interpersonal incompetence, as did the definitions of several other researchers. Doll was one of the first people to realize that social incompetence among retarded persons could and often did emerge in early childhood. It was Doll who developed the Vineland Social Maturity Scale in an attempt to measure social competence, as you may recall. He also reported that mental retardation was not a disease, and was therefore incurable. Doll claimed that children who were identified as mentally retarded and were later found to be functioning normally had been initially diagnosed incorrectly. Doll called such cases instances of "pseudofeeblemindedness." He also argued that mental retardation originated in the person's constitution, a theory that discounted the causative effect of the environment. (The relationship between heredity and environment will be discussed in the section of this chapter concerned with etiology.)

Doll offered a multicriteria definition as an alternative to the trend of that time of defining retardation according to a single criterion, such as an IQ score. He stated:

> We observe that six criteria by statement or implementation have been generally considered essential to an adequate definition and concept. These are (1) social incompetence, (2) due to mental subnormality; (3) which has been developmentally arrested, (4) which obtain at maturity, (5) is of constitutional origin and (6) is essentially incurable [p. 215].

Doll's definition differed little from earlier definitions on the subjects of social incompetency and mental subnormality, but his statements on development and the constitutional origins and incurability of mental retardation were a departure from the thinking of his contemporaries.

Multiple Types of Mental Retardation. Kanner (1948) identified three types of "feeble-mindedness." Different types or levels of retardation were described by other researchers, but Kanner was one of the first to consider the influence of a retarded person's environment in defining retardation. In describing the three types, Kanner stated:

> The [absolute] type consists of individuals so markedly deficient in their cognitive, emotional, and constructively conative potentialities that they would stand out as defectives in any existing culture. . . . They would be equally helpless and ill-adapted in a society of savants and in a society of savages. They are not only deficient intellectually, but deficient in every sphere of mentation.
>
> The [relative] type is made up of individuals whose limitations are definitely related to the standards of the particular cultures which surrounds them. In less complex, less intellectually centered societies they would have no trouble in attaining and retaining equality of realizable ambitions. Some might even be capable of gaining superiority by virtue of assets other than those measured by intelligence tests. . . . They could make successful peasants, hunters, fishermen, tribal dancers. They can, in our own society, achieve success as farm hands, factory workers, miners, waitresses, charwomen. But, in our midst their shortcomings, which would remain unrecognized and therefore non-existent in the awareness of a more primitive cultural body, appear as soon as scholastic curricula demand completion in spelling, history, geography, long division and other preparations deemed essential for the tasks of feeding chickens, collecting garbage, and wrapping bundles in a department store. . . . It is preferable to speak of such people as intellectually inadequate rather than mentally deficient [Kanner, 1957, pp. 70–71].
>
> [The third type is] "apparent" feeblemindedness in which existing potentialities for the acquisition or reproduction of tested information have not been realized fully because of lack of opportunity, physical handicaps . . ., remediable but not as yet remedial specific disabilities, temporary educational blocking, or inadequacies of the person who administers the test [Kanner, 1948, p. 374].

Kanner's definitions mark the beginning of the progression that resulted in the definitions currently used by diagnostic professionals. Kanner's description of "absolute" retardation closely resembles the current definition of moderate to severe retardation, whereas his "relative" type resembles what is now considered mild retardation. His "apparent" classification covers some of the problems now considered learning disabilities, which will be discussed in Chapter 8. It is interesting that Kanner was drawing attention to testing errors in 1948. Inappropriate educational assessment and intelligence testing have resulted in a considerable amount of litigation during the past two decades.

CONTEMPORARY DEFINITIONS OF MENTAL RETARDATION

Two definitions of mental retardation are currently being widely discussed. These are the behavioral definition (Bijou, 1966), and the definition proposed by the American Association on Mental Deficiency (Grossman, 1977), which is the most widely accepted.

Behavioral Definition of Mental Retardation. The articulation of the behavioral definition is generally attributed to Bijou (1966), who stated that "a retarded individual is one who has a limited repertory of behavior shaped by events that constitute his history" (p. 2). In his definition Bijou emphasizes observable behavior and pays little or no attention to nonobservable internal mental processes. Educators who subscribe to the behavioral definition emphasize training retarded children to adapt to and cope with their environment with the skills they possess.

Problems with a Behavioral Definition. The behavioral definition of mental retardation quite often presents problems to special educators who have not been trained in applied behavior analysis. Neisworth and Smith (1978) point out that a major shortcoming of the approach is its failure to quantify what is meant by a limited behavioral repertoire. In other words, the definition does not describe the point at which the limitations in a person's repertoire of behaviors indicate that she is retarded.

MacMillan and Forness (1973) point out that the behavioral model does not take into account some of the concepts that were developed by Piaget and other developmental psychologists. Nevertheless, the behavioral approach has important implications for teaching retarded children, and many educators subscribe to it.

The American Association on Mental Deficiency Definition. The revised 1977 AAMD definition has found the widest acceptance of any, but even this definition is not universally accepted. The AAMD definition has been revised frequently over the past two decades (Grossman, 1973, 1977; Heber, 1959, 1961); in its current form, it represents a compromise between the needs of those who require statistical objectivity (e.g., IQ test scores) and those who require environmental performance data (e.g., adaptive behavior assessment). This is the 1977 AAMD definition of mental retardation:

> Mental retardation refers to significantly subaverage general intellectual functioning existing concurrently with deficits in adaptive behavior and manifested during the developmental period. (Grossman, 1977, p. 5)

The key terms in the AAMD definition can be defined as follows:

— "General intellectual functioning" refers to the results obtained from the administration of an individualized intelligence test.
— A "significantly subaverage" score is one that is more than two standard deviations below the mean for the test.
— "Adaptive behavior" is the effectiveness with which an individual meets the standards of personal independence and social responsibility expected for his age and cultural group.
— The "developmental period" is the period between the child's birth and tenth birthday.

The rationale for including IQ scores as a criterion in the AAMD definition, even though the use of IQ scores for diagnostic purposes had been widely criticized, has been explained by Grossman:

> For several reasons, the upper I.Q. limits (67 on the Stanford-Binet and 69 on the WISC) are proposed as only guidelines rather than rigid limits. The assessment of intelligence is subject to some variation because of such factors as test construction, circumstances of administration and measurement errors. Despite these limitations, intelligence test scores represent more reliable and valid measures of ability and performance than do either adaptive behavior measures or clinical judgment [1977, p. 12].

It should be noted that the AAMD definition described mental retardation in terms of behavioral performance. The causes of mental retardation are not considered, and reference is not made to the disorder's prognosis for change. The definition takes into account the roles of intelligence and adaptive behavior.

PROBE 7-2
Definitions of Mental Retardation

1. The most widely accepted definition of mental retardation is that of the
   a. APA
   b. AMA
   c. AAMD
   d. CEC
   e. ABS

2. What were the three types of mental retardation identified by Kanner?

   a. _____

   b. _____

   c. _____

3. Write the definition of mental retardation proposed by the American Association of Mental Deficiency.

_____

_____

_____

4. A significantly subaverage score is one that is _____ standard deviations below the mean on a standardized test of intelligence.

5. The developmental period is the period between the child's _____ and _____ .

6. What is Bijou's behavioral definition of mental retardation?

_____

_____

7. For the special educator, what is the principal value of a behavioral definition?

_____

8. What is one criticism of the behavioral definition?

_____

9. T   F   Doll's major contribution to a definition of mental retardation is related to the area of social competence.

EDUCATIONAL CHARACTERISTICS OF THE MENTALLY RETARDED PUPIL

You should be able to describe the education and learning characteristics of mentally retarded individuals.

The mentally retarded student almost always presents the same kinds of learning problems as the child who is developing normally. The retarded pupil learns reading skills, motor skills, and other skills in the same fashion as other pupils, but the characteristics of her learning may be different in three areas: the rate of acquisition of skills, the generalization and transfer of recently acquired skills, and paying attention to tasks.

Retarded children develop more slowly than other children. They acquire and use the same skills as children who are developing normally, but they may acquire the skills at a later age. Although skills are developed in the same manner as they are in normal children, the final level of mastery of a skill may not be as refined as it is in other children.

The ability to generalize recently learned skills to new situations is another problem area for the retarded. Generalization and transfer training is an important part of education programs for the retarded, regardless of the pupils' classifications. In educational programs for the moderately and severely retarded, it is not unusual to require the pupil to demonstrate mastery of a skill (1) in reaction to, or in the presence of, at least three different persons; (2) in at least three different natural settings; (3) in response to at least three different sets of instructional materials; and (4) to at least three different appropriate language cues (Brown, Nietupski, and Hamre-Nietupski (1976).

Teachers often find that mentally retarded pupils do not pay attention as well as normal pupils. The retarded pupils' lack of attention can be attributed to their inability to focus on the relevant aspects of a task (House and Zeaman, 1958; Zeaman and House, 1963). The retarded child will require more frequent and lengthier opportunities to practice a task before he can master it. Once the retarded child has mastered the task, however, he can perform it at a rate similar to that of nonretarded children. Zeaman and House (1963) suggest that discrimination problems can be reduced through (1) the use of three-dimensional objects; (2) the sequencing of tasks from the easy to the more difficult; (3) emphasis on the relevant aspects of tasks; (4) increased novelty of the negative and positive stimuli; (5) the avoiding of failure; and (6) establishment of a "set" to attend to relevant dimensions.

Attention problems are more serious in severely retarded children and in those who have multiple handicaps. Baumeister (1967) suggests that the teacher provide specific instruction in how to persevere in problem solving. Turnure (1970) stresses that the retarded should be taught to use contextual and task cues rather than environmental cues in solving problems.

CURRICULAR IMPLICATIONS

The curricula designed for the three most commonly used educational classifications of mental retardation (educable mentally retarded, trainable mentally retarded, and severely/profoundly mentally retarded) differ in both the difficulty of skills taught and the actual skills or subjects covered. Mentally retarded pupils' educational needs vary so greatly that it is virtually impossible to design a single curriculum for one particular subgroup of retarded children. Children at all levels of functioning should be educated for maximal adaptive competency.

The classroom teacher should determine the individual needs of the retarded pupil and use whatever curriculum she can to meet those needs.

CLASSIFICATION OF THE MENTALLY RETARDED

You should be able to describe the different systems used to classify mentally retarded children.

Over the years a number of systems have been used to classify mentally retarded children. Several of these systems have been alluded to in previous sections of this chapter, where terms such as mild, moderate, severe, profound, and absolute, relative, and apparent were used to refer to diagnostic categories.

Gelof reported in 1963 that twenty-three classification systems were being used in English-speaking countries alone. Classification is necessary because the retarded are such a heterogeneous group. Placing those with common characteristics in categories makes communications among professionals more productive. It is also assumed that appropriate classification leads to placement in appropriate treatment and educational programs.

There have been three primary systems of classification, according to etiology, clinical type, and severity of symptoms.

CLASSIFICATION ACCORDING TO ETIOLOGY

It has at different periods been fashionable to classify mentally retarded children according to the cause of their retardation. A number of etiological classification systems simply divided the children into two groups: those for whom a cause of the retardation could be identified, and those for whom a cause could not be identified. Some of the terms used during the past fifty years to classify known and unknown etiologies are given in Table 7–3.

These early etiological classification systems were useless for educational purposes and were often considered offensive by parents. Imagine being told that your child had "garden-variety mental retardation," or that his retardation was "familial in nature."

The cultural-familial classification is still used by educators who believe that mental retardation is often caused by a combination of environmental and hereditary factors. This belief, called the *interaction* hypothesis, is based on the assumption that mental retardation of unknown origin is caused by biological weaknesses and environmental deprivation. Almost all cases of cultural-familial retardation are found in severely economically depressed communities, and many professionals attribute them to the effects of malnutrition and other dietary

Table 7-3
Classification by Etiology

Known Etiology		*Unknown Etiology*	
Extrinsic	Tredgold, 1937	Intrinsic	Tredgold, 1908
Pathological	Lewis, 1933	Subcultural	Lewis, 1933
Exogenous	Strauss and Lehtinen, 1947	Endogenous	Strauss and Lehtinen, 1947
		Garden variety	Sarason, 1953
		Cultural-familial	Zigler, 1967

problems in combination with the psychological effects of poverty. The results of research into the effects of sociocultural factors on intellectual performance are inconclusive. The data do show that environmental factors such as poverty can seriously affect the intellectual development of children, and there is some evidence that heredity sometimes limits intellectual development. The environment a child grows up in clearly influences whether or not she achieves her maximum hereditary potential, a fact that has significant implications for early childhood and parent education.

Retarded children are still classified according to etiology by physicians and psychologists. The AAMD *Manual on Terminology and Classification on Mental Retardation* lists ten medical classifications of mental retardation (Grossman, 1977), including classifications according to the following causes: infections and intoxicants, trauma (injury), metabolism or nutrition, brain disease, conditions due to unknown prenatal influence, chromosomal abnormality, gestational disorders, psychiatric disorders, environmental influences, and others. Many of these causes will be explained in the section of this chapter on etiology.

CLASSIFICATION ACCORDING TO CLINICAL TYPE

Retarded children are also classified according to the clinical type of their retardation. In this classification system an attempt is made to separate the symptoms of the retardation from its causes. Clinical type classification systems are also used primarily by physicians.

The cause of a particular clinical type of retardation may or may not be known. What is more, it is possible that within a given clinical classification the causes of some children's retardation will be known, and the causes of the retardation of others, unknown. For example, some types of cretinism (a thyroid deficiency) are caused by genetic problems, and other types are caused by a lack of iodine in the diet. Children with all these types exhibit similar symptoms, making the identification of the cause difficult.

The word "syndrome" is often used in discussions of classifications according to clinical type. A syndrome is a cluster or constellation of symptoms. Perhaps the most common, with respect to mental retardation, is Down's syndrome, which will be discussed in the section on etiology.

Systems that classify children according to clinical type are of little use to educators. The wide variety of conditions and behaviors that characterize mentally retarded childrem make it impossible to fit them neatly into classifications made in this manner. Most children for whom this classification system is appropriate have distinct physical symptoms that are readily observable by the physician or diagnostician.

CLASSIFICATION ACCORDING TO SEVERITY OF SYMPTOMS

The earliest system that classified retardation according to the severity of its symptoms was developed by the American Association for the Study of the Feebleminded (later to become the American Association on Mental Deficiency) at the turn of the century. This organization used the term "moron" to denote those with IQ scores between 50 and 75; "imbeciles" were those with IQs between 25 and 50; and "idiots" had IQs below 25. Although this derogatory terminology has been eliminated from the professional literature, retarded children are still classified according to the severity of their deficits in intellect and adaptive behavior. You will remember the AAMD classified levels of retardation as mild, moderate, severe, and profound, according to their IQ scores, the number of standard deviations that they fall below the mean on intelligence tests, and their levels of adaptive behavior.

The classification system of the AAMD is the system currently used most widely by diagnosticians, and a system of educational classification that parallels the AAMD categories has evolved. Smith (1971) describes these categories as "educable mentally retarded," "trainable mentally retarded," and "severely and profoundly retarded." (The term "handicapped" is frequently substituted for the term "retarded.") The mildly retarded are called educable and the moderately retarded, trainable. The severely and profoundly retarded categories are the same under both systems.

Although IQ scores are usually one of the criteria used to differentiate the educable mentally retarded (EMR), trainable mentally retarded (TMR), and the severely/profoundly retarded (S/PR), the major difference among these groups for special educators is in their educational needs. Children in different categories require different types of educational programs. As a result, schools set up separate classes and programs for children in different classifications and teachers are trained and certified to work with children at a particular level of functioning. This classification system is currently the most useful one for special education programming.

PROBLEMS WITH CLASSIFICATION SYSTEMS

Each of the classification systems just discussed presents problems. Smith (1971) described three problems encountered in attempts to classify mentally retarded children: "First, one is never able to gain total agreement between people on which dimensions or factors should be classified. . . . A second problem . . . is that of deciding on upper and lower boundaries within subgroups. . . . A third . . . is in the assignment of individuals to a category" (pp. 12–13).

Problems in deciding what program a child should be placed in are particularly difficult when a child is near the cutoff point between the EMR and TMR classifications. Distinctions between the TMR and the S/PR are generally easier to make, but these too can present problems when one is dealing with children in the upper range of the S/PR classification and the lower range of the TMR classification.

It could be argued that it shouldn't matter what category a child is placed in, because the goal should always be to raise the child to a higher level of functioning. As a practical matter, however, it does make a difference, because almost all special education programs provide different kinds of education to those who have been classified as EMR and those who have been classified as TMR. Programs for the EMR generally focus on academic skills such as reading, arithmetic, language, and vocational training. These basic skill areas are taught to prepare the EMR child for independent living. The program for TMR children, on the other hand, generally focuses on the development of self-help skills and the survival skills needed for communication and coping with the demands of a community. The TMR child is prepared for living in a supervised environment and employment in facilities such as sheltered workshops. Placing a child in a program for the trainable mentally retarded would be a grave error if the child was capable of functioning in a program for the educable mentally retarded.

As you will have noted, it is extremely important that decisions about the classification of retarded children be made cautiously. Children should be classified only when classification leads to the development of an appropriate educational program that will meet the needs of the child involved.

INCIDENCE AND PREVALENCE

> **You should be able to describe the incidence and prevalence of mental retardation.**

It is important to know the number of retarded children in our culture to plan for the provision of services, to obtain funding, and to estimate the number of teachers and other professionals needed to serve them.

The prevalence of mentally retarded individuals in our society is difficult to determine accurately. An actual census would be prohibitively expensive. The process of obtaining accurate figures is complicated by differing definitions, public apathy, and the reluctance to label a child as mentally retarded. As a result of these problems, estimates are based on studies of various communities; the results are extrapolated to cover the entire population.

The process of estimating prevalence itself presents many problems. Opinion about the best way to conduct a study varies, and different studies have used different criteria for mental retardation. The situation is complicated by the many geographic, cultural, and social factors that influence estimates. Finding a population that is sufficiently large and that reflects the composition of the entire population is also a problem. These many variables have resulted in prevalence estimates varying from 0.6 percent to 15 percent of the population.

CURRENT ESTIMATES OF MENTAL RETARDATION

Although the actual number of mentally retarded individuals in the population is not known, the consensus is that the *incidence* of mental retardation in the population is 3 percent, and the *prevalence,* 1 percent (Tarjan, Wright, Eyman, and Kiernan, 1973). This means that about 1000 people in a city of 100,000 are mentally retarded. The one percent prevalence estimate has been corroborated in studies conducted by Birch, Richardson, Baird, Horobin, and Illsley (1970); Heber (1970); and by Mercer (1973), who actually conducted a census of a city of 100,000 people.

Many people mistakenly believe that the 3 percent figure is the prevalence of mental retardation. This figure gained credence from reports of the President's Task Force on the Mentally Retarded (1970). As MacMillan (1977) points out, "There is reasonably firm evidence that three percent of newborns in this country will at some time in their lives be diagnosed as mentally retarded. But it is risky to extrapolate from this evidence the conclusion that at any point in time three percent of the population of the United States is mentally retarded" (p. 62). Mercer (1973) pointed out that a one-dimensional definition of mental retardation (e.g., IQ scores only) might yield a prevalence rate approaching 3 percent. The use of multidimensional definitions that include both IQ and adaptive behavior, however, yields a prevalence rate of roughly one percent.

Insofar as the prevalence of different levels of retardation is concerned, Dunn (1973) and Penrose (1966) estimate that the ratio of EMR to TMR to S/PR is 12:3:1, or 75%:20%:5%. This means that of a hundred identified mentally retarded children in the population, seventy-five can be expected to be in the educable range, twenty would be in the trainable range, and five would be in the severely/profoundly retarded range. This ratio was fairly well confirmed by Mercer (1973) in her study of the community of 100,000 people.

PROBE 7-3
Classifications, Incidence, and Prevalence of Mental Retardation

1. List the three major systems used to classify mentally retarded children.

   a. _____

   b. _____

   c. _____

2. *Matching*

   _____ Severely/profoundly   a. EMR

           retarded   b. TMR

   _____ Moderately retarded   c. S/PR

   _____ Mildly retarded

3. Cite two problems in the use of classification systems for retarded children.

   a. _____

   b. _____

4. List the three categories in the classification system that are most useful for special education programming.

   a. _____

   b. _____

   c. _____

5. What is a syndrome? _____

6. T   F   Retarded children should be classified only when classification leads to the development of an appropriate educational program.

7. Incidence is _____

8. Prevalence is _____

9. In a community of 200,000 the projected prevalence of retardation would be _____ percent.

10. In number 9, _____ children would be classified as EMR, _____ as TMR, and _____ as S/PR.

11. T   F   One can place great faith in the use of incidence figures for planning services for the mentally retarded for any given community.

CAUSES AND PREVENTION OF RETARDATION

You should be able to discuss the major causes of mental retardation.

For teachers, the cause of retardation in a particular child is of little importance. The teacher should be concerned more with the child's behavior and other characteristics than with the causes of his retardation. Why, then, have we included a discussion of causes? There are at least two reasons. First, as a teacher you will encounter a number of the terms and diagnostic labels in diagnostic reports, particularly medical ones. Second, you should be able to answer the questions of parents and other lay people. A knowledge of causes will make you a better rounded professional, even if the information is not directly applicable to teaching.

More than 250 causes of mental retardation have been identified. It's hard to believe, but these causes account for only about 10 percent of the cases of mental retardation. In the remaining 90 percent the physical or medical cause of the retardation cannot be pinpointed (Maloney and Ward, 1979). More detailed information on the causes of retardation is available in the texts by MacMillan (1977), Neisworth and Smith (1978), and Robinson and Robinson (1976).

GENETIC IRREGULARITIES

A review of some of the basic concepts of genetics is in order before we proceed to our discussion of retardation caused by genetic problems.

Genes are the basic units of heredity. They direct and control the processes of growth and development that occur in each of our cells. A defect in a gene can interrupt the biochemical processes that occur in the cells, which can in turn affect certain physical and mental characteristics.

The genes are located in chromosomes, of which every body cell has forty-six. At the moment of conception, twenty-three chromosomes from the male sperm cell and twenty-three from the female egg cell are passed on to form a new cell of forty-six chromosomes, which then begins to divide and ultimately forms a new human being.

The genes are arranged along the chromosomes almost like matched strings of beads. When the chromosomes pair up at conception, the genes from both parents that relate to eye color, hair color, etc., are matched up with one another. A dominant gene generally determines a characteristic, regardless of the gene that it is matched up with on its paired chromosome. A recessive gene determines a characteristic only when it is matched up with a similar recessive gene on its paired chromosome. If two recessive genes do not match up, the offspring will not exhibit the trait that they are responsible for; in that case, however, the offspring will be a "carrier" of the trait, and will have the potential of passing it on to future offspring, if the recessive gene does match up with a recessive mate. Additional information on genes is available in the work of Gottesman (1963), from which this account has been taken.

Dominant Gene Defects. Fortunately, mental retardation due to single defective dominant genes is quite rare. Conditions such as tuberous sclerosis and neurofibromatosis are due to dominant genes and result in severe retardation. These conditions are rare because the parents have the disorder themselves, and they frequently cannot pass on the traits because of sterility or lack of opportunity (Telford and Sawrey, 1977). A notable exception is Huntington's chorea, which cannot be identified until the victim is approximately thirty-six years old (Gottesman, 1963).

Recessive Gene Defects. A number of retarded children are born to seemingly normal parents. This is often the result of the inheritance of matching recessive genes from the child's parents. Recessive genes can cause problems in metabolism, endocrine disturbances, and cranial anomalies, any of which can result in retardation. These conditions are relatively rare, however.

Phenylketonuria (PKU) is a recessive gene disorder that affects the metabolism of proteins. PKU can be identified in infants by a simple blood test that should be routinely administered shortly after birth. The probability that the disorder will result in retardation can be reduced through a diet low in phenylalanine. There are several other conditions that affect the metabolism of proteins (Robinson and Robinson, 1976).

Another recessive gene disorder is galactosemia, a condition that affects the metabolism of carbohydrates. If the disease is detected before brain damage has occurred, retardation can be prevented with a milk-free diet. Several other disorders of carbohydrate metabolism can also cause retardation (Telford and Sawrey, 1977).

Tay-Sachs disease affects the metabolism of fats; it is most prevalent in Jewish families. This disease can cause paralysis, blindness, and convulsions; it usually causes death by the time the child is three years old (Robinson and Robinson, 1976).

Cretinism, a disorder of the endocrine system, is characterized by lack of the thyroid hormone. Although this condition is sometimes caused by recessive genes, it can also be caused by a diet that is deficient in iodine. Early treatment with thyroxin can prevent some of the physical symptoms associated with cretinism, but persons with this disorder are almost always retarded (Robinson and Robinson, 1976).

Microcephaly is one of several cranial disorders that can be caused by recessive genes. Microcephalic children are generally short and have small skulls, curved spines, and rather severe retardation. This condition can also be caused by nongenetic factors, such as exposure of the mother to massive dosages of x-rays during pregnancy (MacMillan, 1977).

Chromosomal Aberrations. Retardation is also caused occasionally by improper cell division, which can result in cells that have an abnormal number of chromosomes or chromosomes that have an abnormal structure.

The most common condition involving chromosomal aberrations is *Down's syndrome.* (The term "syndrome," you will remember, means a constellation or cluster of symptoms.) Down's syndrome used to be called "mongolism," primarily because children with this syndrome have almond-shaped eyes that slightly resemble those of the Mongol race. Down's syndrome children have three number 21 chromosomes (called trisomy-21). Children with Down's syndrome constitute about 10 percent of the moderately-to-severely retarded population. The risk of having a Down's child is related to the age of the mother. Between the ages of twenty and thirty, the risk is one in 1500; between forty and forty-five, the risk is one in seventy. A test called amniocentesis can be used to determine whether a pregnant woman is carrying a child with Down's syndrome or other chromosomal aberrations. In this test, a small portion of the amniotic fluid that surrounds the fetus is examined.

PROBLEMS DURING PREGNANCY

A number of factors that can cause retardation can affect a woman during pregnancy. These prenatal factors have the most serious consequences during the first three months of pregnancy, although some factors can endanger the fetus at any point during gestation.

A number of the prenatal factors that can (but sometimes don't) cause retardation have been described by Berlin (1978). Maternal disease such as serious kidney disease or diabetes mellitus is one such factor. It can cause a number of complications during pregnancy. Certain drugs, exposure to large doses of radiation, and poor maternal nutrition can also harm the fetus.

Infections are also a major cause of retardation. Rubella, or German measles, in the first trimester of pregnancy can have disastrous consequences. Rubella can now be prevented with vaccinations. Syphilis is another infectious disease that can injure the fetus.

Rh incompatibility can also have serious consequences. A woman with Rh negative blood who is impregnated by an Rh positive male has a chance of producing a fetus with Rh positive blood. When this occurs, the mother's body produces antibodies that attack the fetus as they would attack a foreign substance that has entered the body. Rh incompatibility rarely affects a first-born child; a vaccine called RhoGam has been developed that prevents Rh factor problems in later pregnancies. In some cases it is necessary to give the child a blood transfusion to eliminate antibodies that are damaging the child's tissues.

There is also some evidence that alcohol, LSD, heroin, and cigarette smoking can negatively affect the fetus (MacMillan, 1977), but a definite link between these drugs and retardation has not been demonstrated. Pregnant women should limit their use of tobacco and alcohol and use only those drugs that are recommended by a physician.

PROBLEMS AT BIRTH

A number of problems that can result in retardation can occur during labor and delivery.

Although there is no direct cause-effect relationship between prematurity and retardation, premature babies are more susceptible to disease and more fragile than full-term babies, and are as a result more susceptible to retardation (MacMillan, 1977). Brain damage can be caused by prolonged or difficult labor, by difficult forceps manipulation, by problems related to the abnormal positioning of the baby in the womb, or by problems related to a mother's small pelvis. Asphyxia, the deprivation of oxygen, may be caused by compression of the umbilical cord or other problems (MacMillan, 1977). This is probably the major cause of cerebral palsy.

Treatment for some genetic disorders must be begun shortly after birth. Children born to mothers with Rh antigens must be monitored to ensure that high levels of bilirubin do not result in brain damage. The blood sugar levels of infants born to diabetic mothers should be monitored to determine whether the child needs treatment. PKU and galactosemia tests should also be conducted, and treatment should be initiated if it is warranted. Surgery may be necessary in cases of spina bifida, as mentioned in the chapter on physical disabilities. Hydrocephaly, a related condition, can also be identified shortly after birth. This condition, which is usually caused by prenatal factors, head injury, tumors, or infections, is characterized by the build-up of cerebrospinal fluid in the skull. If untreated, the head will expand, which results in severe brain damage. Surgical procedures have been developed whereby a shunt can be inserted to drain the fluid into the general circulatory system.

PROBLEMS AFTER BIRTH

Mental retardation can also be caused by problems occurring after the child is born, including head injuries, brain tumors, infectious diseases such as meningitis and encephalitis, hunger and malnutrition, and some food additives. Lead and mercury poisoning can also cause retardation, as can complications arising from childhood diseases such as whooping cough, chicken pox, and measles.

PSYCHOSOCIAL FACTORS

Most of the causes of retardation discussed thus far have involved damage to the central nervous system. The causes of most of these cases can be identified. As mentioned earlier, however, these causes account for only about 10 percent of the mentally retarded population. What is more, the children affected by this type of disorder generally have retardation in the moderate to severe range. What is the cause of the remaining cases of retardation, most of which are relatively mild?

The President's Committee on Mental Retardation (1976) concluded that 75 percent of our mentally retarded children come from urban and rural poverty areas. Although the causes already discussed affect children from poverty areas, too, most cases are of unknown origin. We can only speculate on why so many mildly retarded children come from impoverished environments.

It seems reasonable to assume that malnutrition, inadequate medical and prenatal care, disease-producing conditions, and other health hazards associated with disadvantaged areas all contribute to lowered intellectual functioning. In addition, it appears that a number of other, less readily observable factors help produce mental retardation. These are related to childrearing practices, the home environment, family structure, and similar factors. Causative factors of these types are known as "psychosocial" factors.

The American Association on Mental Deficiency (Grossman, 1973) uses four criteria to determine whether a child's retardation can be attributed to psychosocial disadvantages.

1. Intelligence and adaptive behavior are at retarded levels of functioning.
2. There is retarded intellectual functioning in the immediate family, and usually the larger family circle as well.
3. There is no clear evidence of brain damage in the child.
4. In most instances, the home environment is impoverished.

Mild retardation due to psychosocial factors is almost always difficult to identify in young children. Most of the youngsters in this category appear to develop fairly normally; they are generally only slightly slower than their nonretarded peers. Most of these children are not identified until they reach school age, when it is discovered that they have difficulty with educational tasks.

Most authorities on mental retardation do not believe that intelligence and other characteristics of the personality are caused exclusively by either genetic or environmental factors. The current belief is that these traits are a result of the interaction of genetic and environmental variables. It is believed that intelligence can be limited to a certain range by genetic factors, but within that range an individual's intelligence will be determined by her environment. This means that children who have the genetic potential to be only mildly retarded may have a much lower level of intelligence if they are raised in a very poor environment. As you can see, it is important that children be raised in as rich and stimulating an environment as possible.

PREVENTION

The chances that mental retardation can be prevented improve every time a cause is identified. A number of preventative measures are already known. Among these are

— Vaccination against rubella
— Surgical procedures to correct hydrocephaly
— Amniocentesis to detect chromosomal aberrations in the fetus
— Use of drugs to control the effects of childhood illnesses
— Blood transfusion of Rh-factor babies, and vaccination of Rh-sensitized mothers
— Laws that prohibit the use of lead-based paint on baby toys and furniture
— Dietary treatment of PKU and galactosemia
— Improved maternal nutrition and prenatal health care
— Genetic counseling for persons who are carriers of potential genetic defects
— Enrichment of impoverished environments

Educating the public about the causes of mental retardation and the methods of preventing it is one of the major challenges facing the special educator today.

PROBE 7-4
Causes and Prevention of Retardation

1. T F A knowledge of the causes of retardation can be very helpful to a teacher in the actual instruction of retarded children.

2. T F The causes of most cases of mental retardation cannot be clearly identified.

3. Describe the four criteria used by the AAMD to identify mental retardation due to psychosocial disadvantage.

   a. _____

   b. _____

   c. _____

   d. _____

4. Describe current beliefs about the roles of genetic and environmental factors in determining intelligence and other personality characteristics.

   _____

   _____

5. *Matching*

_____ Dominant gene defect	a. Down's syndrome
_____ Preventable with diet	b. Cretinism
_____ Treated by blood transfusion	c. Cerebral Palsy
	d. Rh factor
_____ Thyroid deficiency	e. tuberous sclerosis
_____ Trisomy-21	f. Hydrocephaly
_____ Small skull	g. PKU
_____ Correctible with surgery	h. Microcephaly
_____ Asphyxia as major cause	

6. List five methods of preventing mental retardation.

a. _____

b. _____

c. _____

d. _____

e. _____

EDUCATIONAL AND SERVICE DELIVERY OPTIONS

You should be able to describe the implications of PL 94–142 for educating mentally retarded children in the least restrictive environment.

The implications of normalization were discussed in Chapter 1. The impetus in the drive for normalization came from parents and professionals concerned about the practice of placing the mentally retarded in large residential institutions that were little more than warehouses for human beings. Because the normalization movement was started by people concerned with the welfare of the mentally retarded, it is not surprising that the most striking changes that have resulted from normalization involve retarded individuals. Important changes have occurred in the care of children in public school programs, as well as in institutional and residential care settings. Some of the currently available options that have resulted from normalization are discussed in the following pages.

EDUCATIONAL SERVICE OPTIONS

The continuum, or cascade, of educational services was described in Chapter 1. It may be helpful to refer back to Figure 1-1 (page 34) to refresh your memory about the educational provisions that are currently available to mentally retarded children. When considering educational options for the retarded, it is important to keep in mind that (1) educational placement should be based on the child's needs; (2) the child should be placed in the most facilitative (or least restrictive) environment; and (3) placement should be flexible enough that a child could be moved to a different setting if the situation warranted it.

The Regular Classroom. You will recall that there are several options available for children placed in the setting at the least restrictive end of the continuum — the regular classroom. EMR children are much more likely to be placed in regular classrooms than TMR children, and most EMR children will require support services. These may involve itinerant teachers who work directly with the child on a part-time basis (e.g., with a child who needs speech therapy); consulting services for the regular classroom teacher; or part-time attendance in a separate resource room staffed by a special education teacher, where the child is usually given extra help in a basic subject such as reading or mathematics.

EMR children in the upper range of the classification are likely to be most successful in the regular classroom. Those with lower intellectual and adaptive behavior levels require more special services. The child with a low level of adaptive behavior is especially likely to present problems in the regular classroom.

The Special Class. There are two special class options in the continuum of educational services: part-time placement and full-time placement. Only those whose academic and adaptive behavior problems preclude placement in the regular classroom should be placed in the special class. It may be best for EMR students with severe academic problems but good adaptive behavior to remain in the special class for academic work and join their regular classmates for physical education, art, music, shop, home economics, and other activities in which academic skills are not crucial. Full-time placement in a special class is warranted only for those children who need intensive instruction in academic areas and adaptive behavior. Some children who have relatively good academic skills but poor adaptive behavior are placed full-time in a special class. When this is the case, every effort should be made to improve the child's adaptive behavior so that he can be moved to a more facilitative environment.

Most TMR and S/PR children will be educated in full-time, self-contained special classes. The emphasis in the TMR classroom is on self-help skills, basic communication skills, and vocational skill development that will eventually permit the child to be employed in a supervised or sheltered job site. Although most TMR people require supervision throughout their lives, it is not unusual for a TMR individual to acquire in school all the life-care skills needed to live independently or in a group home.

Because the full-time pupils in a special class are segregated in their education, it is important that they be allowed other opportunities to participate in the social and nonacademic life of the school. Both EMR and TMR children benefit from social and leisure time interaction with nonhandicapped children. In fact, these children interact most frequently with nonhandicapped children when they are not in school. School personnel should try to foster such interactions, and should attempt to provide the retarded with skills that will permit them to interact successfully.

The Special Day School. The special day school is rapidly disappearing. At one time it was common practice to house all education programs for handicapped children is special schools. Such facilities still exist, but they are generally quite specialized and are appropriate only for children who cannot profit from integration in regular public schools. These schools are generally found only in large metropolitan areas, where the population of severely and profoundly handicapped individuals is large enough to justify the operation of a separate educational facility.

Home-bound Instruction. Home-bound instruction for the mentally retarded is uncommon. This type of instruction is generally provided only to those who cannot attend school because of a medical or physical problem, as when a child requires complete bed care. Most home-bound instruction is short-term, provided only while the child is recuperating from a temporary illness or disorder. The cascade-of-services model requires that the child be moved back into the least restrictive environment as soon as feasible.

Hospitals and Residential Institutions. Children are placed in facilities such as hospitals and residential institutions only when they have a medical problem or are severely retarded. Unless she has severe or dangerous behavioral problems, the EMR child should not be placed in such settings. The placement of a TMR child in such a facility would be justified only after placement in school- and community-based programs had proved ineffective. Although S/PR children are found more frequently in these settings, they, too, should be placed there only after other options have been tried and found inexpedient. As a result of PL 94–142, S/PR children are being served more frequently in public schools. Program options for the S/PR child will be discussed in more detail in Chapter 10.

In summary, the cascade-of-services model has been found to be a workable alternative to the exclusion and segregation of the retarded from public school programs. The success of several derivative or adoptive models has been documented (Adamson, 1970; Taylor and Soloway, 1973; Van Etten and Adamson, 1973). As Deno (1970) points out,

> "The cascade system is designed to make available whatever different-from-the-mainstream kind of setting is required to control the learning variables deemed critical for the individual case. It is a system which facilitates tailoring of treatment to individual needs rather than a system for sorting out children so they will fit conditions designed according to group standards not necessarily suitable for the particular case [p. 233].

COMMUNITY-BASED RESIDENTIAL SERVICES

During the past two decades, especially the 1970s, a movement has grown to provide services to the mentally retarded in their home communities. This is a dramatic change from the former practice of isolating the mentally retarded, particularly the moderately and severely retarded, in large, self-contained residential institutions that offered little or no contact with the outside community.

Why did the large institution model develop? Wolfensberger (1976) claimed it was a result of the way people perceived the mentally retarded. These perceptions included the views that the retarded were sick, subhuman, a menace to society, objects of pity, a burden of charity, or "holy innocents." Although the establishment of institutions was well intentioned, many of them deteriorated into hell holes. Burton Blatt's photo exposé of institutions for the retarded, *Christmas in Purgatory* (1966), contrasts conditions in well-run and badly run institutions.

Wolfensberger suggests that the mentally retarded should be regarded as developing individuals. This role perception of the mentally retarded emphasizes that their behavior is due to developmental retardation, that their behavior can change, and that they are capable of growth and development. Those who subscribe to this developmental model have a positive attitude toward the mentally retarded, one that is reflected in a more humane and realistic approach to the delivery of services. As a result of Wolfensberger's work, a shift away from large institutional "warehouses" for the retarded has occurred.

Principles of normalization in the delivery of services to the retarded are reflected in the following suggestions of Menolascino (1977):

1. Programs and facilities for the mentally retarded should be physically and socially integrated into the community. . . .
2. No more retardates should be congregated in one service facility than the surrounding neighborhood can readily integrate into its resources, community social life, etc. . . . We are doing a disservice to normal children in not allowing them to experience handicapped children in classroom settings. . . .
3. Integration of the mentally retarded — and, therefore, normalization — can best be attained if the location of services follows population density and distribution patterns. . . .
4. Services and facilities for the retarded, if they are to be normalizing in their intent, must meet the same standards as other comparable services and facilities for the non-retarded, not be stricter nor more lenient. . . .
5. Staff personnel working with retarded persons must meet at least the same standards as those working with comparable non-retarded individuals. . . .
6. In order to accomplish maximal normalization, either by encouraging the retarded to emulate the behavior of non-retarded or by endeavoring to improve public perception of the mentally retarded, the retarded must have maximal exposure to the non-retarded population in the community. . . .
7. Daily routines for the mentally retarded should be comparable to those of non-retarded persons of the same age.
8. Services for children and adults should be physically separated, both in order to reduce the probability that children will imitate the deviant behavior of their elders and because services to adults and children tend to be separated in the mainstream of our society. . . .
9. The retarded should be dressed and groomed like other persons their age; they should be taught a normal gait, normal movements, and normal expressive behavior patterns; their diet should be adjusted as to assure normal weight.
10. As much as possible, the adult retardate, even if severely handicapped, should be provided the opportunity to engage in work that is culturally normal in type, quantity, and setting . . . [Adapted from Menolascino, 1977, pp. 79–83].

One important result of normalization has been the movement to build or make use of residential facilities that resemble the housing available to the rest of the community. There are a number of residential alternatives available to the retarded, including houses converted to group homes, apartments where supervision is available, foster family homes, specially built, low-enrollment, residential facilities located within the local community, and nursing homes. In the rest of this chapter we will describe these alternatives in greater detail.

Group Homes. The mentally retarded frequently live in houses that have been renovated to meet fire, health, and multiple occupancy standards. Many communities where municipal codes are very strict have chosen to build houses designed for group use, thereby eliminating the high expense of converting older housing to meet operating standards.

In group homes from six to twelve retarded people live together, share household responsibilities, work, and recreate in the immediate community. Both males and females may live in the group house, but cohabitation is generally not permitted. The group home is usually staffed full-time by live-in personnel, who rotate shifts. Staff members do not generally live permanently in the home, although this practice is followed in some instances — particularly when there are staff shortages.

In many cases the group home is the first arrangement the mentally retarded person lives in after leaving an institution. The group home introduces the individual to independent living and is used as a training site to help the retarded cope with the demands of the community. It is also a good first step outside the immediate family for mentally retarded adults who are leaving home for the first time. Whether he is moving from home or from an institution, the retarded individual should be moved to a different living arrangement, such as an apartment, as soon as he demonstrates the ability to function more independently.

The Eastern Nebraska Community Office of Retardation (ENCOR) was one of the earliest organizations to advocate the use of group homes and of alternative living units (ALUs) that are designed to house six or fewer clients. Many effective, community-based, residential service programs have been designed around the ENCOR model. ENCOR's recent emphasis on the development of ALUs is an effort to reduce the practice of placing the retarded in large group homes, which often resemble mini-institutions (Menolascino, 1977).

Supervised Apartment Living Units. Apartment living is found less frequently than group homes, but it is expected to grow more popular as the ALU arrangement becomes more familiar to the public. At this level of services, one or two retarded individuals rent an apartment just as anyone else would; supervision is provided according to the retarded individual's needs. In some cases the supervisor lives in an adjacent apartment; in others, she visits regularly and is available when needed. In some programs, the apartment ALU begins with the supervisor living with the client in a large three- or four-bedroom apartment, or the retarded people may live in a "cluster" of apartments in a separate part of the same building the supervisor lives in. As the retarded individuals acquire the skills necessary to live independently, they are encouraged to move into an apartment of their own or to share an apartment with an acquaintance. Supervisors drop by at regular intervals. In most ALU programs, the mentally retarded attend a training program that assists them in skill development. The clients should recreate and work independently but remain part of a life-care and counseling program.

Foster Family Homes. To develop adaptive behavior skills, it is extremely important that the retarded child and adolescent grow up in a family. Most foster family arrangements are regulated by state and municipal licensing boards. In most cases, foster parents receive fees, but they do not usually receive training. Supervision of foster care homes is usually less rigorous than it is for group homes or ALUs; in many cases assistance is available only for crises. The ENCOR program mentioned earlier has a "developmental home" plan similar to the foster home plan. In this program, however, the participating parents are trained to deal with the retarded, and supervision is provided.

Residential Care Facilities. When federal funding became available for residential construction (see PL91–517, for example), many private corporations were formed to sponsor construction of residential facilities designed to house 50 to 100 persons. These facilities, known as Intermediate Care Facilities for the Mentally Retarded (ICF/MR), are regulated by the federal government.

Most ICF/MRs are designed to provide total life care for retarded clients throughout their lives. In some instances ICF/MRs are community-based group homes with ALU components available in the array of services, but this practice is as yet fairly uncommon because it requires additional staff and other resources.

It is sometimes difficult to operate a profit-making corporation and provide a normalized service delivery system to the mentally retarded at the same time. There has been some litigation by advocates claiming that services are sacrificed for the sake of profit. Just as there were major court cases during the 1970s involving large institutions for the retarded, it seems likely that there will be cases during the 1980s involving claims that the civil rights of the retarded in the ICF/MRs are being violated.

Nursing or Geriatric Care Facilities. Attention has only recently been focused on providing care for the elderly retarded. The elderly could be "dumped" in large institutions when they were still operating. There were very few programs for the elderly, and they had little opportunity for stimulation or treatment. With today's emphasis on community-based facilities, service for the 5 percent of the mentally retarded population who are over fifty is becoming a major issue. Schapiro and Eigerdorf (1975) describe nine types of arrangements that are appropriate for the older retarded:

1. *Older Adult Apartments:* any apartment complex built or modified to serve the elderly.
2. *Alternative Living Units:* two- or three-bedroom apartments with supervision within the apartment.
3. *Rural Living Arrangements:* provisions for rural housing for the elderly are provided under HUD's Housing Rural Development Act.
4. *Mobile Home Living:* resembles any other mobile home park, but provides supervision and assistance to the elderly retarded.

5. *Congregate Housing:* supervised existing public housing.
6. *Nursing Homes:* public or private; the retarded should be integrated with "normal" elderly patients.
7. *Institutions:* may include hospitals with units designed to provide long-term or life care.
8. *Extra-mural Care:* care provided in the home.
9. *Sheltered Housing:* a situation in which assistance in managing daily activities is provided [in the client's own home]; not a nursing home or apartment setting.

Living arrangements available to the elderly retarded closely resemble those available to younger retarded individuals. There are highly restrictive options (nursing care) and relatively independent options (apartments). The goal is to integrate the elderly retarded into the mainstream of services to the elderly.

PROBE 7-5
Educational and Service Delivery Options

1. What characteristics should an EMR child exhibit to be considered for placement in some variation of the regular classroom? _____

2. T F Most TMR children will be educated in self-contained special classes.

3. Under what circumstances might an EMR child receive home-bound instruction? _____

4. T F Special day schools for the retarded continue to be a popular educational option.

5. What role perception of the mentally retarded has been suggested by Wolfensburger? _____

6. List four principles of normalization.

   a. _____

   b. _____

   c. _____

   d. _____

7. List three living alternatives to institutional placement.

   a. _____

   b. _____

   c. _____

8. What is the major criticism of foster family care for the retarded? _____

_____

_____

9. What type of facility sometimes takes on the characteristics of large institutions for the retarded?

_____

_____

SUMMARY

1. To be diagnosed as mentally retarded, a person must be significantly sub-average in both intelligence and adaptive behavior.
2. IQ scores should be considered in diagnosing mental retardation, but they are of little use in teaching a retarded child.
3. A child's level of adaptive behavior is determined by comparing his performance to the standards of independence and social responsibility that are expected for his age level and cultural group. Adaptive behavior is very difficult to measure.
4. Mental retardation is defined as significantly subaverge general intellectual functioning existing concurrently with deficits in adaptive behavior and manifested during the developmental period (Grossman, 1977, p. 5).
5. Classification systems related to etiology and clinical type are of little use in education. The classification system based on severity of symptoms, which identifies children as educable mentally retarded, trainable mentally retarded, and severely/profoundly retarded, is the system of greatest utility.
6. Children should be classified into diagnostic categories only when classification will lead to the development of an educational program that will meet their needs.
7. The estimated incidence of mental retardation is 3 percent, whereas the estimated prevalence at any given time is closer to one percent.
8. Genetic irregularities, problems during pregnancy, problems at birth, problems after birth, and psychosocial factors can cause mental retardation, but the causes of most cases are unknown.
9. In many cases, mental retardation can be prevented with proper care.
10. EMR children with good adaptive behavior skills can often be successfully integrated into regular classes.

11. TMR children are usually educated in special classes.
12. It is best to regard retarded people as "developing individuals" who are capable of growth and development that can lead to favorable changes in their behavior.
13. Living arrangements such as group homes and alternative living units located in the local community are preferable to large residential institutions.

TASK SHEET 7
Field Experiences in Mental Retardation

Select *one* of the alternatives and complete the assigned tasks:

Program Visitation

Visit a program that serves the mentally retarded, such as a public school, group home, institution, sheltered workshop, or rehabilitation center, and respond to the following:

1. Where did you go?
2. Describe the physical setting.
3. Describe the activities you observed.
4. Interview one of the professionals at the facility about the program and some of the problems he or she encounters.
5. Describe your reactions to this experience.

Professional Interview

Interview a professional who provides services to retarded people. Describe whom you interviewed, the services this person provides, the questions you asked, the person's responses, and what you learned from this experience. (If you can arrange it, you might prefer to interview the parent of a retarded child.)

Reading

Read Burton Blatt's *Christmas in Purgatory* and write a brief paper describing your reactions.

Library Study

Use the library to locate three articles on some aspect of mental retardation, and write a one-page abstract of each.

Design Your Own Field Experience

If you know of a unique experience that you can have with mentally retarded people, discuss your alternative with your instructor and complete the tasks that you agree on.

Probe Answers

Probe 7-1

1. True
2. IQ
3. IQ (intelligence, intellectual functioning) and adaptive behavior
4. mild: 67–52
   moderate: 51–36
   severe: 35–20
   profound: 19 and lower
5. False
6. False
7. a. size of normative sample
   b. restricted sample of behaviors assessed
   c. error of measurement
   d. educational utility of IQ
8. False
9. "The effectiveness or degree to which an individual meets the standards of personal independence and social responsibility expected of age and cultural group" (Grossman, 1977, p. 11).
10. Adaptive behavior measurement is more subjective than measurement of intelligence.
11. a. academic skill
    b. interpersonal skill
    c. social skill
    d. independent functioning

Probe 7-2

1. c
2. a. absolute
   b. relative
   c. apparent
3. "Mental retardation refers to significantly subaverage general intellectual functioning existing concurrently with deficits in adaptive behavior and manifested during the developmental period" (Grossman, 1977, p. 5).
4. two
5. birth; the tenth birthday
6. "A retarded individual is one who has a limited repertory of behavior shaped by events that constitute his history" (Bijou, 1966, p. 2).
7. Its implications for teaching

8. Any one of the following:
   a. It does not define what is meant by a "limited behavioral repertoire".
   b. It does not take into account many variables commonly held by many of the developmental psychologists.
9. True

Probe 7-3

1. a. etiology
   b. clinical type
   c. severity of symptoms
2. c; b; a
3. a. agreeing on the factors that should be classified
   b. deciding on upper and lower boundaries within subgroups
4. a. EMR
   b. TMR
   c. S/PR
5. a cluster or constellation of symptoms
6. True
7. the number of persons who exhibit mental retardation during their lifetime
8. the number of persons at a given point in time who will be assessed as mentally retarded
9. 1
10. 1500; 400; 100
11. False

Probe 7-4

1. False
2. True
3. a. Intelligence and adaptive behaviors must be at retarded levels of functioning.
   b. There must be retarded intellectual functioning in the immediate family and usually the larger family circle.
   c. There must be no clear evidence of brain damage in the child.
   d. The home environment is usually impoverished.
4. These traits are a result of the interaction of genetic and environmental variables.
5. e; g; d; b; a; h; f; c
6. Any five of the following:
   a. vaccination against rubella

b. surgical procedures to correct hydrocephaly
c. amniocentesis
d. drug therapy
e. blood transfusion
f. laws to protect against environmental danger
g. dietary treatment for PKU and galactosemia
h. improved maternal nutrition
i. genetic counseling

Probe 7-5

1. an IQ and adaptive behavior in the upper range of the classification
2. True
3. if there is some medical or physical reason preventing safe use of school facilities.
4. False
5. that of "developing individuals"
6. Any four of the following:
   a. Programs and facilities should not be physically segregated from the community.
   b. No more retardates should be congregated in one service facility than the surrounding community can readily integrate into its resources.
   c. Daily routines taught to the retarded should be similar to those of all other persons in the community.
   d. Grooming and dressing of the retarded should not be significantly different in style or type from that of others in the community.
   e. Work should be provided that is culturally normal in type, quantity, and setting.
   f. Services for adults and children should be separated.
   g. The retarded should be given maximum opportunity for contact with the nonretarded in their community.
   h. Staff working with the retarded should meet the same standards as those providing services to comparable nonretarded persons.
7. a. group home
   b. foster care
   c. apartment living
8. lack of training of foster parents
9. group homes or Intermediate Care Facilities for the Mentally Retarded

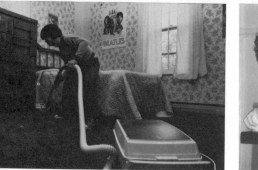

This is a group home for moderately retarded adolescents and young adults. Eight people, four of each sex, live in this large, beautiful community residence. A house director and four staff counselors work with the residents, who range in age from fifteen to twenty-four. The group home provides educational programs for the residents, and several are employed in a local sheltered workshop.

The group home places emphasis on the development of daily living skills, such as self-grooming, shopping, and handling money. Considerable effort is also expended in making the lives of the residents as normal as possible through their integration into community activities. What helps to make these efforts successful is the atmosphere of warmth and caring that exists among staff and residents.

Laura Jane was not the kind of bright-eyed handicapped child you might see on a Madison Avenue poster. She was unkempt, raw-boned, and moved awkwardly. Her voice was loud and harsh, her nearly incoherent speech punctuated with a rasping cough. She always had a runny nose, and often smelled offensive. Her laughter had an empty sound, her eyes a hollow look. She wouldn't pay attention to the teacher's directions, and her response to discipline was a kicking, screaming tantrum. She seemed to be in motion almost all the time, and this was upsetting to the other children in her kindergarten class. She wouldn't sit still to listen to a story. She couldn't tell stories about things the other children shared — a family of dolls, zoo animals, or going to the store. When the teacher asked her a question, she repeated the question rather than giving an answer. She couldn't count or draw a person, didn't know any colors, and couldn't even copy lines or circles. When her teacher tried to help her individually, she wouldn't pay attention.

The doctor said that she had normal vision and hearing and a normal physical examination with some "soft neurological signs." The psychologist said her Binet mental age was 3 years, 9 months. Laura Jane's mother said her rate of learning to walk and talk had been slightly slower than it was for her other six children, and that Laura Jane had had frequent high fevers with some loss of consciousness.

Actually, Laura Jane had a learning disability. She had many of the "classic signs," or characteristics, and after a year of special help, she was sitting and listening, talking and responding, counting to ten, writing her name, and most amazing of all, her IQ score had improved. But if you thought she was mentally retarded, culturally disadvantaged, emotionally disturbed, or if you just couldn't decide, you had lots of company. It would be possible to classify her in many different ways. Her case illustrates the confusion, conflict, and intrigue surrounding what we call "learning disability."

Source: From C. Morsink, The Unreachable Child. Journal of Learning Disabilities, 1971, 4, 33–40. Reprinted by permission.

8

Learning Disabilities

Catherine V. Morsink

Catherine V. Morsink is a Professor and Chairman of the Department of Special Education at the University of Florida. Dr. Morsink's professional experience includes teaching special classes for learning disabled and mentally retarded children and a regular third grade class in which several mildly handicapped children were mainstreamed.

"Learning disabled" (often abbreviated LD) is a label applied to children who, because of severe problems in learning, are eligible for special education services. As can be seen from the discussion of Laura Jane on the facing page, the student exhibiting a learning disability can be easily misunderstood by teachers and parents. Learning disabilities — their diagnosis, cause, and treatment in the schools — is an extremely complex problem confronting today's educator. This chapter will use the words "learning disability" or "specific learning disability" to refer to one type of extreme difficulty in learning (math or handwriting, for example). The many kinds of learning difficulties range in seriousness from the simple to the severe; only the severe problems are called "disabilities." The National Advisory Committee on the Handicapped estimated that there were 1,966,000 LD children aged nineteen or less in 1975 and 1976. Of this number, 1,706,000 (87 percent) were unserved, while 260,000 (13 percent) were receiving services (Logan, 1977).

To understand and help learning disabled individuals, you should be familiar with current identification procedures and the LD definition. You should also be able to recognize the disorder's characteristic behaviors and tell the difference between real disabilities and simple learning difficulties. To do this, you need to view learning disabilities from a broad perspective that includes an understanding of its controversial definition, historical background, and future trends. That's what this chapter is all about.

Learning disabilities are extremely varied and complex; they include severe difficulties in learning to read, write, speak, comprehend — even, in the broadest sense, to find places on a map, tell time, or ride a bicycle. Space limitations make it impossible to address all learning disabilities in depth. For this reason we have opted to focus on one type of learning disability: reading. Reading disability was selected for major (though not exclusive) emphasis because it is the most common, and — educationally — the most debilitating of the learning disabilities. It should be understood, however, that reading disability isn't the only type of learning disability.

DEFINITION OF LEARNING DISABILITIES

You should be able to cite the current definition of the label "learning disabilities" and to explain how a child is identified as learning disabled.

RECENT FEDERAL GUIDELINES

The LD definition adopted by the federal government in December 1977, to provide guidelines for funding programs under Public Law 94–142, reads as follows:

> "Specific learning disability" means a disorder in one or more of the basic psychological processes involved in understanding or in using language, spoken or written, which may manifest itself in an imperfect ability to listen, think, speak, read, write, spell, or to do mathematical calculations. The term includes such conditions as perceptual handicaps, brain injury, minimal brain dysfunction, dyslexia, and developmental aphasia. The term does not include children who have learning problems which are primarily the result of visual, hearing, or motor handicaps, or mental retardation, or of environmental, cultural, or economic disadvantage [*Federal Register*, Dec. 29, 1977, p. 65083].

During 1978 these guidelines were widely discussed, expanded, and modified. Final guidelines for the learning disabilities definition in PL 94–142 were not agreed on until January 1979, although the law was passed in 1975. The original guidelines and definition were so controversial that changes were required.

Many professionals disagree about precisely what constitutes a learning disability, but there is general agreement about some of the disorder's basic dimensions. These dimensions have been summarized by Wallace and McLoughlin (1975):

1. *Discrepancy.* There is a difference between what a child should be able to do and what she is actually doing.

2. *Manifestation.* There is some task others can do that an LD child can't do (such as listen, read, or do arithmetic).
3. *Focus.* The child's problem is centered around one or more of the basic psychological processes involved in using or understanding language.
4. *Integrities.* The child has good eyes and ears, is not disadvantaged or retarded, but still isn't learning.

The most important thing for you to understand about the federal guidelines is that *a team decision* is now required to identify a child as a disabled learner. This team is composed of the child's regular classroom teacher, a person qualified to conduct a diagnostic examination (school psychologist, speech pathologist, reading specialist, etc.), and others as needed. This team must agree that *the child does not achieve* "commensurate with his or her age and ability levels ... when provided with *appropriate learning experiences.*" The team must also agree that the child shows a *"severe discrepancy"* between achievement and ability in one or more of the following areas: oral expression, reading comprehension, basic reading skills, written expression, listening comprehension, math reasoning, or math calculations. The team may not identify a child as LD if the problem is primarily a result of mental retardation, emotional disturbance, a visual, hearing, or motor handicap, or environmental, cultural, or economic disadvantages. At least one team member other than the child's regular teacher must observe the child in his regular classroom. (There are special provisions for children below school age.) The team prepares a written report that describes relevant behavior during the classroom observation and includes a list of medical findings, a statement of whether the child requires special education, and a description of the effects (if any) of environmental and cultural disadvantages.

IDENTIFICATION PROCEDURES

The federal guidelines we have mentioned suggest, in a general way, how to identify an LD student. Guidelines at the state and local levels are usually more specific, but they conform to these general guidelines. It's easier to understand the identification procedure if you have an example — in this case the state guidelines for school-age children for Kentucky. In Kentucky the team that decides whether a child is LD is the Admissions and Release Committee in the child's school. Kentucky's guidelines specify that the team should include:

— The referred child's regular class teacher
— A person qualified to do individual diagnostic testing
— A teacher certified in learning disabilities
— A person qualified to give individual intelligence tests
— Others as needed — speech pathologist, counselor, reading teacher, physician, etc.

The team makes certain that due process procedures and procedural safeguards are followed at each step. This involves obtaining parental permission for assessment, allowing parental access to records, ensuring that tests are not biased, and so forth. (For details, see Council for Exceptional Children, 1977.)

The team *may* determine that a student has a learning disability if

— Her achievement isn't commensurate with age and ability levels when appropriate learning experiences are provided.[1]
— There is a severe discrepancy between achievement and intellectual ability in one or more of the seven areas.
— The discrepancy *isn't* the result of mental retardation, etc. (same as federal guidelines).

First the child is assessed. The following information is gathered:

— A report of the child's specific strengths and weaknesses, written by the person making the referral.
— A report of the child's behavior in the classroom (or elsewhere, if the child is not in school), written by an observer other than the child's teacher.
— The results of individual standardized tests of skills conducted by qualified personnel.
— The results of an individual assessment of intelligence conducted by qualified personnel.
— The results of correctly conducted tests for vision, hearing, and emotional disturbance, if necessary.

The team prepares a written report, which is much the same as that outlined in federal guidelines. Each member certifies in writing that he agrees with the report, or he submits a separate statement. If the team decides the child has a learning disability that requires special education and related services, an individual education plan is prepared (Kentucky Administrative Regulations, 1978).

Several important points related to the assessment of children suspected of having learning disabilities deserve mention. There are some "Catch 22s" as well.

First, it is the responsibility of the person making the referral (usually the classroom teacher) to write a report on the child's specific strengths and weaknesses. This report might say, for example, "This student makes errors on one in every five words when reading orally but is able to answer all comprehension questions correctly when I read the passage out loud to her," or "He can correctly compute the answer to any two- or three-digit addition or subtraction problem that does not include regrouping, but he always makes errors in carrying or borrowing." This kind of report can be extremely helpful in deciding whether a learning disability exists and what the specific disability is.

Next, a good assessment includes an observation of the child's behavior in the actual setting (school or preschool) where education is provided. It is essential to

[1] Achievement in the seven areas named in the federal guidelines; i.e., oral expression, basic reading skills, math reasoning, etc.

know how long and under what conditions the student can concentrate on a given task. This information is far more valuable than the score on a single test, especially if the test was given in a quiet room under one-to-one supervision — a setting quite different from the classroom.

An individualized standardized test of skills — an achievement test in an area such as reading, math, or spelling — is needed to determine how much difficulty the child has in comparison with others who have been through the same curriculum or are at the same grade level. This can be one of the commonly used national tests, such as the *Wide Range Achievement* or *Peabody Individual Achievement Test,* or an achievement test developed and standardized locally for a particular school district or curriculum.

The real "Catch-22" is the need for an individual measure of intelligence. IQ tests are currently the subject of great controversy. They have, for example, been declared unconstitutional in a 1979 court case in California *(Larry P. v. Riles)* on the grounds that they are racially and culturally biased and discriminate against minority-group children. In some states (perhaps nationally, soon) it is at the same time necessary and illegal to measure the IQ of a child referred for special services! You should be aware of the limitations of IQ tests and realize that they should be administered only by qualified persons. You should also be familiar with some alternative methods of determining individual intelligence — records of the child's personal developmental history and adaptive/social behavior, both in and out of school, for example.

Finally, the assessment may include tests for vision, hearing, and in some cases, "emotional disturbance." Tests for sensory problems are usually administered by the school nurse or a physician. Tests for "emotional disturbance," like those for IQ, must be administered by qualified persons, and are quite controversial. (See Chapter 9.)

Remember that assessment is simply a way to determine whether a given child has a learning disability and requires special help. Assessment instruments are helpful tools in the hands of those who know how to use them. Children are protected from being labeled "learning disabled" when they are simply having difficulty in school by requirements for parental permission and involvement, and by the requirement that labeling decisions be made by a team of educators and professionals. As time goes on, educators will continue to improve the instruments and methods used in assessment of learning disabilities.

PROBE 8-1
Definition of Learning Disabilities

1. The National Advisory Committee on the Handicapped estimated that there are approximately _____ children with learning disabilities in the United States, and that approximately _____ percent are not receiving appropriate educational services.

2. T   F   The federal definition of learning disabilities excludes children who are mentally retarded.

3. What are Wallace and McLoughlin's four dimensions of learning disabilities?

   a. _____

   b. _____

   c. _____

   d. _____

4. T   F   The federal definition of learning disabilities is very precise and universally accepted.

5. List the seven academic areas in which an LD child may have a severe discrepancy between ability and achievement.

   a. _____

   b. _____

   c. _____

   d. _____

   e. _____

   f. _____

   g. _____

CONTROVERSY OVER THE LEARNING DISABILITIES DEFINITION

You should be able to explain why the LD definition and label are so controversial.

You may have the impression that identification of an LD student is complicated. It is not only that; it is also highly controversial.

Before 1960 few people had even heard of learning disabilities, and almost nobody knew what a learning disability was. LD children were considered lazy, stubborn, or stupid.

During the early 1970s the pendulum swung the other way. Daily newspapers, popular magazines, and prime-time television shows ran features on learning disability. It became fashionable to say your child had a learning disability. Almost everybody thought he knew what a learning disability was. Every student who had any kind of difficulty in learning was suspected of "being an LD," and far too many children were diagnosed, labeled, and placed in special programs. It seems absurd to suggest that the definition itself is the most controversial issue in learning disabilities, but it's true. You can't really understand learning disabilities until you view them from the perspective provided by the controversy over definition of the term.

WHICH STUDENTS ARE LD?

The current LD definition has generated a lot of controversy (Senf, 1978). For one thing it encompasses only underachievement in strictly academic skills. Since the determination of underachievement is made by the school committee that plans the child's program, it could differ widely from place to place. There is also controversy about inclusion of the child who is achieving at an average level (keeping up with others in the grade) but is extremely gifted. Is this child learning disabled because there is a discrepancy between ability and achievement? The school-based committee will need to decide about both the child who is gifted but stays at grade level and the one whose slightly poor performance seems severely so in comparison with large numbers of classmates who do extremely well. Some schools may judge too many children as eligible, whereas others may fail to identify some of those who need services.

The federal definition was accepted after much discussion about limiting the total number of children who could be labeled as learning disabled. A maximum of 2 percent of the population was suggested, but the limitation was removed. There were also efforts to distinguish children with learning disabilities from children with simple learning difficulties on the basis of their lag in skills. A complicated formula for determining discrepancy was proposed, but it was ultimately rejected. Both proposals addressed the continuing problem of separating the few students who are *really* LD from the large group of students who have difficulty in learning. The difference is in the severity of the problem.

THE PROBLEM WITH LABELS

Another major controversy centers around the exclusion of certain children from the LD definition — those who are retarded, emotionally disturbed, or culturally disadvantaged, for example. The question of excluding the culturally different child is especially important, since large numbers of culturally different children underachieve academically in the public schools (Senf, 1978).

There are three basic objections to labeling a child according to a definition of learning disability: (1) Labels really don't define discrete groups of individuals, since there is considerable overlap between categories of mildly handicapped children (learning disabled, mildly mentally retarded, emotionally disturbed, culturally disadvantaged). (2) There is little evidence that a specific educational treatment is more appropriate for a student labeled one way than another. (3) Worst of all, children are frequently mislabeled and sometimes categorized on the basis of data from biased tests. (Yes, this is against the law.) These three points are illustrated by selections from the literature on reading disability in the discussion that follows.

Labels Don't Define Discrete Groups. Children with reading disabilities are found in great numbers in special classes other than LD classes. It is difficult to estimate the percentage of *educable mentally retarded* (EMR) children who have failed to learn to read. Garrison and Hammill (1971) estimated that 65 percent of the EMR students in their study had failed to meet criteria in reading. Kirk (1964) concluded from his review that many mentally retarded children read below expectancy for their mental age. The "performance below expectancy" idea is a major component of the learning disability concept.

Estimates of the percentages of the *environmentally disadvantaged* who have reading problems range from 5.8 percent, when only disabilities of neurological origin are included (Kappleman et al., 1969), to more than 50 percent, when all who read below expectations are counted (Cohen, 1969).

Estimates of the percentages of *emotionally disturbed* children who have reading problems range from 52 percent (Stone and Rowley, 1964) to 84 percent. Stennett (1966) found that by grades four to six, 30 percent of his sample of disturbed students were in remedial reading classes, and they fell farther behind their classmates as they progressed through the elementary grades. The longitudinal study by Zax, Cowen, Rappaport, Beach, and Laird (1968) confirmed the existence of multiple academic difficulties, especially in reading, within their group of emotionally disturbed children.

An in-depth study of *disadvantaged urban children* (Kappleman, Kaplan, and Ganter, 1969) indicates that learning disability, rather than "cultural deprivation," is often the predominant cause of their school failure. Of the 506 children referred for evaluation, significant learning disabilities were identified in 306. Fifty-six percent of the 306 were diagnosed as having organic learning handicaps and the remaining 44 percent as having functional learning handicaps. Cultural deprivation was judged as the predominant cause of the learning disorder in only 6 percent of the children studied. The authors stress the need for early recognition and proper treatment of learning disabled children and urge that the highly visible handicap of socioeconomic status not be allowed to obscure the existence of the learning disability.

As you can see from these studies, the fact that a child has been placed in one category does not necessarily mean that she does not exhibit characteristics associated with another category. Many children who are not labeled LD do have learning disabilities in reading and other academic areas.

Treatment not Dependent on Label. There is little evidence that children labeled "LD" differ in their educational needs from those labeled "EMR" (Educable Mentally Retarded) or "ED" (Emotionally Disturbed). Instructional programs should be based on the individual needs of children, not on the label given a child, as indicated by the following study by Ensher (1972), and many other reports.

Ensher's study involved forty-two children aged seven through eleven in classes labeled EMR. After administering a battery of seven assessment instruments, she developed and supervised a remedial program based on the skill needs indicated. Using a formula for calculating a learning disability as a discrepancy between the students' expected and measured achievement, Ensher found that many EMR children had "learning disabilities."

The majority of students in the Ensher study improved substantially over a two-year period. Ensher's findings did not support assumptions about "global retardation," the inability of the EMR to accomplish higher academic tasks, the unique characteristics of learning disabilities, or the static rates of knowledge acquisition in the EMR group under observation. Ensher suggested that the achievement gains of students in her study were the result of a constellation of factors, including the nature and severity of the learning disability, the child's cognitive strengths, emotional behavior, total intellectual impairment, and teacher attitude and competence. She cited studies suggesting that the present categorization of EMR children is social, administrative, and legal, but not scientific, educational, or therapeutic in its function.

There is further evidence that categorical labels such as LD and EMR are educationally irrelevant. With increasing frequency, books on exceptionality are combining or associating traditional categories. Reynolds and Birch (1977) have devoted a chapter in their book on exceptional children to "learning disabilities and behavior disorders," while discussing children categorized as "mentally retarded" in a separate chapter. Smith and Neisworth (1975), on the other hand, have chosen to separate learning disabilities from adjustment problems (social/ emotional problems or behavior disorders) and to include both mental retardation and learning disabilities under the generic heading of "learning problems." In this work, retardation is defined as a general learning problem, whereas disability is considered a specific one. Gearheart and Weishahan (1976) discuss learning disabilities and mild mental retardation in different parts of a single chapter, pointing out that the two areas have both presumed differences and apparent overlaps. There seems to be as much confusion about whether learning disability differs from mild mental retardation, emotional disturbance, and cultural disadvantage as there is about what a learning disability is! However a child is labeled, the same instruction techniques may be used to remediate his skill deficits.

Possible Mislabeling Bias. Learning disabilities, then, are found within the categories of educable mentally retarded, emotionally disturbed, and environmentally disadvantaged children. Evidence indicates that the labeling and class placement of children are based on socioeconomic factors, and that many children are mislabeled and placed inappropriately. In the early 1970s it was suspected that children from upper socioeconomic levels who had learning problems were being placed in classes for the learning disabled, whereas those from minority groups were labeled EMR (Franks, 1971). This practice led to a number of legal actions against school districts by parents charging discriminatory practices (see Abeson and Zettel, 1977; Jones, 1976; Ross, DeYoung, and Cohen, 1971).

The Garrison and Hammill study, cited earlier, indicates that labeling and the resultant EMR class placement have often been based on factors other than intellectual retardation. Twenty-five percent of the EMR students in their sample passed four or five of the criterion tests for intellectual normalcy, and over 40 percent passed two or three of them. The study's authors found that the combination of a reading problem and a low score on an IQ test were frequently associated with special class placement, and suggested that many children in EMR classes are inappropriately placed. Rubin, Krus, and Balow (1973) found that less than one-third of the students they studied who scored within the EMR range were placed in EMR classes, and that 28 percent of those in special classes actually scored above the EMR range on an individual intelligence test. They suggested that the child's group behavior and relatively low socioeconomic status were major factors in the placement of children whose IQs alone did not indicate that they belonged in an EMR class. Abeson and Zettell (1977) and Jones (1976) summarized the findings of others regarding mislabeling and misplacement of minority group children in classes for the EMR. They conclude that, in California, for example, three to four times as many Mexican Americans and two to three times as many blacks are placed in special classes as would be expected from their percentage in the general population.

Even when test results are not used arbitrarily, many children are mislabeled and misplaced as a result of the bias inherent in the test instruments themselves. In the California cases of Diana and Larry P., the issue was improper placement in an EMR class based on the results of a test that measured the values of white, middle-class culture and was therefore inappropriate for measuring the intelligence of minority group students. Jones (1976, pp. 235-57) provided some examples of this bias: in the answer keys for IQ tests, policemen were seen as "nice," government as "fair"; and words like casserole, scholar, and observatory were used to indicate intelligence.

The exclusive use of such tests is now expressly forbidden by PL 94-142, to protect the rights of parents and children. Tests must now be given in the child's native language, and they may not be culturally biased. In addition, placement decisions must be based on more than one test, and the child's parents (and the child, when appropriate) must be involved in the placement decision. Parents are now given written notice of meetings, and access to their child's records; they may in addition protest a placement decision or request an impartial hearing. As a result of new legislation, unbiased test instruments are being developed, and procedures to protect the rights of handicapped children and their parents are being implemented. But in the interim, the question of whether to label children as LD, or EMR, is highly controversial.

WHY IS A DEFINITION NECESSARY?

If agreement on a definition is so difficult, and labeling so controversial, why have a definition at all? The primary reason is that defined categories are required by the legislation that funds services. The federal definition is used to identify learning disabled children and to fund their educational programs. This explains the exclusions: programs for children whose primary handicaps are global, sensory, emotional, or the result of cultural differences are allotted separate funds. To provide them with additional funds because they are also learning disabled would give them a disproportionate share of funding.

There are additional reasons to have general guidelines for a state-of-the-art definition. Ross (1976) points out that the term "learning disabilities" is useful in calling attention to a particular problem — it stimulates communication that eventually leads professionals to solutions. A concise definition of learning disabilities would be hard to generate since "learning" itself is a difficult-to-define abstraction. In addition, a given child is said to have a learning disability only when other causes of the learning problem have been eliminated, and eliminating other causes is an almost impossible task (Smith and Neisworth, 1975). Nevertheless, we need a general definition to prevent professionals in various fields from generating separate definitions and intensifying the tendency of each specialty to view the problem from its own perspective. This factionalism is, according to Abrams (1977) and Ringelheim (Senf, 1978), one of the major barriers to progress. The federal definition seems broad enough to encompass all points of view, but it also cautions us against thinking that the learning disabled are a homogeneous group.

Laura Jane's story exemplifies the major issue and the controversy that presently surrounds the definition of "learning disabilities": Our present technology doesn't enable us to differentiate a child with a learning disability from one whose learning difficulties result from mild mental retardation, emotional disturbance, or cultural deprivation. Yet, in order to provide these handicapped children with the special services they require, we must label them and place them in categorical programs.

The federal definition is a good starting point in the effort to determine precisely what a learning disability is. It delineates a general category of exceptional children eligible for these special services. It does *not* describe individual children or explain particular behaviors. And it should not be interpreted as meaning that children whose primary learning problems can be accounted for by guidelines for other categories cannot also have extreme difficulty in learning.

If the question of whether a controversial, tentative definition is better than none makes you want to throw up your hands and say, "Who cares?" consider a final argument by Grossman (1978), who discusses the observations of science historian Thomas Kuhn. Kuhn has observed that there is a pattern to the development of a science: it begins with data collection that leads to concept formation and ultimately to the development of definitions. Once definitions are accepted, all new data are measured against them. This is the form of quality control that separates astronomy from astrology and chemistry from alchemy. The accepted definitions, then, need to be specific enough to exclude the absurd, yet flexible enough to accommodate the creative thought that generates new knowledge. The federal definition seems to contain elements of both specificity and flexibility. That it is controversial and tentative reflects our present state of knowledge: nobody knows exactly what a learning disability is!

PROBE 8-2
Controversy Over the Learning Disabilities Definition

1. T F Special education did not begin to focus on children with learning disabilities until the mid-to-late 1960s.

2. Describe two reasons why the current definition of learning disabilities is so controversial.

   _____

   _____

3. What are the three primary objections to labeling a child as learning disabled?

   _____

   _____

   _____

4. T F The federal definition of learning disabilities excludes children who are disadvantaged or mentally retarded, yet research has indicated that learning disabled children exist within these populations.

5. If there is so much controversy over definitions of learning disabilities, why do we bother to have a definition?

_____

_____

_____

CHARACTERISTICS OF CHILDREN WITH LEARNING DISABILITIES

You should be able to recognize some of the characteristics of learning disabilities and to distinguish them from simple learning difficulties.

The problems you have experienced while trying to learn something difficult are similar to those experienced by disabled learners, though of lesser duration and degree. These difficulties are called "characteristics" when they are severe, resistant to simple remedial teaching methods, and accompanied by serious discrepancies between achievement and ability.

LEARNING PROBLEMS AND LEARNING DISABILITIES

Children with learning disabilities may have trouble with attention, perception, and memory. They may also have difficulty thinking and using language. It is important for the teacher to understand these problems. She should be able to tell the difference between simple learning problems and "real" learning disabilities, which require special help. One way to tell the difference is to *try* some straightforward remedial teaching and to see if it solves the problem. Here are some examples.

Attention. We all occasionally have problems focusing our attention. We may be distracted by other thoughts, or we may not know where to look and what to attend to. Can you read Figure 8-1? If you focused on the words hidden behind the lines, you read, "Are you paying attention?" The question, "Can you read Figure 8-1?" may have given you a clue to look for words. This illustrates an important part of the LD definition — the part about a child not achieving *even* when provided with *appropriate learning experiences.* An appropriate "experience"

Figure 8-1

(method) for you in this case was the verbal cue (the question). It helped you understand what you were to do. Had it not been included, you would not have known what to do, the experience would have been inappropriate, and the "test" of your attention unfair. Many children need special cues from the teacher to help them understand where and how to focus attention. These can be verbal cues, or nonverbal cues, such as pointing. It is also helpful to provide settings and materials that cut down on distractions. And (do you need to be reminded of this?) it helps to provide materials that are interesting instead of dull! If these guidelines are followed and the child still has a persistent, severe attention problem, the child *may* have a learning disability.

Perception. You can understand part of the mystery of "perception" by reflecting on your experiences with visual illusions like the one in Figure 8-2. If you stare at the cube for about ten seconds, it seems to flip over. Your perception of its orientation changes. In a similar manner, some children with learning disabilities seem to be unstable in their perception of images. Johnson illustrates another aspect of differences in perception by presenting three pictures of a lady (1972, pp. 267-69). One seems to be a pretty young lady with a feather in her hat; another, with one or two different lines, looks like a haggard old lady with a shawl. The third picture, which has both kinds of details, can be perceived as either a young or old lady, but the viewer usually perceives it as the image of whichever picture he or she saw first. This experience illustrates a problem some LD children have. Many children have difficulty perceiving either details or whole configurations. They frequently have problems "shifting gears"; that is, they have trouble expanding their original perceptions and seeing things in a different way. If you

Figure 8-2

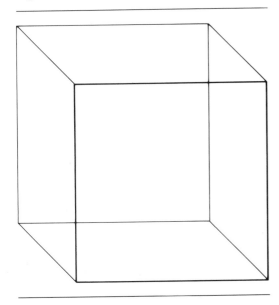

observe that a child often doesn't perceive letters and figures clearly, or that this child has great difficulty learning how to do things in a slightly different manner, the child *may* have a learning disability. You cannot be sure, however, until you have provided appropriate learning experiences — in this case, clear stimuli without irrelevant details, and an explanation of the task's distinctive features.

Memory. What kinds of things are hardest for you to remember? Try this experiment. Look at Figure 8-3 for five seconds. Write what you saw. Now try Figure 8-4. Look for five seconds. Write what you saw. Now check yourself.

Why was BRIOGANTRY easier? Probably because it looked more like a word, and the letters could be placed in larger groups to simplify learning them. Children with learning disabilities don't seem to know how to group things into meaningful parts to help them recall. Many children try to remember things one fragment at a time, just as you did with XTMSLFKBQH. They need help to understand how parts are meaningful and can be grouped. They also need lots of interesting practice and continued reinforcement to achieve mastery. A child who has severe and persistent difficulty remembering abstract symbols *may* need further assessment to determine whether she has a learning disability. But such children should be suspected of having a learning disability only if they've been given appropriate instruction. It is the *teacher* who has a problem if he is asking children to remember long lists of nonsense words, or to learn twenty-five addition facts in a day.

Figure 8-3

Thinking Difficulties. Try this example to see how you respond to problems that require careful thinking. Read this:

> What follows the day before yesterday if two days from now will be Sunday? [Whimbey, 1977, p. 255].

Can you answer the question quickly? What did you try to do when you read this problem? If you're a systematic problem solver, you tried to take it apart and solve it one step at a time. But if you're a "one-shot thinker," as many LD students are, you got confused and just guessed at the answer. Of course, you'd find this problem harder to solve if it was read to you out loud and you had to hold the details in mind while solving each step. That would not be an appropriate learning experience. Many children need assistance in developing strategies to help them remember relevant details and in working through a series of steps. Manipulative materials or concrete aids are helpful in problem solving. If you observe a child who always has great difficulty with thinking skills — he seems to be a one-shot, impulsive guesser — you *may* want to make a referral for a possible learning disability, but only, of course, after you've tried good remedial procedures like using concrete materials, helping the child work through the problem's steps, and providing lots of reinforcement for systematic efforts.

Figure 8-4

Language. Remember when you were little and thought shoe trees were trees that had shoes instead of leaves on them? Actor Fred Gwynne has written a delightful children's book called *A Chocolate Moose for Dinner* (Gwynne, 1976). It illustrates the child's simpler ideas of words which adults know have multiple meanings. It shows, for example, a picture of "shoe trees" and shows how "lions *pray* [prey] on other animals." (Picture that in your mind's eye!) Mort Walker, the creator of the Beetle Bailey comic strip, has also pictured this more concrete level of language in the verbal responses of his character named Zero. Zero is shown using a metal file to smooth down the general's papers after being told to "file these papers," and he goes to ask for the keys to the jeep when the general, in exasperation, moans, "You're driving me to the psychiatrist's couch!" Such difficulties with language are understandable, because our language is filled with abstraction and multiple meanings. Children who lack experience with words should be provided with relevant experiences, and words should be taught with visuals and illustrations. Children who continue to have serious trouble after good teaching techniques have been tried should be suspected of having a learning disability. Whether or not the child does will be decided by the school-based committee.

All of our examples were, of course, vastly oversimplified for the purpose of illustration. They were intended to show that all of us have some of the problems that are often attributed to children with learning disabilities. It is important to remember that they may just be common problems, and not symptoms of learning disabilities, and that the first step is to provide the child with "appropriate learning experiences" such as those suggested. If the problem persists, especially if more than one problem is apparent, procedures for obtaining parental permission for further assessment should be initiated. For students to have a learning disability their problems must have resulted in an inability to learn one or more of the seven areas of the definition. It must also be demonstrated to the committee that there is a *severe* discrepancy between achievement and ability, in spite of the provision of appropriate learning experiences. The committee must also be given evidence that the problem is not primarily the result of mental retardation, emotional disturbance, cultural, environmental, or economic disadvantage, or of a visual, hearing, or motor handicap.

COMMON CHARACTERISTICS OF LEARNING DISABILITIES

LD characteristics are far too complex to be illustrated adequately in a brief explanation. You should, however, have some perspective on the nature and severity of the LD child's difficulties. This section outlines seven common LD characteristics, which have been selected because they are educationally relevant and because most of them resemble the common difficulties you just reviewed. As before, the most common disability, reading disability, is emphasized. The seven educationally relevant characteristics of reading disability to be discussed are

1. Attention difficulty
2. Perceptual problems
3. Poor motivation/attitude
4. Poor sound/symbol association
5. Memory problems
6. Language deficits
7. Transfer difficulties

Each of these characteristics is defined and its research basis summarized.[2]

Attention Difficulty. Many children with serious learning difficulties find it hard to focus their attention on a selected sound, word, number, or line of print (Cruickshank, Betsen, Ratenburg, and Tannhauser, 1961; Strauss and Lehtinen, 1947). Ross (1976) suggests that the major difficulty is an inability to use attention selectively. He explains that children not using selective attention may look at the chalkboard or the fly on the eraser instead of the letter or word they should see. He also maintains that their attention may be overselective — for example, they may focus only on the circular part of the letter "b" and thus be unable to differentiate it from the "d." In a recent study, Hallahan et al. (1978) compared disabled learners to "normal" teenagers on a task involving selective attention. They found that the LD group was deficient in giving selective attention to the central learning task, but not to the incidental details. A possible consequence, then, of an attention problem, is that students may focus on the irrelevant details while missing the central issue. Another possible problem is that children may guess at answers impulsively, without looking at the word, listening to the question, or thinking through their response.

Perceptual Problems. Studies of disabled learners suggest that many of them are confused by words or numbers that look or sound alike. They may have trouble differentiating similar sounds (Wepman, 1960) and recognizing small visual differences (Strauss and Lehtinen, 1947; Cruickshank et al., 1961).

Poor Motivation/Attitude. Many disabled learners have poor attitudes and motivation, partly because they have experienced repeated failure. Fernald (1943) described the negative attitude of the nonreader as a major problem requiring

---

[2] The material presented in this section has been abstracted and adapted from the teacher's guide to a set of instructional materials for disabled readers. (See Morsink et al., *DELTA: A Design for Word Attack,* Tulsa, OK: Educational Development Corporation, 1977.

that the teacher develop entirely new strategies. Cruickshank et al. (1961) observed that disabled learners who had experienced repeated failures had extremely low tolerance for frustration. The result of this characteristic may be that students refuse to try, resorting instead to impulsive guessing, or reacting violently to failure.

Poor Sound/Symbol Association. Although some LD children have trouble receiving information that is presented auditorily or visually, a greater number experience difficulty in associating auditory with visual stimuli (Abrams, 1975; Johnson and Myklebust, 1967). Researchers who compared disabled readers and normal learners in their ability to attach auditory meanings to visual abstract symbols found that the performance of the disabled readers was significantly poorer (Birch and Belmont, 1964; Guthrie, 1974). Steinhauser and Guthrie (in Guthrie, 1974), reporting on a task requiring subjects to indicate whether letter patterns in words looked the same and had the same sound, concluded that disabled readers could match symbols that were visually alike, but that they had trouble matching sounds with visual symbols. Recent research supports the assumption that auditory-visual integration is related to reading ability (Deverensky, 1977; Ward, 1977), but indicates that the variables are related in a complex manner, depending on the students' development, IQ, and economic background.

Memory Problems. "Word blindness," a synonym for reading disability, is used to suggest a severe deficit in visual memory. Such deficits can be intensified by inadequate instruction. That is, if the teacher presents too many words at once or introduces new words before old ones are mastered, the "interference" theory of learning suggests that none of the words will be remembered. There is reason to believe that careful, skill-centered instruction results in better memory for words. Morsink, Cross, and Strickler (1978) compared the abilities of disabled readers and normal learners to recall sequences of "meaningful" (bo, nup, ...) and "meaningless" (fz, sdm, ...) letters. They found that although the disabled readers were poorer in both tasks, they were markedly inferior on "meaningful" recall. This suggests that they didn't know how to simplify the task by grouping meaningful segments, that the segments were not meaningful to them, or both. Gibson's summary (1970) indicates that decoding instruction can improve the recall of abstract symbols, and Otto (1961) has shown that, though poor readers learn the "names" for symbols more slowly, they can remember verbal labels once they have learned them. These findings underscore the importance of careful instruction as an aid to memory.

Language Deficits. According to the definition, LD children have an overall deficit in one or more of the processes involved in language. An increasing number of researchers are suggesting that reading disability is related to overall language facility (Abrams, 1975; Sievers et al., 1963; Vogel, 1974). A frequent observation is that disabled learners continue to use language incorrectly long after it has been mastered by children with comparable education and background. It has also been observed that academic achievement can be predicted from tests of oral language usage. These findings suggest that a general underlying problem with language sometimes extends to difficulty in learning, and imply a need for emphasis on oral language development.

Transfer Difficulties. Bryant (1965) and Abrams (1969) have suggested that disabled learners have extreme difficulty generalizing their knowledge of sound/symbol relationships to new situations. In an interesting study comparing the reading subskills of disabled readers and normal learners, Guthrie (1973) provided evidence that the reading subskills of normal learners are highly interconnected or are derived from an understanding of concepts common to all subskills. Among disabled readers, however, reading subskills may seem unrelated, and each subskill may have to be learned independently.

It should be emphasized that there is a difference between simple learning difficulties and learning disabilities characterized by the problems we have described. The existence of any learning difficulty suggests that the teacher should change the child's instructional program. Obviously, many of these problems are sometimes experienced by "normal" learners. The teacher of a child who is having difficulty in one of these areas should not conclude that she has a learning disability. Only when the child's problems are severe and do not improve with good remedial teaching should the referral be made. And only after careful assessment and the development of a consensus among the school committee should a child be identified as LD.

PROBE 8-3
Characteristics of Children with Learning Disabilities

1. In order to be called a "characteristic," difficulties that children with learning disabilities have must be

   a. _____

   b. _____

   c. _____

2. Match the things that either the child or teacher is doing with the appropriate characteristic that it is designed to remediate.

Characteristic	*Teacher and child behavior*
___ attention problem	a. Teacher uses exercises in problem solving.
___ perception difficulty	b. Child is doing exercises on synonyms.
___ memory deficit	c. Teacher uses verbal and non-verbal cues.
___ thinking difficulty	
___ language deficit	d. Teacher provides positive reinforcement for correct responses.
___ motivation problem	e. Child is doing exercises differentiating "saw" and "was" and "b" and "d."
___ transfer difficulty	
___ sound/symbol association problem	f. Teacher provides practice in reading words in different contexts.
	g. Child is pronouncing words presented on flash cards.
	h. Teacher stresses grouping of meaningful parts of words.

LEARNING DIFFICULTIES AND INSTRUCTION

You should be able to explain the relationship between learning difficulties and instructional factors.

The number of students with real learning disabilities is quite small — probably about 3 percent of the school population (DCLD, 1976). A much larger number of children exhibit "learning disability behaviors," that is, they have difficulty in learning. This is often caused by some aspect of the instructional program.

It has always been assumed that a child who has had no opportunity to learn cannot have a learning disability. In an early definition, Money (1962) stated that children could not be said to have a learning disability unless they had at least been exposed to conventional instruction. The new federal guidelines go even further, indicating that LD students are those who haven't learned in spite of "appropriate instructional opportunities." Samuels' (1970) definition of the disabled reader also includes the requirement that the child not have learned "despite adequate instruction." Otto (1970) has questioned whether adequate reading instruction exists, and whether anyone even knows precisely what it is. Reynolds and Birch (1977) have stated the essence of the problem of instructional factors: "Most pupil behaviors called learning disabilities and behavior disorders are best acknowledged as the consequences of failure to provide enough high quality individualized instruction" (p. 351).

Of course it is difficult for teachers who have large classes to provide this high-quality individualized instruction. It is also difficult, as Otto pointed out (1970), to specifically state all the dimensions of good instruction, since there are a number of theories of learning and a variety of effective techniques. But there are some general guidelines. You can perhaps understand them better if you experience a situation where you are required to learn something new and very difficult. If you fail repeatedly, your teacher's patience may naturally wear a little thin. The difficulty of the subject, combined with the teacher's intensified efforts and your increasing feelings of frustration, may make *you* feel like a disabled learner, even though you're not. Try the simulation exercise in Chart 8-1 and see if you can explain the relationship between learning difficulties and instructional factors.

EVOLUTION OF THE FIELD OF LEARNING DISABILITIES

You should be able to describe the historical background of the LD movement and to explain how the LD concept evolved.

Our understanding of what a learning disability is and how it should be treated has evolved as our knowledge has expanded. Initially, learning disabilities were believed to be organic in origin. Later, training programs based on measurements of theoretical learning processes such as visual memory were developed. At a later stage, we designed treatments that were primarily educational, intended to remediate the child's specific academic skill deficits. Recently, there have been intriguing suggestions that many learning disabilities have an environmental cause, such as radiation or air pollution. At present, our view of LD is primarily, but not exclusively, educational. It emphasizes a transdisciplinary approach in which concerned professionals work together on diagnosis and treatment.

PHYSICAL CAUSES OF LEARNING DISABILITIES

Early in the development of the learning disability concept, many specialists thought that the child's problems resulted from an internal physical deficit. This

Chart 8-1
Teaching Disability Simulation

You have been selected for the high reading group, the "Eagles." You are to try to learn this new code. Pay special attention to the directions on this task sheet, and complete all activities carefully.

Learn these new words and phrases:

MKC	— Kansas City, Missouri
FA	— weather report
Ø4	— fourth day of the month
1852	— time in Greenwich. This is the same as 1252 in Kansas City, 1152 in Denver, or 1052 in Los Angeles.
IA KANS NWRN MO	— Iowa, Kansas, Northwestern Missouri
NEB EXCP PHNDL	— Nebraska except the panhandle
KTS	— knots
8-15 ⊕	— 800-1500 feet, complete overcast
AGL	— above ground level
5HND	— 500
R-F	— light rain and fog
①	— scattered clouds
⑪	— broken clouds

Now learn this rule: Words in this code are spelled by their main consonant sounds. For example:

FLWG	— following
SPRDG	— spreading
CNTRD	— centered
PHDL	— panhandle

Of course there are exceptions, like WX = weather, and V = variable, but you'll just have to learn them separately.

Now that you know the rules, try this little test: How do you think you would write the following words in this code?

Evening _____ Kansas _____ Monday _____

Did you say EVNG, KNS, MNDY? Wrong! It should be EVE, KANS, MON.

If that was too hard for you, try the easier task given to the slower group, the "Robins": *Look at these words and compare them with the code symbols to see what is left out:*

CSDRBL	— considerable. These letters are left out: C-NS-D-R-BL-.
VSBY	— visibility. These letters are left out: V-S-B----Y.

Not bad. Now try a harder one. What is CIGS? _____ Did you say cigars?

Cigarettes? Wrong!!! This is a weather code. CIGS means ceilings — the distance of the clouds above the ground. You'll have to concentrate better than that.

Well, *try one more.* You won't have to move down to the slowest group, the "Sparrows," if you get this one right. What is ① V ⑪ ? Come on, we had all that before! You just weren't paying attention, were you? It's variable scattered to broken clouds. Sorry, you blew it!

So you have a learning disability, do you? The code you were trying to learn is not unlike the English code, with its inconsistent, confusing rules, and symbols that are hard to tell apart. That was part of the problem. But the way the lesson was presented made the code even harder to learn. Describe two of the instructional factors (i.e., what the teacher did and how the material was presented) that exacerbated your problem.

1. _____

_____

_____

_____

_____

2. _____

_____

_____

_____

_____

This task is a modification of a two-part simulation prepared for use in teacher training. The original includes all instructions and a second example of a more effective presentation of the same material. See Morsink, C., LRNG to Read, *Journal of Learning Disabilities,* 1973, *6,* 479–85.

internal deficit could be a constitutional problem present at birth, such as a hereditary, genetic, or congenital abnormality; or it could be a deficit occurring after birth, the result of infections, toxins, poor nutrition, injury, or illness (see Baren, Liebl, and Smith, 1978, for details).

The early literature also suggested that the LD child suffered from neurological impairment. Learners with severe disability were observed to have difficulty recalling the orientation and sequence of letters, a phenomenon that the neurologist Orton (1937) termed "strephosymbolia," or twisted symbols. Strauss and Lehtinen (1947) noted that neurologically impaired children tended to perceive fragmented parts rather than integrated wholes, that they were distracted by extraneous details, and that they did not perceive figures as distinct from their backgrounds. Strauss and Lehtinen also discussed their students' difficulty in relating temporal (sounds) and spatial patterns (the letters in a word which the sounds represent). They suggested further that the students' tendency to perseverate (repeat the same response over and over again) indicated an inability to perceive unfamiliar sequences or relationships. Problems such as these resemble those observed in adults who had suffered strokes. Because these authors reported on a neurologically impaired group of LD children, they inferred that neurological impairment might be the cause of learning disabilities.

In a 1961 report based on observations of brain injured and hyperactive children in an experimental educational program, Cruickshank et al. reported that hyperactive children without brain damage exhibited learning characteristics similar to those of the neurologically impaired. Cruickshank's work also detailed teaching methods that could be used effectively for children with serious learning difficulties, regardless of the cause of the difficulty. New labels such as "minimal brain dysfunction" and "maturational lag" came into use to describe children who had disabilities in the absence of documented neurological impairment.

PSYCHOLOGICAL PROCESS THEORIES

During the same period, others believed that learning disabilities resulted from deficits in the psychological learning processes. This group felt that learning disabled children were a heterogenous group, and that effective teaching required that the individual's learning strengths and weaknesses be identified. This concept provided the impetus for the development of diagnostic tests designed to identify students with difficulties in basic learning processes such as perception, association, and memory. Tests such as the *Marianne Frostig Developmental Test of Visual Perception* (Frostig, 1961) and the *Illinois Test of Psycholinguistic Abilities* — ITPA (Kirk, McCarthy, and Kirk, 1968) emphasized a process approach to remediation. Each of these tests prescribed a remedial program based on the test results.

Although theoretically promising, attempts to measure process deficits, to use test data for remedial programs, and to evaluate the results of remediation have been disappointing. Zach and Kaufman (1972) pointed out that although visual perception deficits were frequently indentified by tests that measured visual-motor performance (copying), their treatment often consisted of training in visual discrimination (matching). Hammill (1972), while acknowledging that training may not have been correctly implemented, concluded that research did not support the theory and questioned whether visual perceptual processes could be improved with training. Hammill and Larsen's (1974, 1978) reviews of the research on remedial programs based on the ITPA implied that the value of these programs had not been demonstrated.

EDUCATIONAL INTERVENTION STRATEGIES

In the early 1970s the learning disability concept began to develop an educational rather than physical or psychological process emphasis. This new emphasis resulted from the acknowledgement that, although there may be differences in the educational and behavioral characteristics of LD children who have brain damage and those who don't, distinctions between the two groups are difficult to make, particularly in the public school setting (Reed, Robe, and Mankinen, 1970). Another factor was the difficulty in determining the validity of the psychological process approach.

Educational programs for LD children had actually been proposed earlier by many educators, including Fernald (1943), Gillingham and Stillman (1960), Bryant (1965), Johnson and Myklebust (1967), and Englemann and Bruner (1969), among others. Kirk, Hegge, and Kirk (1948) developed a similar approach to reading instruction for students labeled mentally retarded. These programs were all designed for children who had extreme difficulty in learning to read. Fernald's method emphasized a kinesthetic approach, in which the child traced words with her finger while looking at the copy and saying the parts of the word aloud. This approach was used because it provided a new method of instruction not associated with past failure. Gillingham and Stillman's program, published in 1960 but developed much earlier, was based on the work of the neurologist, Orton. These researchers broke the reading act into its simplest components, letters and sounds, and emphasized teaching each association separately before putting letters and sounds together in a given sequence to form words. Bryant's method stressed repeated practice, or "overlearning," as a means of helping disabled readers make automatic sound/symbol associations. He also emphasized the importance of making careful lesson plans to ensure that the learner responded correctly, and stated that errors should be corrected immediately. Johnson and Myklebust split reading disability into auditory and visual "dyslexia," and designed special remedial programs for each category. Englemann and Bruner's approach emphasized the teaching of individual sound/symbol associations and the subsequent blending of sounds into words, in combination with a rapid-paced format in which the teacher gives continuous reinforcement. All of these programs were primarily educational in the sense that they stressed a task analysis of the reading act and emphasized instructional techniques.

ENVIRONMENTAL FACTORS

Historically, then, the learning disabilities movement has evolved from a physical and learning process to an educational model. The current emphasis is not exclusively educational, however; a number of professionals view the purely educational approach as simplistic (Abrams, 1977; Hollander, 1977; Senf, 1978).

In addition, there is a growing list of environmental factors that may have some relationship to learning disabilities. Each of these has its own advocacy group, each leads logically to a different treatment approach, and each is based on at least a little research data. Examples and explanations follow.

Consider the following noneducational explanation: learning disabilities may be aggravated by allergies, induced by nutritional deficits, related to biochemical disorders, or intensified by fluorescent lighting (see Hollander's summary, 1977). Baren et al. (1978) add smog, fluoride, radiation, aerosols, and auditory pollution to the list of possible environmental causes for educational problems.

There is some research on these controversial medical and environmental causes and treatments. Feingold (1976) reported that a diet which eliminates artificial food colors and flavors plus salicylates (found, for example, in aspirin and in fresh fruits) reduces the levels of hyperactivity in some children. Ott (1976) has suggested in a report on his studies of first graders that cool white fluorescent lighting intensifies fighting, out-of-seat behavior, and inattention. The installation of bulbs that provide light resembling daylight enhances some children's abilities to study and remain calm and quiet.

Research on these matters is continuing, and the findings cited should be regarded as inconclusive. Sieben (1977), presenting the physician's point of view, suggests caution and discusses the need for more research to validate controversial medical treatments. It should be emphasized that not even the advocates of these theories suggest that they have found either a cause or a treatment for all learning disabilities.

The present extensive use of drugs for LD children is another indication that current emphasis is not exclusively educational, since the use of drug therapy implies that the disability has a physical cause. Abrams (1977) estimates that 200,000 children are being given amphetamines and stimulants, that another 100,000 are receiving tranquilizers and antidepressants, and that the use of drugs to modify behavior may increase. Parents, educators, physicians, and the general public are expressing concern over the massive use of drug therapy.

The need for medication can be determined only by a physician. The effects of medication vary with the individual and are not always predictable. For example, some stimulants allow patients to control their attention and organize activity by assisting them in screening out disruptive stimuli. Tranquilizers sometimes reduce a child's attention span, and anticonvulsants can magnify hyperactivity. In all cases, drug use should be carefully monitored (Baren et al., 1978). In a review of psychostimulant use with children, Whalen and Henker (1976) concluded that they often have positive effects, but that gains may not be maintained when drug use is discontinued. They also point out that there is no way to predict which child will benefit from drug use. The current conclusion about the use of medication, then, is the same as the conclusion about the effectiveness of other treatments: it may be right for some LD children and wrong for others. The extent to which drug use is beneficial can be determined only by more research.

EDUCATIONAL IMPLICATIONS OF VARIOUS THEORIES

As you can see, each of the theories about the cause of learning disabilities could translate into its own treatment program. If, for example, you believed that LD was an organic problem, you might treat the disability with medication. If, on the other hand, you thought it was a disorder in an underlying psychological process, you would design a remedial program that emphasized learning processes such as "memory" and "perception." Few people adhere exclusively to one theory, but each theory has its own educational implications.

PROBE 8-4
Evolution of the Field of Learning Disabilities

Indicate whether each statement suggests an educational (ED), physical (PH), psychological process (PS), or environmental (EN) explanation of learning disabilities.

_____ 1. Since a special diet eliminating salicylates and certain artificial food colors and flavors seems to reduce hyperactivity in some children, the possibility that these substances contribute to learning disabilities should be explored further.

_____ 2. One reason finger-tracing techniques are used in remedial reading is that this method is not associated with past failure.

_____ 3. Some early studies indicated that learning disabled children, as a group, had some basic deficits in their learning processes.

_____ 4. Abnormalities present at birth may cause or contribute to the development of learning disabilities.

_____ 5. It is possible that fluorescent lights in classrooms increase children's inattention to academic tasks.

_____ 6. Careful planning, immediate correction of errors, and repeated practice were among the components suggested for the LD child's instructional program.

_____ 7. Some learning disabled children benefit from certain types of drugs, whereas others don't.

_____ 8. The characteristics of some children in LD programs suggest that they are neurologically impaired.

_____ 9. According to the skill-referenced approach, LD students should receive instruction related directly to the skills they are having difficulty with.

_____ 10. There is a need to develop and validate new tests that can be used to measure various aspects of the learning process.

Describe in 250 words or less, how the concept of learning disabilities has developed. Incorporate the medical, psychological process, environmental, and educational explanations of the problem.

_____

_____

_____

_____

_____

THE LEAST RESTRICTIVE ENVIRONMENT

You should be able to tell how to manage LD children in the least restrictive environment.

The major contemporary issue in learning disabilities is the same as it is in other areas of special education: how can we identify and meet the needs of a broad range of exceptional learners in the least restrictive environment? The question takes an added significance in the field of LD, because there has been so much disagreement over definition of the term and no resolution of the treatment controversy. In the future it will become increasingly important to separate — for treatment purposes — those few students with true disabilities from the much larger group of students with less complicated learning difficulties. Classification may become more important, but it won't be any easier; the fact that learning difficulties range along a continuum from the mild to the severe, and resist clear differentiation, will continue to present problems. In addition, even students with severe disabilities should be served in the regular classroom part of the time.

Two major trends in teaching LD children in the least restrictive environment seem to be emerging:

1. Service to LD children will be provided by a team of professionals rather than a single specialist, and most of it will take place in regular classes.
2. The emphasis will be on preventing learning disabilities by providing instruction in academic skills for all children — those with simple learning difficulties and those with severe disabilities.

THE SERVICE TEAM

There is an increasing awareness among professionals that the needs of the LD child cannot be met by educators, parents, physicians, psychologists, or any other group acting alone — the causes of learning disabilities are too varied and their treatment too complex. This is why the new federal regulations require a group consensus for identification of the LD child. A diagnosis is made only after the results of classroom observations, ability and achievement tests, and related medical evaluations have been presented to the school's admissions and release committee, a transdisciplinary team.

Transdisciplinary Ecological Approach. A transdisciplinary approach is one in which each member of the service team, a specialist in dealing with some aspect of a child's problem, maintains the ability to listen to and negotiate with other specialists. The intent is to reach consensus on a program that responds to the child's total range of needs.

One of the proponents of the "ecological" approach is Hobbs (1978), who defines the term this way:

> The term ecology or ecosystem considers the total life circumstances of the child.... A classification system is needed that can in some way mobilize the people who are important in the life of the child.... An ecologically oriented system is a classification system that is based on the service needs of children and their immediate worlds [p. 495].

Haring and Bateman (1977) suggest that communities should establish systems designed to identify and treat the learning disabled. These systems would coordinate school and community agency services and establish comprehensive files of information on LD individuals, to be used in making treatment decisions. The authors assert that such a comprehensive, coordinated system could

1. Disseminate information describing the LD child to all the agencies requiring such information.
2. Collect information on the recommendations made and how they affected the child's subsequent development.
3. Provide funding for multidisciplinary community screening projects.
4. Develop valid, reliable psychological tests, behavioral objectives, and normative developmental information.

The ecological, transdisciplinary approach is designed to take advantage of aspects of the field that are still evolving. There are exciting developments in medical treatment and in educational approaches, and new concepts in psychology and environmental research. All contribute to our understanding of learning disabilities, but the most effective approaches are derived from the entire range of sources.

New Roles for Special Educators. As the diagnostic practices and treatment of the LD have evolved, the role of the special educator has changed as well. Special educators now act as team members rather than isolated specialists. The requirement that exceptional children be educated in the least restrictive environment has also exerted an influence. The special educator now serves as a collaborator, consultant, and resource person.

Most of the special services provided to mildly handicapped children who remain in the regular class most of the time are provided through a resource or consulting teacher trained in special education and diagnostics. Many model university programs of this kind have already been developed and implemented. In other cases, school districts have developed model programs that emphasize classroom teacher retraining. There are many descriptions of the resource teacher approach; those provided by Wiederholt, Hammill, and Brown (1978) and by Hawisher and Calhoun (1978) are particularly noteworthy.

The special educator's role as a resource person will also be important for the severely disabled learner who requires initial placement in a special education setting. These children will need to be prepared for reentry into the educational mainstream. Reentry is a task that involves collaboration between the regular and special class teachers (Grosenick, 1971).

The new role of the special educator as a team member and resource person will require a new form of training, one that stresses professional interactions. Denemark, Morsink, and Thomas (1980) report that training for professional interactions should include practice in expressing ideas in simple, direct language and experiences in joint planning, team teaching, and collaborative evaluation of educational programs. The LD specialist of the future will have to know not only how to identify and teach the LD child, but how to work cooperatively as a member of a professional team as well.

EMPHASIS ON ACADEMIC INSTRUCTION

Current educational practice emphasizes the identification of skills in which students are deficient. This is done with skill-based or criterion-referenced tests, so called because they are used to identify the child's skill deficits, and because a student's performance is compared to a predetermined criterion. The test measures the academic subskills normally taught in a certain subject (reading or math, etc.) at a particular grade level, and determines whether each student has met a certain criterion level (usually 80 percent or better) indicating mastery of that skill. Those who have not met the criterion are given additional instruction and then retested.

Once a student's skill deficits have been identified, the teacher can plan lessons to help the student master those skills. The first step in lesson planning is to determine an instructional objective that describes exactly what the student needs to learn. This objective should be based directly on the items failed on the test. If, for example, the child had problems with two-digit addition problems involving carrying, the objective would be for the child correctly to compute two-digit addition problems with carrying to the tens column. If the student had trouble reading words that began with the initial "cl"-blend, the objective would be for the child to read correctly words that began with the cl-blend. This kind of specificity helps the teacher translate test results into remedial programs.

Teachers frequently design their own skill-based, criterion-referenced tests by determining what subskills are used in each academic area at a certain grade level and then developing test items to measure the student's achievement of these skills (for suggestions, see Hammill and Bartel, 1977). There are also a number of commercially developed tests on the market. The major skill-based testing and teaching programs in the area of reading instruction have been reviewed by Rude (1974). Many of these programs describe remedial activities for each of the subskills tested. Some of them also provide lists of sources for additional lessons.

The skill-referenced educational approach is appropriate for disabled readers because it presents tasks designed to help resolve specific learning problems. Hartman and Hartman (1973) suggest that remedial programs that stress lower level skills, such as eye-hand coordination, are less effective because the skills learned as a result of training may not be transferred to academic tasks. Another advantage of the skill-referenced approach is that it can be used by teachers who have little time available for work with individual students. During a twenty-minute session, a teacher could give a remedial lesson to a student who, for example, confuses words having similar visual patterns. The teacher could offer direct instruction, such as practice differentiating similar words, or indirect instruction, such as exercises in differentiating forms such as circles and squares. The teacher should pretest the child, and present low-level instruction only if necessary. In any case, low-level instruction would have to be followed with direct instruction using words.

Some research indicates that effectiveness of the skill-based approach depends on the way it is used by the teacher (Morsink and Otto, 1977). Face-to-face instruction is more effective than the use of worksheets that students complete independently. Teachers who select instructional activities carefully, provide enough practice to ensure skill mastery, and show students how to apply the skills they learn, find that their students retain information and generalize better.

Another problem with the purely skill-based approach is that it's too simple. It suggests to some critics that all the teacher needs to do is identify a child's skill deficits and present skill-based instruction. If this were true, it would imply that learning disabilities are no more than unlearned skills, which would suggest that all children who have failed to master the basic skills should be identified as LD. This has happened in some places, resulting in almost half of a school's population being referred for diagnosis of learning disabilities! If the insistence on clearly determined neurological impairment resulted in the identification of too few LD children, the assumption that all skill deficits are learning disabilities has resulted in the identification of too many. Identifying skill needs and providing appropriate instruction is an important part of the treatment of LD children, but these techniques should be based on careful assessment procedures and used in conjunction with other methods when necessary.

A LOOK TO THE FUTURE

This is an exciting time in the education of all children, particularly of those who have learning disabilities. Former United States Commissioner of Education Ernest L. Boyer (1978) has stated that this is a time to provide access to education for all children, to increase our commitment to the quality of education, and to provide leadership in new educational strategies that meet the demands of our changing social context. Grossman (1978) asserts that a crucial "third stage" in the evolution of the learning disability movement has been entered. The first stage, in the early 1960s, was essentially medical in its orientation. During the second stage, from about 1965 to 1970, an educational approach that focused on treating the child in the classroom was emphasized. During stage three, the important issue will be how to distinguish the LD child from those whose learning difficulties are less complex. According to Grossman, at this stage service personnel can no longer afford to waste energy on arguments about theory and definitions. If they do, he argues, the government bureaucracy, rather than teams of concerned professionals will formulate the definition and resolve the issue along budgetary lines. Professionals from all fields must renew our efforts to cooperate if we are to be equal to the magnitude of the task.

SUMMARY

1. The most widely accepted definition of "learning disabilities" is found in federal legislation. It is generally agreed that the LD child does not perform at the level she should be able to.
2. The decision to diagnose a child as a disabled learner is made by a transdisciplinary team.
3. Our present technology does not enable us to differentiate a child with a learning disability from one whose learning difficulties result from mild mental retardation, emotional disturbance, or cultural deprivation.
4. Children with learning disabilities may have serious problems with attention, perception, problem solving, and language skills.
5. Learning disabilities and behavior disorders may occur in part because our schools are unable to provide enough high-quality individual instruction.

6. The current concept of learning disabilities reflects a long history of different interpretations of how persons learn.
7. In contemporary services for the learning disabled, the goal is to provide intense services within the least restrictive environment possible, using a transdisciplinary team approach.
8. The regular classroom teacher should become skilled through in-service training in managing learning disabilities within the mainstream of the school.

TASK SHEET 8
Field Study in Learning Disabilities

Select *one* of the following alternatives and complete the assigned tasks:

Program Visitation

Visit an educational program for children with learning disabilities. Talk with teachers, administrators, or other relevant staff. Describe the facility that you visited, the activities that were being conducted, and any problems that were described by staff. Summarize your reactions to this experience.

Program Comparison

Visit a program for children who have been diagnosed as having learning disabilities. Then visit *either* a regular elementary school program *or* a class for children who have been diagnosed as mildly retarded. Describe each visit and your general impressions of the students and the instructional programs. How were the groups and programs alike and how were they different?

Parent Interview

Interview the parent (or other family member) of a child who has been diagnosed as having a learning disability. Describe the circumstances of the situation. Find out what the reactions were when it was first discovered that the child had a learning disability. Describe the actions taken by the parents in obtaining educational services for the child. Determine the extent of satisfaction with the services that the child is receiving. Describe the problems that have been encountered by the parents.

Definitions

Ask two educators (teachers, principals, college professors, fellow teacher-education students, etc.) to define what a learning disability is. Record their definitions. Analyze each of the definitions according to the four dimensions of learning disabilities described by Wallace and McLoughlin.

Library Study

Read three articles related to the topic of learning disabilities and write a one-page abstract of each.

Design Your Own Field Experience
If none of the above learning activities fits your needs or circumstances, design one of your own after discussing the idea with your instructor.

Probe Answers

Probe 8–1

1. 1,966,000; 87
2. True
3. a. discrepancy
   b. manifestation
   c. focus
   d. integrities
4. False
5. a. oral expression
   b. basic reading skills
   c. math reasoning
   d. written expression
   e. listening comprehension
   f. math calculation
   g. reading comprehension

Probe 8–2

1. True
2. a. The definition encompasses only under-achievement in academic skills.
   b. The definition does not properly account for the underachieving gifted pupil.
3. a. Labels do not really define discrete groups of individuals; they do not account for overlap between categories.
   b. Little evidence exists to support the use of one educational treatment for any particular label.
   c. Biased tests can cause mislabeling.
4. True
5. We use a definition basically for federal funding purposes. Also, the definition calls attention to a particular learning problem and stimulates communication among professionals.

Probe 8–3

1. a. observed consistently over time
   b. resistant to simple remedial teaching methods
   c. accompanied by a significant gap between achievement and ability
2. g; e; c; a; b; d; f; h

Probe 8–4

1. EN	6. ED
2. ED	7. PH
3. PS	8. PH
4. PH	9. ED
5. EN	10. PS

Answer to essay question:

Early practices had a medical orientation that looked for physical (neurological) causes of learning disability. The focus was on brain injury. It was also believed that learning disabilities were caused by impaired psychological processes, and efforts were made to remediate these processes. Environmental factors, such as lighting, smog, and inadequate diet, have been said to cause learning disabilities. Educational explanations for learning disability have included criticism of teaching methods and instructional materials. Current emphasis is on examining the educationally relevant characteristics of learning disabled children and working with these directly.

Peter

His voice is usually high-pitched, rapid, sing-song like:
"What color is your house do you have a dog what's his
name what's your dog's name does he have spots on his
face where's your house do you have a dog what's his
name what's your dog's name what's the color of your
house do you have a dog my dog's name is Choo-Choo
she has spots on her face what's your name your name is
Laurie my name is Peter Lee Eaton Peter Lee Eaton that's
my name you don't have a house you don't have a dog
my dog's name is Choo-Choo my house is white what's
your dog's name your name is Laurie . . ."

Sally

The children are coloring dittos. The teacher has her feet
up on her desk. She is reading a novel. Sally is at her desk
coloring. She begins to whistle a tune.

Teacher: "Please, please, if everyone did that we wouldn't
get our work done."
Sally: Stops a few seconds then begins whistling again.
Teacher: "Sally, stop it. What did I just tell you?"
Sally: Continues whistling but at a lower volume.
Teacher: "Cut it out RIGHT NOW. . . . Do you want to
go to the office?"
Sally: Begins laughing and loud singing.
Teacher: "STOP IT. . . . ALL RIGHT IF YOU WANT
TO GO TO THE OFFICE THE REST OF THE
DAY THAT'S WHAT YOU'LL DO. *RIGHT NOW.*
. . . LET'S GO."
Sally: Gets up and runs across the room.
Teacher: Grabs Sally's arm and takes her back to her seat.
Sally: Sings loudly.
Teacher: Puts her hand over Sally's mouth and whispers in
her ear.
Sally: Resumes coloring quietly while the teacher has her
arm around her.

Source: "Peter" is from L. P. Van Veelan, Cheer Soap Opera,
unpublished manuscript, University of Kentucky, 1975, p. 1. "Sally" is
from B. Ray, Emotionally Disturbed, or "Sit Down, Shut Up and You'll
Stay Out of Trouble," unpublished manuscript, University of Kentucky,
1978, p. 6. Reprinted by permission.

9

Behavior Disorders

C. Michael Nelson

C. Michael Nelson is a Professor in the Department of Special Education at the University of Kentucky. Dr. Nelson has taught special education classes for adolescents, worked as a psychologist, and been involved in camping and residential treatment programs for behaviorally disordered children. He is past President of the Council for Children with Behavior Disorders.

The two children described on the facing page are behaving very differently from one another. Peter is talking almost nonstop, whereas Sally appears to be almost willfully misbehaving. Yet they have something in common: both have been identified and labeled by their school systems as behaviorally disordered or emotionally disturbed.[1]

Almost everybody would agree that something is wrong with the children in these situations — that they are different, strange, and don't fit in with other children, or conform to our conception of "normal" behavior. But exactly what is wrong with them? Why are Peter and Sally different? How did they get that way? How do schools and parents cope with such children, and what happens to them when they grow up? We hope to provide answers to questions such as these in this chapter. You will find as you read that the answers are much more difficult to discern than the questions. The field of behavior disorders is fraught with controversy and conflicting opinions.

Whether you teach in a "regular" or a "special" classroom (for any disability group), you will frequently be involved with children labeled "behaviorally

[1] The terms behaviorally disordered and emotionally disturbed are considered synonymous in this chapter.

disordered." According to Wood and Zabel (1978), 30 percent of the children in any age group are considered by teachers to have behavior problems. Although the proportion of children whose maladaptive behavior persists for a relatively long time is much smaller, it is likely that one or more pupils in any class of thirty will be difficult to manage in the classroom.

DEFINING BEHAVIOR DISORDERS

You should be able to define behavior disorders.

To organize diverse phenomena and group them according to common characteristics, modern society relies heavily on classifying and labeling. Peter and Sally have in common the label "behaviorally disordered." This label might lead one to expect that these two children are similar in more ways than they are different, but they aren't, of course. Like other children, they are different in many respects: age, sex, and other physical attributes, aptitude, achievement, personality, and, importantly, the types of behaviors they display and the frequency with which they display them. The term "behavior disorders" encompasses an almost unlimited variety of behavior. What characteristics, then, do these behaviors have in common?

FUNDAMENTAL CHARACTERISTICS OF BEHAVIOR DISORDERS

Several characteristics are considered in determining whether a child's behavior is disordered. These include (1) the perception that the child's behavior departs from acceptable standards, (2) the degree to which her behavior deviates from these standards, and (3) the length of time the behavior pattern has continued.

Behavior That Departs from Acceptable Standards. In defining behavior disorders by referring to standards of behavior we must ask what normal behavior is, and who decides what is normal or abnormal. The answer to the first question is difficult to determine. The prevalence of behaviors that indicate psychological disorders is very high in population samples of "normal" children — those who have not been referred by their parents or teachers for help because of behavior problems (Lapouse and Monk, 1958; Ross, 1974). The behavior of children considered *disordered* or *disturbed* differs in degree, and not in kind, from that of children considered normal (Quay, 1972; Ross, 1974). In answer to the second question, the judgment of whether a child's behavior is aberrant is made by an adult — a parent or teacher. Peers also make judgments and place labels on children, but these judgments rarely result in "official" action such as referral to a child guidance clinic or a special education program. Adults are responsible for the "official" *deviant* labels some of our children must wear to school every day.

Implicit in an adult's judgment that a child is *behaviorally deviant* is the assumption that the child's actions violate the standards of the culture or subculture. Social standards may be based on such factors as age, sex role, and setting. For example, thumb sucking is considered normal in two year olds, but in an eight year old the same behavior would be considered deviant. A ten-year-old boy who wears dresses and makeup would qualify for a deviant label in the American culture. Running and screaming are considered normal behaviors on a playground, but they are cause for alarm if they occur in church. Since it is adults who interpret these standards and apply them to children's behavior, whether or not a child is labeled deviant is largely a function of adult expectations (Kauffman, 1977).

The tolerance of adults for behavior, as well as their expectations, affects which children are identified as deviant. Thus, an extremely active child might not attract undue attention in teacher *A*'s classroom, but teacher *B*, who values quiet and order, might find the same behavior intolerable. Because of the widespread use of labels, teachers have found that it is quite easy to get their judgments confirmed by mental health professionals. They are thus reinforced for identifying "problem" children by getting them moved from their classrooms into special education programs.

Degree of Deviation from Acceptable Standards. A second element of most definitions of behavior disorders is the judgment that the child's behavior is extreme. Sally is out of her seat too often. Too much of Peter's verbal behavior is repetitive and bizarre. Behavior also can vary to the opposite extreme, as in the case of the child who is excessively isolated and withdrawn, or the child who is grossly deficient in his ability to use language. Extremely high or low rates of behavior call attention to the child, and are likely to result in his being labeled and assigned to a "deviant" category. Remember that it is the degree, or amount, of behavior and not a particular type of behavior, that distinguishes deviant from normal children (Patterson, Shaw, and Ebner, 1969; Quay, 1972). In addition, extremely intense behavior, such as violent tantrums, can result in a child's being labeled deviant, even if such behavior is infrequent.

Duration of the Behavior Pattern. Most definitions of behavior disorders also assume that the problem is chronic rather than transient (Hallahan and Kauffman, 1978). Peter has been strange since he was old enough to walk and talk. Sally's reputation as a behavior problem has extended through several years of school. Everyone is capable of behaving abnormally during periods of stress. The death of a loved one, failure in a marriage or career, or leaving home for the first time can all result in transient disturbances. It is only when such behavior patterns persist long after the stressful situation has passed that an individual is considered disturbed.

In summary, then, a child's behavior may be judged disordered (1) if it deviates from the range of behaviors for the child's age and sex which significant adults perceive as "normal"; (2) if it occurs very frequently or too intensely; or (3) if it occurs over an extended period of time.

WHO "OWNS" THE DISORDER?

The question of "owning" a disorder may at first seem nonsensical. If a child is labeled behaviorally disordered or emotionally disturbed, the problem is apparently that child's. Once again, however, the answer isn't that simple. If deviance is partially determined by environmental expectations, and if these expectations are influenced by adults' tolerance for behavior, it is possible that children could be labeled because the expectations made of them are inappropriate. Children so identified and labeled are just as stigmatized as those "correctly" labeled, and become the targets of interventions designed to remediate or change their presumed behavior disorder. Most theories of psychopathology (e.g., the psychoeducational, behavioral, and biophysical theories) assume that the problem is the child's, and, therefore, that therapeutic change should occur in her (Rhodes, 1970).

In recent years Rhodes (1967, 1970, 1975) has championed another view — that disturbance is the result of interactions between the child and his school, home, and peer group, also known as his "microcommunities." This theory is termed "ecological," because it is concerned with the interrelationships between behavior and environment. The ecological theory has influenced most contemporary definitions of behavior disorder (see, for example, Kauffman, 1977; Ross, 1974), and it has significant implications for treatment. Consider, for instance, how you would approach Sally differently if you viewed her disorder as a problematic interaction between her and her teacher rather than as a "characteristic" owned exclusively by Sally. One might accuse Sally's teacher of incompetence, or even of being behaviorally disordered herself, because her actions deviate from widely accepted standards for teaching behavior. The ecological model, however, rejects the view that disturbance originates from individual psychopathology, either in children or in other significant people in the environment. Although we would like to bring Sally's teacher's behavior up to acceptable standards, our immediate concern would be to reduce the disturbing interactions occurring between her and Sally.

The ecological model stresses that behavior is situation-specific. That is, a child may have a behavior problem in one situation but not in others. If, for example, Sally is disruptive in her third-grade class but isn't when she is on the playground, at home, or in her Sunday School class, is she behaviorally disordered? To label her as such may cause her to be stigmatized in settings in which her social interactions are not disturbing. The application of the label could establish expectations for disordered behavior that would become self-fulfilling prophecies. It would probably be better not to label her, and to confine direct intervention to the setting in which the disturbance occurs. Peter, on the other hand, has disturbing encounters with people in all of his microcommunities. In his case, intervention (and a label, if it aids intervention) would be applied across all social settings. The extent to which intervention should be applied across settings or microcommunities is determined by the process of ecological assessment, which will be discussed later.

DIFFERENCES BETWEEN PSYCHODYNAMIC AND BEHAVIORAL ORIENTATIONS

How one conceptualizes a behavior disorder influences how one defines, identifies, and diagnoses it, and ultimately what kind of intervention one applies to it. The study of children's behavior disorders has been heavily influenced by Freudian psychology, which views mental disorders as disease processes that are essentially the same as physical diseases. According to this model, the disease produces symptoms, which are regarded as behavioral manifestations of the underlying disorder. To cure the disorder one must diagnose and treat the disease process that caused it. According to this view, the elimination of symptoms will result only in the appearance of new symptoms, as happens when a physician treats pneumonia. And, in fact, it has been widely believed for many years that mental disorders should be treated medically. This "medical model" dominated the field from the turn of the twentieth century until the late 1950s and early 1960s.

In 1960 Thomas Szasz challenged the medical model, arguing that an analogy to physical disease is inappropriate when applied to social problems (i.e., those which involve living and getting along with other people). Problems in living cannot readily be traced back to neurological or other biochemical defects, and, moreover, labeling a behavior as a "symptom" of mental illness involves a subjective social judgment, not an objective physical diagnosis. Szasz also criticized the view that social relationships are naturally harmonious, since everyone occasionally has problems in his social environment.

Ullmann and Krasner (1965) also criticized the medical model, offering as an alternative the psychological or behavioral model, which is derived from learning theory. Rather than concentrating on an underlying psychological pathology that is not directly observable, they emphasized the specification and direct treatment of overt behavior; that is, the treatment of symptoms themselves. This model explains behavior in terms of the environmental variables that influence it, particularly those which occur as a consequence of behavior. The behavioral model has had at least as much influence on the field of behavior disorders as Freudian theory. Techniques based on this model have been demonstrated to be very effective with both children and adults.

Nevertheless, the medical, or psychodynamic, model still has its proponents, and the debate between advocates of the two models continues today. An important distinction between the models involves their assumptions about the sources and nature of the child's problem; they also have different implications for the treatment of children in schools, clinics, and residential institutions. The psychodynamic model analyzes internal events and variables. These are termed *hypothetical constructs,* because they are theoretical constructions of what might be going on in the child. For example, Freud developed the concepts of the id, ego, and superego to explain the dynamics of personality development. Their existence cannot be proven, however, because they are theoretical constructions based on assumptions about what is occurring in the child. Within the psychodynamic model, treatment of emotional disorders consists of attempts to resolve conflicts and imbalances among these assumed dynamic internal forces, once the central disorder or disease process has been diagnosed.

The behaviorist's objections to this internal view of the forces behind human behavior have been stated by Skinner (1967):

1. The constructs are vague and their existence has not been scientifically verified.
2. The constructs are not subject to scientific scrutiny, and therefore they cannot be proven, disproven, or revised.
3. There isn't a one-to-one correspondence between inner and outer (observable) events.
4. The inner system isn't the best explanation of overt, or observable, behavior.
5. Outer events cannot be completely explained by reference to inner states, (e.g., "He struck out because he was angry." But what made him angry?).

Skinner argued that because of the present state of the behavioral sciences it is best to attempt to account for behavior without appealing to inner explanatory constructs. This does not mean that the behaviorist views the organism as "empty," however, or that science won't discover actual relationships between inner and outer events. The behaviorist believes, rather, that providing explanations of what can be objectively observed and measured — overt behavior — will lead to greater understanding of both normal and abnormal behavior. One of the advantages of the label "behaviorally disordered" over the label "emotionally disturbed" is that the former implies an emphasis on the child's behavior, rather than on emotional constructs that aren't easily defined or measured.

The psychodynamic, behavioral, and ecological conceptions are by no means the only models influencing work with behavior disorders. The *biophysical* model seeks to explain disordered behavior in terms of biochemical, neurological, or genetic causes. Like the psychodynamic model, this view stresses a medically oriented, treatment approach. The *sociological* model emphasizes conditions in the child's larger social environment (cultures and subcultures) that foster and maintain deviant behavior. Treatment is usually directed toward ameliorating these conditions or increasing the child's resistance to them. Finally, the *counter theory* model rejects theories that attempt to reduce disordered behavior to a limited set of theoretical assumptions. It focuses instead on advocacy for the deviant child and the delivery of effective services. The goal of intervention is often to change the values and expectations of those who consider the child's behavior disordered. Each of these theories has contributed to the understanding and treatment of children's behavior disorders. Rhodes and Tracy (1972) offer more complete explanation of these models.

THE PROBLEM OF LABELING

> Peter Lee has been tested several times and has been given a variety of labels: "severely retarded," "profoundly retarded," "moderately retarded," "hyperactive," "perceptually disordered," "emotionally disturbed." Usually the advice was "Do something about it now or else it will be a serious problem later." Peter knows the tricks of the "I.Q." test. He can draw a man. The last time he went for testing, he wouldn't comply: instead he hung himself upside down in the closet to the puzzlement of the psychiatrist. He yelled, "I'm a *bat!* I'm a *bat!*" (Van Veelan, 1975, pp. 10–11).

The problems inherent in labeling handicapped children have been considered in some detail in Chapter 1. The issue is of particular concern to those who work with behaviorally disordered children, because such children can be labeled in so many different ways. The diagnostic fiasco involving Peter is an example. Children who have severe behavior disorders are especially likely to be given different labels by different diagnosticians and treatment agencies. There is also the problem of which label to apply to a child with multiple problems. For instance, is Peter emotionally disturbed, mentally retarded, or both? If both, which label will result in his getting the best services? The child and his parents are frequently deprived of special services while experts argue about which category the child belongs in.

In addition, labels tend to make us think in circles, and come to be used as explanations for children's behavior (Ross, 1974). When we ask, "Why is Sally out of her seat so much?" the reply, "Because she's hyperactive," is almost automatic. If we then ask why the label "hyperactive" was assigned, a likely response is, "Because she's out of her seat so much." This may seem insignificant, but an unfortunate effect of such circular reasoning is that the child's label is used as an excuse to do nothing to help her. Sally's teacher may know how to keep her in her seat but have no idea how to treat "hyperactivity." This type of circular reasoning helped perpetuate the medical model and promote the alarmingly frequent use of drugs to control children labeled behaviorally disordered (Sulzbacher, 1972).

Children exhibiting severe behavior disorders may be assigned a variety of labels. However, which diagnostic label best "fits" the child is less important than designing a special education program suited to her unique learning needs.

CONCEPTUAL AND EDUCATIONAL DEFINITIONS
OF BEHAVIOR DISORDERS

Now that some of the problems involved in identifying, classifying, and treating children in school have been discussed, you should realize that labeling a child behaviorally disordered or emotionally disturbed may do more harm than good. An understanding of ecological theory, in particular, should lead professionals to reject attempts to define behaviorally disordered children in terms of their alleged "characteristics."

Nevertheless, defining the population of behaviorally disordered children provides a central concept around which to organize information about them, and much of the information about them has been collected on the basis of their differences from other child populations. How can a definition avoid stigmatizing labels on the one hand and provide a useful, if theoretical, understanding of a group of children on the other? The answer is, we need *two* definitions: one to use in summarizing information, and one to guide school practice.

Kauffman's (1977) definition satisfies the need for a conceptual description: "Children with behavior disorders are those who chronically and markedly respond to their environment in socially unacceptable and/or personally unsatisfying ways but who can be taught more socially acceptable and personally gratifying behavior" (p. 23). Although this definition provides guidelines for educational practice and emphasizes the possibility of growth and change, the terms, "chronically," "markedly," "socially unacceptable," and "personally unsatisfying" are ambiguous. This leaves a great deal to the discretion of the person making the judgment. In view of the potential negative consequences of labeling a child in such circumstance, a different "working definition" is in order.

Such a noncategorial definition has been developed by Lilly (1970). He states that his definition is one "in which it is *not* assumed that all school problems are centered in the child and that removal of children from problem situations will be beneficial for everyone involved" (p. 48). Lilly's position is compatible with the ecological view, in that it focuses on factors in the environment as well as within the child and emphasizes that intervention should be directed at problems in the settings where they occur. Lilly replaced disability labels with the term "exceptional school situations": "An exceptional school situation is one in which interaction between a student and his teacher has been limited to such an extent that external intervention (i.e., special support services) is deemed necessary by the teacher to cope with the problem" (p. 48).

Obviously, Lilly's definition doesn't distinguish children with behavior problems from the learning disabled, mentally retarded, or other alleged child populations. This is in keeping with the growing opposition to labeling, which has been nicely described by Lindsley (1971): "It is fast becoming immoral across our land for normal, educated adults to gang up in staffs of three to 12 on one child with classroom problems and to fight over the label they will indelibly tattoo on his cumulative school record," (p. 118). Special education is becoming less diagnostic — less oriented toward discovering "underlying" disorders — and more prescriptive or action-oriented. Labeling the interaction between a teacher and child rather than the child alone reflects our increasing awareness of the importance of ecological factors, and a more humanistic concern for children. It also reflects the special educator's involvement in mainstreaming. Rather than removing the child to a special setting and applying interventions to her alone, support services are being taken to the child and the teacher.

These trends have made it necessary for special educators to move into new roles. Instead of removing children from regular classrooms for the school day, special education teachers are spending more time helping the regular classroom teacher develop individualized approaches to working with all children, normal as well as exceptional (Lilly, 1971; Reynolds and Birch, 1977).

PROBE 9-1
Defining Behavior Disorders

1. A teacher in your school is worried because he has learned that one of his new pupils has been identified as emotionally disturbed. Tell him why it is better to concern himself with specific behaviors and the settings in which they occur than to pay excessive attention to the label.

   _____

   _____

   _____

   _____

   _____

2. Explain why it is better to assume that behavior disorders are characteristics of the interactions between children and other people than it is to assume that they exist exclusively in the child.

   _____

   _____

   _____

   _____

   _____

3. T   F   Professionals typically consider peer evaluation rather than adult opinion in assessing behavior disorders.

4. The three characteristics common to most definitions of behavioral disorders are

   a. _____

   b. _____

   c. _____

TYPES AND CLASSIFICATIONS
OF BEHAVIOR DISORDERS

You should be able to identify different types of behavior disorders.

In view of the preceding discussion, you may be surprised by the suggestion that there are "types" of behavior disorders. You should keep in mind that the reason we discuss the concept in this manner is related more to the organization of the professional literature than to any practical considerations in working with children.

DIAGNOSIS OF BEHAVIOR DISORDERS

The determination of different categories of behavioral disorders begins with diagnosis. Diagnosis, in turn, consists of three steps: (1) initial screening, (2) identification, and (3) assignment to a diagnostic category. The purpose of screening is to identify children who may need special help. The identification process confirms which of the children identified during screening require therapeutic interventions. Diagnosis involves classification for the purpose of planning an intervention strategy.

During *screening,* children who may be having problems are identified by teachers, parents, peers, or in some cases, by self-report. It may involve simply asking which children have trouble getting along with classmates, following directions, or controlling themselves, or which have difficulty in other areas. It can also involve completing a standardized behavioral rating scale, such as the Walker Problem Behavior Identification Checklist (Walker, 1970), the Behavior Problem Checklist (Quay and Peterson, 1967), or the Devereux Child Behavior Rating Scale (Spivack and Spotts, 1966). Teachers who use such devices can judge children's behavior fairly reliably.

Disordered children are *identified* by comparing these judgments or ratings to an external criterion. The most valid criterion for identifying children entails direct observation of behavior, or *target assessment.* The goal of target assessment is the identification of (1) behaviors that are causing problems to the child or others in her social environment, (2) environmental variables that might be influencing the target behaviors, and (3) variables that might be used to change these behaviors (O'Leary, 1972; Worell and Nelson, 1974). A target behavior for Sally might be her disruptive classroom behavior or, more specifically, inappropriate noises and noncompliance. Influential environmental variables one might consider are how the teacher attends to Sally when she is disruptive, and whether the assigned work is appropriate for Sally. If the school had resources to help Sally and her teacher, the diagnostic process could end with target assessment, and the problem could be dealt with directly, without giving Sally a label. The tradition, however, is to continue diagnosis until something wrong with the child is found, and the process often continues to the next step.

The final step in diagnosis consists of assigning the child to a *classification* of behavior disorder and developing an intervention plan. The traditional approach at this level of diagnosis is to refer the child to a clinic for formal diagnostic testing. Generally, a battery of tests, which includes standardized intelligence and achievement instruments and, in some cases, projective techniques, is administered. The last mentioned are used to assess personality constructs that are not directly observable but may be "projected" through responses to ambiguous stimuli, such as ink blots or pictures. Depending on the theoretical persuasion and competence of the clinician, the child may emerge from the diagnostic testing session with any of a number of labels. Some of the more common ones are "hyperkinetic," "obsessive-compulsive," "minimal brain dysfunction," and the ever-popular "adjustment reaction to childhood." Since these labels seldom translate into useful educational prescriptions, however, special educators infrequently use them to assign children to programs. The label "behaviorally disordered" or "emotionally disturbed" is sufficient to get the child into a special education program.

THE ECOLOGICAL APPROACH TO DIAGNOSIS

The ecological model provides a more practical approach to diagnostic assessment. The process begins when someone, usually a teacher or parent, reports a problem. The professional then assesses the problem in detail, focusing on the interaction of the child with those who are experiencing the problem, and not on the child in isolation. In addition to the problem situation, variables related to the school, the home, the child, the peer group, and the child's local community are studied. Intervention plans are developed for situations in which disturbing interactions occur. The ecological assessment process also specifies areas of strength and support that may be useful in planning treatment (Wahler and Cormier, 1970).

Because it carefully assesses environmental variables, the ecological model is especially useful in designing intervention strategies. Another advantage of this type of assessment is that it need not lead to a stigmatizing label; the emphasis is on the situation rather than the presumed underlying pathology of the child. For example, we would observe Sally's behavior in the playground, lunchroom, and gym as well as in her regular classroom. We might also interview other teachers and Sally's parents, to determine the extent of the behavior pattern displayed in her classroom and to identify other problems or potential problems. This would reveal how serious a problem Sally is, and would also indicate whether intervention should be extended outside the major problem situation. In addition, ecological assessment could reveal whether an attempt should be made to change some of Sally's teacher's behavior. It could also uncover persons or activities from other microcommunities that could be incorporated into the intervention. For example, Sally's mother might be willing to give her daughter extra privileges at home when she brings home favorable reports from school. Or perhaps Sally is developing into a fine backgammon player and could get some of the attention she apparently desires by sharing her knowledge with the class.

CLASSIFICATION OF BEHAVIOR DISORDERS

Why do we attempt to classify behavior disorders? Scientists go through the process of classification to organize information, which permits them to make useful statements about the phenomena being classified. In the behavioral sciences these "useful statements" are used to provide treatment to individuals assigned to different categories. This means that one should be able to predict the behavior of individuals placed in a particular category when specific intervention techniques are applied. As was the case in assigning children to the broad category of "behavioral disorders," assigning them to subcategories may create more problems than it solves.

To make useful statements about the children assigned to a category of disordered behavior, it must (1) be demonstrated that the category actually exists; (2) be shown that children can be reliably assigned to that category; and (3) be proven that patterns of disordered behavior are related to their psychological antecedents and consequences. Few of the more than twenty-four proposed classification systems for children's behavior disorders have met these requirements (Quay, 1972).

Clinical Approach. Most of the traditional approaches to diagnostic classification are based on the medical model. Kanfer and Saslow (1967) described three such systems. *Classification by etiology* involves grouping disorders according to their common causes. This works well when the cause is obvious, as it is with tuberculosis, for example. Causes that result in the same patterns of disordered behavior in different children have not been discovered, however. What is more, identical causes do not lead to identical behavior disorders. *Classification by prognosis,* or response to treatment, presents problems because classification cannot be accomplished until treatment is started and responses are observed. Scores from projective personality instruments and psychological tests are traditionally used to predict response to treatment, but the predictive value of such instruments, even with adults, is poor. Another approach is *classification by symptoms,* but here, too, general statements about characteristics have little predictive validity. Diagnosis tends to be derived from behaviors expressed or reported in the clinicians' office, which are often irrelevant to the person's total life pattern (Kanfer and Saslow, 1967). Roughly 70 percent of the children who are clinically diagnosed are classified under the category of "adjustment reaction," which means little more than that the child has a behavior problem (Quay, 1972).

Statistical Approach. In recent years, alternatives to the clinical approach have been developed. Several of these classification systems group clusters of observed behaviors statistically. This approach is better than the clinical methods because its categories are based on observable groups of behaviors. This permits teachers and parents to evaluate children's behavior reliably (Quay, 1972). In numerous studies by Quay and his colleagues, four categories of behavior disorders have been identified:

1. *Conduct disorders* consist of aggressive verbal and physical behavior of an antisocial nature.
2. *Personality disorders* are characterized by withdrawal rather than attack. Included are feelings of distress, fear, and anxiety, as well as physical complaints and expressed unhappiness.
3. *Immaturity* is characterized by age-inappropriate behaviors. It is much less prevalent than the two previous categories.
4. *Socialized delinquency* includes behaviors that may be encouraged by peer pressure or other environmental circumstances. For instance, stealing or fighting may be openly supported by a delinquent peer group (Quay, 1972).

Functional-Analytic Approach. Kanfer and Saslow (1967) developed the functional-analytic approach to classify adult behavior disorders, but it has also worked well with children. It suggests three behavioral categories. *Behavioral excesses* are behaviors that are excessive in frequency, intensity, or duration, or that occur when socially inappropriate. *Behavioral deficits* are behaviors that fail to occur with sufficient frequency, with adequate intensity, in appropriate form, or under conditions in which they are socially expected. *Behavioral assets* are all nonproblematic behaviors. This category reflects the understanding that even highly deviant individuals have areas of strength. The functional-analytic approach can be used especially well with ecological assessment procedures. Derived from the behavioral model, its chief advantage is that it does not result in a label's being applied to a child. Instead, the child's maladaptive behaviors are specified, and strategies for change are suggested. Part of the intervention strategy is the identification of environmental variables that reinforce or maintain the problematic behavior. This approach is the same as target assessment, mentioned earlier.

Classification by Severity. Hallahan and Kauffman (1978) divided the behaviorally disordered into two groups on the basis of the severity of their disorders. Children with *mild and moderate* behavioral disorders can be managed by their teachers and parents with short-term consultation by a specialist. Children with *severe and profound disorders,* on the other hand, require intense and prolonged intervention, usually in a segregated setting. In calling attention to the problems involved in developing diagnostic classifications of children with extreme behavioral deviations Kauffman (1977) stated, "Today neither etiologies nor behavioral characteristics have been found to distinguish subcategories of the severely and profoundly disturbed. *Psychotic, schizophrenic, atypical, autistic,* and *retarded* are examples of labels that at present are, for practical purposes at least, interchangeable," (p. 30). Using the information we have about Peter and Sally, we might consider Peter's disorders as severe and requiring intensive intervention; Sally's problems are probably relatively mild and could be addressed in the regular classroom.

Classification by severity permits the efficient allocation of educational services. But until criteria are established to differentiate children in need of intense and prolonged intervention from those who can profit from short-term help, there is a risk that children will be classified as severely or profoundly disordered merely to get them removed from regular classrooms.

O'Leary (1972) pointed out that the poor reliability and validity of projective techniques renders them useless for classifying children or for predicting their behavior. He also observed that although statistical approaches provide a useful conceptual scheme for organizing deviant child behavior, research has yet to demonstrate the effectiveness of these techniques for predicting child behavior and for planning treatment. The assessment of target behaviors and their ecological contexts, on the other hand, offers several advantages: (1) the child does not have to be labeled as a member of a deviant population; (2) problem behaviors and environmental variables are described in a fashion that leads directly to an intervention plan; (3) problems are assessed where they occur, not in a clinic (O'Leary, 1972); (4) the assets of the child and the situation are considered, not just his problems; and (5) the child's environment, and not just the child himself, is considered a potential cause of the problem. The target assessment or function-analytic approach is thus highly compatible with Lilly's definition of an exceptional school situation.

PROBE 9-2
Types and Classifications of Behavior Disorders

1. A teacher in your school complains about a "behaviorally disordered" child in her class. If you were using an ecological approach to the diagnosis of behavior disorders, would you agree with her use of this term? Why or why not?

_____

_____

_____

2. List two behavior patterns a child diagnosed as having a conduct disorder might exhibit.

   a. _____

   b. _____

3. Why is a functional analytic or target behavior approach to classification unlikely to result in a child being labeled as behaviorally disordered?

   _____

   _____

   _____

   _____

   _____

PREVALENCE FACTORS

You should be able to describe factors that affect the prevalence estimates of behavior disorders.

We stated earlier that teachers perceive 30 percent of their pupils as having behavior problems. State agency estimates of the number of children who warrant the label "behaviorally disordered," based on that intensity and persistence of their problem behavior, range from 0.05 to 15 percent, due to variations in state definitions and terminology (Schultz, Hirshorn, Manton, and Henderson, 1971). Since the estimated prevalence of all handicapped school children is 10 to 12 percent, Wood and Zabel (1978) have suggested that 3 percent of the school-age population is behaviorally disordered. Almost all of these pupils would be considered mildly or moderately disturbed, with severely and profoundly disturbed children accounting for only 0.1 percent (Hallahan and Kauffman, 1978).

Juvenile delinquency is a category of behavior disorder defined by the legal system. The population of children identified as delinquent overlaps the population of behaviorally disordered children. That is, children with behavior problems may or may not get into trouble with the law; adjudicated delinquents may or may not have been labeled behaviorally disordered. If this overlap is disregarded, the delinquency rate among children ages ten to seventeen is approximately 3 percent. In 1972, for example, 1 million cases were handled by the juvenile courts (U.S. Department of Health, Education, and Welfare, 1973).

Behavior disorders are not evenly distributed across ages, sexes, or socioeconomic levels. Although studies do not consistently find more boys than girls with behavior problems, boys tend to be overrepresented in programs for behaviorally disordered children by as much as ten to one (Rich, 1977). Schools have a particularly low tolerance for acting-out (aggressive behavior), which is more often displayed by boys, members of minority groups (Rich, 1977), and children from lower socioeconomic levels (Kauffman, 1977). As girls grow older, their personality problems increase, whereas boys develop conduct problems or exhibit immaturity (Kauffman, 1977).

Two interesting questions about the later adjustment of behaviorally disordered children may be asked: Do behaviorally disordered children become maladjusted adults? and, What happens to children who receive treatment, compared to those who do not? Lewis (1965) reviewed the research on these questions, and found that (you guessed it) the answers aren't simple. With regard to the first question, if the criterion for evaluating adult disturbance is admission to a psychiatric hospital, the answer is no. If however, the criterion is a diagnosed adult psychiatric disorder, the answer is yes. Considering both criteria together, Lewis (1965) concluded, "The extent to which a childhood predisposition to mental illness influences appearance of problems in adult life is not entirely clear, but it is apparently not a determining factor" (p. 472). The child who acts out or has conduct problems is more likely to have serious adjustment problems as an adult than the withdrawn child (Kauffman, 1977; Lewis, 1965).

The answer to the second question (What happens to behaviorally disordered children as a result of treatment efforts?) is disheartening. Approximately two-thirds of behaviorally disordered children improve within two years even without intervention (Ross, 1974). Of those who receive formal professional help in school or elsewhere, two-thirds to three-fourths improve, regardless of the treatment setting, the discipline of the therapist, or the age of the children (Lewis, 1965). Thus, time may be a more important factor than treatment, because roughly the same number of children improve with treatment as without it.

PROBE 9-3
Prevalence Factors

1. T F Severely and profoundly behaviorally disordered school-age children account for approximately 0.1 percent of the total population of behaviorally disordered children.

2. Why do you think more boys than girls are identified as behavior problems?

_____

_____

_____

3. A reasonable estimate of the number of school-age behaviorally disordered children is

   a. 2 percent
   b. 1 percent
   c. 3 percent
   d. 10 percent

4. Knowing that most behaviorally disordered children improve with time, would you advise a concerned parent to "let him grow out of it"? Why or why not?

_____

_____

_____

_____

BIOPHYSICAL AND ENVIRONMENTAL CORRELATES

You should be able to describe the biophysical and environmental correlates of behavior disorders.

The hypothesis that behavior disorders have specific causes is derived from the medical model; the term "etiology" itself refers to the study of the causes of diseases. For the physician, finding the cause of a disease may be helpful in curing it, but that is not the case in the behavioral sciences. In the first place, the causes of disordered behavior may have occurred in the child's remote past, which makes them difficult to discover and impossible to treat. Second, it is usually not necessary to know the cause of a behavioral disorder to provide effective intervention (Kauffman, 1977; Worell and Nelson, 1974). In addition, behavior is the result of the interaction of multiple "causes." As Ross (1974) put it, "Any specific behavior, taking place at any one point, represents the end point of the interaction of genetic-constitutional factors, the current physiological state of the individual, his current environmental conditions and past learning which, in turn was a function of a similar interaction" (pp. 6–7).

Nevertheless, behavioral scientists have been trying to understand causality for many years. There are many studies and much discussion of the subject, but they have yielded little valuable information. This is true largely because of limitations in the ways causal agents can be studied. Whereas medical researchers can isolate a suspected causal agent (a virus or bacterium, for example), inject it into a laboratory animal, and observe its effects while keeping all environmental variables constant, the behavioral scientist has to rely on less precise research strategies. Although Watson and Raynor (1920) developed a generalized conditioned fear response in the infant Albert, thereby establishing a direct cause-effect relationship, the ethics of this kind of research would be severely criticized today and the research halted. Another insurmountable problem is the control of environmental variables, which could be done only by raising experimental subjects in a laboratory.

As a result of these factors, investigations of the causes of children's behavior disorders have usually involved retrospective examination of the case histories of children who have been given similar diagnostic labels. (The assumption that children having the same label are a homogeneous population is false, of course). These studies identify factors that are associated, or correlated, with behavioral disorders. Statistical correlation techniques demonstrate how factors vary together, but it is very important to understand that *they do not establish that one factor causes another.* Behavior disorders have been correlated with poor home environments, inadequate parental discipline, low socioeconomic status, learning problems in school, and other influences, but it would be a mistake to reason that these factors *cause* behavior disorders. Such factors are correlates, not causes, of behavioral disorders.

The relatively high correlation between a variable such as low socioeconomic status and behavior disorders does suggest that the former contributes to the disorder, but there is also a possibility that a mutual relationship between these two conditions and a third unknown variable could account for the correlation. There are many variables associated with low socioeconomic status, such as the absence of a father in the home, the presence of deviant peer models, and membership in a racial minority group (see Nelson and Polsgrove, in press). Correlational studies that fail to take into account the simultaneous influence of such variables may inaccurately conclude that a single cause-effect relationship exists.

Inferences about causes must be made very carefully even when a behavior disorder is consistently related to a biophysical causal agent. For example, Lesch-Nyhan syndrome is a disorder of the nervous system that results in cerebral palsy, mental retardation, and apparently without exception, self-mutilating behavior, such as severe biting of the lips and fingers (Slater and Cowie, 1971). The consistent relationship of self-mutilation to this syndrome could lead one to conclude that Lesch-Nyhan syndrome causes self-mutilation (or more precisely, that the biochemical defect responsible for the syndrome produces all of its symptoms, one of which is self-mutilation). Anderson and Herrmann (1975) studied the effects of punishment, time-out from positive reinforcement, and positive reinforcement of behavior other than self-mutilation on five boys with Lesch-Nyhan. They found that these behavioral techniques quickly eliminated self-mutilation. The authors observed different rates of one subject's self-injurious behavior in the presence of his grandfather, grandmother, and mother. In a fifteen-minute session with another subject, following self-mutilation with social attention caused the behavior's rate of occurrence to triple. Furthermore, they observed that in all subjects the behavior occurred only in the presence of parents. These observations led Anderson and Herrmann to conclude that environmental factors play a role in the maintenance, if not the development, of the disorder.

One cannot assume, however, that because a particular behavior responds to a specific environmental event, the event caused the behavior in the first place. Specifically, that the subjects responded to adult attention does not mean that adult attention was the cause of the behavior's appearance. It does suggest, however, that a particular biochemical condition alone may not be able to produce a behavior disorder.

What are the implications of this for the behavioral scientist? Ross (1974) stated it unequivocally: "The only causal question science can investigate takes the form 'Under what conditions does this phenomenon occur?' " (p. 6). These conditions cannot be identified very accurately outside the laboratory. Accordingly, we discuss etiology in terms of *predisposing causes,* those that set the stage for a potential behavior disorder; *precipitating causes,* those which may trigger a behavior; and *contributing factors,* events that are consistently associated with behavior disorders and that may influence them (Hallahan and Kauffman, 1978). Thus, Lesch-Nyhan may predispose a child to develop self-injurious behavior, the presence of certain adults may precipitate it, and social attention may inadvertently contribute to its development and maintenance. These factors and conditions are not causes, but rather etiological correlates. These can be divided into two groups: biophysical and environmental.

BIOPHYSICAL CORRELATES

Biophysical factors include genetic, neurological, or biochemical conditions. Although the evidence is inconclusive, studies indicate that severe and profound behavior disorders are more frequently of biological origin than are milder disturbances (Kauffman, 1977). Biophysical agents have been linked to a variety of behavioral disorders, including infantile autism and hyperactivity. For example, Rimland (1964) suggested that autism is a defect in relating new stimuli to former experience, caused by lesions in the brain. Because autism tends to occur in children born prematurely, and such children were until recently exposed to pure oxygen, Rimland hypothesized that the cause of the neurological defect was hypersensitivity to oxygen.

A more direct approach to the question of etiology of behavior disorders was taken by Chess, Thomas, and Birch (1967), who monitored 136 children over a ten-year period. Thirty-nine children in their original sample developed behavioral disorders of various types and degrees of severity. From extensive interviews with the mothers of these children the authors developed patterns of reactivity that could be used to characterize three basic temperaments in the children in their sample. The "easy" child was biologically regular, approached new stimuli, adapted quickly and easily to change, and showed a predominantly positive mood. The "slow to warm up" child responded negatively to new stimuli and adapted slowly to new situations. The willingness of parents and teachers to let such a child adapt at her own pace was important to her adjustment. The "persistent" child resisted interference and efforts to divert him from an activity. Arbitrary or forceful adult interference could cause adjustment problems for these children.

Chess et al. (1967) found that behavior problems were most likely to develop in children whose biological functions were irregular, who tended to withdraw when faced with new stimuli, who adapted slowly or not at all to new situations, whose moods were frequently negative, and who tended to react intensely. Whether children with these temperamental patterns acquired behavioral disorders depended on the way they were handled by their parents. The authors cautioned against concluding that the parents had a major role in the development of behavior problems, however. They found no evidence that the parents of difficult infants were different from the other parents studied. It can be concluded that the reciprocal influence of the infant's temperament on the parents and the parents' reaction to the child's temperament are more important in the etiology of disordered behavior than either innate behavioral tendencies or specific parental practices.

ENVIRONMENTAL CORRELATES

Because children spend most of their time in school and at home, the possible contributions of these environments to behavior disorders have been widely discussed.

Home Factors. Ever since the popularization of Freudian theory, parents of behaviorally disordered children have been abused for contributing to the problems of their children. Freud implicated parental discipline and toilet-training techniques, and others have blamed broken homes, maternal deprivation, parental reinforcement patterns, and faulty childrearing practices. Research, however, has not led to discovery of the origins of behavior disorders in family relationships. It is therefore, *"extremely inappropriate for special educators to adopt an attitude of blame toward parents of troubled children"* (Kauffman, 1977, p. 97, italics added).

Patterson, Reid, Jones, and Conger (1975) compared interactions in families with aggressive children to those in families of nonaggressive children. The interactions of the families of aggressive children tended to be hostile, whereas interaction in the families of nonaggressive children tended to be more positive. Studies such as this do *not* show whether the interaction pattern caused the behavior disorder or the behavior disorder was responsible for the disturbing interactions. It is likely that these factors affect each other reciprocally or that aggressive behavior is the result of other factors altogether.

School Factors. As Kauffman (1977) observed, the fact that many children develop behavior problems only after they enter school implies that schools may contribute to the appearance of behavior disorders. Studies of behaviorally disordered children in school indicate that, as a group, they do relatively poorly on tests of intelligence and achievement (Kauffman, 1977). This could lead one to assume that school failure may be a cause of disordered behavior, but it is also possible that behavior disorders cause school failure. Research on this topic has been inconclusive.

Some authorities have argued that schools themselves have become maladaptive social institutions, working in the service of the cultural values of conformity and mediocrity. Reimer (1972), for example, was severe in his criticism of school curricula:

> I do not regard schools as truly educational but, more nearly, as an institutional perversion of education. In my opinion, schools not only prevent true education from occurring, they actually miseducate. They teach not what is relevant and true but what is irrelevant and untrue to the interests of their students. They do this, however, in the service of a society of which they are a central institution and major bulwark. They effectively adjust their students to the requirements of this society [p. 484].

Even if schools were above such criticism, it is clear that they tend to enforce conformity and punish children who violate standards of order and discipline, or who don't fit the pattern expected of the average child (Nelson, 1977). Sally's teacher may not have caused her behavior problems, but she hasn't helped her overcome them either.

That schools sometimes contribute to behavior problems is also indicated by the fact that behavior disorders are more common among boys than girls in school, whereas parents report fewer problems with them at home. Ross (1974) suggests that this may be because boys have more learning difficulties than girls and may as a result find school more difficult. They may respond with behaviors that school personnel regard as hyperactive, aggressive, or antisocial.

The *peer group* may also influence the development of behavioral disorders in school or other microcommunities. There has been little research on this subject, but children undoubtedly influence each other's behavior. This influence may exceed that of parents and other adult models, especially among older children.

The peer group plays an especially influential role in the maintenance of gang delinquency (Stumphauzer, Aiken, and Veloz, 1977). Buehler, Patterson, and Furniss (1966), for example, studied the way staff and peers reacted to delinquent and prosocial behavior in institutions for delinquent girls. In all of the institutions studied, approximately 75 percent of the girls' delinquent behavior was followed by peer approval, whereas peers punished compliance with social norms. Institutional staff members, on the other hand, reacted inconsistently to the girls' behavior. These results do not explain how the deviant behavior was acquired in the first place, but they do suggest that antisocial behavior sometimes becomes deeply ingrained through association with a deviant peer group.

A succinct summation of our understanding of the etiology of behavior disorders has been provided by Kauffman (1977): "The answer to the question 'Why did this child become emotionally disturbed?' is, in most cases, 'No one knows!' " (p. 139). This is true whether one is considering the case of a severely disordered child like Peter or a child such as Sally, who presents classroom management problems. Behavior disorders may be associated with predisposing, precipitating, or contributing factors. Research on the subject does little to increase our understanding because it must rely on correlational methods and because influential variables are almost impossible to control. As research into the causes of behavior disorders continues, additional correlates may be found. Recently, for example, the influence of viewing televised violence on children's aggressive behavior has been documented (Bandura, 1973; Lefkowitz, Eron, Walder, and Huesmann, 1977). Certain food additives also appear to be linked to hyperactivity (Rose, 1978). In the meantime, fortunately, effective intervention can be provided without identifying specific etiologies (Kauffman, 1977).

PROBE 9-4
Biophysical and Environmental Correlates

1. A noted psychiatrist, addressing a professional group of which you are a member, states that all severe mental illnesses are caused in part by genetic factors. You clear your throat, raise your hand, and rise to speak. All eyes turn toward you. What will you say?

_____

_____

_____

2. Environmental correlates that may influence a child to exhibit behavior problems are (circle one):

   a. peers
   b. home
   c. school
   d. all of the above
   e. b and c only

3. What would you say to a parent who was worried that she had caused her child's behavior problem?

   _____

   _____

   _____

   _____

DISTURBING AND DISTURBED BEHAVIORS

You should be able to differentiate "disturbing" and "disturbed" behaviors and discuss intervention strategies for each.

As mentioned earlier, there are many problems in defining a population of children. A "population" is nothing more than a convenient hypothetical construct around which information is organized. Describing children in terms of group averages leads us to think of them stereotypically. The "average" child from any population (whether "normal" or "behaviorally disordered") simply doesn't exist. There are children who meet the criteria of Kauffman's (1977) definition, but they should not be regarded as members of categories such as "hyperactive," "autistic," or "school phobic." They are individuals, and unless descriptions of their characteristics contribute to our understanding of them as individuals, they are of little worth to teachers and child advocates. Accordingly, a few of the exceptional teaching situations that a teacher might encounter in the classroom will be presented in this section.

Consistent with the ecological approach, behaviors will be grouped according to whether they are "disturbing" (i.e., they threaten classroom order and discipline, but tend to be specific to just one ecological setting) or "disturbed" (i.e., they occur with excessive intensity, frequency, or both, across several ecological settings).

DISTURBING BEHAVIORS

Two general types of behavior are "disturbing" to classroom teachers: behaviors that cause management or discipline problems, and behaviors that affect the social climate of the classroom. The first group includes children who talk excessively, leave their seats, don't do their work, don't follow directions, or are generally disruptive. These children are frequently labeled "hyperactive." This label may be appropriate when children are consistently overactive in many different settings, but it is frequently applied to children who present problems only in a particular classroom. This label is so widely misused, and it has such undesirable ramifications, that in most cases target assessment is a preferable alternative.

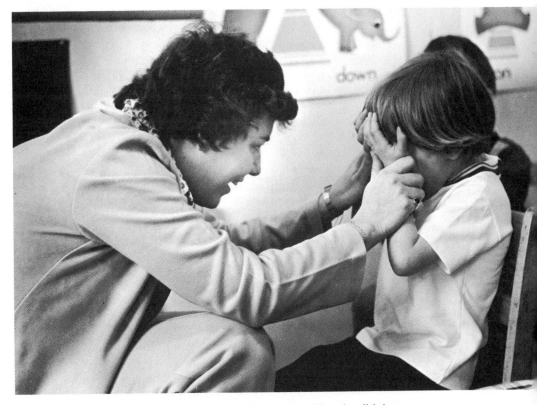

Children exhibiting "disturbed" behavior do so in many settings; "disturbing" behavior occurs with specific environments or persons. In either case, it is most productive to focus on the interaction between the child and those in his environment.

Behaviors that threaten the teacher's authority and control also create management problems. Defiance and aggression toward authority figures are especially likely to alarm teachers and other school officials. Such behavior should be evaluated in the context of the demands and expectations of the adults in authority. Unless these behaviors extend to all authority figures or are extremely intense, as when a child strikes a teacher, it is best to provide intervention where the problem occurs, rather than moving the child to a segregated environment. This is in keeping with ecological strategy of dealing with problems where they happen rather than forcing the child to do all the changing.

Behaviors affecting the classroom social climate are disturbing because the teacher must take time from her normal teaching functions to arbitrate disputes and encourage appropriate interaction with other children. This group of behaviors includes withdrawal and isolation, as well as inappropriate social interactions. The child who fails to play with or talk to his peers, or who does not join group games or class discussions, needs help to participate fully in the social life of his classroom. The child whose bullying or clowning causes classmates to shun or ridicule her also needs help. The teacher often has trouble dealing with such behavior because the variables controlling it (e.g., peer attention) are not under the teacher's control. Nevertheless, intervention is best applied where the problem occurs, because it is the "normal" classroom that the child must adjust to.

An important characteristic of disturbing behavior is that it tends to occur in some situations and not in others. A child who is a severe management problem in one teacher's classroom may be no problem at all in another's. Similarly, a child's behavior may be disturbing to some persons but not to others. During ecological assessment an effort is made to "map" the child's disturbance by determining in which situations the child is perceived as causing problems. Intervention is applied only in those settings where the disturbance occurs. Other settings may contribute resources for the intervention plan, but there is no need to intervene in situations where there are no problems. Disturbing behaviors are clearly the result of reciprocal interactions between the child and others in his environment. A child who is not regarded as a problem in all settings should not be considered the exclusive source of the problem.

The belief that disturbing children should receive intervention in the classroom is based on the assumption that the classroom teacher will be able to manage the child with special education consultation. These children, then, would be considered mildly and moderately disturbed according to Hallahan and Kauffman's (1978) definition. The attitude that a disturbance is the result of the child and her environment is unpopular with many teachers and school administrators, who sometimes use special education programs as dumping grounds for problems that regular educators are unwilling to tackle. As a new special education teacher you should realize that some teachers react defensively to the view that deviance is an interactive problem rather than a characteristic of a child. If you focus on the problem, however, and avoid labeling either the child or the teacher, you should quickly overcome this obstacle, provided of course that you are supported by a school policy that emphasizes teacher consultation and mainstreaming.

DISTURBED BEHAVIORS

It is tempting to characterize "disturbed" behaviors as symptomatic of an underlying pathology. We hope you need no further proof that such a conceptualization would be grossly inaccurate and, in practice, seriously abused. Even if it could be proven that underlying disorders exist, and they could be accurately disgnosed, there still would be the problem of designing effective interventions based on a child's diagnosis.

Children in this category are likely to have severe and profound behavior disorders, according to the Hallahan and Kauffman (1978) definition. "Disturbed behavior" refers to behaviors that occur in diverse ecological settings, i.e., in the presence of different people and in various locations. The child may be said to carry the disturbance with her, and the disturbance affects most or all of her transactions with her social environment. But *it should never be assumed that a child who has been labeled "disturbed" meets this criterion.* The conclusion that a child "owns" a behavior disorder can be made only after his behavior has been assessed in all of his ecological settings, and even then the view that disturbance is a reciprocal phenomenon between the child and the social environment is most useful for intervention. In fact, the term "disturbed" is used here only as a descriptive category. Its use as a label for children's behavior should be specifically avoided. A complete ecological assessment identifies environmental as well as personal variables that should be incorporated into a treatment plan. Interventions for disturbed behavior tend to involve intensive and prolonged treatment and removal of the child from the regular classroom.

A great variety of behaviors may be characterized as disturbed. The behaviors previously described as disturbing could be included if they occur across several ecological settings. The child who defies *all* authority figures, or the child who withdraws from *all* social contacts presents a different treatment problem than the child who acts in these ways only in some situations. Peter and Sally both may say inappropriate things, but Sally's performances tend to take place only in the classroom, whereas Peter babbles meaninglessly in all situations.

Behaviors that do not appear to be controlled by specific environmental stimuli may also be considered disturbed. For example, such self-stimulating behaviors as rocking, hand flapping, and head banging seem to occur without environmental reinforcement. [Recall, however, that Anderson and Herrmann (1975) showed that the severe self-mutilation associated with Lesch-Nyhan may be maintained by subtle environmental factors.] Failure to respond to verbal cues and directions is another example of lack of stimulus control, as anyone who has futilely yelled "stop" to a nonverbal child knows. In cases such as this the problem is one of communication. Verbal commands don't work with the child, because the words don't have stimulus value for him. To respond appropriately to the command "stop," the child must understand what the word means; i.e., he must respond differently when he hears the word "stop" than he does when he hears another word, such as "go." Verbal deficits of this sort are severe and occur across different social settings. The syndrome labeled "autism" is often characterized as a verbal or language disorder, because children given this label often have no functional language, in addition to grossly inappropriate social behavior and low-level or nonexistent self-help skills. Once again, only a complete ecological assessment will reveal whether the failure to respond appropriately to verbal and nonverbal stimuli is generalized or occurs only in specific ecological settings.

Deficits in self-help or daily living skills also qualify as disturbed behavior. Children who do not feed or dress themselves or look after their own toilet needs require intensive educational efforts that extend beyond the school setting. Enuresis (bladder incontinence) and encopresis (lack of appropriate bowel control) are two behavior problems that can keep the child from entering the regular class. It is important to know whether the child is incontinent just before or during school, or at other times as well. The child who wets her pants before reading group, for example, presents a very different problem than the child who has never acquired any bladder control.

PROBE 9-5
Disturbing and Disturbed Behaviors

1. You are a special education consultant, and a child who displays aggressive behavior has been referred to you. Briefly describe the steps you would go through in assessing the problem. (Hint: think in terms of the settings in which you might want to study the behavior, the persons with whom you would talk about the child's behavior, and the kinds of information you would collect.)

_____

_____

_____

_____

_____

_____

2. How would you expect "disturbing" aggressive behavior to differ from "disturbed" aggressive behavior. How would the difference influence your intervention plan?

_____

_____

_____

_____

_____

_____

_____

_____

_____

_____

_____

EDUCATIONAL ENVIRONMENTS

You should be able to describe the implications of PL 94-142 for educating children with behavior disorders in the least restrictive environment.

The educator of behaviorally disordered children is able to draw on a continually expanding array of service delivery options. The current emphasis on providing all school-related services in the least restrictive environment possible has added considerably to the educator's repertoire of intervention strategies. The cascade of services available to the behaviorally disordered individual and her family is vastly different today from what was available even a decade or two ago.

Special education for children with serious behavior problems scarcely existed before the middle of the twentieth century. Early school programs were heavily influenced by psychoanalytic theory. They were also affected by the work of Alfred Strauss and Laura Lehtinen, who pioneered a highly structured approach for children with learning and behavioral disorders (Strauss and Lehtinen, 1947). Strauss and Lehtinen's approach was based on the assumption that children exhibiting hyperactive, impulsive, or distractable behavior were brain injured. Brain damage was assumed to cause disorders in perception and attention as well, which was thought to account for significant learning problems in the same children. This constellation of symptoms or behaviors was termed the Strauss syndrome. The methods developed by Strauss and Lehtinen were later extended by Cruickshank (Cruickshank, Bentzen, Ratzeburg, and Tannhauser, 1961) and were applied by Haring and Phillips (1962) to children labeled emotionally disturbed.

During the 1960s and early 1970s school programs for children exhibiting behavioral disorders expanded rapidly. Most of these programs emphasized the use of self-contained classrooms, the efficiency of which has been questioned in the light of follow-up studies of children returned to the regular classroom (e.g., Vacc, 1972). Critics of the widespread practice of assigning handicapped children to self-contained special classes welcomed the passage of PL 94-142, and its mandate for the least restrictive environment. The following continuum or cascade of services describes the educational environments presently available to children labeled "behaviorally disordered."

1. *Regular Classroom.* Most children with behavior problems are placed in this setting. Increasingly, however, special education consultants are available to help the regular classroom teacher develop and implement Individualized Educational Programs (IEPs).

2. *Resource rooms* are available for children requiring more intensive help with learning or behavior problems than the regular classroom teacher can provide. Some resource teachers also offer both consultation to the regular teacher and direct services to the child.

3. *Self-contained classrooms* accommodate children whose behaviors limit their access to the mainstream to such an extent that they need a highly structured, special environment for most of the school day. Because such classrooms are located within the school building, systematic efforts to mainstream pupils can be accomplished in gradual steps during the school year. The priority placed on serving the severely handicapped by PL 94-142 has prompted the development of public school programs for "autistic" and "psychotic" children. The lower intellectual functioning of these children, their lack of adequate language and self-care skills, and the relatively high frequency with which they exhibit bizarre and inappropriate behavior often dictates placement in a self-contained special class or a special school, the next step up the continuum of services. It should not, however, be assumed that a child labeled autistic, for example, cannot function at all in the mainstream. It is better to locate programs for such children in public schools than in segregated settings, where opportunities to model and learn more normalized behavior patterns are severely limited.

4. *Special day schools* are a relatively unusual option. These may be public or private, and may serve one or several categories of handicapped children. The

child's access to the mainstream is severely restricted by his physical removal from the public school building.

5. *Re-education schools* are a special type of residential school program found throughout the United States. Founded by Nicholas Hobbs (1966), "Re-Ed" is based on the ecological model. The child is removed from the normal school environment only because she requires such extensive intervention. Contact is maintained with the child's natural ecology through intensive liaison work and through the child's home visits, which typically occur every weekend. Furthermore, the child's stay in the residential program is intentionally brief, averaging about six months. Re-Ed support is provided from the time the child leaves the residential program until she and others in her microcommunities (e.g., parents, teachers) can function without it.

6. *Residential treatment programs* provide comprehensive intervention, which may include psychotherapy, chemotherapy, or other medical therapies, in addition to education. The child's stay in such programs is generally relatively long — one or two years — and his contact with his natural ecology more severely limited. The trend today is away from custodial facilities.

In this continuum of services, fewer children and more severe behavior problems will be found as one moves up the continuum away from the least restrictive environment. In theory, children should be moved away from the least restrictive environment one step at a time, and they should be moved back down as soon as feasible (see Reynolds and Birch, 1977). In practice, however, the philosophy of "out of sight, out of mind" prevails, and except for programs like Re-Ed, which provide support systems for transitions from one level to another, there is little evidence that program placement is as flexible as it should be. Recent innovations in educational strategies are helping to overcome such problems, however. For example, the Madison Plan (Taylor, Artuso, Soloway, Hewett, Quay, and Stillwell, 1972; Taylor and Soloway, 1973) divides the resource room into four levels designed to serve children at their level of competence. Children move through the levels and into the mainstream as they demonstrate competencies necessary to succeed at less restrictive levels.

INFORMATION SOURCES

A number of professional and lay organizations provide support for the parent or educator concerned with behaviorally disordered children. Closer Look, the National Information Center for the Handicapped, provides information regarding handicapping conditions and locally available services and programs. The National Society for Autistic Children is a valuable resource for anyone dealing with severely disordered children. Finally, the Council for Exceptional

Children and the Council for Children with Behavior Disorders (a division of CEC) disseminate information through professional journals and conferences and perform advocacy activities affecting children involved in disturbing encounters with their social environment.

CURRENT TRENDS

What does the future hold for the education of behaviorally disordered children? There are several noteworthy trends on the horizon. Of greatest importance is the provision of educational services to unserved children, including those with severe and profound behavioral disorders, preschool children exhibiting behavior problems, secondary age youngsters, and delinquents. The provision of services to children on the basis of their labels is at odds with the philosophy of this chapter but, nevertheless, programs for these children are badly needed. In the near future we hope services will be made available on the basis of children's needs instead of their labels. The practice of restricting special education services to children who meet rigid, formal definitions for categorical disabilities must be abolished before the special and regular educator can work as an effective team to help all children who have learning or adjustment problems (Reynolds and Birch, 1977).

A second promising trend is the increasing diversification of optional learning environments in the educational mainstream. This trend toward "alternative education" reflects greater sensitivity to the individuality of all children and gives the child who deviates from existing standards for "normal" behavior a chance to survive, in the least restrictive appropriate environment (see Nelson, 1977).

In addition, the current emphasis on mainstreaming has started a trend toward in-service teacher training and consultation by special educators, for example, mental health consultation provided by a crisis teacher or helping teacher to children or their teachers (Morse, 1971). Other special educators have expanded the role to include teacher training as well (Knight, 1978; Lilly, 1971; McKenzie, 1976). In her role as a trainer, the special educator can provide a variety of instruction, including formal graduate courses, after-school workshops, demonstration teaching, and informal consultation. Two encouraging consequences of this trend are a reduction in labeling and an increase in the ability of regular classroom teachers to accept and foster individual differences in children. The in-service teacher trainer's role requires less direct intervention with children as regular classroom teachers assume greater responsibility. The special educator helps the teacher acquire the skills to deal with exceptional teaching situations, rather than simply removing one participant in the disturbing interaction. Whether or not this trend becomes established will depend on the work of farsighted educators who realize that the best interests of handicapped children are *not* served by segregating them. You should realize, however, that this trend does not eliminate the need for more restrictive educational environments, such as resource rooms and self-contained classes. But in-service training and teacher consultation do reduce the population of such programs.

Finally, the role of the educator as child advocate is becoming increasingly important. As the roles of special educators become more diversified, so too do the demands placed on them. The in-service teacher trainer must sometimes work with teachers and administration who resist change, the parent counselor or trainer must overcome guilt and denial, and the classroom teacher must deal with children who progress very slowly or who reward him at the end of a long day with verbal abuse. As the efforts of special educators extend beyond traditional school boundaries, it is important to remember that the child is the client, and that one is dealing with microcommunities that have traditionally handled problems by rejecting the child or making her a scapegoat. Advocacy takes more than a strong personality, dedication, and tremendous patience, however; it takes great skill. Today's special educator must be familiar with a complex teaching technology, laws, and statutes affecting the handicapped, and counseling techniques and consultation strategies as well.

PROBE 9-6
Educational Environments

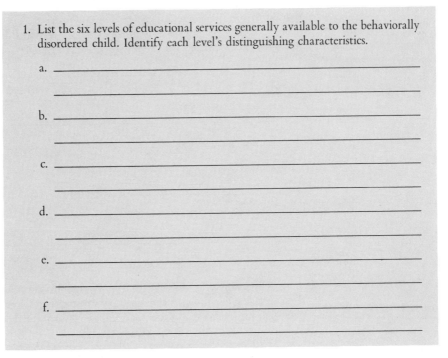

1. List the six levels of educational services generally available to the behaviorally disordered child. Identify each level's distinguishing characteristics.

   a. _____

   _____

   b. _____

   _____

   c. _____

   _____

   d. _____

   _____

   e. _____

   _____

   f. _____

   _____

2. You are the chairperson of a school-based Admissions and Release Committee, which recommends educational placements for exceptional children. For each of the children described, indicate which of the six levels of the educational cascade you would recommend for placement and briefly explain your reasons.

a. Peter: A ten year old with "psychotic" behaviors. He has good speech and language skills but no academic skills. He has violent outbursts and behaves aggressively in many situations without apparent provocation.

   Placement: _____

   Reasons: _____

   _____

   _____

   _____

   _____

   _____

b. Sally: An eight-year-old second grader who has been a discipline problem all year. She is about one year behind her grade level in arithmetic and functions at the readiness level in reading and language arts. Her teacher complains that she does not do assignments without constant supervision and disrupts the class with "silly" behavior.

   Placement: _____

   Reasons: _____

   _____

   _____

   _____

   _____

   _____

   _____

c. Tim: A fourteen year old who spends most of his time in Spanish class sleeping or daydreaming. Although he has better than average intellectual potential, his teacher complains that he hasn't learned a thing.

   Placement: _____

Reasons: _____

_____

_____

_____

_____

_____

d. James: A twelve year old who has been expelled from school for aggressive attacks on a teacher and for vandalism. He already belongs to a street gang, and his parents are unable to control him.

Placement: _____

Reasons: _____

_____

_____

_____

_____

_____

e. Alice: A seventeen year old who is taking algebra (a required college-prep course) for the second time and still failing. Her work in other classes is average or slightly above average. Both Alice and her parents express a desire for her to attend college.

Placement: _____

Reasons: _____

_____

_____

_____

_____

_____

SUMMARY

1. Behavior disorders are best defined by considering characteristics common to the behaviors thought to be disordered.
2. There are a number of conceptual approaches to defining behavior disorders. The psychodynamic and behavioral orientations receive the most attention.
3. The ecological approach to the diagnosis and classification of behavior disorders has found wide acceptance by special educators.
4. Factors such as age, sex, and socioeconomic variables affect prevalence estimates of behavior disorders.
5. Examination of the biophysical and environmental correlates of behavioral disorders is more productive for intervention than traditional investigations of etiological factors.
6. Rather than discuss the "characteristics" of behaviorally disordered pupils, teachers should differentiate "disturbing" behaviors, which tend to be specific to one setting, *and* "disturbed" behaviors, which occur with excessive intensity and/or frequency across several settings.
7. The provision of services to the behaviorally disordered in the least restrictive environment requires that a broad array of services to be available to the individual, the family, and the professionals involved.
8. Current trends in services for the behaviorally disordered person include provision for the previously unserved severely and profoundly disordered, and in-service training of the regular educator to handle behavior problems in the mainstream of the school setting.
9. *Most important, do not label children as behaviorally disordered.*

TASK SHEET 9
Field Experience in Behavior Disorders

Complete *one* of the following alternatives:

Child Observation

Get permission from a building principal and the appropriate teachers to observe a child who has been identified by the school as behaviorally disordered. The child need not have been formally labeled. Observe the child for thirty minutes, if possible, in both a structured situation, such as a group lesson, and during free play.

1. What behaviors make the child "different" from her "normal" peers?
2. How are these behaviors different in terms of their frequency and intensity?
3. How do the teacher and the peer group react to the child's deviant behavior? Does their reaction seem to have anything to do with the behavior being a problem (i.e., do they call attention to it, give in to it, or seem to anticipate it)?

Parent or Teacher Interview

Interview a parent or regular classroom teacher regarding his perceptions of behavior disorders. Find out what he thinks the term means. You may use the term "emotionally disturbed" if you prefer.

1. Whom did you interview?
2. How did he react to the term "behaviorally disordered" or "emotionally disturbed"? What did he think it meant?
3. How would his conception affect the way he reacted to or worked with a child having one of these labels?

Professional Interview

Interview a teacher, psychologist, or counselor who deals with children with behavior disorders. Describe the person you interviewed and her responsibilities. Identify rewards and problems encountered in working with these children.

Library Study

Locate three articles on behavior disorders. Write a one-page critique of each.

Design Your Own Field Experience

If none of the above activities fits your needs, design one of your own after discussing the idea with your instructor.

Probe Answers

Probe 9–1

1. a. A label is a self-fulfilling prophesy (i. e., it sets up negative environmental expectations).
   b. It is circular, and thus may not explain anything.
   c. It may not be the "best" label, in terms of getting the child the most appropriate special services.
   d. It may not be the child's problem.
   e. Using a label will not solve the problem.
2. This assumption avoids harmful labeling; emphasizes the reciprocal nature of behavior problems; is more likely to lead to positive environmental changes; and does not scapegoat the child.
3. False
4. a. the perception that these behaviors depart from acceptable standards
   b. the degree to which the behaviors deviate from these standards

   c. the length of time the behaviors have continued

Probe 9–2

1. You would not agree. The problem may not be "owned" by the child; instead, it may be the teacher's, or (more likely) a product of the interaction between child and teacher. A thorough assessment of the problem behavior, problem situation, and the child's ecological units would have to be done before anyone could be blamed for the problem. Even then, it would be more productive to work on the disturbing interaction than to identify and label the child.
2. a. aggressive verbal behavior
   b. aggressive physical behavior
3. The functional analytic approach identifies a child's behavioral assets; maladaptive behaviors are identified and intervention strategies are suggested.

Probe 9–3

1. True
2. a. Girls are taught to be more conforming than boys.
   b. Adult tolerance for boy's behavior is lower than that for girl's behavior.
   c. More boys than girls have learning problems in school.
3. c
4. This is not advisable. Even though he might improve with time, treatment probably offers him a better chance. The sooner it is provided, the better.

Probe 9–4

1. The evidence for this conclusion is very weak. While there are more indications that biochemical factors cause severe behavior disorders, genetic misfortune is not the only one of these factors. Moreover, problem behavior has been shown to involve the interaction of numerous factors. Therefore etiological links are not as direct as the psychiatrist's statement implies.
2. d
3. The child's problem was no more caused by the parent's behavior than the parent's behavior was caused by the child's problem. The influence is reciprocal, and blaming either child or parent does little to relieve the situation. It is better to start an intervention than to worry about causes at this point. Perhaps the parent can learn to deal with his child more effectively as treatment progresses.

Probe 9–5

1. a. Settings: classroom, playground, gym, lunchroom, bus, home, neighborhood
   b. Persons: teacher, parent, guidance counselor, cafeteria workers, janitor, church or scout leader, peers, siblings
   c. Information: whether the child is a problem in each setting, what kinds of behavior she displays (both acceptable and unacceptable), how persons in these settings react to the problem and to appropriate behaviors, what expectations are made of the child by different adults, how expectations and management vary among adults and settings
2. Disturbing agressive behavior would be limited to specific individuals or situations. For example, it may occur only in the presence of a particular adult, peer, or group engaged in a particular activity (e.g., sports), or a particular event (e.g., taunting). Disturbed aggressive behavior would occur in the presence of a variety of persons and in many situations. The child may be characterized, in this instance, as responding in a generalized manner with aggression. In the case of disturbing behavior, intervention would be directed toward the specific problem situation, and may involve changing an environmental antecedent (e.g., preventing a bully from taunting the child; providing closer supervision in sports activity) as well as teaching the child better alternative responses. In the case of disturbed behavior, it is more likely that intervention would focus on changing the child's behavior (i.e. teaching him to make more adaptive responses, to analyze the behavior of others more accurately, to avoid persons who prompt aggressive behavior). Environmental factors also would be included, but greater emphasis would be placed on the child's behavior itself.

Probe 9–6

1. a. *Regular classroom:* setting for most behaviorally disordered children; special education consultants help regular teachers with IEPs.
   b. *Resource room:* for children needing more help with learning or behavior problems than the regular teacher can offer.
   c. *Self-contained classroom:* located in the regular school building; for children with lower intellectual functioning, inadequate language and self-care skills, and frequent inappropriate behavior; conducive to gradual mainstreaming.
   d. *Special day school:* a fairly unusual placement; limits children's access to the mainstream; may serve one or several categories

of handicapped children.

e. *Re-education school:* type of residential program; for children who need extensive intervention; contact maintained with child's natural ecology through liaison work and home visits; brief stay, averaging about six months.

f. *Residential treatment program:* provides intervention (including psychotherapy and chemotherapy) in addition to education; contact with natural ecology more limited than that in re-education school; relatively long stay — one or two years.

2. a. *Residential treatment.* Peter's behavior problems extend beyond the limits of all schools or Re-Ed and require intensive intervention in a readily managed environment. Peter may need to be closely supervised to protect himself as well as others from his apparently unprovoked violent outbursts.

b. *Resource room, plus consultation for her regular classroom teacher.* Sally needs intensive remediation for her academic difficulties, which probably cannot be provided in the regular classroom. Her teacher also needs to learn more effective management techniques.

c. *Regular classroom, plus consultation for his teacher.* Tim needs better incentives to stay awake and participate; his teacher needs to learn how to motivate him, not only for Tim's good, but for the good of future students. A resource room is not the optimal place to learn a foreign language, even if the resource teacher were qualified to teach it.

d. *Re-Ed.* James's behavior problems extend beyond the limits of the school. Re-Ed employs a treatment model that can address the problems James presents to each of his microcommunities. The focus is on changing James and his environment. He has been expelled from school, which limits what the public schools are willing to do with him. In Re-Ed, he will maintain contact with his natural environment and at the same time receive a structured 24-hour residential program.

e. *Regular classroom or resource room.* Alice requires intensive individualized help with algebra. That she gets this help is most important; less important is where she receives it, although her maximum participation in the regular class environment is desirable.

Jennifer:

The head nurse of a woman's locked ward introduces me to Jennifer. She is lying in a urine-soaked bed under a restraining sheet.

"How long has she been here?"

"Fifteen years. She gets up five to fifteen minutes every day."

"How about meals?"

"She is fed here in bed."

Later in the day I talked with one of the "brighter girls" (state school term), who has worked in the community and now serves the attendants assisting in feeding and cleaning.

"Ann, how long have you been here?"

"A long time."

"How long is that?"

"Seventeen years."

"How long has Jennifer been here?"

"About fifteen years."

"Does she ever get up?"

"Only on Mondays and Thursdays for a bath."

During the three hours I was present, Jennifer was not allowed out of her restraint. That evening another observer was able to see Jennifer's case history, including her medical record. According to that, Jennifer is receiving: Mellaril, 100 mg. three times a day; Valium, 5 mg. three times a day; phenobarbitol, 1 ½ gr. three times a day; and Dilantin sodium, 1 ½ gr. twice a day. . . .

Jennifer, of course, cannot put her own bib on, so it is done for her. Since she is not allowed out of the bed, she must eat lying flat. The urine-soaked bed was not cleaned before she ate lunch, nor was it cleaned before dinner. It has become her way of life.

Source: From Burton Blatt, *Souls in Extremis: An Anthology of Victims and Victimizers.* Boston: Allyn and Bacon, 1973, pp. 32–33. Reprinted by permission.

10

Severe and Profound Handicaps

David L. Gast and Margo Berkler

David L. Gast is Assistant Professor in the Department of Special Education and Coordinator of personnel preparation programs in the area of severely/profoundly handicapped at the University of Kentucky. Current areas of interest include the design of data-based instructional programs with severely handicapped learners. Margo Berkler is Assistant Professor in the Department of Special Education at the University of Idaho. Current activities include the development of instructional strategies for the severely handicapped and training teachers of the severely handicapped.

Children such as Jennifer with severe and profound handicaps have only recently begun to be served in the public education system. Programs for these children have been brought about through court cases, which affirmed their right to education, and through enactment of PL 94-142, which mandated that they receive a free and appropriate public education.

The provision of school programs to the severely and profoundly handicapped presents a number of problems for educators. For one thing, many of these children require training in very basic skills, ranging from toilet training to language development. Public schools have not previously been required to address such needs, so we are just beginning to find ways to teach the severely handicapped effectively. In the past many of these children were routinely placed in institutions, where they received custodial care rather than instruction. Another problem is that there is a shortage of teachers who have been specifically trained to work with the severely handicapped.

As you read this chapter you should realize that many of the concepts we present are newly evolved. There will undoubtedly be changes made as new information becomes available about how best to meet these children's needs. Through continuing research and development, more effective instructional methodologies, curricula, and service delivery systems will be implemented.

Those who plan on working with this population of children will need to read the relevant professional literature to keep abreast of techniques that are being developed.

CHARACTERISTICS OF THE SEVERELY/PROFOUNDLY HANDICAPPED

> **You should be able to describe the characteristics and prevalence of severely and profoundly handicapped children.**

Severely and profoundly handicapped individuals are functionally mentally retarded. As you will remember from Chapter 7, mildly retarded children are hard to characterize precisely. More seriously retarded children exhibit greater behavioral deficits and typically are easier to identify. As mentioned in Chapter 7, severe and profound retardation can be caused by a number of factors, including genetic problems, exposure to radiation, maternal disease, birth injury, chromosomal mutations, drugs, infections, lack of oxygen to the brain, malnutrition, and many others.

In this chapter "severely and profoundly handicapped" children are considered to be those individuals who have disabilities such as severe speech and language disorders, visual impairment, and physical disabilities *in addition to* severe or profound mental retardation. The organization of professionals serving this population is called The Association for the Severely Handicapped (TASH), formerly the American Association for the Education of the Severely/Profoundly Handicapped. Children with multiple disabilities and mild retardation or average or above average intelligence are considered "multiply handicapped."

TOWARD A DEFINITION

Although there is general agreement among professionals about the behaviors that characterize the severely and profoundly handicapped, there is as yet no universally accepted definition of this group. For our purposes, the definition generated by a group of educators from seven southeastern universities, the Southeastern Regional Coalition (1978), will suffice:

> The severely handicapped individual is defined for educational purposes as:
> (1) having serious primary disabilities that are cognitive (e.g., −4 standard deviations below a normal IQ on a standardized test of intelligence such as the Revised Stanford-Binet Test of Intelligence) and/or behavioral (e.g., autistic or childhood schizophrenic), (2) having the high probability of additional physical and/or sensory handicaps, and (3) requiring significantly more resources than

are provided for the mildly and moderately handicapped in special education programs [p. 39].

According to this definition, the individual is described as severely/profoundly handicapped on the basis of her current level of functioning. It is educationally oriented in that it recognizes the need for additional services if effective instruction is to be provided. It also implies that instruction will focus on basic skills such as toileting, communication, and personal hygiene, rather than on academic skills.

PREVALENCE

The number of severely and profoundly handicapped persons in the population is difficult to estimate. According to the United States Office of Education (1975), approximately 2.3 percent of the population is mentally retarded. It is generally estimated that 0.1 percent of the total population can be categorized as severely/profoundly handicapped, although this is not specified in the USOE report. The 0.1 percent figure includes only those with severe and profound cognitive deficits; it does not include persons with severe speech, orthopedic, auditory, or visual impairment.

BEHAVIORAL CHARACTERISTICS

It is important to understand that the problems of the severely/profoundly handicapped differ in degree, not in kind, from the problems of other child populations. That is, it is the extent of the handicaps that results in the child's classification, and not the type of handicap. Many children have visual, auditory, motor, or neurological impairments. Adaptive equipment such as glasses, hearing aids, or braces can correct some children's impairments. But children whose disabilities are so severe that they cannot be corrected with adaptive equipment may be rendered functionally retarded.

Severely/profoundly handicapped children are a heterogeneous population. No two children have the same characteristics. Within this population, we find the following types of children:

> Those who are not toilet trained; aggress toward others; do not attend to even the most pronounced social stimuli; self mutilate; ruminate; self stimulate; do not walk, speak, hear, or see; manifest durable and intense temper tantrums; are not under even the most rudimentary forms of verbal control; do not imitate; manifest minimally controlled seizures; and/or have extremely brittle medical existences [Sontag, Burke, and York, 1973, p. 21].

An elaboration of some of the characteristics in this list will illustrate the wide variety of behaviors that a teacher of the severely/profoundly handicapped may encounter. The meaning of some of these characteristics is clear. The others can be explained as follows:

— *Aggression toward others* refers to behaviors that can inflict bodily harm on other persons, such as biting, kicking, hitting, hair pulling, and throwing things.
— *No attention to even the most pronounced social stimuli* means that the child does not make eye contact with adults and other children, does not look at instructional materials, and does not respond to simple verbal instructions.
— *Self-mutilation* refers to behaviors such as head banging, biting oneself, eye gouging, and hitting oneself on the head.
— *Rumination* refers to self-induced vomiting after which a portion of the vomitus is chewed again and swallowed.
— *Self-stimulation* refers to purposeless, repetitive behaviors, such as body rocking, hand flapping, and finger twirling.
— *Durable and intense temper tantrums* refers to a combination of physical aggression, self-mutilation, or self-stimulation occurring over an extended period.
— *Imitation* is the ability to mimic or repeat a behavior immediately after someone (referred to as the "model") demonstrates it.
— *Extremely brittle medical existence* refers to the presence of life-threatening conditions, such as heart failure, respiratory difficulties, central nervous system disorders, and digestive system malfunctions.

DEAF-BLIND CHILDREN

In 1964 and 1965 the United States was struck by a rubella epidemic.[1] As a result, more than 30,000 children with hearing and visual losses were born. Many had other impairments as well.

To provide for these children, an amendment to Title VI of the Elementary and Secondary Education Act, PL 90-247, Part C, was passed by Congress in 1968. This legislation served several purposes. It defined deaf-blind children as those who have both "auditory and visual handicaps, the combination of which causes such severe communication and other developmental and educational problems that they cannot properly be accommodated in special education programs solely for the hearing handicapped child or for the visually handicapped child." The degree of impairment in these children varies considerably. Very few children are completely deaf and blind.

[1] The authors express their appreciation to Caroline Jones for the information presented in this section.

PL 90-247 also provided for the establishment of ten multistate regional centers designed to serve as models and to coordinate services to the deaf-blind. One of the centers' goals was to develop educational technologies designed specifically to meet the needs of the deaf-blind. In 1976 it was estimated that at least 5050 children had been served by the regional centers and that the total would reach 7000.

Deaf-blindness can be caused by a number of factors other than rubella, although that was the most prevalent cause in the 1960s. Prenatal causes include a variety of infections and toxins that may be passed from the mother to the fetus. Genetic disorders such as Usher's syndrome, Hurler's syndrome, and Tay-Sachs disease can also result in visual and auditory impairments. Trauma to the child during birth can also damage the sensory system. Postnatal diseases such as meningitis and encephalitis may lead to deaf-blindness.

The educational needs of deaf-blind children vary greatly, because these children have varying degrees of visual and auditory impairment. Some children have additional impairments, such as physical disorders, which require specific educational or medical intervention. One should not, however, assume that all deaf-blind children function at low levels. Some of these children overcome their sensory limitations and lead productive lives.

Probably the most important need of this population is a means of communication. Those who can use neither their vision nor their hearing cannot effectively use sign language, verbal speech, braille, or large print. For these children, methods of communication based on the use of the sense of touch have been developed. These methods, which involve delivering manual signals to the hands of the person with whom one is communicating, can involve presenting familiar gestures, Morse code, or other communication codes to the palm. One of the most common approaches makes use of natural gestures and sign language. It is extremely important that deaf-blind children be taught to use a communication system effectively, because so many areas of development depend on the ability to send and receive signals about the environment.

The deaf-blind should be encouraged to develop as great a range of skills as possible. Auditory and visual training help the child make use of residual vision and hearing. Mobility and orientation training may be taught to facilitate independent movement. Hearing aids can often be used to advantage. In addition, the use of the sense of touch to make fine discriminations is also taught. Deaf-blind children should be urged to use all of their senses to interact with the environment. They may develop self-stimulatory behaviors if left alone.

In other areas of education, the needs of the deaf-blind resemble those of other children. Development must be encouraged in all areas — cognitive, motor, and self-help. The methods used in instruction may be similar to those used with other children. If gross motor development is delayed, for example, methods much like those used to teach nonhandicapped children may be used after adaptations are made in the communication system.

The severely/profoundly handicapped present a challenge to the special educator. It should be remembered that these children were being placed in institutions for their entire lives in the recent past. Only during the 1970s was it recognized that they can benefit from being placed in educational programs.

PROBE 10-1
Characteristics of the Severely/Profoundly Handicapped

1. What is the difference between "multiply handicapped" and "severely/profoundly handicapped"?

   _____

   _____

   _____

2. What are the three primary components of the definition of "severely/profoundly handicapped" given in this chapter?

   a. _____

   b. _____

   c. _____

3. T F Education for the severely/profoundly handicapped focuses primarily on the development of basic skills.

4. What is the prevalence of severely/profoundly handicapped children in the general population? _____

5. What is meant by the statement, "severely/profoundly handicapped children differ from other handicapped children in degree, not in kind"?

   _____

   _____

   _____

6. Describe four characteristics commonly found in children enrolled in classes for the severely/profoundly handicapped.

   a. _____

   b. _____

   c. _____

   d. _____

CURRICULUM CONSIDERATIONS

> **You should be able to discuss the primary areas of instruction appropriate for the severely/profoundly handicapped.**

As noted earlier, instructional programs for severely/profoundly handicapped children emphasize the development of basic skills rather than academic skills. Eight areas of basic skills are described in the following section, along with some of the techniques used to teach each of them.

LANGUAGE DEVELOPMENT

Three types of language problem are frequently encountered in severely/profoundly handicapped children (Guess and Horner, 1978):

1. These children frequently have a low level of receptive language and an even lower level of expressive language. This often results in the use of gestures and body movements in an effort to communicate.
2. Unclear speech is also a common problem. People who are not in daily contact with severely/profoundly handicapped children may have difficulty understanding them.
3. Bizarre speech patterns, in which the speech is clear but the content is meaningless, are also found in some children. *Echolalia,* the repetition of everything that someone else says, is also common.

Some children profit from the use of nonverbal communication systems. These may be the only means of communication available to those who cannot communicate verbally, or they may be used as an aid while speech is being developed. Nonverbal communication systems include the use of manual communication (sign language); communication boards with words or pictures on them, to which the child can point (Figure 10-1); and electronic devices, which produce speech electronically through the manipulation of buttons or visual displays. Additional information about communication boards can be found in Vanderheiden (1978) and Vanderheiden and Grilley (1976).

Many instructional programs have been developed to teach speech and language to the severely/profoundly handicapped. Most of these programs (e.g., Guess, Sailor, and Baer, 1976; Miller and Yoder, 1974) emphasize the development of speech and language skills that are specific to the environment in which the children live and that the child can use in her daily life (MacDonald and Hortsmeier, 1978; McDonnell, Fredericks, and Grove, 1977; Tawney and Hipsher, 1972).

Figure 10-1
Examples of Communication Boards

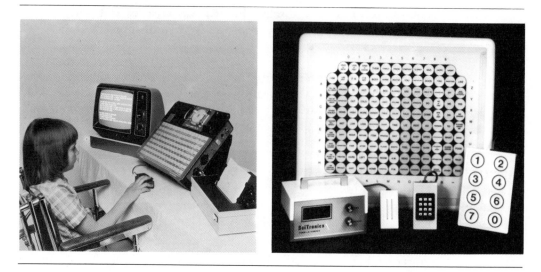

Before teaching language to these children one must frequently develop their prerequisite skills, such as being able to sit in a chair, look at the teacher, and work on a particular task. It may later be necessary to develop the ability to imitate vocal sounds, movements of the teacher, and speech sounds. Bricker, Dennison, and Bricker (1976) have developed a program to teach prerequisites for verbal behavior that is based on the sensorimotor period of development described by Piaget (1952).

SELF-CARE SKILLS

Most severely/profoundly handicapped children lack fundamental self-care skills in the areas of toileting, dressing, eating, and grooming. It is important that these children develop self-care skills so they can become as independent as possible. This also makes their care simpler and more pleasant for parents and teachers.

A number of the instructional programs developed for toilet training have been described by Duncombe, Pacheco, and Quilitch (1977). Some of them are quite imaginative. For example, effective use has been made of signaling devices that buzz when the child urinates or soils his pants. "Rapid" toilet training, which involves increasing the frequency of elimination by having the child drink more fluids, has also been successful (Foxx and Azrin, 1973). *Habit training* is another method. This procedure involves placing the child on the toilet at regular intervals each day. The child gradually learns to void only on the toilet at predictable times.

Most children of average ability know how to get dressed and undressed by the end of their sixth year. The severely/profoundly handicapped frequently take much longer, however, largely because they lack the eye-hand coordination and fine motor skills required to accomplish the necessary tasks. As a result, training in buttoning, lacing, snapping, shoe tying, dressing, and undressing is generally part of the instructional program. A number of the training programs related to dressing have been reviewed by Snell (1978).

Many of these children also have trouble eating. They may have difficulty with tongue movement, sucking, swallowing, and lip closure. They may also have bite and gag reflexes. The teaching of self-feeding skills may be a difficult

By acquiring feeding skills in many small steps and with the help of his camp counselor, this child will eventually learn to feed himself.

and time-consuming task. Children are first taught finger feeding, then drinking from a glass, followed by the use of a spoon, fork, and knife, in that order. These skills are often broken into many small steps (task analyzed) to help the child acquire them as quickly as possible. Specially adapted equipment, such as spoons with large handles and plates with raised edges to prevent spillage, is often used in these training programs. The goal of teaching self-feeding is the development of good table manners and related mealtime skills.

COGNITIVE DEVELOPMENT

Severely/profoundly handicapped children rarely develop sophisticated reading, writing, or mathematic skills. They should, however, be taught cognitive skills that will be useful in their daily lives, including those used to read signs and symbols such as safety signs, restroom signs, and traffic control signals. They should also be taught to tell time by the hour and half hour. The education of younger children will in most cases emphasize the acquisition of preliminary skills, such as paying attention, before cognitive training programs can begin.

The concepts of Piaget, discussed in Chapter 2, are particularly important in the education of the severely/profoundly handicapped. It is currently popular to base the content of programming for these children on Piaget's work, and the methods used to teach the content on the principles of applied behavior analysis.

The cognitive skills emphasized are those generally acquired during the normal child's first two years. This corresponds to Piaget's sensorimotor stage of development and includes the teaching of skills that are often considered reflexes, such as eye-hand coordination. More detailed information can be obtained from Piaget (1954, 1963) and Uzgiris and Hunt (1975).

SENSORY AND PERCEPTUAL SKILLS

Many severely/profoundly handicapped children have sensory and perceptual skill deficits. Those who have acuity problems can often be helped through the use of eyeglasses and hearing aids. Assessment of visual and hearing acuity is very difficult with these children, however, because they may have trouble responding or have limited communication skills.

The perceptual processes (the ways children perceive and interpret their environments) may be even more difficult to assess. The perceptual skills of the severely/profoundly handicapped cannot be assumed to exist, as they are with children who develop normally. For example, simple discriminations between shapes and colors must be systematically taught. Guess and Horner (1978) provide suggestions for teaching perceptual skills.

Swimming is an aid in developing gross motor skills as well as an enjoyable leisure-time activity.

GROSS AND FINE MOTOR SKILLS

Gross motor skills are those which involve the large muscles of the body. These skills are necessary for activities such as hopping, skipping, running, and jumping. Fine motor skills involve the small muscles and include skills such as holding, grasping, catching, and writing. The severely/profoundly handicapped child frequently must be taught these skills. As with other skill areas, it may be necessary to help the child develop prerequisite skills such as head control, sitting up, rolling over, and grasping objects, before beginning instruction in more complex skills. Physical therapists frequently assist in the development of programs to teach gross and fine motor skills. The Bobath (1967) neurodevelopmental therapy program is also quite useful, as are motor development curricula specifically designed for the severely/profoundly handicapped (Bricker, Davis, Wahlin, and Evans, 1977; Farber, 1974; Fredericks, Baldwin, Doughty, and Walter, 1972; Smith, 1973).

SOCIAL AND RECREATIONAL SKILLS

Training in social adjustment is very important for this population. These individuals often appear to be oblivious to other persons, or they interact inappropriately. The importance of social skills is underscored by the recognition that the severely handicapped can often perform the manual skills necessary to function successfully in the home, community, and at work, but they are kept from performing successfully because they lack the necessary social skills.

A typical social interaction training program provides instruction in five areas. Children are taught (1) to recognize the appropriate time and place for a social interaction; (2) how to initiate interactions; (3) how to receive requests for interaction; (4) how to sustain interactions; and (5) how to terminate social interactions. An instructional program to teach these skills has been designed by Williams, Hamre-Nietupski, Pumpian, McDaniel-Marx, and Wheeler (1978).

Social skill training is also concerned with the development of leisure-time activities. The severely/profoundly handicapped frequently spend their leisure time watching television. Wehman (1976) has developed a program to teach leisure activities. It begins with the use of toys and progresses through the use of records, games, and hobbies to active socialization with others.

VOCATIONAL HABILITATION

Vocational habilitation is training designed to lead to employment. The term "habilitation," rather than "rehabilitation," is used because it refers to initial training, rather than retraining. In the past it was widely believed that the severely/profoundly handicapped could not be productively employed. More recently, however, it has been shown that these individuals can be taught to perform rather complex tasks. For example, severely/profoundly handicapped people have learned to assemble a fifty-two-piece cam switch activator (Bellamy, Peterson, and Close, 1976), a twelve-piece bicycle brake (Gold, 1974), an intricate cable harness (Hunter and Bellamy, 1976), and a saw chain (O'Neil and Bellamy, 1978). Training projects such as these have demonstrated that these people can do productive work.

In this area, too, the child is first taught prerequisite skills, called "prevocational training." The goals of this training are the development of manual skills and concern for the quality of work; the construction of small objects; the creation of an awareness of the importance of finishing a task; and the strengthening of work-related personality characteristics (Baroff, 1974). Mithaug, Mar, and Stewart (1978) have developed a training program that can be used to develop such skills.

Another aspect of prevocational training is the assessment of the individual's abilities to determine whether she can perform a particular job. This process also involves determining what skills a job requires. Behavioral checklists have been developed that can be used to assess the skills of potential students in vocational training programs (Walls and Werner, 1977). Once the individual's skills have been assessed, the emphasis should be on training her to perform available work, rather than finding work the individual can perform. In the past these people were given highly repetitive jobs requiring little skill, but recent evidence indicates they can perform complex tasks, as mentioned. Training should ultimately lead to employment in a sheltered workshop, which is an establishment designed to provide jobs for those who require considerable supervision or who cannot hold jobs in regular commercial establishments. Those who are capable of holding jobs outside the sheltered workshop should receive further training.

In the vocational training program itself, training is focused on helping the individual acquire skills and increasing his rate of productivity. The rate at which skills are acquired affects what type of job the person can perform. Most workshops get their work from industry. More complex jobs of course require more intensive training over a longer period of time. The rate of productivity affects the kind of supervision that is required, the cost of production, and the wages that the worker earns. Employees are often paid on the basis of the amount of work that they perform.

Many techniques are used in vocational training. Some of them focus on stimulus discrimination — the ability to make a particular response to a stimulus with specific properties. For example, a student may be taught that a particular ball bearing should be placed on the shaft of a bicycle brake immediately on top of a round washer. Presenting tasks in a progression from the easiest to the most difficult (Irvin, 1976) and the use of teaching techniques that prevent the child from making many errors (Irvin, 1976) are basic methods for teaching stimulus discriminations. Other training procedures involve repeating the desired response several times (Wehman, Schutz, Renzaglia, and Karen, 1976), rewarding successive approximations, priming the response, verbal guidance, modeling, and providing cues, (Bellamy, Peterson, and Close, 1976). Clearly stated performance goals, competition, and reinforcement can help increase productivity (Bellamy, Inman, and Schwarz, 1978).

COMMUNITY LIVING SKILLS

A wide range of skills to be used in community and daily living needs to be taught to the severely/profoundly handicapped. Some, such as cooking, are rather broad, whereas others, such as signing a time card, are quite specific. The individual's living situation determines the kind of skills that should be learned. It would be pointless, for example, to teach a child how to use a television during his leisure time if the child's family had no television.

Specific programs have been developed to teach a variety of skills. Additional training after a skill has been learned may help the child generalize the skill she has acquired. For example, Nietupski, Certo, Pumpian, and Belmore (1976) taught a group of people to shop in a particular grocery store using a card corresponding to the store's arrangement. With training, this skill could be generalized to other grocery stores. Spellman, DeBriere, Jarboe, Campbell, and Harris (1978) developed a symbol system based on pictures, which could be used by nonreaders to learn skills such as cooking. A number of training programs for such skills as toothbrushing, complexion care, and hair washing have been developed by the staff of Project MORE (Lent and McLean, 1976). Other programs teach skills such as how to use the telephone, ride the bus, and groom oneself (Brown, Williams, and Crowner, 1974; Haring and Brown, 1977). Good curriculum guides for teachers concerned with developing community living skills have been developed by Anderson, Hodson, and Jones, 1975; Bender and Valletuhi, 1976; Casa Grande Center, 1978.

PROBE 10-2
Curriculum Considerations

1. T F Children with severe and profound handicaps frequently have delayed speech and language development.

2. List two language problems often found with the severely and profoundly handicapped.

   a. _____

   b. _____

3. Why are nonverbal communication systems used?

   a. _____

   b. _____

4. What is "rapid" toilet training?_____

   _____

5. T F Severely/profoundly handicapped children rarely have difficulty learning how to feed themselves.

6. What kind of reading skills should be taught to the severely/profoundly handicapped?_____

   _____

7. The ____ of programming for the severely/profoundly disabled is based on Piaget's work, whereas the ____ are based on the principles of applied behavior analysis.

8. Differentiate between fine motor and gross motor skills.

   _____

   _____

   _____

9. T F Eyeglasses and hearing aids are useful for correcting deficits in perception.

10. T F The severely/profoundly handicapped do not need to be taught how to use their leisure time.

11. ____ training programs are designed to teach the preliminary skills necessary to do a variety of work tasks.

12. Why do we refer to "habilitation" rather than "rehabilitation" in the education of the severely/profoundly handicapped?

_____

_____

_____

13. T   F   Severely/profoundly handicapped people cannot be taught to do complex tasks in sheltered workshop settings.

14. T   F   Social interaction training is an important aspect of community reintegration.

15. T   F   The severely/profoundly handicapped never work outside sheltered workshops.

TEACHER COMPETENCIES

> **You should be able to describe the skills and knowledge necessary to teach severely/profoundly handicapped children.**

As you have seen, the curriculum for the severely/profoundly handicapped is quite different from that for less seriously handicapped children. As a result, the teachers of these children must develop different skills. These teachers can expect, for example, to spend a considerable amount of time controlling severe behavior problems. A teacher of the mildly handicapped, on the other hand, might spend a considerable portion of her time teaching reading. The skills needed to teach the severely/profoundly handicapped have been studied by many researchers, including Fredericks, Baldwin, Grove, Riggs, Fureg, Moore, Jordan, Gage, Levak, Alrik, and Wadlow (1977), Perske and Smith (1977), and Wilcox (1977). Some of the necessary skills cited by most investigators will be described in this section.

BEHAVIOR MANAGEMENT

Many severely handicapped children exhibit inappropriate behaviors that are called "stereotypic" or "self-stimulatory." Some of these behaviors, such as body rocking, finger twirling, and hand flapping, are not harmful, but others, such as head banging and eye gouging, are self-injurious. Other behaviors — biting, pinching, and hair pulling, for example — can be dangerous to others. These behaviors are common among children who have been institutionalized and who have not been taught to behave more appropriately. These behaviors must be reduced in frequency or eliminated before the teacher can teach effectively. Thus, the teacher must have a thorough understanding of applied behavior analysis, also known as behavior modification.

Many teachers who have only a superficial understanding of behavior modification have been assigned the responsibility of designing behavioral management programs. An awareness of available techniques is not enough for designing effective programs, however. To produce positive results the teacher must be able to select the techniques best suited to the child and his environment, and apply them in a sensitive, systematic, and consistent fashion. The teacher must also be able to assess the program's effectiveness and, when appropriate, make modifications. The teacher should be concerned not only with the elimination of inappropriate behavior; she must also work to develop constructive behavior and help the student generalize what he has learned in the classroom to other settings. Publications by the following authors deal with behavioral management: Gibson and Brown (1976), Kauffman and Snell (1977), and Kiernan and Woodford (1975).

UNDERSTANDING OF NORMAL CHILD DEVELOPMENT

Special educators should understand normal child development. The developmental model, described in Chapter 2, can help the teacher determine what to teach, just as applied behavior analysis provides a methodology. Three fundamental assumptions in the developmental model have significant implications for teaching: (1) behavior in different areas develops in a systematic sequence; (2) the acquisition of behaviors progresses from simple to complex responses; and (3) relatively complex behavior results from the coordination or modification of simpler responses (Haring and Bricker, 1976).

Although the developmental model is helpful in selecting instructional objectives for the severely/profoundly handicapped, it should not be rigidly adhered to. Many severely/profoundly handicapped children do not develop normally and will not attain the same developmental milestones as nonhandicapped children. Teachers should adapt their teaching to emphasize milestones that serve the needs of the individual child. Guides for the use of developmental sequences in the instruction of severely/profoundly handicapped children have been developed by Bricker, Bricker, Iacino, and Dennison (1976) and Cohen, Gross, and Haring (1976).

BEHAVIORAL ASSESSMENT AND EVALUATION

The classroom teacher is responsible for selecting and administering assessment instruments that yield information about instructional objectives. Assessment efforts should be coordinated with people who administer psychological assessments, such as psychologists, psychometrists, and psychiatrists, and with other people who provide diagnostic information, including parents.

A comprehensive educational assessment may take up to four weeks. No single instrument will provide enough information for developing an instructional program, so the assessment should involve several instruments. Some of the instruments that the teacher should know how to administer include

AAMD Adaptive Behavior Scale
Balthazar Scales of Adaptive Behavior
Behavioral Characteristics Progression (BCP)
Brigance Diagnostic Inventory of Early Development
Camelot Behavioral Checklist
Learning Accomplishment Profile (LAP)
Pennsylvania Training Model Individual Assessment Guide
Portage Guide to Early Education
The TARC Assessment Inventory for Severely Handicapped Children
TMR Performance Profile for Severely and Moderately Retarded
Uniform Performance Assessment System (UPAS)

Comprehensive reviews of these instruments and others have been prepared by Du Bose (1978), Haring (1977), and Sailor and Horner (1976).

CURRICULUM SELECTION AND ADAPTATION

There is no "master curriculum" that the teacher can adapt for his entire instructional program, and there never will be one. There are a number of excellent curriculum guides available (Fredericks et al., 1976; Wabash Center for the Mentally Retarded, 1977; Bender and Valletuhi, 1976; Tawney, Knapp, O'Reilly, and Pratt, 1979), but all the curricula suggested will require adaptation by the teacher if they are to meet individual student objectives.

The teacher must be able to select appropriate instructional objectives and materials, an instructional format, and effective teaching methods. The materials used should be familiar to the child; items such as personal clothing, eating utensils, and favorite toys can be used in teaching such skills as concept development, self-care, and language. This helps the child learn to exhibit skills she has learned in her natural environment.

The teacher should also be able to assess a task analysis, to determine whether all the components of the task to be learned have been adequately described. In addition, the teacher should know specifically how his instructional materials will be used to meet individualized objectives, and whether the sequence of objectives corresponds to the sequence of developmental milestones. He must also be certain that all appropriate instructional areas (gross motor skills, self-care, language, etc.) are included in the curriculum. Finally, the teacher must be able to assess the child's progress and make modifications when necessary.

INSTRUCTIONAL ARRANGEMENTS

Because the problems of the severely/profoundly handicapped vary so much in nature and severity, it is very difficult to instruct these children in groups. As a result classes tend to be small. It will be necessary to provide these children with group instruction, but each child should work on individual objectives.

It is important that children learn how to generalize to group situations skills learned in one-to-one instruction. This can be done by providing initial instruction on a one-to-one basis, and moving the child to a group of two to four students after she has mastered the skill. In the small group the teacher can reinforce the skill and, when necessary, provide remedial instruction. The child should also be given the opportunity to demonstrate skills under a variety of conditions. For example, a student who is being taught to respond yes or no might be asked whether she wanted juice at snack time, or a favorite toy during free play. Only when a child has generalized a skill to the natural environment and unstructured activities can the skill be considered learned.

The teacher must also be skilled in classroom design — the arrangement of the classroom, daily activity schedule, and management system to meet the needs of individual students. Two good sources on this subject are the publications by the Allegheny Intermediate Unit (1976) and by Fredericks et al. (1977).

BEHAVIOR ACQUISITION, GENERALIZATION, AND MAINTENANCE

Koegel and Rincover (1977) consider learning a three-phase process. The first phase, *acquisition,* is the process of learning a new behavior or skill. *Generalization* is the ability of the student to use the skill under different conditions. The third phase, *maintenance,* refers to the durability of the skill over time. Brown et al. (1976) claim that the severely/profoundly handicapped child must be taught all three of these phases.

To encourage acquisition, the teacher should be able to use such techniques as behavior shaping, physical prompting, and fading. These techniques, which were described in the introduction to Part III, have been used to teach such diverse skills as wearing glasses (Wolf, Risley, Johnston, Harris, and Allen, 1967) and verbal imitation (Lovaas, Berberich, Perloff, and Schaeffer, 1966). Behavior shaping, although effective, is a slow process, and teachers more frequently use physical prompting and fading. The teacher should also be familiar with more sophisticated procedures, such as time delay (Touchette, 1971) and the system of least prompts (Cuvo, Leaf, and Borakove, 1978).

For teaching to be considered effective, the child must generalize to his natural environment those skills that have been learned in the classroom. Brown et al. (1975) recommend that a behavior be considered learned only after the child has demonstrated the behavior "(a) in reaction to, or in the presence of, at least three different persons; (b) in at least three different natural settings; (c) in response to at least three different sets of instructional materials; and (d) to at least three different appropriate language cues" (p. 13). The teacher can make use of the student's family and personal belongings to enhance behavior generalization.

For a behavior to be maintained, the teacher must gradually transfer control from the classroom to the child's home and community. This requires that the child's family be included in the educational process. In addition, the teacher should systematically decrease the frequency of reinforcement so that the situation in the classroom will approximate the situation in the natural environment. This process is known as "thinning" the schedule of reinforcement.

MEASUREMENT

The teacher must be able to reliably measure student performance. To do so, the teacher must be able to define instructional objectives in observable terms and collect information on whether the child meets an objective. The teacher can base decisions about instruction on the data that have been collected. Measurement can also reinforce teachers for their work and signal the need for program modification as soon as it is necessary.

In practice, it is impossible to measure all of a student's behaviors. Teachers must decide which behaviors or programs need to be monitored on a daily basis (continuous measures) and which can be evaluated through weekly checks (probe measures). Probe measurement often is most appropriate for students who learn slowly. The progress of these students could be measured with weekly probes that record the program step on which the student is working every Friday. If the student is still working on the same step after two weeks, the teacher would recognize that the program might need to be analyzed into smaller instructional steps. Probe measures are less rigorous than continuous measures, but their use is appropriate in some circumstances. One such probe measurement system has been presented by Nelson, Gast, and Trout (1979).

Continuous measurement can provide the teacher with a wealth of information on which to base teaching decisions. According to most instructional programs, the teacher provides a specific number of trials on a task each day. The teacher records whether the student responded correctly on each trial. This collection of information on each trial is an example of continuous measurement. This keeps the teacher in touch with the student's performance on a daily basis and permits her to modify the instructional program immediately. Although continuous monitoring may prove cumbersome at first, it is easily mastered with practice. Examples of various measurement systems are provided by Hall (1971) and Smith and Snell (1978).

MEDICAL AND PHYSICAL MANAGEMENT

Teachers working with children who have medical problems should have a basic understanding of anatomy, physiology, and neurology. This knowledge is useful in working with health personnel such as occupational and physical therapists. The teacher should also know how to deal with common medical emergencies and how to manage convulsive disorders. Training in safety and nutrition are also desirable.

Prosthetic and orthotic devices such as eyeglasses, hearing aids, leg and back braces, and wheelchairs are frequently used by the severely/profoundly handicapped. The teacher must know how these devices work and where in the community they can be obtained. The teacher will also have to take responsibility for modifying the environment so that children using these devices can function more efficiently. For example, ramps, elevators, and handrails may have to be installed. In addition, teachers should know how to create new and inexpensive devices. The teacher's knowledge is often helpful to engineers in designing new, inexpensive devices, and in improving existing devices.

STUDENT AND PROGRAM ADVOCACY

Teachers of the severely/profoundly handicapped are in a position to be effective advocates. They must be prepared to support and explain the components of a student's IEP to persons concerned with the child's education. They must also be prepared to serve as legal and citizen advocates. Teachers are often called on to testify in court cases for these children. Therefore, they must also understand their State Department of Education's commitment to serving the severely/ profoundly handicapped and the laws and regulations that apply to their education. Teachers frequently assist in the drafting of laws, regulations, and local policies and procedures that apply to the education of severely handicapped children.

Finally, teachers of the severely/profoundly handicapped often help secure community-based services for their children. These services may include sheltered workshops, physical therapy, public health services, and transportation. Thus, the teacher should understand the community's needs and priorities and know how to form citizen advocacy groups and to identify human and agency resources. The teacher must also be familiar with the issues involved in reintegrating individuals into the community.

TEACHERS AS SYNTHESIZERS

In addition to the roles we have described, Bricker (1976) has suggested that the teacher of the severely/profoundly handicapped serve as an educational synthesizer: one who incorporates available services into the education programs. This is a very important part of the job, because solving the problems involved in educating the severely/profoundly handicapped frequently requires contributions from a variety of professionals. The teacher must be able to incorporate information from a variety of disciplines and to develop cooperative relationships with specialists. In the role of educational synthesizer, the teacher serves as an evaluator, coordinator, and trainer. She must be able to identify specific child disabilities, make use of appropriate resources and specialists, communicate effectively, incorporate programming suggestions into daily activities, and evaluate the effectiveness of the intervention program.

Because the severely/profoundly handicapped have such serious problems, many people assume that they need only to be cared for. This attitude has perpetuated the practice of warehousing many of these individuals in institutions. As you have seen, however, these children present a major challenge to special educators, one that can result in genuine progress if met with the methods we have described.

PROBE 10-3
Teacher Competencies

1. Why do teachers of the severely/profoundly handicapped require different skills than teachers of mildly handicapped children?

   _____

   _____

2. What is stereotypic behavior?_____

   _____

3. T F Behavioral management is used only to suppress undesirable behaviors in the classroom.

4. Describe five skills that teachers of the severely/profoundly handicapped should have.

   a. _____

   b. _____

   c. _____

   d. _____

   e. _____

5. How can an understanding of normal child development be helpful in the education of the severely/profoundly handicapped?

   _____

6. T   F   It is sometimes only necessary to use one assessment instrument to obtain enough information to plan instruction.

7. A comprehensive assessment of a severely/profoundly handicapped child may take as long as _____.

8. T   F   There is no "master curriculum" for the severely/profoundly handicapped.

9. Under what circumstances might a teacher choose to use a probe measure rather than a continuous measure?

   _____

   _____

10. T   F   The severely/profoundly handicapped should never be educated in groups.

11. What are the three phases of learning described by Koegel and Rincover?

    a. _____

    b. _____

    c. _____

12. What three criteria can a teacher use to determine whether a skill has been learned?

    a. _____

    b. _____

    c. _____

13. Why should a teacher be able to perform task analysis?

_____

_____

14. T F It is helpful for teachers of the severely/profoundly handicapped to have a knowledge of first aid.

15. What are three ways a teacher can serve as an advocate for the severely/profoundly handicapped?

   a. _____

   b. _____

   c. _____

16. An important role of teachers of the severely/profoundly handicapped is that of educational _____.

DELIVERING EDUCATIONAL SERVICES

> You should be able to describe the implications of the least restrictive environment clause of PL 94–142 for the education of the severely/profoundly handicapped.

REFERRAL

Children have been placed in classes for the severely handicapped for a number of reasons that have nothing to do with their ability to learn: the child had a physical problem; the child had never been to school; the child was not toilet trained; the child was nonverbal and therefore presumed retarded; it was the only class with an available opening; or a standardized intelligence test report was returned stamped "untestable."

Placement on the basis of factors such as these is, of course, unjustified. Sontag, Sailor, and Smith (1977) have proposed that children be assigned to programs on the basis of their educational needs. Children would be assigned to programs for the severely handicapped *only* if assessment showed that the child's primary area of need was in *basic skills*. Those who could be taught *academic* skills would be placed in other programs. According to Sontag et al., basic skills consist of (1) self-help skills; (2) fine and gross motor skills; (3) beginning communication development; (4) beginning social skill development; and (5) beginning cognitive or preacademic skills.

Referral based on the child's educational needs will not end inappropriate placement, but it could reduce its frequency. Some children could benefit from aspects of both kinds of programs and might be best served by dividing their time between them.

EDUCATIONAL PROVISIONS

There are now thousands of severely handicapped students in this nation who live with their nonhandicapped parents, play with nonhandicapped siblings and nonhandicapped friends in their neighborhoods, wait in the waiting rooms of physicians along with nonhandicapped citizens, attend church with nonhandicapped worshippers, and lie in the sand next to nonhandicapped bathers. However, these same handicapped individuals are segregated from nonhandicapped citizens in what is presumably the major education force in the life of any child — THE SCHOOL [Brown, Wilcox, Sontag, Vincent, Dodd, and Gruenewald, 1977, p. 195].

The phrase *least restrictive alternative* came into use in 1975 with the passage of PL 94–142. As you know from previous chapters, the phrase is used to imply that "the educational service delivery models used for severely handicapped students must closely approximate the best available educational service delivery models used for nonhandicapped students" (Brown et al., 1977, p. 197). The phrase "least restrictive educational opportunity" was proposed by Kenowitz, Zweibel, and Edgar(1978), who suggested that three factors should be considered in providing this opportunity: the physical setting, the individual education plan (IEP), and interaction with nonhandicapped children.

The Physical Setting. Most severely handicapped students in the United States are currently receiving educational services in one of three types of centers (Kenowitz, Zweibel, and Edgar, 1978):

1. Isolated segregated centers, such as institutions, state schools, and state hospitals. In the past, many of these institutions did not provide education. Those which now provide education frequently fail to meet the student's needs because of lack of funds, poorly trained teachers and staff, and a variety of other factors.
2. Community-based segregated centers are special education centers administered by the public school that serve only handicapped children. These centers group special services in a central location; thus, they do not comply with the concept of the least restrictive educational opportunity.
3. Segregated classrooms in regular schools allow flexibility in educational experiences and permit interaction with nonhandicapped students. Severely handicapped students may be integrated with nonhandicapped students for part of their day, during lunch and recreation periods, for example.

Brown et al. (1977) listed five disadvantages of segregated education centers which should be considered before placing a severely handicapped child:

1. There is little or no exposure to nonhandicapped students.
2. Severely handicapped students tend to learn the skills, attitudes, and values of the handicapped, rather than those of the rest of society.
3. Teachers tend to spend their time resolving handicapping problems at the expense of developing community-referenced skills.
4. Student performances are compared to "handicapped" criteria rather than the criteria used to judge those who are not handicapped.
5. Nonhandicapped children are not exposed to the severely handicapped, which decreases the probability that their attitudes will become more tolerant and constructive.

Ideally, all handicapped students should be served in integrated settings. Whether this goal is achieved will depend on the commitment of teachers, parents, and the community.

The Individual Education Plan (IEP). The child's education is guided by the IEP, which explains the rationale for the child's placement and educational program. To develop the IEP, the student must be assessed, goals must be set, and instructional procedures and curricula must be selected. Placing the child in the least restrictive environment is the responsibility of the interdisciplinary team who develop and implement the IEP.

Interactions with Nonhandicapped Persons. If severely handicapped students are to be prepared to live in public, minimally segregated, heterogeneous communities, we must provide them with educational services that will help prepare them for integrated living. Many parents fear that interaction with nonhandicapped peers will lead to ridicule and rejection. Although problems sometimes do occur, more and more successful interactions are being reported. The public school programs in Madison, Wisconsin, have demonstrated that the interaction of severely handicapped students and regular education students can be mutually beneficial.

Many professionals contend that integration is most likely to be successful at the preschool age level, and the number of integrated preschool programs is increasing rapidly. This does *not* mean, however, that we should not attempt to increase the interaction of older handicapped and nonhandicapped peers.

Interaction should occur in the community as well as the school. Severely handicapped students must learn to ride a bus, recognize danger signs, obey traffic lights, purchase necessities, and perform other tasks of daily living; the community must learn to accept these handicapped individuals and be willing to assimilate them. As Sailor and Haring (1978) have stated, "The inevitable consequence of exposure of severely handicapped children in public settings is public education" (p. 13).

TRANSPORTATION

The expense of transporting severely handicapped children often dictates whether they will be educated in an isolated, segregated, or integrated setting. Special arrangements must be made for the safety of the transportation and for getting the child into and out of the vehicle. Specialized equipment such as hydraulic lifts, wheelchair lifts, and special seat belts may be needed. In addition, bus drivers and aids must be trained to deal with the children's medical problems, such as seizures, as well as their behavioral problems. The combination of these factors may make the cost of transportation so high that severely handicapped children may be placed in segregated facilities even when it is not appropriate.

CLASSROOM GUIDELINES

Should the severely handicapped be placed in centers that serve the handicapped exclusively, or should they be placed in segregated classes in regular education buildings? Those who believe they should be placed in segregated centers argue that such grouping makes the delivery of specialized services more efficient. Proponents of the other position advance all arguments used in the defense of integration, and argue that it is just as easy to provide services to students in classrooms "clustered" in the regular school building as it is to provide them in isolated centers (Sherr, 1976). This clustering, however, is not strictly in line with the concept of integration. Thus, many argue for the "dispersal" model — spreading classes for the severely handicapped throughout several schools in a district. Besides providing greater possibility for reintegration into the community, this model also reduces transportation problems, since students are likely to be close to home.

In addition to the location of the building for the classroom, the location of the classroom itself must be considered. The building must be totally accessible (i.e., doorways and halls wide enough to accommodate wheelchairs, ramps where necessary, lowered drinking fountains, etc.). Classrooms should be on the ground floor to increase accessibility. These classrooms should *not* be the rejects of all the other teachers (i.e., near the boiler room, the most unattractively decorated, the coldest or hottest, etc.). Finally, it is crucial that no handicapped students be excluded from participating in any activities because of inaccessibility of facilities.

The physical environment of the classroom must be carefully planned. Not only should it be on the ground floor; it should also be a large room at least partially carpeted, and have accessible toilets and sinks. Lighting should be appropriate and the noise level easily controlled.

The environment should facilitate engaging the child. This can be accomplished through the use of appropriate adaptive (orthotic and prosthetic) equipment. Such equipment should include: (1) positioning equipment such as pillows, wedges, sandbags, special chairs, supports, and standing tables; (2) facilitation equipment such as specialized wheelchairs, walkers, crawlers, and adapted scooters and bicycles; (3) special equipment for self-help skills; (4) equipment designed to facilitate cognitive tasks — such as head pointers, and adapted typewriters — and to aid communication — various types of augmentative systems such as communication boards.

If all teachers and administrators come to believe as did Lindsley (1964) that "children are not retarded, only their behavior in average environments is sometimes retarded" (p. 62), then we will see increased application of these guidelines for classrooms for the severely handicapped. We hope that, as a result of improved environments, we will see a concomitant improvement in the children's skills.

PROBE 10-4
Delivering Educational Services

1. T F Children whose needs are primarily academic should not be placed in classes for the severely handicapped.

2. Children needing _____ skill development can generally be placed appropriately in classes for the severely handicapped.

3. T F Children who need both basic skill and academic training may be best served by spending time in more than one type of educational program.

4. What three factors should be considered in providing the least restrictive educational opportunity?

   a. _____

   b. _____

   c. _____

5. T F Moderately and severely handicapped students benefit most from being placed in isolated, community-based centers.

6. Define the "dispersal" model.

   _____

   _____

   _____

   _____

7. List four characteristics of the physical environment that are desirable when establishing classrooms for the severely handicapped.

   a. _____

   b. _____

   c. _____

   d. _____

8. T F The problems involved in transporting the severely handicapped may inappropriately dictate segregation rather than integration.

9. Name three types of positioning equipment that are used by the severely handicapped.

   a. _____

   b. _____

   c. _____

SUMMARY

1. Severely and profoundly handicapped children are a heterogeneous population. Characterized by low cognitive abilities, they have a high probability of suffering additional behavioral, physical, and sensory handicaps.
2. A person who works with the severely and profoundly handicapped is likely to encounter a wide variety of behaviors including aggression toward others, temper tantrums, self-mutilation, and failure to respond to social stimuli.
3. Curriculum areas in which severely and profoundly handicapped children should receive instruction include language development, cognitive development, sensory and perceptual skills, gross and fine motor skills, social and vocational skills, community living skills, and self-care skills.
4. Teachers of severely and profoundly handicapped children must be able to carry out the many aspects of instruction, to handle severe behavior problems, and to understand and manage a wide range of medical and physical problems.
5. Because of the demands of educating the severely and profoundly handicapped, the teacher must be able to utilize information from a variety of disciplines and the skills of different specialists.
6. Like other exceptional children, the severely and profoundly handicapped should be educated in the least restrictive environment.

TASK SHEET 10
Field Experiences with the Severely/Profoundly Handicapped

Select *one* of the alternatives and complete the required tasks. Write a report of no more than three pages about your activities.

Parent Interview

Interview the parents of a severely/profoundly handicapped child. Using great tact, try to determine some of the problems the parents have encountered in rearing their child and placing him or her in programs. Try to find out what other services the parents would find helpful.

Observation

Visit an educational program for the severely/profoundly handicapped, and talk with administrators, teachers, parents, aides, or other staff members. Describe the physical setting, the type of program, and the activities that you observed. Also, answer the following questions about the provision of the "least restrictive opportunity":

Facility

— Is the facility placed near the center of community activity?
— To what extent does the facility isolate children from other handicapped and nonhandicapped children?
— How effectively are ancillary services such as physical therapy, speech therapy, and medical services delivered in each classroom?
— What architectural barriers did you observe?

Opportunities for Normal Integration

— What opportunities are the students given to practice skills learned in the classroom in the community?
— What opportunities are there for students to interact with less severely handicapped and nonhandicapped peers? How frequently are these opportunities offered?

Appropriate Educational Programming

Use your observations to comment on the training of the staff, the staff expectations for student performances, assessment procedures, the goals established for the children, adequacy of instruction, and evaluation procedures.

Participation

Volunteer your services at a facility serving severely handicapped individuals and record your activities, impressions, and questions. Describe the areas in which you think handicapped children would require intensive training before they could function in the community.

Library Study

Use the library to identify at least three articles related to the education of severely/profoundly handicapped children. Write a one-page critique of each.

> **Design Your Own Field Experience**
> If none of these alternatives appeals to you or you have an opportunity to perform some other task with the severely/profoundly handicapped, design your own field experience. Check with your instructor to determine its acceptability.

Probe Answers

Probe 10-1

1. The primary difference between "multiple handicapped" and "severely/profoundly handicapped" is cognitive. Both imply multiple disabilities while only the latter implies severe mental retardation.
2. a. The primary disability is cognitive and/or behavioral.
   b. There is a high probability of additional physical and/or sensory deficits.
   c. They require significantly more resources than the moderately and mildly handicapped.
3. True
4. .1 percent
5. The extent of a severely handicapped child's disability differentiates him from other children, not the particular type of handicap (auditory, visual, motor).
6. Any four of the following:
   a. failure to attend
   b. self-stimulation
   c. rumination
   d. lack of imitation
   e. no response to simple instructions
   f. seizure activity
   g. sensory impairments (deafness, blindness, deaf-blindness)
   h. aggression toward others
   i. inability to dress independently
   j. lack of speech
   k. motor impairments

Probe 10-2

1. True
2. a. delayed speech and language

b. problems in speech clarity
3. a. to provide the nonverbal individual with a means of communication
   b. to serve as an aid while speech is being developed
4. increasing the fluid intake of the child thus increasing the frequency of elimination
5. False
6. functional reading skills, which refers to teaching them to read everyday signs and symbols (restroom signs, traffic signals)
7. content (what to teach); methodologies (how to teach)
8. Gross motor skills are associated with the large muscle groups and include running, hopping, and jumping. Fine motor skills involve the small muscles and include grasping, catching, and writing.
9. True
10. False
11. Prevocational
12. Habilitation refers to teaching skills that have not previously been in a child's repertoire. Rehabilitation refers to retraining or to reorganizing skill patterns.
13. False
14. True
15. False

Probe 10-3

1. The behaviors exhibited by severely/profoundly handicapped students are more severe and require a different curriculum.
2. Stereotypic behavior consists of repetitive, purposeless movements, such as body rocking, finger twirling, and hand flapping.

3. False
4. Any five of the following:
   a. behavior management
   b. knowledge of normal child development
   c. assessment, curriculum selection and adaptation
   d. instructional arrangements
   e. behavior acquisition
   f. generalization and maintenance
   g. measurement
   h. medical and physical management
   i. advocacy.
5. A normal development model provides the necessary structure and guidance for determining what to teach.
6. False
7. four weeks
8. True
9. when student progress is slow
10. False
11. a. acquisition
    b. generalization
    c. maintenance
12. a. generalization to different natural environments/settings
    b. skills performed with different sets of materials
    c. skills performed with different language cues.

13. Task analysis is an important teacher competency in adapting curriculum to meet individual student learning styles.
14. True
15. a. developing the individual education plan
    b. participating in drafting laws, regulations, and local policies and procedures
    c. helping to secure cummunity-based services
16. synthesizers

Probe 10–4
1. True
2. basic
3. True
4. a. physical setting for education
   b. individual education plan
   c. interaction with nonhandicapped students
5. False
6. The "dispersal" model refers to placing special education units in regular elementary and secondary schools throughout a district.
7. a. ground floor
   b. large room
   c. partially carpeted floor
   d. toilets and sinks in the room
8. True
9. a. wedges
   b. sandbags
   c. special chairs

No ordinary handbook on child care could possibly have prepared Richard and Sally Hunter for their first baby. When he was just six months old, Kam Hunter began speaking in complete sentences. By the time he was 3, he had taught himself to read. As a first grader, he was allowed to enroll in Spanish courses at a high school near his elementary classroom in Ionia, Mich.; within a year, at the age of 7, he was a full-time high-school student. Today, Kam is a sophomore in the Honors College of Michigan State University. He is only 12 years old. "I just want to be treated like any other college student," says the handsome, blond youngster. "But I know that's probably not possible."

Kam Hunter is one of the gifted children — roughly 2.5 million young Americans who are endowed with academic, artistic or social talents far beyond those of their peers. They are not just the diagnosed geniuses, but comprise a widely varied group whose gifts range from prodigious prowess in chess or music to extraordinary facility in language, mathematics or the visual arts: a toddler in Seattle who amassed (and read) a library of more than 100 books before she was 2 years old; an 8-year-old chess champion from New York City who is well on his way to becoming a grand master; an inner-city 12-year-old from Baltimore whose paintings already hang in public galleries.

"They come from all levels of society, all races and both sexes," says Dr. Harold Lyon, former director of the Federal Office for the Gifted and Talented. "These are the future Beethovens, the Newtons, the Jeffersons, the Picassos, Baldwins and Martin Luther Kings. And like other minorities, they need help."

Source: From *Newsweek,* October 23, 1978. Copyright 1978, by Newsweek, Inc. All Rights Reserved. Reprinted by Permission.

11

Gifted and Talented Children

Edwina D. Pendarvis

Edwina D. Pendarvis is Assistant Professor and Coordinator of the certification program for teachers of gifted children at Marshall University in Huntington, West Virginia. She has teaching experience in regular elementary and secondary classrooms and in a resource room serving gifted children in kindergarten through junior high school.

It may seem strange that Kam Hunter, and children like him, need special education. They have the ability to succeed at virtually any intellectual task they undertake. But ability is not the only factor in success; there are many factors that influence a child's development and performance. The purpose of this chapter is to help you gain insight into the nature of giftedness and the educational provisions that can help actualize gifted children's potential.

DEFINITIONS AND NEED FOR PROGRAMS

> **You should be able to define giftedness and explain why gifted children should be provided with special education.**

BARRIERS TO SPECIAL EDUCATION FOR GIFTED CHILDREN

The education of the gifted has been characterized as one of "benign neglect." Despite growing recognition of the importance of modifying instruction for gifted children, bright youngsters still spend much of their time in school practicing what they already know, reading books that are too easy for them, and answering questions that require little mental effort.

The difficulty in convincing educators and the public that special programs are needed arises from several widespread misconceptions about gifted children. Many people believe that special programs are unnecessary because gifted children will succeed anyway. There are two flaws in this argument. First, the exceptional talents of gifted children are frequently unrecognized, so there is no way of knowing whether they do become successful. Second, research has shown that many gifted children are *not* successful in their academic efforts.

History offers many examples of persons whose talents went unrecognized during their school years but who later became eminently successful. Some of these famous people are mentioned in a recent biography of Thomas Edison (R. W. Clark, 1977):

> Here he [Thomas Edison] showed what has almost become a sign of genius: After only three months he returned home in tears, reporting that the teacher had described him as "addled." This was in fact no cause for alarm. Leonardo daVinci, Hans Anderson and Niels Bohr were all singled out in their youth as cases of retarded development; Newton was considered a dunce; the teacher of Sir Humphrey Davy commented, "While he was with me I could not discern the faculties by which he was so much distinguished"; and Einstein's headmaster was to warn that the boy "would never make a success of anything" [p. 9].

These gifted men did "make it" anyway, but how many equally gifted persons have failed to succeed? One study of high school dropouts showed that there was almost as great a percentage of gifted dropouts as can be found in the total school population; another found that over half of the gifted children studied were achieving far below their capabilities (Marland, 1971). Children such as these are far less likely to excel today than they would have been in Edison's time, because success in most fields now requires many years of intensive study.

Another barrier to special provisions is the belief that programs for the gifted are elitist and promote intellectual snobbery. Contributing to this argument is the misconception that gifted children come only from middle- and upper-class families. But as Shirley Chisholm pointed out at a conference on gifted minority students, special programs benefit the many gifted children who come from disadvantaged backgrounds as well (Education of the Handicapped, 1979). It is likely that a much larger proportion of talented children will be found in culturally different environments as techniques for identifying the gifted are improved.

If we subscribe to the belief that education should help all students develop to their full potential, we have yet another reason to provide special programs for the gifted. It would be unfair to deny these children the chance to become all they are capable of being. Because of the many technological and social problems facing us today, and the ability of these children to enrich the lives of others, it might be considered irresponsible as well.

DEFINITIONS OF GIFTEDNESS

Many people equate giftedness with a high IQ score, but it can be defined in many ways. One of the first to define giftedness was Sir Francis Galton (1962). In *Hereditary Genius,* written in the nineteenth century, Galton proposed that the elements necessary to achieve eminence were (1) capacity, or ability; (2) zeal, or enthusiasm; and (3) the power to do laborious work. Galton's conception of giftedness was quite broad, and his study included many types of gifted persons: scientists, poets, musicians, statesmen, oarsmen, and wrestlers.

The term "gifted" became associated with a high IQ in the late 1920s, when Lewis Terman began an important longitudinal study of gifted children. Terman used a high intelligence quotient as a criterion for including children in his study. This association of giftedness with high IQ scores prevailed until the 1950s, when research on intelligence such as that conducted by J. P. Guilford (1967) showed that many important intellectual abilities are not measured by intelligence tests. It became apparent that creative abilities were not reflected by an IQ, and educators came to question the validity of a definition that failed to include children with creative promise.

Concern for children who are gifted in the arts and children who show leadership potential has led to the broad definition of giftedness adopted by the United States Office of Education (USOE). As set forth in Section 902 of the Gifted and Talented Children's Act of 1978 (PL 95-561), this definition is as follows:

> The term *gifted and talented children* means children and, whenever applicable, youth who are identified at the preschool, elementary, or secondary level as possessing demonstrated or potential abilities that give evidence of high performance capabilities in areas such as intellectual, creative, specific academic, or leadership ability, or in the performing and visual arts, and who by reason thereof, require services or activities not ordinarily provided by the school.

It has been estimated that, in applying the broadened definition of giftedness, we would find approximately 3 to 5 percent of the total school age population to be eligible for special programs. This percentage includes the future artists, dancers, political leaders, and others who would have been excluded under the narrow, high-IQ definition of the first half of this century.

PROBE 11-1
Definitions and Need for Programs

1. T F Gifted children drop out of school at about the same rate as that of the total school population.

2. T F Only a small number of disadvantaged children are gifted.

3. T F Gifted children are easily identified because they consistently excel in school.

4. T F IQ tests measure most important intellectual abilities, including creativity.

5. List two common misconceptions about gifted children that result in opposition to programs for the gifted.

   a. _____

   b. _____

6. Following the work of Lewis Terman in the 1920s, giftedness was sometimes determined solely on the basis of _____.

7. What are the five areas in which children may demonstrate high performance as cited in the USOE definition of the gifted and talented?

   a. _____

   b. _____

   c. _____

   d. _____

   e. _____

CHARACTERISTICS OF GIFTED CHILDREN

You should be able to describe the distinctive characteristics of gifted children.

No two children are alike, and some educators contend that gifted children vary in more ways than any other group. Nevertheless, there are some traits that many gifted children have in common; an understanding of these characteristics can be helpful in identifying the gifted and placing them in the most appropriate programs.

As you read this section you should keep in mind that most of the studies designed to identify characteristics of gifted children have been based on samples composed largely of white, middle- or upper-class children. Until further research is done comparing gifted children from different socioeconomic levels, we must realize that many of the characteristics of high-achieving gifted children from upper socioeconomic levels may be less common in underachieving gifted children who come from different segments of society.

INTELLECTUAL ABILITY

Intellectually gifted children have many abilities that make them likely to succeed academically. They can memorize rapidly and retain what they've learned; they read at an early age and with superior comprehension; they see relationships among ideas; and they have an advanced vocabulary (Terman and Oden, 1947). These abilities, combined with superior facility in communication (Renzulli and Hartman, 1971) enable them to master the basic school curriculum more quickly than other children. Educators have a responsibility to challenge bright students by teaching material not included in the basic curriculum.

Other characteristics of gifted students suggest changes that should be made in their educational programs. Many gifted children have an almost insatiable curiosity about a variety of subjects (Terman and Oden, 1947). Because of this inquisitiveness, they may welcome instruction on such topics as astronomy, archaeology, and electronics, which are not usually included in the regular school program. The high levels of independence (Lucito, 1964) and motivation (Terman and Oden, 1947) of these students suggest that they are capable of initiating and carrying out projects on their own, and they should be given opportunities for independent study. Their ability to solve problems that demand complex thinking skills such as analysis (identifying relationships) and synthesis (forming new relationships) suggest that they be given assignments that involve identifying causes, establishing categories, and generating and testing hypotheses (Clark, 1979). Modifications such as these will be discussed at greater length later in the chapter.

The social and emotional development of intellectually gifted children generally equals or exceeds that of other children of the same age. Research indicates that they are physically well developed, interested in many extracurricular activities, and well liked by their peers, and that they have a good sense of humor (Terman and Oden, 1947). They show an early concern for morality and may be more likely to raise ethical questions than other children (Gallagher, 1975).

These positive traits should not lead you to believe that gifted children are "superchildren"; they have all the problems of other children and may have additional problems resulting from feelings of being unusual and from having unrealistically high standards for themselves and others. A teacher of gifted children in St. Petersburg, Florida, reports, "They very often get pressure because they're bright or different. They are not the elitists they're criticized for being. They're struggling for their own identities" (Maunder, 1977, p. 8). Pressure to conform and outright hostility may threaten the gifted child's social and emotional adjustment. The teacher must try to counteract these influences and ward off bitterness and frustration such as is evident in this remark by a highly gifted student: "If I offend people just by existing, that is not my fault." (Nevin, 1977, p. 81).

Gifted children sometimes contribute to their own alienation by being harshly critical of others. These children should be taught that consideration for the feelings of others and tempering judgments with diplomacy and tact are important elements of social interaction. By the same token, many gifted children are too hard on themselves. These children need help in accepting failure as a valuable part of the learning process; failure signals the need for renewed effort and suggests directions for the new effort to take. In short, gifted children need encouragement and guidance to cope with the special problems that may accompany their unusual ability.

CREATIVITY

> They sought it with thimbles, they sought it with care;
>   They pursued it with forks and hope;
> They threatened its life with a railway-share;
>   They charmed it with smiles and soap.
>   "The Hunting of the Snark"
>   — Lewis Carroll

The nature of the creative process is almost as elusive as Lewis Carroll's imaginary creature, the mysterious snark.

In spite of many years of diligent research, scientists still don't understand the relationship between intelligence and creativity. A child who has high levels of the abilities measured by IQ tests, such as memory, comprehension, and reasoning, may not be creative. In fact, some experts believe that, given average or slightly above average intelligence, creativity may be a function of personality rather than mental ability (Welsh, 1975).

Creative adults have been found to be committed to their work, sensitive to the problems in their field, and able to pull together many apparently unrelated pieces of information to solve problems (Taylor, 1964). Young children do not, of course, possess expertise in a particular field. How, then, can we recognize children who have unusual creative potential?

Children's creativity is often measured with tests of divergent thinking ability. Divergent thinking is characterized by the ability to produce a large number of possible solutions to a problem. High scorers on tests of divergent thinking can think of many unusual answers to questions that have no single answer, such as "List the ways you can think of to change children's books to make them more fun," or "List inventions that could be designed by combining some of the elements of a tape recorder and a typewriter."

For a solution or product to be judged creative, it should be unusual or novel; it should solve a problem; and the original insight should be fully developed (MacKinnon, 1962). Divergent thinking is probably most important for contributing novelty; other mental abilities, such as judgment or evaluation, may be more important for the other two components. Since it is novelty, or originality, that is most important to our concept of creativity (the terms "original" and "creative" are often used synonymously) it seems appropriate to consider children who are good divergent thinkers as having creative potential.

Children who are divergent thinkers share several characteristics. They may have a reputation for wild, silly ideas; their responses are unusual and clever; and they show intellectual playfulness as well as humor (Torrance, 1962). Nonconformity, independence, and willingness to take risks are also typical of creative children (Torrance, 1962). Unfortunately, these characteristics may cause the students to be unpopular with teachers (Getzels and Jackson, 1962).

Creative children generally prefer loosely structured, open-ended learning activities, which allow them to develop and express their own ideas (Torrance, 1974). Strom and Torrance (1973) found that creative children expressed a strong dislike for highly structured programmed instruction and learned less from it than less creative children. Not surprisingly, creative children sometimes become impatient with the routine in the regular classroom. As one highly creative child put it, "It's amazing how difficult a subject can become if you study it slowly enough" (Aschner and Bish, 1965, p. 223). Teachers can accommodate this group's learning preferences by including "open-ended" activities that permit the child to inquire and discover on her own.

SPECIAL TALENTS

Although the terms "giftedness" and "talent" have been used here interchangeably, "talent" is often considered to be specialized ability. Although many talented children have high general intelligence or creativity, many show only average intellectual or creative ability. As in the two groups just discussed, the characteristics of talented children suggest the types of programs they may benefit from most. Brief summaries of the behaviors that indicate talent in particular areas are provided in Table 11-1.

Table 11-1
Characteristics of Children with Special Talents

Talent Area	Abilities	Characteristics
Mathematics	Ability to manipulate symbolic material more effectively and more rapidly than classmates	Highly independent Enjoy theoretical and investigative pursuits Effective in social interactions Less conforming than general population (girls)
Science	Ability to see relationships among ideas, events, and objects Elegance in explanation; the ability to formulate the simplest hypothesis that can account for the observed facts	Highly independent "Loners" Prefer intellectually rather than socially challenging situations Reject group pressures Methodical, precise, exact Avid readers
Language Arts	Capability of manipulating abstract concepts, but sometimes inferior to the high general achiever in working with mathematical material Imagination and originality	Highly independent Social and aesthetic (girls) Theoretical and political (boys) Greatly enjoy reading
Leadership	Ability to effect positive and productive change Good decision-making ability Proficiency in some area, such as athletics or academics Ability to communicate	Empathetic Sensitive Charismatic — can transform the group through their enthusiasm and energy
Psychomotor Ability	Gross motor strength, agility, flexibility, coordination, and speed Excellence in athletics, gymnastics, or dance Fine motor control, deftness, precision, flexibility, and speed Excellence in crafts — jewelry-making, model-building, mechanics, working with electronic equipment, etc. Ability to use complicated equipment with little or no training	Enjoy and seem to need considerable exercise Competitive Like outdoor activity Interested in mechanics, electronics, or crafts Have hobbies such as model-building, origami, pottery

Table 11-1
Continued

Talent Area	Abilities	Characteristics
Performing Arts	Ability to disregard traditional methods in favor of their own original ones Resourcefulness in use of materials Ability to express their feelings through an art form Attention to detail in their own and others' artwork	Self-confident Competitive Ambitious Prefer working alone Sensitive to their environment Gain satisfaction through expressing their feelings artistically

Sources: Ellison, Abe, Fox, Coray, and Taylor, 1976; Keating, 1976; Kough and DeHaan, 1958; Kranz, n.d.; Lindsay, 1977; Passow and Goldberg, 1962; Renzulli and Hartman, 1971; Roe, 1953; Stanley, George, and Solano, 1977.

Children who are gifted in a specific academic area, such as mathematics, science, or language arts, should be considered for cross-grade placement. They should be allowed to attend classes well above their grade level, including college courses, in the subjects in which they excel. Their assignments should involve advanced concepts and skills, and they should be instructed by teachers who are experts in their subjects. Their teachers should be skillful in matching the rate of instruction to the child's capabilities and in developing lessons that require analysis and creative problem-solving. Children with special talent in one area may need extra support and guidance to stimulate interest and learning in other subjects. Children with exceptional scientific ability may be inclined to introversion. These children should be given many opportunities for positive interaction with classmates.

To assist in the development of leadership, the teacher should provide many small-group activities in which leaders can emerge. Children who show special promise should be taught verbal and nonverbal communication skills; strategies for planning, organizing, and decision-making; and the dynamics of group processes. The moral development of those who may affect the values of others can be improved through values clarification activities.

Artistic or psychomotor ability is developed primarily in music, art, and athletic programs. These should be supplemented by clubs and special interest classes for subjects such as drama, photography, film making, and electronics.

Kam Hunter is a twelve-year-old sophomore in the Honors College of Michigan State University. Obviously too young to play football, he participates as a student manager.

Mentor programs, which bring experts from the community into the classroom, are an excellent means of teaching children with exceptional ability in a particular area. Outstanding achievement in athletics has been recognized for many years; surely outstanding achievement in academic subjects, leadership, and artistic ability deserves recognition as well.

PROBE 11-2
Characteristics of Gifted Children

1. T   F   Most intellectually gifted children are smaller and less physically fit than nongifted children.

2. The personality trait shared by children with high intellectual ability, children with specific academic ability (in mathematics, science, or language arts), and creative children is that they are _____.

3. Which of the following questions requires divergent thinking?
   a. As president of the United States, what would you do to solve the energy shortage problem?
   b. What were Mercutio's final lines in his famous death scene in "Romeo and Juliet"?
   c. What were the major causes of the "Great Depression"?

4. How could appropriate instruction be provided to a first-grade student who was reading at the sixth-grade level?

   a. _____

   b. _____

5. Identify which kind of giftedness the following statements typify:
   a. Among his activities were membership on the Student Council, in the debating society, and in National Honor Society, and football, swimming, and band.

   _____

   b. When asked what procedure should be followed, she had well-organized, goal-oriented suggestions to offer.

   _____

   c. Classmates are often critical of her original, sometimes bizarre ideas and behavior.

   _____

6. T   F   The relationship between intelligence and creativity has been clearly established.

IDENTIFICATION PROCEDURES

You should be able to describe methods of identifying gifted children.

One of the most important tasks facing educators interested in developing talent is the identification of the gifted. It is difficult because no single test or procedure will identify all different types of gifted children.

For many years, the only way a student could gain entrance to a gifted program was by getting a high score on an IQ test. Although IQ scores are still used in combination with other methods, their use as the single, determining factor in identification has come under harsh criticism for a number of reasons. There is evidence that the tests are biased against children who are not from the white middle class; there are sometimes discrepancies between children's scores on group IQ tests and their scores on more reliable individual IQ tests; there is a test bias against children with physical, sensory, communication, or behavioral problems; and IQ tests fail to measure many important abilities, such as creativity and leadership.

As a result of the failures of intelligence tests, several alternatives have been developed, including interest inventories, creativity tests, evaluation of student work samples, and behavior checklists that reflect parents', teachers', or peers' judgments of students' abilities. Experts recommend the use of several methods of evaluation, and the adoption of a case study approach to identification (Martinson, 1974; Renzulli and Smith, 1977).

In the case study approach, the first step is to screen the student population by reviewing and collecting easily obtainable information, such as grades, awards, and achievement and intelligence test scores. Teachers, parents, and students may be given questionnaires or checklists on which to record their perceptions of a child's abilities. The names of children who have high test scores, many awards, good grades, or positive evaluations by teachers, parents, or peers are submitted to a committee, which may be composed of school administrators, teachers, the guidance counselor, and a specialist in gifted education. This committee reviews the information on each child and makes its recommendations. Some children can generally be placed in the gifted program on the basis of screening information, whereas others may be eliminated or referred for more individual evaluation, such as creativity or special aptitude tests. Some students may be asked to submit a sample of their creative work to be evaluated by persons with expertise in art, music, or other subjects.

Table 11-2 contains a brief summary of the advantages and disadvantages of some of the methods of evaluation used most frequently. The case study ap-

Table 11-2
Summary of Commonly Used Methods of Evaluation

Method	Strengths	Limitations	Comments
Teacher evaluation via behavior checklists or questionnaires	Familiar with student's work. Familiar with "normal" performance for grade level.	Teacher perceptions may be influenced by irrelevant factors such as appearance, willingness to conform, and attitudes toward classwork.	Teachers may fail to recognize as many as half of the gifted students. Teacher nomination may be improved through in-service training on the characteristics of gifted children.
Peer evaluation via behavior checklists or questionnaires	Familiar with student's work. May be aware of interests or abilities of which the teacher is unaware.	Student perceptions may be influenced by whether they like or dislike their classmate, and whether the teacher appears to like their classmate.	Little research has been done on the effectiveness of peer evaluation. It may be most useful in identifying leadership potential.
Parent evaluation via behavior checklists or questionnaires	Familiar with child's development, interests, and abilities.	Parents tend to overnominate (i.e., to nominate children who would not be eligible for a gifted program). Parents may not know how their child's behavior compares with that of other children of the same age.	In kindergarten and at the primary level, parents may be better than teachers at identifying gifted children.
Grades	Availabile information.	Review of grades fails to identify underachievers and children who are gifted in nonacademic areas.	Referral of children with an average of "B" or better results in the inclusion of more gifted children than teacher referral, but more nongifted children are referred as well. *(continued on following page)*

Table 11-2 Continued

Method	Strengths	Limitations	Comments
Work samples	Can be collected in all talent areas, including the visual or performing arts.	Requires availability of experts such as music teachers and art teachers to judge the work sample.	Work samples reflect both the student's ability and commitment.
Interest Inventories	Seem to be more "culture fair" than IQ or achievement tests.	Ability level may not be as high as interest level.	One of the few measures that reflect commitment to an area of art or science.
Achievement Tests	Indicate academic aptitude in particular subject areas. Test scores are usually on record in children's cumulative folders. They are a readily available source of information.	May fail to identify underachievers, especially children from culturally different environments and gifted handicapped children.	Success on most achievement tests requires superior verbal comprehension.
Group Intelligence Tests	Can indicate aptitude even when achievement is low. Test scores are often on record in children's cumulative folders.	If high cutoff points (e.g., 130 IQ or above) are used, as many as half of the gifted children may be overlooked. Fails to differentiate the highly gifted from the moderately gifted.	For screening purposes, a relatively low cutoff point such as 115 IQ can reduce the number of gifted children missed.
Creativity Tests	Tap abilities not measured by IQ or achievement tests. Usually considered more "culture fair" than IQ or achievement tests.	Administration and interpretation often require special personnel. May be difficult to distinguish "original" but relevant responses from "bizarre" irrelevant responses.	The relationship between ability to do well on a creativity test and consistent, outstanding creative performance hasn't been established.

Table 11-2 Continued

Method	Strengths	Limitations	Comments
Individual Intelligence Tests	Most reliable single indicator of intellectual giftedness in middle- and upper-class socioeconomic levels. Many individual tests measure both verbal and nonverbal ability.	Are expensive. Require special personnel for administration and interpretation. Can be biased against minority groups and gifted handicapped children. Fail to assess important abilities such as creativity, leadership, and artistic talent.	Interpretation of the quality and character of responses by a competent tester can provide considerable insight into a child's ability.

proach permits the use of many evaluative measures so that no gifted child is overlooked because of limitations in measurement devices.

Just as no single test can be relied on to identify giftedness, no single combination of methods will reveal the talents of all children. The case study approach permits educators to determine which combination of assessment methods is most appropriate for the individual child. The combination most useful in identifying the intellectually gifted suburban child will probably not be the best one to identify the creatively gifted inner-city child. Factors such as the age, background, personality, and type of ability of the child must be weighed against the strengths and weaknesses of the different methods to find the combination best suited to the individual child.

PROBE 11-3
Identification Procedures

1. T   F   No single test or combination of tests can be used to identify all gifted children.

2. Two methods of identification that may miss as many as half of the gifted students are _____ and _____.

3. Three procedures may be used to identify children's interests of which teachers may be unaware:

   a. _____

   b. _____

   c. _____

4. The most reliable single indicator of intellectual giftedness among children from middle- or upper-class families is _____

   _____.

5. Distinguishing original, relevant response from bizarre, irrelevant responses may be a problem in measuring _____.

6. For very young children, _____ is often more effective than teacher nomination in identifying the gifted.

7. What are the major steps in the case study approach to identification?

   a. _____

   b. _____

   c. _____

EDUCATIONAL PROVISIONS FOR GIFTED CHILDREN

You should be able to describe the educational practices that are appropriate for gifted children.

PROGRAMS FOR GIFTED CHILDREN

Although there are many kinds of programs for gifted children, most of them have similar goals. Whether gifted children are placed in special schools, sent to

Chart 11-1
Programs for Gifted Children

HORIZONTAL PROGRAMS	*VERTICAL PROGRAMS*
Exploration Often used with students in kindergarten through third grade; allows the student to explore different subject areas according to his or her level of interest and ability. Emphasis is placed on encouraging enthusiasm for learning and stimulating curiosity. As in all gifted programs, higher levels of cognitive learning are encouraged.	*Acceleration* Offers students the opportunity to move through their school career at the pace that is most suitable to their rate of learning. This may involve skipping several grades, early entrance to kindergarten, and early entrance to college. Advanced classes and honors programs are often considered forms of acceleration.
Enrichment Expands students' experiential and informational base by exposing them to areas of study which they do not encounter in the regular curriculum. In this program, the stress is often on motivating the students to use their learning potential.	*Independent Study* Allows students to explore areas of particular interest. The teacher puts the students in touch with resources and helps them define their goals and outline strategies for reaching them.
Executive Internship Offers students an opportunity to learn about areas of interest in the world of work. For example, a high school student interested in photography might spend a semester working in a photographer's studio.	*Mentorship* Matches experts in the community with students who are interested and talented in similar areas. Arrangements are made for the mentors to share their experience, skills, and knowledge with the students.

resource rooms for part of the day, or given special assignments in the regular classroom, educational modifications are designed to

— Quicken the pace of learning by moving the student through activities faster than would be appropriate for children of average ability.
— Broaden the range of experiences and knowledge of gifted children by teaching subjects not offered in the regular curriculum.
— Develop problem-solving and research skills so that gifted children can become producers of knowledge rather than merely knowledge consumers.
— Provide opportunity for concentrated, in-depth study of areas in which the students are especially interested or able.

As you will see from the descriptions of some of the most common types of programs in Chart 11-1, some programs emphasize one goal more than others. Programs that emphasize broadening the student's knowledge base can be described as *horizontal*. *Vertical* programs increase the pace of instruction or allow students to examine subjects more deeply than usual in the regular program. Development of problem-solving and research skills is generally an important element of both types of program. It should be recognized that these programs are categorized according to their major emphasis; no program consists entirely of horizontal or vertical experiences.

Children can be grouped in programs that take place (1) full-time, as in a special class or school; (2) part-time, by sending the children to a resource room or learning center for part of the school day; or (3) in the regular classroom. Most educators favor part-time programs because they allow gifted children and their classmates to interact, and at the same time permit intensive, specially designed instruction, which is difficult to provide in the classroom. Ideally, every school district would offer a variety of programming options, because no single program can meet the needs of the variety of talented children likely to be found in a district. This will require more support and funding than are currently available, however. In the meantime, increasing educators' understanding of the philosophy of education for the gifted should improve the programs that exist today.

INSTRUCTION FOR THE GIFTED

> Building educational experiences around student interests is probably one of the most recognizable ways in which special programs for gifted and talented students differ from the regular curriculum [Renzulli and Smith, 1979, p. 8].

Most educators of the gifted subscribe to a humanistic philosophy of education that finds intrinsic value in the individual (Stanley, George, and Solano, 1977). Inherent in this view are concern for the rights of the individual and the desire to nurture the qualities that make a person unique. This respect for individual preferences implies that programs for the gifted should provide freedom of choice and a free and open learning environment (Renzulli, 1977).

This student-centered approach suggests that the teacher should serve as a facilitator of learning. Qualities considered important to this role are flexibility and creativity; the ability to admit mistakes; a sense of humor; sympathy with the problems of gifted children; and enjoyment in working with gifted children (Maker, 1975). In addition, the teacher should be willing to take risks. This willingness might stem from self-confidence, a feeling of security, and openness to experience. This quality is important because gifted children need role models who are willing to risk failure if they are to accept the difficult challenge necessary to emotional and intellectual growth.

Should teachers of the gifted be gifted themselves? This question is the source of much controversy. Many people argue that it is sufficient for teachers of the gifted to be gifted at *teaching*. Others contend that the teachers should be gifted themselves if they are to empathize with the problems of gifted children, provide sufficiently challenging instruction, and even keep up with them as they learn. Some compromise suggestions are that teachers of the gifted should be above average in intelligence but not necessarily gifted; that teachers of elementary gifted children need not be gifted, but teachers of gifted high school students should be; and that teachers, whether gifted or not, should be familiar with many subjects and expert in at least one.

As you can see, this issue hasn't been resolved, in part because gifted adults are as difficult to identify as gifted children. In addition, teacher-educators are reluctant to use procedures that could exclude persons capable of becoming excellent teachers of the gifted. A more pragmatic approach is to define the abilities and skills the teacher of the gifted should have and base teacher preparation on these.

According to Renzulli (1977), the first function of the teacher is to help students identify and expand their interests; the second is to help students acquire and use the skills and resources needed to pursue their interests; and the third is to help students evaluate the results of their studies. The three activities involved in such an approach are (1) enrichment and exploration; (2) skill building; and (3) investigation.

The primary purpose of *enrichment and exploration activities* is to assist children in identifying interests. Enrichment can be provided through a variety of means. The teacher can bring audiovisual and printed material to the classroom. Learning centers that focus on topics not covered in the regular curriculum, such as astronomy, archaeology, and science fiction, can be established. Autoinstructional learning packages can be made or purchased. Field trips can be arranged. Volunteers from the community can be invited to the classroom to share their interests or hobbies. Children can be invited to share their knowledge with others.

The second function of the teacher, *skill building*, involves teaching students research and problem-solving skills. These include learning ways to discover many possible solutions to a problem; how to observe, classify, and evaluate data; and practice in complex thinking skills such as analysis (identifying relationships) and synthesis (using learned information to create new information or new combinations of information). Skill-building activities may involve inquiry training, brainstorming, simulation games, and games that require logic or other deductive thinking strategies.

Investigation activities are often conducted through independent study or in small groups. Renzulli (1977) stresses that actual problems should be investigated, and that the investigation should result in a new product or solution. In the sense intended here, a trip to the library to look up information already known would not be considered investigation. This type of investigation might yield a very different result than traditional independent study. Rather than a research paper, the product might be a student-made film, a newspaper article, a plan for making more efficient use of school facilities, or an attitudinal survey.

NEW TRENDS IN GIFTED PROGRAMS

Although the general trend in gifted education is toward *more* programs, the effectiveness of existing programs has been evaluated as well. Some enrichment programs have been criticized for being more entertaining than educational (Renzulli, 1977). Such criticisms have led educators to increase the use of acceleration and to develop IEPs for the gifted, in an effort to ensure high-quality education.

In the past, acceleration has been viewed with distrust by many educators, but the work of Julian Stanley and his coworkers in their study of Mathematically Precocious Youth has compelled educators to take a new look at this method. Stanley has shown that unusually capable children who are eager to move ahead can meet the demands of college courses without suffering the social and emotional maladjustment predicted by opponents of acceleration (Stanley, Keating, and Fox, 1974). It is important to bear in mind, however, that acceleration should be contingent not on ability alone, but on desire to move ahead in school as well. Seven of the children accelerated in Stanley's program, interviewed for an article in *Smithsonian* magazine, were all eager to get on with their studies, and they all placed a high value on intellectual pursuits. One of the youths, Michael Kotschenreuther, "burns to discover something 'that hasn't been known before' " (Nevin, 1977, p. 81).

Studies of early entrants to kindergarten indicate that this is another avenue that should be open to gifted children. Bright children who enter kindergarten six months to a year early compare favorably to their older classmates. Hobson (1963) found that early entrants graduated from high school with honors more frequently than similar children who entered school at the usual age. They also participated in more extracurricular activities, including social activities and athletics. The academic achievement and social acceptance of early entrants has been found to equal that of other children of similar intellectual ability (Birch, Tisdall, Barney, and Marks, 1965). Findings such as these imply a need for greater flexibility in admissions and promotions procedures through elementary and secondary school.

Educators agree that acceleration alone will not meet the needs of gifted children. Renzulli and Smith (1979) recommend compacting and streamlining the regular curriculum so that more time can be spent providing instruction. They suggest that student achievement in the regular curriculum be assessed, which would permit the development of individual plans allowing students to skip units they've already mastered and substitute activities tailored to their interests and abilities. By carefully assessing student achievement and involving students in educational decision making, acceleration can be combined with alternatives such as enrichment, independent study, and mentorships in an approach that offers much promise for meeting the needs of gifted children.

Individualized education programs (IEPs) are an effective vehicle for designing and implementing the combination of alternatives most suitable for the gifted child. IEPs for gifted children ensure that they are not simply placed in an honors, enrichment, or other special program for part of the day; instead, each child has a program designed specifically for her. In addition to individualized programs and increased acceleration, there are other new trends that promise to improve the education of the gifted.

IEPs for gifted children differ from IEPs for handicapped children in several ways, because their purposes are different. The primary purpose of educational programs for gifted children is not to remediate problems but to develop strengths in complex behaviors (Renzulli and Smith, 1979). Because students are usually highly capable in many areas, more emphasis is paid to student interests than is typical in developing IEPs for the handicapped. The complexity of the skills being taught usually results in broader, less precisely stated objectives (Henson, 1976). In addition, the sequencing of skills and overall implementation of IEPs is relatively unstructured, because a highly structured approach in teaching complex skills may inhibit one of the most important goals of gifted education, the creative application of what is learned (Renzulli and Smith, 1979).

PROBE 11-4
Educational Provisions for Gifted Children

1. Following are some of the program goals and objectives established for a gifted child. Identify the type of activity that would be most appropriate for accomplishing the goal or objective by writing E for enrichment, S for skill-building, or I for investigation.

   _____ To provide an opportunity for experiences that extend the student's experiential horizons.

   _____ The student will be able to form a reasonable hypothesis based on available information.

   _____ The student will complete a photographic essay depicting the ethnic composition of the classroom.

   _____ To provide an opportunity for the student to utilize his or her initiative, self-direction, and originality in dealing with problems.

   _____ To provide an opportunity for the student to apply his or her skills in decision-making, planning, and communication.

2. Check your knowledge of gifted programs by matching the following items:

_____ A broad term for programs that expand students' experience or knowledge base.

_____ A program usually offered children in kindergarten through third grade.

_____ A program that matches gifted students with local experts.

_____ Grade skipping.

_____ A vertical learning program that permits a student to study in-depth a subject of special interest.

a. Vertical
b. Mentor
c. Horizontal
d. Exploration
e. Independent Study
f. Acceleration

BARRIERS TO ACHIEVEMENT

You should be able to describe barriers to achievement and strategies for counteracting their effects.

"CLASSIC" UNDERACHIEVERS

Damon is in the sixth grade. His unusual intellectual capacity is reflected by his high IQ score, 130 on the Stanford-Binet Intelligence Scale, and by his ready grasp of abstract ideas, reasoning ability, and insight into relationships between facts. However, Damon does C or D work in most of his subjects; since the second grade, his work has fallen far short of his intellectual capability.

Damon's written work is messy and almost always incomplete. He resents having to redo his papers and uses any excuse to get out of going to school. His parents and teachers have tried punishing, encouraging, coaxing, and lecturing to get him to try harder. When asked why he doesn't do well in class, Damon usually responds that classwork is boring, the teacher doesn't like him, and that he isn't all that smart anyway.

Damon is typical of a group of underachievers considered "classic" because they were the first to be the subject of a great deal of research. More recently other groups of underachievers, as well as low achievers and potential underachievers, have been studied. Most of the research on the "classic" underachiever was conducted during the period from the 1920s to the early 1960s, when definitions of giftedness were based largely on intelligence test scores. Because the children studied had IQ scores in the ninetieth percentile and above, researchers looked for factors that affected the children's motivation and commitment to achieving in school. Among the factors investigated were personality traits, parent-child interactions, and attitudes toward school.

Although most of Terman's gifted children grew up to be outstandingly productive adults, some of his subjects had a history of underachievement that began in the primary grades and continued throughout their lives. These students could be consistently differentiated from gifted achievers in four qualities: (1) inability or unwillingness to persist to achieve goals; (2) lack of integration of goals, and a tendency toward purposelessness; (3) lack of self-confidence; and (4) feelings of inferiority (Terman and Oden, 1947).

Other studies have confirmed Terman's results. For example, in a study reported in *Able Misfits* (Pringle, 1970), lack of confidence was found to be the personality trait most frequently associated with underachieving gifted children. Some other personality traits associated with underachievement are impulsiveness, lack of initiative (Clasen and Robinson, 1978), solitariness, and unsociability (Crow and Crow, 1963; Pringle, 1970). A study of highly intelligent dropouts found that the male dropouts were more assertive, more independent, and more rebellious than equally bright boys who stayed in school (Gowan and Torrance, 1971).

The reasons for the underachievers' negative attitude toward school have not been established, but poor parent-child relationships appear to be a contributing factor. Parents of gifted underachievers are often rejecting and inconsistent in their methods of discipline; they are usually either too permissive or too demanding (Raph, Goldberg, and Passow, 1966). Fathers are demanding or nonsupportive, and mothers tend to be low in dominance and unassertive (Gallagher, 1975). Counseling of parents and their children does not consistently result in improved performance, perhaps because so many factors can be involved in underachievement.

The best way to remove the barriers to achievement may be to use a combination of methods. The Cupertino School District in California combined peer counseling, behavior modification, techniques of self-control, and a stimulating curriculum in a warm, cooperative setting to create a program that has met with unusual success (Whitmore, 1977). The results of this program and others have suggested some "dos" and "don'ts" for teachers (Gallagher, 1975; Whitmore, 1977):

— Don't give the students lectures or "pep talks" to get them to try harder. This has been shown to have detrimental effects on achievement.
— Don't set up rigid standards or use authoritarian techniques; these may only increase feelings of rebellion.
— Show warmth, support, and respect for the student.

— Encourage cooperation, rather than competition, in the classroom.

— Reward small gains in achievement, and don't expect quick success.

GIFTED CHILDREN FROM DIFFERENT CULTURES

Because of cultural biases in testing and instruction, many gifted children who are not from the white middle class are not identified and don't receive instruction that could develop their talents. Torrance (1977) suggests that these children should not be expected to exhibit the same strengths as white, middle-class children; we should instead seek strengths that reflect the special "creative positives" of culturally different children. These creative positives may include the ability to improvise with commonplace materials, responsiveness to concrete materials, expressiveness in speech and "body language," and fluency in nonverbal media. An example of the creative expressiveness of a young Appalachian student in a program for culturally different gifted children is provided in Hauck and Freehill's *The Gifted — Case Studies* (1972):

The Worst Punishment for a Man
by
Junior _____

Sitting here at my desk, it seems that the day will never end. It's just now 3:30 P.M. and I have a conference with the Secretary of State at 4:00 P.M., at 5:00 P.M. a conference with Mike Mansfield and Senator Long. Oh God, I am tired. I'm not as young as I once was. The pages of history may contain but a paragraph about my life or my work, but at least I sure's hell have won the paragraph. "More critics than any U.S. President ever" — that's what the papers say. It seems nobody's satisfied with what I do. Viet Nam is really a hellava mess — and guess who gets all the blame for everything — me: Damn it! When will those demonstrators with the long hair and low morals and the intellectuals with no common sense learn that if we leave that little nation we are breaking our word, breaking our commitments, giving the communists another base of strength? Oh, damn it! Nobody listens to me . . . and this election coming up — McCarthy, Wallace and all the other S.O.B.'s who disapprove of the Great Society and how I try to run it. God help them though. Let one of 'em win — please. That's the worst punishment I can think of for a man — to be President of the United States [p. 99].

The ability to see things from an unusual perspective, the concern for social issues, and the intellectual playfulness apparent in this composition illustrate the creativity sometimes found among children who come from environments not conducive to success in school. Special efforts must be made to counteract factors that can inhibit the performance of these children. These factors include: (1) inexperience with the concepts and vocabulary of middle-class society; (2) the low expectations of many educators for culturally different children;

(3) the children's expectations of failure (Baldwin, Gear, and Lucito, 1978); and (4) the fact that achievement in school may conflict with peer loyalty (Hauck and Freehill, 1972).

The achievement of children from culturally different environments can sometimes be improved by providing intensive individual guidance, and instruction in study skills (Hildreth, 1966). These children should also receive help in reconciling conflicts between school values and the values of their peers. Exercises in values clarification should be provided to help children develop a system of values that allows them to maintain the beliefs of their culture and at the same time incorporate other values that encourage achievement.

GIFTED HANDICAPPED CHILDREN

Children can of course be both gifted and handicapped: Thomas Edison was deaf; Aldous Huxley was blind; Elizabeth Barrett Browning suffered from spinal injuries; and, according to some researchers, Einstein had learning disabilities. There is no handicapping condition that precludes giftedness. Talent has been found in every group, including the retarded. A recent discovery of giftedness among the handicapped was that of a Japanese boy with a reported IQ of 40, Yoshihiko Yamamoto (Figure 11-1), who won international acclaim for his artwork (Morishima, 1974). Are cases such as this rare? Probably not. Using a broad definition of giftedness, June Maker, author of *Providing Programs for the Gifted Handicapped* (1977), suggests that the incidence of giftedness among the handicapped is 3 to 5 percent, about the same as in the nonhandicapped population.

Gifted handicapped children are often unusually difficult to identify, because a handicapping condition can mask unusual potential. For example, Krippner (1967) describes the case of a deaf boy who was in a school for the mentally handicapped until he was seventeen. Then he was discovered to be gifted — but the discovery was made only by accident. An employee of the institution happened to leave a transistor radio kit on a work table and the handicapped youngster assembled it with ease.

The low expectations of many educators contribute to this failure to recognize giftedness. Low expectations not only prevent recognition of talent, they can destroy students' faith in their abilities. The low self-esteem that can result seems to be caused in part by the discrepancy between the extremely high goals gifted children set for themselves and the low expectations of others. Gifted handicapped adults suggest that educators who want to improve the performance of gifted handicapped children must expect more than mediocre performance (Maker, 1977).

The education of the gifted handicapped has only recently begun to interest many educators. More information on this area is available in June Maker's

Figure 11-1
Nagoya Castle, Produced by Yamamoto in the Ninth Grade

Providing Programs for Gifted Handicapped (1977). This book offers an excellent review of research and programs for the gifted handicapped.

GIFTED GIRLS

Research has yet to establish consistent differences in the intellectual ability of girls and boys, but there are significant differences in their achievement. Until puberty, when both boys and girls become more role conscious, girls do better in school than boys. Then the situation reverses and boys do better than girls, especially in math and science, which are traditionally masculine pursuits. In math, the gap in achievement continues to widen with age (Keating, 1976). As girls grow up they yield progressively more to boys in achievement and leadership. Many researchers feel that social stereotypes and expectations are responsible for women's failure to pursue advanced study and careers commensurate with their ability (Clark, 1979). Despite the feminist movement, girls are still expected to be more conforming and less assertive than boys.

High general achievers and high arithmetic achievers are self-confident and assertive (d'Heurle, Mellinger, and Haggard, 1959), but gifted girls tend to be less self-confident than gifted boys. One study found that IQ was positively correlated with expectations of success among boys, but the brighter a girl was, the less well she expected to do (Morse, 1971). This lack of self-confidence may result from a conflict between characteristics of giftedness and society's perceptions of how a girl should behave. A recent research study (Solano, 1976) on teacher and pupil stereotypes of gifted boys and girls showed that although gifted boys are viewed favorably by their peers, gifted girls are viewed quite unfavorably. Disapproval by peers and teachers would shake anyone's confidence; educators should encourage acceptance of individual differences among all their students. Especially important to the achievement of gifted girls are avoidance of sex-role stereotyping, rewarding intellectual risk-taking, providing suitable role models, and increasing awareness of career alternatives. The following passage by Amelia Earhart typifies this concern:

> It has always seemed to me that boys and girls are educated very differently. Even from the early grades, they take different subjects. For instance, boys are usually put into woodworking classes, and girls into sewing or cooking — willy-nilly. I know many boys who should, I am sure, be making pies and girls who are much better fitted for manual training than domestic science. Too often little attention is paid to individual talent. Instead, education goes on dividing people according to their sex, and putting them in little feminine or masculine pigeonholes. Outside of school, similar differences are noticeable, too. In the home, boys and girls usually follow the pursuits which tradition has decreed for the one and the other. As different as what they do are ways of doing it. Girls are shielded and sometimes helped so much that they lose initiative and begin to believe the signs "Girls don't" and "girls can't" which mark their paths. Mrs. Bertrand Russell puts this fact very forcibly when she says women are bred to timidity. . . . Probably the most profound deterrent of all is tradition which keeps women from trying new things and from putting forth their whole effort.

PROBE 11-5
Barriers to Achievement

1. T F The incidence of giftedness among handicapped children is lower than the incidence in the general population.

2. Reread the "case study" of Damon at the beginning of this section. Identify four characteristics that are typical of "classic" underachievers or that contribute to underachievement.

a. _____

b. _____

c. _____

d. _____

3. Suggest some strategies that could be used to improve Damon's academic performance:

a. _____

b. _____

c. _____

4. Identify two factors that contribute to underachievement among the gifted handicapped.

a. _____

b. _____

5. T   F   Values clarification activities should be used to help culturally different gifted children incorporate elements of the middle-class value system while maintaining their own cultural identity.

6. The personality trait consistently found among gifted underachieving boys and gifted girls is _____.

EDUCATING GIFTED CHILDREN IN THE LEAST RESTRICTIVE ENVIRONMENT

You should be able to explain what the principle of education in the least restrictive environment means for gifted children.

The principle of education in the least restrictive environment is based on the belief that segregated settings impair the progress of handicapped children, in part because of the absence of nonhandicapped children to serve as models from whom they can learn appropriate behavior. In other words, educators hope to normalize the behavior of handicapped children. An awareness of this principle has caused some people to question whether gifted children should spend even part of the day away from the regular classroom. It is probably as important for the gifted to be educated in the least restrictive environment as it is for the handicapped, but what *is* the least restrictive environment for gifted children? Do we want the behavior of gifted children to be like that of other students? Full-time placement in the regular classroom may meet the goal of normalization, but in the case of gifted children it may not be appropriate. Many gifted children in regular classrooms are already "normalizing" themselves by hiding their abilities so that they will be accepted by teachers and classmates (Clasen and Robinson, 1978).

The gifted should undoubtedly interact with children of varying degrees of ability. Their social growth requires that they play with children of their own age. Their potential for outstanding performance, however, may demand a different goal, one of *denormalization*. The learning characteristics of gifted children are different from those of other children, but they are positive differences and should be nurtured. For the realization of learning potential, the regular classroom can be the *most* restrictive environment for highly gifted children.

Consider the problems of programming for David, a kindergarten-age child who "speaks a half-dozen languages, says his main interest is comparative philology, calculates mathematical equations, does chemistry experiments, studies the violin, reads the *New York Times* and college textbooks" (Bentsen, 1979). The regular elementary curriculum is as unsuitable for David as it would be for a profoundly handicapped child. The elementary teacher is unlikely to have the specialized knowledge necessary to help David pursue his interests independently, and it is unrealistic to suppose that experts can be brought into the classroom daily. David's education will probably require coordination of high school and college courses, independent study guided by teachers who are experts in his areas of interest, social experiences with children his own age, and counseling to help him deal with his "differentness."

Children like David are very rare; most gifted children will benefit from a more balanced combination of outside learning experiences and instruction in the regular classroom. The decision about how much instruction should be provided in the regular classroom should be based on the ability of the teacher to provide individual instruction for the gifted, the support services and materials available, and the child's abilities and social and emotional development.

Because most gifted children will be instructed in both the regular classroom and in a special class, the classroom teacher and the teacher of gifted classes share the responsibility for their education. The classroom teacher is in a position to observe the gifted child's work in all subjects. In some subjects the gifted child may be at the same level as the other children, or he may even need remedial work. In other subjects, the teacher may find that the child has already mastered the material more rapidly than other children. The teacher of the gifted can assist in these subjects by planning activities and finding materials for enrichment and advancement. Together, the teachers can plan many alternative learning experiences involving independent study, autoinstructional materials, and learning centers.

Alternatives such as these can be used to provide individual instruction to all children, not just identified gifted children. The teacher may find that these learning experiences result in the discovery of previously unrecognized talent. As mentioned earlier (Stanley, 1976), giftedness may be overlooked if regular learning activities are not difficult enough to allow gifted children to display their exceptional ability. By providing advanced work, the teacher may find some students capable of accomplishing much more than was expected.

The regular classroom teacher plays a crucial role in the social and emotional development of gifted children. It is a difficult role, and the responsibilities involved may be accomplished more readily when the teacher has a strong conviction of the unique worth of every child in the classroom. The climate of support and recognition for individual differences that is based on such a conviction will forestall resentment of gifted children by their classmates and intellectual arrogance among the gifted. The teacher who rewards a whole range of qualities, such as effort, honesty, generosity, humor, and imagination, will make the classroom safe for gifted children because every child will be "gifted" in some way.

In summary, the least restrictive environment for gifted children is that which provides instruction commensurate with ability and which includes provisions for social and emotional development. The variety of social, emotional, and instructional needs of gifted children requires a continuum of alternative settings, ranging from support in the regular classroom to full-time placement in a special school or college. The key to finding and providing the least restrictive environment for each gifted child is commitment to the idea of shared responsibility. Through the combined efforts of general and gifted education personnel we can identify talented children and change their education from one of benign neglect to one of productive action.

PROBE 11-6
Educating Gifted Children
in the Least Restrictive Environment

1. Why may education in a regular classroom *not* be the least restrictive environment for gifted children?

_____

_____

2. T   F   Learning activities for gifted children should be difficult enough to allow them to display their abilities.

3. Describe at least three ways that the classroom teacher can facilitate education of gifted children in the regular classroom.

a. _____

b. _____

c. _____

SUMMARY

1. Common arguments against special provision for the gifted are based on misconceptions about gifted children.
2. The concept of giftedness includes many kinds of ability.
3. Characteristics common to gifted children suggest the need for special educational provisions.
4. The identification of gifted children is best accomplished through the combined use of a variety of evaluative methods.
5. Gifted programs typically seek to accelerate learning, broaden experience, develop problem-solving skills, and provide opportunity for in-depth study.
6. A humanistic, student-centered approach is characteristic of gifted programs.
7. Acceleration is a desirable alternative for many gifted students.
8. IEPs for gifted children differ from IEPs for handicapped children in several respects.
9. Poor parent-child interaction patterns, social stereotypes, and learning, behavior, physical, or sensory handicaps inhibit the achievement of many gifted students.
10. Full-time placement in the regular classroom may be the *most* restrictive environment for many gifted children.

TASK SHEET 11
Field Study on Gifted Children

Select *one* of the following alternatives and complete the assigned tasks:

Definitions

Ask five people to define "giftedness." Record their answers and respond to the following questions:

1. What did the definitions have in common?
2. What was the narrowest definition?
3. What was the broadest definition?
4. How many definitions fell in each of the following categories?
   a. Very restrictive — few abilities would be included.
   b. Moderate — several or many abilities would be included.
   c. Broad — most or all abilities would be included.

Write your definition of giftedness.

Interview on Acceleration

Interview an educational administrator, a teacher, and a parent regarding their views on acceleration. Ask each to give at least two reasons supporting her views. Record the views and reasons given by each, and respond to the following:

1. Were the majority for or against acceleration?
2. Were some of the reasons given similar? If so, what were they?
3. On the basis of your reading and interviews, summarize and defend your position on acceleration.

Program Visitation

Visit a program for gifted children in a public or private school. Report on your visit, answering the following questions:

1. Where did you visit?
2. When were you there and for how long?
3. What activities did you observe?
4. What types of programming were used?
5. What did you observe that helped you categorize the program?
6. What did you learn, and what was your reaction to the visit?

Political Action

Write a letter to one of your legislators expressing your belief that gifted children need special education provisions. Submit a copy of the letter and the legislator's response. What was your reaction?

Library Study

Read three articles related to the gifted and write a one-page abstract of each *or* read a biography of a gifted person. Describe the characteristics of that person which are typical of the gifted. List any atypical characteristics. If you were the person's teacher, what modifications in educational programming would you have suggested? Why?

Design Your Own Field Experience

If you know of a unique experience you can have with gifted people, or do not want to do any of the above alternatives, discuss your idea with your instructor and complete the tasks that you agree on.

Probe Answers

Probe 11–1

1. True
2. False
3. False
4. False
5. a. Gifted children will succeed without special provisions.
   b. Gifted programs are elitist, serving only middle- and upper-class youngsters.
6. high IQ scores
7. a. general intellectual ability
   b. specific academic ability
   c. creativity
   d. leadership
   e. ability in the visual and performing arts

Probe 11–2

1. False
2. very independent
3. a
4. a. by placing the child in a higher grade for reading instruction
   b. by locating or developing materials to individualize the child's reading program
5. a. general intellectual ability
   b. leadership
   c. creativity
6. False

Probe 11–3

1. True
2. group intelligence testing; teacher nomination
3. a. peer evaluation
   b. parent evaluation
   c. interest inventories
4. the individual intelligence test
5. creativity
6. parent evaluation or nomination
7. a. screening
   b. review of information obtained in the screening process
   c. further evaluation as needed to determine eligibility for placement in a gifted program

Probe 11–4

1. E; S; I; I; I
2. c; d; b; f; e

Probe 11–5

1. False
2. a. lack of persistence to achieve goals
   b. unsuccessful efforts by parents and teacher to coax the child into better performance
   c. poor attitude toward school
   d. lack of confidence (reflected in Damon's assertion that he "isn't all that smart anyway")
3. a. Make a point of showing your respect and support for him. For example, ask for his opinion and give him many opportunities for input into his educational program.
   b. Encourage cooperation in the classroom by offering opportunities for students to work and study together.
   c. Praise him for even small improvements in academic performance.
4. a. society's lowered expectations for handicapped persons
   b. society's failure to recognize and make provisions for superior ability in the handicapped population
5. True
6. lack of self-concept

Probe 11–6

1. The goal of the least restrictive environment is generally the normalization of handicapped children. However, many gifted children in regular classrooms "normalize" themselves by hiding their abilities so that they will be accepted by their peers. To realize their potential for outstanding performance gifted children may require "denormalization," since the regular classroom can be the *most* restrictive environment for them.
2. true
3. a. The teacher can plan alternative learning experiences that make use of independent

studies, autoinstructional materials, and learning centers.

b. The teacher can support the unique worth of every child in the classroom and in this way prevent or reduce resentment of the gifted students.

c. By initiating alternative learning experiences to provide individual instruction to all children, the teacher may discover previously unrecognized giftedness.

IV

Complementing Special Education Services

As the field of special education grew during the 1970s, the number and quality of complementary services increased as well. Many of these services were designed to draw parents into active involvement in educating their children, to help the handicapped adjust to life after graduation, or to assist the community in assimilating the handicapped. These services can often benefit students without handicaps as well. Because of space limitations, we cannot discuss all of the ancillary services in detail, but several of them are discussed in the first two chapters in this section.

Just as the education of students should continue after they graduate, so should the education of teachers. In the last chapter we discuss the importance of having a cogent philosophy of special education, and suggest methods of lifelong professional development.

Career Education. Today's special education programs should address the vocational and ca-

reer needs of the children they serve. In this chapter, the circumstances that lead to the development of career education are discussed and career education is defined and differentiated from vocational education. Several models for providing career education are described, with particular emphasis on the model most appropriate for the handicapped, the competency-based model. In addition, several instructional approaches, methods, and activities are illustrated, particularly as they are used in secondary-level career preparation. Finally, the effect of career education on the work of the special educator is described.

Working with Parents. Parents have always played an important part in the education of exceptional children, but since the passage of PL 94–142, their involvement is mandated by law. In this chapter, effective relationships between parents and professionals are described, as are some of the problems encountered by parents of the handicapped. The effects on a family of having a handicapped child are discussed, and different types of parent programs presented. Also included is a discussion of ways to involve parents in the education of their exceptional children. The chapter closes with a description of how professional people should work with parents and parent groups.

Continuing Professional Development. For special education services to be effective, they must be provided by highly competent professionals. This chapter underscores the importance of continuing to develop professional skills after formal education is completed. A model that can be used by professionals to guide their development is presented, and the application of the model explained. Also included is a list of resources that may be used to facilitate professional development.

Merideth Moore is forcing down the unemployment rate — for the retarded. . . .

The mentally retarded men and women she places are trained at Metro Industrial Services of the Blue Grass Association for Mental Retardation, where Ms. Moore is a placement specialist.

"The employers really talk to one another," she said. "We have people who work out well in many jobs that previously have been high turnover positions."

The six people from (Metro Industrial Services) are far better than employees I get off the street," said Doug Miller, manager of the Lafayette Club in Lexington. "There's a work-related attitude these people have — I am really amazed when I see someone nowadays who truly wants to work. . . ."

The supervisors say the people referred by the service get along well with other workers.

And the supervisors say they treat their retarded workers no differently than other employees — the service cautions employers not to do so.

"I'm satisfied," says James Burnell, the head steward. "I tell them what needs to be done and they do it."

Carlton Scully, the executive director of the Blue Grass Association for Mental Retardation, said the cost of training workers is about $13 a day, compared to about $100 a day for the care of a person placed in a residential institution. . . .

At the industrial service . . . workers are trained in different kinds of production. At the beginning, many work on projects where speed is not emphasized, so they can learn how to do the job. Others are placed in the Vocational Development Program, where high productivity is stressed — similar to the type of pressure they would face in a factory or other business. . . .

The trainees also learn about being punctual, paying attention to their work and getting along with supervisors and fellow employees. . . .

Source: From Eileon Levy, "Training of Mentally Retarded Employees Met with Praise, Job Offers." Lexington *Herald-Leader,* February 11, 1979. Reprinted by permission.

12

Career Education

Patricia Thomas Cegelka

Patricia Thomas Cegelka is Professor and Chairman of the Department of Special Education at San Diego State University. Dr. Cegelka has been a teacher of secondary special education, a methods and materials consultant for learning disabled children, and a school psychologist. Her areas of professional interest include career and vocational education, secondary special education, personnel development, mental retardation, and learning disabilities.

The article on the facing page describes some of the practices involved in preparing one part of the special education population for employment. Although work training practices may be a part of career education for anyone — the moderately or severely handicapped, the learning disabled, and the so-called normal student — career education is much more than preparing people to get jobs. Furthermore, it should begin when the child enters the education system as a child and continue throughout the child's school career.

The notion of a continuum of career education experiences is rapidly becoming accepted in regular public school programs. For the handicapped, however, the continuum often does not exist or else favors noncompetitive and sheltered work settings. A range of career education experiences is essential if exceptional students are to be valued, full partners in the community.

In this chapter, career education will be defined, and the forces that have influenced the field's development will be explained. The different models for career education in the school will be presented, and the stages in career education will be described. Several instructional approaches will also be discussed, with particular emphasis on the competency-based model often used with special education students. Finally, we will discuss the implications of PL 94-142 on providing career education in the least restrictive environment.

CAREER EDUCATION PRECEDENTS

> **You should be able to identify the major factors in the development of the career education movement.**

RATIONALE FOR CAREER EDUCATION

The emphasis on career education in our country's schools began in the early 1970s. It reflects a change in the focus and goals of education, away from a narrowly academic emphasis to a concern with the overall quality of life adjustment.

The rationale for career education was first articulated by the United States Commissioner of Education in 1971. The concept was designed to address problems causing frustration and dissatisfaction in many parts of the population. Students were frustrated because they thought their schoolwork was irrelevant to what they would do after graduation. Educators were dismayed by the high dropout rate. Workers were dissatisfied with meaningless occupations, and employers were frustrated by having to deal with poorly prepared, discontented, and poorly motivated workers. Many people attributed these problems largely to the education system, and changes in the system were suggested to solve them. Career education was devised to correct the following shortcomings (Hoyt, 1975):

1. Too many students were leaving the education system deficient in the basic academic skills required to adapt in our rapidly changing society.
2. Education appeared to be oriented toward preparation for further education, and to be irrelevant to other aspects of life.
3. Widespread worker alienation was considered the result of educational practices that provided inadequate preparation for adult work roles.
4. The educational system virtually ignored the career education of various special groups, such as the disadvantaged, minorities, women, and the handicapped.
5. The growing need for the continuing education of adults was not being met.
6. Insufficient attention was being paid to the learning opportunities existing outside the structure of formal education.
7. The general public, including parents and the business-industry-labor community, was not participating sufficiently in the formulation of educational policy.

Career education seeks to resolve these problems by combining occupational and academic education. It emphasizes that the basic purpose of education is preparation for living and that implicit in that purpose is preparation for *making* a living. The commissioner of the United States Office of Education and other proponents of career education have suggested that the primary goal of education should be to prepare every graduating student "to be ready to enter higher education or to enter useful and rewarding employment" (Marland, 1971).

By emphasizing the relationship of subject matter to various careers and occupations, by providing opportunities for students to explore specific occupations, and by developing needed work skills, career education seeks to make education more relevant, to better prepare students to successfully assume their adult roles, and to help restore the work ethic in American society. These goals have received widespread public support. A 1973 Gallup survey of public attitudes toward the schools found that "few proposals receive such overwhelming approval today as the suggestion that the schools give more emphasis to the study of trades, professions, and businesses to help students decide on their careers." Nine out of every ten persons surveyed indicated their support for this objective. A national study found that 75 percent of the high school juniors polled desired help in this area, with half of them indicating that little or no such help was available in their schools.

HISTORICAL AND LEGISLATIVE ORIGINS

Despite the recency of the interest in career education, the roots of this type of education run deep. Vocational goals have long been a part of the American education system: Two hundred years ago Ben Franklin's Academy was combining liberal education with training in practical skills in an effort to facilitate the success and mobility of the middle classes. During the late nineteenth and early twentieth century, the combined influences of rising industrialism, increasing immigration, and expanding numbers of students attending secondary schools brought about the development of vocational education programs. The Smith-Hughes Act of 1917 provided further support for vocational education in the secondary schools.

During this century the need for education that was not designed exclusively to prepare students either for college or for jobs has become increasingly apparent. The first legislation developed specifically to provide career education was passed by Congress as part of the Education Amendments of 1974. Three basic career education policies were described in this act:

1. Every child should, by the time he or she has completed secondary school, be prepared for employment and for full participation in society, according to his or her ability.
2. It is the obligation of each local educational agency to provide that preparation for all the children in the school district, including those who are handicapped or otherwise disadvantaged.

3. Each state and local educational agency should provide a program of career education designed to prepare each child for maximum employment and participation in our society according to his or her ability (Educational Amendments of 1974, PL 93-380).

Ten million dollars per year were appropriated to carry out these policies. A number of other measures designed to promote career education were also initiated. The United States Office of Career Education and the National Advisory Council for Career Education were established; a study of current education programs and practices was authorized, grants were made available to state departments of education for the development of state career education plans, and a research and demonstration grants program was authorized. It is important to note that the handicapped are specifically mentioned as beneficiaries of these laws and services.

The Career Education Incentive Act, passed in 1977, authorized the expenditure of over $400 million over a five-year period to improve and expand career education at the local level. Although the funding actually appropriated has been less than that authorized, this legislation has supported many activities, including program planning and curriculum development; in-service training of teachers; the assessment of community needs; cooperative efforts among schools, industry, business, and labor; guidance counseling; placement and follow-up services among teachers, parents, counselors, and community personnel; work experience programs for students; the purchase of materials; the development of resource centers; and the payment of salaries.

This money was made available to state departments of education, which then distributed the funds. Each state developed a plan to provide local career education programs and appointed both state and local career education coordinators. At present more than half of the 17,000 school districts in the United States provide career education.

PROBE 12-1
Career Education Precedents

1. List two of the events that led to an increasing vocational orientation to education.

   a. _____

   _____

   b. _____

   _____

2. List six societal concerns that contributed to the development of the career education movement.

   a. _____

   b. _____

   c. _____

   d. _____

   e. _____

   f. _____

3. T F   The idea that career education should be a part of the American education system was first conceived in the 1970s.

4. Which of the following are *not* true about the Career Education Incentive Act?
   a. It authorized $400 million for career education.
   b. It provides money directly to school districts based on applications to the United States Office of Career Education.
   c. All of the money authorized was actually provided to programs.
   d. It provides money for a variety of career education efforts at the local level.

CAREER EDUCATION CONCEPTS AND DEFINITIONS

You should be able to discuss the various concepts and definitions of career education.

To encourage schools and other educational agencies to develop programs to best meet their own needs, the United States Office of Education did not define "career education" until 1975. As a result, many different conceptualizations of career education have evolved, ranging from those which are narrowly oriented toward job training to those which encompass a great variety of skills. One of the narrower conceptualizations states, "There is nothing mysterious or esoteric about Career Education. If it means anything at all, it means preparing for entry into the world of work. We can theorize it to death, or we can get down to the business of giving people job skills" (Dellefield, 1974, p. 11).

A broader definition is that of Goldhammer and Taylor (1972), who defined career education as "a systematic attempt to increase the career options available to individuals and to facilitate more rational and valid career planning and preparation" (p. 6). This resembles the official USOE definition, finally formulated in 1975, which states, "Career education is the totality of experience through which one learns about and prepares to engage in work as part of his or her way of living" (Hoyt, 1975).

Within this conceptualization, *career* is broadly defined as the "totality of work one does in his or her lifetime," and *work* is defined as "any conscious effort aimed at producing benefits for oneself and/or for oneself and others." A *vocation* is the primary work role one is engaged in at any particular time; it includes both unpaid work roles, such as student, housewife, volunteer, or hobbyist, and paid work roles, such as plumber, doctor, and bus driver. A person's *career* encompasses all of his work and vocational roles. It generally begins before one enters first grade and continues throughout one's life.

Another writer has defined *career* as "the sequence of major positions occupied by a person throughout his pre-occupational, occupational and post-occupational life, including work-related roles such as those of a student, employee, and pensioner, together with complementary avocational, familial, and civic roles" (Super, 1978, p. 18). According to this definition, career education would be "properly synonymous in meaning with *education*. Or to put it differently, all education, in addition to whatever else it may be, should be career education" (McMurrin, 1973, p. 19). This comprehensive approach to career education is further elaborated by Miller (1973):

> What does career education include? Reading, writing, arithmetic — certainly! What skills could be more appropriate on most jobs? Attitudes and values, effective human relations, study skills — essential characteristics of a good employee. Art, music, foreign language — these will be a part of the total life work of some pupils. To hear many describe the scope of career education, it can and should embrace all of education [pp. 153-55].

One of the broader conceptualizations of career education is that of the Council for Exceptional Children (CEC), the major professional organization for special educators. Presented in its entirety in Chart 12-1, this approach has been aptly summarized by Brolin (1978), who defined career education as "all of education systematically coordinating all school, family, and community components together to facilitate each individual's potential for economic, social, and personal fulfillment" (p. 7). The CEC position advocates goals that have been promoted by educators of the handicapped for more than twenty years. These goals, or *life functions,* as they were termed in the 1958 *Illinois Curriculum Guide,* relate to:

1. Citizenship
2. Communicating
3. Home and family
4. Leisure time
5. Management of materials and money
6. Occupational adequacy
7. Physical and mental health
8. Safety
9. Social adjustment
10. Travel

Chart 12-1
Council for Exceptional Children
Position Statement on Career Education

Career education is the totality of experiences through which one learns to live a meaningful, satisfying work life. Within the career education framework, work is conceptualized as conscious effort aimed at producing benefits for oneself and/or others. Career education provides the opportunity for children to learn, in the least restrictive environment possible, the academic, daily living, personal-social and occupational knowledges and specific vocal work skills necessary for attaining their highest levels of economic, personal, and social fulfillment. The individual can obtain this fulfillment through work (both paid and unpaid) and in a variety of other societal roles and personal life styles including his/her pursuits as a student, citizen, volunteer, family member, and participant in meaningful leisure time activities.

Exceptional children, i.e., those whose characteristics range from profoundly and severely handicapped to those who are richly endowed with talents and/or intellectual giftedness, include individuals whose career potentials range from sheltered to competitive work and living arrangements. Exceptional children require career education experiences which will develop to the fullest extent possible their wide range of abilities, needs, and interests.

It is the position of CEC that individualized appropriate education for exceptional children must include the opportunity for every student to attain his/her highest level of career potential through career education experiences. Provisions for these educational experiences must be reflected in an individual educational program for each exceptional child which must include the following:

— Non-discriminatory, on-going assessment of career interests, needs, and potentials which assures the recognition of the strengths of the individual which can lead to meaningful, satisfying careers in a work-oriented society. Assessment materials and procedures must not be discriminatory on the basis of race, sex, national origin, or exceptionality.
— Career awareness, exploration, preparation, and placement experiences in the least restrictive school, living, and community environments which focus on the needs of the exceptional individual from early childhood through adulthood.
— Specification and utilization of community and other services related to the career development of exceptional individuals (e.g., rehabilitation, transportation, industrial and business, psychological, etc.).
— Involvement of parents or guardians and the exceptional student in career education planning.

Career education must not be viewed separately from the total curriculum. Rather, career education permeates the entire school program and even extends beyond it. It should be an infusion throughout the curriculum by knowledgeable teachers who modify the curriculum to integrate career development goals with current subject matter, goals, and content. It should prepare individuals for the several life roles which make up an individual's career. These life roles may include an economic role, a community role, a home role, an avocational role, a religious or moral role, and an aesthetic role. Thus, career education is concerned with the total person and his/her adjustment for community working and living.

An approach that encompasses all of these areas is clearly life preparation, not merely training for a job. The distinction is important: many people confuse career education with vocational education. Although vocational education may be provided in secondary school and later, career education is a much broader concept. The *life-centered* approach to career education focuses on social and personal as well as economic fulfillment, and includes career development experiences from early childhood through adulthood to prepare the person for a large variety of roles.

PROBE 12-2
Career Education Concepts and Definitions

1. Give several examples of both paid and unpaid work.

   _____

   _____

   _____

   _____

2. T   F   Career education is basically the same as vocational education.

3. List five aspects of career education not related to occupational training.

   a. _____

   b. _____

   c. _____

   d. _____

   e. _____

CAREER EDUCATION MODELS

> **You should be able to identify the characteristics common to most school-based career education models.**

At the time that it introduced career education, the United States Office of Education provided $15 million for the development of four experimental models for career education. These four models were (1) the rural-residential based model, (2) the home-community based model, (3) the employer-based model, and (4) the school-based model. Although all of these models have been extensively tested, the latter two are the most common, probably because they more closely resemble traditional education programs. The employer-based model, renamed Experience Based Career Education (EBCE), provides a highly individualized, highly structured, community-oriented alternative to traditional secondary education. This model will be discussed in a later section of the chapter, dealing with secondary programming in career education.

The school-based model is the one that has had the greatest effect on education. As conceived by Marland (1971), Hoyt (1975), and others, the focus of the school-based model is on adult occupational adjustment. This model has three overlapping stages, which are described in detail in Chart 12-2. During the *career awareness* stage, children are introduced to the values and the different types of paid work. In the next stage, *career orientation and exploration,* they learn more about job options and explore areas they are interested in. Finally, during *career preparation* they prepare for a technical or vocational occupation, or for college. Included in the third stage are adult and continuing education. This reflects the fact that people today are choosing to start second careers and getting additional training and education with increasing frequency.

Chart 12-2
School-Based Model: Career Education Stages

Career Awareness. Children should examine the world of work for the first time during elementary school. Through an understanding of the relationship between work and the rest of life, children can be encouraged to develop work values and an appreciation of the worth of good work habits. Children should examine the work roles of members of their families and be able to differentiate occupations. They might also examine the work roles of school staff members. Field trips to a dairy, zoo, or factory would expose them to the various occupations involved in production or in maintaining the facility. A wide array of career options should be presented to the students. It is also important that children be provided with a variety of role models — representatives from business, labor, and industry as well as the children's parents.

Career Orientation and Exploration. Career orientation, generally provided to students in seventh and eighth grades, permits students to examine a variety of specific occupations. The characteristics certain types of jobs have in common are emphasized, with particular attention being paid to the fifteen occupational clusters identified by the USOE. In ninth and tenth grades, students explore jobs through observation and experience with actual jobs, often in simulated work environments. Career guidance becomes increasingly important in organizing exploratory experiences around students' interests and abilities. The effects of various career choices on family life, leisure activities, and other life situations are also stressed at this stage, as are the relationships between occupation and societal values and beliefs.

Career Preparation. The preparatory stage of the school-based program, provided for students in eleventh and twelfth grades, is designed to ensure that every student acquires a saleable skill before graduation and is prepared to either obtain a job or enter a postsecondary instruction program. Students should focus on areas of particular interest and explore several jobs in depth. At this stage some students participate in work experience programs, whereas others enroll in specific vocational training programs or explore postsecondary training opportunities. Basic academic skills are still emphasized, but attention is also paid to the skills needed for family life, avocational pursuits, and citizenship.

Many adults return to formal education programs to enhance their nonoccupational lives as well. Numerous educators have adopted the life-centered approach to career education to stress aspects of the school-based model that are unrelated to jobs. This approach emphasizes important life goals such as avocational skills, civic participation, family development, and personal values, attitudes, and habits, in addition to occupational preparation.

Brolin (1978) has developed a life-centered approach to career education for the mildly handicapped that specifies 22 competencies and 102 subcompetencies in three curriculum areas: (1) daily living skills, (2) personal-social skills, and (3) occupational guidance and preparation skills. (See Chart 12-3.) According to this approach, the mildly handicapped student should have all these skills before he leaves school. Because the competency statements encompass the skills everyone needs to succeed in community living, they are useful for other groups as well, from the nonhandicapped to the severely handicapped. Furthermore, they are broadly enough stated that they can be applied to all levels of instruction, from the primary grades through high school. They can also be taught using a variety of subject matter.

Brolin provides suggestions for teachers in *Life Centered Career Education: A Competency-Based Approach* (1978). The curriculum plan details student objectives for each subcompetency, suggests instructional activities, and recommends ways that families and people in the community can assist in competency devel-

Chart 12-3
Career Education Competencies

A. *Daily Living Skills Curriculum Area*
 1. Managing Family Finances
 2. Caring for and Repairing Home Furnishing and Equipment
 3. Caring for Personal Needs
 4. Raising Children, Family Living
 5. Buying and Preparing Food
 6. Buying and Making Clothing
 7. Engaging in Civic Activities
 8. Utilizing Recreation and Leisure
 9. Mobility in the Community

B. *Personal-Social Skills Curriculum Area*
 10. Achieving Self-Awareness
 11. Acquiring Self-Confidence
 12. Achieving Socially Responsible Behavior
 13. Maintaining Good Interpersonal Relationships
 14. Achieving Independence

 15. Making Good Decisions, Problem Solving
 16. Communicating Adequately with Others

C. *Occupational Guidance and Preparation Curriculum Area*
 17. Knowing and Exploring Occupational Possibilities
 18. Making Appropriate Occupational Decisions
 19. Exhibiting Appropriate Work Behaviors
 20. Exhibiting Sufficient Physical and Manual Skills
 21. Acquiring a Specific Saleable Job. Skill is not included because the subcompetencies would be unique to the particular skill being acquired.
 22. Seeking, Securing, and Maintaining Satisfactory Employment

opment. The following paragraphs illustrate methods of emphasizing competencies at all levels of instruction.

The daily living skills curriculum area emphasizes the skills needed to care for oneself, to participate in family living, and to manage a home and personal finances. One of the subcompetencies for Competency 3, "Caring for Personal Needs," is "Dress Appropriately." At the elementary career awareness stage, the importance of appropriate dress could be emphasized — what clothes to wear in what weather, and to what activities, for example. During exploration, methods of buying and caring for clothes could be taught. At the career preparation stage, clothes construction and fashion could be studied, and more advanced methods of caring for clothes could be taught.

The personal-social curriculum area focuses on skills that foster self-understanding and independence. One of the subcompetencies involved in Competency 16, "Communicating Adequately with Others," is "Read at Level Needed for Future Goals." Students at the career awareness level might be taught to read and interpret important signs, such as traffic, safety, and restroom signs. At the next stage, students might begin studying the types of information provided in the newspaper and locating businesses and agencies by using the telephone book. At the career preparation stage, students could use help-wanted ads, newspaper advertisements, and the Yellow Pages to plan for real or simulated occupational or recreational pursuits.

Occupational guidance and preparation skills include competencies that can be developed at all instructional levels (Competencies 17, 18, and 19), and competencies that should be emphasized primarily at the high school level (Competencies 20, 21, and 22). The understanding of job classifications can be taught at all levels. During the career awareness stage the emphasis can be on the variety of jobs that are available in the school and community. At the career exploration level students can identify general job categories and discuss the ways jobs are classified: by salary, type of work, level of skill and training required, and location of work, for example. At the career preparation stage students can participate in actual job training.

The Competency-Based Model for Infusing Career Education into the Curriculum (see Figure 12-1) illustrates the fact that all the stages of career education (awareness, exploration, preparation, placement, and follow-up) for each of the twenty-two competencies can be taught in conjunction with material from other subject areas. The model also indicates that the educational experiences can occur in the family, the school, or the community. It further emphasizes that career education is a cooperative venture, a "process of systematically coordinating all school, family, and community components to facilitate each individual's potential for economic, social, and personal fulfillment" (Brolin, 1978, p. 96).

Current mainstreaming practices have resulted in the increasing participation of the handicapped in the career education experiences of regular school programs. Special educators must be certain, however, that these experiences are

Figure 12-1
Competency-Based Model for Career Education

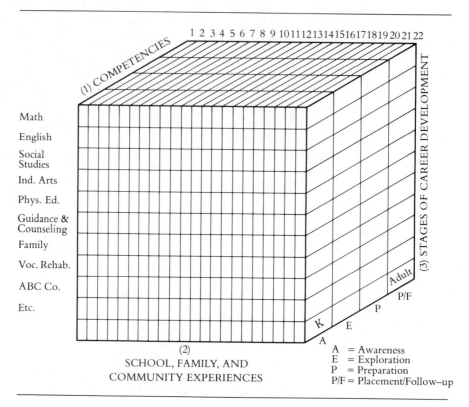

compatible with the goals stated in the student's IEP, and that they are developmentally appropriate for the student. Handicapped students with developmental lags may not be ready for experiences and concepts that are appropriate for the regular classroom student. In such cases the special or regular education teacher should adapt instruction for the handicapped student or see that the student receives career education in a setting other than the regular classroom.

PROBE 12-3
Career Education Models

1. Briefly describe the focus of each of the three curriculum areas, and think of one elementary- and one secondary-level activity for each area.

   a. Daily Living _____

   _____

Elementary Activity _____

_____

Secondary Activity _____

_____

b. Personal/Social _____

_____

Elementary Activity _____

_____

Secondary Activity _____

_____

c. Occupational _____

_____

Elementary Activity _____

_____

Secondary Activity _____

_____

2. Indicate the grade level at which each stage would be emphasized and list some
   probable program features of each stage.

Stage	*Grades*	*Program Emphasis*
Career Awareness	____	a. _____
		b. _____
		c. _____
Career Orientation and Exploration	____	a. _____
		b. _____
		c. _____
Career Preparation	____	a. _____
		b. _____
		c. _____

INSTRUCTIONAL APPROACHES IN CAREER EDUCATION

> **You should be able to identify the instructional approaches used in career education programs.**

THE INFUSION AND SEPARATE PROGRAMMING APPROACHES

There are two basic approaches to career education instruction: the *infusion approach* and the *separate programming approach*. The infusion approach integrates career education and the existing curriculum. Separate programming can involve (1) developing a separate curriculum devoted to career education (the EBCE program discussed later in this chapter is an example of separate programming); (2) developing separate career education classes; or (3) providing separate units devoted specifically to career education within courses on other subjects. The last approach is the one used most frequently.

Clark (1979) suggests that students are served best through the use of a combination of the infusion and separate programming approaches. Infusion does not require that course or units be added to an already crowded curriculum, and separate programming ensures that career education will be systematically approached. This combination approach permits a balance between academic skills and career education skills, providing a unique opportunity to tie together the two sets of competencies (Clark, 1979).

The ratio of separate programming to infusion found in any school program will be determined by such factors as the preparation and orientation of the teachers involved and the school's commitment to career education. The students' grade level, their degree of handicap (if any), and the instructional setting are also considered. Clark (1979) has developed a schematic representation of career education delivery options based on these three considerations; it is shown in Table 12-1. You will notice that separate programming is generally used for more severely handicapped children and for those in special class settings. In the regular classroom, career education is usually provided through infusion and unit teaching. Visually or hearing impaired children and the severely learning disabled may need separate career education courses in addition to that which has been infused into the regular class coursework.

The infusion approach relates curriculum content to adult careers, thereby increasing the relevance of education for the learner. In Brolin's Life-Centered Career Education program, career education competencies are considered the primary goals, with academic skills playing a supportive role. Although basic academics are taught, instructional content is selected according to its value in facilitating the acquisition of competencies.

Table 12-1
Delivery Systems for Career Education

	Mildly Handicapped		Moderately to Severely Handicapped	
	K-3	*4-6*	*K-3*	*4-6*
Regular Class or Resource Room	Infusion and unit teaching	Infusion and unit teaching	Infusion and separate subject	Infusion and separate subject
Special Class	Infusion and separate subject	Infusion and separate subject	Total curriculum	Total curriculum

Source: Clark, G. M. *Career Education for the Handicapped Child in the Elementary Classroom*, p. 165. Copyright 1979 by Love Publishing Company. Reprinted by permission.

Another method of infusing career education involves stressing the relevance of regular subjects to the problems of earning a living and other aspects of life after graduation. With this method, the focus of instruction is the academic subject matter. Here is a list of suggestions for ways that this type of instruction might be implemented:

Math: Emphasize the kinds of information communicated by numbers: age, weight, height, sizes of clothing, addresses, phone numbers, social security numbers, license numbers, and so on. Demonstrate practical applications of mathematical processes as in measuring, money management, construction plans, and computing wages and deductions. Have students interview adults to discover how they use math in their jobs and at home. Investigate how mathematics is used in the school cafeteria — altering recipes, determining the prices that should be charged, ordering food, and tallying receipts, for example. Use a token economy.

Language Arts: The children can be acquainted with how people use language in different occupations through activities involving role-playing. Application blanks, classified ads, résumés, and tax forms can be examined. Students can practice writing business and thank-you letters and using the telephone. The psychology of advertising can be studied.

Social Studies. Study the history and future of a particular job, business, or industry. Examine the variety of jobs and services available in a community. Teach map reading as an aid to student mobility, and explain how it can be useful in occupations such as delivery man or taxi driver. In the study of history or of different cultures, needs common to all people can be emphasized.

Health, Physical Education, and Fine Arts. Jobs and other pursuits that require strength, dexterity, and endurance can be discussed. The relationship between nutrition and exercise, and good health can be studied. Oral hygiene, cleanliness, and appropriate dress can be emphasized. The appreciation of the arts and of aesthetics can be taught as a leisure-time activity.

Unit Instruction. Unit instruction can be used with either the infusion or separate programming approach. Meyen (1976) has defined it as a "highly generic approach that allows skills and concepts to be couched in the context of themes meaningful to students." This means that a single instructional experience is used to meet content, career development, and academic skill goals. A particular unit could emphasize the acquisition of information or the development of a specific skill, or it could be centered around a particular activity.

The experience unit is probably the most appropriate for infusing career education concepts into the total instructional program. Kirk and Johnson (1951), in an early book on teaching the mentally retarded, suggested that a portion of the daily instruction be organized around a unit theme, with tool subjects (reading, writing, and arithmetic) and other activities (art, music, and recreation) connected with that theme. Meyen (1976) goes further and recommends that experiences in each of six core areas be incorporated into each unit, regardless of the unit's topic. The core areas he suggests are arithmetic, social competencies, communication skills, safety, health, and vocational information. A particular unit might emphasize one core area more than the others, depending on the topic, but experiences in all the core areas should be planned for each unit. For example, a unit on manufacturing could cover mathematics, science, health and safety, language arts, and other academic subjects. Mathematical skills could be related to wages, salaries, prices, and hours worked. Scientific principles could be explained in terms of machinery observed on a field trip. Health and safety could be approached through a discussion of special clothing worn by workers, company safety rules, and health services available at a factory. Interviewing, reading, films, sociodrama, and role-playing could be related to language arts.

A unit devoted to career education could focus exclusively on that subject (such as Community Helpers), or it could be designed to help students meet other educational objectives as well. It could include such topics as community services, good work habits, and self-awareness. The unit approach is especially helpful to teachers of the handicapped, because it permits students to learn information and develop concepts by means other than reading, and it provides many opportunities for remediation. As mentioned earlier, the teacher may have to provide alternative methods of career education to handicapped students if they are not at the same developmental stage as the nonhandicapped.

In any group instruction, it is important for the teacher to remember that although the group may be focusing on a particular theme, there is room for individualization of objectives within that theme. Indeed, whether the student is mainstreamed or is in a self-contained setting, it is essential that objectives and activities be varied to meet the individual student's needs. A good way to ensure that both individual and group objectives are met is to include them in the daily lesson plan. This helps the teacher use time effectively, and leaves her a record of her approach to the unit, which can be used in subsequent years and shared with other teachers.

INSTRUCTIONAL METHODS AND ACTIVITIES

A number of techniques and activities can be used in career education. One of the best is to invite family members and persons from business, industry, and social groups to visit the classroom and discuss their work and social activities. A panel

Individualized instruction in specific work skills is often the most effective form of training for the severely and moderately handicapped. Above, a teacher demonstrates a simple assembly program to a workshop client.

of several persons is an interesting forum for such discussions. Field trips to places of employment, community service agencies, and recreation facilities can also be effective. Field trips should be carefully planned around a set of objectives, and they should be integrated with activities in the classroom.

Within the classroom, role-playing, sociodramas, and simulation are excellent methods of developing specific career education concepts. Students can practice for situations such as riding a bus, making a date, or interviewing for a job, and they can develop sociodramas for acting out various social or occupational situations. Simulation can provide a realistic opportunity to learn about a particular occupation, business, or community agency. In special education settings, assembly lines, stores, banks, corporations, and restaurants have all been simulated successfully. A school for moderately and severely retarded students even "simulated" a restaurant that served hot lunches and snacks. Employment situations can be simulated through the use of time clocks, by designating work areas, and by assigning worker roles such as line-leader, shade-puller, and blackboard-cleaner on a rotating basis. At the high school level Junior Achievement gives students the opportunity to develop their own companies, produce and sell products, and divide the profits. Class discussions, demonstrations, and inquiry or problem-solving techniques can be used effectively at both the elementary and secondary levels.

Learning Centers. A learning center is an instructional area where children teach themselves. These centers can be designed to teach a skill or concept that is being emphasized in an instructional unit. They can be developed for use by either individuals or groups.

Centers should focus on specific instructional objectives; they should provide direct sensory experiences through which concepts and learning skills can be developed (Beach, 1977). They should include a variety of activities — reading, listening, discussing, and watching, for example. Each center should offer activities appropriate for students at different levels.

The use of learning centers offers several advantages:

> Learning centers can help you to personalize and individualize instruction. They can give children a choice. They can provide different modes of learning. They can buy time, time for you to say to a child, face to face: "My, I like that. Tell me about it." Centers can have specific activities for specific skills. They can be self-checking. They can provide activities that are open-ended and that encourage divergent thinking [Davidson et al., 1976].

Another important aspect of learning centers is that they foster self-management, which is itself an important skill in career development. If the instructions for the center's use are clearly stated, students can enter the center and select an activity with little or no help from the teacher. The provision of more than one activity in the center will encourage children to exercise their ability to make choices.

EDUCATION FOR LEISURE

Career education has been conceptualized to include both paid and unpaid productive efforts. The concept extends beyond economic factors to encompass one's total life style, including leisure time. People have more leisure time than ever before, and there is an increasing emphasis on the meaningful use of this time. Improved technology has given us a shorter work week and more unemployment, and has created highly specialized jobs that are often uninvolving, uncreative, and unfulfilling. Increasingly, people are seeking satisfaction through their leisure-time activities.

Educating the handicapped for leisure can help them overcome many of the social, economic, and attitudinal barriers that might otherwise keep them from enjoying the social and recreational life of the community. Some of the goals of leisure education of particular relevance to the handicapped are:

— Appreciation of the wide diversity of leisure choices and lifestyles.
— Recognition that understanding and appreciation of leisure experiences will be enhanced through direct exploration and participation.
— Development of specific skills necessary for participation in a variety of leisure time activities.
— Understanding of the contributions that leisure time provides for self-expression and physical and intellectual development.
— Development of interests and problem-solving skills that will facilitate independent pursuits of leisure in the home, school, and community [Leisure Information Service, 1976, pp. 42–43].

Some of the most popular leisure education activities take place out of doors. Instructional programs for the handicapped have been designed in backpacking, nature study, camping, and outdoor sports. Project EXPLORE (Expanding Programs and Learning in Outdoor Recreation and Education) provides a competency-based, skill-oriented curriculum designed to provide individualized, systematic, and direct instruction to handicapped children. Instructions have been developed in the areas of (1) camping and self-maintenance; (2) sports, games, and physical development; (3) arts and crafts; (4) safety and survival, and (5) nature study and development. The curriculum has been used successfully in special education classrooms, summer camps, and outdoor education programs with children whose handicaps ranged from mild to severe. Special instruction programs have also been developed for teaching swimming, bowling, skiing, horseback riding, wheelchair basketball, and other sports. The Special Olympics

Learning to compete in leisure activities aids the personal adjustment of handicapped people. The competitive skills learned may then carry over into other areas of their lives.

for the mentally retarded have increased public acceptance of the fact that everyone can benefit from participating and competing in sports.

Another recent focus of leisure education is on the arts. Since the mid-1970s, the National Committee ★ Arts for the Handicapped (NCAH) has been promoting arts programming. The NCAH sponsors state and local Very Special Arts Festivals across the nation, funds exemplary Model Site programs, supports a variety of Special Project programs, and serves as a resource for information and technical assistance on arts and the handicapped. These activities are based on the recognition that children can learn by working in and observing the arts, and that arts experiences promote social, emotional, and intellectual growth.

An example of a program that provides both art and leisure education is the Appalachian Folkcrafts Project for the Handicapped. In this project, curriculum materials were developed to teach handicapped children folkcrafts as a leisure-time activity. There was already a well-established crafts industry in Appalachia, so the development of these skills was a natural means of mainstreaming handicapped youngsters into the leisure activities of the region. Learning folkcraft processes permitted the participants to develop a sense of regional pride, learn something about art, and attend social activities at craft fairs and associations. A set of guidelines for using this approach in other geographic areas was developed by the personnel of this project (Cegelka, 1979).

PROBE 12-4
Instructional Approaches in Career Education

1. What are two methods of infusing career education into the regular curriculum?

    a. _____

    _____

    b. _____

    _____

2. Which of the following statements are true?
    a. Infusion is a method in which both career education and academic skills are systematically developed.
    b. An alternative to infusion is the unit approach to teaching.
    c. Career education is best taught with a combination of infusion and separate programming.
    d. Separate programming may be necessary to develop some career education concepts.
    e. Some subject area content cannot be taught adequately through career education infusion.

3. For one career education competency, develop a sociodrama or role-playing activity.

    _____

    _____

    _____

    _____

4. Explain why leisure education is important for the handicapped.

    _____

    _____

    _____

    _____

    _____

    _____

5. List six leisure activities or resources in your community that the handicapped could participate in. Do not include activities the handicapped could merely observe.

_____

_____

_____

_____

_____

_____

CAREER EDUCATION IN THE LEAST RESTRICTIVE ENVIRONMENT

You should be able to describe the provision of career education according to the principles of the least restrictive environment.

SECONDARY PROGRAMMING FOR THE HANDICAPPED

Until recently, most career education was provided at the high school level. In special education the majority of services have been provided to the educable mentally retarded, and have involved work-study experience. The traditional model for work experience was developed in the 1960s through cooperative vocational rehabilitation/special education programs supported with federal funds.

Although programs varied, they generally involved exploration activities during the sophomore and junior years and supervised work study or job placement during the senior year. During the sophomore year, students would typically spend part of the day in one of a series of job settings learning basic employment expectations, such as keeping busy, following directions, and being on time. These experiences would also give students the opportunity to practice mobility skills such as using public transportation. During the junior year, students would be placed for part of the day in three to five different jobs for four to six weeks each. They would generally be paid for their work. During these jobs, occupational behavior would be evaluated. As seniors, students were required to hold a full-time job for one semester or a part-time job for the entire school year. Students were generally integrated with regular classes for activities such as physical education, shop, home economics, art, or music, but they were otherwise self-contained. This permitted the special education teacher to incorporate efforts to remediate work-related problems noted during on-the-job observation into the instructional programs.

Rehabilitation counselors served as work-study coordinators for some of these programs, working closely with the students and their teachers from the time they entered tenth grade until graduation. The work of these counselors was instrumental in making these programs successful. A counselor from the Kansas Work-Study Program published an excellent book on obtaining employer cooperation for on-the-job training; here is an excerpt from that book:

Several years ago I was hired as a vocational rehabilitation counselor and I can readily recall my first day on the job. I was assigned a caseload of handicapped clients and my major responsibilities were too numerous and varied to list.... I was instructed to read the policy manual and find the clients.

"What do you mean, 'find the clients?' " I responded.

"The last counselor left unexpectedly and the first thing you need to do is find out who and where your clients are," I was matter-of-factly told....

...I picked the folder lying on top and arbitrarily chose this person to be my first client. After reading the folder, I decided to go to the restaurant where the client was listed as working. I pulled up to the restaurant in a state car and entered the place of business to find I had arrived at a busy time. Since the manager wasn't available to talk, I decided to have lunch. After eating, I was approached by the manager who informed me that the client had walked off the job four months ago. I hope counselors [will learn] to understand business routine, *schedule,* and business thinking.

It took me four days to find the client. He was at home, unshaven, watching television, and feeling sorry for himself. He was living in a place which smelled like urine and looked like a pigsty. I hope [that counselors will learn] about *people.*

Within a year under my counseling and guidance, this client was placed on, and walked off of, five different jobs. I hope [that counselors learn] something about *evaluation* and *training.*

One time I remember driving around the block three times to build up enough courage to talk with a hostile employer. He was mad and he had a right to be. My client lost his temper and broke the front window in the store. I hope [that counselors will learn] about *how to approach* an employer.

I once knew an eager counselor who placed six clients on jobs in one day. He thought he really had done something. During a follow-up session one month later, he couldn't find any of them — they all had been fired. I hope [that counselors will learn] about *follow-up.*

I heard of a client placed at the local humane society to care for animals. During the second week he felt sorry for the caged up animals and went around opening up all the pens. There were dogs all over the county. It took over two weeks to round up the dogs. Yes, I hope [that counselors will understand] *people's feelings.*

I once worked with a client who had spent considerable time in jail for stealing bicycles. I took him to a grocery store to be interviewed for a job. Things were going fairly well until he spotted a bicycle shop across the street. I couldn't get his nose away from the window. He just keep muttering, "I want to work in a bicycle shop." I gave up at the grocery store, grabbed his arm, and quickly went across the street to inquire about a job in the bicycle shop. I don't know how, but the client somehow got a job that very day and worked there for several years before he was sent to prison for breaking into houses. You know, I hope [that counselors] really [do learn] about people, *all types of people.*

I have had clients hug me, laugh with me, cry with me, curse me, throw things at me, and spit on me. I have experienced joy and sorrow, success and failure. I have worked with clients I enjoyed seeing come into my office and I have worked with clients I enjoyed seeing walk *out* of my office. At times I really liked working for vocational rehabilitation and at other times I couldn't stand it [Payne, Mercer, and Epstein, 1974].

Although there is no longer the same type of cooperative funding, work-study programs are still used to prepare the handicapped for careers. Vocational rehabilitation counselors help arrange placement in some school districts; in others, the salaries of work-study coordinators are paid from local or state vocational education funds.

An important feature of job tryouts is the opportunity they provide for careful evaluation of student behaviors and interactions while at work. Unfortunately, school personnel often assume that the student needs only minimal attention at this stage. By using the job tryout stage to assess the student's interests, promptness, job attendance, ability to follow directions, and other job-related skills, the instructor can plan remedial efforts for the part of the program occurring in the school.

Increasingly, the more capable handicapped students are being mainstreamed into regular vocational education programs. Frequently, a special needs coordinator works in these programs as a liaison between special education and vocational education. This individual may be instrumental in recommending placement of students into various vocational programs and may assist the teacher in adapting their curriculum, equipment, or instruction as well as provide individual tutoring for students. Training for specific skilled occupations can greatly enhance the vocational adjustment of the handicapped.

In addition to vocational education and work study options, both college preparatory and general studies curricula might be appropriate. This option might be used with children who do not have intellectual handicaps, such as those with specific learning disabilities, behavior disorders, or visual or auditory handicaps. Work evaluation or work adjustment program options may be appropriate for children who are less capable intellectually, such as those who are likely to be placed in a community rehabilitation facility or sheltered workshop.

The various options discussed are not mutually exclusive, of course. Students could participate in two or more career preparation experiences. For example, a student in the college preparatory curriculum might choose to participate in a work evaluation center during a summer session in an effort to better understand his occupational aptitudes and preferences.

Another option that is frequently used in conjunction with other forms of career education is the Experience-based Career Education program (EBCE). This program provides an alternative to educational programs located entirely within the schools. Designed for students between the ages of thirteen and eighteen, it draws on academic, general, and vocational curricula in an effort to increase the relevance of education to the world of work and to reduce student alienation.

This type of career education makes use of banks, publishing houses, factories, travel agencies, hospitals, and other such settings. The experiential component of the program involves a series of community placements of one to three hours a day for between two and thirteen weeks each. Each student's individual program is designed by a learning coordinator, who works with the student in selecting community experiences and relevant academic classes. A person at each occupational site is responsible for providing the student with opportunities for observation and experience doing job-related tasks.

Because this program is at the same time highly structured and highly individualized, it is especially good for both the handicapped and the nonhandicapped. The federal guidelines state that these programs should be designed for students with all levels of academic ability, and that they should offer education throughout the year. In addition, the guidelines state that these programs should provide open entry and exit and the opportunity for students to return to the traditional school program. EBCE can be provided in conjunction with college preparatory, general education, or vocational education curricula, or it can provide an alternative to high school for some students. It can also be adopted as a refinement of a cooperative work-study program. Research for Better Schools, Inc., has concluded that EBCE could play an important role in developing closer relationships between societal and educational planning (Burdke, Beths, and Beasley, 1973).

FINDING THE LEAST RESTRICTIVE ENVIRONMENT

Career education can benefit persons of all ages in all types of educational settings. As pointed out earlier, the goals of career education have long been advocated in slightly different form, as goals for the handicapped. Special education tends to become "normalized" as teachers incorporate career education into their curricula and all students come to share the same goals.

A word of caution is needed, however. Although the skills and objectives of a career education curriculum are appropriate for both handicapped and non-handicapped youngsters, developmental lags of the former group could mean that somewhat different learning experiences are required within a given instructional program. The special education teacher can be a valuable resource to the regular class teacher in modifying career education programs so that the handicapped student can be successfully incorporated. In addition, at the secondary level particularly, the curricular focus of the regular academic classes may not be and often is not supportive of the career development needs of the mildly handicapped. There is frequently little about the lowest-track academic class to recommend it as attractive or even appropriate to the career development needs of slow students. Nonprescriptive mainstreaming can result in limiting the options of the special education student. Care must be taken by the student's IEP Committee to ensure that she is placed only in those settings which facilitate the development of specific competencies and that all career education competencies are developed.

Opportunities for handicapped students to participate in a variety of mainstream career preparation programs have expanded considerably in the past several years. PL 94-142, guaranteeing appropriate education for all handicapped children, specifically mentioned vocational education as appropriate for many handicapped individuals. The Vocational Education Act of 1963 and its amendments have provided that 10 percent of the research and demonstration monies that each state received under this legislation be used for providing vocational education to the handicapped. In addition, the Vocational Rehabilitation Act of 1973 guarantees handicapped individuals access to all educational programs receiving federal money. These legislative efforts have greatly expanded the opportunities afforded the handicapped to obtain appropriate career preparation at both the secondary and postsecondary levels.

It is important that the full range of placements, from the completely segregated to the completely integrated, be considered for each child. Unfortunately, many educators interpret the "least restrictive environment" clause of PL 94-142 as meaning that students should be placed in the least restrictive environment *currently available*, without considering whether the environment meets the career education needs of the student. The lowest academic track in a school's secondary program may provide few benefits to the student with significant academic handicaps. Another half-grade level of achievement in reading or arithmetic may be less useful to the student than daily living, personal-social, and occupational skills.

The best approach is to place students in classes on the basis of their need to acquire specific skills. Brolin (1974) suggests that student progress be carefully monitored, and that the student remain in a particular setting only until he attains specifically prescribed competencies. Segregated settings may be more frequently appropriate for students with severe or multiple handicaps, but even students with mild handicaps may need educational experiences available only through separate specialized programming efforts.

Whether the student is in a self-contained or a mainstream setting, the overall career education model has important implications for the level of achievement students attain. Carefully sequenced educational experiences at the elementary and junior high levels permit education at the secondary level to focus, when appropriate, on the development of specific occupational skills. The acquisition of desirable personal characteristics and attitudes is an important goal of all levels of career education. Education programs that combine training in academic, personal-social, daily living, and occupational skills hold great promise for developing the individual to his or her full potential.

PROBE 12-5
Career Education in the Least Restrictive Environment

1. The cooperative work–study programs of the 1960s had which of the following features?
   a. Vocational rehabilitation counselors worked with the schools in placing and evaluating the student during on-the-job training.
   b. The programs provided highly integrated, mainstream career education experiences.
   c. The programs provided a graduated sequence of occupational exploration experiences.
   d. As part of the program, problems observed during on-the-job training were remediated in the classroom.
   e. They were supported jointly with funds from vocational rehabilitation and special education projects.

2. List four types of career preparation programming available today.

   a. _____

   b. _____

   c. _____

   d. _____

3. Would the EBCE program be appropriate for a handicapped secondary student? Why?

   _____

   _____

   _____

4. Describe two ways that career education facilitates the mainstreaming of mildly handicapped students.

_____

_____

_____

5. Describe the detrimental effect that inappropriate mainstreaming can have on the career development of handicapped students.

_____

_____

SUMMARY

1. Career education is designed to improve the overall quality of life adjustment of all people, regardless of age, ability level, or handicap.
2. Career education developed out of a recognition that our educational, social, and economic systems failed to prepare students for life as working adults.
3. The career education movement has received considerable support from state and federal legislation.
4. There are many definitions of career education, ranging from those which are narrowly occupational to those which encompass overall life adjustment.
5. The career development stages are career awareness, career orientation and exploration, and career preparation. These stages both are sequential and overlap.
6. Two common approaches to career education are the infusion approach and the separate programming approach. Most successful programs make use of both approaches.
7. A number of different techniques and exercises have been used successfully to teach career education, including unit teaching, learning centers, guest speakers, field trips, sociodramas, class discussions, demonstrations, and simulations.
8. In the past, the cooperative vocational rehabilitation/special education program was the model for career education in secondary special education.
9. Today the educational options for career preparation include the college preparatory or general studies curriculum, vocational education, experience-based career education, work-study programs, and work evaluation and adjustment programs.

10. The importance of preparing persons for the nonoccupational aspects of adult life is reflected in the provisions of programs designed to develop avocational skills.
11. Special programs have been started in outdoor education, sports, and arts activities for the handicapped.

TASK SHEET 12
Field Experiences with Special Career Education

Select *one* of the following alternatives and complete the required tasks.

Workplace Visit

Visit one of the following and write a paper of no more than three pages about your experiences:
   a. a sheltered workshop
   b. a public school work-study program

Interview on Employment

Interview one of the following people and write a three-page paper on the substance of your interview:
   a. A secondary work-study teacher
   b. A vocational rehabilitation counselor
   c. A sheltered workshop employee
   d. An employer who hires handicapped persons

Interview on Work Problems

Interview a handicapped person about the problems associated with employment. Write a three-page paper describing this person's responses.

Library Study

Use the library to locate three articles on career education for the handicapped and write a one-page critique of each.

Design Your Own Field Experience

If you know of a unique experience you can have in the area of career education, or do not want to do any of the above alternatives, discuss your idea with your instructor, and complete the tasks that you agree on.

Probe Answers

Probe 12-1

1. a. the education amendments of 1974
   b. the Smith-Hughes Act of 1917
2. a. Many students upon completion of their education lacked basic academic skills needed to cope with our rapidly changing society.

b. Education seemed directed only toward preparation for further education.
c. Education contained minimal career preparation for such groups as the disadvantaged, minorities, women, and the handicapped.
d. Adult continuing education was not adequately provided for in the educational system.
e. Sufficient use was not made of learning opportunities outside the structure of formal education.
f. The general public did not have a great enough voice in educational policy making.
3. False
4. b and c

Probe 12-2

1. Paid: factory worker, lawyer, bus driver
   Unpaid: student, volunteer, hobbyist
2. False
3. a. effective use of leisure time
   b. management of materials and money
   c. physical and mental health
   d. social adjustment
   e. citizenship

Probe 12-3

1. a. *Daily living* emphasizes skills needed to care for oneself, to participate in family living, and to manage a home and personal finances. Elementary: dressing appropriately. Secondary: buying and caring for clothes.
   b. *Personal/social* focuses on skills that foster self-understanding and independence. Elementary: reading and interpreting important signs. Secondary: learning to use the telephone book and the newspaper to locate business and agencies.
   c. *Occupational* includes competencies that cover specific vocational task areas as well as skills related to seeking employment. Elementary: knowing and exploring occupational possibilities. Secondary: identifying general job categories.

2. Career Awareness: grades K–6
   a. relationship of work to total life process
   b. work values
   c. variety of occupations
   Career Orientation and Exploration: grades 7–10
   a. commonalities of different jobs
   b. job observation
   c. hands-on live or simulated job experiences
   Career Preparation: grades 11–12
   a. acquisition of usable skills
   b. participation in work experience
   c. enrollment in specific vocational preparation programs

Probe 12-4

1. a. the unit method of instruction or the experience unit of instruction
   b. "real world" emphasis, where career education is an integral, not a separate part, of all education
2. c, d, and e
3. For the competency of appropriate work behaviors, an employment situation can be simulated by using time clocks, designating work areas, and assigning different worker roles on a rotating basis.
4. Leisure education fosters appreciation of the many different types of leisure activities and lifestyles, develops specific skills needed to participate in a variety of leisure activities, and teaches how leisure time enhances self-expression and intellectual development.
5. Possibilities include swimming, wheelchair basketball, horseback riding, arts and crafts, backpacking, and nature study.

Probe 12-5

1. a, b, c, and d
2. a. work study
   b. vocational education
   c. college preparatory
   d. work evaluation/adjustment program

3. The EBCE program would be appropriate, because it is highly individualized and highly structured, which permits a wide degree of application based on the student's needs.

4. a. Experiential activities (such as job placements) are normalizing experiences.

   b. Many vocational programs do not rely heavily on academic skills; consequently, handicapped students can compete in them.

5. Often a handicapped student is placed in the least restrictive environment currently available, which is not necessarily the most supportive of the student's career education needs. For example, a student placed in the lowest academic track of a secondary school simply because it is the least restrictive environment may not acquire the daily living, personal/social, and occupational skills he needs.

I always felt ... that handicapped children only belonged to, oh, I don't know, "weird" people. They had one eye in their forehead, and they were either half-retarded themselves, or they were poor. It couldn't happen to a normal middle class person like myself.

I think there were definite stages, at least I went through definite stages of accepting Heather. The first one was disbelief. I just couldn't believe that she was not coming along normally. People would ask me in the store, you know, they could sense after she got so old that there was something wrong. I'd say, "Oh, she's just a little slow." But I would try to hide it from people, and I would just not believe it and not accept it.

And then, the second stage came where she was undeniably handicapped. I couldn't say any longer "she's a little slow." It got to where it was unquestionable. And then I got to where I resented other healthy kids. This was a really bad stage for me. You'd see mothers wailing on their kids at the supermarket [and] I wanted to shake them, and say: "Look what you've got, you've got a beautiful, healthy, normal child. What are you doing? You know you don't appreciate her."

And I think a lot of people stay in that stage, and that's sad because they're very bitter, and all they can think of is feeling sorry for themselves — they're at this stagnant point in life.... If you get past that, and pull yourself up, and say: "O.K., it's nobody's fault, I'm not going to blame myself anymore." ... I'm not being punished. Where can I go from here? What can I do for my child? What kind of a future can I plan for her? ... I'm not helping her sitting here crying in my beer. What can I do now? I have to go on. Right now, there's no room in my heart for bitterness. I have to go on. You could destroy yourself if you sit around like that.

Source: Adapted from English, R. W., and Olson, K. K. *Parenting handicapped children: Earliest experiences. Center paper No. 106.* Eugene, Oregon: Rehabilitation Research & Training Center in Mental Retardation, 1976, 10-11.

13

The Role of Parents

James A. McLoughlin

James A. McLoughlin is Associate Professor in the Department of Special Education at the University of Louisville, and a staff member in the Parent Education Project. Dr. McLoughlin has taught in both special and regular education and is the author of many articles on the topic of parents of exceptional children.

Raising children successfully is never an easy task, but the parents of exceptional children may find it especially difficult, as the profile on the facing page indicates. In recent years, parents and special educators have been working together to meet the challenges presented by exceptional children. Parents are becoming increasingly involved in planning and carrying out their children's educational programs. To cooperate effectively, educators must understand the special needs of parents of exceptional children, some of which are described in the following pages.

EFFECTS OF THE HANDICAPPED ON FAMILIES

You should be able to describe how a handicapped child can affect his family.

PARENTAL REACTIONS

The reactions of parents to the birth of a handicapped child vary greatly. Such factors as religion, socioeconomic status, severity of handicap, parental knowledge, and order of birth can all affect parental responses. A variety of descriptions of the emotional stages parents pass through before they accept their child's handicap have been offered, but they are highly speculative. Most parents, however, appear to experience periods of frustration, fear, guilt, disappointment, and uncertainty.

According to Kroth (1975), the initial reaction of parents is one of *shock,* even though they frequently suspect that their child has a problem before it is confirmed by professionals. Then parents typically go through a period of *denial.* They may seek other professional opinions during this stage, hoping for a more promising diagnosis. Although parents' lives are often thrown into a state of confusion and turmoil, they may deny that the handicap has an emotional effect. Denial may also take the form of unrealistic planning for the child. This stage is the result of a number of factors, including cultural pressure for the "ideal" child, the level of success expected by the parent, and parental identification with the handicapped child — that is, regarding the child's problem as a problem in oneself. The denial reaction is illustrated in the following quotes, which, like the others in this section of the chapter, are taken from interviews with parents of children with Down's syndrome.

> "The doctor said it wasn't our fault. I know God didn't make her this way but he permitted it to be; it was the only way I could have been brought to God; I used to swear and drink.... By God's permission I expect some day Alice will be healed — I really do."

> "With the progress Martha's making, we feel she isn't severely retarded and may outgrow the condition. I really feel she'll be all right.... We moved out here in order to put her in school. It was the big sacrifice in comparison to how little she's learning. I think we should be looking for a private school" [Kramm, 1963, p. 12].

After the denial stage, feelings of *guilt* often appear. Parents may blame themselves, circumstances, other people, or God. The effects of this fault finding may be felt by physicians, teachers, family members, and other people in the community.

During the period of adjustment to the handicap, parents may experience a number of emotions. They may feel *sorrow* and have a tendency to *withdraw* into themselves. They may also develop *fear* of the future. This may result in *overprotectiveness* expressed through excessive attention and care. Parents may try to keep the child on an infantile level, as illustrated in this quote:

> "Rose is sometimes so good and sometimes so bad. She runs around in the stores touching everything and calling attention to herself. She throws stones at the children. Her father wants to protect her. He carries her around, and wants to do everything for her. He never says no to her. He's strict with the boys but he lets Rose get away with everything. Sometimes the younger boy teases her. Once he called her 'Nosy-Rosey.' My husband got very angry and said, 'Don't let me ever hear you say that again!' I told him if he took that stand the boys would get to hate Rose" [Kramm, 1963, p. 15].

Another possible reaction is *rejection* of the child. In some cases this is overt, and the child is openly resented. Society or professionals may be blamed for the child's handicap. The following examples illustrate overt rejection:

> The father of a ten-year-old said:
> "This kind of child brings only worry and sacrifice. If it's just work and physical care that's involved, you can take it — you know it will come out all right in the end — but not this — if you have your faculties you have everything — but when you don't have them. . . ."

> The mother of a fifteen-year-old said:
> "What use is it to have children when you have this kind? What good are they? They change your life and personality. You become flat. They take everything from you and give nothing in return. They tie you down and there is no one to help you. It takes a lot out of you. You become a machine. Everything has to be done in a routine order to train them. It's not just doing the same thing over and over. It's that there's so little progress to show for the effort."

> The mother of a twenty-two-year-old said:
> "I have some allergies I didn't have before. He just about ruined my life. Just when he should be taking me around, I have to take him. I just wonder how much longer it will last" [Kramm, 1963, p. 39].

Rejection can also be *disguised*, as when parents consider the handicap a disgrace. Resentment can be concealed by an overly solicitous attitude:

> "I wonder if I'm really doing right by placing Dorothy. Especially now that she's in school and doing so nicely. I feel quite guilty. I'm going to miss her. She's always so happy to see me when she comes home from school. . . . All my relatives feel she should be placed. My mother said, 'You'll just have to put her away.' My sister doesn't ask to have her visit them. She only asks John. I feel by placing Dorothy we will avoid embarrassment for John when he dates — also loss of family friends who might stay away on account of her" [Kramm, 1963, p. 29].

Rejecting parents may set low expectations for the child and, in extreme cases, ignore or even abandon her.

Finally, many parents reach the stage of *acceptance*. They admit that the child has a disability but feel no guilt and do not resent society. Some parents reach this stage quickly, some slowly, and some never really face the realities of a handicapping condition. The parents must face these realities over and over again. As any parent will tell you, they go to bed with them and they wake up with them. Both denial and acceptance are positive reactions, because they permit the child to grow and develop. The following statement from the mother of a moderately retarded child exemplifies the process of acceptance:

> "Just at first it was hard taking Tony out. Not that I was ashamed — I guess I was just mad at society for not knowing that these things can happen. Now I don't mind the staring. At first I felt bitter — But not for long. Tony has added

more to this home than he has taken from it. Life without children would be empty. I would like to have Tony normal, but since that can't be, I want more children and normal ones" [Kramm, 1963, p. 41].

These emotional stages often overlap, of course (Sommer, 1944). Furthermore, spouses may react differently to the handicap, as this father indicated:

"[My wife] was more, well, geared, I would say, to accept that David was handicapped. I didn't want to accept it at all. I felt, 'Wow,' you know. Here we have a handicapped child, and I found myself being defensive. I didn't care to take him out in public. It just struck me as . . . I just didn't know how to really act with him out in public. My wife, she'd stop and explain, and to me, it tore me apart to have somebody ask me a question: 'What's wrong with him?' But then we became involved here with the group. This is when I finally came to the point where I could finally accept that: 'Well, gee, there are other families that are in the same position as we are — they have a handicapped child also'" [Adapted from English and Olson, 1976, pp. 14–15].

Parental reactions are especially important because they can affect the handicapped child's behavior (Symonds, 1947). If accepted by parents, exceptional children may have more socially acceptable behavior and be more cooperative, friendly, honest, emotionally stable, and cheerful. If not accepted, they may be emotionally unstable, restless, resentful, and excessively active. Overprotective parents can cause their children to be overly dependent and can impair their motivation.

Alternative suggestions about the emotional stages that parents of handicapped children pass through can be found in Chinn, Winn, and Walters (1978); Stewart (1978); Turnbull and Turnbull (1978); and Wolfensberger (1967).

REACTIONS OF OTHER FAMILY MEMBERS

Like parents, other members of the family must adjust to the handicapped child's condition (Wolfensberger, 1967). Many families have successfully integrated a handicapped member into the full range of family activities, but it takes lots of love and a high level of commitment, communication, and work.

In large part, siblings adopt the attitudes of their parents toward the handicapped child (Klein, 1972). Unless the family is well integrated, the handicapped child may become the scapegoat for the family's problems. Siblings may resent excessive attention given to the disabled child if they become neglected in the process. Sibling responses are most favorable when the family is close and shares the same goals. Families with relatively independent children are generally better at accepting the handicapped. Grossman (1972) found positive reactions among some of the nonhandicapped siblings he interviewed.

According to Cansler and Martin (1974) sibling concerns may include (1) curiosity about the cause of the handicap and its effect on them, (2) inability to

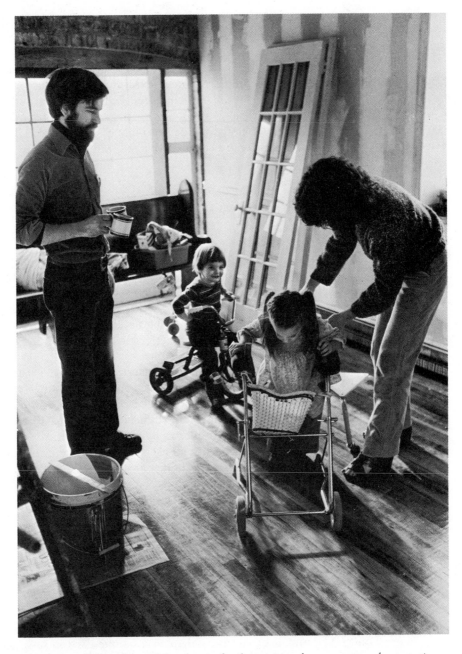

By including their handicapped daughter in family activities, these parents are demonstrating their acceptance of her. This will have a positive effect on the attitude that their nonhandicapped son will develop toward his sister.

talk to their parents about the handicapped child, in spite of their desire to do so, (3) worry about the reactions of their friends, and (4) worry about whether they will have to care for the handicapped child in the future.

A number of authors have addressed the subject of the handicapped child's interaction with the family. Moore and Morton (1976) suggest a number of books for children to read about handicaps. Landau, Epstein, and Stone (1978) have compiled an anthology of popular writings about the handicapped. Grossman (1972) has interviewed the normal siblings of retarded children and provides information useful in a cooperative family effort to integrate a handicapped child.

PARENTAL NEEDS

For parents to understand and adapt to their child's handicap, they must generally learn a considerable amount of new information. Although certain kinds of handicaps require specific knowledge, many needs are common to the parents of all handicapped children (English and Olson, 1976; Kanner, 1953; McLoughlin and Kershman, 1979; Stewart, 1978; Turnbull and Turnbull, 1978; Wolfensberger, 1967).

Understanding the Handicap. The first concern of most parents is to understand their child's problem. This often involves becoming familiar with diagnostic procedures. Finding the appropriate specialists can present problems, and once they are discovered it is sometimes difficult to get unanimous opinions. A frequent complaint is that diagnostic information has been withheld, or that information is presented in professional jargon that is difficult to understand.

The etiology of the disorder is another area of interest, particularly in the case of genetic disorders, such as Down's syndrome. Parents may also wonder whether exceptionalities such as learning disabilities and emotional disturbance will affect other children they may have planned to have. A knowledge of prenatal, perinatal, and postnatal causes of disabilities will be useful to parents who are genuinely interested in discovering whether they are responsible for their child's problem. Some exceptionalities, such as emotional disturbance, are influenced by environmental factors. When this is true, parents may be relieved to discover that they can do something about the problem.

An important area of parental concern is the child's potential for development. This will be determined by such factors as the disability's severity and age of onset. The parents of young children may be interested in such developmental areas as speech and language. Later concerns may involve academic achievement and school behavior. The parents of exceptional adults may have questions about their child's employability and what approach to take regarding sexual relations.

A list of publications of interest to parents of handicapped children has been prepared by Moore and Morton (1976).

Services and Resources. Parents of exceptional children frequently do not know what services are available to them and where to get them. Here are some important questions that are asked about services:

1. How does one go about finding the specialists appropriate to the child's needs? Exceptional children may need assistance in a number of areas, such as language, academic skills, motor skills, vocational training, and social and emotional behavior. Each area has its own specialists. For example, children with motor problems may be served by physical therapists.
2. What medical treatments and adaptive devices would benefit the child? Parents may have questions about drugs, vitamin therapy, diet control, sterilization, and other medical techniques. They may also be interested in finding out about the maintenance, use, and repair of braces, wheelchairs, hearing aids, glasses, and other devices.
3. How much will meeting the needs of the child cost? Specialists, medication, adaptive devices, and special schools are all expensive. Although PL 94-142 guarantees a free and appropriate education to all handicapped children, the cost of additional services can be substantial.
4. What school programs are available? Parents should be familiar with the various options available in the public schools and with their educational methods and materials. Some parents will be interested in home-based programs. In consultation with professionals, parents must decide which program is most suitable for their child.
5. Should the child be placed in a residential facility or kept at home? This is one of the most difficult decisions parents face. To determine the best course parents must learn about the facility's financial requirements, planning and evaluation procedures, accreditation, program objectives, administrator and teacher qualifications, philosophy and structure, and recreational and social facilities.
6. What governmental agencies, laws, and regulations can be of use to the parents of the handicapped? Parents should know how to lobby for support and services, and how to make the public aware of the needs of the handicapped.
7. What parent organizations and training groups are available, and what services do they provide? These organizations can provide assistance and information about transportation, babysitting, camps, and other services and activities.

Parents may find that the necessary special services are not available, or that they are very expensive and yield few discernible benefits. In addition, parents frequently complain that they are not included in decision making, that they aren't informed about their child's progress, and that they have to maintain constant vigilance to ensure that the child is receiving the necessary services. Professionals should realize that parental anger is caused by society's frequent insensitivity and incompetence in meeting the needs of the handicapped. It should be remembered that the enactment of PL 94–142 was largely the result of the activism of concerned parents.

Other Considerations. In addition to the concerns already mentioned, parents must make other adjustments and resolve other types of problems. Child management is an area of concern for many parents. They will be interested in the child's behavior problems at school and may want to learn strategies to be used in the home. Problems may arise in feeding, toileting, discipline, sexual activity, dating, and other areas. Parents should be familiar with scheduling techniques, the design of barrier-free environments, planning methods, and so forth.

Parents must also decide what to tell the handicapped child's siblings about his condition, and be prepared to explain his behavior to friends, neighbors, and relatives. Finding playmates may be difficult, particularly if the child has a behavior problem. There may also be difficulties in taking the exceptional child to shopping and recreational facilities. In addition, parents must generally search for understanding and competent doctors, dentists, and other specialists.

Parents must also take time for their own fulfillment. It is sometimes difficult to find acceptable babysitters and care centers. Some parents have to learn how to seek support from other people, such as relatives or professionals.

Some problems are encountered only by the parents of children with a particular kind of problem. Reference works that describe the needs of these parents include: for the learning disabled, Wallace and McLoughlin (1979); for the autistic, Warren (1978); for the emotionally disturbed, Park and Shapiro (1976); for the multiply handicapped, Gordon (1977); for the retarded, Chinn et al. (1975); for the deaf and blind, Kakalik, Brewer, Doughtery, Fleischauer, and Genesky, 1973); for the physically handicapped, Joel (1975) and Finnie (1975); for the blind, Lowenfeld (1971); for the deaf, Bloom (1970); and for the speech and language impaired, Schreiber (1973).

PROBE 13-1
Effects of the Handicapped on Families

1. T   F   Parents should not discuss their handicapped child with their non-handicapped children.

2. Name four of the typical emotional stages the parents of a handicapped child may pass through before they accept their child's condition.

    a. _____

    b. _____

    c. _____

    d. _____

3. What are three problems that the parents of exceptional children may encounter in searching for services?

    a. _____

    b. _____

    c. _____

4. Name six areas about which the parents of exceptional children may need to find information.

    a. _____

    b. _____

    c. _____

    d. _____

    e. _____

    f. _____

PARENTAL INVOLVEMENT

You should be able to describe ways to involve parents in the education of their exceptional children.

The parents of exceptional children have played an important role in the initiation and development of special education programs. They have supported every major effort to develop services. It was not until after World War II that parents began to organize on behalf of their handicapped children. Groups such as the National Association for Retarded Citizens, the United Cerebral Palsy Association, and the Association for Children with Learning Disabilities have become very effective forces in determining policies and establishing programs for the handicapped.

In spite of the many contributions of parents, they have frequently been excluded from crucial aspects of the programs for their children. For the most part, education has been left to the professionals. Recently, however, parents have begun to assume a broader role in the educational process. Educators have realized that parents must participate in programs if they are to be as effective as possible.

Professional educators have been hesitant to involve parents in educational programs for a number of reasons (Kelly, 1974; Schulz, 1978). One reason is that they are sometimes reluctant to admit they need help, and that they do not have all the answers. Professionals have also claimed that parents are frequently uncaring or overprotective. Uncaring parents refuse to get involved, and overprotective parents cannot be objective. Some professionals also contend that the educational process is too complex for parents to understand, and that contact between the two groups should be limited to parent conferences several times a year. Finally, there have been claims that parents are incompetent in raising their children, and that they would add little to educational programs if they became involved in them.

Fortunately, attitudes are changing and more positive approaches to working with parents are emerging. This is due largely to the enactment of PL 94-142, which mandates increased parent involvement. However, some negative attitudes still prevail, and the educator should be on the alert to ensure that they do not interfere with cooperative efforts with parents.

Professionals often overlook ways in which parents can assist in education. Listed in Table 13-1 are some of the ways in which parents can become involved in the various stages of the educational process, and some suggestions that professionals could use to facilitate parental activities.

INTERACTING WITH PARENTS

Parents can provide valuable information and assistance to teachers at every stage of the education process. Some of the considerations that are important to teachers in interacting with the parents of exceptional children are described in the following sections.

Identification and Referral. For reliable early identification of exceptional children parents must be well informed. The parents of children referred for special education services should be interviewed to obtain information useful in diagnosing the child's problem. Parents are familiar with a great deal of information about the child that would otherwise be unavailable to the diagnostician, including the child's personal traits, interests, health history, behavior when interacting with adults and other children, and attitudes. Information such as this is necessary for a complete, valid diagnosis.

In seeking information from parents, it is important to be sensitive to parents' feelings. Only information relevant to the child's disability and the educational program should be solicited. Kroth and Simpson (1977) have suggested some guidelines for interviewing parents: (1) The interview should be conducted in a quiet, private setting. (2) The interview should be held in a positive atmosphere; at the same time, however, the interviewer should be prepared for hidden motivations and agendas. (3) Careful attention should be paid to the parents' nonverbal behavior as well as their verbal responses; by the same token, the interviewer should be aware of the messages she is sending. (4) In sharing the information obtained, the interviewer should respect the parents' right to privacy. Pleasant, constructive interaction with parents in the early stages of identification can contribute to effective cooperative efforts later on.

Assessment. Parents can assist in assessment in a number of ways. They are the primary source of information for the *Vineland Social Maturity Scale,* which, as you may remember from Chapter 7, is an instrument used to determine children's levels of adaptive behavior. Case histories are also gathered from parents.

Parents can also collect specific information by observing their child in the home. Many examples of how parents can gather such information and implement successful education programs at home are provided by Cooper and Edge (1978). Parents are infrequently involved in the administration of standardized tests, but Kroth and Simpson (1977) have found that parent-administered standardized tests yield about the same results as tests administered by teachers. McLoughlin and Lewis (1981) provide specific suggestions for involving parents in the assessment process.

Planning and Implementation. The law requires that parents be involved in developing their handicapped child's IEP. The involvement of parents at this stage serves several purposes. First, it permits parents to understand their child's program better, which may be reflected in a more positive attitude toward the program at home. This attitude may have a positive influence on the child. Second, parents are more likely to be interested in a program they are familiar with and helped to develop. Third, parental involvement eliminates the confusion and disagreement that may arise from misinformation and differing priorities. Fourth, parents are encouraged to serve as volunteers, and they can provide valuable help and permit teachers more time for individual instruction.

In implementing programs, parents can offer a number of important services. They can assist in transportation, fund-raising projects, the construction of instructional materials, and classroom activities such as dressing and feeding. Volunteer programs must be well planned and coordinated; volunteers should be trained for specific responsibilities and be carefully supervised.

Table 13-1
Areas for Parent and Professional Interaction

Stages	Parental activities	Professional facilitation
Identification	Be alert to early warning signs Be aware of etiology Be aware of services Refer child to proper service Talk to other parents	Be aware of community resources Use public service media Make information available Offer parent education groups Assure adequate funding Make services available
Assessment	Maintain a developmental log Respond to interview questions and written questionnaires Cooperate with teachers and other professionals Be a team member Agree to assessment Attend committee conferences Supply relevant information from previous evaluations	Avoid jargon Be interdisciplinary Conduct conferences slowly and clearly Be realistic Be positive Supply samples of a child's work Write understandable reports Supply assessment reports
Programming	Consider appropriate placement options and program goals Choose a placement site and program goals cooperatively Identify and choose goals for own use Attend committee conferences Visit classrooms Read parents' literature Review materials	Encourage classroom observation Explain educational curriculum Demonstrate strategies and materials Design and supply parent activities Explain placement alternatives Point out goals for parents (if advisable)

Parents can also serve as tutors and teaching aides at home and in the classroom. In this capacity parents can be of help in almost every area of instruction. Shearer (1976) suggests that professionals should provide goals that can be met in a short time when establishing parent volunteer programs. Parents should be shown what to do and how to do it and should be given an opportunity to practice the skill under supervision. The criteria for completion of instruction should also be explained. Parents should, of course, be reinforced for their participation.

There are several resources useful in guiding parental instruction and involvement. Manuals to assist parents in improving social skills have been developed by Patterson and Gullion (1971), Becker (1971), Patterson (1975), Smith and

**Table 13-1
Continued**

Stages	Parental activities	Professional facilitation
Implementation	Be a classroom aide Join parent organizations (PTA, ACLD, etc.) Support efforts of professionals Model good attitude toward program Be a tutor Reinforce child's skills at home	Supply parent education groups Support parents' organizations Supply discussion groups Maintain home programs Design materials and activities for parent use Design formal parent intervention progams in school and home
Evaluation	Hold professionals accountable Be accountable Supply feedback to professionals Help evaluate educational plans Serve on parent advisory boards Support parent activism (ACLD)	Supply parent training programs Establish parent advisory boards Support parents' organizations Include parents' contributions in evaluation procedures Facilitate communication with parents

Source: McLoughlin, J. A., Edge, D., and Strenecky, B. Perspective of parent involvement in the diagnosis and treatment of learning disabled students. *Journal of Learning Disabilities,* 1978, *11,* p. 295. Reproduced with permission of publisher.

Smith (1976), and Cooper and Edge (1978). These guides explain behavior management techniques based on the principle of applied behavioral analysis. Activities for the home in language arts and mathematics are provided by Cooper and Heron (1978). Wallace and Kauffman (1978) offer specific suggestions for remediating problems in the social-emotional and visual-motor areas, and in spoken language, written language, reading, and arithmetic. Ideas for informal assessment are arranged according to common problem areas, such as "Does the child have difficulty following directions?"

A Guide for Better Reading by Granowsky, Middleton, and Mumford (1977) describes one school system's program to improve reading. In this program teachers assess reading skills and explain the findings to parents. The parents refer to the guide for activities to use in helping their child. Ideas for evaluation are also included.

Buist and Schulman (1969) have compiled a list of toys and games that can be used with exceptional children. They are described by age in four disability categories: perception, retention and recall, conceptualization, and expression. The play format permits parents to assist their exceptional children in a pleasant fashion. Finally, Moore and Morton (1976) offer a list of readings about parents working with their exceptional children. For each area of exceptionality many examples are provided of parents assisting their children, in some cases without professional support.

Evaluation. Parents are required by law to be involved in at least one review of the child's individual education program a year. These evaluations are used to determine whether the program has been effective and whether changes in goals, objectives, placement, or procedures need to be made.

The effectiveness of parental involvement in an annual evaluation is determined largely by the extent of communication between teachers and parents during the school year. Communications with parents can be accomplished in a number of ways. Daily or weekly progress reports, graphs of child progress, and report cards that describe the child's skill levels rather than providing grades have all been used effectively (Kroth, 1975). "Smiley faces" can be used to reinforce children for meeting objectives. What is most important is that parents and teachers remain in regular contact, whether through phone calls, school conferences, written notes, home visits, casual meetings in the community, or parent groups. Every available opportunity should be used to share constructive comments about the child's behavior.

Parents can also be involved in the evaluation of their child's program by serving on advisory boards and steering committees. In these groups the opinions of parents can be solicited about a wide range of matters related to the education of exceptional children and ways of encouraging productive interaction between professionals and parents.

PROBE 13-2
Parental Involvement

1. T   F   Parents should not be involved in efforts to identify and refer handicapped children.

2. Describe three of the attitudes you might encounter among teachers opposed to parental involvement in the education of their handicapped children.

   a. _____

   b. _____

   c. _____

3. For each of the following stages of the educational process, describe a way in which parents can be of assistance, and how a professional could facilitate that particular parental effort.

   a. *Identification*

   Parent _____

   Professional _____

   b. *Assessment*

   Parent _____

   Professional _____

   c. *Programming*

   Parent _____

   Professional _____

   d. *Implementation*

   Parent _____

   Professional _____

   e. *Evaluation*

   Parent _____

   Professional _____

4. Give three reasons that parents should be involved in the education of their handicapped children.

   a. _____

   b. _____

   c. _____

PARENTS AND THE LEAST RESTRICTIVE ENVIRONMENT

You should be able to discuss implications, for parents, of educating children in the least restrictive environment.

There are several considerations involved in placing children in the regular classroom, special class, hospital setting, institution, or other administrative arrangement. The educator must meet certain legal requirements, develop parent organizations and training programs, and develop a plan for conducting parent conferences.

LEGAL RESPONSIBILITIES OF THE SCHOOLS

The parents of exceptional children have a number of rights guaranteed by law, which will be repeated here for your review.

1. The parents of the handicapped must receive written notice in their native language that the school is considering a change in their child's education program.
2. They must give permission for their child to be tested for the purpose of determining whether he should be placed in a special education program.
3. Parents have the right to an independent evaluation if they are dissatisfied with the evaluation performed by school personnel.
4. They have the right to be actively involved in the development of the child's individualized educational program.
5. They must specifically approve the placement of their child.
6. They have the right to examine all school records related to their child, and to remove inaccurate or misleading data from the child's file.
7. They may request an impartial due process hearing if they disagree with procedures or decisions relative to the placement of their child. The hearing officer may not be an employee of the school district. The parents have the right to legal counsel, and they may examine witnesses, present evidence, and obtain a written record of the hearing and findings. The hearing must be held no more than forty-five days after it is requested.
8. Parents may appeal the results of the due process hearing to the state Department of Education, which must review the appeal within thirty days. Parents can further appeal decisions to the federal courts if they are dissatisfied with the results of their appeal to the state Department of Education.

School officials must ensure that proper procedures are established to notify parents about testing placement, nonbiased assessment, record keeping, and timetables. The information collected must be kept confidential. Although the regulations mentioned were mandated specifically for the handicapped, the quality of education would be improved if they were applicable to all students.

PARENT PROGRAMS

An important part of the program for the exceptional child should be the development of a parent program. In many cases parents will be involved with the school as part of the regular parent-teacher organization. In other cases it may be desirable to establish separate groups to deal with the needs of parents of exceptional children, or to create formal programs to involve parents in the direct instruction of their children. Regardless of the type of program, the goal is to improve the educational process for everyone involved: parents, teachers, students, and administrators.

Purposes of Parent Programs. Parent programs are generally designed to provide parents with social and emotional support. By talking to parents who have similar problems and to professionals who can be of assistance, parents can learn to cope with feelings such as those described at the beginning of the chapter.

Parent programs can also provide a forum for the exchange of information. This can involve scheduling guest speakers, maintaining a lending library, or publishing a newsletter.

Parent programs frequently offer parents an opportunity to participate in their child's programs as teacher aides, volunteers, tutors, data collectors, behavior managers, or field trip monitors. A major goal of all parent programs should be to improve the interactions between parents and their exceptional child. Parent groups can help parents develop appropriate expectations for their children and strategies for better communication (Lillie and Trohanis, 1976).

Several programs have been developed that involve parents intensively in their children's education. The Portage Project, for example, provides for a teacher to visit the child's home for one and a half hours a week. During these visits, objectives for the child are developed and teaching strategies are demonstrated. The parents provide the child with the actual lessons and collect information on performance, which is reviewed the next time the teacher visits (Shearer and Shearer, 1977). The PEECH project, on the other hand, trains parents to provide instructional assistance in the classroom (Karnes and Zehrbach, 1977).

Parent Training. The development of parent programs should be a cooperative effort between parents and professionals. According to Cooper and Edge (1978), problems in parent training groups are frequently caused by unprepared group leaders, by parents who do not comply with training procedures, by difficulties in group interaction, by parents with personal problems, and by people attempting to use the group for other purposes. Before the programs are begun, parental needs should be assessed to determine what type of training is needed. Evaluations should be conducted following the training programs to determine their effectiveness and provide information for improving future training sessions. A useful annotated bibliography of training materials appropriate for the parents of exceptional children has been prepared by Strenecky, Strenecky, and Dare (1978).

Parent Conferences. In addition to the conferences held to develop the IEP, meetings should be held at intervals to discuss such factors as the child's progress, school-home cooperative programs, and other issues of concern to parents and teachers. In all professional interactions it is important that professionals communicate candidly and clearly: parents complain that information is sometimes withheld from them and that educators use jargon that they cannot understand.

Losen and Diament (1978) have listed some rules that teachers should follow when speaking to parents:

1. Do not act in an authoritarian manner.
2. Be empathetic and listen without making judgments.
3. Ask questions which open up the discussion rather than limit it.
4. Be considerate of parents' potential vulnerability about their child's problems.
5. Accord the same rights and respect to all parents that is given to parents respected as professional colleagues [p. 40].

By following these guidelines, teachers and parents can improve the chances that conferences will be conducted in an atmosphere of cooperation and increase the likelihood of success.

When considering the educational placement of the handicapped child, the advantages and disadvantages of the various service arrangements should be carefully explained to parents. Parental objections to certain kinds of classes or teachers must be taken into account in making the placement decision. The consequences of diagnostic labels and the possible reactions of others to such labels should also be explained to parents.

School personnel must be as supportive of parents as possible, because parents must give their consent to the placement decision. Parents should be made to feel comfortable in the IEP conference. Their opinions should be solicited, and they should be encouraged to make suggestions about their child's needs. School personnel should express an interest in the child, and ample time should be provided to conduct the meeting. Finally, the staff should realize that the IEP conference can be very trying for parents, and they should be prepared to deal with parents' possible emotional reactions.

PROBE 13-3
Parents and the Least Restrictive Environment

1. As a school official, describe three policies that you would establish to ensure that the legal rights of parents are protected.

   a. _____

   _____

   b. _____

   _____

   c. _____

   _____

2. Describe four purposes served by parent programs.

   a. _____

   b. _____

   c. _____

   d. _____

3. T F Because professionals are familiar with the needs of parents, they should have the major responsibility in developing parent training programs.

4. T F Assessment of parental needs is the first step in developing a parent training program.

5. T F In conducting a parent conference, professionals should try to be as nonauthoritarian as possible.

SUMMARY

1. Although reactions vary, the parents of handicapped children may experience periods of shock, denial, guilt, fear, overprotectiveness, overt rejection, and disguised rejection before reaching the stage of acceptance.
2. The attitudes of parents can improve or adversely affect the behavior of their handicapped children.
3. The siblings of handicapped children largely adopt the attitudes of their parents toward the handicapped child.

4. The parents of handicapped children need a great deal of information about such subjects as diagnosis, treatment, management, and support services.

5. The relationship between parents and professionals concerned with handicapped children is gradually improving. Successful relationships depend on mutual trust and understanding.

6. Parents can assist in the identification, assessment, and programming of their children and in the implementation and evaluation of their children's programs.

7. Parents have the legal right to be involved in all decisions regarding the education of their handicapped children. They also have the protection of due process if they are dissatisfied with the educational program that has been provided.

8. Parent programs should provide emotional support, a forum for the exchange of information, an opportunity to participate in the child's program, and parent–child interaction training.

9. Professionals should be candid with parents and communicate in a nonauthoritarian manner. Parents should be treated with consideration and sensitivity.

TASK SHEET 13
Field Experiences with Parents of Exceptional Children

Select *one* of the following alternatives and complete the required tasks. Write a report of no more than three pages about your activities.

Parent Interview

Interview the parents of a gifted or handicapped child. Using great tact, ask about their reactions when they learned that their child was exceptional. Try to determine the problems that the parents encountered in attempting to obtain services. If the parents have gone through the due process procedures mandated by PL 94–142, determine how they reacted to the experience.

Observation

Observe the meeting of a placement committee in your local school district. Describe how the professionals interacted with the parents at the meeting, and how the parents participated. Determine whether the parents' rights were correctly observed. What was your reaction to the procedure?

Professional Interview

Interview a professional person about her experience with the parents of exceptional children. If the professional participates in parental involvement programs, ask her to describe them.

Participation

Offer your services to a parent training program or other program in which parents are involved.

Library Study

Use the library to identify at least three articles related to the parents of the handicapped. Write a one-page critique of each.

Design Your Own Field Experience

If none of these alternatives is attractive to you, or if you have the opportunity to perform some other task with parents of exceptional children, design your own field experience. Check with your instructor to determine its acceptability.

Probe Answers

Probe 13–1

1. False
2. Any four of the following:
   a. shock
   b. denial
   c. guilt
   d. fear
   e. sorrow
   f. withdrawal
   g. rejection
3. a. not knowing whom to go to
   b. not getting understandable information
   c. getting varying opinions
4. a. locating specialists
   b. available medical treatment
   c. cost of care and treatment
   d. available school programs
   e. appropriate placement
   f. laws that apply

Probe 13–2

1. False
2. a. Teachers are trained professionals and do not need parental help.
   b. Parents do not care about their handicapped children and do not want to get involved.

   c. Parents are overprotective of their children and lack objectivity to help them.
3. a. *Identification*
      Parent: being alert to early warning signs
      Professional: making information available
   b. *Assessment*
      Parent: responding to interview questions and written questionnaires
      Professional: writing understandable reports
   c. *Programming*
      Parent: identifying and choosing goals for own use
      Professional: encouraging classroom observations
   d. *Implementation*
      Parent: being a classroom aide
      Professional: designing materials and activities for parental use
   e. *Evaluation*
      Parent: supplying feedback to professionals
      Professional: establishing parent advisory boards
4. a. Parents are required to participate in the IEP process.
   b. Parents are a valuable source of information about behavior seen most often in the home setting.

c. Early identification of problems may be up to parents.

Probe 13–3

1. Any three of the following:
    a. Give parents prior written notice in their native language of any program change. Develop the necessary forms. Maintain documentation.
    b. Obtain parental permission before testing a child. Maintain suitable records.
    c. Let parents know they have a right to an independent evaluation. Supply information about where they can get it done.
    d. Alert parents to the time, place, and purpose of the conference at which the child's individualized educational program is developed. Involve them at the actual meeting.
    e. Get parental approval of placement in special education. Prepare the necessary forms and maintain suitable records.
    f. Inform parents of their right to examine the child's school records. Also, explain the procedures for changing the records.
    g. Inform parents of impartial due process hearing procedures in case they disagree with any procedures or decisions.
    h. Inform parents of procedures to appeal the results of the due process hearing to the State Department of Education. Parents should also know that they can file a lawsuit if they are still dissatisfied after a state department review.
2. a. providing social-emotional support
    b. fostering exchange of information
    c. encouraging parental participation in the child's program
    d. developing better parent-child interaction
3. False
4. True
5. True

1. Teachers each day will fill lamps, clean chimneys, and trim wicks. Wash windows once each week.

2. Each teacher will bring in a bucket of water and a scuttle of coal for the day's session.

3. Make pen nibs carefully. You may whittle nibs to your individual tastes.

4. Men teachers will be given one evening off each week for courting purposes, or two evenings off a week if they go regularly to church.

5. After ten hours in school, the teacher should spend the remaining time reading the Bible and other good books.

6. All teachers are encouraged to take complete baths with soap at least every week, and change underclothing frequently to avoid offending others.

7. Women teachers who marry or engage in unseemly conduct will be dismissed.

8. Every teacher should lay aside from each pay a goodly sum of his earnings for his benefit during his declining years so that he will not become a burden on society.

9. Any teacher who smokes Spanish cigars, uses liquor in any form, or frequents pool and public halls or gets shaved in a barber shop, will give good reason to suspect his worth, intentions, integrity and honesty.

10. The teacher who has performed his labor faithfully and without fault for five years will be given an increase of five cents per day in his pay, providing the Board of Education approves.

14

Continuing Professional Development

A. Edward Blackhurst

A. Edward Blackhurst is a Professor and past Chairman in the Department of Special Education at the University of Kentucky. Dr. Blackhurst has directed projects on special education instructional materials, the uses of communication satellites in special education, scholarship programs for special education teachers, and the training of special education administrators. He was also instrumental in developing Teaching Exceptional Children, *a journal for special education teachers.*

The rules for teachers listed on the facing page are said to have been posted by the principal of a New York school in 1872. They probably reflect the attitudes and expectations of society toward teaching at that point in history. Fortunately, times have changed. Although teachers are still expected to conduct their personal lives in a fashion that is consistent with prevailing community standards, there is now more concern with their professional competence than their personal habits.

When you complete your formal education, you should be competent to begin teaching. You should realize, however, that you will have to continue to develop your professional skills throughout your career. The field of special education is developing so rapidly that teachers must work diligently to keep up with new information, diagnostic instruments, instructional materials, and teaching methods.

In 1975 the Council for Exceptional Children (CEC) adopted a set of ethical standards to guide professionals who work with exceptional children. These contrast sharply with the "Rules for Teachers" written a little more than a century before. One of these guidelines reads as follows:

> Responsibility and accountability for the continuing professional development and performance of special education personnel rest mainly with the individual. Preparation and employment agencies should support, assist, and encourage

ongoing professional development. Assuming that the opportunities for continuing professional development are present, the responsibility for using the opportunities rests with the individual [*Guidelines for Personnel in the Education of Exceptional Children*, 1976, p. 49].

In this chapter a model will be presented that can be used to develop a personal program of professional development. The various elements that should be considered will be described, and suggestions will be made for the application of the principles that are discussed. These suggestions should be useful to both the beginning special education student and the practicing professional. Teachers can use the information to plan for future professional growth, and students can use it to analyze their abilities and the quality of their education. In fact, the information presented here can be used to evaluate your entire special education training program.

DESIGNING A PROFESSIONAL DEVELOPMENT PROGRAM

You should be able to design a personal program of professional development in special education.

Much of the professional development of teachers occurs in a rather haphazard fashion. Although almost all special educators are members of professional organizations and attend in-service training programs, they may participate only when it is convenient, or when attendance is required by school administrators. Few professionals systematically appraise their needs and develop a plan to meet them. The pressures of work, home, family, and social obligations often relegate professional development to a position of low priority. Although almost everyone has said, "I must learn how to do this," or "I must learn more about that topic," the time and the initiative are frequently lacking.

One reason for this desultory approach is that the subject of professional development is seldom approached systematically. To use time and resources efficiently, it is necessary to design a specific plan and carry out planned activities. This process should involve a number of activities, including those illustrated in Figure 14-1.

To use this model of professional development you would begin with the task to the left of the model, "Develop and Maintain Philosophy," and proceed in sequence through the others. The long block at the bottom simply indicates that you must continually evaluate, revise, and refine your program if your approach to professional development is to remain flexible.

In the following pages the elements of the model and how to use them will be

Figure 14-1
Professional Development Model

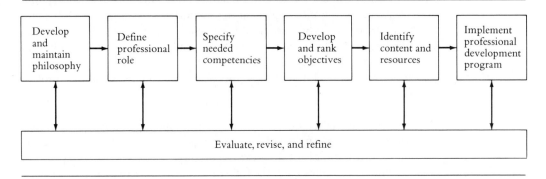

| Develop and maintain philosophy | Define professional role | Specify needed competencies | Develop and rank objectives | Identify content and resources | Implement professional development program |

Evaluate, revise, and refine

explained. You should note that the successful use of the model is based on three suppositions: (1) that you will apply principles described in a systematic fashion; (2) that you will analyze your abilities and needs; and (3) that you will maintain the initiative to conduct the required activities. If these three rules are followed, you should be able to develop a program of professional development that will effectively meet your needs.

ELEMENT ONE: DEVELOP AND MAINTAIN A PHILOSOPHY

The first element in the model involves developing a personal philosophy. A "philosophy" can be defined as "an integrated personal view that serves to guide the individual's conduct and thinking" (Good, 1959, p. 395).

The development of a philosophy is very important: as the definition implies, it can serve as the conceptual foundation for all professional activities. In most teacher education programs, however, little attention is paid to it. Although many teacher training programs expose students to a variety of philosophical viewpoints, and attempts are often made to encourage students to adopt the philosophy held by the program's faculty, little emphasis is usually placed on the student developing her own philosophy. Neither students nor professionals are often asked to articulate or demonstrate their philosophy of special education.

It is very difficult to design guidelines for the development of a philosophy, because so many variables are involved. A person's philosophy is a reflection of his values, ethics, logic, aesthetics, and perceptions of knowledge, reality, and truth. There are, however, four criteria that can be used by everyone in the development of a philosophy, regardless of their philosophical orientation:

1. Develop your philosophy to the point where you can articulate it concisely

for other professionals. You should also be able to explain it to parents and other people who may not have training in special education.

2. You should be able to defend your philosophy. This entails understanding what aspects of the philosophy can be supported with logic and facts, and which aspects are derived from your values.
3. Be flexible. You should be receptive to new information, and be willing to modify your philosophy in light of new experiences.
4. Demonstrate your philosophy by applying it in your personal and professional life.

If you meet these criteria, and share with other special educators a commitment to improving the quality of life for exceptional children, your particular philosophical orientation is of no great importance.

In analyzing your philosophy, the following questions may help you focus on some of the basic issues:

— What are the responsibilities of society in providing for exceptional children?
— What are the responsibilities of the professionals concerned with the welfare of exceptional children?
— What should the relationship be between the special and general educator? How should they interact?
— What are the goals for the group of exceptional children I am working with?
— What theories of learning and instruction do I subscribe to and use in working with exceptional children?
— What is my position on issues such as normalization, human rights, institutionalization, mainstreaming, sterilization, individualized instruction, intelligence testing, genetic counseling, abortion, behavior modification, professional accountability, etiologies, labeling, and other contemporary issues?
— What is my rationale for doing each of my professional activities in one way rather than another?

Many other questions could be posed about the roles of schools and other agencies, about the education profession, and about specific teaching techniques. If you cannot answer a question or are dissatisfied with your answer, you should involve yourself in experiences that will permit you to develop or refine your thoughts about the subject of the question.

Experience shows that the most competent special educators are those who have a well-developed philosophy. They are the most effective teachers, they have the most self-confidence, and they are the most comfortable and secure in their professional activities. The first priority of those who do not have a solid philosophical base should be to develop one.

One point deserves to be reemphasized: it is not enough merely to be able to articulate your philosophy; you must be able to demonstrate it in your life as well. It is hypocritical to articulate one philosophical position and act according to the dictates of another, but unfortunately some people do just that.

This teacher's philosophy of special education calls for educating handicapped children with nonhandicapped children to the greatest extent possible. As can be seen, her actions reflect her philosophy.

ELEMENT TWO: DEFINE PROFESSIONAL ROLES

The second element of the professional development model involves the definition of the roles and functions of the special educator. This type of analysis is given surprisingly little thought, even by students in the field. An undergraduate might plan on teaching the mildly or moderately retarded; a masters student might hope to become a resource room teacher or diagnostic-prescriptive specialist; or a doctoral candidate might express an interest in special education administration or college teaching.

Too frequently, students pay little attention to the unique functions that must be performed in assuming any of these roles. As they are about to be graduated, students often express concern about their ability to assume these roles. Part of the reason for their concern, of course, is that they are suddenly faced with the fact that reality is confronting them. Of equal importance, however, is that they never really took the time to analyze the specific tasks or functions that they would be required to perform after they assumed a new position. The student who has made the effort to identify responsibilities that will be required will not be caught unprepared to assume these responsibilities.

Let us assume that you are interested in becoming a resource teacher for children with mild learning and behavior disorders. One of your most important activities would be to identify the tasks you must be able to perform to do your job successfully. You could do this in a number of ways. You could talk to resource teachers and experts, and observe resource teachers at work. You could research the job in the library. The result might be a list of the tasks the resource teacher must be able to do, such as this one:

— Assess learner behavior.
— Design and implement instruction programs.
— Select and use instructional materials.
— Manage the learning environment.
— Provide for the needs of children with sensory and physical impairments.
— Initiate resource teacher programs.
— Implement due process safeguards.
— Work effectively with parents.
— Maintain student records.
— Demonstrate appropriate professional behavior [Blackhurst, McLoughlin, and Price, 1977].

Although this list might not apply to all resource teaching arrangements, it does provide a general guideline for the job's responsibilities. If you were already a resource teacher and planned to stay in that position, you would simply list your job's responsibilities.

ELEMENT THREE: SPECIFY NEEDED COMPETENCIES

Once the responsibilities of the job are defined, you should ask yourself two questions: (1) Which responsibilities am I completely unprepared for? and (2) In which do I need additional experience? The answers would provide the general topic areas for your professional development program.

The next step would be to determine what competencies are needed in each of the topic areas. As part of this process you would also discover more detailed information about the general responsibilities identified in the previous step. This would be accomplished by determining what competencies are involved in each general responsibility (Blackhurst et al., 1977). This process is illustrated in the following pages.

Chart 14-1
Competencies Required to Assess Learner Behavior

Special education teachers should be able to:

1. administer, score, and evaluate the results of standardized individual and group achievement tests.
2. use the results of standardized psychological assessment instruments.
3. administer, score, and evaluate the results of formal and informal diagnostic and prescriptive instruments to determine the students' abilities in each major area of instruction.
4. use direct observation techniques to evaluate student performance and identify behaviors that need to be modified.

Assessment of Learner Behavior. Special educators must be able to use assessment procedures and instruments to identify exceptional children. They must also be able to use in-depth diagnostic procedures to identify the educational strengths and weakness of children who are referred. The results provide the basis for the child's IEP. Because there are few published tests that are appropriate for exceptional children, the special educator must also be skilled in informal assessment and in direct observation. For the competencies required in assessment see Chart 14-1.

Design and Implementation of Instructional Programs. Once the child's educational needs have been assessed, the special education teacher must design an appropriate individual education program that specifies exactly what type of instruction is required (Chart 14-2). Then, in the least restrictive educational setting, instruction is begun.

Selection and Use of Instructional Materials. The variety of available instructional materials has grown dramatically during the past ten years. The quality of these materials varies considerably, however, and the special education teacher must be able to select and use those which are most effective (see Chart 14-3). If appropriate materials are not available, the teacher should be able to design her own.

Management of the Learning Environment. A major responsibility of the special educator is to provide individual instruction. To do so, the educator must be able to manipulate the many variables in the learning environment (see Chart 14-4). This is often accomplished through the use of behavioral management techniques.

Chart 14-2
Competencies Required to Design and Implement Instructional Programs

Special education teachers should be able to:
1. derive educationally relevant information from formal and informal assessment instruments.
2. identify and describe long-term educational goals and short-term behavioral objectives for each student.
3. perform task analyses.
4. organize student objectives in sequence from the easy to the more difficult in each instructional area.
5. design instructional programs that match the objectives for each student.
6. implement the instructional programs.
7. use instructional procedures appropriate to the learning task.
8. provide individualized instruction for students.
9. monitor educational progress systematically and continuously.
10. make use of the principles of applied behavioral analysis in instructional programs.
11. modify existing instructional programs or devise new ones based on the results of your program evaluation.

Provide for the Needs of Children with Sensory and Physical Impairments. Special educators frequently work with children who have impaired vision, hearing, speech, or physical functioning. They must be able to modify their instructional approaches to accommodate the special needs of these children (see Chart 14-5). Children with impairments are increasingly being educated in the regular classroom, so the resource teacher must also be able to advise the regular classroom teacher on ways to modify instructional programming to improve these children's integration.

Chart 14-3
Competencies Required to Select and Use Instructional Materials

Special education teachers should be able to:
1. evaluate instructional materials to determine their quality.
2. select and adapt instructional materials to meet specific objectives.
3. select and use a variety of instructional equipment.
4. use programmed and autoinstructional materials.
5. design, construct, and use teacher-made instructional materials when necessary.
6. identify, locate, and use professional literature, and demonstrate a knowledge of informational services.
7. match the materials to the needs of the learners.
8. identify and implement measurement techniques to evaluate the effectiveness of the materials used.

Chart 14-4
Competencies Required to Manage the Learning Environment

Special education teachers should be able to:
1. adjust the learning environment to facilitate learning, particularly for children who are distractible or hyperactive.
2. establish rapport with students.
3. use a positive approach in managing the classroom through the use of such techniques as preventive discipline, behavior modification, active listening, and contingency contracting.
4. manage behavior through the use of nonverbal signals.
5. use verbal communication effectively. State directions clearly, ask appropriate questions, use good grammar, and develop positive, negative, and neutral inflections.
6. use clinical and precision teaching techniques.
7. manage individual, small-group, and large-group instructional settings.

Implement Resource Teacher Programs. Only teachers who work with the mildly handicapped have the responsibility of implementing resource teacher programs, because these children spend most of the school day in the regular classroom. In addition to having the competencies listed in Chart 14-6, the resource teacher must be able to get along well with others. It is also important that she be mature, because she will frequently be required to work closely with general education teachers who have many more years of experience.

Chart 14-5
Competencies Required to Meet the Needs
of Children with Sensory and Physical Impairments

Special education teachers should be able to:
1. modify the environment of the classroom to meet the needs of children with sensory or physical disabilities.
2. deal with seizures in the classroom.
3. adapt materials for use by children who use prosthetic devices.
4. identify, obtain, and operate adaptive and assistive equipment.
5. lift and transfer physically impaired children safely.
6. provide classroom support for programs in adaptive physical education and physical therapy.
7. provide opportunities for sensory and physically impaired children to interact socially with their peers.
8. provide support for children suffering from emotional stress as a result of their impairments.
9. use devices designed to compensate for low vision or hearing.

Chart 14-6
Competencies Required to Implement Resource Teacher Programs

Resource teachers should be able to:
1. obtain cooperation from school administrators and general education faculty.
2. explain the principles and practices of mainstreaming to other educators.
3. coordinate scheduling.
4. share materials, approaches, equipment, and ideas.
5. counsel, support, and encourage regular teachers to facilitate the integration of the handicapped child into the regular classroom.
6. perform effectively as part of an interdisciplinary team, and know how to assist in assigning staff members to students, in obtaining information about students for ancillary personnel, and in referring students to specialists.
7. use the services of ancillary personnel and appropriate referral procedures.

Implement Due Process Safeguards. Special education teachers and school systems are considered legally responsible if the rights of disabled children or their parents are violated. Great care should be exercised in protecting these rights (see Chart 14-7), but special educators should carry liability insurance to cover them in the event of an inadvertent violation. Such insurance is available through professional organizations such as The Council for Exceptional Children.

Work Effectively with Parents. Good parent-teacher interactions are especially important in the education of exceptional children. Children can be educated more efficiently if parents provide reinforcement; by the same token, children may progress slowly if parents and teachers work at cross-purposes. See Chart 14-8 for the competencies you will need in this area.

Maintain Student Records. Accurate, up-to-date records are an important tool in the development of the IEP required by federal law. Adequate record keeping also makes it easier to work with parents. The competencies required in this area are listed in Chart 14-9.

Chart 14-7
Competencies Required to Implement Due Process Safeguards

Special education teachers should be able to:
1. follow local, state, and federal laws, regulations, and guidelines.
2. use unbiased procedures for screening, assessing, and placing exceptional children.
3. design individual education plans for exceptional children.
4. adhere to the regulations related to the confidentiality of student records.

Chart 14-8
Competencies Required to Work Effectively with Parents

Special education teachers should be able to:
1. establish rapport with parents.
2. deal with the handicapped child's problems in a sensitive way.
3. develop channels of communication with parents.
4. conduct parent conferences.
5. offer constructive suggestions and support to the child's parents.
6. develop and supervise instruction and management programs for use by parents.

Demonstrate Appropriate Professional Behavior. Although the competencies in Chart 14-10 are less specific than some of the previous ones, they are among the most important. These general principles provide the foundation for effective teaching.

The competencies in Charts 14-1 through 14-10 would be equally applicable to general education teachers. This emphasizes the fact that, just as exceptional children resemble other children in more ways than they differ from them, special education teachers resemble general education teachers in many of their responsibilities. Special educators generally have a greater depth of knowledge and more specific skills because they are more highly educated. In addition, they may have responsibilities such as operating resource rooms and providing consultation services, and they have been trained to teach children who present more difficult educational problems.

To plan a professional development program you would analyze your ability to perform each of the competencies. You might be interested in comparing this list with the courses you plan to take during the rest of your educational program, to see whether the courses provide the necessary training. If formal instruction is not available, you might be able to plan independent study or bring about a change in your college curriculum.

Chart 14-9
Competencies Required to Maintain Student Records

Special education teachers should be able to:
1. collect, organize, and maintain records of academic performance.
2. develop a system for evaluating student performance, using direct measurement and charting of student behavior.
3. prepare clear, concise, objective, and diplomatic progress reports and referrals.
4. maintain anecdotal records about student's emotional development and behavior.

Chart 14-10
Competencies Required to Demonstrate
Appropriate Professional Behavior

Special education teachers should be able to:
1. develop an educational philosophy and demonstrate it in their professional activities.
2. facilitate the activities of others in a sensitive, humanistic fashion.
3. maintain flexibility and be receptive to educational change.
4. engage in a continuing program of professional and personal development.
5. use the community agencies and professional resources that provide services to exceptional children, their parents, and those who work with them.
6. conduct professional activities in an ethical fashion.

ELEMENT FOUR: DEVELOP AND RANK OBJECTIVES

Once you have determined which competencies you need to work on, you may need to develop specific objectives to guide the remainder of the program, and rank these objectives in order of importance.

Some competencies will have been stated clearly enough in the previous stage that it will not be necessary to make them more specific. For example, the fourth competency involved in working effectively with parents is "Be able to conduct parent conferences." This description alone might be explicit enough to direct activities for some people. For others, however, it may still be too general, in which case it will be necessary to break it down into more specific areas of interest. One might ask questions such as these:

1. How can one establish rapport with parents?
2. Are there general rules for what one should or should not do in conferences?
3. What are some of the common concerns of the parents of exceptional children?
4. How can one make constructive criticisms of parents without being threatening?
5. What should be done when parents obviously disagree with each other about what should have been done with their child in a particular situation?

Such questions can be used to develop very specific program objectives. Some people require more specific objectives than others. More experienced persons typically prefer to use relatively general objectives, because they are familiar with the task and are familiar with their own educational strengths and weaknesses. What is most important is that the list of objectives be specific enough to provide an orientation for future activities.

The most important considerations in determining the priorities of objectives are probably the immediacy of the problem and the amount of prior experience. For example, if you identified a need for additional work in reading instruction and in conducting parent conferences, and your reading program was progressing smoothly but you were soon to begin parent conferences, the latter would be your top priority. As you can see, setting priorities is determined subjectively, according to one's perception of the area of greatest need.

Although it is customary to think of objectives as including clearly defined conditions, behaviors, and criteria (Mager, 1962), these factors are not crucial to the use of this professional development model. What is most important is that you know what you need to accomplish and when you need to accomplish it.

It is also important not to overlook development in areas for which objectives are difficult to establish, such as affective development or experiential learning. An example of an experiential development activity would be sitting in on another teacher's classes, or observing an interdisciplinary meeting to assign staff to a particular student. Activities of this sort might provide insight into personal behavior or into the circumstances that affect an educational situation.

ELEMENT FIVE: IDENTIFY CONTENT AND RESOURCES

Once the professional development program's objectives have been identified and priorities have been established, it is necessary to identify the materials needed to attain the objectives.

An obvious source of information is other people, including colleagues, supervisors, people from related professions, university professors, and librarians. There are also many state and local agencies that can provide information, including those concerned with health and mental health, education, rehabilitation, and welfare. Private agencies, such as associations for retarded citizens, sheltered workshops, and clinics are also valuable sources.

A number of federal agencies can provide valuable information, particularly about the federal resources that are available to support services to exceptional children. These include such agencies as the President's Committee on Mental Retardation, the President's Committee on Employment of the Handicapped, the Secretary's Committee on Mental Retardation, the National Institute of Mental Health, the Office of Child Development, and the Office of Special Education in the federal Department of Education.

Another source of information is the reference section of most college libraries. References relevant to working with exceptional children include *Exceptional Child Education Resources; Mental Retardation Abstracts; Deafness, Speech, and Hearing Abstracts; Language and Language Behavior Abstracts; Psychological Abstracts; Education Index; Current Index to Journals in Education; and Dissertation Abstracts.*

Whatever source you use to find information, it is important that you know exactly what you are looking for. Librarians and people who work in agencies are best able to deal with specific requests. An important tool in making specific requests is the *Thesaurus of ERIC Descriptors,* which is available in most college libraries. This publication lists and defines many terms, some very broad and some very specific. These terms, or *descriptors,* are used in most organizations and reference works to organize and retrieve information. The use of appropriate descriptors will increase the speed and improve the results of most searches for information.

In addition to the sources already mentioned, many others have been developed during the last ten years, some of which are listed in Table 14-1. Information retrieval services are changing rapidly. Although the information included in the table was accurate in late 1978, the services, addresses, and fees may have changed by the time this book is published.

ELEMENT SIX: IMPLEMENT PROFESSIONAL DEVELOPMENT PROGRAM

The implementation of your professional development program will depend on your objectives and personal circumstances and will, as a result, be highly subjective. There are, however, three general guidelines that apply to everyone.

First, professional development activities should be approached systematically. If you have carefully followed the previous steps in this model, you should know what the results of each activity will be. This will be helpful in planning a program of course work, in selecting in-service or continuing education programs, and in developing independent enrichment or study activities.

Second, you should join the appropriate professional organizations, most of which publish journals, conduct training courses, and provide other benefits. These organizations have been responsible for many of the recent improvements in the education of exceptional children, through legislation, litigation, and professional negotiations.

Another benefit of belonging to a professional organization is related to mental health. Special education teaching is difficult work, and it provides different challenges than teaching in the regular classroom. For example, teachers of the severely and profoundly handicapped must often be content with small improvements in their students' skills, and they must have a high tolerance for repetitive teaching and for working with children who may have very limited language skills. What is more, the special education teacher frequently works without interacting with other special education colleagues. As a result of these factors the teacher often becomes frustrated and depressed. The author knows of a number of teachers and administrators who have reported feeling "burned out" after a few years of work in this type of situation. Participation in a professional organization can provide you with opportunities to interact with colleagues who

Table 14-1
Agencies Providing Information Search and Retrieval Services in Special Education

Information Needs	Name and Address	Form and Content of Data Base	Product
Professional literature and research.	[a] Council for Exceptional Children Information Center 1920 Association Drive Reston, VA 22091 Toll free phone: (800) 336-3728	Computer-stored abstracts of professional literature from *Exceptional Child Education Resources, Resources in Education, Current Index to Journals in Education,* Exceptional Child Bibliography Series, ERIC Clearinghouse on Exceptional Children, and other sources. The CEC can also search other data bases including: Educational Resources Information Center (ERIC), Social Sciences Citation Index (SSCI), Psychological Abstracts, Smithsonian Science Information Exchange (SSIE), Dissertation Abstracts (DATRIX II), and National Technical Information Service (NTIS).	Computer printouts of abstracts and literature packets containing reprints of CEC Journal articles, brochures, bibliographies, documents, abstracts, and newsletters.

(continued on following page)

[a] Fees were charged for services in 1978.
Information for this table was compiled by Elisabeth Churchill, whose assistance is gratefully acknowledged.

Table 14-1 Continued
Agencies Providing Information Search and Retrieval Services in Special Education

Information Needs	Name and Address	Form and Content of Data Base	Product
Locations of agencies and schools for the handicapped — by state and/or handicapping condition Information on resources for parents	Closer Look Box 1492 Washington, DC 20013	Information service to locate services for handicapped children. Information on handicapping conditions.	Computer listing. *Closer Look* (bimonthly newsletter). Parent packets.
Access to doctoral dissertations and master's theses.	[a] University Microfilms DATRIX II (Direct access to Reference Information) University Microfilms 300 N. Zeeb Road Ann Arbor, MI 48106 PH: (313) 761-4700	Dissertations. Key words must be identified. *High Frequency Keyword Lists* and search order forms are available at universities or from DATRIX, University Microfilms.	Bibliography — title of dissertation; author's name and degree, and university; date of publication; and page and volume in *Dissertation Abstracts*. Microfilms of entire dissertations can also be purchased.
Information about handicapping conditions and services for the handicapped.	Office of Handicapped Individuals (OHI) Clearinghouse Room 3517 Switzer Bldg. 330 C Street, SW Washington, DC 20201	Draws from all information sources in the Department of Education and other departments of the federal government, and the private sector.	Written answer that may include copies of material and references to laws, programs, or services.
Instructional media and materials for special education.	National Instructional Materials Information System *(NIMIS)* NICSEM/NIMIS II University of Southern California Los Angeles, CA	Computerized data base of instructional media and materials.	Listing of instructional media and materials with bibliographic information and an abstract of each item. Catalogs and indexes of materials and media for various handicaps. Newsletter.

Table 14-1
Continued

Information Needs	Name and Address	Form and Content of Data Base	Product
Government and the education of handicapped children. Federal and state laws, rules, and regulations.	State/Federal Information Clearinghouse on Exceptional Children (SFICEC) c/o The Council for Exceptional Children 1920 Association Drive Reston, VA 22091	Computer-based information system. Draws information from the law, administrative literature, attorney general's opinions, and actual litigation pertaining to handicapped children and special education programs.	SFICEC develops and distributes various information products. Also conducts searches to answer specific individual information requests.
Literature pertaining to human communication and its disorders.	[a] Information Center for Hearing, Speech, and Disorders of Human Communication 310 Harriet Lane Home Johns Hopkins Medical Institutions Baltimore, MD 21205	Computer. Specializes in literature on hearing, language, speech, and disorders of human communication (effective from 1967).	Topical bibliographies.
Literature about basic and applied research on visual impairment.	[a] International Research Information Service (IRIS) American Foundation for the Blind 15 West 16th Street New York, New York	Descriptor index of basic and applied research in areas of visual impairment. Gathered from scientific literature, project reports, acquisition lists, unpublished materials, and conference and seminar proceedings.	Publications based on review of literature, bibliographies, and state-of-the-art reports and evaluations.

(continued on following page)

Table 14-1 Continued
Agencies Providing Information Search and Retrieval Services in Special Education

Information Needs	Name and Address	Form and Content of Data Base	Product
Information on medical fields and related areas.	MEDLINE (MEDLARS On-Line) Medical Literature Analysis Retrieval System MEDLINE National Library of Medicine 8600 Wisconsin Avenue Bethesda, MD 20014	One-line bibliographic search services. Citations from biomedical journals. (Request search through nearest MEDLINE Center or Library.)	Computer printout of bibliography. NLM Literature Search Series.

may have similar problems, to share ideas, to discuss alternative methods of dealing with situations, and to receive support for your efforts.

The third guideline relates to the CEC Professional Guidelines, mentioned earlier. Guideline 4.4 states, in part, "Special educators should undertake only those activities which they consider ethical and helpful to exceptional persons" (p. 51).

ELEMENT SEVEN: EVALUATE, REVISE, AND REFINE

A program of professional development should be flexible. This means that the professional must continually evaluate his activities and plans and make modifications when necessary. But how does one engage in self-evaluation? Two procedures can be suggested. The first involves examining each of the competency statements in this chapter and asking yourself how well you can do the task and whether you should learn how to do it better. You could also obtain the forms used to evaluate student teachers or regular school teachers, and assess your performance in each of the areas mentioned.

Although the emphasis in this model has been on self-evaluation, you can also benefit by enlisting the assistance of colleagues. CEC Professional Guideline 4.2 states, "Special education personnel have a professional responsibility to participate in the objective and systematic evaluation of themselves, colleagues, services,

The best special education teachers are those who are continually involved in activities to improve their professional skills. Systematic planning, self-evaluation, and initiative are necessary for a successful professional development program.

and programs for the purpose of continuous improvement of professional performance" (p. 50). Some school systems have successfully implemented a system of peer assistance in planning and evaluating professional development programs.

This provides mutual support and fosters greater objectivity in evaluating the elements described in this model.

CONCLUSION

The best special educators engage in an ongoing program of professional development. They become involved in their professional organizations, participate in continuing education programs, and constantly look for ways to improve their professional performance. To begin an effective development program, one must analyze one's strengths and weaknesses, locate the necessary resources and information, and efficiently manage time, energy, and personal resources. The approach to such a program should be systematic, and, as the CEC professional guidelines state:

> Members of a profession define themselves as such not only by the body of knowledge and skills that are essential to and distinguish their occupation but also, and perhaps more importantly, by the practice of the occupation in a manner which is generally recognized as professional, that is, in accord with the methods and standards of the profession [*Guidelines for Personnel in the Education of Exceptional Children*, 1976, p. 1].

The model described in this chapter is a practical approach to professional development. The use of this plan and adherence to the CEC Continuing Professional Development Guidelines can result in improved services to exceptional children.

SUMMARY

1. Special educators have a responsibility to design educational programs that continue to develop their professional competence after they have completed their formal education.
2. A well-developed philosophy serves as the foundation for success as a special educator.
3. Professional development efforts are most successful if they are approached on a well-planned and systematic basis.
4. The seven steps in designing a professional development program are to develop a philosophy, define your professional role, specify competencies that are needed to perform that role, develop and rank objectives for meeting the competencies, identify content and resources related to the objectives, implement the program, and evaluate, revise, and refine your efforts.
5. Special educators should become active members of their professional organizations and abide by the standards and ethics of their profession.

TASK SHEET 14
Philosophy of Special Education

This text has been designed to help you begin the development of a philosophy of special education. For the area you are interested in, write your current philosophy of special education. It may be helpful to refer to the section of this chapter (pp. 561–562) that deals with the development of a philosophy.

Glossary

Acceleration: Any of a number of educational provisions used to move students through the curriculum more rapidly than usual, e.g., early school admission, grade-skipping, accelerated classes.

Adaptive behavior: The effectiveness or degree with which an individual meets the standards of personal independence and social responsibility expected for age and cultural group.

Addition: Articulation disorder where a sound or sounds are added in normally nonoccurring positions in a word.

Advocacy (and consumerism): A trend in which parents and professionals are working in an assertive fashion to gain better services for handicapped persons.

Affricate: A sound that is a combination of a plosive and a fricative sound (t, ʃ, dʒ).

Agnosia: Inability to attach meaning to sounds, words, or visual experiences.

Air conduction test: A pure-tone hearing test using earphones.

Alchemy: a pseudoscience that alleges to create gold from other chemical compounds.

Amblyopia (lazy eye): A condition in which the brain will not tolerate double vision and suppresses what is being transmitted by the weaker eye.

Amniocentesis: A test that may be done during pregnancy to identify certain genetic disorders in the fetus. It consists of extracting a small amount of amniotic fluid, which surrounds the fetus in the womb, for examination.

Anoxia: Lack of oxygen.

Anterior: Refers to the front of the body.

Anvil (or incus): One of the bones of the middle ear that carries vibrations across the middle ear cavity.

Aphasia: Acquired language impairment caused by brain damage.

Apraxia: Difficulty with voluntary or purposeful muscular movement with no evidence of motor impairment.

Aqueous humor: Watery substance between the cornea and the lens of the eye.

Architectural barrier: A condition of the physical environment that can inhibit or prevent handicapped persons from using facilities or moving about.

Arthritis: Condition affecting the joints and muscles, causing pain, stiffness, and inflammation.

Arthrogryphosis: A congenital disease in which the muscles may be poorly developed with crooking or contraction of the joints.

Articulation: The movements of the vocal system that result in the production of speech sounds and words.

Articulation disorder: A communication disorder associated with substitutions, omissions, distortions, and/or additions of speech sounds.

Asthma: Chronic condition characterized by wheezing or labored breathing caused by a constriction of the air passages in the bronchial tubes and by an increased amount of thick secretions in the air tubes of the lungs.

Astigmatism: Blurred vision caused by uneven curvature of the cornea or lens.

Ataxia: A type of cerebral palsy in which lack of muscle coordination results in loss of coordinated movements, especially those relating to balance and position.

Athetosis: A form of cerebral palsy characterized by involuntary, jerky, purposeless, repetitive movements of the extremities, head, and tongue.

Atrophy: The degeneration or death of tissue.

Audiogram: A graphic portrayal of the results of hearing testing.

Audiologist: A specialist in evaluation and remediation of auditory disorders.

Audiology: A science concerned with hearing

impairments, including their detection and remediation.

Auditory analysis: Ability to isolate components of an auditory message.

Auditory cortex: The portion of the brain covering that is associated with the hearing sense.

Auditory discrimination: Ability to detect the differences between sounds.

Auditory figure-ground perception: Ability to isolate a particular sound or a word from other sounds or words occurring simultaneously.

Auditory integration: Ability to associate a sound or sound combinations (word and sentences) with other experiences.

Auditory nerve: Cranial nerve VIII that carries auditory impulses from the cochlea to the brain.

Auditory perception: Use of the auditory channel to identify and attach meaning to specific recurring experiences (words) that are heard.

Auditory training: Training designed to teach a hearing impaired person to make best use of residual hearing.

Auditory-visual integration: Ability of the child to combine sound with symbol in understanding of, for example, phonetic symbols.

Aura: A condition that occurs in some individuals with epilepsy just before a seizure. The person may see unusual colors, hear ringing sounds, smell peculiar odors, or experience other phenomena during this time.

Auricle (pinna): The externally visible, flaplike, cartilaginous structure on the side of the head.

Autism: A severe behavioral disorder characterized by extreme withdrawal and self-stimulation, requiring intense and prolonged intervention, usually in a segregated setting.

Behavior checklists: A list of traits or behaviors that research has shown to be characteristic of a group of children. These checklists are often used to rate children to determine whether they should be referred for special services.

Behavior disorders: Disorders in which behavior deviates from a normal range, occurs over an extended period of time, and is extreme in terms of intensity and frequency.

Behavioral excesses: Behaviors that are excessive in terms of frequency, intensity, duration, or occurrence under conditions when their socially sanctioned frequency is close to zero.

Behavioral model: Assumptions that behavior disorders are primarily a result of inappropriate learning and that the most effective preventative actions and therapeutic interventions will involve controlling the child's environment in order to teach appropriate behaviors.

Behavior modification: See introduction to Part III for list of concepts and their definitions.

Bilabial sounds: Those sounds made with both lips (p, b, m, w).

Biophysical model: Assumptions that behavior disorders are primarily a result of dysfunction of the central nervous system due to brain lesions, neurochemical irregularities, or genetic defects and that the most effective preventative actions and therapeutic interventions will involve prevention or correction of such biological defects.

Blind: Those whose visual acuity is 20/200 or less in the better eye with the best possible correction or a restriction in the field of vision to an angle subtending an arc of 20 degrees or less. These people must use braille, and tactile and auditory materials in their education.

Bone conduction test: A hearing test that measures the response of the sensorineural mechanism in the inner ear bypassing the outer and middle ear system.

Braille: A code developed for blind persons in which a system of raised dots allows the person to read with the fingertips.

Buckley Amendment: Guarantees parents control of the school records of their children.

Career: The totality of work one does in his or her lifetime.

Career awareness: Program emphasized during elementary years that examines the relationship of work to the total life process and emphasizes basic work values.

Career education: The totality of experiences through which one learns about and prepares to engage in work as part of his or her way of living.

Cascade of services: A hierarchy of educational service alternatives for handicapped persons, ranging from the least restrictive regular classroom to the highly restrictive hospital or institutional setting.

Casefinding: Activities designed to make initial contact with the target populations.

Cataract: Clouding of the lens of the eye that obstructs the passage of light.

Caudal: Reference to the tail-end or hind part of the body.

Central auditory disorder: Disorder of auditory comprehension, perception, and discrimination where there is no disorder or damage to the peripheral hearing mechanism.

Central nervous system (CNS): The part of the nervous system to which the sensory impulses are transmitted and from which motor impulses develop.

Cephalad: Reference to the head or anterior end of the body.

Cephalocaudal development: Development that proceeds from the head downward.

Cerebellum: An area of the brain which, if damaged, results in an inability to maintain balance and coordinated movement, or ataxia type cerebral palsy.

Cerebral palsy: An abnormal alternation of human movement or motor functioning arising from a defect, injury, or disease of the tissues of the central nervous system.

Cerumen: Bitter-tasting, waxlike material secreted by glands in the skin lining along the outer two-thirds of the auditory canal.

Chemotherapy: Administration of drugs to control or aid a problem.

Child find: A concerted effort by state and local educational agencies to identify all handicapped children in need of special education services.

Choroid: Layer of the eye between the sclera and retina that contains blood vessels that provide nourishment to the retina.

Cineflouroscopy: X-ray motion pictures.

Circular pursuit: Visually following a moving object in a circular pattern.

Clubfoot: A congenital abnormality in which the foot is turned downward and inward at the ankle.

Cochlea: Snail-shell shaped auditory part of the inner ear. The sense organ of hearing.

Cognition: Awareness or understanding of information.

Concept: Thought, opinion, idea, or mental image.

Conduct disorder: A behavioral disorder characterized by a pattern including both verbal and physical aggressive behavior of an antisocial nature.

Conductive hearing loss: Hearing disorder caused by blockage or damage to the structures of the outer or middle ear.

Congenital condition: Condition present at birth.

Conjugate eye movement: Moving both eyes together in a coordinate manner.

Conjunctiva: Thin transparent layer that lines the eyelids and covers the front of the eye and prevents dust or other particles from entering.

Cornea: Transparent cover in front of the iris and pupil that refracts light rays.

Cretinism: Congenital thyroid deficiency that can stunt physical growth and cause mental retardation.

Criterion-referenced test: A test of academic achievement in which a student's performance is compared to pre-established level of items correct.

Cyanosis: A blue discoloration of the skin caused by a lack of oxygen in the blood.

Cystic fibrosis: A disease affecting mucous glands in the body causing respiratory and digestive problems.

Decibel: A dimensionless unit expressing the logarithmic ratio of two amounts of pressure, power, or intensity; measure of loudness of a particular sound. Abbreviated dB.

De-institutionalization: Term used to describe the movement away from placing handicapped people in large residential institutional facilities.

Developmental model: A model of development based on normal developmental milestones.

Diabetes: A metabolic disorder in which the body is not able to properly utilize carbohydrates in the diet because of a failure of the pancreas to secrete an adequate supply of insulin.

Diabetic coma: A condition in which enough insulin is not available to help the body convert the intake of glucose.

Digital grasp: Grasping an object using the fingers (digits), rather than the whole hand.

Diphthong: Speech sound made with voicing that is a combination of two vowels coming together in the same syllable.

Disability: A condition due to the reduction of function or absence of a particular body part or organ (e.g., paraplegic, amputee); synonymous with disorder or dysfunction.

Discriminative stimulus: A stimulus which is consistently paired with reinforcement.

Disfluency: Speech marked by repetition, hesitation, prolongations, and in general, a lack of flow which calls attention to itself; referred to by some as stuttering.

Distal: Away from the body or trunk.

Distortion: Articulation disorders wherein an acceptable sound is replaced by a sound that doesn't exist in a given language.

Divergent thinking: Production of many different solutions to a problem or question which has no "right or wrong" answers.

Dysarthria: Term referring to any speech disorder that has as its base an impairment of the central or peripheral nervous system.

Dyslexia: A severe disability in learning to read.

Eardrum (tympanic membrane): The semi-transparent membrane which separates the outer and middle ear.

Echolalia: Imitation of the sounds of others.

Educational synthesizer: A teacher who incorporates available resources such as physical therapists into daily educational programs.

Electroencephalogram: Graphic record of the electrical output of brain waves.

Emmetropic eye: The normal eye; one that is perfectly focused for distance so that the image of an object focuses directly on the retina.

Encephalitis: A condition that causes inflammation of the brain which may result in brain damage.

Encopresis: Lack of bowel control.

Enrichment: Educational experiences not usually included in the curriculum, e.g., opportunities to study archaeology, filmmaking, etc.

Enuresis: Lack of bladder control.

Epilepsy: A chronic condition of the central nervous system, characterized by periodic seizures accompanied by convulsions of the muscles, and, with more severe attacks, loss of consciousness.

Etiology: The causes or origins of a disease or condition.

Eustachian tube: Tubelike structure connecting the middle ear and the naso-pharynx.

Exceptional children: Those who have physical, mental, behavioral, or sensory characteristics that differ from the majority of children to such an extent that they require special education and related services in order to develop to their maximum capacity.

Expressive language: Ability to encode language and present it orally or in a written or gestural form.

Extensor muscle: Those muscles that are used to extend the arm, such as in reaching.

External auditory canal: An irregularly shaped, tubelike passage extending from the inside of the head to the middle ear. Approximately 1″ long in adults.

Fading: Gradual removel of additional stimuli such as prompts.

Fine motor skills: Use of small muscles for reaching, grasping, and manipulation of objects such as puzzles, formboards, cubes, and drawing materials.

Flexor muscles: Muscles used to pull your arm toward your body as if one were flexing the muscles.

Frequency: The number of vibrations which occur at the same rate over a period of time in a sound wave. Measured in Hertz (Hz).

Fricative: A sound that is produced when the contact of the articulators does not completely halt air flow, but merely dams it in a manner that causes the air to escape with a friction-like noise (f, v, θ, ϑ, s, z, ʃ, h).

Functional hearing loss: "Hearing loss" which has a psychological, as opposed to organic, cause.

Functional learning handicap: Handicap in

learning that develops as a result of prolonged stress or environmental problems.

Generalization: Process of a skill being performed in different environments with different persons, different instructional materials, and different language cues.

Gifted: A term used to refer to children with outstanding ability or potential. The term is usually applied to children who perform in the top three to five percent on measures of aptitude or achievement in such areas as general intellectual ability, specific academic aptitude, creativity, leadership or artistic ability.

Glaucoma: Severe disorder that occurs when the aqueous fluid does not circulate properly and results in an elevation of pressure in the eye.

Glide: A sound that is the result of movement of the articulators during its pronunciation (w, r, l).

Global retardation: Profound, inclusive difficulty in learning, as opposed to specific difficulty in a single area such as reading or math.

Glottal: Sounds made by action of vocal folds.

Gower's sign: A symptom of Duchenne type of muscular dystrophy in which the child is seen "walking up" his lower limbs with his hands.

Grand mal seizure: A severe type of convulsive disorder involving loss of consciousness and extreme convulsions.

Gross motor skills: Use of large muscles for walking, running, and other whole body movements.

Habilitation: refers to the training of skills and attitudes which are not part of an individual's past experiences.

Half-way house: A small residential facility established to bridge the gap from institution to community.

Handicap: refers to problems that impaired or disabled people have as a result of interaction with their environment (e.g., inability of deaf person to hear a telephone or person in wheelchair to use a revolving door).

Hemiplegia: Paralysis of the extremities on one side of the body.

Horizontal programming: Instructional approach used with gifted children which broad-

ens knowledge through the use of enrichment activities, exploration or internship experiences.

Hydrocephalus: A condition of excess cerebrospinal fluid in the brain that results in an enlargement of the head and mental retardation.

Hyperactivity: Excessive physical/muscular activity characterized by excessive restlessness and mobility; sometimes associated with learning disabilities.

Hyperopia (farsightedness): A condition that occurs when the eye is too short and the rays of light from near objects are not focused on the retina.

Hypertonicity: Refers to heightened state of excessive tension. Muscles are tight and tense.

Hypotonicity: Refers to flaccid muscle tone or inability to maintain tension or resistance to stretch.

Impairment: A condition resulting from diseased or defective tissue (e.g., cerebral palsy, birthmark, nearsightedness).

Individual educational program (IEP): A component of Public Law 94-142 that requires a written plan of instruction for each child receiving special services; the IEP must include a statement of the child's present levels of educational performance, annual goals, short-term objectives, specific services needed by the child, dates when these services will begin and be in effect, and when the child should be reevaluated.

Incidence: Refers to the estimates of the numbers of individuals in the population who may exhibit a particular characteristic at some time during their lifetime.

Incus (anvil): The second or middle bone in the chain of bones in the middle ear joining the malleus and stapes; anvil shaped.

Infusion approach: An approach to career education which stresses that career education should not be approached as a separate content area, but infused into the existing curriculum.

Insulin: A protein hormone produced by the pancreas and secreted into the blood where it regulates carbohydrate metabolism.

Intelligence-quotient (IQ): Score on a test designed to measure intellectual abilities, such as memory, comprehension, and reasoning. The average score for the general population is usually 100.

Inter-individual differences: The differences between students.

Intra-individual differences: The differences within students.

Iris: Colored part of the eye that expands or contracts depending upon the amount of light passing through the eye.

Juvenile rheumatoid arthritis: A chronic condition common to school age children beginning with general fatigue, stiffness and aching of the joints.

Kinesthetic approach: An instructional technique that utilizes sensations derived from the student's muscles or movement sensations.

Kyphosis: A condition in which the back around the shoulder area is rounded.

Labio-dental: Sound produced as a result of contact with the *lower* lip and teeth (f, v).

Language: The systematic manner in which a people agree to symbolically represent their environment, thoughts, and emotions. This symbolic systems depends on speech and consists of word and word combinations.

Laryngectomy: Removal of all or part of the larynx.

Lateral sound: A sound produced by the air stream passing around the sides of a fixed articulator (l).

Lens: Structure of the eye that refines and changes the light rays passing through the eye.

Lingua-alveolar: Sound produced as a result of contact between the tongue and alveolar ridge (t, d, m, s, z, t ʃ, d ʒ, r, l).

Lingua-dental: Sound produced as a result of contact between the tongue and teeth (ð, θ).

Lingua-palatal: Sound produced as a result of contact between the tongue and hard palate (j, ʃ).

Lingua-velar: Sound produced as a result of contact between the tongue and soft palate (h, g ŋ).

Linguistic functioning: Ability to use language.

Lordosis: A condition in which the spine is curved inward, resulting in a swayback and/or protruding abdomen.

Mainstreaming: The educational placement of the child in the least restrictive educational setting.

Malleus (hammer): The first of a chain of three small bones in the middle ear extending from the eardrum to the incus; hammer shaped.

Manual communication: Communication which relies on hand signs or finger spelling.

Masking: The stimulation of one ear of a subject by controlled noise to prevent the hearing with that ear of the tone or speech being presented to the opposite ear.

Meningitis: Inflammation of the membranes that surround the brain and spinal cord.

Meningocele: A sac-like pouch that protrudes through an opening in the skull or spinal column.

Mental retardation: Significantly subaverage general intellectual functioning existing concurrently with deficits in adaptive behavior and manifested during the developmental period.

Microcephaly: A cranial disorder characterized by the development of a small head with a sloping forehead; retardation results from lack of space for brain development.

Minimal brain dysfunction: (controversial definition) Applies to children of average or above average intelligence who have learning disabilities associated with functional problems of the central nervous system.

Mixed hearing loss: Hearing disorder as the result of a combination of conductive and sensori-neural loss.

Monoplegia: Paralysis of one limb.

Multiple sclerosis: A disease or progressive deterioration in which the protective sheath surrounding the nerves degenerates and causes failure of the body's neurological system.

Muscular dystrophy: A hereditary disorder that causes a loss of vitality and progressive deterioration of the body as a result of death of muscle tissue.

Myopia (nearsightedness): Occurs when the eye is too long and the rays of light from distant objects are not focused on the retina.

Nasal sound: A sound produced by the blocking of the oral cavity, the opening of the velum and the emission of air via the nasal cavity (m. n, ŋ).

Neurologically impaired: Associated with problems in the functioning of the central nervous system.

Normalization: The concept that all handicapped persons should be provided with the opportunity to live according to the patterns and conditions of everyday life, which are as close as possible to the norms and patterns of the mainstream of society.

Norm-referenced test: Shows student's performance in comparison to the group of people on which the test was standardized.

Occipital lobe: A portion of the brain where visual stimuli are interpreted and "seeing" takes place.

Omission: Articulation disorder wherein a sound or sounds are omitted from words.

Operant conditioning: Changing behavior by altering its consequences; altering the future probability of the occurrence of a response by providing reinforcement or punishment as a consequence.

Ophthalmologist: A physician that specializes in treatment of the eye.

Optic nerve: The nerve that sends impulses to the occipital area of the brain where visual stimuli are interpreted.

Optician: A specialist trained to grind lenses to prescription.

Optometrist: A professional person who examines the eye for defects and/or refractive errors and prescribes corrective lenses.

Oral method: A method of teaching the hearing impaired that concentrates on teaching the child to speak and depend on lipreading or speech reading.

Organic learning handicap: Inherent, inborn, or constitutional handicap in learning.

Orthopedically handicapped: A disabling condition caused by physical impairments especially those related to the bones, joints, and muscles.

Ossicles: Three small bones of the ear that transfer sound waves from the eardrum.

Osteogenesis imperfecta: A congenital bone disease resulting in very fragile bones (often called brittle bone disease).

Otitis media: Middle ear infection.

Otosclerosis: Condition of the middle ear where a bony growth develops around the base of the stapes, impeding its movement.

Otolaryngologist: A physician who specializes in diseases of the ear and throat.

Otologist: A physician who specializes in diseases of the ear.

Otoscope: Small light used to examine the auditory canal and eardrum.

Paraplegia: Paralysis of the lower half of the body including both legs.

Partially seeing: Those whose visual acuity is between 20/200 and 20/70 in the better eye with the best possible correction or who in the opinion of an eye specialist need either temporary or permanent special education facilities. Partially seeing people can use ink print in their education.

Perceptual skills: Ability to select, organize, and interpret the stimuli that surround us.

Perinatal: Refers to the time during birth.

Petit mal seizure: A mild form of convulsive disorder characterized by dizziness and momentary lapse of consciousness.

Phenylketonuria (PKU): A genetic disorder which, if undetected, may cause mental retardation. May be detected at birth.

Phocomelia: A type of congenital deformity in which the hands and/or feet are directly attached to the torso and may resemble "seal flippers." Commonly found in children whose mothers took thalidomide to control morning sickness.

Pitch: The psychological attribute of auditory sensation by which man perceives the highness or lowness of a sound.

-plegia: Latin suffix referring to paralysis or inability to move.

Plosive sound: A sound that is produced by building pressure behind a complete articulatory closure and suddenly releasing it in an explosive manner (p, b, t, d, k, g).

Poliomyelitis (polio or infantile paralysis):

An acute disease that inflames nerve cells of the spinal cord or brain stem and leaves a residual paralysis or muscular atrophy; is preventable through vaccination.

Postnatal: After birth.

Prehension: Grasping skills in fine motor development.

Prenatal: Occurring or existing before birth.

Prevalence: The number of individuals in the population who currently exhibit a particular characteristic.

Proximal: Refers to close to the body or trunk.

Proximodistal development: Development proceeds from the trunk outward.

Psychomotor: A term used to describe operations which combine cognitive and physical processes, e.g., playing a violin, playing tennis, handwriting, etc.

Psychomotor seizure: A seizure characterized by many automatic, stereotyped movements.

Pupil: The contractive opening in the middle of the iris.

Pure tone air conduction test: An audiometric test utilizing pure tones of varying frequencies which are presented through ear phones.

Pure tone bone conduction test: An audiometric test utilizing pure tones of varying frequencies which are presented through a vibrator.

Pyramidal tract: Area of the brain located between the motor and sensory areas of the cortex. Damage in this area results in spastic cerebral palsy.

Quadriplegia: Paralysis involving all four of the body extremities.

Receptive language: Ability to receive and understand transmitted language.

Refraction: The bending of light rays.

Rehabilitation: The retraining or reorganizing of skill patterns in individuals.

Retina: Back portion of the eye, containing nerve fibers connected to the optic nerve.

Retrolental fibroplasia: Eye disorder caused by too much oxygen in incubators of premature babies.

Rh incompatibility: A condition in which the fetus has Rh positive blood and the mother has Rh negative blood. The mother consequently builds up antibodies that attack the fetus, resulting in birth defects.

Rheumatic fever: Disease usually following a streptococcal infection that is characterized by acute inflamation of the joints, fever, chorea, skin rash, nosebleeds, and abdominal pains. It often damages the heart by scarring its tissues and valves.

Rigidity cerebral palsy: A type of cerebral palsy in which hypertension of the muscles creates stiffness.

Rubella (German measles): A communicable disease transmitted by a virus; infection of a woman during early stages of pregnancy produces a high probability of severe handicaps of the offspring.

Schizophrenia: A disorder characterized by split or dual personality, flights of ideas, distorted thought processes, and misconception of reality.

School phobia: Intense fear of the teacher, a classroom, peers, or any other aspect of the school. When it is time to go to school the child develops psychosomatic symptoms.

Sclera: Tough outer layer of eyeball which protects the contents as well as holding contents in place.

Scoliosis: Muscle weakness allowing a serious abnormal curvature of the spine which may be corrected with surgery or the use of a brace.

Seizure: An impairment of consciousness which may or may not be accompanied by active disruption of the motor state.

Semicircular canals: Three canals within the inner ear that function to maintain balance.

Sensorineural hearing loss: Hearing disorder caused by damage or dysfunction of the cochlea or VIII auditory nerve.

Severely handicapped individual: One who has serious primary disabilities that are cognitive, and/or behavioral, has the high probability of additional physical and/or sensory handicaps, and requires significantly more resources than are provided for the mildly and moderately handicapped in special education programs.

Shaping: Reinforcement of successive approximations or better and better attempts of the target response.

Snellen chart: A white background with black letters or symbols of graded size used to test distant field visual acuity.

Spasticity: A type of cerebral palsy characterized by muscular incoordination resulting from muscle spasms, opposing contractions of muscles, and paralytic effects.

Special education: Instruction that is designed to meet the needs of children who cannot profit from the regular curriculum.

Specific learning disability: Disorder in one or more of the basic psychological processes involved in understanding or in using language, spoken or written, which may manifest itself in an imperfect ability to listen, think, speak, read, write, spell, or to do mathematical calculations.

Speech: The physical process involved in producing the sound and sound combinations of a language.

Speech reading: Interpreting the movements of the lips, face, head, and gestures as an aid to communication; also called lip reading or visual hearing.

Speech reception threshold (SRT): The lowest intensity at which a person can repeat two syllable words at least 50 percent of the time.

Spina bifida: Congenital defect, caused by a failure of the bony elements of a portion of the spine to close completely.

Spinal muscular atrophy: Disease that affects the spinal cord and results in progressive degeneration of motor nerve cells.

Stapes (stirrup): The last or innermost bone in the chain of bones in the middle ear extending from the incus to the oval window; stirrup-shaped.

Strabismus: A condition in which the two eyes fail to move in a coordinated fashion, resulting in what appears to be crossed eyes.

Standardized tests: Tests that are available from a test publisher that have been administered to a number of people under identical conditions.

Stereotypic or self-stimulatory behavior: Repetitive, bizarre behaviors that serve no observable function, e.g., body rocking, finger flipping.

Stoma: Opening at the base of the neck created to allow air to pass to the lungs of a laryngectomized person.

Stroke, or CVA (cerebral vascular accident): Sudden interruption of blood flow to the brain.

Stuttering: *See* disfluency.

Substitution: Articulation disorder where one sound of a language is replaced by another sound of that language.

Syndrome: A cluster or constellation of symptoms.

Syntax: The part of a grammar system that deals with the arrangement of word forms to show their mutual relations in the sentence.

Talented: A term often used synonymously with "gifted"; or to refer to superior ability in a specific area, e.g., talented musically, artistically, etc.

Task analysis: Breaking down of a skill into component behaviors, subskills, or subtasks.

Thalidomide: A drug taken as a relaxant that can cause congenital deformities when taken by pregnant women.

Threshold of hearing: The minimal value of sound wave pressure that will produce the sensation of sound; the point at which the person just begins to hear a sound.

Time delay procedure: Procedure used during acquisition of a response in which the presentation of the cue is systematically delayed.

Total communication: Philosophy of educators of the hearing impaired which recognizes the advantages of oral and manual systems and tries to blend them into a larger system.

Triplegia: Paralysis of three of the body's limbs.

Tuberculosis: An infectious disease characterized by the formation of small nodules in the tissue of the lungs.

Underachiever: Any child whose scholastic performance is below that suggested by performance on IQ tests or other indicators of aptitude.

Validity: Refers to the extent to which a test measures what it purports to measure.

Vertical programming: Instructional approach used with gifted children which moves children up the curriculum ladder more rapidly than usual or deeper into subject matter than in the regular school program.

Visual acuity: Sharpness or clearness of vision.

Visual field (peripheral vision): Side vision which is measured in terms of degrees of visual arc.

Vitreous: A jelly-like clear substance in the center of the eyeball which helps hold the shape of the eye and has slight refractive power.

Vocation: Primary work role in which one is engaged at any particular time.

Voice disorder: Occurs when an individual's voice does not present an appropriate and consistent sound as a result of misuse of the voice structures or tissue change in the vocal tract.

Voiced sound: All sounds that use vocal fold vibration.

Work: Conscious effort aimed at producing benefits for oneself and/or others.

References

Chapter 1

ABESON, A., and BALLARD, J. State and federal policy for exceptional children. In F. J. Weintraub, A. Abeson, J. Ballard, and M. L. LaVor (Eds.), *Public policy and the education of exceptional children.* Reston, Va.: Council for Exceptional Children, 1976, 83–95.

AIELLO, B. (Ed.). *Places and spaces: Facilities planning for handicapped children.* Reston, Va.: Council for Exceptional Children, 1976.

ARAGON, J. Cultural conflict and cultural diversity in education. In L. A. Bransford, L. Baca, and K. Lane (Eds.), *Cultural diversity and the exceptional child.* Reston, Va.: Council for Exceptional Children, 1973, 24–31.

BLATT, B., and KAPLAN, F. *Christmas in purgatory.* Boston: Allyn and Bacon, 1966.

CRUICKSHANK, W. M., and JOHNSON, G. O. (Eds.) *Education of Exceptional Children and Youth* (3rd Ed.). Englewood Cliffs, N. J.: Prentice-Hall, 1975.

DENO, E. *Instructional alternatives for exceptional children.* Reston, Va.: Council for Exceptional Children, 1973.

DIANA v. STATE BOARD OF EDUCATION. Civil Action No. C-70 37RFP (N.D. Cal. January 7, 1970).

DOLL, E. A historical survey of research and management of mental retardation in the United States. In E. P. Trapp and P. Himelstein (Eds.), *Readings on the Exceptional Child.* New York: Appleton-Century-Crofts, 1962.

GEARHEART, B. R. *Organization and administration of educational programs for exceptional programs.* Springfield, Ill.: Charles C. Thomas, 1974.

GILLUNG, T. B., and RUCKER, C. H. Labels and teacher expectations. *Exceptional Children,* 1977, *43,* 464–465.

HOBBS, N. *The future of children.* San Francisco: Jossey-Bass, 1975.

ITARD, J. M. *The wild boy of Aveyron.* (G. Humphrey & M. Humphrey, trans.) New York: Appleton-Century-Crofts, 1932. (Originally published, 1894.)

KANNER, L. *A history of the care and study of the mentally retarded.* Springfield, Ill.: Charles C. Thomas, 1964.

THE KENTUCKY ASSOCIATION FOR RETARDED CHILDREN ET AL. v. KENTUCKY STATE BOARD OF EDUCATION ET AL. Civil Action No. 435 E. D., KY, filed September 12, 1973.

KESSALBRENNER v. ANONYMOUS, 33 N. Y. 2d 161, 305 N. E. 2d 903, 350 N. Y. S. 889 (1973).

KINDRED, M., COHEN, J., PENROD, D., and SHAFFER, T. *The mentally retarded citizen and the law.* New York: Free Press, 1975.

KLINE, D. F. *Child abuse and neglect: A primer for school personnel.* Reston, Va.: Council for Exceptional Children, 1977.

LANE, H. *The wild boy of Aveyron.* New York: Bantam Books, 1976.

LARRY P. v. RILES, Civil No. C-71-2270, 343F. Supp. 1306 (N.D. Cal., 1972.)

LAU v. NICHOLS, 94 S. Ct. 786 (1974), dicta on appropriateness of education.

MARTIN, S. Discrimination in special education. In B. Bogatz (Ed.), *With bias toward none: Proceedings of a national planning conference on non-discriminatory assessment for handicapped children.* Lexington: University of Kentucky, Department of Special Education, c. 1976.

MARYLAND ASSOCIATION FOR RETARDED CHILDREN v. STATE OF MARYLAND, Equity No. 100-182-77676 (Circuit Court, Baltimore, MD, 1974).

MILLS v. BOARD OF EDUCATION OF THE DISTRICT OF COLUMBIA, 348 F. Supp. 866 (D. D. C., 1972).

NAZZARO, J. N. *Exceptional timetables: historic events affecting the handicapped and gifted.* Reston, Va.: Council for Exceptional Children, 1977.

NIRJE, B. The normalization principle and its human management implications. In R. B. Kugel and W. Wolfensberger (Eds.), *Changing patterns in residential services for the mentally retarded.* Washington, D. C.: U. S. Government Printing Office, 1969, 231–240.

NONDISCRIMINATION ON BASIS OF HANDICAP. *Federal Register,* Vol. 42, No. 86, Wednesday, May 4, 1977.

PAYNE, J. S., KAUFFMAN, J. H., PATTON, J. R., BROWN, G. B., and DEMOTT, R. H. *Exceptional children in focus.* Columbus, OH: Charles E. Merrill, 1979.

PENNSYLVANIA ASSOCIATION FOR RETARDED CHILDREN v. COMMONWEALTH OF PENNSYLVANIA 343F. Supp. 279 (E. D. Pa., 1972), Consent Agreement.

REID v. BOARD OF EDUCATION OF THE CITY OF NEW YORK, Administrative Procedure No. 8742 before the State Commissioner of New York, decision rendered November 16, 1973.

SAETTLER, H. CBTE and the handicapped: A Washington perspective, In J. J. Creamer and J. T. Gilmore (Eds.), *Design for competence based education in special education.* Syracuse: Division of Special Education and Rehabilitation, Syracuse University, 1974, 8–10.

SATCHELL, M. Ladies, start your engines. *Parade,* May 6, 1979.

STEVENS, G. *Taxonomy in special education for children with body disorders: The problem and a proposal.* Pittsburgh: University of Pittsburgh, 1962.

TAYLOR, O. Language, cultural contrasts, and the black American. In L. A. Bransford, L. Baca, and K. Lane (Eds.), *Cultural diversity and the exceptional child.* Reston, Va.: Council for Exceptional Children, 1973, 34–41.

WALLACE, G. and LARSEN, S. C. *Educational assessment of learning problems: Testing for teaching.* Boston: Allyn and Bacon, 1978.

WEINTRAUB, F. J. and ABESON, A. New education policies for the handicapped: The quiet revolution. In F. J. Weintraub, A. Abeson, J. Ballard, and M. L. LaVor (Eds.), *Public policy and the education of exceptional children.* Reston, Va.: Council for Exceptional Children, 1976, 7–13.

WEINTRAUB, F. J., ABESON, A. R., and BRADDOCK, D. L. State law and education of handicapped children: Issues and recommendations. Arlington, Va.: Council for Exceptional Children, 1971.

WEINTRAUB, F. J., ABESON, A., BALLARD, J., and LaVOR, M. L. (Eds.), *Public policy and the education of exceptional children.* Reston, Va.: Council for Exceptional Children, 1976.

WESTLE, C. M. A bicentennial declaration of human rights for handicapped persons. Central Michigan University, Office of Career Development for Handicapped Persons, 1976.

WIECK, P. R. Vans meet handicapped regulations for now. *Albuquerque Journal,* March 1, 1979.

WOLF V. LEGISLATURE OF UTAH, Civ. No. 182464 (3rd Dist., Salt Lake City., Jan. 8, 1969).

WOLFENSBERGER, W. *The principle of normalization in human services.* Toronto: National Institute on Mental Retardation, 1972.

WYATT V. ANDERHOLT Vol. 503 Federal Reporter, 2nd Series, 1305.

WYATT V. STICKNEY, 325 F. SUPP. 781, 784 (M. D. ALA. 1971).

Chapter 2

ACKERMAN, P. R., and MOORE, M. G. Delivery of educational services to preschool handicapped children. In T. D. Tjossem (Ed.), *Intervention strategies for high risk infants and young children.* Baltimore: University Park Press, 1976.

ADELSON, E., and FRAIBERG, S. Gross motor development in infants blind from birth. In B. Z. Freidlander, G. M. Sterritt, and G. E. Kirk (Eds.), *Exceptional Infant, Vol. 3: Assessment & Intervention.* New York: Brunner/Mazel, 1975.

ALLEN, K. E., HOLM, V. A, and SCHIEFELBUSCH, R. L. (Eds.). *Early intervention — A team approach.* Baltimore: University Park Press, 1978.

APPELL, M. W. Infant stimulation programming for the deaf-blind. In E. L. Lowell and C. C. Rouin (Eds.), *State of the art.* Sacramento: California State Department of Education, 1977.

BARRAGA, N. Prevention of deficits: Preschool intervention. Lecture presented at Project PAVE Special Study Institute, Louisville, July 1978.

BATTELLE CENTER FOR IMPROVED EDUCATION. Final report on evaluation of Handicapped Children's Early Education Program (HCEEP). (Report to Bureau of Education for the Handicapped, U.S. Office of Education.) Columbus, Ohio: Author, 1976. Cited in J. B. Jordan and others (Eds.), *Early childhood education for exceptional children.* Reston, Va.: Council for Exceptional Children, 1977.

BECK, R. The need for adjunctive services in the management of severely and profoundly handicapped individuals: A view from primary care. In N. G. Haring and L. Brown (Eds.), *Teaching the Severely Handicapped, Vol. 2.* New York: Grune and Stratton, 1977.

BLOOM, B. *Stability and change in human characteristics.* New York: John Wiley & Sons, 1964.

BOWER, T. G. R. *A primer of infant development.* San Francisco: W. H. Freeman and Co., 1977.

BRAUN, S. J., and EDWARDS, E. P. *History and theory of early childhood education.* Worthington, Ohio: Charles A. Jones Publishing Co., 1972.

BRONFENBRENNER, U. Is early intervention effective? In B. Z. Friedlander, G. M. Sterritt, and G. E. Kirk (Eds.), *Exceptional Infant, Vol. 3: Assessment & Intervention.* New York: Brunner/Mazel, 1975.

BRONFENBRENNER, U. Introduction. In H. Chauncey (Ed.), *Soviet preschool education. Vol. I: Program of instruction.* New York: Holt, Rinehart and Winston, 1969.

BRONFENBRENNER, U. *Two worlds of childhood: U.S. and U.S.S.R.* New York: Simon and Schuster, 1970.

BRUNER, J. S. *The relevance of education.* New York: Norton, 1971.

BRUNER, J. S. *The process of education.* Cambridge, Mass.: Harvard University Press, 1960.

CALDWELL, B. M. Impact of interest in early cognitive stimulation. In H. Rie (Ed.), *Perspectives in psychopathology.* Chicago: Aldine-Atherton, 1971.

CALDWELL, B. M. Arbitration between the child and the family. In V. C. Vaughan III and T. B. Brazelton (Eds.), *The family — Can it be saved?* Chicago: Year Book Medical Publishers, Inc., 1976.

CALDWELL, B. M., and STEDMAN, D. J. (EDS.). *Infant education.* New York: Walker and Co., 1977.

CONFERENCE ON NEWBORN HEARING SCREENING — PROCEEDINGS SUMMARY AND RECOMMENDATIONS. San Francisco: Maternal and Child Health Service, Health Services and Mental Health Administration, Public Health Service, Department of Health, Education and Welfare, 1971.

CONNOR, F. P., WILLIAMSON, G. G., and SIEPP, J. M. *Program guide for infants and toddlers with neuromotor and other developmental disabilities.* New York: Teachers College Press, 1978.

CORTER, C. M. Brief separation and communication between infant and mother. In T. Alloway, P. Pliner, and L. Krames (Eds.), Attachment behavior: *Advances in the study of communication and affect, Vol 3.* New York: Plenum Press, 1977.

CROSS, A. Diagnosis. In L. Cross and K. W. Goin (Eds.), *Identifying handicapped children.* New York: Walker and Co., 1977.

CROSS, L. Casefinding. In L. Cross and K. W. Goin (Eds.), *Identifying handicapped children.* New York: Walker and Co., 1977 (a).

CROSS, L. Identification of young children with handicaps. In N. E. Ellis and L. Cross (Eds.), *Planning programs for early education of the handicapped.* New York: Walker and Co., 1977 (b).

CUTSFORTH, T. D. The unreality of words to the blind. *Teachers Forum,* 1932, *4,* 86–89.

DAY, M. C., and PARKER, R. K. (Eds.). *The preschool in action.* Boston: Allyn and Bacon, 1977.

DeVries, R., and Kohlberg, L. Relations between Piagetian and psychometric assessments of intelligence. In L. G. Katz (Ed.), *Current topics in early childhood education.* Norwood, N.J.: Ablex Publishing Corporation, 1977.

DeWeerd, J., and Cole, A. Handicapped Children's Early Education Program. *Exceptional Children,* Nov. 1976, *43,* (3), 155–157.

DeWeerd, J. Introduction. In J. B. Jordan et al. (Eds.), *Early childhood education for exceptional children.* Reston, Va.: Council for Exceptional Children, 1977.

DuBose, R. Identification. In M. Snell (Ed.), *Systematic Introduction of the Moderately and Severely Handicapped.* Columbus: Charles E. Merrill Publishing Co., 1978.

Ellis, N. E., and Cross, L. (Eds.). *Planning programs for early education of the handicapped.* New York: Walker and Co., 1977.

Ensher, G. L., Blatt, B., and Winschel, J. F. Head start for the handicapped: Congressional mandate audit. *Exceptional Children,* Jan. 1977, *43,* 202–10.

Enzer, N. B., and Goin, K. W. (Eds.). *Social and emotional development: The preschooler.* New York: Walker and Co., 1978.

Erhardt, R. P. Sequential levels in development of prehension. *American Journal of Occupational Therapy,* 1974, *28,* (10), 592–6.

Erickson, M. L. *Assessment and management of developmental changes in children.* St. Louis: C. V. Mosby Co., 1976.

Evans, E. D. *Contemporary influences in early childhood education.* New York: Holt, Rinehart and Winston, 1971.

Finnie, H. R. *Handling the young cerebral palsied child at home.* New York: E. P. Dutton & Co., 1975.

Flavell, J. *Cognitive development.* Englewood Cliffs, N.J.: Prentice-Hall, 1977.

Fraiberg, S. Intervention in infancy: A program for blind infants. In B. Z. Friedlander, G. M. Sterritt and G. E. Kirk (Eds.), *Exceptional Infant, Vol. 3: Assessment & Intervention.* New York: Brunner/Mazel, 1975.

Francis-Williams, J. *Children with specific learning difficulties.* Oxford: Pergamon Press, 1974. Cited in N. E. Ellis and L. Cross (Eds.), *Planning programs for early education of the handicapped.* New York: Walker and Co., 1977.

Frankenburg, W. K. Considerations for screening. In N. E. Ellis and L. Cross (Eds.), *Planning programs for early education of the handicapped.* New York: Walker and Co., 1977.

Freedman, R., Warner, D. D., and Cook, P. *Exemplary programs for the handicapped, Volume III: Early childhood education.* Cambridge, Mass.: Abt Associates, 1973.

Furth, H. G. *Piaget for teachers.* Englewood Cliffs, N.J.: Prentice-Hall, 1970.

Garfunkel, F. Early childhood special education for children with social and emotional disturbances. In H. H. Spicker, N. J. Anastosiow, and W. L. Hodges (Eds.), *Children with special needs: Early development and education.* Minneapolis, Minn.: Leadership Training Institute/Special Education, 1976.

Gesell, A., and Amatruda, C. S. *Developmental diagnosis.* New York: Harper and Row, 1947.

Gesell, A., and Ilg, F. *Infant and child in the culture of today.* New York: Harper and Row, 1943.

Gesell, A., and Thompson, H. Learning and growth in identical infant twins: An experimental study by the method of co-twin control. *Genetic Psychology Monograph,* 1929, *6,* 1–125.

Good, C. V. *Dictionary of education.* New York: McGraw-Hill, 1959.

Guralnick, M. J. (Ed.), *Early intervention and the integration of handicapped and nonhandicapped children.* Baltimore: University Park Press, 1978.

Harbin, G. Educational assessment. In L. Cross and K. W. Goin (Eds.), *Identifying handicapped children.* New York: Walker and Co., 1977.

Hart, V. *Beginning with the handicapped.* Springfield, Ill.: Charles C. Thomas, 1974.

Hayden, A. H. Perspectives of early childhood education in special education. In N. G. Haring (Ed.), *Behavior of exceptional children.* Columbus, Ohio: Charles C. Merrill, 1974.

Hayden, A. H. Early childhood education. In K. E. Allen and others (Eds.), *Early intervention — A team approach.* Baltimore: University Park Press, 1978.

Hayden, A. H., and Dimitriev, V. The multidisciplinary preschool programs for Down's syndrome children at the University of Washington model preschool center. In B. Z. Friedlander, G. M. Sterritt, and G. E. Kirk (Eds.), *Exceptional Infant Vol. 3: Assessment & Intervention.* New York: Brunner/Mazel, 1975.

Hayden, A. H., and Edgar, E. B. Identification, screening, and assessment. In J. B. Jordan and others (Eds.), *Early childhood education for exceptional children.* Reston, Va.: Council for Exceptional Children, 1977.

Hayden, A. H., and Gotts, E. A. Multiple staffing patterns. In J. B. Jordan and others (Eds.), *Early childhood education for exceptional children.* Reston, Va.: Council for Exceptional Children, 1977.

Hayden, A. H., and Haring, N. D. Early intervention for high risk infants and young children. In T. D. Tjossem (Ed.), *Intervention strategies for high risk infants and young children.* Baltimore: University Park Press, 1976.

Hayden, A. H., and McGinness, G. D. Bases for early intervention. In E. Sontag, J. Smith and N. Certo (Eds.), *Educational programming for the severely and profoundly handicapped.* Reston, Va.: Division on Mental Retardation, Council for Exceptional Children, 1977.

Hayden, A. H., Morris, K., and Bailey, D. *The effectiveness of early education.* (Final report to the Bureau of Education for the Handicapped, U.S.O.E.). University of Washington, Seattle: Model Preschool Center for Handicapped Children, 1977. Cited in K. E. Allen and others (Eds.), *Early intervention — A team approach.* Baltimore: University Park Press, 1978.

Hein, G. E. Evaluation in open classrooms. In S. J. Meisels (Ed.), *Special Education and development.* Baltimore: University Park Press, 1979.

Hendrick, J. *The whole child: New trends in early education.* St. Louis: C. V. Mosby, 1975.

Hicks, D. E. Children with hearing impairments. In J. J. Gallagher (Ed.), *The application of child development research to exceptional children.* Reston, Va.: Council for Exceptional Children, 1975.

Higgins, S., and Barresi, J. The changing focus of public policy. *Exceptional Children,* Jan. 1979, *45* (4), 270–277.

Hirshoren, A., and Umansky, W. Certification for teachers of preschool handicapped children. *Exceptional Children,* Nov. 1977, *44* (3), 191–3.

HORTON, K. B. Early intervention for hearing impaired infants and young children. In T. I. Tjossem (Ed.), *Intervention strategies for high risk infants and young children.* Baltimore: University Park Press, 1976.

HUNT, J. McV. *Intelligence and experience.* New York: Ronald Press, 1961.

HUNT, J. McV, PARASKEVOPOULOS, J., SCHICKEDANZ, D., AND UZGIRIS, I. C. Variations in the mean ages of achieving object permanence under diverse conditions of rearing. In B. Z. Friedlander, G. M. Sterritt and G. E. Kirk (Eds.), *Exceptional Infant, Vol. 3: Assessment & Intervention.* New York: Brunner/Mazel, 1975.

ILLINGWORTH, R. S. *The development of the infant and young child.* Baltimore: Williams and Wilkins, 1972.

JOHNSON, D. J. Children with communication disorders. In J. J. Gallagher (Ed.), *The application of child development research to exceptional children.* Reston, Va.: Council for Exceptional Children, 1975.

JORDAN, J. B., HAYDEN, A. H., KARNES, M. B., and WOOD, M. M. (Eds.), *Early childhood education for exceptional children.* Reston, Va.: Council for Exceptional Children, 1977.

KAKALIK, J. S., BREWER, G. D., DOUGHERTY, L. A., FLEISCHAUER, P. D., and GENENSKY, S. M. *Services for handicapped youth.* (Report to the Department of Health, Education and Welfare, Washington, D. C. Office of the Assistant Secretary for Planning and Evaluation.) Santa Monica, Cal.: Rand Corporation, 1973.

KAMII, C. A sketch of the Piaget-derived preschool curriculum developed by the Ypsilanti Early Education Project. In B. Spodek (Ed.), *Early childhood education.* Englewood Cliffs, N. J.: Prentice-Hall, 1973.

KARNES, M. B., and ZEHRBACH, R. R. Alternative models for delivering services to young handicapped children. In J. B. Jordan and others (Eds.), *Early childhood education for exceptional children.* Reston, Va.: Council for Exceptional Children, 1977 (a).

KARNES, M. B., and ZEHRBACH, R. R. Early education of the handicapped: Issues and alternatives. In B. Spodek and H. J. Walberg (Eds.), *Early childhood education: Issues and insights.* Berkeley, Cal.: McCutchan Publishing Corp., 1977 (b).

KEOGH, B. Early identification of children with potential learning problems. *Journal of Special Education,* 1970, *4,* (3), 307–66.

KIRK, S. A. *Early education of the mentally retarded.* Urbana: University of Illinois Press, 1958.

KIRK, S. A. General and historical rationale for early education of the handicapped. In N. E. Ellis and L. Cross (Eds.), *Planning programs for early education of the handicapped.* New York: Walker and Company, 1977.

KLAUS, R. A. & GRAY, S. W. The early training project for disadvantaged children: A report after five years. *Monographs of the Society for Research in Child Development,* 1968, *33* (4, Serial No. 120).

KNOBLOCK, H., and PASAMANICK, B. (Eds.). *Gesell and Amatruda's Developmental Diagnosis.* New York: Harper & Row, 1974.

KOCH, F. P. A nursery school for children with cerebral palsy: Five-year follow-up study of thirteen children. *Pediatrics,* 1958, *22,* 329–335.

LACROSSE, E. L. The contribution of the nursery school. In R. Koch and J. C. Dobson (Eds.), *The mentally retarded child and his family* (2nd ed.). New York: Brunner/Mazel, 1976.

LAVECK, B. V. V. The developmental psychologist. In K. E. Allen and others (Eds.), *Early intervention — A team approach.* Baltimore: University Park Press, 1978.

LEWIS, M., and ROSENBLUM, L. A. (Eds.), *The development of affect.* New York: Plenum Press, 1978.

LILLIE, D. L. *Early childhood education: An individualized approach to developmental instruction.* Chicago: Science Research Associates, Inc., 1975.

LILLIE, D. L. Screening. In L. Cross and K. Goin (Eds.), *Identifying handicapped children.* New York: Walker and Company, 1977 (a).

LILLIE, D. L. Identifying and planning services for children. In N. E. Ellis and L. Cross (Eds.), *Planning programs for early education of the handicapped.* New York: Walker and Company, 1977 (b).

LILLIE, D. L., and TROHANIS, P. L. (Eds.). *Teaching parents to teach.* New York: Walker and Company, 1976.

LOWREY, G. H. *Growth and development of children.* Chicago: Year Book Medical Publishers, 1973.

LUTERMAN, D. M. A parent-oriented nursery program for preschool deaf children — A follow-up study. *Volta Review,* Feb., 1971, *73* (2), 106–112.

McCARTHY, J. McR. Children with learning disabilities. In J. J. Gallagher (Ed.), *The application of child development research to exceptional children.* Reston, Va.: Council for Exceptional Children, 1975.

MEIER, J. H. *Developmental and learning disabilities: Evaluation, management, and prevention in children.* Baltimore: University Park Press, 1976.

MOORES, D. F. Early childhood special education for hearing handicapped children. In H. H. Spicker, N. J. Anastasiow, and W. L. Hodges (Eds.), *Children with special needs: Early development and education.* Minneapolis, Minn.: Leadership Training Institute/Special Education, 1976.

MOSS, J. W., and MAYER, D. L. Children with intellectual subnormality. In J. J. Gallagher (Ed.), *The application of child development research to exceptional children.* Reston, Va.: Council for Exceptional Children, 1975.

MYKLEBUST, H. R. *The psychology of deafness.* New York: Grune & Stratton, Inc., 1960.

NATIONAL SOCIETY FOR THE PREVENTION OF BLINDNESS, INC. *Home eye test for preschoolers.* New York: Author, 1975.

NEILON, P. Shirley's babies after fifteen years: A personality study. *Journal of Genetic Psychology,* 1948, *73,* 175–186.

NORRIS, M., SPAULDING, P. J., and BRODIE, F. H. *Blindness in children.* Chicago: University of Chicago Press, 1957.

NORTHCOTT, W. H. *Curriculum guide: Hearing impaired children — birth to three years — and their parents.* Washington, D. C.: The Alexander Graham Bell Association for the Deaf, 1972.

NORTHCOTT, W. H. Implementing programs for young hearing impaired children. *Exceptional Children,* March 1973, *39* (6), 455–463 (a).

NORTHCOTT, W. H. (Ed.), *The hearing impaired child in a regular classroom: Preschool, elementary, and secondary years.* Washington, D. C.: The Alexander Graham Bell Association for the Deaf, 1973 (b).

NORTHCOTT, W. H. Integrating the preprimary hearing-impaired child: An examination of the process, product, and rationale. In M. J. Guralnick (Ed.), *Early intervention and the integration of handicapped and nonhandicapped children.* Baltimore: University Park Press, 1978.

PIKLER, E. Learning of motor skills on the basis of self-induced movements. In J. Hellmuth (Ed.), *Exceptional Infant, Vol. 2: Studies in abnormality.* New York: Brunner/Mazel, 1971.

PUBLIC LAW 90-538, *Handicapped Children's Early Education Assistance Act,* September 30, 1968.

PUBLIC LAW 93-380, *Education Amendments of 1974,* August 21, 1974.

PUBLIC LAW 93-644, *The Head Start, Economic Opportunity, and Community Partnership Act of 1974,* January 4, 1975.

RAMSDELL, D. A. The psychology of the hard-of-hearing and the deafened adult. In H. Davis and S. R. Silverman (Eds.), *Hearing and deafness.* New York: Holt, Rinehart and Winston, 1965.

SAFFORD, P. L. *Teaching young children with special needs.* St. Louis: C. V. Mosby, 1978.

SCHERZER, A. L. Early diagnosis, management, and treatment of cerebral palsy. *Rehabilitation Literature,* July 1974, *35* (7), 194–199.

SCHLESINGER, H. S., and MEADOW, K. P. *Sound and sign: Childhood deafness and mental health.* Berkeley: University of California Press, 1972.

SHEARER, M. S. and SHEARER, D. E. Parent involvement. In J. B. Jordan and others (Eds.), *Early childhood education for exceptional children.* Reston, Va.: Council for Exceptional Children, 1977.

SIGEL, I. Concept formation. In J. J. Gallagher (Ed.), *The application of child development research to exceptional children.* Reston, Va.: Council for Exceptional Children, 1975.

SKEELS, H. M. Adult status of children with contrasting early life experiences: A follow-up study. *Monographs of the Society for Research in Child Development,* 1966, *31* (39, Serial No. 105).

SKEELS, H. M., and DYE, H. B. A study of the effects of differential stimulation on mentally retarded children. *Proceedings and Addresses of the American Association on Mental Deficiency,* 1939, *44* (1), 114–136.

SPECIAL REPORT: Public Policy, NAEYC–EPSDT. Early and Periodic Screening, Diagnosis, and Treatment. *Young Children,* September, 1976, *31* (6), 486.

STEPHENS, B. Piagetian approach to visually handicapped education: Research review. Lecture presented at Project PAVE Special Study Institute, Louisville, July, 1978.

TJOSSEM, T. D. (Ed.), *Intervention strategies for high risk infants and young children.* Baltimore: University Park Press, 1976.

TORRANCE, E. P. Broadening concepts of giftedness in the 70's. In S. A. Kirk and F. E. Lord (Eds.), *Exceptional children: Educational resources and perspectives.* Boston: Houghton Mifflin, 1974.

UMSTED, R. G. Children with visual handicaps. In J. J. Gallagher (Ed.), *The application of child development research to exceptional children.* Reston, Va.: Council for Exceptional Children, 1975.

WADSWORTH, B. J. *Piaget for the classroom teacher.* New York: Longman, Inc., 1978.

WALLACE, G., and McLAUGHLIN, J. A. *Learning disabilities: Concepts and characteristics.* Columbus, Ohio: Charles E. Merrill, 1975.

WARREN, D. H. *Blindness and early childhood development.* New York: American Foundation for the Blind, 1977.

WARREN, N. Cultural variation and commonality in cognitive development. In J. Oates (Ed.), *Early cognitive development.* New York: John Wiley & Sons, 1979.

WINDSOR, C. E., and HURTT, J. *Eye muscle problems in childhood: A manual for parents.* St. Louis: C. V. Mosby, 1974.

VAUGHAN, D., ASBURY, T., and COOK, R. *General ophthalmology.* Los Altos, Cal.: Lange Medical Publications, 1971.

ZEHRBACH, R. R. Determining a preschool handicapped population. *Exceptional Children,* October 1975, *42* (2), 76–83.

Chapter 3

BARRE-BLACKEY, S., MUSSELWHITE, C., and ROGISTER, S. *Clinical oral language sampling: A handbook for student clinicians.* Danville, Ill.: Interstate Printers & Publishers, 1978.

BLOODSTEIN, O. *A handbook on stuttering.* Chicago: National Easter Seal Society for Crippled Children and Adults, 1975.

BLOOM, L., and LAHEY, M. *Language development and language disorders.* New York: John Wiley & Sons, 1978.

CULATTA, R. Fluency: The other side of the coin. *American Speech and Hearing Association,* 1976, *18,* 795–800.

CULATTA, R., and RUBIN, H. A program for the initial stages of fluency therapy. *Journal of Speech and Hearing Research,* 1973, *16,* 556–569.

CURTIS, J. (Ed.) *Processes and disorders of human communication.* New York: Harper & Row, 1978.

DARLEY, F., and SPRIESTERSBACH, D. *Diagnostic methods in speech pathology* (2nd ed.). New York: Harper & Row, 1978.

DAVIS, D. M. The relation of repetitions in the speech of young children to certain measures of language maturity and situational factors. *Journal of Speech Disorders,* 1939, *4,* 303.

DEUPREC, M. The muscles of voice and speech. In L. Travis (Ed.), *Handbook of speech pathology and audiology.* New York: Appleton-Century-Crofts, 1971.

DIEDRICH, W., and YOUNGSTROM, K. *Alaryngeal speech.* Springfield, Ill.: Charles C. Thomas, 1966.

Human Communication and its disorders: An overview. Report of the National Advisory Neurological Diseases and Stroke Council, National Institute of Health, Public Health Services, Bethesda, Maryland. Department of Health, Education and Welfare, 1969.

JOHNSON, W. *The onset of stuttering.* Minneapolis: University of Minnesota Press, 1959.

JOHNSON, W., BROWN, S. F., CURTIS, J. F., EDNEY, C. W., and KEASTER, J. *Speech handicapped school children.* New York: Harper & Row, 1967.

KENT, L. A retraining program for the adult who stutters. *Journal of Speech and Hearing Disorders,* 1961, *26,* 141–144.

MILISEN, R. The incidence of speech disorders. In L. Travis (Ed.), *Handbook of speech pathology and audiology.* New York: Appleton-Century-Crofts, 1971.

PERKINS, W. *Speech pathology: An applied behavioral science* (2nd ed.). St. Louis: C. V. Mosby, 1977.

RUBIN, H., and CULATTA, R. A point of view about fluency. *American Speech and Hearing Association,* 1971, *13,* 380–384.

RUBIN, H., and CULATTA, R. Stuttering as an aftereffect of normal developmental disfluency. *Clinical Pediatrics,* 1974, *13* (2), 172–176.

SHAMES, G. H. Dysfluency and stuttering. *Pediatric Clinics of North America,* 1968, *15,* 691.

TOMBLIN, J. B. *Processes and disorders of human communication.* (Curtis, Ed.) New York: Harper & Row, 1978.

TRAVIS, L. (Ed.). *Handbook of speech pathology and audiology.* New York: Appleton-Century-Crofts, 1971.

VAN RIPER, C. *Speech correction: Principles and methods* (6th ed.). Englewood Cliffs, N.J.: Prentice-Hall, Inc., 1978.

WEST, R. The neurophysiology of speech. In L. Travis (Ed.), *Handbook of speech pathology and audiology.* New York: Appleton-Century-Crofts, 1971.

WILLIAMS, D. A point of view about "stuttering." *Journal of Speech and Hearing Disorders,* 1957, *22,* 390–397.

WILLIAMS, D. Stuttering. In J. Curtis (Ed.), *Processes and disorders of communication.* New York: Harper & Row, 1978.

Chapter 4

ADES, H. W. Central auditory mechanisms. In J. Fields, H. W. Magoun, and V. E. Hall (Eds.), *Handbook of physiology,* Vol. 1. Washington, D. C.: American Physiological Society, 1959.

BERGER, K. W. *Speechreading: Principles and methods.* Baltimore: National Education Press, Inc., 1972.

CARHART, R. Development and conservation of speech. In H. Davis & S. R. Silverman (Eds.), *Hearing and deafness.* New York: Holt, Rinehart & Winston, 1970.

DAVIS, H., & SILVERMAN, S. R. *Hearing and deafness* (3rd ed.). New York: Holt, Rinehart & Winston, 1970.

DUFFY, J. K. Hearing problems of school age children. In I. S. Fusfeld (Ed.), *A handbook of readings in education of the deaf and postschool implications.* Springfield, Ill.: Charles C. Thomas, 1967.

FURTH, H. G. *Deafness and learning: A psychosocial approach.* Belmont, Ca.: Wadsworth, 1973.

GARRETSON, M. D. The need for multiple communication skills in the education process of the deaf. *Rocky Mountain Leader,* 1963, *62,* 1–8.

HOLM, V. A., and KUNZE, L. H. Effect of chronic otitis media on language and speech development. *Pediatrics,* 1969, *43,* 833.

KELLER, H. *Helen Keller in Scotland.* London: Methuen & Co., Ltd., 1933.

LENNEBERG, E. H. *Biological foundations of language.* New York: John Wiley & Sons, 1967.

LEWIS, N. Otitis media and linguistic incompetence. *Archives of Otolaryngology,* 102, 1976, 387–390.

MARTIN, F. N. *Introduction to audiology.* Englewood Cliffs, N.J.: Prentice Hall. 1975.

McCONNELL, F. Children with hearing disabilities. In L. M. Dunn (Ed.), *Exceptional children in the schools: Special education in transition* (2nd ed.). New York: Holt, Rinehart & Winston, 1973.

MEADOW, K. P. Development of deaf children. In E. M. Hetherington (Ed.), *Review of child development research* (Vol. 5). Chicago: University of Chicago Press, 1975.

MEADOW, K. P. Sociolinguistics, sign language and the deaf sub-culture. In T. J. O'Rourke (Ed.), *Psycholinguistics and total communication: The state of the art.* Washington, D. C.: American Annals of the Deaf, 1972.

MENYUK, P. *The development of speech.* Indianapolis, Ind.: Bobbs-Merrill Co., 1972.

MICHELSON, R. P., MERZENICH, M., and SHINDLER, R. The cochlear implant. *Audiology and Hearing Education,* 1, 2, October-November, 1975, 29.

MYKLEBUST, H. R. *The psychology of deafness* (2nd ed.). New York: Grune & Stratton, 1964.

NEEDLEMAN, H. Effects of hearing loss from recurrent otitis media on speech and language development. In B. F. Jaffe (Ed.), *Hearing Loss in Children.* Baltimore: University Park Press, 1977.

NEWBY, H. A. *Audiology.* New York: Appleton-Century-Crofts, 1972.

NORTHERN, J. L., & DOWNS, M. P. *Hearing in children.* Baltimore: Williams and Wilkins, 1974.

PAPARELLA, M. Use and abuse of tympanostomy tubes. *Otitis Media.* Publication of the Second National Conference on otitis media. Columbus: Ross Laboratories, 1979, 86–99.

PAPARELLA, M., & JUHN, S. R. Otitis media: Definition and terminology. *Otitis Media.* Publication of the Second National Conference on otitis media. Columbus: Ross Laboratories, 1979, 2–8.

PARADISE, J. L. Medical Treatment of acute otitis media: A critical essay. *Otitis Media.* Publication of the Second National Conference on otitis media. Columbus: Ross Laboratories, 1979, 79–84.

PINTNER, R. The deaf. In R. Pintner, J. Eisenson, and M. Stantom (Eds.), *The psychology of the physically handicapped.* New York: Appleton-Century-Crofts, 1941.

PINTNER, R., and REAMER, J. F. A mental and educational survey of schools for the deaf. *American Annals of the Deaf,* 65, 1920, 451.

PORTER, T. H., LYNN, M. S., and MADDOX, H. E. The cochlear implant. *Texas Journal of Audiology and Speech Pathology,* 4, 3, Fall-Winter, 1979, 24–27.

PROCTOR, C. A., and PROCTOR, B. Understanding hereditary nerve deafness. *Archives of Otolaryngology,* 1967, *85,* 23–40.

QUIGLEY, S. P. Some effects of impairment upon school performance. Manuscript prepared for the Division of Special Education Services, Office of the Superintendent of Public Instruction for the State of Illinois, 1970.

RAMSDELL, D. A. The psychology of the hard-of-hearing and the deafened adult. In H. Davis and S. Silverman, *Hearing and deafness.* New York: Holt, Rinehart & Winston, 1970, 435–446.

REPORT OF THE AD HOC COMMITTEE TO DEFINE DEAF AND HARD OF HEARING. *American Annals of the Deaf*, 120, 1975, 509–512.

RUBIN, M. *Hearing aids: Current developments and concepts.* Baltimore: University Park Press, 1976.

SANDERS, D. A. *Aural rehabilitation.* Englewood Cliffs, N.J.: Prentice-Hall, 1971.

SILVERMAN, S. R. The education of deaf children. In L. E. Travis (Ed.), *Handbook of speech pathology and audiology.* Englewood, Cliffs, N.J.: Prentice-Hall, 1971.

U. S. DEPARTMENT OF HEALTH, EDUCATION, AND WELFARE. HEW *Monthly Vital Statistics Report. Advance Report: Final Natality Statistics, 1963.* Washington, D. C: U.S. Department of Health, Education, and Welfare, Public Health Service, National Center for Health Statistics, 1964.

VERNON, M., and BROWN, D. A guide to psychological tests and testing procedures in the evaluation of deaf and hard of hearing children. *Journal of Speech and Hearing Disorders*, 29, 1964, 414–423.

WILLIAMS, B. R., and VERNON, M. Vocational guidance for the deaf. In H. Davis and S. R. Silverman (Eds.), *Hearing and deafness* (3rd ed.). New York: Holt, Rinehart & Winston, 1970.

WRIGHTSTONE, J. W., ARANOW, M. S., and MOSKOWITZ, S. Developing reading test norms for deaf children. *American Annals of the Deaf*, 108 1963, 311–316.

Chapter 5

ABESON, A., BOLICK, N., and HAFF, J. *A primer on due process: Education decisions for handicapped children.* Reston, Va.: The Council for Exceptional Children, 1976.

ALBER, M. B. (Ed.). *Listening: A curriculum guide for teachers of visually impaired students.* Springfield, Ill.: Specialized Educational Services Department, Materials Development and Dissemination Section, State Board of Education, 1978.

ALLEN, J. H. *May's diseases of the eye* (23rd ed.). Baltimore: Williams and Wilkins, 6, 1963.

AMERICAN FOUNDATION FOR THE BLIND. *Facts about blindness.* New York: American Foundation for the Blind, 1976.

AMERICAN FOUNDATION FOR THE BLIND. *Itinerant teaching services for blind children.* New York: American Foundation for the Blind, 1957.

AMERICAN FOUNDATION FOR THE BLIND. *A teacher education program for those who serve blind children and youth.* New York: American Foundation for the Blind, 1961.

AMERICAN PRINTING HOUSE FOR THE BLIND. *Distribution of January 6, 1979, Quota registrations by school, grades and reading media.* Author, 1979.

AMERICAN PRINTING HOUSE FOR THE BLIND. *English braille American edition*, 1959. Louisville, Ky.: Author, 1972.

ASHCROFT, S. C. Blind and partially seeing children. In L. M. Dunn (Ed.), *Exceptional Children in the Schools.* New York: Holt, Rinehart & Winston, 1963.

BARRAGA, N. C. *Increased visual behavior in low vision children.* New York: American Foundation for the Blind, 1964.

BARRAGA, N. C. (Ed.). *Visual efficiency scale for low vision kit.* Louisville, Ky.: American Printing House for the Blind, 1970.

BATEMAN, B. *Reading and psycholinguistic processes of partially seeing children.* (CEC Research Monograph, Series A, No. 5.) Arlington, Va.: Council for Exceptional Children, 1963.

BATEMAN, B. The modifiability of sighted adults perceptions of blind children's abilities. *New Outlooks for the Blind*, 1964, *58*, 133–135.

BATEMAN, B. Visually handicapped children. In N. G. Haring and R. L. Schiefe (Eds.), *Methods in special education.* New York: McGraw-Hill, 1967, 257–301.

BAUMAN, M. K. Group differences disclosed by inventory items. *International Journal for the Education of the Blind*, 1974, *13*, 101–106.

BAUMAN, M. Blind and partially seeing. In M. V. Wisland (Ed.), *Psychoeducational diagnosis of exceptional children.* Springfield, Ill.: Charles C. Thomas, 1977.

BENDER, Q., and ANDERMANN, K. Brain damage in blind children with retrolental filmoplasia. *Archives of Neurology*, 1965, *12*, 644–649.

BIRCH, J. W., TISDALL, W., PEABODY, R., and STERRETT, R. *School achievement and effect of type size on reading in visually handicapped children.* (Cooperative Research Project No. 1766, Contract No. OEC-4-10-028.) Pittsburgh, Pa.: University of Pittsburgh, 1966.

BLEDSOE, C. W. The family of residential schools. *Blindness*, 1971. Washington, D. C.: American Association of Workers for the Blind, 1971.

CARROLL, T. J. *Blindness: What it is, what it does and how to live with it.* Boston: Little, Brown and Co., 1961.

CATON, H., and BRADLEY, E. L. A new approach to beginning braille readings. *Education of the Visually Handicapped*, 1978–79, *10*, 66–71.

CATON, H., and RANKIN, E. Variability in age and experience among blind students using basal reading materials. *Journal of Visual Impairment and Blindness.* Submitted August, 1978.

CATON, H. A primary reading program for beginning braille readers. *Journal of Visual Impairment and Blindness*, 1979, *73*, 309–313.

CHALKLEY, T. *Your eyes: A book for paramedical personnel and the lay reader.* Springfield, Ill.: Charles C. Thomas, 1974.

CHASE, T. B. Developmental assessment of handicapped infants and young children: With special attention to the visually impaired. *AFB Practice Report.* New York: American Foundation for the Blind, 1977.

COWEN, E. L., UNDERBERG, R., VERRILLO, R. T., and BENHAM, F. G. *Adjustment to visual disability in adolescence.* New York: American Foundation for the Blind, 1961.

CUTSFORTH, T. D. *The blind in school and society: A psychological study.* New York: American Foundation for the Blind, 1951.

DAUTERMAN, W. L., SHAPIRO, B., and SWINN, R. M. Performance of intelligence for blind reviewed. *International Journal for the Education of the Blind*, 1967, *17*, 8–16.

DAVIS, C. J. *New developments in intelligence testing of blind children.* Proceedings of the conference on new approaches to the evaluation of blind persons. New York: American Foundation for the Blind, 1970.

DEMOTT, R. Visually impaired. In N. G. Haring (Ed.), *Behavior of exceptional children: An introduction to special education.* Columbus, Ohio: Charles E. Merrill, 1974, 529–563.

EAKIN, W. M., PRATT, R. J., and McFARLAND, T. L. *Type size research for the partially seeing child.* Pittsburgh: Stanwix House, 1961.

FRIEDMAN, J., & PASNAK, R. Attainment of classification and seriation concepts by blind and sighted subjects. *Education of the Visually Handicapped*, 1973, *5*, 55–62.

GALTON, L. New devices to help the blind and near-blind. *Readings in Visually Handicapped Education.* Guilford, Conn.: Special Learning Corporation, 1978.

GOLDMAN, H. Psychological testing of blind children. *Research Bulletin*, American Foundation for the Blind, 1970, *21*, 77–90.

GOTTESMAN, M. A. A comparative study of Piaget's developmental schema of sighted children with that of a group of blind children. *Child Development*, 1971, *42*, 573–580.

GOTTESMAN, M. A. Conservation development in blind children. *Child Development*, 1973, *44*, 824–827.

GOTTESMAN, M. A. Stage development of blind children: A Piagetian view. *New Outlook for the Blind*, 1976, *70*, 94–100.

GOWMAN, A. G. *The war blind in American social structure.* New York: American Foundation for the Blind, 1957.

GRAHAM, M. D. Wanted: A readiness test for mobility training. *New Outlook for the Blind*, 1965, *59*, 157–162.

HAMMILL, P., CRANDELL, J. M., and COLARUSSO, R. The slossen intelligence test adapted for visually limited children. *Exceptional Children*, 1970, *36*, 535–536.

HANNINEN, K. A. *Teaching the visually handicapped.* Columbus, Ohio: Charles E. Merrill, 1975.

HARLEY, R. K. Children with visual disabilities. In L. M. Dunn (Ed.), *Exceptional children in the schools* (2nd ed.). New York: Holt, Rinehart & Winston, 1973.

HARLEY, R. K., and LAWRENCE, G. A. *Visual impairment in the schools.* Springfield, Ill.: Charles C. Thomas, 1977.

HATLEN, P. H. Visually handicapped children with additional problems. In B. Lowenfeld (Ed.), *The visually handicapped child in school.* New York: John Day, 1973.

HAYES, S. P. *Contributions to a psychology of blindness.* New York: American Foundation for the Blind, 1941.

HIGGINS, L. C. *Classification in congenitally blind children.* New York: American Foundation for the Blind, 1973.

JONES, J., and COLLINS, A. *Educational programs for visually handicapped children.* Washington, D. C.: U. S. Government Printing Office, 1966.

KENTUCKY STANDARDS FOR PROGRAMS FOR VISUALLY IMPAIRED CHILDREN. Frankfort, Kentucky Bureau for Education of Exceptional Children, Kentucky State Department of Education, 1978.

KIRK, S. A., and GALLAGHER, L. T. Children with visual impairments. In *Educating exceptional children* (3rd ed.). Boston: Houghton Mifflin, 1979, 237–279.

KURZWEIL COMPUTER PRODUCTS. *The Kurzweil Report*, Spring 1979, pp. 1–2.

KURZWEIL COMPUTER. *The Kurzweil Report*, Summer 1978, *2*, 1–2.

LAWRENCE HALL OF SCIENCE. *SAUI Update: Science activities for the visually handicapped.* Berkeley, Ca.: Author, 1978.

LIVINGSTON, J. S. Evaluation of enlarged test form used with partially seeing. *Sight Saving Review*, 1958, *28*, 37–39.

LOWENFELD, B. *Our blind children, growing and learning with them* (3rd ed.). Springfield, Ill.: Charles C. Thomas, 1971.

LOWENFELD, B. History of the education of visually handicapped children. *The visually handicapped child in school.* New York: John Day, 1973.

LOWENFELD, B. *The changing status of the blind: From separation to integration.* Springfield, Ill.: Charles C. Thomas, 1975.

LOWENFELD, B., ABEL, G., and HATLEN, P. *Blind children learn to read.* Springfield, Ill.: Charles C. Thomas, 1969.

LYNDON, W. T., and McGRAW, M. L. *Concept development for visually handicapped children.* New York: American Foundation for the Blind, 1973.

MEYEN, E. L. *Exceptional children: An introduction.* Denver: Love Publishing Co., 1978.

MILLER, C. K. Conservation in blind children. *Education of the Visually Handicapped*, 1969, *12*, 101–105.

MONTGOMERY, J. R. *Congenital rubella: Baylor study.* Forty-ninth Biennial Conference, Association for the Education of the Visually Handicapped, 1969, 1–7.

NAPIER, G. D. Special subject adjustments and skills. In B. Lowenfeld (Ed.), *The visually handicapped in school.* New York: John Day, 1973, 221–227.

NATIONAL SOCIETY FOR THE PREVENTION OF BLINDNESS. *Vision screening in schools* (Publication No. 257). New York: National Society for the Prevention of Blindness, 1969.

NOLAN, C. Y. The visually impaired. In E. Meyer (Ed.). *Exceptional children and youth: An introduction.* Denver: Love Publishing Co., 1978.

NOLAN, C. Y. Thoughts on the future of braille. *Journal of Visual Impairment and Blindness*, 1979, *73*, 333–335.

O'BRIEN, R. *Alive . . . aware . . . a person: A development model for early childhood services with special definition for visually impaired children and their parents.* Rockville, Md.: Montgomery County Public Schools, 1976.

PARKER, J. Adapting school psychological evaluation of the blind child. *New Outlook for the Blind*, 1969, *63*, 305–311.

PEABODY, R. L., and BIRCH, J. W. Educational implications of partial vision: New findings from a national study. *Sight Saving Review*, 1967, *37*, 92–96.

PINTNER, R. J., EISENSON, J., and STANTON, M. *The psychology of the physically handicapped.* New York: F. S. Crofts, 1941.

SCHOLL, G. Understanding and meeting developmental needs. In B. Lowenfeld (Ed.), *The visually handicapped child in school.* New York: John Day, 1973.

SCHOLL, G., and SCHNUR, R. *Measures of psychological, vocational, and educational functioning in the blind and visually handicapped.* New York: American Foundation for the Blind, 1976.

SILVERMAN, W. W. Prematurity and retrolental fiberoplasia. *New Outlook for the Blind*, 1970, *64*, 232–236.

SIMPKINS, K., and STEPHENS, B. Cognitive development of blind subjects. *Proceedings of the 52nd Biennial Conference of the Association for the Education of the Visually Handicapped*, 1974, 26–28.

SMITH, E. W., KROUSE, S. W., and ATKINSON, M. M. *Educators encyclopedia.* Englewood Cliffs, N.J.: Prentice-Hall, 1961.

SOCIAL SCIENCE CONSORTIUM. Project MAVIS materials adaptations for visually impaired students in the social studies. Boulder, Col., 1978.

SPIVEY, S. A. *The social position of selected children with a visual loss in regular classes in the public schools of Atlanta, Georgia.*

Specialist in education thesis. George Peabody College for Teachers, 1967.

SPUNGIN, S. J., and SWALLOW, R. Psychoeducational assessment. Rate of psychologist to teacher of the visually handicapped. *AFB Practice Report.* New York: American Foundation for the Blind, 1977.

SWALLOW, R. Assessment for visually handicapped children and youth. *AFB Practice Report.* New York: American Foundation for the Blind, 1977.

SWALLOW, R., MANGOLD, S., and MANGOLD, P. Informal assessment of developmental skills for visually handicapped students. *AFB Practice Report.* New York: American Foundation for the Blind, 1978.

SYKES, K. S. A comparison of the effectiveness of standard print and large print in facilitating the reading skills of visually impaired students. *Education of the Visually Handicapped,* 1971, *3,* 97–106.

TAYLOR, J. L. Educational programs. In B. Lowenfeld (Ed.), *The visually handicapped child in school.* New York: John Day, 1973.

TAYLOR, J. L. Selecting facilities to meet educational needs. In B. Lowenfeld (Ed.), *The blind preschool child.* New York: American Foundation for the Blind, 1947.

TELESENSORY SYSTEMS. *Optacon training.* Palo Alto, Cal.: Author, 1973.

TILLMAN, M. H., and OSBORNE, R. T. The performance of blind and sighted children on the Wechsler Intelligence Scale for children: Interaction effects. *Education of the Visually Handicapped,* 1969, *1,* 1–4.

TOBIN, J. J. Conservation of substance in the blind and sighted. *British Journal of Educational Psychology,* 1972, 42:2, 192–197.

U. S. DEPARTMENT OF HEALTH, EDUCATION AND WELFARE, PUBLIC HEALTH SERVICES, NATIONAL INSTITUTE OF HEALTH. *Interim Report of the National Advisory Eye Council 1976.* (DHEW Publication No. 76-1098), 1976.

VAUGHN, D., and ASBURY, T. *General opthalmology* (7th ed.). Los Altos, Cal.: Lange Medical Publications, 1974.

WARREN, D. H. *Blindness and early childhood development.* New York: American Foundation for the Blind, 1977.

WORMALD INTERNATIONAL SENSORY AIDS. *Electronic Travel Aids.* Bensenville, Ill., 1979.

Chapter 6

AIELLO, B. (Ed.). *Places and spaces: Facilities planning for handicapped children.* Reston, Va.: The Council for Exceptional Children, 1976.

ALLEN, R. M., and JEFFERSON, T. W. *Psychological evaluation of the cerebral palsied person: Intellectual, personality, and vocational applications.* Springfield, Ill.: Charles C. Thomas, 1962.

BENDER, E., SCHUMACHER, B., and ALLEN, H. A. *A resource manual for medical aspects of disabilities.* Carbondale, Ill.: Rehabilitation Counselor Training Program, Rehabilitation Institute, Southern Illinois University, 1976.

BLECK, E. E. Anatomy-basic parts and terms of the nervous and musculo-skeletal systems. In E. E. Bleck and D. A. Nagel (Eds.), *Physically handicapped children: A medical atlas for teachers.* New York: Grune & Stratton, 1975, 1–14.

BLECK, E. E. Arthrogryposis. In E. E. Bleck and D. A. Nagel (Eds.), *Physically handicapped children: A medical atlas for teachers.* New York: Grune & Stratton, 1975, 21–23.

BLECK, E. E. Cerebral palsy. In E. E. Bleck and D. A. Nagel (Eds.), *Physically handicapped children: A medical atlas for teachers.* New York: Grune & Stratton, 1975, 37–89.

BLECK, E. E. Muscular-dystrophy: Duchene type. In E. E. Bleck and D. A. Nagel (Eds.), *Physically handicapped children: A medical atlas for teachers.* New York: Grune & Stratton, 1975, 173–179.

BLECK, E. E. Myelomeningocele, meningocele, spina bifida. In E. E. Bleck and D. A. Nagel (Eds.), *Physically handicapped children: A medical atlas for teachers.* New York: Grune & Stratton, 1975, 181–192.

BLECK, E. E. Osteogenesis imperfecta. In E. E. Bleck and D. A. Nagel (Eds.), *Physically handicapped children: A medical atlas for teachers.* New York: Grune & Stratton, 1975, 205–208.

BLECK, E. E. Traumatic paraplegia and quadriplegia. In E. E. Bleck and D. A. Nagel (Eds.), *Physically handicapped children: A medical atlas for teachers.* New York: Grune & Stratton, 1975, 209–214.

BLECK, E. E., & NAGEL, D. A. (Eds.) *Physically handicapped children: A medical atlas for teachers.* New York: Grune & Stratton, 1975.

CAPUTE, A. J. Cerebral palsy and associated dysfunctions. In R. H. A. Haslam and P. J. Valletutti (Eds.), *Medical problems in the classroom: The teacher's role in diagnosis and management.* Baltimore: University Park Press, 1975, 149–163.

CATHEY, M. L., AND JANSMA, P. Mainstreaming orthopedically disabled individuals in various activities, Part I. *The Directive Teacher,* 1979, *2,* 9, 29.

DENHOFF, E. Cerebral palsy: Medical aspects. In W. M. Cruickshank (Ed.), *Cerebral palsy: Its individual and community problems* (2nd ed.). Syracuse: Syracuse University Press, 1966, 24–100.

EPILEPSY FOUNDATION OF AMERICA. *Answers to most frequent questions people ask about epilepsy.* Washington, D. C.: Epilepsy Foundation, 1977.

FORD, F. R. *Diseases of the nervous system: In infancy, childhood and adolescence* (5th ed.). Springfield, Ill.: Charles C. Thomas, 1966.

HALLAHAN, D. P., and KAUFFMAN, J. M. *Exceptional Children: Introduction to special education.* Englewood Cliffs, N. J.: Prentice-Hall, 1978.

HARVEY, B. Asthma. In E. E. Bleck and D. A. Nagel (Eds.), *Physically handicapped children: A medical atlas for teachers.* New York: Grune & Stratton, 1975, 1–14, 25–26.

HOHMAN, L. B., and FREEDHEIM, D. K. Further studies on intelligence levels in cerebral palsied children. *American Journal of Physical Medicine,* 1958, *37,* 90–97.

HOPKINS, T. W., BICE, H. V., and COLTON, K. C. *Evaluation and education of the cerebral palsied child.* Arlington, Va.: International Council for Exceptional Children, 1954.

JOHNSTON, R. B., and MAGRAB, P. R. (Eds.) *Developmental disorders: Assessment, treatment, education.* Baltimore: University Park Press, 1976.

KEATS, S. *Cerebral palsy.* Springfield, Ill.: Charles C. Thomas, 1965.

KLIMENT, S. A. *Into the mainstream: A syllabus for a barrier-free environment.* Washington, D. C.: U. S. Government Printing Office, Superintendent of Documents, 1976, 38–44.

Koehler, J. Spinal muscular atrophy of childhood. In E. E. Bleck and D. A. Nagel (Eds.), *Physically handicapped children: A medical atlas for teachers.* New York: Grune & Stratton, 1975, 255–259.

Livingston, S. *Living with epileptic seizures.* Springfield, Ill.: Charles C. Thomas, 1963.

Mace, R., and Iaslett, B. *An illustrated handbook of the handicapped section of the North Carolina state building code.* Raleigh, N. C.: The North Carolina State Building Code Council and the North Carolina Department of Insurance, 1977.

Melichar, J. F. *ISAARE*, Vols. 1 to 7. San Mateo, Cal.: Adaptive Systems Corp., 1977.

Melichar, J. F. ISAARE, a description. *AAESPH Review,* 1978, *3*, 259–268.

Miller, J. J. Juvenile rheumatoid arthritis. In E. E. Bleck and D. A. Nagel (Eds.), *Physically handicapped children: A medical atlas for teachers.* New York: Grune and Stratton, 1975, 233–240.

Myers, B. R. The child with a chronic illness. In R. H. A. Haslam and P. J. Valletutti (Eds.), *Medical problems in the classroom: The teacher's role in diagnosis and management.* Baltimore: University Park Press, 1975, 97–127.

Peirce, R. L. Epileptics share a world of uncertainty and secrecy because of public's ignorance. *The Courier-Journal,* March 6, 1979.

Sharrard, W. J. W. Spina bifida and its sequelae. *South African Medical Journal,* 1968, *42,* 915–918. In D. D. Peterson (Ed.), *The physically handicapped: A book of readings.* New York: MSS Educational Publishing Company, 1969, 207–210.

Taylor, A. R. *The study of the child.* New York: D. Appleton and Company, 1898.

Walshe, F. *Disease of the nervous system.* Baltimore: Williams and Williams, 1963.

Wolf, J. M. Historical perspective of cerebral palsy. In J. M. Wolf, *The results of treatment in cerebral palsy.* Springfield, Ill.: Charles C. Thomas, 1969, 5–44.

Part III Introduction

Bettelheim, B. *Love is not enough.* New York: Macmillan, 1950.

Bettelheim, B. *The empty fortress.* New York: Free Press, 1967.

Fenichel, C. Psychoeducational approaches for seriously emotionally disturbed children in the classroom. In P. Knoblock (Ed.), *Intervention approaches in education for emotionally disturbed children.* Syracuse: Syracuse University Press, 1966.

Haring, N. G. and Schiefelbusch, R. L. (Eds.), *Teaching Special children.* New York: McGraw-Hill, 1976.

Hewett, F. M. *The emotionally disturbed child in the classroom.* Boston: Allyn and Bacon, 1968.

Hobbs, N. Helping the disturbed child: Psychological and ecological strategies. *American Psychologist,* 1966, *21,* 1105–1115.

Hobbs, N. Nicholas Hobbs. In J. M. Kauffman and C. D. Lewis (Eds.), *Teaching children with behavior disorders: Personal Perspectives.* Columbus, Ohio: Charles E. Merrill, 1974.

Knoblock, P. Open education for emotionally disturbed

children. *Exceptional Children,* 1973, *39,* 358–365.

MacMillan, D. L. and Forness, S. R. Behavior modification: Savior or servant? In R. K. Egman, P. E. Meyer, and G. Tarjan (Eds.) *Sociobehavioral studies in mental retardation.* Washington, D. C.: A. A. M. D., 1973.

O'Leary, K. D. and O'Leary, S. G. *Classroom management: The successful use of behavior modification.* New York: Pergamon Press, 1972.

Reeves, R., and Kauffman, J. M. The behavior disordered. In N. G. Haring (Ed.), *Behavior of Exceptional Children* (2nd Ed.). Columbus, Ohio: Charles E. Merrill, 1978, pp. 123–154.

Chapter 7

Adamson, G. *Final report of the Educational Modulation Center.* Olathe, Kansas: Olathe Public Schools, 1970.

Baumeister, A. A. Problems in comparative studies of mental retardates and normals. *American Association on Mental Deficiency,* 1967, *71,* 869–875.

Berlin, C. M., Jr. Biology and retardation. In J. T. Neisworth and R. M. Smith (Eds.), *Retardation: Issues, assessment and intervention.* New York: McGraw-Hill, 1978, 117–137.

Bijou, S. W. A functional analysis of retarded development. In N. R. Ellis (Ed.), *International review of research in mental retardation,* Vol. 1. New York: Academic Press, 1966, 1–19.

Birch, H. R., Richardson, S. A., Baird, D., Horobin, G., and Illsley, R. *Mental abnormality in the community: A clinical and epidemiological study.* Baltimore: William and Wilkins, 1970.

Blatt, B., & Kaplan, F. *Christmas in purgatory.* Boston: Allyn and Bacon, 1966.

Brown, L., Nietupski, J., and Hamre-Nietupski, S. Criterion of ultimate functioning. In A. Thomas (Ed.), *Hey, don't forget about me!* Reston, Va.: Council for Exceptional Children, 1976.

Bruner, J. S. The course of cognitive growth. *American Psychologist,* 1964, *19,* 1–15.

Cattel, R. B. *Abilities: Their structure, growth, and action.* Boston: Houghton Mifflin, 1971.

Deno, E. Special education a developmental capital. *Exceptional Children, 37,* 1970, 229–237.

Doll, E. A. *Measuring social competence: A manual for the Vineland Social Maturity Scale.* Minneapolis: Educational Test Bureau, 1953.

Dunn, L. M. Children with moderate and severe general learning disabilities. In L. M. Dunn (Ed.), *Exceptional children in schools* (2nd ed.). New York: Holt, Rinehart and Winston, 1973.

Fogelman, C. J. (Ed.) *AAMD Adaptive behavior scale manual* (Rev. ed.). Washington, D. C.: AAMD, 1975.

Gelof, M. Comparisons of systems of classifications relating degrees of retardation to measured intelligence. *American Journal of Mental Deficiency,* 1963, *68,* 297–317.

Gottesman, I. I. Genetic aspects of intelligent behavior. In N. R. Ellis (Ed.), *Handbook of mental deficiency.* New York: McGraw-Hill, 1963, 253–296.

Grossman, H. (Ed.) *Manual on terminology and classification in mental retardation.* Washington, D. C.: American Association on Mental Deficiency, 1970.

GROSSMAN, H. *Manual on terminology and classification in mental retardation* (rev. ed.). Washington, D. C.: American Association on Mental Deficiency, 1973.

GROSSMAN, H. *Manual on terminology and classification in mental retardation.* (rev. ed.) Washington, D. C.: American Association on Mental Deficiency, 1977.

GUILFORD, J. P. The structure of the intellect. *Psychological Bulletin,* 1956, 53, 267–293.

HAYWOOD, H. C. What happened to mild and moderate mental retardation. *American Journal of Mental Deficiency,* 1979, 83, 427–431.

HEBB, D. O. The effect of early and late brain injury upon the test scores, and the nature of adult intelligence. *Proceedings of the American Philosophical Society,* 1942, 85, 275–292.

HEBER, R. F. *Epidemiology of mental retardation.* Springfield, Ill.: Thomas, 1970.

HEBER, R. F. *A manual on terminology and classification in mental retardation.* Washington, D. C.: AAMD, 1959.

HEBER, R. F. *A manual on terminology and classification in mental retardation.* Washington, D. C.: AAMD, 1961.

HOUSE, B. T., and ZEAMAN, D. Visual discrimination learning in imbeciles. *American Journal of Mental Deficiency,* 1958, 63, 447–452.

KANNER, L. *Child population* (3rd ed.). Springfield, Ill.: Charles C. Thomas, 1957.

KANNER, L. Feeblemindedness, absolute, relative and apparent. *Nervous Child,* 1948, 7, 365–397.

KAUFFMAN, J. M. and PAYNE, J. S. (Eds.) *Mental retardation: Introduction and personal perspectives.* Columbus, Ohio: Charles E. Merrill, 1975.

LeFEVRE, D. B. *Blue Grass Association for Mental Retardation News.* Lexington, Ky.: June-July, 1978.

LEWIS, E. D. Types of mental deficiency and their social significance. *Journal of Mental Science,* 1933, 79, 298–304

MACMILLAN, D. L. *Mental retardation in school and society.* Boston: Little, Brown and Co., 1977.

MACMILLAN, D. L. and FORNESS, S. R. Behavior modification: Savior or servant? In R. K. Eyman, P. E. Meyer, and G. Tarjan (Eds.), *Sociobehavioral studies in mental retardation.* Washington, D. C.: AAMD, 1973.

MALONEY, M., and WARD, M. P. *Mental retardation and modern society.* New York: Oxford University Press, 1979.

MENOLASCINO, F. J. *Challenges in mental retardation: Progressive ideology and sources.* New York: Human Services Press, Inc., 1977.

MERCER, J. R. The myth of three percent prevalence. In R. K. Eyman, C. E. Meyers, and G. Tarjan (Eds.), *Sociobehavioral studies in mental retardation, monographs of the AAMD,* 1973.

MERCER, J. R. *Labeling the mentally retarded.* Berkeley: University of California Press, 1973(a).

MERCER, J. R. System of multicultural and pluralistic assessment (SCMPA)-Technical Manual. New York: Psychological Corporation, 1979.

NEISWORTH, J. T., and SMITH, R. M. (Eds.) *Retardation: Issues and assessments, and interventions.* New York: McGraw-Hill, 1978.

NIHIRA, K., FOSTER, R., SHELLHARS, M., and LELAND, H.

American Association on Mental Deficiency: Adaptive behavior scale. Washington, D. C.: American Association on Mental Deficiency, 1974.

PENROSE, L. S. The biology of mental defect (2nd rev. ed.). New York: Grune and Stratton, 1966.

PIAGET, J. *The psychology of intelligence.* New York: Harcourt, Brace, 1950.

Presidents committee on mental retardation: Trends in state services. Washington, D. C.: U. S. Government Printing Office, 1976.

Presidents task force on the mentally handicapped: Action against mental disability. Washington, D. C.: U. S. Government Printing Office, 1970.

ROBINSON, N. M., AND ROBINSON, H. B. The mentally retarded child: A psychological approach (2nd ed.). New York: McGraw-Hill, 1976.

SALVIA, J. Perspectives on the nature of retardation. In J. T. Neisworth and R. M. Smith (Eds.), *Retardation-issues, assessment, and intervention.* New York: McGraw-Hill, 1978, 27–47.

SARASON, S. B. *Psychological problems in mental deficiency* (2nd ed.). New York: Harper & Row, 1953.

SCHAPIRO, J., and EIGERDORF, V. Options in living arrangements, workshop report F. In J. C. Hamilton and R. M. Segal (Eds.), *Proceeding — a consultation conference on the gerontological aspects of mental retardation.* Ann Arbor: University of Michigan, Institute of Gerontology, 1975.

SLOAN, W., AND BIRCH, J. A. A rationale for degrees of retardation. *American Journal of Mental Deficiency,* 1955, 66, 262.

SMITH, R. M. *An introduction to mental retardation.* New York: McGraw-Hill, 1971.

STRAUSS, A. A. and LEHTINEN, L. E. *Psychopathology and education of the brain-injured child (Vol. I).* New York: Grune & Stratton, 1947.

TARJAN, G., WRIGHT, S. W., EYMAN, R. K., and KIERNAN, C. C. National history of mental retardation. Some aspects of epidemiology. *American Journal of Mental Deficiency,* 1973, 77, 369–379.

TAYLOR, F. D., and SOLOWAY, M. M. The Madison School plan: A functional model for merging the regular classrooms. In E. N. Deno (Ed.), *Instructional alternatives for exceptional children.* Minneapolis: Leadership Training Institute/Special Education, University of Minnesota, 1973, 145–155.

TELFORD, C. W., and SAWREY, J. M. *The exceptional individual* (3rd ed.). Engelwood Cliffs, N. J.: Prentice-Hall, 1977.

TERMAN, L. M., & MERRILL, M. A. *The Stanford Binet Intelligence Scale* (3rd rev.). Boston: Houghton Mifflin, 1973.

TREDGOLD, A. F. *A textbook of mental deficiency* (6th ed.). Baltimore: William Wood and Co., 1937.

TURNURE, J. E. Distractibility in the mentally retarded: Negative evidence for an orienting inadequacy. *Exceptional Children,* 1970, 37, 181–186.

VAN ETTEN, G., and ADAMSON, G. The fail save program: A special education service continuum. In E. Deno (Ed.), *Instructional alternatives for exceptional children.* Reston, Va.: Council for Exceptional Children, 1973.

WECHSLER, D. *Wechsler Intelligence Scale for Children: A manual.* New York: Psychological Corp., 1974.

WOLFENSBERGER, W. Will there always be an institution? II: The impact of new service models. *Mental Retardation,* 1971, 9 (6), 31–38.

WOLFENSBERGER, W. *The principle of normalization in human services.* Toronto: National Institute on Mental Retardation, 1972.

WOLFENSBERGER, W. The origin and nature of our institutional models. In R. B. Kugel and A. Shearer (Eds.), *Changing patterns in residential services for the mentally retarded* (Rev. ed.). Washington, D. C.: President committee on mental retardation, 1976.

ZEAMAN, D., & HOUSE, B. J. The role of attention in retardate discriminative learning. In N. R. Ellis (Ed.), *Handbook of mental deficiency.* New York: McGraw-Hill, 1963, 159–223.

ZIGLER, E. Familial mental retardation: A continuing dilemma. *Science,* 1967, 155, 292–298

Chapter 8

ABESON, A., and ZETTEL, J. The quiet revolution: The handicapped children act of 1975. *Exceptional Children,* 1977, *44,* 115–128.

ABRAMS, J. Further considerations on the ego functioning of the dyslexic child: A psychiatric point of view. In G. Spache (Ed.), *Reading disability and perception.* International Reading Assoc., 1969.

ABRAMS, J. Minimal brain dysfunction and dyslexia. *Reading World,* 1975, *14,* 219–227.

ABRAMS, J. The myths and realities of severe reading and related learning disabilities. In P. D. Pearson and J. Hansen (Eds.), *Reading: Theory, research, & practice,* Twenty-sixth yearbook of National Reading Conference. Clemson, S. C.: NRC, 1977, 150–157.

BAREN, M., LIEBEL, R., and SMITH, L. *Overcoming learning disabilities: A team approach.* Reston, Va.: Prentice-Hall, 1978.

BIRCH, H., and BELMONT, L. Auditory-visual integration in normal and retarded readers. *American Journal of Orthopsychiatry,* 1964, *34,* 852–861.

BOYER, E. L. A conversation with E. Boyer: Priorities of the USOE. *Exceptional Children,* 1978, *44,* 570–574.

BRYANT, N. D. Some principles of remedial instruction for dyslexia. *The Reading Teacher,* 1965, *18,* 567–572.

COHEN, S. A. *Teach them all to read: Theory, methods and materials for teaching the disadvantaged.* New York: Random House, 1969.

CRUICKSHANK, W., BETSEN, F. A., RATENBURG, F. H., and TANNHAUSER, M. T. *A teaching method for brain injured and hyperactive children.* Syracuse, N. Y.: Syracuse University Press, 1961.

DCLD COMMITTEE OF DEFINITION, IDENTIFICATION, AND INCIDENCE OF LEARNING DISABILITIES: Recommendations of the first Invitational caucus on Learning Disabilities. Council for Exceptional Children; *DCLD Newsletter,* 1976, *1,* 9.

DENEMARK, G., MORSINK, C., and THOMAS, C. Accepting the challenge for change in teacher education. In M. Reynolds (Ed.), *A common body of practice for teachers: The challenge*

of P. L. 94–142 to teacher education. Washington, DC: AACTE, One Dupont Circle, 1980.

DEREVENSKY. J. Cross modal functioning and reading achievement. *Journal of Reading Behavior,* 1977, *IX,* 233–251.

ENGLEMANN, S., and BRUNER, E. *DISTAR Reading I.* Chicago: Science Research Assoc., 1969.

ENSHER, G. *A diagnostic study of reading disabilities of children enrolled in six public school classes for the mentally retarded.* Unpublished doctoral dissertation, Boston University, 1972.

FEINGOLD, B. Hyperkinesis and learning disabilities linked to the ingestion of artificial food colors and flavors. *Journal of Learning Disabilities,* 1976, *9,* 551–559.

Federal Register, Dec. 29, 1977, *42* (163), p. 65083.

FERNALD, G. *Remedial techniques in basic school subjects.* New York: McGraw-Hill, 1943.

FRANKS, P. Ethnic and social status characteristics of children in EMR and LD classes. *Exceptional Children,* 1971, *37,* 537–538.

FROSTIG, M. *Marianne Frostig Development Test of Visual Perception.* Palo Alto, Cal.: Consulting Psychologists Press, 1961.

GARRISON, M., and HAMMILL, P. Who are the retarded? *Exceptional Children,* 1971, *38,* 13–20.

GEARHEART, B., and WEISHAHAN, M. *The handicapped child in the regular classroom.* St. Louis: C. V. Mosby, 1976.

GIBSON, E. Learning to read. In H. Singer & R. Ruddell (Eds.), *Theoretical models and processes of reading.* Newark, Del.: International Reading Association, 1970, 315–334.

GILLINGHAM, A., and STILLMAN, B. *Remedial training for children with specific disability in reading, spelling, and penmanship.* Cambridge, Mass.: Educator's Publishing Service, 1960.

GROSENICK, J. Integration of exceptional children into regular classes: Research and procedure. *Focus on Exceptional Children.* October 1971, *3,* (5), 1–8.

GROSSMAN, R. LD and the problem of scientific definitions. *Journal of Learning Disabilities,* 1978, *11,* (3), 120–123.

GUTHRIE, J. *Identification and instruction of children with reading disability.* Second Annual Report to the Spencer Foundation, July 1974. (ERIC Document 098 516)

GUTHRIE, J. Models of reading and reading disability. *Journal of Educational Psychology,* 1973, *65,* 9–18.

GWYNNE, F. *A chocolate moose for dinner.* New York: Windmill Books, 1976.

HALLAHAN, D., GAJAR, A., COHEN, S., and TARVER, S. The learning disabled as an inactive learner. *Journal of Learning Disabilities,* 1978, *11,* 231–236.

HAMMILL, D. Training visual perceptual processes. *Journal of Learning Disabilities,* 1972, *5,* 552–559.

HAMMILL, D., & BARTEL, N. *Teaching children with learning and behavior problems* (2nd ed.). Boston: Allyn and Bacon, 1978.

HAMMILL, D., & LARSEN, S. The effectiveness of psycholinguistic training. *Exceptional Children,* 1974, *41,* 5–15.

HAMMILL, D., & LARSEN, S. The effectiveness of psycholinguistic training: A reaffirmation of position. *Exceptional Children,* 1978, *44,* 6, 402–417.

HARING, N., & BATEMAN, B. *Teaching the learning disabled child.* Englewood Cliffs, N. J.: Prentice-Hall, 1977.

HARTMAN, N., & HARTMAN, R. Perceptual handicap or reading disability? *The Reading Teacher,* 1973, *26,* 684–695.

HAWISHER, M., and CALHOUN, M. The resource room: An

educational asset for children with special needs. Columbus, Ohio: Charles Merrill, 1978.

Hobbs, N. Classification options: A conversation with N. Hobbs on exceptional child education. *Exceptional Children,* 1978, *44,* 494–497.

Hollander, S. K. A multidisciplinary approach to the etiology and management of learning disability. In P. D. Pearson and J. Hansen (Eds.), *Reading: Theory, research and practice,* 26th Yearbook of National Reading Conference. Clemson, S. C.: NRC, 1977, 150–157.

Johnson, D. *Reaching out.* Englewood Cliffs, N. J.: Prentice-Hall, 1972, 267–269.

Johnson, D., and Myklebust, H. *Learning disabilities: Educational principles and practices.* New York: Grune & Stratton, 1967.

Jones, R. Evaluating mainstream programs for minority children. In R. Jones (Ed.), *Mainstreaming and the Minority child.* Minneapolis: Leadership Training Institute, 1976, 235.

Kappleman, M., Kaplan, E., and Ganter, R. A study of learning disorders among disadvantaged children. *Journal of Learning Disabilities,* 1969, *2,* 261–269.

Kentucky Administrative Regulations, (707 KAR 1:05B. Sect. 4,) Frankfort, KY Dept. of education (pp. 8-6), December 6, 1978.

Kirk, S., Hegge, T., and Kirk, W. *Remedial reading drills.* Ann Arbor, Mich.: George Wahr, 1948.

Kirk, S., McCarthy, J., and Kirk, W. *The Illinois test of psycholinguistic abilities.* Urbana: University of Illinois, 1968.

Kirk, S. Research in education. In H. Stevens and R. Heber (Eds.), *Mental retardation: A review of research.* Chicago: University of Chicago Press, 1964, 57–99.

Larry, P. v. Riles, Civil Action N. C. — 71-2270, 343F. Supp. 1306 N.D. Cal., 1972.

Money, J. *Reading disability: Progress and research needs in dyslexia.* Baltimore: John Hopkins Press, 1962.

Morsink, C. Learning to read: A simulation for teacher training. *Journal of Learning Disabilities,* 1973, *6,* 479–485.

Morsink, C. The unreachable child: A teacher's approach to learning disabilities. *Journal of Learning Disabilities,* 1971, *4,* 33–40.

Morsink, C. (Ed.). *DELTA: A design for word attack.* Tulsa, Oklahoma: Educational Development Corporation, 1977.

Morsink, C., & Otto, W. Special considerations in teaching LD children to read. In P. D. Pearson and J. Hansen (Eds.), *Reading: Theory, research, & practice,* Twenty-sixth yearbook of the National Reading Conference. Clemson, S. C.: NRC, 1977, 163–167.

Morsink, C., Cross, D., and Strickler, J. How disabled readers try to remember words. *Reading Horizons,* 1978, *18,* 174–180.

Orton, S. *Reading, writing and speech problems in children.* New York: W. W. Norton, 1937.

Ott, J. Influence of fluorescent lights on hyperactivity and learning disabilities. *Journal of Learning Disabilities,* 1976, *9,* 417–422.

Otto, W. The acquisition and retention of paired associates by good, average, and poor readers. *Journal of Educational Psychology,* 1961, *52,* 241–248.

Otto, W. *Educational factors involved in reading disability.*

Paper presented at Annual Convention of the International Reading Association, April 20, 1970. Madison: University of Wisconsin, Wisconsin Research and Development Center for Cognitive Learning.

Reed, J., Robe, E., and Mankinen M. Teaching reading to brain damaged children: A review. *Reading Research Quarterly,* 1970, *5,* 379–401.

Reynolds, M. C., and Birch, J. W. *Teaching exceptional children in all America's schools.* Reston, Va.: Council for Exceptional Children, 1977.

Ross, A. *Psychological aspects of learning disabilities and reading disorders.* New York: McGraw-Hill, 1976.

Ross, S., DeYoung, H., and Cohen, J. Confrontation: Special education placement and the law. *Exceptional Children,* 1971, *38,* 5–12.

Rubin, R. A., Krus, P., and Balow, B. Factors in special class placement. *Exceptional Children,* 1973, *39,* 525–532.

Rude, R. Objective-based reading system: An evaluation. *The Reading Teacher,* 1974, *28,* 169–175.

Samuels, S. J. Reading disability? *The Reading Teacher,* 1970, *24,* 267.

Senf, G. A conversation with Daniel Ringelheim: Coming face to face with the impersonal numbers game. *Journal of Learning Disabilities,* 1978, *10,* 8.

Senf, G. Implication of the final procedures for evaluating specific learning disabilities. *Journal of Learning Disabilities,* 1978(a), *11,* 3.

Sieben, R. Controversial medical treatments of learning disabilities. *Academic Therapy,* 1977, *13,* 133–147.

Sievers, D., et al. (Eds.). *Selected studies on the Illinois Test of Psycholinguistic Abilities.* Madison, Wisconsin: Photo Press, 1963.

Smith, R., and Neisworth, J. *The exceptional child: A functional approach.* New York: McGraw-Hill, 1975.

Stennett, R. Emotional handicap in the elementary years: Phase or disease? *American Journal of Orthopsychiatry,* 1966, *36,* 444–449.

Stone, F., and Rowley, V. Educational disability in emotionally disturbed children. *Exceptional Children,* 1964, *30,* 423–426.

Strauss, A. A. and Lehtinen, L. E. *Psychopathology and education of the brain-injured child.* New York: Grune & Stratton, 1947.

Vogel, S. Syntactic abilities in normal and dyslexic children. *Journal of Learning Disabilities,* 1974, *1,* 103–109.

Wallace, G., and McLoughlin, J. A. *Learning disabilities: Concepts and characteristics.* Columbus, Ohio: Charles Merrill, 1975.

Ward, L. Variables influencing auditory-visual integration in normal and retarded readers. *Journal of Reading Behavior,* 1977, *IX,* 290–295.

Wepman, J. Auditory discrimination, speech, and reading, *Elementary School Journal,* 1960, *60,* 325–333.

Whalen, C., and Henker, B. Psychostimulants and children: A review and analysis. *Psychological Bulletin,* 1976, *83,* 1113–1130.

Whimbey, A. Teaching sequential thought: A cognitive-skills approach. *Phi Delta Kappan,* 1977, *59,* 225.

Wiederholt, J. L., Hammill, D. D., and Brown, V. *The*

resource teacher: A guide to effective practice. Boston: Allyn and Bacon, 1978.

ZACH, L., and KAUFMAN, J. How adequate is the concept of perceptual deficit for education? *Journal of Learning Disabilities,* 1972, *5,* 351–356.

ZAX, M., COWEN, E., RAPPAPORT, J., BEACH, D., and LAIRD, J. Follow-up of children identified early as emotionally disturbed. *Journal of Consulting and Clinical Psychology,* 1968, *32,* 369–374.

Chapter 9

ANDERSON, L. T., and HERRMANN, L. Lesch–Nyhan Disease: A specific learning disability? Paper presented at the ninth annual convention of the Association for the Advancement of Behavior Therapy, San Francisco, December, 1975.

BANDURA, A. *Aggression: A social learning analysis.* Englewood Cliffs, N.J.: Prentice-Hall, 1973.

BUEHLER, R. E., PATTERSON, G. R., and FURNISS, J. M. The reinforcement of behavior in institutional settings. *Behavior Research and Therapy,* 1966, *4,* 157–167.

CHESS, S., THOMAS, A., and BIRCH, H. G. Behavior problems revisited: Findings of an anterospective study. *Journal of the American Academy of Child Psychiatry,* 1967, *6,* 321–331.

CRUICKSHANK, W. M., BENTZEN, F., RATZEBURG, F., and TANNHAUSER, M. *A teaching method of brain-injured and hyperactive children.* Syracuse, N.Y.: Syracuse University Press, 1961.

HALLAHAN, D. P., & KAUFFMAN, J. M. *Exceptional children: Introduction to special education.* Englewood Cliffs, N.J.: Prentice-Hall, 1978.

HARING, N. G. and PHILLIPS, E. L. *Educating emotionally disturbed children.* New York: McGraw-Hill, 1962.

HOBBS, N. Helping the disturbed child: Psychological and ecological strategies. *American Psychologist,* 1966, *21,* 1105–1115.

KANFER, F. H., & SASLOW, G. Behavioral analysis: An alternative to diagnostic classification. In T. Millon (Ed.), *Theories of Psychopathology,* Philadelphia: W. B. Saunders, 1967.

KAUFFMAN, J. M. *Characteristics of children's behavior disorders.* Columbus, Ohio: Charles E. Merrill, 1977.

KNIGHT, M. F. Vermont's consulting teacher model for in-service training of educational personnel. In C. M. Nelson (Ed.), *Field-based teacher training: Applications in special education.* Minneapolis: Department of Psychoeducational Studies, University of Minnesota, 1978 (in press).

LAPOUSE, R., and MONK, M. A. An epidemiologic study of behavior characteristics in children. *American Journal of Public Health,* 1958, *48,* 1134–1144.

LEFKOWITZ, M. M., ERON, L. D., WALDER, L. O., and HUESMANN, L. R. *Growing up to be violent.* Elmsford, N. Y.: Pergamon Press, 1977.

LEWIS, W. W. Continuity and intervention in emotional disturbance: A review. *Exceptional Children,* 1965, *31,* 465–474.

LILLY, M. S. A training based model for special education. *Exceptional Children,* 1971, *37,* 745–749.

LILLY, S. M. Special education: A teapot in tempest. *Exceptional Children,* 1970, *37,* 43–49.

LINDSLEY, O. R. The beautiful future of school psychology:

Advising teachers. In M. C. Reynolds (ed.), *Proceedings of the conference on psychology and the process of schooling in the next decade: Alternative conceptions.* Minneapolis: Leadership Training Institute/Special Education, 1971, 116–120.

MCKENZIE, H. S. Higher education's role in mainstreaming: An example. In S. Jordon (Ed.), *Teacher please don't close the door: The exceptional child in the mainstream.* Reston, Va.: Council for Exceptional Children, 1976, 112–133.

MORSE, W. C. The crisis or helping teacher. In N. J. Long, W. C. Morse, and R. G. Newman (Eds.), *Conflict in the classroom settings.* Monograph No. 1. Eugene, Oregon: Depart-

NELSON, C. M. Alternative education for the mildly and moderately handicapped. In R. D. Kneedler and S. G. Tamer (Eds.), *Changing perspectives in special education.* Columbus, Ohio: Charles E. Merrill, 1977, 185–207.

NELSON, C. M., and POLSGROVE, L. The etiology of adolescent behavior disorders. In G. B. Brown, R. L. McDowell, and J. Smith (Eds.), Educating adolescents with behavior disorders. Boston: Little, Brown and Co., in press, (9) 9.

O'LEARY, K. D. The assessment of psychopathology in children. In H. C. Quay and J. S. Werry (Eds.), *Psychopathological disorders of children.* New York: John Wiley & Sons, 1972, 234–272.

PATTERSON, G. R., REID, J. B., JONES, R. R., & CONGER, R. E. *A social learning approach to family intervention (Vol. I: Families with aggressive children).* Eugene, Ore.: Castalia, 1975.

PATTERSON, G. R., SHAW, D. A., and EBNER, M. J. Teachers, peers and parents as agents of change in the classroom. In A. K. Benson (Ed.), *Modifying deviant social behaviors in various classroom settings.* Monograph No. 1. Eugene, Oregon: Department of Special Education, University of Oregon, 1969, 13–48.

QUAY, H. C. Patterns of aggression, withdrawal and immaturity. In H. C. Quay and J. S. Werry (Eds.), *Psychopathological disorders of childhood.* New York: John Wiley & Sons, 1972, 1–29.

QUAY, H. C., & PETERSON, D. R. Manual for the behavior problem checklist. Unpublished manuscript, University of Illinois, 1967.

REIMER, E. Unusual ideas in education. In W. C. Rhodes & M. R. Tracy (Eds.), *A study of child variance. Vol. 1: Conceptual models.* Ann Arbor, Michigan: Institute for the study of Mental Retardation and Related Disabilities, 1972, 481–502.

REYNOLDS, M., and BIRCH, J. *Teaching exceptional children in all America's schools.* Reston, Va.: Council for Exceptional Children, 1977.

RHODES, W. C. A community participation analysis of emotional disturbance. *Exceptional Children,* 1970, *36,* 309–314.

RHODES, W. C. *A study of child variance. Vol IV: The future.* Ann Arbor, Michigan: Institute for the Study of Mental Retardation and Related Disabilities, 1975.

RHODES, W. C., and TRACY, M. L. (Eds.). *A study of child variance. Vol. I: Conceptual models.* Ann Arbor, Mich.: Institute for the Study of Mental Retardation and Related Disabilities, 1972.

RHODES, W. C. The disturbing child: A problem of ecological management. *Exceptional Children,* 1967, *33* 449–455.

RICH, H. L. Behavior disorders and school: A case of sexism and racial bias. *Behavioral Disorders,* 1977, *2,* 201–204.

RIMLAND, B. *Infantile autism.* New York: Meredith, 1964.

Rose, T. L. The functional relationship between artificial food colors and hyperactivity. *Journal of Applied Behavior Analysis,* 1978, *11,* 439–446.

Ross, A. O. *Psychological disorders of children.* New York: McGraw-Hill, 1974.

Schultz, E. W., Hirshorn, A., Manton, A. B., and Henderson, R. A. Special education for the emotionally disturbed. *Exceptional Children,* 1971, *38,* 313–319.

Skinner, B. F. What is psychotic behavior? In T. Millon (Ed.), *Theories of psychopathology.* Philadelphia: W. B. Saunders, 1967, 324–337.

Slater, E., and Cowie, V. *The genetics of mental disorders.* London: Oxford University Press, 1971.

Spivack, G., and Spotts, J. *Devereux Child Behavior (DCB) Rating Scale.* Devon, Pa.: Devereux Foundation, 1966.

Strauss, A. A., and Lehtinen, L. E. *Psychopathology and education of the brain injured child.* New York: Grune & Stratton, 1947.

Stumphauzer, J. S., Aiken, T. W., and Veloz, E. V. East side story: Behavioral analysis of a high juvenile crime community. *Behavioral Disorders,* 1977, *2,* 76–84.

Sulzbacher, S. I. Behavior analysis of drug effects in the classroom. In G. Semd (Ed.), *Behavior analysis and education — 1972.* Lawrence, Kansas: University of Kansas Support and Development Center for Follow Through, Department of Human Development, 1972, 37,-52.

Szasz, T. S. The myth of mental illness. American Psychologist, 1960, *15,* 113–118.

Taylor, F. D., Artuso, A. A., Soloway, M. M., Hewett, F. M., Quay, H. C., and Stillwell, R. J. A learning center plan for special education. *Focus on Exceptional Children,* 1972, *4*(3), 1–7.

Taylor, F. D., and Soloway, M. M. The Madison School Plan: A functional model for merging the regular and special classrooms. In E. Deno (Ed.), *Instructional alternatives for exceptional children.* Reston, Va.: Council for Exceptional Children, 1973.

Ullmann, L. P., and Krasner, L. (Eds.). *Case studies in behavior modification.* New York: Holt, Rinehart & Winston, 1965.

U. S. Department of Health, Education and Welfare, Office of Incidence Youth Development. *Juvenile court statistics: 1972.* Washington, D. C.: U. S. Government Printing Office, 1973.

Vacc, N. C. Long term effects of special class intervention for emotionally disturbed children. *Exceptional Children,* 1972, *39,* 16–22.

Van Veelan, L. P. Cheer soap opera. Unpublished manuscript. University of Kentucky, 1975.

Wahler, R. G., and Cormier, W. H. The ecological interview: A first step in out-patient child behavior therapy. *Journal of Behavior Therapy and Experimental Psychiatry,* 1970, *1,* 279–289.

Walker, H. M. *Walker problem behavior identification checklist.* Los Angeles: Western Psychological Services, 1970.

Watson, J. B., and Raynor, R. Conditioned emotional reactions. *Journal of Experimental Psychology,* 1920, *3,* 1–14.

Wood, F. H., and Zabel, R. Making sense of reports on the incidence of behavior disorders/emotional disturbances in school-aged children. Psychology in the Schools, 1978, *15,* 45–51.

Worell, J., and Nelson, C. M. *Managing instructional problems: A case study workbook.* New York: McGraw-Hill, 1974.

Chapter 10

Allegheny, Intermediate Unit. *Special techniques for teaching the severely and profoundly retarded.* Pittsburgh, Pa.: Allegheny Intermediate Unit, 1976.

Anderson, D. R., Hodson, G. D., and Jones, W. G. *Instructional programming for the handicapped student.* Springfield, Ill.: Charles C. Thomas, 1975.

Baroff, G. D. *Mental retardation: Nature causes and management.* Washington, D.C.: Hemisphere, 1974.

Bellamy, G. T. Habilitation of the severely and profoundly retarded: A review of research on work productivity. In G. T. Bellamy (Ed.), *Habilitation of the severely and profoundly retarded: Reports from the specialized training program.* Eugene: University of Oregon, Center on Human Development, 1976.

Bellamy, G. T., Inman, D. P., and Schwarz, R. H. Vocational training and production supervision: A review of habilitation techniques for the severely and profoundly retarded. In N. G. Haring and D. D. Brecker (Eds.), *Teaching the severely handicapped (Vol. 3).* Seattle: AAESPH, 1978.

Bellamy, G. T., Peterson, L., and Close, D. W. Habilitation of the severely and profoundly retarded: Illustrations of competence. *Education and Training of the Mentally Retarded,* 1976, 10(3), 174–186.

Bender, M., and Valletuhi, P. J. *Teaching the moderately and severely handicapped* (Vols. 1, 2, 3). Baltimore: University Park Press, 1976

Bobath, B. The very early treatment of cerebral palsy. *Developmental Medicine and Child Neurology,* 1967, *9,* 373–390.

Bricker, D. Educational synthesizer. In M. Thomas, *Hey, don't forget about me!* Reston, Va.: Council for Exceptional Children, 1976.

Bricker, D., Bricker, W., Iacino, R., and Dennison, L. Intervention strategies for the severely and profoundly handicapped child. In N. Haring and H. Brown (Eds.), *Teaching the severely handicapped.* New York: Grune & Stratton, 1976.

Bricker, D., Dennison, L., and Bricker, W. A. *A language intervention program for developmentally young children.* Miami, Fla.: University of Miami. Mailman Center for Child Development Monograph Series, 1976, No. 1.

Bricker, D., Davis, J., Wahlin, L., and Evans, J. *A motor training program for the developmentally young.* University of Florida. Mailman Center Monograph Series, 1977, No. 2.

Brown, L., Crowner, T., William, W., and York, R. (Eds.) *Madison's alternative for zero exclusion: A book of readings.* Madison, WI: Madison Public Schools, 1975.

Brown, L., Williams, W., and Crowner, T. (Eds.). *A collection of papers and programs related to public school services for severely handicapped students* (Vol. 4). Madison, Wis.: Madison Public Schools, 1974.

Brown, L., Nietupski, J., and Hamre-Nietupski, S. Criterion of ultimate functioning. In M. S. Thomas (Ed.) *Hey, don't forget about me.* Reston, Va.: Council for Exceptional Children, 1976.

BROWN, L., WILCOX, B., SONTAG, E., VINCENT, B., DODD, N., and GRUENEWALD, L. *Toward the realization of the least restrictive educational environments for severely handicapped students.* AAESPH Review, 2 (4), 1977, 195–201.

CASA GRANDE CENTER, *Independent living skills curriculum.* Petaluma, Cal.: CASA Grande Center, 1978.

COHEN, M., GROSS, P., and HARING, N. Developmental pinpoints. In N. Haring and H. Brown (Eds.), *Teaching the severely handicapped.* New York: Grune & Stratton, 1976.

CUVO, A., LEAF, R., and BORAKOVE, L. Teaching janitorial skills to the mentally retarded: Acquisition, generalization, and maintenance. *Journal of Applied Behavior Analysis,* 1978, *11,* 345–355.

DUBOSE, R. F. Development of communication in nonverbal children. *Education and Training of the Mentally Retarded,* 1978, *13,* 37–41.

DUNCOMBE, B., PACHECO, R., and QUILITCH, R. Review of procedures for toilet training the retarded. In M. A. Thomas (Ed.), *Developing skills in severely and profoundly handicapped children.* Reston, Va., Council for Exceptional Children, 1977.

FARBER, S. *Sensorimotor evaluation and treatment procedures for the allied health personnel.* Indiana University, Purdue University, Indianapolis Medical Center, Occupational Therapy Program, 1974.

FOXX, R. M., and AZRIN, N. H. *Toilet training the retarded.* Champaign, Ill.: Research Press, 1973.

FREDERICKS, H. D., BALDWIN, V. C., DOUGHTY, P., and WALTER, J. *The teaching research motor development scale.* Springfield, Ill.: Charles C. Thomas, 1972.

FREDERICKS, H., ANDERSON, R., BALDWIN, V., GROVE, D., MOORE, W., MOORE, M., and BEARCH, J. *The identification of competencies of teachers of the severely handicapped.* Monmouth, Ore.: Teaching Press, 1977.

FREDERICKS, H., BALDWIN, V., GROVE, D., RIGGS, C., FUREG, V., MOORE, W., JORDAN, E., GAGE, M., LEVAK, L., ALRIK, G., and WADLOW, M. *A data-based classroom for the moderately and severely handicapped.* Monmouth, Ore.: Instructional Development Corp., 1977.

FREDERICKS, ET AL. *The teaching research curriculum for moderately and severely handicapped.* Springfield, Ill.: Charles C. Thomas, 1976.

GIBSON, D., and BROWN, R. (Eds.). *Managing the severely retarded.* Springfield, Ill.: Charles C. Thomas, 1976.

GOLD, M. W. Redundant cue removal in skill training for the retarded. *Education and Training of the Mentally Retarded,* 1974, 9(1), 5–8.

GUESS, P. D., and HORNER, R. D. The severely and profoundly handicapped. In E. L. Meyer (Ed.), *Exceptional children and youth: An introduction.* Denver: Love Publishing Co., 1978.

GUESS, D., SAILOR, W., and BAER, D. M. *Functional speech and language training for the severely handicapped.* Laurence, Kansas: H. & H. Enterprises, 1976.

HALL, R. V. *Managing behavior — behavior modification: The measurement of behavior.* Lawrence, Kansas: H & H Enterprises, 1971.

HARING, N. G. From promise to reality. *AAESPH Review,* 2, 1977, 307.

HARING, N. G., and BRICKER, D. Overview of comprehensive services for the severely/profoundly handicapped. In N. G. Haring and L. J. Brown (Eds.), *Teaching the severely handicapped* (Vol. 1). New York: Grune & Stratton, 1976.

HARING, N. G., and BROWN, L. J. *Teaching the severely handicapped* (Vol. 2). New York: Grune & Stratton, 1977.

HUNTER, J. D., and BELLAMY, G. T. Cable harness construction for severely retarded adults: A demonstration of training techniques. In G. T. Bellamy (Ed.), *Habilitation of the severely and profoundly retarded: Reports from the specialized training program.* Eugene: University of Oregon Center, 1976.

IRVIN, L. K. General utility of easy to hard discrimination training procedures. In G. T. Bellamy (Ed.), *Habilitation of severely and profoundly retarded: Reports from the specialized training program.* Eugene: University of Oregon Center on Human Development, 1976.

KAUFFMAN, J., and SNELL, M. Managing the behavior of severely handicapped persons. In E. Sontag (Ed.), *Educational programming for the severely and profoundly handicapped.* Reston, Va.: Council for Exceptional Children, 1977.

KENOWITZ, L. A., ZWEIBEL, S., and EDGAR, E. Determining the least restrictive educational opportunity handicapped. In N. Haring and D. Briekner (Eds.), *Teaching the severely handicapped* (Vol. 3). Seattle: AAESPH, 1978.

KIERNAN, C., AND WOODFORD, F. (Eds.). *Behavior modification with the severely retarded.* The Hague, Netherlands: Mountont & Co., 1975.

KOEGEL, R., and RINCOVER, A. Research on the difference between generalization and maintenance in extra-therapy respendings. *Journal of Applied Behavior Analysis,* 1977, *10,* 1–12.

LENT, J. R., and McLEAN, B. M. The trainable retarded: The technology of teaching. In N. G. Haring and R. L. Schiefelbusch (Eds.), *Teaching special children.* New York: McGraw-Hill, 1976.

LINDSLEY, O. R. Direct measurement and prosthesis of retarded behavior. *Journal of Education,* 1964, *147,* 62–81.

LOVAAS, O., BERBERICH, J., PERLOFF, B., and SCHAEFFER, B. Acquisition of imitative speech by schizophrenic children. *Science,* 1966, *151,* 705–707.

MacDONALD, J. D., and HORTSMEIER, D. S. *Environmental language intervention program.* Columbus, Ohio: Charles E. Merrill, 1978.

McDONNELL, J. J., FREDERICKS, H. D., and GROVE, D. R. *Initial expressive language program.* Monmouth, Ore.: Teaching Research Publications, 1977.

MILLER, J. L., and YODER, D. E. An ontogenetic language teaching strategy for retarded children. In R. Schiefebusch & L. Lloyd (Eds.), *Language perspectives: Acquisition, retardation and intervention.* Baltimore: University Park Press, 1974.

MITHAUG, D. E., MAR, D. K., and STEWART, J. E. *Matchsort-assemble.* Seattle: Exceptional Education, 1978.

NELSON, C. M., GAST, D. L., and TROUT, D. A charting system for monitoring student performance on instructional programs. *Journal of Special Education Technology,* 1979, *3,* 43–49.

NIETUPSKI, R., CERTO, N., PUMPIAN, I., and BELMORE, K.

Supermarket shopping: Teaching severely handicapped students to generate a shopping list and make purchases functionally linked with meal preparation. In L. Brown, N. Certo, K. Belmore, and T. Crounder (Eds.), *Selected papers related to secondary programming with severely handicapped students* (Vol. 6), part 1. Madison: Madison Public Schools, 1976.

O'NEILL, C. T., and BELLAMY, G. T. Evaluation of a procedure for teaching saw chain assembly to a severely retarded woman. *Mental Retardation,* 1978, 16(1), 37–41.

PERSKE, R., and SMITH, J. (Eds.). *Beyond the ordinary.* New York: Random House, 1977.

PIAGET, J. *The origins of intelligence in children.* New York: W. W. Norton, 1952.

PIAGET, J. *The construction of reality in the child.* New York: Ballantine, 1954.

PIAGET, J. *The origins of intelligence in children.* New York: W. W. Norton, 1963.

PUBLIC LAW 90-247. *Elementary and Secondary Education Ammendments of 1967,* January 2, 1968.

SAILOR, W., and HARING, N. G. Progress in the education of the severely/profoundly handicapped. In N. G. Haring and D. D. Bricker (Eds.), *Teaching the severely handicapped* (Vol. 3). Seattle: AAESPH, 1978.

SAILOR, W., and HORNER, R. Educational assessment strategies for the severely handicapped. In N. Haring and L. Brown (Eds.), *Teaching the severely handicapped.* New York: Grune & Stratton, 1976.

SHERR, R. D. Public school programs. In M. A. Thomas (Ed.), *Hey, don't forget about me!* Reston, Va.: CEC, 1976.

SMITH, D. H. (Ed.). *Motor-academic-perceptual curriculum guide for the early childhood education of the multiply handicapped.* Indiana, Pa.: Arin Intermediate Unit #28, 1973 (ERIC Document Reproduction Service No. ED083775).

SMITH, D., and SNELL, M. Intervention strategies. In M. Snell (Ed.), *Systematic instruction of the moderately and severely handicapped.* Columbus, Ohio: Charles E. Merrill, 1978.

SNELL, M. E. Self-care skills. In M. E. Snell (Ed.), *Systematic instruction of the moderately and severely handicapped.* Columbus, Ohio: Charles E. Merrill, 1978(a).

SNELL, M. E. Functional reading. In M. E. Snell (Ed.), *Systematic instruction of the moderately and severely handicapped.* Columbus, Ohio: Charles E. Merrill, 1978(b).

SONTAG, E., BURKE, P., and YORK, R. Considerations for serving the severely handicapped. *Education and Training of the Mentally Retarded,* 1973, 8, 20–26.

SONTAG, E., SAILOR, W., and SMITH, J. The severely/ profoundly handicapped: Who are they? Where are we? *Journal of Special Education,* 1977, 11(1), 5–11.

SOUTHEASTERN REGIONAL COALITION. Issues in certification for teachers of the severely handicapped. In National Association of State Directors of Special Education, *Special Education Programs for Severely and Profoundly Handicapped Individuals: A Directory of State Education Agency Services.* Washington, D. C.: NASDSE, 1979, 32–50.

SPELLMAN, C., DeBRIERE, T., JARBOE, D., CAMPBELL, S., and HARRIS, C. Pictorial instruction: Training daily living skills. In M. E. Snell (Ed.), *Systematic instruction of the moderately and severely handicapped.* Columbus, Ohio: Charles E. Merrill, 1978.

TAWNEY, J., and HIPSHER, L. *Systematic instruction for retarded children: The Illinois program (Part II) Systematic language instruction.* State of Illinois, Office of the Superintendent of Public Instruction, 1972.

TAWNEY, J., KNAPP, D., O'REILLY, C., and PRATT, S. *Programmed environments curriculum.* Columbus, Ohio: Charles E. Merrill, 1979.

U. S. OFFICE OF EDUCATION. *Estimated number of handicapped children in the United States, 1974–75.* Washington, D. C.: Bureau of Education for the Handicapped, 1975.

TOUCHETTE, P. Transfer of stimulus control: Measuring the moment of transfer. *Journal of Experimental Analysis of Behavior,* 1971, 15, 347–354.

UZGIRIS, I. C., and HUNT, J. *Assessment in infancy: Ordinal scales of psychological development.* Urbana: University of Illinois Press, 1975.

VANDERHEIDEN, G. C. *Non-vocal communication resource book.* Baltimore: University Park Press, 1978.

VANDERHEIDEN, G. C., and GRILLEY, K. *Non-vocal communication techniques and aids for the severely physically handicapped.* Baltimore: University Park Press, 1976.

WABASH CENTER FOR THE MENTALLY RETARDED. *Guide to early developmental training.* Boston: Allyn and Bacon, Inc., 1977.

WALLS, T., and WERNER, S. J. Vocational behavior checklists. *Mental Retardation,* 1977, 15(4), 30–35.

WEHMAN, P. H. A leisure time activities curriculum for the developmentally disabled. *Education and Transfer of the Mentally Retarded,* 1976, 11(4), 309–313.

WEHMAN, P., SCHUTZ, R., RENZAGLEA, A., and KARAN, O. Use of positive practice to facilitate increased work productivity and instruction following behavior in profoundly retarded adolescents. *Habilitation Practices with Severely Developmentally Disabled* (Vol. 1). Madison: Research and Training Center in Mental Retardation, University of Wisconsin, 1976.

WILCOX, B. Competency-based approach to preparing teachers of the severely and profoundly handicapped: Perspective I. In E. Sontag (Ed.), *Educational programming for the severely and profoundly handicapped.* Reston, Va.: Council for Exceptional Children, 1977.

WILLIAMS, W., HAMRE-NIETUPSKI, S., PUMPIAN, I., McDANIEL-MARX, J., and WHEELER, J. Teaching social skills. In M. E. Snell, *Systematic instruction of the moderately and severely handicapped.* Columbus, Ohio: Charles E. Merrill, 1978.

WOLF, M., RISLEY, T., JOHNSTON, M., HARRIS, F., and ALLEN, E. Application of operant conditioning. Procedures to treat the behavior problems of an autistic child: A follow-up and extension. *Behavior Research and Therapy,* 1967, 5, 103–111.

Chapter 11

ASCHNER, M. J., and BISH, C. E. (Eds.). *Productive thinking in education.* Washington, D.C.: National Education Association, 1965.

BALDWIN, A. Y., GEAR, G. H., and LUCITO, L. J. (Eds.). *Educational planning for the gifted overcoming cultural, geographic, and socioeconomic barriers.* Reston, Va.: Council for Exceptional Children, 1978.

BENTSEN, C. The brightest kids. *New York,* June 18, 1979, 12 (25), 36–40.

BIRCH, J. W., TISDALL, W. J., BARNEY, W. D., and MARKS, C. H. *A field demonstration of the effectiveness of feasibility of early admission to school for mentally advanced children.* Pittsburgh, Pa.: University of Pittsburgh, 1965.

CARROLL, L. *The complete works of Lewis Carroll.* New York: The Modern Library.

CLARK, B. *Growing up gifted.* Columbus, Ohio: Charles E. Merrill, 1979.

CLARK, R. W. *The man who made the future.* New York: G. P. Putnam's Sons, 1977.

CLASEN, R. E., and ROBINSON, B. *Simple gifts, the education of the gifted, talented and creative: Book of readings.* Madison: University of Wisconsin, 1978.

CROW, L. D., and CROW, A. *Educating the academically able: A book of readings.* New York: David McKay Co., 1963.

D'HEURLE, A., MELLINGER, J., and HAGGARD, E. Personality, intellectual and achievement patterns in gifted children. *Psychological Monographs,* 1959, *73*(13), 1–28.

EDUCATION OF THE HANDICAPPED: The Independent Biweekly News Service on Federal Legislation, Programs and funding for Special Education. Washington, D. C.: Capitol Publications, Inc., *4*(11), 4–5, 1979.

ELLISON, R., ABE, C., FOX, D., CORAY, K., and TAYLOR, C. Using biographical information in identifying artistic talent. *The Gifted Child Quarterly,* Winter, 1976, XX (4), 402–413.

GALLAGHER, J. J. *Teaching the gifted child* (2nd ed.). Boston, Massachusetts: Allyn and Bacon, 1975.

GALTON, F. *Hereditary Genius.* London: Spottiswoode, Ballantyne & Company, Fontana Library, 1962.

GETZELS, J. W., and JACKSON, P. W. *Creativity and intelligence explorations with gifted students.* New York: John Wiley & Sons, 1962.

GOWAN, J. C., and TORRANCE, E. P. (Eds.). *Educating the ablest: A book of readings on the education of gifted children.* Itasca, Illinois: F. E. Peacock Publishers, 1971.

GUILFORD, J. P. *The nature of human intelligence.* New York: McGraw-Hill, 1967.

HAUCK, B. B., and FREEHILL, M. F. *The gifted: Case studies.* Dubuque, Iowa: William C. Brown, 1972.

HENSON, F. O. *Mainstreaming the gifted.* Austin, Texas: Learning Concepts, 1976.

HILDRETH, G. H. *Introduction to the gifted.* New York: McGraw-Hill, 1966.

HOBSON, J. R. High school performance at underage pupils initially admitted to kindergarten on the basis of physical and psychological examination. *Educational and Psychological Measurement,* 1963, 23, 159–170.

KEATING, D. P. (Ed.). *Intellectual talent: Research and development.* Baltimore, Md.: The Johns Hopkins University Press, 1976.

KOUGH, H., and DeHAAN, R. *Teachers' guidance handbook,* Vol. 1. Elementary Edition. Chicago, Ill.: Science Research Associates, 1958.

KRANZ, B. *Multidimensional screening device for the identification of gifted/talented children* (3rd ed.). Fairfax, Va.: Fairfax County Public Schools.

KRIPPNER, S. Characteristics of gifted and talented youth. Paper presented at a workshop sponsored by Science Research Associates. Published by the U.S. Department of Health, Education, and Welfare, Office of Education. ERIC Document, ED 015503, 1967.

LINDSAY, B. Leadership giftedness: Developing a profile. *Journal for the Education of the Gifted.* 1977, *11* (1), 63–69.

LUCITO, L. Independence-conformity behavior as a function of intellect: Bright and dull children. *Exceptional Children,* 1964, 31 (1), 5–13.

MacKINNON, D. W. The nature and nurture of creative talent. *American Psychologist,* 1962, *17*, 484–495.

MAKER, C. J. *Providing programs for the gifted handicapped.* Reston, Va.: Council for Exceptional Children, 1977.

MAKER, C. J. *Training teachers for the gifted and talented: A comparison of models.* Reston, Va.: Council for Exceptional Children, 1975.

MARLAND, S. P. *Education of the gifted and talented.* Washington, D. C.: U. S. Office of Education, DHEW, 1971.

MARTINSON, R. A. *The identification of the gifted and talented.* Ventura, Ca.: Office of the Ventura County Superintendent Schools, 1974.

MAUNDER, J. Using one's gifts. *The Floridian,* August 28, 1977, St. Petersburg, Fl.: The Times Publishing Company, 6–11.

MORISHIMA, A. "Another Van Gogh of Japan:" The superior artwork of a retarded boy. *Exceptional Children,* 1974, *41*, 92–96.

MORSE, J. A. *Gifted women: Barriers to development of potential.* Paper presented as the Annual International Convention of the Council for Exceptional Children. Miami Beach, Fla., April 18–24, 1971.

NEVIN, D. "Young prodigies take off under special program." *Smithsonian,* October 1977, 76–82.

PASSOW, A. H., and GOLDBERG, M. L. The Gifted: Digests of major studies. Manuscript prepared for the Council on Exceptional Children, NEA. ERIC document, ED 001303, 1962.

PRINGLE, M. L. *Able misfits.* London, England: Longman Groups, Ltd., 1970.

RALPH, J., GOLDBERG, M., and PASSOW, A. *Bright underachievers.* New York: Teachers College Press, Columbia University, 1966.

RENZULLI, J. S., and HARTMAN, R. K. Scale for rating the behavioral characteristics of superior students. *Exceptional Children,* 1971, *38*, 243–248.

RENZULLI, J. S. *The enrichment triad model: A guide for developing defensible programs for the gifted and talented.* Wethersfield, Conn.: Creative Learning Press, 1977.

RENZULLI, J. S., and SMITH, L. H. Two approaches to identification of gifted students. *Exceptional Children,* 1977, *43* (8), 512–518.

RENZULLI, J. S., and SMITH, L. H. *A guidebook for developing individualized educational programs (IEP) for gifted and talented students.* Mansfield Center, Conn.: Creative Learning Press, 1979.

ROE, A. *The making of a scientist.* New York: Dodd, Mead, 1953.

SOLANO, C. H. *Teacher and pupil stereotypes of gifted boys and girls.* Paper presented at the 84th annual conference of the American Psychological Association, Washington, D. C.: September, 3–7, 1976.

STANLEY, J. S. The case for extreme educational acceleration in intellectually brilliant youths. *Gifted Child Quarterly,* 1976, *20* (1), 66–75.

STANLEY, J. C., GEORGE W. C., and SOLANO, C. H. *The gifted and the creative: A fifty-year perspective.* Baltimore, Md.: The Johns Hopkins University Press, 1977.

STANLEY, J. C., KEATING, D. P., and FOX, L. H. (Eds.). *Mathematical talent: Discovery, description, and development.* Baltimore, Md.: The Johns Hopkins University Press, 1974.

STROM, R. D., and TORRANCE, E. P. *Education for affective achievement.* Chicago, Ill.: Rand McNally, 1973.

TAYLOR, C. (Ed.). *Creativity: Progress and potential.* New York: McGraw-Hill Book Company, 1964.

TERMAN, L. M., and ODEN, M. H. *Genetic studies of genius; (Vol. 4) The gifted child grows up.* Stanford, Cal.: Stanford University Press, 1947.

TORRANCE, E. P. *Guiding creative talent.* Englewood Cliffs, N.J.: Prentice-Hall, 1962.

TORRANCE, E. P. *Norms-technical manual: Torrance tests of creative thinking.* Lexington, Mass.: Ginn and Company, 1974.

TORRANCE, E. P. *What research say to the teacher: Creativity in the classroom.* Washington, D.C.: National Education Association, 1977.

WELSH, G. S. *Creativity and intelligence: A personality approach.* Chapel Hill, N.C.: Institute for Research in Social Science, University of North Carolina at Chapel Hill, 1975.

WHITMORE, J. R. *Identifying and programming for highly gifted underachievers in the elementary school.* Paper presented at the second world conference on gifted and talented. San Francisco, Cal.: July 27-August 2, 1977.

Chapter 12

BEACH, D. R. *Reaching teenagers: Learning centers for the secondary classroom.* Santa Monica, Cal.: Goodyear Publishing Co., 1977.

BROLIN, D. E. *Life centered career education: A competency-based approach.* Reston, Va.: Council for Exceptional Children, 1978.

BROLIN, D. E. *"Programming Retarded in Career Education."* (Project PRICE Working Paper) University of Missouri, Columbia. September, 1974 (ED 096 777).

BROLIN, D. E., & KOKASKS, C. J. *Career education for handicapped children and youth.* Columbus, Ohio: Charles E. Merrill, 1979.

CEGELKA, P. C. Education for leisure. *Exceptional Teacher,* 1979, 1, 3-5.

CLARK, G. M. *Career education for the handicapped child in the elementary classroom.* Denver: Love Publishing Co., 1979.

DELLEFIELD, C. Wanted: A working definition of career education. *Educational Leadership,* 1974, 13, 11.

GOLDHAMMER, K., & TAYLOR, R. E. *Career education: Perspective and promise.* Columbus, Ohio: Charles E. Merrill, 1972.

HOYT, K. B. *An introduction to career education: A policy paper of the U. S. Office of Education.* Washington, D. C.: Office of Education, 1975.

KIRK, S. A., & JOHNSON, G. O. *Educating the retarded child.* Boston: Houghton Mifflin, 1951.

LEISURE INFORMATION SERVICE. *A systems model for developing a leisure education program for handicapped children and youth (K-12).* Washington: Hawkins and Associates, 1976.

MARLAND, S. P. *Career education now.* Speech presented by the Convention of the National Association of Secondary School Principals in Houston, Texas. January 23, 1971.

McMURRIN, S. M. Toward a philosophy for career education. In L. McClure and C. Baun (Eds.), *Essays on career education.* Portland, Oregon: Northwest Regional Educational Laboratory, 1973.

MEYEN, E. C. *Developing instructional units: Applications for the exceptional child.* Dubuque, Iowa: W. C. Brown, 1976.

MILLER, A. J. The school-based comprehensive career education model. In J. H. Margisor (Ed.), *Career education: The third annual yearbook of the American Vocational Association,* 1973.

PAYNE, J. S., MERCER, C. D., & EPSTEIN, M. H. *Education and rehabilitation techniques.* New York: Behavioral Publications, 1974.

SUPER, D. E. *Career education and the meanings of work.* Monographs on Career Education, U. S. Department of Health, Education and Welfare, Washington, D. C., U. S. Government Printing House, 1978.

Chapter 13

AVERY, C. B. The education of children with impaired hearing. In W. Cruickshank & G. Johnson (Eds.), *Education of Exceptional Children and Youth.* (2nd ed.). Englewood Cliffs, N.J.: Prentice-Hall, 1967, 343-388.

BECKER, W. C. *Parents are teachers.* Champaign, Ill.: Research Press, 1971.

BIKLEN, D. Advocacy comes of age. *Exceptional Children,* 1976, 42, 308-314.

BLACKHAM, G., and SILBERMAN, A. *Modification of child behavior.* Belmont, Cal.: Wadsworth Publishing Co., Inc., 1971.

BLOOM, F. *Our deaf children.* Washington, D. C.: Alexander Graham Bell Association, 1970.

BRIGANCE, A. *Brigance Diagnostic Inventory of Early Development.* Woburn, Mass.: Curriculum Associates, 1978.

BROWN, L., and HAMMILL, D. *Behavior rating profile.* Austin, Texas: PRO-ED, 1978.

BUIST, C., and SCHULMAN, J. *Toys and games for educationally handicapped children.* Springfield, Ill.: Charles C. Thomas, 1969.

CANSLER, D., and MARTIN, G. *Working with families: A manual for developmental centers.* Reston, Va.: Council for Exceptional Children, 1974.

CHINN, P. C., DREW, C. J., and LOGAN, D. R. *Mental retardation.* St. Louis: C. V. Mosby Co., 1975.

CHINN, P. C., WINN, J., and WALTERS, R. H. *Two-way talking with parents of special children.* St. Louis: C. V. Mosby Co., 1978.

CLEMENTS, J. E., and ALEXANDER, R. N. Parent training: Bringing it all back home. *Focus on Exceptional Children,* 1975, 7, 1-12.

COOPER, J. O., and HERON, T. Educational materials and strategies for home use. In D. Edge, B. Strenecky, and S. Mann (Eds.), *Parenting learning-problem children.* Columbus, Ohio: NCEMMH, Ohio State University, 1978, 55-70.

COOPER, J. V., and EDGE, D. *Parenting: Strategies and educational methods.* Columbus: Charles E. Merrill, 1978.

CRUICKSHANK, W. *The brain-impaired child in home, school*

and community. Syracuse, N.Y.: Syracuse University Press, 1967.

DICKERSON, D., SPELLMAN, C. R., LARSEN, S., and TYLER, L. Let the cards do the talking: A teacher-parent communication program. *Teaching Exceptional Children*, 1973, 170–176.

DOLL, E. *Vineland social maturity scale*. Circle Pines, Minn.: American Guidance Service, 1965.

DREIKURS, R., and GREY, L. *A parent's guide to child discipline*. New York: Hawthorn Books, 1970.

DUNN, L. M., and MARKWARDT, F. C. *Peabody Individual Achievement Test*. Circle Pines, Minn.: American Guidance Service, 1970.

ENGLISH, R. W., and OLSON, K. K. *Parenting handicapped children: Earliest experiences, center paper no. 106*. Eugene, Ore.: Rehabilitation Research and Training Center in Mental Retardation, 1976.

FELLENDORF, G., and HARROW, I. *Parent counseling*. Volta Review, 1970, *72*, 51–57.

FINNIE, N. *Handling the young cerebral palsied child at home*. New York: E. P. Dutton, 1975.

FREDERICKS, H. D., BALDWIN, V. L., and GROVE, D. A home-center-based parent-training model. In D. Lillie & P. Trohanis (Eds.), *Teaching parents to teach*. New York: Walker and Company, 1976, 107–130.

GEARHEART, B. R., and LITTON, F. W. *The trainable retarded: A foundations approach*. St. Louis: C. V. Mosby, 1975.

GOODMAN, L., and HAMMILL, D. *Basic school skills inventory*. Chicago: Follett, 1975.

GORDON, R. Special needs of multi-handicapped children under six and their families: One opinion. In E, Sontag (Ed.), *Educational programming for the severely and profoundly handicapped*. Reston, Va.: Council for Exceptional Children, Division of Mental Retardation, 1977, 61–71.

GORDON, T. *Parent effectiveness training*. New York: Peter W. Wyden, 1970.

GRANOWSKY, A., MIDDLETON, F., and MUMFORD, J. *A guide for better reading*. Asheville, N.C.: Tarmac, Inc., 1977.

GREENFIELD, J. *A place for Noah*. New York: Holt, Rinehart and Winston, 1978.

GROSSMAN, F. K. *Brothers and sisters of retarded children*. Syracuse: Syracuse University Press, 1972.

HARING, N. G. *Behavior of exceptional children* (2nd ed.). Columbus, Ohio: Charles E. Merrill, 1978.

HARING, W., and BATEMAN, B. *Teaching the learning disabled*. Englewood Cliffs, N.J.: Prentice-Hall, 1977.

HAYES, J., and HIGGINS, S. T. Issues regarding the IEP: Teachers on the front line. *Exceptional Children*, 1978, *44*, 267–274.

HUDSON, F., and GRAHAM, S. An approach to operationalizing the IEP. *Learning Disability Quarterly*, 1978, *1*, 13–32.

JELINEK, J., and KASPER, A. K. Exchanging information. In D. Lillie & P. Trohanis (Eds.), *Teaching parents to teach*. New York: Walker and Co., 1976. 49–64.

JOEL, G. *So your child has cerebral palsy*. Albuquerque, N. M.: University of New Mexico Press, 1975.

KAKALIK, J. F., BREWER, G. D., DOUGHERTY, L. A., FLEISCHAUER, P. D., and GENESKY, S. M. *Services for handicapped youth: Report to the Department of Health, Education and Welfare*. Santa Monica, Ca.: Rand Corporation, 1973.

KANNER, L. Parents' feelings about retarded children. *American Journal of Mental Deficiency*, 1953, *57*, 375–389.

KELLY, E. J. *Parent-teacher interaction*. Seattle, Wa.: Special Child Publications, 1974.

KLEIN, S. D. Brother to sister: Sister to brother. *Exceptional Parent*, 1972, *2*, 10–15 & 26–27.

KRAMM, E. R. *Families of mongoloid children*. Washington, D. C.: U. S. Department of Health, Education and Welfare, Children's Bureau, publication number 401-1963, 1963.

KROTH, R. *Target behavior*. Olathe, Kansas: Select-Ed, 1972.

KROTH, R. C. *Communicating with parents of exceptional children*. Denver: Love Publishing Co., 1975.

KROTH, R. L., and SIMPSON, R. L. *Parent conferences as a teaching strategy*, Denver: Love Publishing Co., 1977.

LANDAU, E., EPSTEIN, S., and STONE, A. *The exceptional child through literature*. Englewood Cliffs, N.J.: Prentice-Hall, Inc., 1978.

LILLIE, D. L., and TROHANIS, P. L. (Eds.). *Teaching parents to teach*. New York: Walker & Company, 1976.

LITCHER, P. Communicating with parents: It begins with listening. *Teaching Exceptional Children*, 1976, *8*, 66–75.

LOSEN, S. M. and DIAMENT, B. *Parent conferences in the schools*. Boston: Allyn and Bacon, 1978.

LOVITT, T. C. *In spite of my resistance I've learned from children*. Columbus, Ohio: Charles E. Merrill, 1977.

LOWENFELD, B. *Our blind children: growing and learning with them*. Springfield, Ill.: Charles C. Thomas, 1971.

McLOUGHLIN, J. A. Roles and practices of parents of children with learning and behavior problems. In D. Edge, B. Strenecky, & S. Mour (Eds.), *Training parents of children with learning problems: An educator's perspective*. Columbus, Ohio: Ohio State University Press, 1979.

McLOUGHLIN, J. A., EDGE, D., and STRENECKY, B. Perspective of parent involvement in the diagnosis and treatment of learning disabled children. *Journal of Learning Disabilities*, 1978, *11*, 291–296.

McLOUGHLIN, J. A., and KERSHMAN, S. Mainstreaming in the preschool: Strategies and resources for including the handicapped. *Young Children*, in press.

McLOUGHLIN, J. A., and KERSHMAN, S. *Parents of exceptional children: A great natural resource for early childhood educators*. Unpublished manuscript. Louisville, Ky.: University of Louisville, 1979.

McLOUGHLIN, J. A., and LEWIS, R. *Assessing special students: Strategies and procedures*. Columbus, Ohio: Charles E. Merrill, 1981.

McWHIRTER, J. *The learning disabled child: A school and family concern*. Champaign, Ill.: Research Press Co., 1977.

MOORE, C., and MORTON, K. *A reader's guide for parents of children with mental, physical and emotional disabilities*. Rockville, Maryland: U. S. O. E., Bureau of Community Health Services. D. H. E. W. Publication no. (HSA) 77-5290, 1976.

MUNSEY, B. The parent's right to read. *Journal of Learning Disabilities*, 1973, *6*, 392–394.

NETICK, A., and BULLOCK, L. School-based parent-teacher interaction. In D. Edge, B. Strenecky, and S. Mann (Eds.) *Parenting learning-problem children*. Columbus, Ohio: NCEMMH, Ohio State University, 1978, 29–34.

NOLAND, R. L. (Ed.). *Counseling parents of the mentally retarded.* Springfield, Ill.: Charles C. Thomas, 1970.

PARK, C., and SHAPIRO, L. *You are not alone.* Boston: Little, Brown and Co., 1976.

PATTERSON, G. R. *Families: Applications for social learning to family life.* Champaign, Ill.: Research Press, 1975.

PATTERSON, G. R., and GULLION, M. E. *Living with children: New methods for parents and teachers.* Champaign, Ill.: Research Press, 1971.

REYNOLDS, M., and BIRCH, J. *Teaching exceptional children in all America's schools.* Reston, Va.: Council for Exceptional Children, 1977.

ROBINSON, N. M., and ROBINSON, H. B. *The mentally retarded child: A psychological approach.* New York: McGraw-Hill, 1976.

ROOS, P. Parents of mentally retarded children: Misunderstood and mistreated. In A. Turnbull & H. Turnbull, III (Eds.), *Parents speak out.* Columbus, Ohio: Charles E. Merrill, 1978, 12–27.

RUTHERFORD, R., and EDGAR, E. *Teachers and parents: A guide to interaction and cooperation.* Boston: Allyn & Bacon, 1979.

SCHREIBER, F. *Your child's speech.* Westminster, Md.: Ballantine Books, 1973.

SCHULZ, J. The parent-professional conflict. In A. Turnbull & H. Turnbull, III (Eds.), *Parents speak out.* Columbus, Ohio: Charles E. Merrill, 1978, 28–37.

SHEARER, M. S. A home-based parent-training model. In D. Lillie & P. Trohanis (Eds.), *Teaching parents to teach.* New York: Walker and Co., 1976. 131–148.

SHEARER, M. S., and SHEARER, D. E. Parent involvement. In J. Jordan, A. Hayden, M. Karnes, and M. Wood (Eds.), *Early childhood education for exceptional children.* Reston, Va.: Council for Exceptional Children, 1977, 208–235.

SLOMAN, L., and WEBSTER, S. Assessing the parents of the learning disabled child: A semistructured interview procedure. *Journal of Learning Disabilities,* 1978, *11,* 73–79.

SMITH, J., and SMITH, D. *Child management.* Champaign, Ill.: Research Press Co., 1976.

SOMMERS, V. S. *The influence of parental attitudes and social environment on the personality development of the adolescent blind.* New York: American Foundation for the Blind, 1944.

STEWART, J. C. *Counseling parents of exceptional children.* Columbus, Ohio: Charles, E. Merrill, 1978.

STRENECKY, B., MCLOUGHLIN, J. A., and EDGE, D. Parental involvement: A consumer perspective. *Education and Training of the Mentally Retarded,* 1979, *14,* 54–56.

STRENECKY, M., STRENECKY, B., and DARE, G. Parent involvement in the education of children with learning problems: an annotated bibliography. In D. Edge, B. Strenecky, and S. Mann (Eds.), *Parenting learning-problem children.* Columbus, Ohio: NCEMMH, Ohio State University, 1978, 127–134.

SYMONDS, P. B. Case-study and testing methods. In E. Harms (Ed.), *Handbook of Child Guidance.* New York: Child Care Publications, 1947, 266–314.

TAWNEY, J. W. Programmed environments for the mentally retarded. In P. Mann (Ed.), *Mainstream special education.* Reston, Va.: Council for Exceptional Children, 1974, 146–153.

TELFORD, C. W., and SAWREY, J. M. *The exceptional individual.* Englewood Cliffs, N.J.: Prentice-Hall, 1967.

TURNBULL, A., and TURNBULL, H. *Parents speak out.* Columbus, Ohio: Charles E. Merrill, 1978.

WALLACE, G., and KAUFFMAN, J. *Teaching children with learning problems (2nd Ed.)* Columbus, Ohio: Charles E. Merrill, 1978.

WALLACE, G., and MCLOUGHLIN, J. A. *Learning Disabilities: Concepts and characteristics* (2nd ed.). Columbus, Ohio: Charles E. Merrill, 1979.

WARREN F. A society that is going to kill your children. In A. P. Turnbull and H. R. Turnbull, III (Eds.), *Parents speak out.* Columbus, Ohio: Charles E. Merrill, 1978, 176–197.

WOLFENSBERGER, W. Counseling the parents of the retarded. In A. Baumeister (Ed.), *Mental retardation.* Chicago: Aldine Publishing Co., 1967, 329–400.

Chapter 14

BLACKHURST, A. E., MCLOUGHLIN, J. A., & PRICE, L. M. Issues in the development of programs to prepare teachers of children with learning and behavior disorders. *Behavior Disorders,* 1977, *2,* 157–168.

GOOD, C. V. (Ed.) *Dictionary of Education,* Second Edition. New York: McGraw-Hill, 1959.

Guidelines for Personnel in the Education of Exceptional Children. Reston, Va.: Council for Exceptional Children, 1976.

MAGER, R. F. *Preparing Instructional Objectives.* Belmont, Cal.: Fearon, 1962.

ROLES OF THE RESOURCE TEACHER. Nebraska: Department of Education, undated.

CREDITS *(continued from page iv)*

permission. *Figs. 3–2, 3–3, and 3–4:* From Charles Van Riper, *Speech Correction: Principles and Methods,* 6th ed. © 1978. Reprinted by permission of Prentice-Hall, Inc., Englewood Cliffs, New Jersey. *Fig. 3–5 (left):* I. Kenneth Adisman. *Fig. 3–5 (right):* From Harold Westlake and D. Rutherford, *Cleft Palate,* © 1966. Reprinted by permission of Prentice-Hall, Inc., Englewood Cliffs, New Jersey. *Fig. 3–6:* From W. C. Grabb, S. W. Rosenstein, and K. R. Bzoch (eds.), *Cleft Lip and Palate* (Boston: Little, Brown and Co., 1971), pp. 201-202. Photo courtesy of Dr. D. Ralph Millard, Jr. *Fig. 3–8:* Courtesy of Western Electric.

Part II opening photo: Reprinted by permission of Camp Kysoc, Kentucky Easter Seal Society. Photo by W. J. Wells.

Chapter 4. *Fig. 4–2:* From William W. Green, *Your Health After Sixty.* Copyright © 1979 by Sanders-Brown Research Center on Aging. Reprinted by permission of the publisher, E. P. Dutton. *Figs. 4–3 and 4–4:* William W. Green. *Chart 4–1:* William H. Green. *Fig. 4–6:* Courtesy of the National Association of the Deaf.

Photo essay, pp. 204–205: Alan Carey.

Chapter 5. *Fig. 5–4:* From the National Society to Prevent Blindness, New York, N.Y. by permission. *Fig. 5–5:* Courtesy of Histacount Corporation. *Fig. 5–6:* Courtesy of Wormald International. *Fig. 5–8:* Courtesy of Telesensory Systems, Inc. *Fig. 5–9:* Courtesy of American Printing House for the Blind, Inc. and Howe Press of Perkins School for the Blind. Photo by Rick Friedman. *Figs. 5–10 and 5–11:* Courtesy of American Printing House for the Blind, Inc. *Fig. 5–12:* Courtesy of Telesensory Systems, Inc.

Chapter 6. *Photo, p. 289:* Courtesy of Canadian Rehabilitation Council for the Disabled. *A Trip to the Dentist:* From Barbara Aiello (ed.), *Places and Spaces: Facilities Planning for Handicapped Children,* Council for Exceptional Children, Reston, Va., 1976; and Ronald I. Mace and Betsy Laslett (eds. and illus.), *An Illustrated Handbook of the Handicapped Section of the North Carolina State Building Code,* North Carolina Dept. of Insurance, 1977.

Photo essay, pp. 300–301: Alan Carey.

Part III opening photo: Alan Carey.

Chapter 7. *Fig. 7–2:* From C. J. Fogelman (ed.), *AAMD Adaptive Behavior Scale Manual,* rev. ed., 1975, pp. 14-15. Reprinted by permission. *Fig. 7–3:* From Donald E. MacMillan, *Mental Retardation in School and Society,* Fig. 2-1. Copyright © 1977 by Little, Brown and Company (Inc.). Reprinted by permission. *Excerpt, p. 344:* Adapted from F. L. Menolascino, *Challenges in Mental Retardation: Progressive Ideology and Sources,* 1977, pp. 79-83. Reprinted by permission.

Photo essay, pp. 352–353: Alan J. Brightman.

Chapter 9. *Photo, p. 398:* Alan J. Brightman. *Photo, p. 415:* Alan Carey.

Chapter 10. *Fig. 10–1 (left):* Courtesy of Prentke Romich Co. *Fig. 10–1 (right):* Courtesy of SciTronics, Inc. *Photos, pp. 439 and 441:* Reprinted by permission of Camp Kysoc, Kentucky Easter Seal Society. Photo by W. J. Wells.

Chapter 11. *Photo, p. 472:* Andrew Sacks. *Fig. 11–1:* Courtesy of Akira Morishima.

Part IV opening photo: Reprinted by permission of Camp Kysoc, Kentucky Easter Seal Society. Photo by W. J. Wells.

Chapter 12. *Fig. 12–1:* From Donn E. Brolin and Charles J. Kokaska, *Career Education for Handicapped Children and Youth,* p. 107. Copyright © 1979 by Bell & Howell Company. Reprinted by permission. *Photo, p. 519:* Alan J. Brightman. *Photo, p. 522:* Alan Carey. *Excerpt, pp. 525–526:* Adapted from the Foreword to J. S. Payne, C. D. Mercer, and M. H. Epstein, *Education and Rehabilitation Techniques.* Copyright 1974 by Behavioral Publications. Reprinted by permission of Human Sciences Press.

Chapter 13. *Photo, p. 539:* Alan Carey.

Chapter 14. *Fig. 14–1:* A. Edward Blackhurst. *Photo, p. 563:* Alan Carey. *Photo, p. 577:* Alan Carey.

Name Index

Subject Index